The Law and Politics of Global Competition

The Law and Politics of Global Competition

Influence and Legitimacy in the International Competition Network

CHRISTOPHER TOWNLEY, MATTIA GUIDI,
AND MARIANA TAVARES

OXFORD
UNIVERSITY PRESS

OXFORD
UNIVERSITY PRESS

Great Clarendon Street, Oxford, OX2 6DP,
United Kingdom

Oxford University Press is a department of the University of Oxford.
It furthers the University's objective of excellence in research, scholarship,
and education by publishing worldwide. Oxford is a registered trade mark of
Oxford University Press in the UK and in certain other countries

First Edition published in 2022

Impression: 1

Published in the United States of America by Oxford University Press
198 Madison Avenue, New York, NY 10016, United States of America

British Library Cataloguing in Publication Data
Data available

Library of Congress Control Number: 2021946689

ISBN 978–0–19–885978–9

DOI: 10.1093/oso/9780198859789.001.0001

Printed and bound in Great Britain by
Clays Ltd, Elcograf S.p.A.

To Inma, thank you—Christopher Townley
To my parents—Mattia Guidi
To Chris, with infinite gratitude—Mariana Tavares

Endorsements

1. **Michal S. Gal** - Faculty of Law, University of Haifa, and President of ASCOLA, the international association of competition law scholars
2. **Spencer Weber Waller** - John Paul Stevens Chair in Competition Law, Loyola University Chicago School of Law
3. **Umut Ayd** - Associate Professor, Institute of Political Science, Pontificia Universidad Católica de Chile

Prof. Michal S. Gal, Faculty of Law, University of Haifa, and President of ASCOLA, the international association of competition law scholars

In this book, Townley, Guidi, and Tavares shed light on an important yet often-overlooked aspect of global competition law: the political dynamics behind the actions taken by the International Competition Network. The importance of their analysis stems from the fact that the ICN, which is comprised of national competition authorities the world over, plays a significant role in global debates concerning competition law issues. Furthermore, as the book shows, its recommendations have significant influence on national competition law systems.

One of the many strengths of "Law and Politics of Global Competition" is that it dispels the assumptions often wrongly made with regard to how the ICN's agenda is determined. Given its nature as a voluntary body with no top-down administration, and its consensus requirement, it is widely assumed that the ICN only furthers agendas that benefit all jurisdictions. Yet the authors make a compelling case to the contrary, arguing that in some cases influential actors use their influence to favour their own interests, ignoring conflicting ones of other jurisdictions. To do so, they provide a meticulous analysis of interests and actual influences, based on a quantitative as well as qualitative analysis. They also challenge the voluntariness of the policy recommendations made by the ICN.

Their thought-provoking analysis clears the way for a fresh discussion of the actual role that the ICN plays in the global competition law arena, and the way to strengthen its legitimacy, efficiency, and effectiveness. It is a must-read for anyone interested in global competition law. It may also serve as a case study for anyone interested in the politics of voluntary international cooperation in informal transnational networks.

Spencer Weber Waller
John Paul Stevens Chair in Competition Law, Loyola University Chicago School of Law

Law and Politics of Global Competition is an impressive analysis of the successes, failures, and unintended consequences of the International Competition Network

(ICN). The ICN is one of three international entities that work on issues of competition law and policies. The OECD and UNCTAD are both traditional international organizations with member states, physical headquarters, large secretariats with expert staff, and which work on many issues in addition to competition law and policy.

The ICN prides itself on being different – a virtual organization where National Competition Authorities (NCAs) come together to work exclusively on competition matters and integrate Non-Governmental Advisers (NGAs) into the formulation and implementation of non-binding best practices on a consensus basis. In short, the ICN is all competition, all the time, with a growing membership of the staff of the government competition authorities and private sector experts.

These unique features provide a rich topic for investigation of how the ICN actually operates in the real world. The authors explore the work product of the ICN, the existing literature, political and economic theory, unique survey data about the composition of the NCAs and NGAs, and a great deal of common sense. They succeed in giving us the best available analysis of how the soft law generated by the ICN functions in the real world and produces winners and losers, rule makers and rule takers. More economically advanced NCAs created the ICN and often set and execute the agenda of the ICN on an ongoing basis. Similarly, the bulk of the NGAs come from law firms and businesses in these same more economically advanced jurisdictions and have the additional incentives to push for outcomes favoring their private interests.

The authors are careful to note the benefits newer and less developed jurisdictions receive from participation in the ICN. At the same time, the authors carefully document the important and diverse ways where formal equality in a consensus-based organization producing soft law recommendations does not always manifest itself in an agenda or outputs that favor less powerful interests.

Law and Politics of Global Competition makes important points about the legitimacy, effectiveness, and efficiency of the ICN. It raises important questions about whether the ICN in action meets its stated goals and demonstrates the disparate impact the ICN agenda, structure, and outputs have in the real world and provide sensible recommendations for improvement. This is the most thorough and up-to-date analysis of an important and powerful transnational network whose real world impact would otherwise often operate in the shadows.

Umut Aydin
Associate Professor, Institute of Political Science, Pontificia Universidad Católica de Chile

As it enters its third decade, the International Competition Network is still a black box for those on the outside. Townley, Guidi and Tavares skillfully open this black box and present us with an insightful and rigorous analysis of what goes on inside this transnational network of competition agencies. Why did the ICN take the form that it did? Who wields more influence in this network? Which actors benefit most from it? Through an interdisciplinary perspective and incorporating an original survey of the ICN members, the authors compellingly demonstrate that despite the soft law nature of its recommendations and consensus requirement in its decision-making, a narrow group of advanced industrial economies have been able to exercise a powerful influence in the organization, promoting competition rules that benefit their jurisdictions, and their multinational corporations and law firms. This book is a must-read for anyone interested in the international dimensions of competition policy, and questions of power and legitimacy within transnational regulatory networks.

Acknowledgements

The authors would like to thank Jagoda Klimowicz and Erica Arcudi for their research assistance, as well as the Law School, King's College London for generous research leave and allowances. In addition, we would like to thank those that invited us to present early versions of our work, including the 14th ASCOLA Conference, organized by Professor David Bosco and his team, 'Challenges to Assumptions in Competition Law', 27–29 June 2019 (Aix-en Provence) and the workshop organized by Christel Koop and Tim Büthe, 'The Global Diffusion of Competition Policy: Causes, Consequences and Challenges', 28 October 2020 (London and virtual). Thanks particularly to Umut Aydin, Tim Büthe, and Christel Koop for their helpful feedback.

Contents

Introduction

An 'important and growing' phenomenon is that businesses and their value chains increasingly affect several countries.[1] So do anti-competitive arrangements that they adopt. Private barriers to market access are increasingly obvious as public ones fall.[2] More than 120 legal systems now have competition rules; this number exploded in the 1990s, accompanied by the establishment of competition authorities (NCAs)[3] worldwide.[4] There are a bewildering array of substantive and procedural competition rules for businesses to follow. This has costs, in terms of a loss of efficiency, for companies operating across different countries. It can also have benefits from a democratic and public interest perspective, as each jurisdiction can (try to) protect the values that it holds dear.[5]

Jurisdictions have sought wider influence through extraterritorial application of their competition rules. Another approach has been to try to develop joint substantive and/or procedural competition rules or working procedures. Sometimes this happened through bilateral discussions, such as between the USA and the EU from the 1990s.[6] There were also several (largely unsuccessful) attempts to develop multilateral competition rules, such as the EU-inspired effort to introduce competition rules into the World Trade Organization. Many international organizations have entered the competition arena—such as the Organisation for Economic Co-operation and Development (OECD) and the United Nations Conference on Trade and Development (UNCTAD). These initiatives encouraged dialogue between NCAs, but they were not always sufficient to remove tensions; think of the aborted mergers of GE and Honeywell or Boeing and McDonnell Douglas. Although infrequent, such tensions were high profile.

Many in the competition community thought that things could be better, and a new approach was needed. The result was the International Competition Network

[1] John Fingleton, 'Competition Agencies and Global Markets: The Challenges Ahead' in Paul Lugard (ed), *The International Competition Network at Ten: Origins, Accomplishments and Aspirations* (Intersentia 2011) 174–75.

[2] Merit Janow and James Rill, 'The Origins of the ICN' ibid 22.

[3] NCAs means one or more of the national competition authorities in a particular jurisdiction. For example, in the European Union (EU) this would include the competition authorities of the Member States as well as the European Commission.

[4] J Jordana, D Levi-Faur and X Fernández i Marín 'The Global Diffusion of Regulatory Agencies Channels of Transfer and Stages of Diffusion' (2011) 44 Comparative Political Studies 1343–69.

[5] Christopher Townley, *A Framework for European Competition Law: Co-ordinated Diversity* (Hart 2018) ch 1.

[6] Bruno Zanettin, *Cooperation between Antitrust Agencies at the International Level* (Hart 2002).

The Law and Politics of Global Competition. Christopher Townley, Mattia Guidi, and Mariana Tavares, Oxford University Press.
 DOI: 10.1093/oso/9780198859789.003.0001

(ICN), launched in 2001. The ICN is a transnational network of most NCAs from around the world (including some of the most influential, such as those from the USA and the EU). The ICN focuses exclusively on competition law and policy, both substance and procedure. Non-governmental actors (NGAs), such as major corporations, the law firms that support them, and academics, also contribute to ICN discussions. International organizations, such as the World Bank, UNCTAD, and the OECD, are often involved too. However, only NCAs can be ICN members.

The ICN is a forum where competition experts discuss ways to improve competition policy. The ICN also produces many work products, including an array of surveys, guides, model forms, and principles. ICN work products and proposals for new workstreams are adopted by consensus of all ICN members. States then decide whether to implement them back home.

This book has four core tasks. First, given the lack of transparency of the ICN and how it really works, a key aim is to more clearly chart what happens there. Despite the formal requirement of consensus, Chapter 1 argues that some NCAs (and even some NGAs) have considerably more influence, over the ICN agenda, which work products are produced and their content, than others. Influential actors tend to be from advanced industrialized nations, such as the EU and the USA. Sometimes their interests (and those of their states) diverge quite radically from those of other NCAs (and their states). Yet, these influential actors often use their influence to favour their own interests, and often ignore others' interests, especially when they conflict with the interests of the advanced industrialized nations. Chapter 1 also explains how these actors exert such influence given the ICN's consensus requirement. An important part of this has been for the influential actors to (intentionally or not) drive a wedge between the interest of some NCAs and the interests of their states.

In addition, despite the rhetoric on the implementation of ICN work products being voluntary for states, Chapter 2 argues that, in fact, as the ICN turns its focus to the implementation of its work products, many states face considerable (and increasing) pressure to implement them, particularly the recommended practices. Further, moving to second-order considerations, if one considers political dynamics and the impact of institutions in time, ICN provides policy entrepreneurs with new resources for intervening in and influencing domestic political struggles among groups hoping to influence market rules. Once again, this is likely to be particularly important if a wedge has been driven between the interests of an NCA and its state. States can no longer presume that their NCAs are acting in the states' best interests.

The theoretical findings in Chapters 1 and 2 are supported by a survey that we conducted on NCAs and NGAs (see Chapter 3). Taken together, these three chapters demonstrate a powerful mechanism for transmitting influence for a narrow group of actors. In our view, and acting in their own self-interest, some (often rich, economically advanced) states use the ICN to push specific competition rules (and their interpretations of them) onto some (often weaker) states. We show that this has happened even when the recipient states resist this (and even when it is not necessarily in their best interests).

While improvements could be made, many believe that the ICN and its work products have significantly increased the efficiency and effectiveness of the competition system worldwide. The second core task of this book, specifically Chapter 4, is to critically examine such claims. This is important work. Not only is the ICN widely lauded by the competition community, but it is often cited as a model that other areas should follow.[7]

The ICN is preoccupied with efficiency and effectiveness, making significant (increasing) efforts to assess them. As far as we know (and, as explained below), the ICN has never clearly articulated how it trades its many conflicting goals off against each other (such as tensions between effectiveness and efficiency). This essentially makes it impossible to assess whether the ICN efficiently and effectively achieves its goals. So, as a second-best assessment, we ask how efficiently and effectively the ICN achieves some of its different aims. In some areas, such as the production (and, to a lesser extent, the implementation) of its work products, it can be argued that the ICN is both effective and efficient, although it does not achieve all of its goals equally (and it is difficult to be certain given the ICN's methodologies of assessment). Nevertheless, for an organization that claims to be 'results-based', the ICN spends remarkably little time and effort assessing the results of its actions (eg when its work is implemented by NCAs/states, do superior outcomes occur there and at what cost?). Furthermore, different actors have different aims for the ICN (not all of which align with explicit ICN goals). Despite the 'consensus requirement', the ICN's main focus is on a narrow set of goals, principally in favour of advanced industrial economies. So, we also ask, whose effectiveness and efficiency is pursued here?

The rise of 'informal' transnational networks, like the ICN, has become pervasive over the last 40 years in many areas (not just competition policy). This rise has been largely driven by economically advanced states in the EU and the USA. This might not matter so much if these informal structures had been optimally designed to solve the problems that they confront. However, as Section I.2 explains, recent research suggests that network design is often driven by regulators (such as NCAs) from economically advanced states trying to more effectively project their own power; and to preserve their autonomy from domestic political actors whose views may conflict with regulators' 'expert perspectives' of how best to act.[8]

[7] See, for example, Anne-Marie Slaughter, *A New World Order* (2004) ch 1; Eleanor Fox, 'Linked-in: Antitrust and the Virtues of a Virtual Network' in Lugard (n 1); Youri Devuyst, 'Transatlantic Competition Relations' in Mark Pollack and Gregory Shaffer (eds), *Transatlantic Governance in the Global Economy* (Rowman & Littlefield 2001) 127.

[8] This is not to say that all individuals participating in the ICN (or even all those from the economically advanced states) are consciously working to some nefarious agenda. Many believe that they are

However, participation in the ICN is voluntary. ICN work products are adopted by consensus and need not be actually implemented. So, one might ask whether there is a need to look any more widely (than efficiency and effectiveness) for justifications for bodies like the ICN. We believe that this is important. As noted above, some NCAs have particular influence over the focus and content of ICN work products and they push many others to follow them. This matters because, given their different cultures, socio-economic backdrops, and legal and institutional endowments, ICN work products principally designed by experts from advanced industrial economies (which largely reflect the categories and approaches there),[9] are unlikely to be optimal for other states, such as developing countries, for example. So, the third core task of this book is to argue that efficiency and effectiveness are not enough. Using insights from law, political science, and international relations theory (and from Chapter 3's survey) Chapter 4 assesses the system's legitimacy too (and trade-offs between legitimacy, effectiveness, and efficiency). Legitimacy has been largely ignored in discussions about the ICN. States are likely to assess the need for 'political input' into competition policy in different ways. So, rather than declaring the ICN legitimate (or not) we highlight several potential legitimacy issues that we hope some states will find useful when making their own assessments of the ICN (which is something that we encourage).

Legitimacy concerns are likely to be particularly acute for states whose economies are very different from those key influencers in the ICN that automatically adopt ICN work products without wider scrutiny (perhaps through their NCAs); and even more so for countries dependent upon assistance from ICN actors (especially those with weak institutions of domestic accountability).[10] As we explain below, the ICN's design means that states may not be able to trust their NCAs to act in (or ICN work products to be in) their national interest.

Things do not need to be like this. States can demand access to the ICN and more transparency for the work done there and who exercises influence. This could allow them to conduct more informed political scrutiny of ICN work products before they are used in the state concerned. They might even introduce more political oversight into the ICN (by insisting on a reformulation of its membership from NCAs to states). States might (also) achieve this through more political scrutiny of their NCAs (both their work within the ICN and also 'back home'), perhaps through reducing their independence. How states actually respond will depend, in part, on each jurisdiction's view of legitimacy's importance (and how they define

doing good (and this may often be true). That is partly the point. Once the 'right institutions' are in place, then individual agendas matter less, because discordant voices are less influential (by design).

[9] Yane Svetiev, *Experimentalist Competition Law and the Regulation of Markets* (Hart 2020) 166.

[10] See, for example, Pierre-Hugues Verdier, 'Transnational Regulatory Networks and Their Limits' (2009) 34 Yale Journal of International Law 113, 121; Robert Keohane, Stephen Macedo and Andrew Moravcsik, 'Democracy-Enhancing Multilateralism' (2009) 63 International Organization 22, 27.

legitimacy). They may also need to consider how such demands may affect the viability of the ICN.

Fourth, this book also argues for a change in the way we think about competition rules. Legal and economic insights have been extremely valuable and will continue to be so. However, many in the competition community have lost sight of the redistributive impact of these rules (Section I.3 seeks to set the record straight in this regard). When reminded, they say that this is an issue for other areas of law to deal with. This may be an appropriate response in some legal orders. However, we believe that the competition community needs to move away from the idea that there is a one-size-fits-all system of competition. Many competition systems are possible (many bad ones are too). When considering whether to use ICN work products, 'states' ought to work out what impact they are likely to have in their own legal orders and to reflect upon whether that is desirable in the context of their own systems, norms, culture, and traditions. Competition rules need to be re-politicized, as they are not just technical rules, democratic processes followed, winners and losers considered (not ignored), diversity actively explained, acknowledged, and (more often) accepted. Then, states may choose to amend (or even ignore) many ICN outputs.

The ICN is now entering its third decade. In the ICN's 2020 Annual Conference its Chair, Andreas Mundt, announced the Third Decade Project.[11] A 'top-to-bottom review of the ICN's working methods and substantive coverage with recommendations for the future of the network'.[12] He encouraged all members, NGAs, and others to contribute to this project. It is hoped that this book provides a useful, critical perspective of the ICN that will help NCAs, NGAs, states, and others as they input into what could prove to be a fundamental review.

As can be seen above, there are many potential issues. The Third Decade Project is a great opportunity to have a joint, deep, and far-reaching reflection upon these points. Likely differences will emerge. While offering minor tweaks, some will probably tell us that there are no realistic alternatives to the current structures. It is worth reflecting upon this (as well as thinking about who makes these claims and what they have to fear from change). This is not just an issue for competition policy and enforcement. Wider questions of the role of transnational networks of this kind, whose interests those working in national regulators should be pursuing, and the way that transnational networks interact with majoritarian state actors now exist across many regulatory fields.

This Introduction starts by setting out the background to the ICN's establishment, mission, structure, and how it works. Next, it discusses the rise of informal

[11] The relevant speech is in the introductory session to Day 4 of the ICN 2020 Virtual Conference, 17 September 2020. Video of this conference is available at <www.ftc.gov/news-events/audio-video/video/international-competition-network-2020-virtual-conference-day-4> accessed 7 October 2021.

[12] <www.internationalcompetitionnetwork.org/2020vac/> accessed 7 October 2021.

transnational networks (like the ICN) and briefly discusses possible reasons for this. The following section explains why this is important by highlighting the highly redistributive nature of competition policy (and the ensuing enforcement). Then, working definitions of legitimacy, effectiveness, and efficiency are introduced. As noted above, we suggest that each state more actively assess ICN work products and other support under all three heads in order to judge the costs and benefits of using them in its own system. To conclude we introduce the 'state of the art' in the area and explain the methodology that we have adopted in a little more detail.

I.1 The ICN: establishment, mission, structure, and how it works

In 1997, the US Attorney General established a committee, the International Competition Policy Advisory Committee (ICPAC), to pay particular attention to three things:

> multijurisdictional merger review; the interface of trade and competition issues; and future directions in enforcement co-operation between US antitrust authorities and their counterparts around the world.[13]

ICPAC lasted two years. Members heard from scholars, lawyers, and private business executives (mainly from the EU and the USA).[14] ICPAC delivered its report in February 2000. It sought to provide an environment conducive to the expansion of international trade, to be tolerant to different nations, and to enhance world welfare. Having said that, as one might expect from a US report, it also sought to remove barriers to market access stemming from anti-competitive private barriers to trade around the world. To do this, it advised pushing nations to apply their competition rules in a non-discriminatory manner, to not apply 'non-competition factors' in merger review (with limited exceptions), and to establish independent NCAs. This advice is likely indirectly discriminatory in favour of major firms penetrating new markets (exposing incumbents).[15] The preponderance of US firms in the *Fortune 500* (and equivalent indices) makes them likely beneficiaries of this strategy.

[13] ICPAC, *Final Report* (2000), Executive Summary 1. The Committee was made up of five business people (all from US firms), two lawyers in law firms, a charity (focusing on knowledge diffusion in the USA), four academics, and one state employee (from Fannie Mae). For further insights, see Janow and Rill (n 2); Fox (n 7) 113–17; <www.justice.gov/atr/charter-international-competitiveness-advisory-committee> accessed 7 October 2021.

[14] David Gerber, *Global Competition: Law, Markets and Globalisation* (OUP 2010) 115.

[15] ICPAC (n 13) 3, 5–6.

In order to achieve these goals, the ICPAC report recommended that the USA, among other things, explore the creation of a new global competition initiative (a transnational network) where:

> government officials, private firms and non-governmental organisations could consult on antitrust matters. ICPAC recommended that this Global Competition Initiative be directed toward 'greater convergence of competition law and analysis, common understanding, and common culture'.[16]

The ICPAC report proved highly influential.[17] US and EU competition officials expressed their support for a transnational network in September 2000.[18] In February 2001 the International Bar Association called a meeting of over 40 of the world's senior competition officials and practitioners which supported the idea of 'establishing a new organisation directed exclusively at international antitrust enforcement'.[19] From an early stage, it was clear that major businesses and law firms were prepared to offer money and analytical resources to support this initiative.[20] The ICN was established in October 2001 by a group of competition authorities from around the world:

> In October 2001, competition authorities from 14 jurisdictions launched the International Competition Network (ICN) as an international forum of enforcement authorities exclusively devoted to competition issues.[21]

[16] <http://internationalcompetitionnetwork.org/about/history.aspx> See also ICPAC (n 13) Executive Summary 23, 29; Janow and Rill (n 2) 29.

Please note that since research on this book started, the ICN has fundamentally redesigned its website, changing some page links, and removing many documents that were originally available. The ICN's website itself provides a link for the 'Archived Old ICN Website' (http://old.internationalcompetitionnetwork.org), but this link does not work (we reported this to the ICN but there was no change before this book went to press). Where possible, we have replaced the old links with new ones (or referred to newer ICN documents making the same point). Where we have been unable to find the new links for documents, we have left the old ones as they may help readers locate the documents in cached sites. In this case we signal that this is what we have done by writing "broken ICN link, see discussion in Introduction, n 16" after the relevant link.

[17] François Souty, 'From the Halls of Geneva to the Shores of the Low Countries: the origins of the International Competition Network' in Lugard (n 1) 50; Hugh Hollman and William Kovacic, 'The International Competition Network: Its Past, Current and Future Role' in Lugard (n 1) 73–74; Daniel Sokol, 'The ICN in the Context of International Antitrust Institutions' in Lugard (n 1) 156–57.

[18] Janow and Rill (n 2) 32–34.

[19] <http://internationalcompetitionnetwork.org/about/history.aspx>

[20] Janow and Rill (n 2) 35. Lawyers and business were intimately involved in the development of the ICN from the start: Frederic Jenny, 'The International Competition Network and the OECD Competition Committee: Differences, Similarities and Complementarities' in Lugard (n 1)100 (see also the contributions of E Fox (ibid 115–16) (although NCAs refused some assistance to preserve 'government agency control'); D Sokol (ibid 157); D Lewis (ibid 209); D Anderson (ibid 278).

[21] ICN, *ICN Statement of Achievements 2001–2013* (2013) 3. The jurisdictions involved were: Australia, Canada, the EU, France, Germany, Israel, Italy, Japan, Korea, Mexico, South Africa, the UK, the USA, and Zambia. Half of these are in North America or the EU. However, there is a spread of other jurisdictions, some with established competition systems, as well as some newer regimes.

The ICN has grown considerably since 2001. By 2013 it included '128 agency members from 111 jurisdictions, making it the most extensive network of competition authorities worldwide'.[22] Only NCAs can be ICN members. All prospective members must accede by letter to the ICN's 'Mission and Activities'.[23] Members include the most influential NCAs worldwide, such as those in the USA and the EU. Nevertheless, all members enjoy 'the same rights and privileges of membership'.[24] In addition, NGAs, such as major corporates, law firms, and academics play a role. Similarly, international organizations, such as the World Bank, UNCTAD, and the OECD are often involved in ICN work, on a formal or informal basis. Unlike NCAs, NGAs and international organizations are not ICN members.

The ICN focuses exclusively on competition law and policy, both substance and procedure.[25] It describes its mission in the following terms:

> to advocate the adoption of superior standards and procedures in competition policy around the world, formulate proposals for procedural and substantive convergence, and seek to facilitate effective international cooperation to the benefit of member agencies, consumers and economies worldwide.[26]

In its efforts to achieve these goals, the ICN produces many different work products. In this book we often focus on recommended practices, because these are the 'gold standard' for ICN work products, but there are many others too, such as good practices (often set out in manuals and workbooks) and informative and comparative reports.[27]

[22] ibid 3. 140 NCA members are listed in 2021 <www.internationalcompetitionnetwork.org/members/> accessed 7 October 2021.

[23] ICN, *ICN Operational Framework* (2012) 1.

[24] ibid 2.

[25] ICN, *ICN Factsheet and Key Messages* (2009) 1.

[26] ICN (n 21) 3. Similarly, ICN, *ICN Statement of Achievements 2001–2012* (2012) 4 (the ICN has 'strengthened its mission'); ICN, *NGA Toolkit* (2012) 1.

[27]

> 'Recommended Practices'... are the ICN's 'gold standard' for network approved consensus recommendations, intended as a resource to benchmark agency rules and practices and a driver of convergence ... Next, working groups developed a category of work that includes 'good practices' and other practical work product (often with titles such as guides, manuals, or workbooks) that often are more focused on day-to-day investigative choices. These guides are reference tools for agency staff to enable them to evaluate and compare their own approaches. They detail practices that work well for some, or even many, members but may not be readily applicable for all. More is written in the annals of ICN's work product for the front-line investigator than any other audience ... Finally, a majority of ICN work makes up a category of informative or comparative reports—often the first line of work when the ICN explores a new topic. These reports often articulate different approaches in different jurisdictions but do not present a consensus recommendation. Examples (just a few) include reports on the objectives of unilateral conduct laws, merger remedies, market studies, competition advocacy, vertical mergers, cartel settlements, merger filing fees, obstruction of justice, and waivers of confidentiality in merger investigations.
>
> Maria Coppola and others, '(Nearly) a Century with the ICN' (2020) Competition Policy International

As we have seen, the ICN promotes non-discriminatory practices by NCAs, ignores 'non-competition' goals in its work products, and favours greater independence of NCAs. The similarity of these aims with those originally proposed by ICPAC is striking. We also have information on how the ICN works and the way that it comes to 'decisions'. The ICN is a:

> project-oriented, consensus-based, informal network of antitrust agencies from developed and developing countries that will address antitrust enforcement and policy issues of common interest and formulate proposals for procedural and substantive convergence through a results-oriented agenda and structure.[28]

ICN work is project-driven. The two key ICN 'institutions'[29] are the Steering Group and the Working Groups. The Steering Group chooses which projects to pursue, setting timetables and work plans for them. Its powers include:

- *Selection of ICN Chair:* the Steering Group chooses the ICN Chair, and three vice chairs, from among its members.[30]
- *ICN Membership:* approving new NCAs as ICN members.[31] Note that NGAs are normally appointed by their local NCA.
- *Working Groups:* establishing Working Groups in areas of need;[32] selecting and designating Working Group Chairs;[33] inviting Working Group Chairs to provide updates of their progress;[34] and reviewing and approving Working Group annual work plans.[35]
- *ICN work products (including recommended practices):* identifying subjects of potential interest to ICN members (to be run by Working Groups or by

[28] ICN, *Memorandum on the Establishment and Operation of the International Competition Network* (2002) 1.

[29] There are other more minor bodies within the ICN, such as the ACPC, which manages the planning and coordination of the ICN annual conference: ICN (n 23) 7–8. There is also an ICN Secretariat, which invites ICN members to the Annual Meeting, etc, <www.internationalcompetitionnetwork.org/uploads/library/doc990.pdf> 1 (broken ICN link, see discussion in n 16).

[30] The vice chairs are 'responsible for projects on outreach, international coordination, and advocacy and implementation'. <www.internationalcompetitionnetwork.org/uploads/library/doc608.pdf> 6 (broken ICN link, see discussion in n 16).

[31] <www.internationalcompetitionnetwork.org/uploads/library/doc996.pdf> 2 (broken ICN link, see discussion in n 16).

[32] ICN (n 23) 2.

[33] ibid 2–3. There is a new process for getting these chairs for Working Groups. First, expressions of interest are taken, so people can volunteer. It seems as though the Steering Group then try to accommodate all such requests (we assume that this is only where they are considered appropriate), for example, <www.internationalcompetitionnetwork.org/uploads/library/doc990.pdf> 2 (broken ICN link, see discussion in n 16).

[34] <www.internationalcompetitionnetwork.org/uploads/library/doc1001.pdf> (broken ICN link, see discussion in n 16).

[35] <www.internationalcompetitionnetwork.org/uploads/library/doc1001.pdf> (broken ICN link, see discussion in n 16).

Steering Group members);[36] approving draft recommended practices from the Working Groups.[37]

- *Cooperation with international bodies working in competition law and policy:* inviting (and approving) international organizations to contribute to ICN activity;[38] and hearing reports from ICN–OECD liaison.[39]

Much ICN work is done by working groups, established for specific purposes by the Steering Group. Working Groups' powers include:

- *determining the nature and ambit of their work* within the Steering Group's mandate;
- they may *invite other participants* including, but not limited to, NGAs and international organizations to provide support on issues related to their work;
- *drafting work plans* to be discussed and agreed by the Steering Group;
- *allocate drafting and other leadership tasks* (to NCAs or NGAs) in relation to producing recommended practices, or other work products, in their domain;
- *drafting and approving recommended practices* (and other work products) in their area (subject to final approval by the Steering Group and Annual Conference);
- *arranging teleconferences and workshops* in their area;

[36] ICN (n 23) 2.

[37] Eduardo Pérez Motta, 'A Network of Competition Advocates' (UOKiK's Second International Competition Forum) 2; <www.internationalcompetitionnetwork.org/uploads/library/doc995.pdf> 1 (broken ICN link, see discussion in n 16).

[38] ICN (n 23) 6; <www.internationalcompetitionnetwork.org/uploads/library/doc998.pdf> 2 (broken ICN link, see discussion in n 16).

[39] <www.internationalcompetitionnetwork.org/uploads/library/doc990.pdf> 2 (broken ICN link, see discussion in n 16). The Steering Group also has other financing tasks, such as: facilitating the financing of ICN activities by establishing an appropriate institutional framework (ibid 2); hearing the annual financial update from the Secretariat on the ICN Specified Purpose Account (Section 4 of the Resolution of the International Competition Network Steering Group and Undertaking between Canada and International Competition Network Steering Group; <www.internationalcompetitionnetwork.org/uploads/library/doc1001.pdf>) (broken ICN link, see discussion in n 16); considering and approving expenditures associated with technological improvements to the ICN website (ibid 9); reviewing ICN travel funding applications from ICN members (ibid 2). The Steering Group also controls the hosting of ICN events. It chooses an NCA to host the Annual Conference or other ICN sponsored conferences or workshops (ibid 8–9). These decisions are 'based on the criteria outlined in the Operational Framework'; <www.internationalcompetitionnetwork.org/uploads/library/doc994.pdf> 2 (broken ICN link, see discussion in n 16); although the criteria and balancing of them are not set out in the Steering Group minutes; deciding who can be sponsors and sponsorship terms (Sponsorship is allowed, but 'non-governmental sponsorship should not give rise to the perception of a conflict of interest' ibid 9. For an example of the Steering Group assessing this, see <www.internationalcompetitionnetwork.org/uploads/library/doc998.pdf> 3 (broken ICN link, see discussion in n 16); hearing updates from the NCA charged with planning and organizing the Annual Conference (<www.internationalcompetitionnetwork.org/uploads/library/doc1001.pdf> (broken ICN link, see discussion in n 16); based on 'the advice of the Annual Conference Planning Committee ("ACPC"), approves the agenda, invitations for special guests, and the ICN approach to non-member participants at the Annual Conference' (ibid 2).

- Working Group Chairs can *comment on the Steering Group Chair's suggestions* for new Chairs of the (other) Working Groups.[40]

The current substantive working groups are: advocacy, agency effectiveness, cartels, mergers, and unilateral conduct.[41]

In terms of outputs, ICN recommended practices are of particular importance. As noted above, Working Groups draft recommended practices in their area of competence. Once agreed by the Working Group, recommended practices are sent up to the Steering Group for approval. Approved recommended practices are sent to all ICN members for vetting and then on to the ICN Annual Conference. There they are adopted unless any NCA objects (ie consensus).[42]

ICN activities are voluntary. They rely on the goodwill of NCAs and NGAs, and their staff. There is an ICN annual conference and individual project meetings, 'teleconferences, web-based tools, and workshops'.[43] The annual conference and some workshops are held in person, in varying locations. Most other meetings are held via telephone conference, or online.

Formally speaking, the ICN does not have a rule-making function. It makes recommended practices through consensus. Then, individual states (and their NCAs) 'decide whether and how to implement the recommendations, through unilateral, bilateral or multilateral arrangements, as appropriate'.[44] Although Chapter 2 shows a different practice.

I.2 The rise of transnational networks (like the ICN) and possible reasons for this

In 1945, there were about 110 active international organizations, worldwide. By 2005, there were over 600. According to Roger, in 1945, the vast majority of these (93%) were formal organizations, such as the United Nations.[45] For every five formal international organizations created in the next 30 years, there was only one informal one (such as the Basel Committee on Banking Supervision, set up in 1974 to enhance financial stability).[46] In the 1970s the ratio of informal international

[40] See, respectively, ibid 5; ICN–Unilateral Conduct Working Group, *Unilateral Conduct Working Group Questionnaire* (2006) 1; Pérez Motta (n 37) 2; <www.internationalcompetitionnetwork.org/uploads/library/doc995.pdf> 1 (broken ICN link, see discussion in n 16).

[41] Previous working groups that have now been closed are antitrust enforcement in regulated sectors (2003–05), and telecommunications (2005–06). There are also Operational Working Groups, dealing with membership, and other operational matters. They focus on 'fostering a greater understanding of the ICN, its mission and objectives' and 'the constitution of the Steering Group and the funding needs of the Network'.

[42] Pérez Motta (n 37) 2.

[43] ICN (n 25) 4–5.

[44] ICN (n 28) 1.

[45] <www.un.org/en/> accessed 7 October 2021.

[46] <www.bis.org/bcbs/index.htm> accessed 7 October 2021.

organizations, compared to formal ones, started to rise. This trend accelerated, particularly at the end of the 1980s. By 2005, while still in a minority, informal bodies accounted for almost one-third of all active international organizations.

Here, we start by defining what is meant by a formal and an informal international organization. We classify the ICN as an informal international organization. One might reasonably ask whether this rise in informal international organizations matters. Some have suggested that the choice of formal or informal structures is made to better achieve the organization's desired ends. If true, one might not be concerned by the rise of informal international organizations. In fact, we cite studies which show that power is likely to have a lot to do with this choice too. This is important. Section I.3 highlights the highly distributive nature of competition policy and enforcement. Section I.4 looks at the implications of such choices for legitimacy, effectiveness, and efficiency. Together they explain why informality might matter.

Scholars define formal and informal international organizations in different ways.[47] For Roger, the focus is on arrangements between states, widely understood. By 'state' he means a ministry or the executive, but Roger also includes departments and state agencies of 'humbler provenance', such as finance ministries, central banks, and NCAs. He does not include regional or municipal actors though; nor does he include arrangements between companies and other non-governmental organizations, such as charities and pressure groups.[48]

Roger sees two key differences between formal/informal international organizations. Formal actors usually have functionally separate bodies from their members. This is typically a secretariat with some bureaucratic independence.[49] Informal international organizations often do not have secretariats, headquarters, or similar features. However, there is a spectrum here. Some informal organizations might

[47] Peter Holcombe Henley and Niels M Blokker, 'The Group of 20: A Short Legal Anatomy from the Perspective of International Institutional Law' (2014) 14 Melbourne Journal of International Law 580. For example, many start from the Correlates of War definition of a formal international organization: it must be a formal entity; with at least three states as members; and 'possess a permanent secretariat or other indication of institutionalization such as headquarters and/or permanent staff'. Jon CW Pevehouse and others, 'Tracking Organizations in the World: The Correlates of War IGO Version 3.0 Datasets' (2019) 57 Journal of Peace Research 492, 494. In contradistinction, Vabulas and Snidal suggest three features of informal international organizations: there must be an explicitly shared expectation about its purpose, although not in a formal agreement; this must be between explicitly associated state members, which they define as being ministers or the executive; who participate in regular meetings, without an independent secretariat or other significant institutionalization, such as, for example, permanent staff and/or a headquarters, Felicity Vabulas and Duncan Snidal, 'Organization without Delegation: Informal Intergovernmental Organizations (IIGOs) and the Spectrum of Intergovernmental Arrangements' (2013) 8 Review of International Organizations 197–99. As these authors point out, there is no bright line between these two 'ideal type' classifications.

[48] Charles Roger, *The Origins of Informality: Why the Legal Foundations of Global Governance Are Shifting, and Why It Matters* (OUP 2020) 24–28.

[49] Think of the World Health Organization, employing over '7,000 people from more than 150 countries working in 150 country offices, in 6 regional offices and at … [its] headquarters in Geneva' <www.who.int/about/who-we-are> accessed 7 October 2021.

have such bodies but, if they do, they will likely be small. The size of the secretariat is relevant as it could be a proxy for independence from state interests (which may affect states' ability to reform such organizations as well as their cost). As a result, informal bodies have less scope to act autonomously from their members.[50]

Second, for an international organization to be considered formal, Roger demands that its 'founding document' be 'legally binding'.[51] This is not necessary for informal organizations. The Vienna Convention on the Law of Treaties 1969 defines a treaty as:

> an international agreement concluded between States in written form and governed by international law, whether embodied in a single instrument or in two or more related instruments and whatever its particular designation.[52]

As discussed in Section I.1, when NCAs accede by letter to the ICN's 'Mission and Activities' they sign up to the ICN's constitution and procedural rules, where all members enjoy 'the same rights and privileges of membership'. In consequence, there seems to be an agreement between many actors from around the world. However, several formalities are needed to produce a binding international treaty under the above definition from the Vienna Convention. For example, there must be an agreement between *states*.[53] Who can sign on behalf of each state is a matter for that state. However, a person seeking to sign on behalf of a state must produce 'full powers', unless she falls within certain defined categories, such as a Head of State, Head of Government, or a Minister of Foreign Affairs (but not normally other ministers).[54] Furthermore, the international treaty must be in written form

[50] Roger (n 48) 6 and 28–29.

[51] Roger does not explain how this should be assessed. For simplicity, we focus on the criteria from the 1969 Vienna Convention on the Law of Treaties. However, while this convention often reflects customary international law, it can at times be either wider or narrower, see for example, International Law Commission, *Yearbook of the International Law Commission* (United Nations 1966) 187. As a result, other public international law tests for whether or not there has been an international treaty could be wider or narrower than that stipulated in the 1969 Vienna Convention. Many international organizations have been concluded through means other than international treaties, see, for example, Henry G Schermers and Niels M Blokker, *International Institutional Law: Unity within Diversity* (Brill 2011) 37–39.

[52] The 1969 Vienna Convention on the Law of Treaties <https://treaties.un.org/doc/Treaties/1980/01/19800127%2000-52%20AM/Ch_XXIII_01.pdf> art 2(1)(a).

[53] There are two issues here when it comes to the ICN. First, the 1969 Vienna Convention on the Law of Treaties only applies to the relations between states (although other actors can be present), see art 3(c). The 1986 Vienna Convention on the Law of Treaties between States and International Organizations or between International Organizations, <https://legal.un.org/ilc/texts/instruments/english/conventions/1_2_1986.pdf> art 2(1)(a) has a similar definition of treaty and likely covers agreements between states and some other non-state bodies, such as the EU. However, this 1986 Convention has not yet come into force though because an insufficient number of states parties have ratified it. That said, it may still be useful as a reflection of the position under international customary law.

Second, although the dividing line is not always clear, 'agreements between branches of different governments or between particular public authorities [perhaps including NCAs] do not normally create international organizations'. Schermers and Blokker (n 51) 37. Nevertheless, as we have seen, Roger's classification allows NCAs to make formal agreements.

[54] The 1969 Vienna Convention on the Law of Treaties, art 7, has a more precise definition.

(whether or not it is in a single document). The parties must also have intended to legally bind themselves through this agreement.[55] On the other hand, an informal international organization is constituted by an agreement outside of 'the traditional boundaries of international law'. It may merely be seen as a political understanding. This might be in some kind of non-binding arrangement, or oral agreement, for example, which likely delimits the organization's aims, procedural rules, etc.

While Roger's classification can be criticized,[56] the ICN is an informal international organization under his test (and he explicitly classifies it as such). It does not have its own secretariat, headquarters, or similar. The Canadian Competition Bureau (an NCA) provides such services to the ICN. Second, the ICN was not established by an international binding treaty within the terms of the Vienna Convention on the Law of Treaties. For example, NCAs' action would not normally be seen as state action for these purposes.[57] Second, when NCAs acceded separately by letter to the ICN's 'Mission and Activities'[58] many did not produce 'full powers', see above (although this can be remedied retroactively).[59]

[55] Malcolm N Shaw, *International Law* (8th edn, CUP 2017) 686.

[56] This is because some parts of the test are not entirely clear; and allocating international organizations to the formal or informal category may be controversial, given the judgement involved. In relation to the clarity of the specified tests, confusion arises on at least two levels. Should we be checking for a binding international treaty, or also for the binding creation of an international organization? Roger does not explain. The International Court of Justice has stated that a treaty creating an international organization is just a normal treaty. However, in addition, 'the constituent instruments of international organizations are also treaties of a particular type; their object is to create new subjects of law endowed with a certain autonomy, to which the parties entrust the task of realizing common goals'.*Legality of the Use by a State of Nuclear Weapons in Armed Conflict*, Advisory Opinion, ICJ Reports 1996, 66, 75. More generally, ibid 949; Schermers and Blokker (n 51) 36 and following. Roger ignores the first criterion (new subject of law) and the second criterion (certain autonomy) relates to the secretariat point, which Rogers has already included as a separate criterion (see above). Given the overlaps, we assume that Roger is merely asking whether there is a legally binding international treaty. This seems to mirror the definition from the Correlates of War dataset, which inspired Roger's work. 'The first component of this definition simply posits that IGOs must be formed by an internationally recognized treaty.' Jon CW Pevehouse, Timothy Nordstrom and Kevin Warnke, 'The Correlates of War 2 International Governmental Organizations Data Version 2.0' (2004) 21 Conflict Management and Peace Science 103. That said, Roger's widening of his classification to include bodies such as NCAs as 'states' does introduce unfortunate inconsistency.

Second, and partly as a result of the first issue, allocating at least some international organizations into one of Roger's two (formal/informal) categories is likely to be controversial. Although Roger presents his binding–non-binding distinction as quite a stark one ((n 48) 6 and 29–30), this is not necessarily always so. Furthermore, judgement may be needed to allocate an organization into the appropriate category. For example, did the parties intend 'to legally bind themselves', or is the organization's secretariat small enough (or lacking sufficient independence) to still be considered informal? This could lead to disagreement about whether an international organization should be classified as formal or informal.

[57] See the discussion in n 53. The ICN could still have been established by an international binding treaty outside of the terms of the Vienna Convention on the Law of Treaties (ie through customary law). It is possible that the ICN members established a treaty under international customary law, for example in relation to the ICN's constitutional and procedural rules (such as votes by consensus). Yet, we ignore this issue as we are following Roger's actual classification.

[58] See the text at n 23.

[59] The 1969 Vienna Convention on the Law of Treaties (n 52) art 8.

Furthermore, even if DG COMP had full powers to act for the EU, the EU is not a state.[60]

One might reasonably ask whether this rise in informal international organizations matters. The most common theoretical approach to understanding the creation and actions of international organizations is functionalism. According to functionalists:

> when states create international institutions, they fashion them to resolve the specific problems they encounter in the most efficient way. Cross border problems are expected to vary in their underlying structure, and this should make certain institutional designs more appropriate, or 'rational', than others.[61]

Stone adds that, in international relations theory, we often see functionalism combined with a transaction-cost approach in order to explain organizational design.[62]

Scholars have suggested that informal international organizations will be better at resolving some problems than formal ones. Perhaps more flexibility is desirable (if there is uncertainty about the state of the world, the nature of the problem, or how to solve it). Functionalists expect international organizations to exhibit informal characteristics in areas where such problems predominate. Slaughter, for example, lauds informal networks, such as the ICN, as she says they offer:

> a flexible and relatively fast way to conduct the business of global governance, co-ordinating and even harmonising national government action while initiating and monitoring different solutions to global problems. Yet they are decentralised and dispersed, incapable of exercising central coercive authority.[63]

Functionalism makes sense. It would be strange if states did not try to devise efficient structures that adequately solve the problems that they face. If functionalism is right, then perhaps one does not need to be concerned about the rise in informal international organizations, like the ICN, that we have highlighted above—in fact, it may be positive.

[60] There is a specific treaty for treaties between states and international organizations (see discussion at n 53). But an insufficient number of states have ratified it for it to have been brought into force. The UK has ratified it, but the EU has neither ratified it nor formally confirmed it as an international organization, <https://treaties.un.org/pages/ViewDetailsIII.aspx?src=TREATY&mtdsg_no=XXIII-1&chapter=23&Temp=mtdsg3&clang=_en>

[61] Roger (n 48) 12, see also 53–54. The focus is on what things they think informal organizations are better at doing (Vabulas and Snidal (n 47) 209–10).

Chapter 1, Section 1.2.1.1.2 discusses functionalism and power-based theories in more detail, as well as Roger's empirical analysis and his ideas regarding domestic political constraints.

[62] Randall W Stone, 'Informal Governance in International Organizations: Introduction to the Special Issue' (2013) 8 Review of International Organizations 121, 123.

[63] Slaughter (n 7) 11.

By way of contrast, Patrick fears that informality might: not help solve tough negotiation problems; undermine formal institutions whose legitimacy and technical resources are needed long term; allow rich states to pivot among institutions that they think favour their desired outcomes; and raise wider concerns about legitimacy, accountability, and equity.[64]

In fact, functionalism does not seem to provide the whole answer. One major problem that it faces is empirical. If the nature of organizations tracks the problems that they face, one would expect a strong correlation between the problems that these international organizations face and their level of formality. Yet, one can find international organizations, with different levels of informality, addressing almost the same problems, around the world.[65]

That implies that something else must also be at work. This is not a surprise either. As Stone points out, focusing on transaction costs ignores conflicts of interest. 'Lowering barriers to trade [or, in our case, competition] creates winners and losers, and even equally efficient arrangements can have greatly differing distributional consequences.'[66] By way of contrast, power-based theories rely on a very different kind of argument to functionalist theories. Power-based theories concentrate on the distribution of power (and interests) between states:

> Powerful states are hypothesized to prefer informal solutions that enable maximum flexibility while less powerful states prefer formal ones that more effectively bind. Both, however, are willing to compromise to some degree in order to achieve cooperation of some kind [eg the powerful accept some binding rules to get voluntary cooperation of weaker states], so the process can play out in different ways and lead to different levels of informality. Scholars making these kinds of arguments predict that an organization's informality will be determined by power inequalities [more informality as power inequality rises] and the level of conflict that prevails within specific constellations of states [more informality as the level of conflict rises].[67]

The rise of informal international organizations could (also) be linked to conflicting interests between states and power inequalities. If states push for solutions that favour them and their stakeholders, at the expense of others, then the rise in informal

[64] Stewart Patrick, 'The New "New Multilateralism": Minilateral Cooperation, But at What Cost?' (2015) 1 Global Summitry 115.

[65] Think of cooperation between tax authorities or money laundering, for example, Roger (n 48) 57.

[66] Stone (n 62) 123.

[67] Roger (n 48) 13, see also 55–56. That said, some functionalists admit to the importance of other criteria too. 'The scholar who did the most to popularize functionalism and the transaction–cost approach in international relations, Robert O Keohane, also took pains to point out their characteristic blind spots. Keohane (1984) argued that international institutions are created in order to facilitate cooperation by reducing transaction costs, but he argued that they were created by the most powerful states for their own purposes, and were generally skewed to favor their interests', Stone (n 62) 123–24; similarly, see Slaughter (n 7) ch 6. Stone's reference to Keohane is RO Keohane, *After Hegemony: Cooperation and Discord in the World Political Economy* (Princeton UP 1984).

institutional organizations, like the ICN, may raise cause for concern (especially as it has largely been driven by 'advanced industrial states in North America and Europe').[68] Are informal international organizations, like the ICN, well matched to their tasks or is their form (also) about favouring certain constituents?

Unfortunately, some concern seems justified. Roger's empirical work shows that, while some informal bodies are well matched to the underlying problems that they face, many are not. He calculates that almost 46% of informal international organizations are not well matched. Furthermore, 74% of mismatched international organizations are informal (and this number rises as the number of informal international organizations grows).[69] Key drivers of the rise of informality are independent regulatory institutions (many NCAs are independent) and increased political dissonance within states. Both are increasingly common in economically advanced nations. The scope for opportunism and increased conflicts between states also appear to have a significant impact on this move towards informality.[70]

I.3 Why this matters: the redistributive nature of competition policy

Competition policy and enforcement are highly redistributive. Given their different preferences, cultures, socio-economic backdrops, and legal and institutional endowments, ICN work products, principally designed by experts from advanced industrial economies (largely reflecting their categories and approaches), may not work optimally in other kinds of states. There is a significant amount of scholarship arguing that, to perform well, the nature and interpretation of a state's competition rules should take account of multiple issues, such as: the size and shape of its economy;[71] its 'model of capitalism';[72] whether its constitutional framework impels the competition rules to have multiple goals;[73] whether the state is a net importer, or a net exporter;[74] and whether the state prefers to deal with competition through

[68] Roger (n 48) 8–9 and 42–43.

[69] ibid 208–09.

[70] ibid 72–73, 79, and 104–06.

[71] Newer regimes might have quite specific substantive and procedural problems (concentrated markets, less experienced staff, difficulty to collate basic data), Michal Gal, *Competition Policy for Small Market Economies* (Harvard UP 2003); Michal S Gal, 'When the Going Gets Tight: Institutional Solutions When Antitrust Enforcement Resources are Scarce' (2009) Antitrust: Antitrust Law & Policy eJournal.

[72] See the discussion around n 91.

[73] One might think of the single market goal in EU competition law, Christopher Townley, *Article 81 EC and Public Policy* (Hart 2009) chs 1 and 3; or the social function of private property in Chile, Colombia, and Mexico: Andrés Palacios Lleras, 'Competition Law in Latin America: 100 Years of Solitude' in Swethaa Ballakrishnen and Sara Dezalay (eds), *Invisible Institutionalisms: Collective Reflections on the Shadows of Legal Globalisation* (Hart 2021) 182–87.

[74] Andrew Guzman, 'Antitrust and International Regulatory Federalism' (2001) 76 NYU L Rev 1142, 1152–55.

'government licensing of behaviour' or through private litigation.[75] Others go further and question whether a western development model is desirable at all.[76]

Svetiev notes that many states that merely adopted competition rules through legal transplants from mature jurisdictions (often the EU or the USA) do little with them. However, some states have worked hard, often through an international benchmarking process (and often assisted by NCAs from the EU or the USA), to adapt rules to their specific culture and context. These efforts can be further supported by involving wider stakeholders, such as consumers and employees, in discussions about the scope and content of the rules. States that have done this 'have typically had greater success in enlivening domestic competition enforcement and even becoming rule promoters or rule makers who develop innovative approaches'.[77] There are many examples, but South Africa and China are important reference points.[78]

It is also likely important, for the ongoing acceptance and legitimacy of the rules, that efforts to tailor them to the national context and to engage wider stakeholders continue through time (for example through suggestions for their interpretation in NCA policy guidelines and wider input into these). Once again, there are many examples here, both of the problems of not deeply considering changes, and also of seeking to impose changes on stakeholders rather than engaging with them. One such example may be seen in the adoption of leniency regimes harbouring major ethical choices (although we will see that the ICN's work products makes little effort to articulate the choices they make). The 'leniency regime' advocated in ICN recommended practices (perhaps favouring enforcers over consumers, for example) may not be well matched to the local contexts of many Latin American countries, for example.[79]

As we have seen, this diversity makes it unlikely that there can be one better or best competition system and questionable whether procedural and

[75] See the discussion around n 118.

[76] Usha Natarajan, 'Mirrors, Mirages, and the Development Myth' in Ballakrishnen and Dezalay (n 73) 199 and 203–05.

[77] Svetiev (n 9) 167.

[78] For example, South Africa started with an international benchmarking exercise of competition rules. However, the outputs of that exercise were then debated within the National Economic Development and Labour Council, which brings together government officials responsible for economic policy, with employers and employees. Although none of the competition ideas that it ultimately adopted were unique to South Africa, they were given a local 'twist' (for example the goal to 'promote a greater spread of ownership, in particular to increase the ownership stakes of historically disadvantaged persons'). These efforts to make the competition rules relevant in South Africa, alongside the deeper discussion with relevant stakeholders, gave the competition rules more legitimacy and may be one of the reasons why these rules were 'mainstreamed' more quite quickly there.

Svetiev and others make similar comments about the substantive, procedural, and institutional design of the competition rules in China, Lei Wang and Ivo Krizic, 'Beyond Legal Transplant: China's "Shopping Around" Approach and the Formation of Anti-Monopoly Law' (2017) 40 World Competition, especially 521–24; Lei Wang and Yane Svetiev, 'Competition Law Enforcement in China: Between Technocracy and Industrial Policy' (2016) 79 Law and Contemporary Problems.

[79] Palacios Lleras (n 73) ss II and III.

substantive convergence of competition policy and enforcement would necessarily be appropriate or optimal. Despite this, these are core parts of the ICN's 'mission'.[80] Furthermore, implementing highly uniform rules without changes (and without engaging local stakeholders), is unlikely to lead to optimal outcomes. It may even undermine the legitimacy of the whole competition (or even the wider) system. Despite what it says, there is evidence of the ICN doing this too. In fact, it seems likely that different competition systems are needed (substantively, procedurally, and institutionally). That said, a discussion forum facilitating effective international cooperation could be helpful (although other fora, such as the OECD and UNCTAD, do this already—and did in 2001).

This discussion starts by identifying three kinds of (reasonable) disagreements that exist in relation to competition policy and enforcement. This helps explain why diversity might exist. Then, it confronts arguments in favour and against diversity in competition policy and enforcement. Uniformity can be beneficial (diversity can have costs), but diversity can be beneficial too. The highly redistributive nature of competition policy and enforcement makes the degree of diversity a major political choice. In addition, rich states (and their firms) have incentives to push others to adopt their competition models. This is not always to the benefit of these conforming states (although it might be beneficial for their NCAs). The combination of these points highlights why we believe that many states would benefit from taking the ICN's impact upon them seriously and doing a full (legitimacy, efficiency, and effectiveness) evaluation of whether ICN work products should be adopted there (even by its NCA).

Some say that national preferences are less valuable in competition law and policy today, given increasing agreement on competition's meaning and what benefits it brings. Neoclassical economics postulates that competition is positive,[81] as it pushes firms to innovate and become more efficient, so that their products and services cost less. Successful firms can undercut, and thus eliminate, their rivals (while providing consumers with better goods/services at lower prices).

The assumption that competition is good and more competition is even better has reached the status of a mantra among competition policymakers, business people, and academics. Never before has faith in competition enjoyed such an exalted, almost religious, standing and never before have more dimensions of social reality been immersed with its logic.[82]

[80] The ICN's Mission is extracted in the text at n 28.

[81] eg Neumann has said that from 'day to day there are both winners and losers. Still in the long run all can become winners unless the right to participate in market activities is curtailed. Freedom to join the competitive process must therefore be safeguarded by law.' Manfred Neumann, *Competition Policy: History, Theory and Practice* (Edward Elgar 2001) 3.

[82] Hubert Buch-Hansen and Angela Wigger, *The Politics of European Competition Regulation: A Critical Political Economy Perspective* (Routledge 2011) 1.

However, the neoclassical paradigm tends to ignore that competition can create losers (whom states might want to protect and might have different preferences of how to do so):[83]

> Competition control is located at the interface between enabling and constraining the scope of freedom enjoyed by market players. It constitutes a sensitive area where a great variety of interests clash. As an instrument of public market intervention *par excellence*, it needs to be understood in terms of established legal and economic philosophies that influence policy objectives and conceptions of how to interpret and enforce competition law.[84]

Campbell points out that, in order for markets to exist at all, economic action must be '"confined to certain directions by our general social institutions" ... This is to say that, at root, the welfare enhancing private market is a publicly constituted and endorsed institution, which takes its shape from continuing, extensive regulation'.[85] Without public goods (provided by political organizations, ie states) like security, enforcement of private property rights, a functioning banking system, money, what we call 'markets' simply wouldn't exist. These include the competition rules. Indeed, Cini and McGowan call competition policy 'the most important organizing principle in the capitalist world'.[86]

Legislatures might choose to organize competition in their jurisdictions in different ways. This might require different competition rules. Furthermore, many competition rules leave a wide margin of interpretation for competition authorities

[83] The arbitrary nature of inheritance, and one's own genetic natural gifts mean that success is not necessarily something all can enjoy: Thomas Piketty, *Chronicles on Our Troubled Times* (Penguin 2016) 59–61. Monbiot writes that:

> Attempts to limit competition are treated as inimical to liberty. Tax and regulation should be minimised, public services should be privatised. The organisation of labour and collective bargaining by trade unions are portrayed as market distortions that impede the formation of a natural hierarchy of winners and losers. Inequality is recast as virtuous: a reward for utility and a generator of wealth, which trickles down to enrich everyone. Efforts to create a more equal society are both counterproductive and morally corrosive. The market ensures that everyone gets what they deserve. We internalise and reproduce its creeds. The rich persuade themselves that they acquired their wealth through merit, ignoring the advantages—such as education, inheritance and class—that may have helped to secure it. The poor begin to blame themselves for their failures, even when they can do little to change their circumstances.
>
> George Monbiot, 'Neoliberalism—the Ideology at the Root of All Our Problems' *The Guardian* (London, 15 Apr 2016) <www.theguardian.com/books/2016/apr/15/neoliberalism-ideology-problem-george-monbiot> 1–2, accessed 7 October 2021.

[84] Angela Wigger and Andreas Nölke, 'Enhanced Roles of Private Actors in EU Business Regulation and the Erosion of Rhenish Capitalism: The Case of Antitrust Enforcement' (2007) 45 Journal of Common Market Studies 490.

[85] David Campbell, 'The End of Posnerian Law and Economics' (2010) 73 Modern Law Review 305. Similarly, Joseph Stiglitz, *The Price of Inequality* (Penguin 2012) s 1.

[86] Michelle Cini and Lee McGowan, *Competition Policy in the European Union* (St Martin's Press 1998) 2.

and courts, and this can be used for policy purposes too.[87] The way in which rules work in different places can make a big difference:

> Depending on whether or not the antitrust rules apply to certain practices in a market economy, wealth is either transferred from one group to another, or remains with one group instead of being transferred to another.[88]

Townley points to three sets of disagreements that can arise in the design and implementation of competition rules.[89] First, there are disagreements relating to competition law's substantive goals. Three issues are relevant here: the definition of competition itself, different conceptions of consumer welfare, and the relevance of public policy criteria. Second, even if one could agree on the appropriate competition law goals, there may still be disagreement about the best methods to achieve these goals. We call these disagreements on methods. Third, there are disagreements on procedures and optimal institutional structures. These three sets of disagreements are all interrelated. We will see that the potential impacts of competition are different in different states, there are different ways of seeing the world and dealing with complexity, and these issues have a varying political salience around the world. So, it is unsurprising that different states might want different competition rules and interpret them differently. As the World Bank acknowledges more generally, we need to get away:

> from formulae and the search for elusive 'best practices'... [and get] a better understanding of non-economic factors—history, culture, and politics—in economic growth processes.[90]

Let's start with disagreements on aims. There are many types of capitalism. Economic prosperity can be achieved in different ways. States help through establishing structures to enforce property rights, manage the economy, etc. This helps to protect the legitimacy of markets, by protecting people from their risks and insecurities.[91] The 'varieties of capitalism' literature finds patterns in how

[87] Hans Ullrich, 'International Harmonisation of Competition Law: Making Diversity a Workable Concept' in Hans Ullrich (ed), *Comparative Competition Law: Approaching an International Antitrust System of Antitrust Law* (Nomos 1998) 72–74.

[88] Okeoghene Odudu, 'The Distributional Consequences of Antitrust' in Philip Marsden (ed), *Handbook of Research in Trans-Atlantic Antitrust* (Edward Elgar 2007) 605.

[89] Townley (n 5) ch 1. More detail on the arguments relating to these three 'disagreements' and further references to the literature can be found there.

[90] World Bank, *The Political Economy of Reform: Issues and Implications for Policy Dialogue and Development Operations* (World Bank 2008) vii. Similarly, Imelda Maher, 'Networking Competition Authorities in the European Union: Diversity and Change' in Claus Dieter Ehlermann and Isabela Atanasiu (eds), *Constructing the EU Network of Competition Authorities* (Hart 2002) 225.

[91] Dani Rodrik, *The Globalisation Paradox: Democracy and the Future of the World Economy* (Norton 2011) xviii; Marie-Laure Djelic and Sigrid Quack, 'The Missing Link: Bringing Institutions back into the Debate on Economic Globalisation' (2002) Discussion Paper FS I 02-107 Wissenschaftszentrum

market actors coordinate their actions in economically advanced states. Nations can be grouped based on how much market actors rely on 'market (liberal market economies, LMEs), strategic (coordinated market economies, CMEs) or intermediate, often state-led modes of coordination to pursue their goals'.[92] The UK and the USA are often used as examples of LMEs. Firms exchange goods and services through arm's-length contracts under competitive conditions. Firms tend to employ people for shorter durations, there is less of a role for the state (except in setting the basic market framework), and a predominance of short-term capital markets for finance. Germany and the Scandinavian countries are often grouped as CMEs. There labour, business, and government share economic governance. Firms have social responsibilities that override pure, short-term profit-maximization goals (such as agreements on welfare or training).[93] This provides firms a lot of protection from hostile takeovers, encouraging longer-term investments in research and training. This often leads to higher levels of skill, but less flexibility than LMEs.

As a key organizing principle, one can easily see how competition policy in an LME might be different from that needed in a CME.[94] In an LME, competition policy might push firms to maximize short-term consumer welfare. As long as prices remain competitive and there are economies of scale, an 'LME competition policy' might permit increases in firm size. The focus is less on concentration and more on collusive agreements between firms with clear negative effects on short-term consumer welfare, such as cartels. Whereas, a 'CME competition policy' might find collaboration between firms more desirable, particularly where it leads to a good diffusion of technological innovation. There might also be more focus on enabling small and medium-sized firms to operate in the economy, providing more consumer choice and more opportunities for people to participate. Economic and political power are more dispersed. For CMEs, ordoliberalism might be a better organizing idea than consumer welfare.

Second, even if we all agreed that consumer welfare were the best goal for competition policy in all economies, there is considerable disagreement about its specific focus. For example, there might be disagreement about whether to focus on long-term or short-term consumer welfare. A focus on short-term consumer welfare ignores 'the inherent tension between consumers' immediate interests and producers' incentives to sustain innovation and productive efficiency.[95] It

Berlin für Sozialforschung; Stephen Wilks, *The Political Power of the Business Corporation* (Edward Elgar 2013) 30.

[92] Mattia Guidi, *Competition Policy Enforcement in EU Member States: What Is Independence For?* (Palgrave Macmillan 2016) 80. These are obviously 'ideal types' and some aspects of one economy can sometimes be found in others.

[93] Wigger and Nölke (n 84) 490; Wilks (n 91) 26.

[94] Wigger and Nölke (n 84) 491–93; Oliver Budzinski, 'Monoculture versus Diversity in Competition Economics' (2008) 32 Cambridge Journal of Economics 295; Wilks (n 91) 453–59.

[95] Joseph Brodley, 'The Economic Goals of Antitrust: Efficiency, Consumer Welfare, and Technological Progress' (1987) 62 New York University Law Review.

disregards efficiency gains that drive productivity growth and innovation and that could easily benefit consumers in the long run ... '[96] There are, of course, many other choices that need to be made when applying a consumer welfare standard. They include, whether to favour price, choice, or quality, as these are often in tension (and largely incommensurate);[97] whether the focus should be on consumers or customers,[98] whether economic benefits need be direct or whether indirect benefits can also be considered,[99] and whether consumer welfare gains in one relevant market can justify losses in another.[100] The consumer welfare standard itself is agnostic as to which of these choices are made. However, these choices will be highly redistributive and require major value judgements.

As noted above, the third issue concerning 'disagreements about competition law's substantive goals' relates to whether public policy considerations should be directly considered in competition assessments (and, if so, which goals, what weight should they be given, and when in the analysis). All of these choices will impact on the outcome in some cases (and so will be, once again, redistributive). Considering public policy goals in competition law has several benefits. It opens the door to gains that consumers might otherwise be denied; competition law becomes part of wider public policy rather than blocking other goals, this may encourage corporate social responsibility; it increases consistency with standard cost–benefit analyses, which adds more rigour and introduces fewer distortions in policymaking; and it supports market integration and harmonious development.[101] Finally, it allows states to organize their economies as they like—for example, they can choose whether to protect environmental, animal, and social standards through legislation and/or by encouraging firms (and others) to act and then allowing this in the competition law framework.[102]

On the other hand, considering public policy within competition law raises many problems. It is not easy to measure public policy impacts or to compare them

[96] Katalin Cseres, 'The Controversies of the Consumer Welfare Standard' (2007) 3 Competition Law Review 125. Similarly, Michael Porter, 'Competition and Antitrust' (2001) 46 Antitrust Bulletin 922ff.

[97] Neil Averitt and Robert Lande, 'Using the Consumer Choice Approach to Antitrust Law' (2007) 74 Antitrust Law Journal; Ariel Ezrachi and Maurice Stucke, 'The Curious Case of Competition and Quality' (2015) 3 Journal of Antitrust Enforcement.

[98] Victoria Daskalova, 'Consumer Welfare in EU Competition Law: What Is It (Not) About?' (2015) TILEC Discussion Paper; Townley (n 73) 263–73.

[99] OFT, *Article 101(3)—A Discussion of Narrow versus Broad Definition of Benefits* (2010).

[100] Christopher Townley, 'The Relevant Market: An Acceptable Limit to Competition Analysis?' (2011) ECLR 490.

[101] Christopher Townley, 'Which Goals Count in Article 101 TFEU?: Public Policy and Its Discontents' (2011) ECLR 442–46; Suzanne Kingston, *Greening EU Competition Law and Policy* (CUP 2011) ch 3.

[102] See, for example, the fascinating discussion about the insurance industry in Germany and the EU Court's efforts to open up the industry to competition, undermining German public policy goals, in Michelle Everson, 'The German Federal Supervisory Authority for Insurance' in Giandomenico Majone (ed), *Regulating Europe* (Routledge 1996) 217–23.

to competition harm. This may increase the inconsistency of the application of competition provisions and undermine legal certainty. Independent NCAs may not be the best fora for balancing public policy goals and competition.[103] Finally, distorting competition may not be the most efficient way of achieving public policy goals.[104]

There can be reasonable disagreement about what a 'superior standard' is on any of these dimensions (and thus what standard(s) the ICN should be advocating). The ICN has largely been able to avoid arguments on this issue by opaquely specifying its goals, through the use of terms like 'competition'. Nevertheless, sometimes these conflicts come out into the open. Early discussions in the Unilateral Conduct Working Group (UCWG) provide a great example of this. It originally sought agreement on the best goals of unilateral conduct rules.[105] As Fox notes in her report on the first ICN Annual Conference in 2002, this issue boiled over into a discussion of the goals of competition policy more generally and the relevance of context:

> John Vickers concentrated his presentation on consumer and efficiency goals, highlighting the UK [merger] reform which moved from a public policy standard to the substantial lessening of competition standard. David Lewis defended the public interest criteria used in South Africa's law, particularly its affirmative action in favor of the long excluded black majority, as necessary and important in the context of his country's experiences ... Other speakers and interveners were more skeptical of a role for public interest in the competition law, and some preferred a model entrusting the public interest decision to a minister who is politically accountable for his or her actions.[106]

[103] Having said that, even a consumer welfare test requires significant political choices, as we have seen above, and one can always increase the relevant skills and political accountability of NCAs if this sort of balancing is considered desirable (Townley (n 5) ch 3 discusses this in more detail). Even a 'pure' consumer welfare test is unlikely to generate much legal certainty.

[104] Townley (n 101) 446–48; Townley (n 73) ch 1. Nevertheless, Atkinson, for example, is in favour of explicitly using competition policy for distributional issues. He understands that this cannot achieve fine-tuned redistribution. However, there are: '[D]istinct limits to what can be achieved by second-best taxes and transfers, and, if we wish to make a significant reduction in inequality, there has to be recourse to a whole range of measures that have a—less than perfectly targeted—equalising impact. All forms of distributional intervention are less than ideal.' Anthony Atkinson, *Inequality: What Can Be Done?* (Harvard UP 2015) 127.

[105] The UCWG was established in 2006. Its mission (which has not really changed) is to: 'examine the challenges involved in analyzing unilateral conduct of dominant firms and firms with substantial market power, facilitate greater understanding of the issues involved in analyzing unilateral conduct, and to promote greater convergence and sound enforcement of laws governing unilateral conduct'. The UCWG is currently co-chaired by the European Commission (DG COMP), the Japan Fair Trade Commission, and the South Africa Competition Commission. More information is available at <www.internationalcompetitionnetwork.org/working-groups/unilateral-conduct/> accessed 7 October 2021. For a discussion, see Cynthia Lewis Lagdameo and Andrew Heimert, 'The Unilateral Conduct Working Group' in Lugard (n 1) 287–96.

[106] Eleanor Fox, *A Report on the First Annual Conference of the International Competition Network* (2002) 4.

In other words, David Lewis is saying, the answer about whether to consider public policy in competition rules might be different depending upon the social and economic context in each country. In this case, a claim that there is one 'superior norm' that the ICN can proclaim seems unlikely. Furthermore, he also notes that, in fact, many regimes inject the consideration of public policy factors into their competition rules through different procedural processes (whether this is through carveouts, balancing, or use of politicians to do this work). Nevertheless, many competition experts consider that superior norms would ignore public policy concerns, focusing on 'pure competition factors'.[107]

States themselves might also benefit (or be harmed by) certain kinds of competition rules. This is because competitive outcomes can depend on 'structural features' (which are different in each state), such as whether an economy's growth model is import- or export-driven;[108] or the type of capitalism favoured there.[109] With such different economies, and such different demands for competition as an organizing principle,[110] it is hard to see how there could be one best substantive competition policy. Fundamental value choices are triggered when deciding to move from one economic model (CME to LME, for example) to another.[111] Major value premises are also needed for the other two issues related to disagreements on aims discussed here (which consumer welfare and the relevance of public policy). The normative frameworks that we construct from our value premises are not easily displaced by international competition harmonization,[112] like the ICN's recommended practices and other work.

We said that there were three kinds of disagreements. We have discussed disagreements on aims; there are also disagreements on methods. Even if we could all agree what the aims of competition policy and enforcement should be, there would remain (reasonable) disagreement on how best to achieve these aims. For example, even if consumer welfare were our sole competition goal, economists disagree about how much innovation would maximize consumer welfare. In 2011, the Dutch NCA (in collaboration with the ICN) did a study asking NCAs and others about the emphasis that they place on innovation in their consumer

[107] See Townley (n 5) 30–44.

[108] Guzman (n 74) 1152–55.

[109] Wigger and Nölke (n 84); Thomas Cheng, 'How Culture May Change Assumptions in Antitrust Policy' in Ioannis Lianos and Daniel Sokol (eds), *The Global Limits of Competition Law* (Stanford Law Books 2012) 206; Budzinski (n 94) 298.

[110] As well as one's preferred economic model for achieving this end, Wouter Wils, 'The Judgment of the EU General Court in Intel and the So-Called More Economic Approach to Abuse of Dominance' (2014) 37 World Competition 405.

[111] Not least because states straddling LMEs and CMEs tend to have worse economic performance, Peter Hall and Daniel Gingerich, 'Varieties of Capitalism and Institutional Complementarities in the Political Economy: An Empirical Analysis' (2009) 39 British Journal of Political Science 465–73. Similarly, Guidi (n 92) 100.

[112] Ullrich, 'International Harmonisation of Competition Law' (n 87) 12; Wolfgang Fikentscher, 'Competition, Culture, and Economic (De-)regulation' in Ullrich, *Comparative Competition Law* (n 87) 62–63.

welfare analysis. There was little consensus.[113] This is because the relationship between competition and innovation is complex and controversial (with little agreement between economists). Furthermore, differences also arise on topics like: the importance of vertical restraints;[114] the relevance of recoupment in predatory pricing;[115] the pros and cons of high pricing;[116] the need for states to support private restrictions; and the appropriate role of compulsory licensing for undertakings with dominant intellectual property rights.[117] In the end, the choices here will be based on expertise. But they will also be based on choices such as which economic theory and models to follow and the likely impact in different economies, given the culture, history, and traditions. These, once again, require deep policy choices with redistributive consequences.

The third kind of disagreement is about procedures and institutional structures. As with disagreements on aims, the varieties of capitalism literature postulate tendencies towards different procedures and institutional structures in different types of economies. For example, in LMEs one expects to see courts used as the normal arbiter of competition disputes. Courts in this structure apply competition law as if it were normal substantive law, the 'application and enforcement of generally applicable norms by neutral decision-makers'.[118] The logic is quite different in CMEs. There, competition rules involve 'the execution of economic policy decisions by administrative officials',[119] and so it seems more appropriate for an administrative decision-making process to be adopted. Under this conception of competition law, rules are interpreted by reference to the current economic policy of the relevant 'government'. Competition rules may be interpreted in different ways, from time to time, as a country's 'economic constitution' changes. As a result, those in charge of competition policy and enforcement have a wide range of discretionary 'licensing' powers.[120] This provides firms with the stability they need for long-term planning and investment.

One can see both of these systems in the EU, for example.[121] One can also see, in the EU, NCAs with different levels of independence.[122] There may also

[113] See NMa and ICN, *Competition Enforcement and Consumer Welfare: Setting the Agenda* (2011) 11–14, 25–31. For examples and further discussion, see Christopher Townley, 'Remembering Those Not Yet Born: Inter-Generational Impacts in Competition Analysis' (2011) ECLR 580.

[114] See the 2008 and 2019 reports of the Swedish Competition Authority, <www.konkurrensverket.se/en/competition/knowledge-and-research/the-pros-and-cons> accessed 7 October 2021.

[115] Barbara Gabor, *Regulatory Competition in the Internal Market* (Edward Elgar 2013) 205.

[116] See n 114.

[117] Budzinski (n 94) 302–03.

[118] David Gerber, 'Two Models of Competition Law' in Ullrich, *Comparative Competition Law* (n 87) 107.

[119] ibid 108.

[120] Wigger and Nölke (n 84) 495.

[121] Katalin Cseres, 'Comparing Laws in the Enforcement of EU and National Competition Laws' (2010) 3 European Journal of Legal Studies; Firat Cengiz, *An Academic View on the Role and Powers of National Competition Authorities: Background to the ECN Plus Project* (2016) 19–26.

[122] Although European Parliament and Council, Directive 2019/1/EU to empower the competition authorities of the Member States to be more effective enforcers and to ensure the proper functioning of

be a relationship between these diverse levels of independence and the underlying variety of capitalism in a state. Guidi hypothesizes that this is also related to system coherence within a country, which he thinks might be important for enhanced economic performance (making uniformity a potential cost or even a problem).[123] It seems likely that these institutional differences, related to the use of courts or NCAs, and varying degrees of independence (based on context-specific factors, such as history, culture, politics, and the forces of path dependency) will exert 'significant influence and constrain the potential for full substantive and procedural convergence of competition law regimes'.[124] There are some major differences in national procedural regimes too.[125] This generates tensions which might lead to disagreements. This is also important because different procedural contexts can also generate different substantive decisions in similar cases.[126] Once again, taking the EU as an example, some NCAs have less financial and human capital than others. To compound this, the ability of NCAs to adopt administrative priority rulings varies considerably.[127] This affects where they can focus their resources. In addition, some NCAs have fewer enforcement tools than others. For example, some cannot gather electronic evidence stored on computers and mobile phones. Diversity also exists in the power to seal evidence in premises, the limits of legal privilege, the ability to sanction breaches of the NCAs' powers, and the standard of proof.[128] Moreover, the level of fines between Member States can vary greatly.[129] Some use criminal sanctions.[130] Finally, there are differences in the leniency programmes in the EU. The EU has made recent efforts to try to reduce many of these differences, nevertheless, the fact that they have sought to do this demonstrates the importance (in terms of outcomes) that some of these differences can generate.

the internal market (2019) ch III, seeks to guarantee the independence of national administrative competition authorities when applying certain EU competition rules.

[123] Mattia Guidi, 'Delegation and Varieties of Capitalism: Explaining the Independence of National Competition Authorities in the European Union' (2014) 12 Comparative European Politics 343.

[124] Eleanor Fox and Michael Trebilcock, 'The Design of Competition Law Institutions and the Global Convergence of Process Norms: The GAL Competition Project' (2012) New York University Law and Economics Working Papers IV.

[125] In relation to the EU, for example, Cengiz (n 121) s 2.

[126] Annetje Ottow, *Market and Competition Authorities: Good Agency Principles* (OUP 2015) 34, 90, and 96; Fox and Trebilcock (n 124) IIA and IV.

[127] Michael Wise, *Competition Law and Policy in the European Union* (2007) 40–48; and Wouter Wils, 'Competition Authorities: Towards More Independence and Prioritisation?' (New Frontiers of Antitrust, 8th International Concurrences Review Conference) 36–38.

[128] Olle Rislund, 'Legal Professional Privilege in EU Competition Proceedings—Time for Legislation?' in Martin Johansson, Nils Wahl and Ulf Bernitz (eds), *Liber Amicorum in Honour of Sven Norberg: A European for all seasons* (Etablissements Emile Bruylant 2006).

[129] Ioannis Lianos and others, 'An Optimal and Just Financial Penalties System for Infringements of Competition Law: a comparative analysis' (2014) CLES Research Paper No 3/2014.

[130] Wise (n 127) 72; Wouter Wils, *Efficiency and Justice in European Antitrust Enforcement* (Hart 2008) 155–201.

This 'need' for diversity stands in stark contrast to 'technocratic' projects like the ICN which (despite what they say) seek to push one best or better answer to many competition problems, often without mentioning the values compromised or sacrificed on the altar of uniformity. This phenomenon is not restricted to this area. For example, Koskenniemi points to similar arguments in public international law, which also produces many moral and political choices and produces unequal impacts. However, he says, without political institutions, these choices are made by:

> experts and advisors, economists, technicians, scientists and lawyers, all having recourse to the technical vocabularies of ad hoc accommodation, co-ordination and optimal effect. Utilitarianism is the political constitution of the de-politicised world.

He adds that we need to (re-)politicize governance:

> to re-think the activity of expert institutions not as the technical production of pre-determined decisions by some anonymous logic, but choices by well-placed men and women . . . where power happens.[131]

In other words, even if our focus is a technical one, technocrats (including competition officials) make choices which can have highly redistributive consequences for society. This is why some believe (especially those outside the competition community) that competition needs to be 'controlled' or 'limited' to protect the losers to some degree. There are different models of capitalism, and states are entitled to pick their preferred model. Some might prefer to redistribute resources during competition enforcement itself; others might prefer to wait until after the competitive process has taken place; others, might like to mix these two approaches. Some competition policy approaches might focus on principles that go beyond consumer welfare (such as social sustainability, employment). Even if diversity undermines efficient competition enforcement (eg extra costs of business, and externalities), citizens may still want it where it allows local NCAs to implement local preferences (for 'controls' or 'limits'). This should increase legitimacy at the national level (assuming this is where intervention occurs).[132]

The influence of the epistemic community seeking a more technocratic focus in competition policy and enforcement (maximizing efficiency through free markets and separating out efficiency and equity) is growing. We have seen this debate arising within the ICN already. Within the UCWG the fact that a strong character,

[131] Martti Koskenniemi, *The Politics of International Law* (Hart 2011) 359–60.

[132] Similar positions emerge in international trade (Rodrik (n 91)) and EU projects, such as the euro (Joseph Stiglitz, 'The Problem with Europe is the Euro' *The Guardian* (10 August 2016) <www.theguardian.com/business/2016/aug/10/joseph-stiglitz-the-problem-with-europe-is-the-euro?page=with%3Aimg-3> Accessed 7 October 2021. See also the discussion in Townley (n 5) Introduction.

David Lewis, from a relatively rich 'developing country', was involved meant he was able to withstand the criticism and difference in ways that many others would not have felt able to tolerate. We also saw that there are many reasons why different states might (reasonably) disagree on what competition policy works best for them. To be fair to the ICN, there is clear and repeated emphasis that it is not mandatory for its member states to adopt ICN recommended practices. Implementation is up to the individual state involved. Having said that, as we also saw, the ICN is (increasingly) placing emphasis on ensuring the implementation of its recommended practices (Chapter 2 has more details).

'Imposing' one uniform competition system on diverse states, without reflecting upon the implications on the ground in each case, is likely to cause major redistributive problems (not all of which can be remedied after the event (and doing this can, itself, be costly), even if there were the political will to do so, which there is often not). Embracing diversity also allows widespread experimentation with different approaches to competition worldwide. This can generate more effectiveness and legitimacy benefits, over time.[133] It also facilitates comparisons. In the words of Kerber and Budzinski:

> [G]overnments, competition authorities staff, and citizens (as voters) can use the experiences of other countries to reassess their own competition regimes. This allows for correcting errors, imitating superior rules, enforcement mechanisms, theories and practices, or simply avoiding mistakes that others have made.[134]

However, there is a deeper reason why allowing and even encouraging difference may be important. There are many economic theories and societal systems. Understanding them is highly complex and contingent. We can never be sure that we know what the best practices are, given the fallibility of human knowledge. If we allow the world economic system to remain open to different opinions and theories, then we produce more flexible and innovative competition systems (less prone to systemic failure). As Budzinski explains:

> Decentralisation of competences enhances both the reaction flexibility (resonance ability) and the innovation permeability (openness to knowledge inflow) of the competition regime. The reason is not that each local agency and institution is inherently more adaptable. Instead, the decisive effect is that institutional and agential diversity (i) offers additional channels for the injection of new ideas and (ii) allows for mutual learning due to parallel experimentation with different

[133] Scharpf links problem solving power and legitimacy more generally: Fritz Scharpf, *Governing in Europe: Effective and Democratic?* (OUP 1999) 1.

[134] Wolfgang Kerber and Oliver Budzinski, 'Towards a Differentiated Analysis of Competition of Competition Laws' (2003) ZWeR—Journal of Competition Law 411, 419.

> practices, concepts, ideas, institutional solutions, etc.[135] The existence and interaction of a horizontal (ie on the same jurisdictional level) and vertical (ie on upstream or downstream jurisdictional levels) variety and plurality represents an evolutionary value.[136]

These benefits can improve the quality, flexibility, and robustness of our economic systems.

Having said that, diversity does have costs. Different legal systems can shield firms from competition when we do not want that, it can also raise costs of firms seeking to enter new markets (and thus raise prices for consumers and reduce their choice where market entry is discouraged).[137] In addition, given the power that firms have in playing states off against each other and so pushing them to manipulate economic regulation in the ways they want, one might believe that if all states agreed the same economic rules (including competition), then this might offer some protection against such effects.[138] However, Chapter 1 gives reason for caution for those having confidence in such processes or outcomes.

So, both uniformity and diversity bring potential benefits. Furthermore, as Rodrik explains, democracy, national determination, and economic globalization are in tension.[139] Globalization, which is what the ICN is pushing for, demands politics that are less domestic: 'The greater the emphasis on deep economic integration, the less the room for national differences in social and economic arrangements, and the smaller the space for democratic decision making at the national level.'[140] This is particularly important given the space for (and presence of) disagreements in the highly redistributive competition rules; and the fact that, many informal transnational networks are not optimally designed to solve the problems they face (see above).

I.4 Definitions (legitimacy, effectiveness, and efficiency)

Political philosophers discuss what makes governance by political orders 'good'. For a long time, work focused on 'legitimacy'; however, Weber also introduced the

[135] A uniform, centralized regime, on the other hand, can theoretically only test alternative practices sequentially. This slows down learning processes about best practices and benchmarks. Moreover, sclerotic institutions that refuse to deal with innovation are more probable in centralized regimes.

[136] Oliver Budzinski, 'An Economic Perspective on the Jurisdictional Reform of the European Merger Control System' (2006) 2 European Competition Journal, 126–27. Similarly, see Roger Van Den Bergh, 'Economic Criteria for Applying the Subsidiarity Principle in the European Community: The Case for Competition Policy' (1996) 16 International Review of Law and Economics 363, 366.

[137] OECD, *A Single Market for Europe* (OECD Publishing 2012) 37.

[138] Stiglitz (n 132) 1; Scharpf (n 133) 40; Bob Jessop, 'Multi-level Governance and Multi-level Metagovernance' in Ian Bache and Matthew Flinders (eds), *Multi-Level Governance* (OUP 2004) 66.

[139] Rodrik (n 91) xviii.

[140] ibid 205; see also 189–90 and 200.

concept of 'effectiveness', which is less of a normative standard.[141] Börzel and Panke highlight two dimensions of 'effectiveness':

> Firstly, effective governance produces policies that solve problems and satisfy the demands they were designed to cope with (goal attainment; problem-solving capacity). Secondly, effective governance requires the production of sufficient policy output without delays or deadlocks at reasonable cost (efficiency). Like legitimacy, effectiveness is a standard for good governance, because it contributes to the maintenance of political systems.[142]

This book discusses all three of these criteria: legitimacy, effectiveness, and efficiency. So, we need to specify what we mean by each criterion; and whose perspective we adopt when assessing them.[143] Here we provide working definitions of these concepts to aid readers of Chapters 1–3. Chapter 4 provides more depth, as that becomes necessary.

Let's start with effectiveness. Héritier and Lehmkuhl call 'policy effectiveness' the extent to which a policy achieves the goals defined at the start.[144] 'Effectiveness' is an important governance criterion. Governance mechanisms that are unable to solve problems and achieve their goals are hard to justify, from a functional perspective.[145] Note that 'effectiveness' does not ask about the rationality or appropriateness of the goal(s) set, nor how well they link with other policies, etc.[146]

So, how should one assess the ICN's effectiveness? Early on, one needs to decide whether the focus should be on the ICN's effectiveness as a discussion forum, learning about insights that others have had, comparing methods and systems, debating what is best? Or, should the focus be on whether the ICN produces policies and generates changes that solve the problems that it was designed to address? This is a process-versus-outputs discussion, although they are likely to interrelate to some degree. To answer the 'outputs' question, we would also need to know what the ICN's goals are, whether they are clearly specified and how they are supposed

[141] Max Weber, *Economy and Society* (University of California Press 1978).

[142] Tanja Börzel and Diana Panke, 'Network Governance: Effective and Legitimate?' in Eva Sørensen and Jacob Torfing (eds), *Theories of Democratic Network Governance* (Palgrave MacMillan 2008) 157.

[143] Patrick Kenis and Keith Provan, 'Towards an Exogenous Theory of Public Network Performance' (2009) 87 Public Administration 442.

[144] Adrienne Héritier and Dirk Lehmkuhl, 'Governing in the Shadow of Hierarchy: New Modes of Governance in Regulation' in Adrienne Héritier and Martin Rhodes (eds), *New Modes of Governance in Europe: Governing in the Shadow of Hierarchy* (Palgrave Macmillan 2011) 66.

[145] Börzel and Panke (n 142) 157.

[146] Snyder defines 'effectiveness' in another way, by looking at who is affected by a process. According to him, law matters if 'it has effects on political, economic and social life outside the law—that is, apart from simply the elaboration of legal doctrine'. Francis Snyder, *New Directions in European Community Law* (Weidenfeld & Nicolson 1990) 3. In a study of competition rules, Scharpf uses another criterion to assess effectiveness (how widely laws are applied), Fritz Scharpf, 'Notes Towards a Theory of Multi-level Governing in Europe' (2000) MPIfG Discussion Paper 00/5, 16. However, our focus is policy outcomes, compared to the original goals set.

to interrelate when they conflict. A second aspect of an 'outputs' assessment relates to the extent and nature of ICN outputs. On the one hand, there is an issue of speed and quantity. Has the ICN effectively produced sufficient policy output in a timely manner? On the other hand, the value of the ICN outputs is also relevant. For example, the ICN might be effective at generating consensus in a few 'easy' areas. Is it also able to achieve meaningful consensus where disagreements run deeper? A third set of issues arises when measuring 'output' effectiveness. Is mere production of ICN recommended practices and other work products sufficient? Or is implementation of these ICN outputs needed too (implementation might become more important as it becomes a more central ICN preoccupation)? At a further level of abstraction, is the issue of evidence. Can we simply assume that states achieve their goals with ICN work products if they use them? In other words, are we content to assume ICN benefits once its outputs are used, or do we want evidence that ICN outputs actually improve NCA effectiveness? If we demand evidence, empirical or even anecdotal, how accurately should (or can) this be assessed? These discussions of effectiveness are also linked. It may be, for example, that the ICN finds it relatively easy to agree recommended practices (it might be that those in the competition community think in similar ways, for example). However, if the views of the competition community, rightly or wrongly, do not reflect the views of wider society then implementation of ICN recommended practices in states might be much harder to achieve (especially when changes are not just reliant on NCAs).

In our effectiveness assessment, we isolate various goals that the ICN has set itself. We then assess the ICN on each of these goals. This is not always easy. Many ICN goals are not clearly specified. There is also a general lack of transparency about how ICN goals are prioritized when they conflict. We point to flaws in the way the ICN gathers evidence of effectiveness too. Finally, for an organization that claims to be 'results-based', the ICN spends remarkably little time and effort assessing the efficiency and effectiveness of its actions (eg when its work is implemented by NCAs/states, do superior outcomes occur there and at what cost?).

Turning to 'efficiency', the costs of the process for generating ICN work products need to be assessed. Can savings be made (in time or money) while still achieving a certain level of effectiveness in these outputs? We also need to check whether, using ICN work products, NCAs achieve a certain level of effectiveness more quickly and/or cheaply than would otherwise be the case.[147] Efficiency has several dimensions; so, optimally efficient structures are unlikely to be unique, but a result of trade-offs.[148] For example, it may be more efficient for competition experts to outline 'best practice' competition policy and enforcement techniques. If this is

[147] Similarly, in a network study on the higher education policy sector in Sweden, see Annica Sandstöm and Lars Carlsson, 'The Performance of Policy Networks: The Relation between Network Structure and Network Performance' (2008) 36 Policy Studies Journal 502.

[148] Liesbet Hooghe and Gary Marks, 'Does Efficiency Shape the Territorial Structure of Government?' (2009) 12 Annual Review of Political Science 226–27.

correct, relying on policies produced by these experts may also lead to better competition decisions, and thus fewer appeals and disputes (and thus more efficient competition enforcement too).

If one were to rely solely on competition experts to devise competition policy, this might include all those working in the NCAs (perhaps also those working in the ICN's NGAs?). Certainly, this community could be much more efficient than devising competition policy in parliaments, for example, in the sense that those in the competition community often have quite similar backgrounds and beliefs, making it easier for them to come to agreement. Some might think that it could be even more efficient to restrict input to an even smaller, more homogeneous, group of experts, rather than involving the wider ICN community. Many in the competition community believe that it would be better to exclude public interest criteria from competition decisions (considering environmental and other policy issues elsewhere); but this is not unanimous.[149] As we show below, disagreements exist on many dimensions. On the other hand, if actors that have not been consulted are less likely to accept ICN recommended practices, any increased disputes may, in the long term, reduce systemic efficiency. Even if a political order can solve problems and achieve its goals effectively, if the costs of doing this are prohibitively expensive, then we may question that order's efficiency and it might have to be reorganized.

As we have already noted, a political order's stability does not only depend on its 'effectiveness' and 'efficiency', but will in the end be judged by individuals' compliance with collectively binding rules. This is a function of legitimacy. According to Börzel and Panke:

> Legitimacy is conducive to the maintenance and stability of political order, since the attribution of rightness to the existence of a political system institutionalises compliance as a norm, which guides individual action even in cases of incompatible interests … Should individuals disobey, a legitimate political order enjoys the generalised support of the vast majority of its subjects, in exercising the use of coercive force as the last resort for restoring compliance.[150]

For the purposes of this discussion, legitimacy ultimately involves ensuring that the level and type of competition enforcement reflects the current competition policy within a jurisdiction; and that the current competition policy represents the wishes of the citizens that it affects.[151] The normal way for ensuring this in a democracy is majoritarian control. There are many choices here, such as removing NCA discretion through precise laws or, directly electing the leaders of the NCA.

[149] See the discussion about South Africa's competition goals, around n 78.
[150] Börzel and Panke (n 142) 160.
[151] Yannis Papadopoulos, *Accountability and Multi-level Governance* (OUP 2014) 274.

In many states, democratic (participatory) accountability is an important social value in and of itself and so more direct intervention might be desired.

Now, an initial response is likely to be that one does not need to worry about legitimacy and the ICN. This is for two reasons. First, as we have seen, ICN work products are only accepted as official ICN statements once they have been agreed by consensus within the ICN (or, to put it another way, as long as no NCA has objected to it). However, we have asserted above (and Chapters 1 and 3 support this assertion both theoretically and empirically), that the consensus rule is unlikely to effectively protect newer NCAs (or their states). Nevertheless, even if this is correct, there is a second reason why some might say that one does not need to worry about legitimacy and the ICN. ICN work products are not binding. It is up to states whether or not they choose to implement them. However, while this is formally true, Chapter 2 shows how this rule is unlikely to effectively protect newer NCAs (or their states) either. Once again, Chapter 3's interview responses supports this empirically.

So, if we are to consider legitimacy and the ICN, how should one do this? Two issues arise when seeking to apply majoritarian logic to an entity like the ICN which deals with the production of competition policy. The first is that, as a transnational organization involving actors from around the world, it is unclear what sort of majoritarian oversight could be invoked. There is, after all, no global parliament. The second issue arises because the trend today is to reduce majoritarian control over NCAs even within national orders (in fact, this is one of the policies that the ICN encourages). So, it could be that it is not appropriate to demand majoritarian control for the production of competition policy (and even less its enforcement) involving competition officials (and their NCAs) from around the world. This is an issue that reasonable people (and states) might (and do) disagree about.[152]

Part of one's view of the legitimacy of such processes links to one's understanding of democracy. Democracy comes in many guises and there are many different ways of legitimizing these processes (some of which overlap). An important insight of this book is that legitimacy may be insufficiently considered in relation to the ICN. We believe that each state must assess the ICN and its outputs (as well as how they should be used in that state) through a legitimacy lens shaped by that state's understanding of democracy. As so many states use ICN work products, each with different versions of democracy, many legitimacy assessments are potentially relevant. They may also change over time. So, we consider it more useful to provide states (and others) with a toolbox which they can use to make their own legitimacy assessments. Morgan and Yeung call this 'middle level' theorizing.[153] Baldwin uses

[152] For example, Townley argues that independence is not normally appropriate for NCAs (n 5). Guidi, though not against independence in principle, warns that its supposed benefits must be thoroughly checked and not taken for granted (see Guidi (n 92)). See also Mariana Tavares, 'The ICN: One of the Many International Priorities' in Lugard (n 1).

[153] Morgan Bronwen and Karen Yeung, *An Introduction to Law and Regulation* (CUP 2007) 222–28.

this distinction when he urges us to work out the role of normative political theories and legitimacy assessments. For Baldwin, normative political theories (different versions of democracy) 'make statements about the way that society or government ought to be organized and will commonly attempt to derive such statements from premises allegedly immune from contention'. Legitimacy assessments (logics of justification) are different and operate at a distinct level. Legitimacy assessments involve judgements about 'the merits of legitimacy claims' but they can be thought of as an intermediate discourse. This is because legitimacy assessments allow 'a discussion of legitimacy to take place without immediate linkage to any particular vision of democracy'.[154]

In the absence of direct majoritarian control, Baldwin offers five factors that independent authorities often invoke to demonstrate the legitimacy of their interventions. He is speaking about independent regulatory authorities more generally, but his comments seem applicable to NCAs. For Baldwin, independent authorities can use a legislative argument, claiming a mandate for their actions from a majoritarian body (eg a parliament); there is an accountability rationale, highlighting control of the authority by representative groupings (as power increases, so does the need for accountability);[155] the due process rationale, argues that fair procedures are used; the expertise rationale says that the decisions were reached by experts, in the public interest; and the efficiency rationale says that the independent mandate is being pursued efficiently and effectively.[156] Claims under each of Baldwin's five heads can be contentious. For example, the legislative mandate might leave room for discretion, or it might be hard to show that the experts act in the public interest, in fact. It is the combination of these factors that Baldwin thought should be considered, rather than merely relying on one, alone.[157]

Many of Baldwin's factors do not make immediate sense when applied to a transnational network like the ICN. For example, which majoritarian body could have given it a mandate, who could control it, and what notions of due process would one resort to here? One way out of this cul-de-sac may be for states to examine the legitimacy of the ICN indirectly. They might do this by considering the legitimacy of their own NCAs' actions when setting up, joining, and acting in the ICN. States might also consider the legitimacy of ICN claims that it is creating 'superior' norms

[154] Robert Baldwin, *Rules and Government* (Clarendon Press 1995) 54.

[155] OECD, *Annex to the Summary Record of the 122nd Meeting of the Competition Committee Held on 17–18 December 2014* (2015) 15.

[156] Robert Baldwin, 'Regulatory Legitimacy in the European Context: The British Health and Safety Executive' in Majone (n 102) 90.

[157] Colin Scott, 'Governing without Law or Governing without Government? New-ish Governance and the Legitimacy of the EU' (2009) 15 European Law Journal, 161.

Note that Baldwin includes efficiency and effectiveness as dimensions of legitimacy, whereas in this book we have separated them out. We have done this because efficiency and effectiveness are widely accepted as relevant factors (by the competition community) for assessing regulatory systems. Given the way that these terms are used among this community, we have found it clearer to separate them out. Whether or not one does this should not alter final discussions in any material way.

in the light of both the ways that the underlying ICN goals have been set; and the power dynamics that are at work within the ICN itself. Each state must also decide whether it is legitimate for it to directly incorporate these 'superior ICN norms' into its own legal order (either through legislative change or by allowing its NCA or courts to do this without legislative change). Linked to these issues, as further explained in Chapter 1, states might also have reason to consider the influence that foreign legal orders have on their own order through training and other programs.

Our focus thus far has been on legitimacy, effectiveness, and efficiency as separate phenomena. However, all three phenomena, might interact in new, different ways. For example, it might be much more efficient (in terms of time and resources) for a group of multinational companies and their lawyers to sit down with NCA officials from a small group of rich states (who often have a similar perspective as many trained in these firms) and draft ICN recommended practices. However, this more limited set of inputs into the production of these drafts might mean that they are unaware of particular policy or enforcement differences in countries that are not actively involved in producing these drafts. This might mean that drafts produced in this way, even if agreed upon in the ICN, might be less effective and legitimate in certain places. Of course, while dealing with a wider group of NGAs and NCAs might be more effective, it might not be the most efficient and legitimate way of getting such information (perhaps only some stakeholders are allowed into ICN meetings or can afford to attend them). Perhaps better mechanisms can be explored. Trade-offs are possible on all dimensions. Dynamic improvements can also be important; so, they also need to be considered.

A point about the transparency of the ICN also should be mentioned here. This affects the assessment of (and one's ability to assess) the ICN's legitimacy, efficiency, and effectiveness. At first sight, the ICN seems incredibly transparent. It has a website which is rich with descriptions of the various working groups, papers from the various conferences, and timings for the various meetings that will be held or have been held. However, in our view, this 'transparency' conceals real opacity.[158] Some information on the ICN's website is conspicuous by its absence. For example, there is nothing on the names of those who participated in each session and their role. There is general information on who leads specific working groups, but nothing on who was involved in specific projects and what they did there.[159] No indication is given of where ideas have come from for certain recommended practices or other initiatives and whether these ideas were tested with other stakeholders (and with whom). We do not know who was asked to write the first draft (a tremendously influential position); nor do we know who suggested changes, and why they were

[158] Similarly, in relation to the ICN and other similar transnational networks, see Verdier (n 10) 118.
[159] For example, ICN documents often do not list an author, nor are they dated. In addition, Steering Group mandates and other documents only started being reported in May 2011, whereas they are referred to and seem influential well before then, *Unilateral Conduct Working Group—Mandate* (2006) 1.

rejected, or not. Nor is there any indication of who, if anyone, was left out of consultations (or, more likely, who was sidelined, or only heard, but not listened to). The problems that this book highlights are exacerbated by this lack of transparency.

When arguing for a better system (or analysing how good an existing system is), one must consider legitimacy, effectiveness, and efficiency. If all agree that any of these three can be improved without undermining the other two, the system is likely to be 'better' for the change. Outside of this exceptional case, the best balance of different values will vary under different visions of democracy. Once again, this demands value judgements that cannot be dodged through a pivot to 'expertise'. It is for this reason that we advise any state using ICN products to assess the balance of legitimacy, effectiveness, and efficiency for itself and its own system.

I.5 State of the art and methodology

In terms of the 'state of the art', many competition books are currently available. They often start from the premise that competition is a good thing, benefiting everyone. It is common in competition scholarship to find interdisciplinary work combining law and economics. They aim to provide better rules to encourage competition more completely. There is a reasonable amount of work at the political science–competition law interface, but there remains a lot to do. This is especially true in the space that considers the value-laden nature of competition policy, where power lies in the choosing (or exclusion) of values and norms, and who is likely to win and who to lose from these choices. This is important work because there are winners and losers.

Back in 2010 Gerber said the ICN is new and has not been systemically studied.[160] A decade later, it is less new, but systematic study remains sparse. There are very few books or other literature critically examining the ICN. The best examples to our knowledge are *The International Competition Network at Ten* (2011),[161] which focuses on the ICN's origins, accomplishments, and aspirations. This is a largely uncritical and historical work by various authors (including Dr Tavares). More widely, there is an interesting article by Djelic and Kleiner, focusing on ICN history and placing that in the wider context of transnational governance.[162] Verdier and Gaus also write more general theoretical pieces discussing the ICN and other informal networks.[163] More recently, Roger has done a similar thing in relation to the

[160] Gerber (n 14) 115.

[161] Lugard (n 1). An updated edited ICN book from Paul Lugard came out in 2021, which includes an earlier version of Chapter 1 in this publication.

[162] Marie-Laure Djelic and Thibaut Kleiner, 'The International Competition Network: moving towards transnational governance' in Marie-Laure Djelic and Kerstin Sahlin-Andersson (eds), *Transnational Governance: Institutional Dynamics of Regulation* (CUP 2009).

[163] Verdier (n 10); Alexander Gaus, 'Speaking Truth to Power and Control in Transgovernmental Networks' (ICPP 2015 International Conference on Public Policy).

creation of informal international organizations. He also specifically uses the ICN as a case study.[164] Even more recently, Svetiev examines the ICN (and other organizations) from an experimentalist governance perspective.[165]

Most of these works suffer from at least one of two main problems. On the one hand, they have not managed to get deep inside the ICN, in order to concretely understand the complexities of what is going on (although this is not so of many of the writers in *The International Competition Network at Ten*).[166] This is a core contribution that our book makes (and an important one, given the opacity of the ICN and how it really works). As with these other works, the methodology that we have adopted primarily uses the materials available on the ICN's own website (www.internationalcompetitionnetwork.org). We supplement these with library-based reading of the theoretical approaches in, particularly, law, political science, and international relations theory that predict what is likely to happen and why. In addition, we have tested these readings in three ways. First, with a survey conducted between May and August 2018 among members of competition authorities participating in the ICN and ICN NGAs (Roger does this too; Verdier and Gaus also conduct interviews). Chapter 3 describes our findings from this survey. Second, Dr Tavares has been present in many ICN meetings and has an intimate knowledge of the ICN from the inside, from a time when she was a representative of the Portuguese Competition Authority there. Third, these insights have also been tested in discussions with our many friends and colleagues who have contributed to the establishment of the ICN and its work (see also Svetiev and Djelic and Kleiner). We hope that this combination leads to useful insights. On the other hand, more recent ICN reforms, including the composition of NGAs and the new focus of the ICN on implementation rather than new policy instruments, mean that earlier contributions on the ICN are increasingly out of date. Further, by bringing together empirical and qualitative techniques, from both law and political science, we hope to bring a new richness to the discussion.

[164] Roger (n 48).

[165] Yane Svetiev, 'The Limits of Informal International Law: enforcement, norm generation, and learning in the ICN' in Joost Pauwelyn, Ramses Wessel and Jan Wouters (eds), *Informal International Lawmaking* (OUP 2012). See also Svetiev (n 9) ch 5.

[166] On the importance of this for such work see, for example, Verdier (n 10) 165 and the references there.

1

Influence in the ICN

Who seeks it, how do they do this, and why?

1.1 Introduction

Some have proposed policy networks as a form of governance. Börzel notes a common:

> [U]nderstanding, a minimal or lowest common denominator definition of a policy network, as a set of relatively stable relationships which are of non-hierarchical and inter-dependent nature linking a variety of actors, who share common interests with regard to a policy and who exchange resources to pursue these shared interests acknowledging that co-operation is the best way to achieve common goals.[1]

Transnational networks (like the ICN) involve domestic officials from different countries, specializing in a certain area or issue (rather than being supervised by diplomats, for example).[2] The last 50 years have seen an explosion in the number of transnational policy networks (overlapping with the rise of informal international organizations, discussed in the Introduction). We call these networks 'transnational' because they involve officials from different countries. The network actors agree to search together for the best solutions to their common goals. Network actors, and their states, are then (often) free to decide whether, or not, to adopt the solutions found (although various pressures to implement may apply, in fact).

At least four factors seem to be driving this push towards networks today. First, states often struggle with similar matters, such as controlling fast-moving

[1] Tanja Börzel, 'What's So Special about Policy Networks? An Exploration of the Concept and Its Usefulness in Studying European Governance' (1997) 1 European Integration Online Papers, 1. Similarly, see Grahame Thompson, *Between Hierarchies and Markets: The Logic and Limits of Network Forms of Organization* (OUP 2003) 30–31.

[2] 'They allow domestic officials to interact with their foreign counterparts directly, without much supervision by foreign offices or senior executive branch officials, and feature "loosely structured, peer-to-peer ties developed through frequent interaction rather than formal negotiation"' Kal Raustiala, 'The Architecture of International Co-operation: Transgovernmental Networks and the Future of International Law' (2002) 43 Virginia Journal of International Law 1, 5; Anne-Marie Slaughter and Thomas Hale, 'Transgovernmental Networks and Multi-Level Governance' in Henrik Enderlein, Sonja Wälti and Michael Zürn (eds), *Handbook on Multi-Level Governance* (Edward Elgar 2010) 358.

The Law and Politics of Global Competition. Christopher Townley, Mattia Guidi, and Mariana Tavares, Oxford University Press.
 DOI: 10.1093/oso/9780198859789.003.0002

technologies or pollution. The widespread lowering of trade barriers has led to increasing interdependence between countries. States often cannot control or eliminate problems that they face by themselves. This pushes them to explore different ideas of how to solve common problems (or to explain why they are acting in a certain way in their jurisdiction). For example, lowering tariffs between states increases competition between them, which might encourage international cartels. Should they be stopped? If so, how best to share information and policy choices in order to do this? Second, while states may have different substantive rules in such areas, state structures are often similar, which means that similar bodies working on particular issues are often available (national competition authorities (NCAs), for example). This facilitates contacts and cooperation between officials facing common policy and enforcement problems. Third, independent network exchanges may be further facilitated where regulators in a certain area are commonly insulated from political influence. This is often the case in the competition field, for example. Independence means that the regulators are used to operating without consulting others. The opaque boundaries of their independence also make other actors nervous of interfering with NCAs (an attitude that NCAs have worked hard to foster). Fourth, technological innovations (such as the internet) make this sort of cooperation faster, cheaper, and easier today.[3]

Some see policy networks, like the ICN, as a good way of dealing with transnational problems, supplementing normal national democratic institutions.[4] Such networks enhance states' ability to influence (even if they cannot control) what happens beyond their borders. This can improve efficiency and effectiveness at both a global and a local level. As we will see, the ICN also claims that being a diverse, consensus-led body enhances its legitimacy too.

However, a wealth of political science and international relations literature warns us not to focus solely on formal decision-making processes when analysing networks. Networks are often portrayed neutrally, but (like all institutions) networks are political. They facilitate and constrain actors and outcomes,[5] creating winners and losers, depending upon how they are designed and how they are used. They can sometimes reduce legitimacy, effectiveness, and efficiency too.[6]

[3] Raustiala (n 2) 12–15.

[4] For example, RAW Rhodes, *Understanding Governance: Policy Networks, Governance, Reflexivity and Accountability* (Open UP 1997) 9.

[5] ibid 11, see also 160. Specifically in relation to the European Competition Network (ECN), Wilks and Sturm argue that networks are political structures and Schaub and Tesauro protest at this characterization, Claus Dieter Ehlermann and Laraine Laudati (eds), *European Competition Law Annual 1997: Objectives of Competition Policy* (Hart 1998) 15, 34–35, 66, 77, 79, and 172–73.

[6] Tanja Börzel, 'Organising Babylon—On the Different Conceptions of Policy Networks' (1998) 76 Public Administration Review 253, 253; Beate Kohler-Koch, 'Interdependent European Governance' in Beate Kohler-Koch (ed), *Linking EU and National Governance* (OUP 2003) 140–41.

So, when we analyse a network like the ICN, it is important to determine who is inside and who is outside the network. It is also important to see who is influential in the network, as well as why and how they seek this influence there.

Many stakeholders are (potentially) affected by the substantive and procedural content of the competition rules. Some seem positive about the diversity of ICN participants.[7] We are less sanguine. We list relevant stakeholders here. Only those in *italics* are currently represented in the ICN: *consumers* (in all the various states);[8] parliaments (as their rules are affected); courts; *the national competition authorities*; *big* and small *businesses*; *big* and small *law firms*; *economic consultants*; *international organizations in favour of* (or rejecting) *such rules*; those whose separate system is affected by the competition rules (eg due to externalities that clash with competition provisions, such as intellectual property or environmental norms).

Furthermore, as Fox argues, developed countries are the most active (and influential) in setting the ICN's agenda and designing the content of its recommended practices.[9] Similarly, Ng says:

> Due to the power dynamics that are inherent in the institutions and mechanisms that formulate and propagate international competition law norms [in part through the ICN], they are heavily influenced by and reflect the perspectives and practices of the United States, European Union and developed countries more generally.[10]

This chapter explores two main issues: Section 1.2 describes who is present in the ICN (NCAs, rather than states, and NGAs), and it discusses why they are there and whose interests they are protecting; Section 1.3 analyses how some influence the ICN's agenda and work product.

We will see that many ICN structures and practices potentially (and, in fact, do) favour a narrow set of advanced economies. Additionally, ICN systems and outputs also favour multinational firms (and their advisers) from these same states. This is because these actors manipulate ICN network structure and practices to their advantage. Theory predicts that rules about unanimous decision-making will not be a strong enough bulwark against such efforts. As we will see, many in the ICN agree that some actors are more equal than others. Chapter 2 explores a linked issue, that is how free are network members (and their states) to ignore ICN solutions (ICN rules explicitly say they are free to ignore them).

[7] Daniel Sokol, 'The ICN in the Context of International Antitrust Institutions' in Paul Lugard (ed), *The International Competition Network at Ten: Origins, Accomplishments and Aspirations* (Intersentia 2011) 157–58.

[8] Some consumers are represented, however these consumers' NGAs represent a minority and do not include consumers from many states, <www.icnblog.org/?p=130> accessed 7 October 2021.

[9] Eleanor Fox, 'Linked-In: Antitrust and the Virtues of a Virtual Network' in Lugard (n 7) 106.

[10] Wendy Ng, 'Changing Global Dynamics and International Competition Law: Considering China's Potential Impact' (14th ASCOLA Conference) 5.

1.2 Influence: who is present in the ICN (and who is not) and why

Political theorists underline networks' power to influence. Influence might mean developing new ideas or legitimizing certain courses of conduct. According to Schmidt and Radaelli, networks are particularly influential where their discourse 'contains cognitive arguments that demonstrate the policy programme's relevance, applicability and coherence: and normative arguments that resonate with long-standing or newly emerging values'.[11] Wilks says that the:

> programme of activities 'intended to foster the creation of a common competition culture' ... matches the discourse concept rather neatly. It is primarily co-ordinative, it embraces a cognitive framework drawing on competition law and economics, and it has a strong normative thrust in pursuit of the perceived benefits of competition.[12]

The composition of those present in the ICN (and those who are not) is important in terms of who has (the potential for) influence there. NCAs are key actors in the ICN. They are the focus of Section 1.2.1. We start by asking whether it matters that this is an organization of competition authorities rather than states (Section 1.2.1.1). Then, we look more specifically at which competition authorities are present in the ICN (as well as which are not there) and ask why this might be (Section 1.2.1.2). Each subsection starts by cataloguing the relevant categories of actors; looks at what reasons they give for their engagement in the ICN; and then compares these reasons to the academic theories of influence (as well as what other ICN actors say).

At this point, the ICN may look like an organization made up of a balanced group of NCAs with almost global reach. However, NCAs are not the only actors that are keen to be involved. In fact, the ICN has always been open to a group of private actors too. In the ICN's own words:

> While it is primarily a network of competition authorities, the ICN has always sought to reach out to the entire competition community and take on additional expert advice through the engagement of Non-Governmental Advisors

[11] Vivien Schmidt and Claudio Radaelli, 'Policy Change and Discourse in Europe: Conceptual and Methodological Issues' (2006) 27 West European Politics 188.

[12] Stephen Wilks, 'Agencies, Networks, Discourses and the Trajectory of the European Competition Enforcement' (2007) 3 European Competition Journal 437, 430 (this was in relation to proposals for a European Competition Network, but similar points apply to the ICN). Similarly, Sonja Wälti, 'Multi-Level Environmental Governance' in Enderlein and others (n 2) 416; Frans van Waarden and Michaela Drahos, 'Courts and (Epistemic) Communities in the Convergence of Competition Policies' (2002) 9 Journal of European Public Policy 913, 933.

> ('NGAs')... NGAs are private practitioners, representatives of non-governmental international organizations, members of industry and consumer groups, and academics, who volunteer to contribute to the ICN's work.[13]

So, Section 1.2.2 charts the involvement of NGAs, breaking this down by the types of actor (businesses, service providers, consumers, individuals), the geographic origin of these actors, and their area of expertise (lawyers, economists, etc). We will see that many NGAs are multinational firms (and their advisers). They often hail from economically advanced states and favour competition rules founded on a narrow, neoliberal paradigm. Like NCAs, NGAs claim to be acting in the public interest. However, we hypothesize that this group of actors has the ability and incentive to influence ICN work products in their own self-interest.

One final point on something not covered in this section: epistemic communities. These can be really influential and are networks of professionals 'with recognised expertise and competence in a particular domain and an authoritative claim to policy relevant knowledge within that domain or issue-area'.[14] We could have introduced the competition epistemic community here,[15] because understanding it and its presence within the ICN helps to explain why individuals in the NCAs and NGAs take part in the ICN. However, as the epistemic community is an important mechanism for organizing (and transmitting) power and influence, we have decided to wait until Section 1.3 to discuss it further.

1.2.1 States

Section 1.2.1.1 asks whether it matters that the ICN is a network of competition authorities rather than states. Then, we focus more specifically upon which competition authorities are present in the ICN (as well as which are absent) and ask why this might be (Section 1.2.1.2). NCAs are obviously state actors, but they are a different kind of state actor. This matters. It drives a wedge between NCAs (and their states), to the extent that an NCA can no longer be presumed to act in its own state's interests (although advanced NCAs are more likely to do so).

[13] CSN SG Working Group, *NGA Toolkit* (2012) 1, https://www.internationalcompetitionnetwork.org/portfolio/icn-nga-toolkit/ accessed 7 October 2021.

[14] Peter Haas, 'Introduction: Epistemic Communities and International Policy Coordination' (1992) 46 International Organization 1.

[15] We refer to '*the* competition epistemic community'. However, several communities may compete for influence (from inside and outside the ICN). Internally they may not even be uniform either, Marie-Laure Djelic and Sigrid Quack, 'Transnational Communities and Governance' in Marie-Laure Djelic and Sigrid Quack (eds), *Transnational Communities: Shaping Global Economic Governance* (CUP 2012) 25–26.

1.2.1.1 States or their NCAs?

We have seen four drivers towards networks in the last 50 years. This section starts by outlining the reasons that NCAs give for making the ICN an informal network of competition authorities rather than states. Then, we look at academic theories that might reveal other plausible explanations for such actions. Finally, we compare the two approaches.

1.2.1.1.1 The reasons NCAs give for making the ICN an informal network of competition authorities

Under the ICN's operational framework, only a 'national or multi-national competition agency' can be an ICN member.[16] So, it is the NCA and not its state that is the member. This is unlike some other international organizations, such as the OECD, for example, where the states themselves are members, even when competition law and policy is being discussed.

The ICN describes its current mission in the following terms:

> to advocate the adoption of superior standards and procedures in competition policy around the world, formulate proposals for procedural and substantive convergence, and seek to facilitate effective international cooperation to the benefit of member agencies, consumers and economies worldwide.[17]

One might ask whether the ICN was necessary at all in order to do this. When the ICN was established, there were at least three major multinational competition initiatives already in existence. Officials (both state and NCA) from member states of the Organisation for Economic Co-operation and Development (OECD) already met to discuss competition policy and enforcement in the Competition Law and Policy Committee of the OECD (CLP).[18] The OECD produces recommendations and best practices on competition law and policy. It runs best practice roundtables too. When asked, its representatives also provide detailed critique of national competition regimes and suggest specific improvements. Second, the United Nations Conference on Trade and Development (UNCTAD) brings together officials (both state and NCA) from around the world.[19] Once again, discussions are on recent developments in competition policy and enforcement. It also provides a network of support and encouragement for competition officials. Finally, the World Trade Organization (WTO) had considered an initiative to prepare an international system of competition law standards.

[16] ICN, *ICN Operational Framework* (2012) 1.

[17] ICN, *ICN Statement of Achievements 2001–2013* (2013) 3.

[18] <www.oecd.org/competition/> accessed 7 October 2021.

[19] UNCTAD includes Intergovernmental Group of Experts (IGE) on Competition Law and Policy meeting annually, <https://unctad.org/topic/competition-and-consumer-protection/intergovernmental-group-of-experts-on-competition-law-and-policy> accessed 6 September 2021.

Most of the founding members of the ICN are members of the OECD, UNCTAD, and the WTO. So, the question remains, why not simply use or adapt one of them? The US ICPAC explicitly confronted this issue. It noted that the OECD's CLP had worked well for promoting soft convergence among OECD members (principally rich countries) and for the provision of technical assistance more widely. However, ICPAC argued that the CLP:

> has not, however, achieved much success in rule making or dispute settlement. Moreover, numerous jurisdictions that have competition laws or policies in place or that are considering the introduction of such policy measures are not members of the OECD. And the specialized needs of new competition regimes may not yet be fully integrated into the deliberations and analysis of the OECD.[20]

The logic here is slightly confusing. The ICN (as it is, but also as principally conceived of by ICPAC) is not a rule-making body or a place for dispute settlement either. Furthermore, while it is a fair point that many states are not OECD members, ICPAC might be criticized when it highlights the lack of consideration of the specialized needs of new competition regimes. As ICPAC's members would likely have been aware, in 2001 (the year after the ICPAC report) the OECD created the Global Competition Forum (for all states, not merely the 36 OECD members).[21] It might have made more sense to try using the Global Competition Forum instead of creating a new body. In any event, given the fact that ICPAC did not even consider the possibility of using UNCTAD as a relevant forum (UNCTAD's principal focus is encouraging and supporting new competition regimes), these may well have merely been crocodile's tears.

The WTO also has a more inclusive membership than the OECD. However, ICPAC notes that it is primarily focused on trade. Not all competition problems are trade problems. It might also be pointed out that it was the USA that refused to include competition policy in the Seattle round of trade negotiations, making the WTO a questionable forum for this US committee. Furthermore, ICPAC continues, somewhat in contradiction to its critique of the OECD:

> Moreover, the traditional mandate of the WTO—negotiation of rules that are then subject to dispute settlement—may be inappropriate for competition issues, which instead need to be discussed broadly and in a consultative manner. Only a

[20] ICPAC, *Final Report* (2000) 283.

[21] 'Over 100 competition authorities, international organisations and invited experts worldwide participate in the Global [Competition] Forum every year. Participation is by invitation only and restricted to officials from competition authorities, government agencies and international/regional organisations. Representatives of the business community and trade movements can contribute to the discussions', <www.oecd.org/competition/globalforum/> accessed 7 October 2021.

> limited range of competition matters, if any, are likely to bear fruit in any organization that requires a binding commitment from nations.[22]

So, the OECD is objectionable because it is not a rule-making body or a place for dispute settlement; and the WTO is objectionable because it is a rule-making body and a place for dispute settlement. ICPAC did not even deign to discuss UNCTAD as an appropriate forum.

If ICPAC's arguments are unpersuasive here, can we learn more about the reasons for setting up the ICN elsewhere? Turning to the ICN itself, the ICN website states that:

> Government officials and members of the antitrust bar recognized that the best way to promote sound and effective antitrust enforcement in the wake of economic globalization was through the establishment of a network of competition authorities and international competition specialists.[23]

Some believe that restricting the ICN to a network of NCAs and NGAs, excluding lawmakers and policymakers, is what made the ICN so effective in its first ten years.[24] NCAs may have more common interests and want to focus on competition policy. The more similar those involved are (in terms of interests, outlook, and sense of problem) the more quickly and easily they are likely to find common ground. Von Finckenstein (founding Chairman of the ICN) adds:

> The ICN formula works because: participants are involved as experts, not as representatives of governments; discussions focus on the production of optimal practices without the immediate concern for implementation; we are also able to avoid defensive posturing which leads to a lowest common denominator approach; public and private sectors, and member agencies from developing and developed economies, participate on an equal footing.[25]

Populating the ICN with competition experts from NCAs and NGAs, puts 'expert argument' front and centre. It may also speed up discussions, where permissions do not have to be sought elsewhere.[26] The explicit belief seems to have been that a body made up of these experts would be better able 'to promote sound and

[22] ICPAC (n 20) 282–83. There was also some evidence that ICPAC objected to the possible politicization of the competition rules that might result from agreeing them through state bargaining. It might also undermine the autonomy of the NCAs, ibid 264; Charles Roger, *The Origins of Informality: Why the Legal Foundations of Global Governance Are Shifting, And Why It Matters* (OUP 2020) 180.

[23] <www.internationalcompetitionnetwork.org/about/> accessed 7 October 2021.

[24] Pieter Kalbfleisch, 'From Ditchley Park to the Hague: A Journey Worthwhile' in Lugard (n 7) 4.

[25] Konrad von Finckenstein, 'Introductory Remarks' (2003) 3–4, previously available at <http://www.internationalcompetitionnetwork.org/uploads/library/doc554.pdf> (broken ICN link, see discussion in Introduction, n 16).

[26] Gaining approval for one's stance from other ministries can take time, Hugh Hollman and William Kovacic, 'The International Competition Network: Its Past, Current and Future Role' in Lugard (n 7) 75.

effective antitrust enforcement'. Of course, the risk is that this is just a faster way of excluding relevant voices and getting things 'wrong'.

1.2.1.1.2 Academic theories of influence

We have seen von Finckenstein emphasizing the inclusion of participants as competition experts, rather than as 'representatives of governments'. Why might this matter and how did NCAs do it? There are two reasons why we think that the NCAs that established the ICN might not have wanted to involve states. First, discussions between NCAs, rather than states, helps keep the focus on 'technical', rather than political, differences. This better aligns with how many working in NCAs view competition policy (and, as we discuss in Section 1.2.1.2, technical discussions is likely to favour many of the advanced NCAs involved in establishing the ICN). Second, excluding states helps to more effectively preserve NCAs' autonomy, enhancing their power and their ability to focus ICN discussions on areas of importance to NCAs using solutions they favour. After discussing these issues, we ask why theory suggests informal, rather than formal, international organizations of this kind might have been adopted here.

Networks are controversial (or we think that they should be). Their rise has been 'aided by the perception that many regulatory issues are technocratic'.[27] In part, this are because many of the actors there do not see themselves as involved in a political exercise, but a technical one, designing the 'best' rules. Yet, whether or not competition officials are motivated by redistributional aims, networks (and the rules that they propagate) facilitate and constrain actors and outcomes,[28] creating winners and losers. The Introduction to this book argued that competition policy (and the resulting enforcement) is highly redistributive. This is even true in the rare cases where a policy is Pareto-optimal, as some may 'win' more than others.

An international organization's 'constitutional moment' can be extremely important. At that point in time, several highly redistributive decisions are often hard baked into its DNA. Choosing to use a network, deciding who can participate in it and on what basis, all have redistributive consequences. For example, the 'constitution' may demand a network of state trade ministers, as in the WTO, or a network of expert technical officials.[29] The way that network actors perceive their own roles is also extremely important. For example, Ossege finds that involving *national* experts in EU committees tends to increase the focus on national interests. However, national interests are considered much less relevant if the primary self-perception

[27] Raustiala (n 2) 24.

[28] Rhodes (n 4) 11, see also at 162. Similarly, see the argument between Wilks and Sturm (emphasizing power in networks and how they are not value neutral) and Schaub and Tesauro (arguing that networks are not about power), Ehlermann and Laudati (n 5) 15, 34–35, 66, 77, 79, and 172–73.

[29] Mark Bevir and RAW Rhodes, 'Decentred Theory, Change and Network Governance' in Eva Sørensen and Jacob Torfing (eds), *Theories of Democratic Network Governance* (Palgrave MacMillan 2008) 80–82.

of these actors is as experts with accountability to their 'profession' (or epistemic community) rather than as actors negotiating on their state's behalf.[30] Once the constitutional issues have been decided, then the motivations of ICN actors will likely become less important. This is because who is present and the way they are likely to act often has a major impact.

How actors seek to 'persuade' others to change their standards is likely to be different in a network of NCAs, rather than states. This is because states normally negotiate through political bargaining (or force), whereas the 'regulators' tend to focus upon 'expert argument'. Keeping states out of the network and pushing participants to see themselves as technical experts (rather than state representatives) is the way many NCAs think competition policy should be decided.[31] Many others might not agree that this is the best way to organize this highly redistributive policy area. Chapter 4 discusses this issue in more detail.

There is a second reason why regulators establishing a transnational network might not want to involve states: a network without states more effectively preserves regulators' autonomy, enhancing their power. This gives them more scope to focus network discussions on areas of importance to regulators and rely on solutions they favour (even if their states might disagree). In the words of Singer:

> Political intervention, in its various guises, is the bane of a regulator's existence ... When politicians attempt to influence regulatory policy directly ... they threaten the agency's autonomy and prestige ... Regulators will use all strategies at their disposal to minimise the possibility of intervention.[32]

If a regulator can preserve its autonomy, then it should be better able to ensure that the decisions that it makes are made on the basis of its expert authority (rather than through bargaining or relying on some other goals of area of expertise it might disagree with). Similar motivations likely apply to decisions about setting up a regulatory policy network. In fact, there is some empirical support for this view. As we discussed in the Introduction to this book, Roger recently conducted an empirical study on establishing international organizations since 1945 (including the ICN). He found that involving independent (non-majoritarian) regulators in the creation of international organizations, such as transnational networks, makes it much more likely that informal institutions will evolve (ie they successfully avoid political 'interference').[33]

[30] Christoph Ossege, *European Regulatory Agencies in EU Decision-Making* (Palgrave Macmillan 2016) 34–35.

[31] This reflects those reasons given by the ICN's founding Chairman in the text around n 25.

[32] David Singer, *Regulating Capital: Setting Standards for the International Financial System* (Cornell UP 2007) 22.

[33] Roger (n 22) 9–10, 62–63, and 92–93. This finding is statistically significant. He adds that these 'contrasting domestic implications can be just as significant as the functional properties of these institutions when it comes to explaining why states, and actors within states, want to create them' (ibid 7). Roger also adds that formal agreements could also achieve this end. However, as they demand political

For NCAs there is a third benefit from pushing network actors to see themselves as part of an epistemic community. As Section 1.3.1.2 explains, membership of such a community is a powerful mechanism for encouraging a similar vision of how to understand world problems and possible solutions. This makes it easier to agree on these solutions which, in turn, leads to less public disagreements between regulators which might become politically costly.[34]

We have seen that the involvement of independent regulators often has considerable influence on the adoption of an *informal* international organization. The final point that we want to discuss here is whether qualitative or quantitative studies suggest other possible influences. In the Introduction to the book, we saw that the most common theoretical approach to explaining organizational design is functionalism (often combined with a transaction cost approach). The idea being that the formality (or informality) of an international organization is selected as a result of analysing what is the best, most efficient, structure to perform the relevant tasks.[35]

Several theoretical reasons have been suggested for when informal international organizations might be preferable to formal ones. Of relevance here are: more flexibility, risk of opportunism, secrecy, and lower costs. If there is a lack of clarity about the state of the world, what problems are and what solutions might be most efficient and effective, then international organizations may need to be flexible while we learn more or conditions change. For example, today's best economists and lawyers may agree that there is no place for environmental considerations in competition policy. This may not be such a widespread view in the future. Furthermore, flexibility may also help where the distributional consequences of an arrangement are unclear, especially if this arrangement is to last for a long time.[36]

involvement (and thus risk compromise), regulators would prefer to avoid formal arrangements if they can adequately achieve their goals alone (ibid 63).

[34] As convergence between competition regimes increases, there are fewer conflicts between them. So, the value-laden nature of competition policy and enforcement comes to the attention of politicians less often. This, in turn, makes them less likely to interfere with their NCAs, Chad Damro, 'The New Trade Politics and EU Competition Policy: Shopping for Convergence and Co-operation' (2006) 13 Journal of European Public Policy 867, 871–72; Chad Damro, *Cooperating on Competition in Transatlantic Economic Relations: The Politics of Dispute Prevention* (Palgrave Macmillan 2006) 21 and 71.

[35] Felicity Vabulas and Duncan Snidal, 'Organization without Delegation: Informal Intergovernmental Organizations (IIGOs) and the Spectrum of Intergovernmental Arrangements' (2013) 8 Review of International Organizations 193, 209–10; Randall W Stone, 'Informal Governance in International Organizations: Introduction to the Special Issue' (2013) 8(2) The Review of International Organizations 121–36, 123. Note that, strictly speaking, Stone is not principally discussing a choice between formal and informal international organizations. He is discussing a choice between using formal and informal mechanisms *within* a formal international organization. However, his theoretical insights seem of likely relevance to both processes.

[36] Vabulas and Snidal (n 35) 209–10; Barbara Koremenos, Charles Lipson and Duncan Snidal, 'The Rational Design of International Institutions' (2001) 55 International Organization 761, 792–95; Anne-Marie Slaughter, *A New World Order* (Princeton University Press 2004) 11.

Often mechanisms for change in both formal and informal organizations require consensus or some kind of super majority. This can make change hard, slow, and expensive. Where only non-binding commitments result, states may be more likely to allow recommendations that others want, as they will not feel trapped into following them. Actors may also be more open to organizational changes for a similar reason. More flexible structures (with lower majorities) might also be preferable to allow for change as we learn. This might be easier to agree in non-binding orders. Informal meeting can, over time, breed trust and allow for the sharing of information and ideas. This can often mean that actors start to better understand each other and even generate common ways of seeing the world (and how to solve problems there). It can also make actors less wary of the risk of opportunism by others (and make this less likely). The large secretariats that are often found in formal international organizations can be a powerful force to be reckoned with. Members might find it hard to resist them when they want to change (or they do not), even where many members disagree with them. Roger's empirical analysis of international organizations found no statistically significant effect here, however.[37]

There is also a tension between the autonomy of members and collective oversight of the institutional order to ensure compliance. The smaller secretariats of informal international organizations may be sufficient to help states to pool and share information and experience and then coordinate their response where the incentive to 'cheat' on agreed arrangements is low. However, where the risks of opportunism dominate, informal organizations are less well equipped to provide monitoring and oversight. Formal organizations may be able to provide this extra level of support, but that comes at a cost to state autonomy. There is also the literal cost of paying for a large secretariat to do this extra work.[38] Roger's empirical analysis of international organizations found a statistically significant effect here.[39] Cheating might be less problematic in an area with a strong epistemic community.

A perceived need for secrecy may push states towards informality. Participation in a formal international organization could lead to a perceived need for greater openness about who contributes, in what capacity, and what they are contributing.[40] Unexpectedly, Roger's empirical analysis found the opposite of this proposed relationship to a statistically significant degree.[41]

[37] Roger (n 22) 90–93.

[38] Vabulas and Snidal (n 35) 210; Koremenos and others (n 36) 790.

[39] As 'functionalists predict . . . an international organization is less likely to be informal as the potential for opportunism grows' Roger (n 22) 92.

[40] 'States sometimes use informal transparency rules to limit access and maintain secrecy among a select group of members . . . Other times, states use the lack of formal transparency to provide more open access to interested parties such as non-state actors that can advance the [informal international organization's] . . . mission without having to adhere to overly rigorous accreditation procedures', Vabulas and Snidal (n 35) 210–11. See also Roger (n 22) 32–33.

[41] As 'the need for secrecy increases, an international organisation is less likely to be informal. This is the opposite of what functionalists have thus far predicted' Roger (n 22) 92.

The costs of informal international organizations can also be lower. In large part this is due to fewer direct costs, given their smaller secretariats (or even lack of one). However, it is also linked to the general costs of bureaucracy that formal organizations might bring. On the other hand, large, formal organizations can often accomplish more complex tasks (think of the United Nations with over 9,000 staff, for example). They can also support states more comprehensively, through joint research, norm production, coordination, etc.[42]

We have seen the relevance of the independence of regulators in this process and the failure to find statistically significant impacts for some of these functionalist suggestions. This implies that while functionalist theories are relevant to the amount of informality, they are not the whole story.[43] The other main theoretical base here is rationalist (or power-based) theories.[44]

Power-based theories concentrate on the distribution of power (and interests) between states. The idea is that powerful states will prefer informal organizations and rules because they allow maximum flexibility. Weaker states, on the other hand, prefer formal rules that bind the strong. That said, both may compromise if this means cooperation of value to them is achieved where it would otherwise not be. For example, powerful states may accept some binding rules, in order to get wider voluntary cooperation of weaker states, and vice versa.

> Scholars making these kinds of arguments predict that an organisation's informality will be determined by power inequalities [more informality as power inequality rises] and the level of conflict that prevails within specific constellations of states [more informality as the level of conflict rises].[45]

The rise of informal international organizations could (also) be linked to conflicting interests between states and power inequalities. A powerful state may, for example, choose a route that imposes negative externalities on other states (and feel able to do that even if there is a risk of retaliation, because that threat seems small). Note too that once there is a power imbalance, it may not even be necessary for the powerful to threaten to impose their will. Others, operating in the shadow of (perceived) threats may accommodate the powerful state's wishes anyway, in order to get the strong to participate (or keep participating).

[42] Vabulas and Snidal (n 35) 211.

[43] The Introduction to this book raised another major problem. If international organizations' nature tracks the problems that they face, functionalists predict a strong correlation between these problems and organizations' level of formality. However, international organizations addressing almost the same problems around the world can have different levels of informality (Roger (n 22) 57).

[44] See, for example, Stephen D Krasner, 'Global Communications and National Power: Life on the Pareto Frontier' (1991) 43 World Politics 336; Randall W Stone, *Controlling Institutions: International Organizations and the Global Economy* (CUP 2011).

[45] Roger (n 22) 13, see also 55–56.

> Powerful countries have advantages over weaker states in exerting informal power, including superior information, immediate access to key personnel, and greater cooperation with their requests. In addition, they can generally rely on deference from other states, which prefer to avoid confrontations when their own key interests are not engaged.[46]

Having a wide range of different fora to choose between seems to favour powerful states too.[47]

Roger's empirical analysis also looked at the relevance of power-based theories for explaining the formation of international organizations since 1945. Interestingly, he found that where states have conflicting views and levels of trust are low, states are wary of formally binding themselves in ways which might advantage others. However, he also found that power differences between states do not exert an independent influence on the level of informality.[48] Roger does not conclude from this that power is irrelevant, but he warns that a more nuanced understanding of it is necessary. In fact, his empirical work provides support for the idea that, at least parts, of functionalism and power-based theories correlate with what we actually see. So, he suggests a two-step model to predict whether a formal or an informal international organization is likely to be chosen in the light of the specific context. Step One looks at preference formation *within* states; Step Two at preference aggregation *between* states.[49]

When it comes to preference formation within states, Roger starts by looking at why there is demand for cooperative governance. This might be because certain state actors are facing social, political, or economic externalities in their work. It might (also) be because firms or other stakeholders are facing them and are putting pressure on state actors to take action. Then, building on the idea that states are not unitary actors, Roger asks which state body (or bodies) is (are) contemplating co-operative governance and the political salience of the matter. Do the problems fall on a niche regulator and nobody else cares, for example? Or do they fall on society as a whole and this is a major political issue of general and widespread importance?

According to Roger, different state actors have different baseline preferences. To simplify matters, and following the distinction from Majone,[50] he divides state

[46] Stone, 'Informal Governance in International Organizations: Introduction to the Special Issue' (n 44) 125. Given Stone's focus on choices within formal organizations, see also Vabulas and Snidal (n 35) 213–14, extending Stone's comments to choices between formal and informal international organizations.

[47] Patrick talks of the USA's 'unmatched capacity to "pivot", not only among different regions but among diverse frameworks of international cooperation' Stewart Patrick, 'The New "New Multilateralism": Minilateral Cooperation, But at What Cost?' (2015) 1 Global Summitry, 126.

[48] Roger (n 22) 92–93 and 200.

[49] The discussion here comes from ibid ch 3.

[50] Giandomenico Majone, 'Non-Majoritarian Institutions and the Limits of Democratic Governance: A Political Transaction-Cost Approach' (2001) 157 Journal of Institutional and Theoretical Economics 57.

actors into majoritarian institutions (political ones like a ministry) and non-majoritarian (independent regulatory with some autonomy from political actors) bodies. The distinction is 'fundamentally shaped by the different positions actors occupy in the domestic institutional structures of states and are bound up with the domestic implications'.[51] For Roger, political institutions tend to prefer:

> formal co-operation that helps those in charge to demonstrate leadership [formal are more prestigious] and lock in their policy preferences more effectively [as costlier to create, join and exit]. Legalization can make promises to the domestic audiences that politicians depend on more credible and can improve their electoral prospects.[52]

On the other hand, politicians may be put off by the domestic demands of setting up or joining an international organization. The costs of formal organizations tend to be higher than informal ones, in terms of the political, legal, or budgetary hurdles. For example, they might require more formal action (perhaps involving both the legislature and the executive) to establish and monitor participation in the organization. Formal cooperation efforts might still be worthwhile for politicians, despite these extra 'costs', where issues have a high political salience.

As we saw above, Roger thinks that, principally in order to protect their autonomy and prestige (and to keep the focus of decision-making on their expert authority), independent regulatory agencies prefer informal cooperation, on balance.[53] It should also be added that there is a continuum from formal to informal, but bodies tend to cluster at opposite ends of the spectrum.

The 'basic' preferences of these two sets of actors are just a rule of thumb. Other issues might intervene to change them. For example, where an issue has significant domestic opposition then politicians' use of informality might rise (as this might make it hard to get formal legislative approval through the legislature, for example). Independent regulators' ability to select their informal preference may also be undermined, especially where others are affected by their work (for example the issue might cut across two different state regulatory regimes), an informal route is blocked, or the policy issues become more politically salient for some reason.

After preference formation *within* states, Step Two looks at preference aggregation *between* states to see what sort of organization is likely to emerge. Where all participating states have the same preference formation, it should be easy to predict the resulting organizational structure. Where states have different preferences, prediction is more complex. One has to consider how aligned states' preferences are as well as their power. Power may come from the structure of the relationship,

[51] Roger (n 22) 9.
[52] ibid 9–10.
[53] See the discussion around n 32.

or other options that the 'strong state' has, for example. As he explains, Roger's idea is based on bargaining theories. All else being equal:

> states preferring informality may have a bargaining advantage, since their preference is by nature much closer to the prevailing status quo. This preference can give them power over others, since they can more easily hold out and veto more ambitious formal approaches ... However, the theory also allows for other possibilities if a state's bargaining partners are able to remove the initial status quo as an option, either by threatening to 'go it alone' with others, applying sanctions, or providing side benefits of various kinds.[54]

Roger then proposes a structured approach to predicting the likelihood of formality in international organizations. It relies on insights from both functionalism and power-based theories. However, it seeks to structure the impact of power in ways which are more nuanced. Roger found strong empirical support for his two-step test.[55]

1.2.1.1.3 Comparing reasons given by these actors to the academic theories of influence

We compare the likely motivations for setting up the ICN by the NCAs involved, to the reasons they have given. Then, we apply Roger's two-step theory to preference formation *within* states, and then preference aggregation *between* states to the ICN.

We have suggested that the reasons that ICPAC explicitly gave for creating a new institution, rather than merely using/adapting the OECD or UNCTAD are unpersuasive. Since that report, two justifications have been highlighted on several occasions. First, the importance of a community where competition experts from around the world meet (working as experts rather than government representatives); and particular emphasis on the needs of new jurisdictions. Time and time again, we are also told that, in the ICN, competition experts meet as equals.

It is obvious why these are helpful justifications for those that wished to establish the ICN. Reinforcing them must also help with encouraging widespread participation in the ICN. However, as we have seen, theories from political science and economics hint that two other reasons may more accurately explain the creation of the ICN by those original NCAs (in fact Section 1.2.1.2 discusses even more benefits for them). First, it helps keep the focus on 'technical', rather than political, differences. This better aligns with how many working in NCAs view competition policy. Second, excluding states helps to more effectively preserve NCAs' autonomy, enhancing their power and their ability to focus on areas of importance to them.

[54] Roger (n 22) 11, see also 66–71.
[55] ibid especially ch 4.

In the OECD and UNCTAD, competition officials are often accompanied by state officials from outside the NCA. This can include officials from the Ministry of Business or the Foreign Office, for example. Even where this does not happen, NCAs may be bound to circulate national contributions to each international organization more widely within their state. Importantly, competition officials participate in these formal international organizations as state officials. This emphasizes wider state interests and that impinges upon the freedom of competition officials to intervene in ways that they might like. Note that this also applies to officials in 'advanced NCAs', such as officials from the EU, the USA, and Germany.

Setting up the ICN is a way for NCAs to avoid wider control from their own states.[56] In addition, in fora such as the OECD, NCAs' control over the focus and content of discussions is also challenged by a powerful participation by academics and wider state officials.

By shutting out or better controlling other state actors in the ICN, NCAs can better focus the debate on matters of interest to them, even in ways that their states might dispute.[57] For example, consider NCA responses to ICN questionnaires (inputs). Sometimes, NCAs seem to be promoting a vision of how they think things *should be*, rather than how they *are*. In 2006, the ICN's Unilateral Conduct Working Group (UCWG) asked NCAs and NGAs various questions about the objectives of unilateral conduct laws, the assessment of dominance/substantial market power, and state-created monopolies.[58] The UCWG report that followed noted that DG COMP (the EU NCA) spoke of three EU competition goals: consumer welfare, market integration, and ensuring an effective competitive process as a means to other goals, as well as a goal itself.[59] Yet, the EU courts regularly rely on wider public policy goals.[60] Removing state scrutiny and control from within the ICN, may give NCAs more leeway to rewrite stories in keeping with their own ideology.

[56] Indeed, some states have gone to great lengths to get access to ICN discussions. For example, the Ministry of Development, Industry and Trade (Brazil) has even registered as an NGA; see ICN, *The Future of the ICN in Its Second Decade—Final Report* (2016) Annex 3, <https://www.internationalcompetitionnetwork.org/wp-content/uploads/2018/09/ICN2dDecade2016.pdf> accessed 7 October 2021.

[57] This may be the implication of Dan Sjöblom and Monica Widegren, 'ICN Membership: Opportunities and Challenges for a Competition Authority' in Lugard (n 7) 353, for example.

[58] ICN—Unilateral Conduct Working Group, *Unilateral Conduct Working Group Questionnaire* (2006).

[59] ICN—Unilateral Conduct Working Group, *Report on the Objectives of Unilateral Conduct Laws, Assessment of Dominance/Substantial Market Power, and State-Created Monopolies* (2007) Annex A.

[60] Christopher Townley, *Article 81 EC and Public Policy* (Hart 2009) Part B; Giorgio Monti, 'Article 81 EC and Public Policy' (2002) 39 Common Market Law Review. Similarly, the UK's NCA (the CMA, then the OFT) isolated the same goals, with the exception of market integration, for the Competition Act 1998. This does not seem to be correct, or there is at least reasonable room for doubt: Christopher Townley, 'The Goals of Chapter I of the UK's Competition Act 1998' in Piet Eeckhout and Takis Tridimas (eds), *Yearbook of European Law*, vol 29 (Clarendon Press 2010) 307.

Building on such distortions, ICN recommended practices might advocate 'best practices' which are highly redistributive and not quite as widespread (or acceptable to states, rather than NCAs) as they are made to appear.

We said that there are two dimensions to why NCAs might want to shut states out of the ICN. We have highlighted the benefits (for NCAs) of reducing control (by their own states) of their actions. In addition, framing competition discussions as technical hunts for best practice, rather than negotiations between states, implies that the choice of 'best practices' is a value-neutral exercise. This is, of course, a fiction. The selection of best practices involves choices. The most 'technically competent' will be better able to push others (through peer pressure) to accept these practices. All of this is much easier if discussions are seen as being 'right or wrong' rather than invoking bargaining, where everyone should be seen to benefit. Increasing actor homogeneity within the ICN should also make it easier for participants to agree best practices (it also becomes harder for them to rebel, as they have more to lose).

This, in fact, was likely a clear reason why ICPAC felt that the OECD, UNCTAD, and WTO were inappropriate fora. There, states meet as states, rather than merely as competition experts (although such experts from NCAs are often involved alongside normal state officials). Such networks involve political bargaining and competition officials are subject to far greater control (even the US competition officials are subject to significant control by their own (non-competition) state officials) than they would be in a forum where they can act alone.

Some studies suggest that the primary allegiance of many NCAs (and their employees) is changing. According to Gerber, NCAs in the EU (the EU also has a policy and enforcement network for NCAs) are now often guided by what they think is best for the EU, rather than specifically their own states 'because they identify their own interests and/or the interests of the institutions in which they function with the "success" of European integration'.[61] Similar effects seem likely in the ICN too.[62] Some NCAs may resist peer pressure where they see conflicts with their national interests. Section 1.2.1.2 shows that resistance is not easy and the ICN's consensus requirement is unlikely to protect state (rather than NCA) interests. Over time, resistance likely becomes even harder, due to the network's socialization effect (Section 1.3.1.2).

[61] David Gerber, 'Modernising European Competition Law: A Developmental Perspective' (2001) 22 European Competition Law Review 122, 125.

[62] For example, Andreas Mundt, the ICN Chair, developed the idea of the 'primary allegiances' of ICN NCA members (he also thought that their allegiance was different to consumers in their states). According to Mundt, ICN members do not care about 'my country first but by competition first in our respective country but not only for our country, it's for consumers world-wide consumer in Berlin in Deli, Washington, Jonesburg or Sidney'. See his opening speech at the ICN 2018 Annual Conference in India, <http://webcast.gov.in/icn/> Although, for an early study that disagreed, see Pierre-Hugues Verdier, 'Transnational Regulatory Networks and Their Limits' (2009) 34 Yale Journal of International Law 162.

Given the importance of the composition of international networks, their focus and members' allegiance, the lack of a general, widespread 'political moment' at the ICN's inception may be of particular concern. It would have been one thing if politically accountable state actors (not just NCAs) had elected to establish the ICN in this way (states established the composition of the OECD, for example). Many that favour transnational networks see the 'constitutional moment' as crucial for legitimacy.[63] Some jurisdictions explicitly demand direct liberal political oversight when deciding to join or participate in organizations like the ICN—Chapter 4 discusses this (for example, the correct EU procedures do not seem to have been followed).

Let us turn now to apply Roger's two-step theory to ICN formation, first, to preference formation *within* states, and then preference aggregation *between* states for the ICN. When looking within states, Roger suggests that majoritarian actors may prefer formal transnational relations, whereas regulators may have a preference for informal arrangements. We examine preference formation in the USA and the EU (key players in the ICN's formation). We will see that NCAs in both regions had a strong preference for informal arrangements. Competition had a low political salience in the USA and so politicians were not intervening there; as we explain, others became involved in the EU (we treat the EU as a state here).

When it comes to preference formation within states, one needs to understand the pressures they face. US competition law (and its NCAs' interpretation of it) was the clear 'market leader' entering the 1990s. Four factors contributed to this.[64] First, the quality of the US competition regime. For many, it was the starting point for regime analysis. US commentators often criticized other regimes, including the EU.[65] Second, markets have a gravitational pull based on their relative economic value and diversity.[66] The size and diversity of the US economy meant that it could often focus on domestic needs and politics (rather than following others). This pull of the US market often encouraged others to follow the USA's regulatory lead. This made it easier for these other states' firms to operate in the USA (helping local firms); and made it less expensive for US firms to do business in these other states (lowering consumer costs there). In any event, when negative externalities were low from the application of their competition rules, the USA did not care whether others followed its regulatory lead or not. So, it had little need for a multinational

[63] See, for example, Robert Keohane, Stephen Macedo and Andrew Moravcsik, 'Democracy-Enhancing Multilateralism' (2009) 63 International Organization 1, 1–2.

[64] Similarly, changes in EU/US power in international accountancy standards are documented in Elliot Posner, 'Sequence as Explanation: The International Politics of Accounting Standards' (2010) 17 Review of International Political Economy 639. More generally, see also, David Bach and Abraham Newman, 'The European Regulatory State and Global Public Policy: Micro-Institutions and Macro-Influence' (2007) 14 Journal of European Public Policy 827; Slaughter (n 36) 175–77; Raustiala (n 2) 76.

[65] The literature is extensive here, see the reference around n 75.

[66] Daniel Drezner, 'Globalisation, Harmonisation, and Competition: The Different Pathways to Policy Convergence' (2005) 12 Journal of European Public Policy 841, 842–50.

response.[67] Third, the highly centralized nature of the US competition regime (there are only two key national US NCAs, although US states have a role too) made it easier to speak with a clear voice.[68] This centralized voice also made it harder for firms and others to play the relevant NCAs off against each other. Finally, a wide interpretation of the jurisdictional reach of its competition rules meant that the USA could (and often did) impose its own rules on actions by US, or non-US, actors that had little link with the USA.[69]

However, as business internationalized and the number of competition regimes exploded (in the 1950s fewer than ten jurisdictions had competition rules, today over 130 do),[70] externalities caused by the potential application of myriad regulatory standards to the same arrangements became more noticeable. This was causing problems for US firms. First, trying to comply with the rising number of competition rules as they traded around the world was increasing the costs for US multinationals. In addition, competition rules could be used to open up new markets to outside firms. Yet, many countries were not using their competition rules in this way. This was protecting their home industry and (in the minds of US firms) was a missed opportunity to aid their quest to enter new markets. Many US firms started to lobby US politicians and the US NCAs to get other states to align their competition rules (and their interpretation of them) to better match the US standards. Furthermore, the different interpretation of competition rules around the world was generating more direct issues for the US NCAs. They were finding that their own decisions were conflicting with those in other jurisdictions. This was undermining the US NCAs' power and prestige. It also clashed with their way of understanding the world (and how best to solve competition problems).

The two US NCAs have both achieved a high level of independence from political control.[71] When Congress established the Federal Trade Commission (FTC), it wanted to insulate it from direct political control. The FTC had five commissioners each with a fixed seven-year term. They could only be removed for cause. The FTC has authority to develop norms of business conduct through administrative adjudication. This includes an ability to prioritize certain economic areas of activity. The FTC is also able to gather information and prepare reports outside of individual cases. It also writes policy guidelines to explain how it thinks that certain areas of its enforcement powers should be enforced, substantively and

[67] Making similar points in relation to capital market regulation, see Beth Simmons, 'The International Politics of Harmonisation: The Case of Capital Market Regulation' (2001) 55 International Organization 589, 592–95.

[68] This is not to deny that the two federal US NCAs have disagreed sometimes: William Kovacic and Marc Winerman, 'The Federal Trade Commission as an Independent Agency: Autonomy, Legitimacy, and Effectiveness' (2015) 100 Iowa Law Review 2085.

[69] Muthucumarawamay Sornarajah, 'The Extraterritorial Enforcement of US Antitrust Laws: Conflict and Compromise' (1982) 31 International and Comparative Law Quarterly 127.

[70] <http://unctad.org/en/Pages/DITC/CompetitionLaw/ResearchPartnership/Benchmarking-Competition.aspx>

[71] See, for example, Kovacic and Winerman (n 68).

procedurally. The other US federal NCA is the Department of Justice (DoJ), specifically its Antitrust Division. As part of the law enforcement arm of the executive branch, the DoJ appears more political. In fact, it too has, as a matter of custom, 'a substantial degree of political independence'.

From the outset, the US NCAs exhibited a preference for informal international arrangements with other NCAs. This has the benefit of more flexibility and secrecy with lower costs.[72] There is also evidence of 'a more concerted effort to export US-style antitrust laws and economics abroad'.[73] Similarly, given the well-established independence of US NCAs, over many years, even when firms lobbied US politicians, they principally turned to US NCAs to ask them what they were going to do about the 'problem', rather than seeking to intervene themselves.

The position of DG COMP (the EU entity that joined the ICN) is different. The European Commission, among other things, promotes the EU's general interest. It is steered by a group of 27 commissioners, known as 'the college'. The college decides the Commission's political and strategic direction and ensures the application of EU law, under the EU courts' control. The Commission is organized into policy departments, known as directorates-general (DGs). The DGs do the day-to-day work in their policy area. DG COMP deals with competition. However, it is the college, as a whole, that signs off on final competition policy statements and takes enforcement decisions, not DG COMP. Some say that for many competition matters, other DGs provide little scrutiny. It is hard to see inside the college to verify such claims.

EU firms were confronting similar problems to US firms due to the rising number of competition arrangements around the world. DG COMP faced similar problems to the US NCAs. DG COMP would certainly have liked to enter into informal competition arrangements to ease these issues. However, there was a legal problem. Member States want to retain some control over EU external relations. So, the EU treaties prohibit direct formal international agreements between DG COMP and non-EU NCAs (and probably even informal ones). The Commission, the European Parliament, and even the Member States (through the Council) must all be involved in these arrangements.[74] Second, while DG COMP did a lot to embrace US competition law, particularly during the efforts to 'modernize' EU

[72] Bruno Zanettin, *Cooperation between Antitrust Agencies at the International Level* (Hart 2002), shows how reaching the limits of the unilateral and extraterritorial application of 'national' competition rules led to more interdependence between the EU and USA. Their NCAs started to cooperate more actively. At first, just avoiding conflicts in their enforcement. Over time they became more ambitious, aiming at better coordinating joint investigations of international competition cases.

[73] Anu Bradford, Adam Chilton and Filippo Lancieri, 'The Chicago School's Limited Influence on International Antitrust' (2020) 87 (2) University of Chicago Law Review 297, <https://scholarship.law.columbia.edu/faculty_scholarship/2512>

[74] We know that because, as Zanettin describes (see reference in n 72), the Commission made 'informal competition arrangements' with the US NCAs which, in 1994, the EU courts held that it lacked the power to do. The Annex to Chapter 4 provides a more detailed discussion of these issues.

competition law (starting in the 1990s), it was still heavily criticized, both substantively[75] and procedurally.[76] Although DG COMP was growing in confidence, many still saw the US system as better. Perhaps as a result of this, getting new leadership, and as a way to try to 'constrain' US competition law, DG COMP changed tack and proposed a more formal competition arrangement within the WTO to strengthen international cooperation in competition policy and enforcement.[77] Third, the competition problems that firms were facing was not solely falling on DG COMP. They also touched the portfolio of another powerful Commission DG: DG TRADE. DG TRADE develops trade policy inside and outside of the EU. Competition and trade policy are closely interlinked. Bringing competition issues within the WTO remit, could help to increase trade (by reducing the costs and burdens for multinational firms), including improving market access.[78] By 1996, the EU was formally trying to include competition on the WTO agenda.

The second part of our discussion is to examine preference formation *between* states (once again focusing on the EU and the USA).[79] Roger has suggested that most powerful state often has an advantage, especially where it favours the status quo ante, as happened here. Despite encountering resistance from the USA in 1996, the EU again pushed hard for the inclusion of competition on the WTO agenda in the Seattle round of negotiations in 1999. Once again, there was little appetite for such an expansion among WTO members, including the USA.[80] The USA favoured the status quo (ie simply not adding competition to the WTO rules) and, given the need for unanimity to agree new WTO rules, it could block this EU initiative.

The EU could not force the adoption of a formal international arrangement through the WTO (its first preference). So, it sought influence in other ways. At

[75] For example, the EU never followed anything like a Chicago School economic model, Bradford and others (n 73) 15; Anu Bradford and others, 'The Global Dominance of European Competition Law over American Antitrust Law' (2019) 16 Journal of Empirical Legal Studies 731, <https://scholarship.law.columbia.edu/faculty_scholarship/2513>. Arguments about regulatory standards might seem abstract. However, they are really fights over the kinds of society that we want and who will win and who will lose in those societies (making a similar point in relation to accounting standards, Posner (n 64) s 1. In other words, these fights matter.

[76] See, for example, the influential piece, Barry Hawk, 'System Failure: Vertical Restraints and EC Competition Law' (1995) 32 Common Market Law Review 973.

[77] In 1994, the new Commissioner van Miert of DG COMP ordered this report from a group of experts, Report of the Group of Experts, Competition Policy in the New Trade Order: Strengthening International Co-operation and Rules (1995), COM(95) 359 final, <https://op.europa.eu/en/publication-detail/-/publication/8fff7d91-3130-409b-b81b-aa1ea0fa78ac/language-en>

[78] European Commission, Communication from the Commission to the Council: Towards an International Framework of Competition Rules (1996), COM(96) 284 final, <http://aei.pitt.edu/3971/>, especially 4–6.

[79] See, for example, Yane Svetiev, 'Scaling Experimentalism: From Convergence to Informed Divergence in Transnational Competition Policy' in Jonathan Zeitlin (ed), *Extending Experimentalist Governance? The European Union and Transnational Regulation* (OUP 2015) s 7.2; Verdier (n 62) 150–57; Roger (n 22) ch 7.

[80] Raustiala (n 2) 27, see also 16. Roger charts how the USA and many other states were opposed to an extension of the WTO rules to competition ((n 22) 183–89).

first, the USA felt able to rebuff, or even ignore, such initiatives.[81] However, by the start of the new century (and for the first time ever) the EU blocked a merger that a US NCA had cleared on the same facts and markets.[82] As the EU grew more confident in its competition rules (and increasingly worried about US regulatory power here and elsewhere), it started to assert itself more. It sought to bolster the reputation of the EU competition rules; and more openly attacked the US rules, in areas of disagreement. The EU also more actively encouraged other states to adopt competition rules based on the EU system.[83] These efforts coincided with a rapid expansion of competition regimes around the world. Most states based their competition systems on either the EU or the US model (developing new rules is hard).

Clashes between the EU and US competition systems were becoming more pronounced and public (EU and US firms were increasingly affected by these clashes). By about 2000, the US hegemony in relation to competition was under real threat. The EU had been more successful than the USA at persuading states to follow its competition system.[84] Raw (economic and political) power no longer seemed enough for the USA to get its way. Yet, US firms still wanted US NCAs to help reduce the costs from having to comply with so many conflicting competition systems worldwide.[85] They also wanted US NCAs to help open new markets for them.

The USA needed a new industrial policy strategy here. Gerber sees the ICPAC as the USA's seeking to reassert 'control of the agenda of transnational competition law development'.[86] Time was ripe for change for the EU too. It had insufficient power to act alone; and, its preferred strategy, adoption of competition rules into the WTO, had been blocked.

If the EU and USA were to pool their resources and act together, might there be a better way of achieving their aims—especially in the many areas where their

[81] The *Boeing McDonnell Douglas* merger decision 1997 is one example. The USA cleared the merger, in part due to US defence interests. The EU Commission looked as though it would block it. However, under pressure from the USA, it allowed the merger, subject to commitments in some commercial markets. In the end, the US firms and NCAs prevailed, but this was seen as a major flexing of the EU's wings.

[82] In its *GE/Honeywell* merger decision of 2001, the EU Commission blocked a merger between two US firms which the US Department of Justice had just cleared. Most relevant markets were worldwide in their geographic scope (so the EU and US NCAs came to different decisions on the same facts).

[83] Sometimes, market forces were enough to achieve this; otherwise the EU exerted *political* pressure. For example, some trade deals were only signed once the third country agreed to adopt competition rules based on the EU model: David Gerber, *Global Competition: Law, Markets and Globalization* (OUP 2010). The EU also offered extensive support to other states, drafting competition rules, and training the local NCA.

[84] Bradford and others (n 73) 15; Bradford and others (n 75).

[85] From an EU/US perspective it makes sense to find ways to put pressure on 'foreign' NCAs to be more active, and to be active in line with EU and US trade ideas: ICPAC (n 20) Executive Summary 23–24 makes a similar point, from a US perspective. See also, Hollman and Kovacic (n 26) 80; John Fingleton, 'Competition Agencies and Global Markets: The Challenges Ahead' in Lugard (n 7) 191.

Another problem arises when an NCA uses its competition rules, but with 'bad approaches and techniques'. This can retard economic progress in that state, as well as in other states, Hollman and Kovacic (ibid) 55–56. What is regarded as a 'bad approach' is often value-laden, even if it is dressed up in 'technical clothes'.

[86] Gerber (n 83) 115.

competition policy and enforcement were largely aligned?[87] Historically, the USA has been supportive of a network approach.[88] The EU Commission had also been developing a network of NCAs within the EU. This European Competition Network (ECN) was generating positive signals. So much so that the EU Commission was thinking of further strengthening it.[89] Could a transnational competition network, involving NCAs from around the world, focusing on areas of EU/US consensus (rather than differences), be more fruitful for them (as well as more flexible, cheaper, more secretive, and a great platform for them to influence others)?

It certainly could. Agreeing to a competition network would allow the EU and the USA to work on areas of joint interest together (vetoes ensured that areas of disagreement between them would be ignored). The ICN may not have been the first preference of NCAs in either the EU or the USA. The EU wanted an international organization with formal rules. The USA may have preferred to go it alone, although ICPAC shows that unilateralism was increasingly less useful to the USA. However, it seems that the ICN's structure was an innovative way of trying to achieve the wishes of the EU and the USA and further projecting their influence (as we go on to explain), without compromising their control in areas of disagreement. Given the other NCAs involved in 2001, there was clearly a wide overlap of such perceptions. The major risk seems to lie with DG COMP, by joining the ICN without involving the correct institutions, it now seems to be acting outside of its powers. The Annex to Chapter 4 provides more details on the legal position and shows that DG COMP is not alone. In the last 20 years, many DGs in the EU Commission have sought to evade the EU treaties similarly. Given their reasons for turning to informal networks, their outputs (such as ICN work products) may not be in the interests of the states that these NCAs are purportedly working for.

1.2.1.2 NCAs

This section discusses which competition authorities are present in the ICN (as well as which are absent). Then it asks why this might be. The last section alluded to advantages for technically well-resourced NCAs participating in the ICN. These are likely to be greater the more that they can control the agenda for the production of ICN work products and the production of these work products themselves. In addition, some benefits might arise from participation in ICN activities by less well-resourced NCAs. Obviously, there are not just these two groups of NCAs (the technically well-resourced and the less-well resourced)—there is a continuum

[87] 'it is important not to overstate the degree of competition between the U.S. and EU. There is significant cooperation between the EU and the U.S. on cases of shared interest, and, some argue, convergence in policies as well' (Raustiala (n 2) 42).

[88] Slaughter (n 36) 175.

[89] Stephen Wilks, 'Understanding Competition Policy Networks in Europe: A Political Science Perspective' in Claus Dieter Ehlermann and Isabela Atanasiu (eds), *Constructing the EU Network of Competition Authorities* (Hart 2002).

(and some NCAs may be in one grouping on certain issues, but not others)—but we use two groups to add clarity to the analysis.[90]

1.2.1.2.1 Categories of actors

The ICN has built an incredibly wide membership of NCAs in under twenty years. Today, it includes 140 NCAs from over 100 jurisdictions around the world. However, it should be emphasized that mere presence in the ICN does not equate to influence. Section 1.3 explains that activity is an important indicator of influence. So, here we look at activity within the ICN Steering Group, as well as ICN Working Groups. While ICN membership is extremely wide, influence in these two groups is less widespread. Some NCAs (most notably those from China) have not joined, so we also discuss why this might be and what it means.

Let us start by discussing the ICN's Steering Group. Only NCAs can be proper members of the Steering Group (the same is true of the Working Groups too). NGAs and international organizations are purely there by invitation only and can be removed at any time.

There is a widespread view among NCAs and NGAs that membership of the Steering Group is a key path to influence within the ICN. In our survey, we asked respondents if they thought that membership of the Steering Group enabled its participants to have more control on the ICN's agenda and on its work products; 86 per cent of respondents answered that members of the Steering Group have more influence than other members on the ICN agenda; 69 per cent also said that they have more influence over the ICN work product compared to other NCAs.

Originally, there were no formal rules about which NCAs could be in the Steering Group. When the UK led the ICN in 2012 it suggested more formal rules. The rules that were agreed contain process and substantive elements.[91] In terms of process, outgoing Steering Group members recommend the composition of the new Steering Group. The affinity bias (an unconscious bias that we all have to a greater or lesser degree) makes it likely that outgoing members will recommend those like them (from similar states with similar backgrounds).[92] The Annual

[90] Our survey, discussed in Chapter 3, points to the existence of at least one further NCA cluster (thanks also to Umut Aydin for her helpful insights here). NCAs in this 'middle group' may no longer need basic training, networking, or protection from their own state. However, while these NCAs often still participate in the ICN, they are not leaders there. They may prioritize other fora where they are treated more as equals and can get the specific assistance that they feel they need. They also seem to appreciate the regular meetings in person that these other fora provide as well as the prestige. Given their scarce resources, especially with senior staff time, the NCAs in this group have to focus more on the benefits fora bring. This approach does not prejudice the other two groups of NCAs.

[91] These are set out in ICN (n 16) 3.

[92] The affinity bias 'is the tendency to gravitate toward and develop relationships with people who are more like ourselves and share similar interests and backgrounds. This leads people to invest more energy and resources in those who are in their affinity group while unintentionally leaving others out. Due to the prevalence of affinity bias, the legal profession [and the same applies in other areas] can best be described as a "mirrortocracy"—not a meritocracy', Kathleen Nalty, 'Strategies for Confronting Unconscious Bias' (2016) 45 Colorado Lawyer 45, 46.

Conference confirms this selection, by consensus. We are not aware of particular discussion of these choices in that context.

In terms of substantive membership rules, all elected Steering Group members should meet the following criteria: (a) they must be able to make a significant resource commitment to the ICN, mindful of the relative size of the member agency; and (b) they must have made consistent and effective ICN participation, which may include, but is not limited to: Working Group co-chair experience; leadership of an ICN time-specific or ongoing project; or a substantial contribution to the overall work of the ICN. In addition, the Steering Group composition should be representative, as the members of the outgoing Steering Group are required to select the new members 'with a view to reflecting the geographic and economic diversity of ICN members'. One can understand the logic here. But, once again, these rules embed a bias towards those that have been in the ICN longer, from bigger NCAs, with more time and money to invest. This logic chimes with our survey's findings (see Chapter 3).

Upon first impression, geographic diversity seems to be largely respected in the Steering Group. Since the first Steering Group, over half of the NCAs were from Europe and North America, whose competition agencies make up just over half of the ICN membership (about 51 per cent).[93] Asia (20 per cent) has three or four seats; Africa (16–17 per cent) one; South America tends to have two or three seats (its agencies make up approximately 9 per cent of ICN memberships); and Australia is almost always present (Oceania makes up for approximately 3 per cent of members).

However, the Steering Group members have been rotationally the same 20 or so jurisdictions. This is most likely the result of both resource availability and the Steering Group outgoing members selecting the incoming ones themselves, which effectively enables them to perpetuate their power. Furthermore, as the years pass, their level of experience in leading the ICN increases, which makes it harder for other agencies to challenge the composition of the Steering Group. The lack of diversity in Steering Group membership carries the risk that the only (or main) issues discussed will be the ones of importance to the richest countries in the world, given the Steering Group's power over the ICN agenda. Perhaps this was the point?

In addition, the ICN rules also demand 'economic diversity' for Steering Group members. The lack of economic diversity is much harder to justify and explain. There is clearly domination by the richer, more technically advanced, NCAs

[93] People from 24 different NCAs were involved in the Steering Group between 2006 and 2015. Of these, 13 were from the EU (Belgium, EU, France, Germany, Italy, the Netherlands, Poland, Portugal, Spain, Sweden, UK) and North America (Canada and USA). The remainder were from new jurisdictions (Barbados, Brazil, Mexico, Morocco, South Africa, South Korea, and Turkey) and others (Australia, Japan, Russia, and Singapore). We only compiled the list until 2015 because some gaps appear in the ICN Steering Group membership lists after that. The current Steering Group membership list is available at—<www.internationalcompetitionnetwork.org/working-groups/icn-operations/steering-group/steering-group-members/> accessed 7 October 2021.

(especially of those that started the ICN in the first place). Could it be argued that North America and Europe are the most affected by competition law? If so, might this justify their disproportionate influence? This seems unlikely. Along with globalization and the spread of multinational corporations must come the realization that these corporations inevitably affect all the countries that they touch, either by directly operating in them or through the indirect results of their actions. Furthermore, anti-competitive activity can have a disproportionate impact on poorer consumers (including in poorer countries).[94]

The third category of membership to discuss (after general ICN membership and membership of the ICN Steering Group), is leadership of the ICN Working Groups. Any NCA can join any Working Group, so there is not an issue about Working Group membership. So, what becomes important is how influential an NCA is (or can be) in a specific Working Group. Similar to what we saw for Steering Group membership, 87 per cent of the respondents to our survey consider that the Working Groups' co-chairs have more influence than other members in determining the ICN agenda; 74 per cent also think that they are more influential in shaping work products.

Particular influence comes through being a Working Group co-Chair. Working Group Chairs are appointed by the Steering Group. By way of example, looking at the Chairs of the UCWG from when it was established in 2006 until today, we show the results in Table 1.1.

Table 1.1 Representation of Chairs of the unilateral conduct working group over time

2006–09	2009–12	2013–18	2018–19	2020–23
Germany	Germany	Turkey	Australia	EU (DG COMP)
USA	USA	UK	Italy	South Africa
Mexico		Sweden	South Africa	Japan

Once again, we see the power of the EU and North America with eight chairs (out of 14 this is 57 per cent); compared to the rest of the world: Australia, Mexico, and Turkey all had one chair, South Africa chaired twice). This is not entirely representative in terms of its make-up.[95] Given the membership composition outlined above in fact, to be representative at least geographically, half of the seats should

[94] Alan Winters, Competition and Poverty Reduction (OECD 2013), DAF/COMP/GF(2013)5. <https://www.oecd.org/officialdocuments/publicdisplaydocumentpdf/?cote=DAF/COMP/GF(2013)5&docLanguage=En> especially 21–23, accessed 7 October 2021.

[95] 'Although open to competition officials and their advisors from any country, US and European participants tend to play the central roles in the working groups and annual meetings' Gerber (n 83) 116. Agreeing that there needs to be a better rotation of Steering Group and Working Group Chairs, Mariana Tavares, 'The ICN: One of the Many International Priorities' in Lugard (n 7) 346.

be given to countries outside of North America and Europe (they got 43 per cent). Of these chairs, only Sweden and Turkey were not founding members of the ICN.

We are also told that there is a broad participation of NCAs and NGAs in the UCWG, in the full-range of activities.[96] Again, without attendance sheets, it is not possible to identify which stakeholders are represented in the discussions and who is merely in passive attendance.[97] On the positive side, the UCWG itself has determined to make more efforts to broaden out participation to those that have been less active. Specifically, they mention a demand for economists.[98] It will be interesting to see how that works out.

This lack of diversity in the UCWG co-chairs means that (in its appointment of these officers) the Steering Group fails on both the geographical and economic fronts, to select members 'reflecting the geographic and economic diversity of ICN members', as requested in the ICN Operational Framework.[99] It is unclear why. Perhaps EU and North American agencies took up the co-chair roles so often because other agencies did not volunteer for the position due to lack of resources? If this is the reason, then perhaps the ICN needs to make more active efforts to achieve balanced representation (such as financial compensation).

1.2.1.2.2 The reasons these actors (and others) give for their ICN engagement

ICN cooperation is disarmingly aimed at proposing superior standards and procedures in competition policy; proposing substantive and procedural convergence; and aiding international cooperation.[100] Typically, two potential beneficiaries of

[96] For example, on the active role of NGAs in the UCWG, see Calvin Goldman, Robert Kwinter and Navin Joneja, 'A Perspective on the Role and Contribution of NGAs at the ICN' in Lugard (n 7) 388.

[97] Although we know of no relevant statements from the UCWG, two indicators from elsewhere make us sceptical of 'broad participation' claims. First, the Merger Working Group has stated that the preparation of its Merger Guidelines Workbook was concentrated in very few hands (11 NCAs, all founding members of the ICN and NGAs from six states, all founding members), ICN Merger Working Group, ICN Merger Guidelines Workbook (2006) 2, <https://www.internationalcompetitionnetwork.org/wp-content/uploads/2018/05/MWG_MergerGuidelinesWorkbook.pdf> accessed 7 October 2021. Second, examining recent assessments of what powerful NCAs, such as the US Federal Trade Commission, have done within the ICN also paints a picture of concentrated power. See, for example:

> The FTC was a founding member of the ICN and has maintained its participation in the network as a top priority for the agency's international program. With the support of successive agency heads and a major resource commitment, the FTC has: helped lead the ICN's strategic thinking as part of the Steering Group; led the Merger, Unilateral Conduct, and Agency Effectiveness Working Groups as well as the ICN's implementation work and its Training on Demand project; led or co-led the development of recommended practices on merger review procedures, merger analysis, the assessment of dominance, and agency investigative process; organized and co-hosted seven ICN workshops; and participated in dozens of projects across the ICN.

Maria Coppola and others, '(Nearly) A Century with the ICN' [2020] Competition Policy International, the quotation comes from the Introduction, available online only at <https://www.competitionpolicyinternational.com/nearly-a-century-with-the-icn/> accessed 7 October 2021.

[98] Cynthia Lewis Lagdameo and Andrew Heimert, 'The Unilateral Conduct Working Group' in Lugard (n 7) 294–95.

[99] ICN (n 16) 6.

[100] See reference at n 17.

ICN work are mentioned, ie NCAs and consumers. For example, in 2010, Fingleton (a former head of the ICN), said that:

> the ICN must continue to develop its model of governance to ensure that its work addresses the needs of competition agencies and serves the interests of consumers in each member jurisdiction.[101]

Some statements point to benefits for other beneficiaries too:

> to facilitate the task of firms and their representatives in working with several competition agencies simultaneously, especially with regard to merger notifications. Antitrust enforcement at times may impose unnecessary costs and uncertainty on the business community and marketplace. The ICN works to promote sound and principled procedural and substantive standards that help minimize such burdens and leave pro-competitive, efficiency enhancing conduct free to flourish.[102]

'Unnecessary costs and uncertainty' might undermine the interests of consumers by leading to higher prices (although it seems unlikely that any such effect would be very pronounced). However, this quote's focus does not seem to be on ensuring consumer benefits, in particular.

The ICN justifies its value to NCAs by highlighting the dissemination of antitrust experience (enforcement policies, analytical approaches, and investigative techniques), and exchanges of recommended practices on topical issues, that it facilitates. This aids convergence between NCAs in their interpretation and application of competition rules (insofar as this is permissible in their national orders). Even where this is not possible, it leads to a better understanding of other NCAs' actions, which facilitates better cooperation between them. The ICN is quick to note that it is of value to both established and newer NCAs. It explains that the ICN provides:

> a forum for newer agencies to draw on the experiences and support of more established agencies, for example as they seek to advocate a competition culture in their jurisdiction, where there may face vested local interest groups.[103]

[101] John Fingleton, *The International Competition Network: Planning for the Second Decade* (2010) 8, <https://www.internationalcompetitionnetwork.org/wp-content/uploads/2020/01/SpeechChairFingleton2010.pdf> accessed 7 October 2021. Fingleton also references 'economies benefiting', but where does this come from?

[102] ICN, *A Statement of Mission and Achievements up until May 2006* (2006) 1, previously available at <http://www.internationalcompetitionnetwork.org/library.aspx?page=37> accessed 7 October 2021. Similarly, ICN, A Statement of Mission and Achievements up until May 2005 (2005) 1, previously available at <http://www.internationalcompetitionnetwork.org/uploads/library/doc547.pdf> (in the case of both website addresses cited here, the links are broken, see discussion in Introduction, n 16).

[103] ICN, *ICN Factsheet and Key Messages* (2009) 7, see also 3.

As if NCAs and NGAs in the ICN were not themselves vested local interest groups.

Participants have offered several ideas of the benefits that the ICN might bring. Sometimes the achievement of some of these benefits may clash with achieving others. There may, for example, be a clash between benefits for firms and customers, or between benefits for customer groups in different states. No system has been offered to explain what hierarchy should be followed in such cases. Even the existence of such clashes is barely acknowledged.

1.2.1.2.3 Academic theories of influence

Regulators, such as NCAs, can find themselves dealing with complex problems. The best ways of solving these problems may not be easy to ascertain. They may even depend upon the actions of consumers, firms, and regulators in other states, where externalities are present.

Transnational networks (like the ICN) can be effective and efficient places in which to discuss what the best solutions to common problems are and how to achieve them. Wide-reaching networks like the ICN include experts from around the world, which collects a lot of experience together. They provide a forum for regulators to share stories about the problems that they have faced and what worked and what did not. This helps to build a community. On a personal level, it can be comforting to realize that others face similar problems and frustrations. It can also be illuminating to hear about the solutions that others have devised. This sharing (and the ensuing discussions) can also save time, by eliminating 'solutions' that did not work elsewhere. Such exchanges can also lead to individual, or even group, learning. They may also result in improved, agreed policy guidelines or approaches for all. Doing such work in networks can be an efficient way to proceed (compared to acting in isolation, or even bilaterally). Over time these efficiencies can grow, community spirit can lower the costs of coordinating actions across different states, by developing relationships and trust, etc.[104]

There are many different network theories. Functionalist accounts focus on the efficiency of the network for achieving members' goals. Bradford, for example, says that an informal competition network was chosen because it offers 'a better path for international antitrust convergence'. 'Convergence' is an interesting core goal to highlight, given the ICN's lack of emphasis on implementation. She adds: 'Given the nature of the collective action problem in antitrust co-operation, binding arrangements and formal institutions remain largely unnecessary and undesirable.'[105] These are major claims given the likely implications of using an informal network. On the other hand, a rationalist account of networks sees institutions, like

[104] Slaughter and Hale (n 2) 363–64; Fingleton (n 85) 191–92. More generally on how networks work and their power, see Börzel (n 1) 1; Thompson (n 1) 30–31.

[105] Anu Bradford, 'International Antitrust Co-operation and the Preference for Non-Binding Regimes' in Andrew Guzman (ed), *Co-operation, Comity and Competition Policy* (OUP 2011) 322.

the ICN, as a reflection of state power and interests. The strong create institutions to serve their wants.[106] If this is the case, then one would expect ICN membership to bring particular benefits to strong NCAs. When analysing the relational aspects between network actors and their interaction more generally (not in relation to the ICN), Kahler has said:

> Under a political lens, networked governance, too often represented as inherently consensual, reveals distributional and status conflicts that are often resolved through the introduction of centralization and hierarchy, within or outside the network. These insights from political analysis serve to revise network approaches to international relations and to expand their scope.[107]

Yet, Gaus counsels us not to just assume that powerful states are also powerful within networks.[108] In his study, which focused on the ICN itself, Gaus locates power more diffusely. NCAs that are 'presumed to dominate the ICN due to their position in the international system are not able to do so without concessions to much smaller, "second-tier" members'.[109]

We think that power is important in the ICN and NCAs' influence is unequal there. Gaus is right when he says we should not just assume power within the network, because of its existence outside. However, as we explain in more detail below, our own experience inside the ICN itself suggest that significantly more influence and power rests with a few powerful NCAs (and NGAs), rather than in a more diffuse power relation that Gaus highlights. As we explain in Section 1.3, this is because we think he overestimates the importance of informal power (the ability to get desirable outcomes outside the normal channels of power) and allocates this informal power too widely and permanently.[110] Gaus may also be too 'trusting' in those he surveyed in relation to the idea that weaker states exercise control over NGAs.[111]

[106] Arthur Stein, 'Neoliberal Institutionalism' in Christian Reus-Smit and Duncan Snidal (eds), *The Oxford Handbook of International Relations* (OUP 2008) 206.

[107] Miles Kahler, 'Networked Politics: Agency, Power, and Governance' in Miles Kahler (ed), *Networked Politics: Agency, Power, and Governance* (Cornell UP 2009) 9.

[108]

> Following the existing theories when explaining the location, sources and directions of power and control in TGNs [trans-governmental networks], we are either left to alternate between outright neglect of these issues or an oversimplification driven by IR [international relations] research that equates power and control in networks with member states that are also the most powerful and resource-rich in the international system.
>
> Alexander Gaus, 'Speaking Truth to Power and Control in Transgovernmental Networks' (ICPP 2015 International Conference on Public Policy) 9

See also his further discussion of the international relations, sociology, and political science literatures (ibid 4–8).

[109] ibid 9.

[110] See the discussions around nn 157 and 170.

[111] Gaus (n 108) 18.

Scholars have long debated under which conditions soft law (ie 'non-binding' rules, such as ICN recommended practices) emerges. Soft law facilitates cooperation where there is mutual interest in finding common ground, harmonizing different national regulatory environments.[112] Some contend that, as they are produced in a setting that is participatory, deliberative, and non-binding, soft law should generate higher acceptance of common standards.[113] Others are less convinced, arguing that only a small subset of issues can be solved by international soft law, that is 'coordination games'. In coordination games, actors just want to find common standards that can facilitate economic and intellectual exchanges between them, but they are indifferent to the particular type of standard that is chosen.[114] Although true coordination games exist in competition, they are rare.[115] In many instances in which public and private actors interact at international level, standards already exist (although this may be less true in newer regimes).

It is true that the consensus requirement implies that (absent individual or collective mistake) all ICN action must be a Pareto improvement. Here, we explain how the ICN's structure and format help widen the space for agreement beyond narrow coordination games. They do this through focusing on the benefits to NCAs (rather than states) and technical issues (rather than state bargaining). First, networks must benefit *each network member*.[116] For NCAs that do not anticipate network benefits, it may be hard to justify the expense of ICN participation. The need for individual benefits is worth emphasizing. Many of those participating in the ICN state that this is a selfless exercise of world betterment. This is unlikely to be the case. While the ICN *may* generate positive externalities, each NCA must also perceive individual benefit in order for it to use its limited resources for such work.[117] Having said that, as Section 1.2.1.2.4 explains in more detail, benefits

[112] See Kenneth Abbott and Duncan Snidal, 'Hard and Soft Law in International Governance' (2000) 54 International Organization 421; Slaughter (n 36).

[113] David Trubek and Louise Trubek, 'Hard and Soft Law in the Construction of Social Europe: the role of the Open Method of Co-Ordination' (2005) 11 European Law Journal 343.

[114] This situation occurs for example when new standards have to be set: the different actors have no intense preferences as to which option has to be chosen, but they all prefer the establishment of a common standard over regulatory divergence, Tim Büthe and Walter Mattli, *The New Global Rulers: the privatization of regulation in the world economy* (Princeton UP 2013); Simmons (n 67).

[115] Verdier (n 62) 123–24.

[116] Walter Powell, 'Neither Market Nor Hierarchy: Network Forms of Organisation' in Grahame Thompson and others (eds), *Markets, Hierarchies and Networks* (SAGE 1991) 272; Burkard Eberlein, 'Policy Co-ordination without Centralisation? Informal Network Governance in EU Single Market Regulation' in Ehlermann and Atanasiu (n 89) 149; Rhodes (n 4) 161.

[117] Advanced NCAs and newer NCAs are unlikely to be seeking the same thing from a network. NCAs must also assess the costs (compared to the benefits) of network membership. Network relationships often take a lot of resources to establish and maintain, Patrick Kenis and Keith Provan, 'Towards an Exogenous Theory of Public Network Performance' (2009) 87 Public Administration 440, 440. One needs to consider the actual costs of participation as well as the opportunity costs (participation in the network takes time and so may mean that an NCA has less time for running cases or doing advocacy, for example). The costs and benefits for an NCA (as well as between NCAs) may arise at different times. Resource interdependencies may undermine distinctions between competition enforcement and policy. Powerful enforcers may gain influence at the policy setting stage (agreeing ICN recommended

come in many guises. Advanced NCAs' greater resources mean that they can make participation worthwhile for newer NCAs (because they benefit from newer NCAs' participation), while still ensuring that most benefits fall to the advanced NCAs.[118]

Network actors and their employees prioritize certain networks over others. All have limited time and resources. If NCAs no longer feel that network benefits outweigh the costs of participating in the network, they may seek to change the network. If they do not succeed, then they might leave the network, or at least invest considerably less time and resources in it.[119] In this way we agree with Gaus that all ICN members must feel that membership benefits them. As we will see, powerful and influential NCAs are able to distort these benefits.

When we say that each network member (i.e., an NCA) must benefit, we need to be clear about what this means. Benefits might accrue directly *for the NCA itself* (such as making enforcement tasks easier). Or, benefits may come indirectly to the NCA by generating gains for stakeholders that the NCA considers valuable (such as an easier investment climate for national firms abroad).[120] As noted in Section 1.2.1.1, by making the ICN's focus technical rules rather than state interests, NCAs are encouraged not to consider the impact of ICN activities and work products in terms of the distribution of benefits between states (such as on firms, employees, and other stakeholders in their jurisdictions—other than consumers).[121] Some NCAs may still consider that the distribution of such benefits towards their own states is important. However, as we explain below, regular contact with the network (and the epistemic community) is a powerful mechanism for aligning actors' focus on 'technical issues'. All of this, along with the widespread independence of NCAs, potentially drives a wedge between NCAs' interests and their states' interests, such that we (and states) cannot assume they overlap very well.

The third issue to consider here is how benefits might be allocated between network participants (and others). Collective action will not necessarily maximize

practices, for example) as others know that these enforcers will not invest resources in policies that they disagree with, Firat Cengiz, *Antitrust Federalism in the EU and the US* (Routledge 2013) 41–42.

118 Similarly, Andrés Palacios Lleras, 'Competition Law in Latin America: 100 Years of Solitude' in Swethaa Ballakrishnen and Sara Dezalay (eds), *Invisible Institutionalisms: Collective Reflections on the Shadows of Legal Globalisation* (Hart 2021) 195.

119 Wise NCAs would consider whether network benefits can be achieved more effectively and cheaply in other ways, perhaps through bilateral negotiations with other NCAs, for example, David Marsh and Martin Smith, 'Understanding Policy Networks: Towards a Dialectical Approach' (2000) 48 Political Studies 4, 9.

120 NCA (and NGA) employees can also benefit from network activity. Rewards may come from a feeling of participating in something greater (based on a belief in the 'competition religion'). Bringing a successful technique back from the ICN may also be an easy way of getting social capital in one's own NCA. This may be valuable from a career perspective, either at home or abroad—see Section 1.3.1.2. Individual benefits of this kind may lead to complex interactions between network effects and those from relevant epistemic communities. At the extreme, this may mean that benefits only accrue to NCA or NGA employees. In this case, these benefits need to be reframed as accruing to the NCA/NGA itself.

121 For a similar point based on the agency problem, see Verdier (n 62) 170.

public goods either for the whole world, or even for ICN members. As regards global welfare, Section 1.2.1.1.3 shows that networks are political institutions, benefiting their members, while those outside of the network may suffer, even if they have relevant interests.[122] As regards maximizing the welfare of ICN members as a whole, Olson shows that:

> unless the number of individuals in a group is quite small [which is not the case for the ICN], or unless there is coercion or some other special device to make individuals act in their common interest, *rational, self-interested individuals will not act to achieve their common or group interests.*[123]

So, while all ICN members must benefit, welfare is unlikely to be maximized (although Section 1.3.1.2 argues that the epistemic community may affect this to some degree).[124] Nor is it likely that the benefits generated by the ICN are equally divided across all ICN members (and their states). One might expect each NCA to seek to maximize the benefits to itself (directly or indirectly) through its ICN participation.[125] Formally ICN members have equal power. ICN decision-making is via consensus. However, in practice, NCAs have radically different amounts of power within the ICN. This means that different NCAs may benefit from the ICN to radically different degrees. This is also the perception of ICN actors.

1.2.1.2.4 Compares reasons given by these actors to the academic theories of influence

It is hard to argue with the ICN's aims 'proposing superior standards and procedures in competition policy; proposing substantive and procedural convergence; and aiding international co-operation' (at least the first and third aim). However, the idea of what might be a 'superior standard' overflows with (unspecified) normative content. The issue deserves special attention because, as pointed out in the Introduction to this book, competition policy (and the ensuing enforcement) is a

[122] Wilks in Ehlermann and Atanasiu (n 89) 15, 70, 78; L Schaap and M van Twist, 'The Dynamics of Closedness in Networks' in Walter Kickert, Erik-Hans Klijn and Joop Koppenjan (eds), *Managing Complex Networks: Strategies for the Public Sector* (Sage 1997) 72.

[123] Mancur Olson, *The Logic of Collective Action* (Harvard UP 1965) 2 (emphasis as original).

[124] Olson did not think that epistemic communities would normally have much influence in larger groups (ibid 60–65), but there is reason to believe that their power is stronger in the competition community.

[125] In principle, the consensus rule allows NCAs to block ICN outputs, even if they are Pareto efficient. There is a lot of evidence from political science that individuals often block Pareto-efficient deals that they consider to be inequitable. For a discussion of this in relation to the GATT, see Richard Steinberg, 'In the Shadow of Law or Power? Consensus-Based Bargaining and Outcomes in the GATT/WTO' (2002) 56 International Organization 339, 346. As we explain below, blocking an ICN work product that is supported by NCAs from the EU and the USA would be a major step for an NCA; see the discussion about the *consensus rule* (Section 1.2.1.2.4). Few will feel able, in fact, to do this, even if ICN rules clearly allow it.

highly redistributive exercise, with winners and losers. The ICN makes no effort to explain how clashes within or between the interests of NCAs, consumers, law firms and their clients, or different economies, might be resolved.

There are two broad types of changes that experts might seek in order to achieve the kinds of competition rules that they want (in their own or other states). There may be a need for legislative change to alter divergent national competition rules themselves. Such changes are not normally within the gift of an NCA (although they may effectively lobby their own states to make such changes). However, NCAs can often have major substantive and procedural impacts without involving wider state actors. Competition rules tend to be widely drafted, leaving lots of room for different interpretations in the grey spaces where the rules are unclear. This creates opportunities for some NCAs to push for alignment by others.

So, it is important to ascertain which NCAs have the most power within the ICN and whether they can impact who 'benefits generated by the ICN' accrue to. We also need to see whether the consensus rule provides an adequate break here. In fact, we argue that, while the consensus rule implies that NCAs can protect their own state's interests, not only may this be untrue (in fact), but NCAs might not seek out their own state's interests at all.

Advanced NCAs (especially the NCAs from the EU and the USA) There are several reasons to believe that those that are likely to benefit most from transnational networks are those that establish and run them. This tends to be actors from advanced economies, such as the NCAs from the EU and the USA. First, networks are fora for sharing their knowledge and insights with officials facing similar problems worldwide. This provides opportunities for advanced NCAs to learn (although, realistically, this mainly comes from other advanced NCAs).[126] The ICN also provides them with regular, repeated opportunities to engage with other NCAs and to persuade them of the benefits of their rules.[127] The ICN is also a relatively cheap route for advanced NCAs to try to push other NCAs to change the interpretation of their competition rules (or even push these NCAs to push their states to change their competition rules) to be more like the systems in the EU and the USA.[128]

There are many reasons why advanced NCAs from the EU and the USA might want others to follow the competition systems of the EU and the USA. As the Introduction to this book pointed out, competition rules based on principles used by advanced NCAs (such as non-discrimination, only competition goals

[126] The informal nature of these exchanges tends to 'entrench the hegemony of established regimes' Yane Svetiev, *Experimentalist Competition Law and the Regulation of Markets* (Hart 2020) 163.

[127] Svetiev (n 79) 183–84.

[128] Katja Weber, *Hierarchy Amidst Anarchy: Transaction Costs and Institutional Choice* (U of New York Press 2000); van Waarden and Drahos (n 12) 932; Stein (n 106) 209. It also facilitates exchanges between NCAs on eg specific cases, due to the contacts made through the ICN: Sjöblom and Widegren (n 57) 354.

and independent NCAs) likely favour multinational firms from these jurisdictions. Convergence of the competition rules globally also helps EU and US firms to expand into new jurisdictions, as they are familiar with the (new) rules to be applied in the 'reforming states'.[129] More uniform rules across different states reduces multinationals' costs.[130] Furthermore, there are several potential benefits for the EU and US NCAs themselves if their own rules are used, as they do not have to learn new rules. There is also less risk that other NCAs engaged in similar activities will undermine the efforts of these advanced NCAs.[131]

The competition rules of the advanced NCAs seem likely to be followed given the decisions taken in the ICN's 'constitutional moment', network pressures, and advanced NCAs' special influence in the ICN. First, the 'advanced NCAs' establishing the ICN took several 'constitutional decisions', based on competition theories that they like, which help to ensure that ICN work products favour their rules and stakeholders (even at others' expense). These theories are adapted to working in these advanced economies (and may not work so well elsewhere).[132] For example—'formally non-discriminatory'—EU/US competition rules should

[129] As one NCA points out:

> The continuous integration of Member States' economies within a consistent competition framework has been mirrored by the advocacy efforts of the Commission to promote common competition principles internationally. In an ever more globalised economy, ensuring a more level playing field on the world stage has become an essential objective of competition policy. This led the Commission, starting from the 1990s 'to seek to encourage the application of similar policies by the Community's main trading partners, by means of bilateral agreements or through multilateral negotiation. [fn Report on Competition Policy 1992, 15]. Consequently, the Commission pursued a twofold strategy: it developed and strengthened direct bilateral relations with main trading partners and it invested substantially in multilateral bodies such as the OECD or the International Competition Network (ICN).

European Commission, *Commission, Report on Competition Policy* (2010) para 26. Similarly, as a former employee of DG COMP (the part of the EU Commission which is an ICN member) says, 'Cooperation with other competition agencies can be expected to bring significant benefits for the EU: direct benefits in terms of more effective/efficient enforcement of EU competition rules, but also indirect benefits, such as fair treatment of EU companies in non-EU markets, and the creation of a level-playing field between EU companies and foreign competitors', Eva Valle Lagares, 'International Agreements Regarding Co-operation in the Field of Competition: the new strategy of the European Commission' (2010) 1 Journal of European Competition Law and Practice 155, 155. Similar statements have been made about the work of the US NCAs. For example:

> Like SEC officials, DOJ and FTC regulators claim that networking with foreign regulators, technical assistance efforts, and the accompanying export of U.S. regulation directly benefit the U.S. For example, former FTC Chairman Janet Steiger argued that the competition reforms pursued by the FTC and DOJ abroad 'not only benefit the citizens of the region, but will enhance the competitiveness of American industry by helping to open new markets and investment opportunities. [fn Justice Department, *FTC Receive Funds to Support Competition Counseling Aid*, 8 Int'l Trade Rep. (BNA) 871 (1991)]. Raustiala (n 2) 41.

[130] ICPAC (n 20) Executive Summary 21, see also 22–25. Similarly, ICN Unilateral Conduct Working Group, *State-Created Monopolies Analysis Pursuant to Unilateral Conduct Laws* (2006) 1; Hollman and Kovacic (n 26) 55–56; Joaquín Almunia, *A New Decade for the International Competition Network* (2011) 2–4.

[131] Similarly, Palacios Lleras (n 118) 195, referring to leniency regimes, for example.

[132] See the discussion around n 149.

help to open up new markets to EU/US firms.[133] Similarly, large multinationals strongly advocate ignoring 'non-competition' policy goals (eg industrial policy and environmental protection) in competition decisions. The ICN has embraced this too, benefiting large multinationals (disproportionately from the economically advanced states that were central in establishing the ICN). It considerably simplifies the competition rules. This might not matter too much in states with other ways of achieving these public policy goals. However, poorer states may find this hard. So, such a policy stance is likely to have very different implications in such jurisdictions. Yet, focusing on expertise and technical solutions, rather than political bargaining, encourages participants to ignore winners and losers (making agreement easier) (see Section 1.2.1.1).[134]

As Section 1.3.1.2 explains, it is also worth reflecting on the specific individuals involved in the ICN and their preferences. As noted, they will appreciate the autonomy from political influence and the emphasis on technical expertise rather than state bargaining. They are also likely to appreciate the bringing together of many experts in their own field (likeminded people often have interesting discussions), the possibility of recursivity that this brings,[135] the opportunity to further improve ICN work products in the future, the sense of community, and the flexibility for change. There is also a widespread intellectual belief, among the epistemic community of 'competition people', that the neoliberal paradigm that many propagate is positive for states large and small. This adds an important, almost evangelical, dimension to support the work of these individuals. Such sentiments might even push these individuals to seek more benefits for developing NCAs than one might otherwise expect (see also Section 1.3.1.2). All of this within a network structure where, formally at least, all are treated as equals.[136] The advanced NCAs

[133] For example, 'In the merger review process, jurisdictions should not discriminate in the application of competition laws and regulations on the basis of nationality' ICN Merger Working Group, *Guiding Principles for Merger Notification and Review* (2002) principle 3, <https://www.internationalcompetitionnetwork.org/portfolio/guiding-principles-for-merger-notification-review-procedure/> accessed 7 October 2021.

[134] Wilks (n 12) 437ff.

[135] Svetiev (n 79) 185. There is some evidence of the ICN seeking to do this. At the start of its second decade it spoke of reformulating existing recommended practices and other work products, dynamically. See, for example, ICN, *The ICN's Vision for Its Second Decade* (2012), <https://www.internationalcompetitionnetwork.org/wp-content/uploads/2018/07/ICN2dDecade2011.pdf> accessed 7 October 2021. This sort of exercise does not seem to have been hard-wired into the ICN system though, Svetiev (n 126) 160 and 170–73 (and it would be hard to achieve this too, given the size of the network and the diversity in membership).

[136] Even those with different visions may conform over time. Networks are powerful media for developing consensus through similar ways of seeing the world. According to Schmidt and Radaelli, networks are particularly influential where their discourse 'contains cognitive arguments that demonstrate the policy programme's relevance, applicability and coherence: and normative arguments that resonate with long-standing or newly emerging values' Schmidt and Radaelli (n 11) 188. Wilks says that the 'programme of activities "intended to foster the creation of a common competition culture"... matches the discourse concept rather neatly. It is primarily coordinative, it embraces a cognitive framework drawing on competition law and economics, and it has a strong normative thrust in pursuit of the perceived benefits of competition' Wilks (n 12) 430 (this was in relation to proposals for a European Competition

that set up the ICN likely saw it as a first step on the road to convergence around their own standards for competition law and policy worldwide (at least the ones they agree with).[137]

There are some costs that counterbalance these benefits. First, there is the cost of setting up and supporting the ICN itself. These costs have been kept small by not having a permanent secretariat and having most meetings online (although the annual meeting of all NCAs is done in person). Many of the costs have been borne by the richer NCAs, at least at the start (especially Canada). Second, there are the costs of participating in ICN activities, such as the Steering Group, or on the various Working Groups. This can involve a lot of resources.[138] Demand for technical assistance and training also comes via contacts with ICN members. Presumably, these costs require a diversion of funds from other activities that the EU and US NCAs might want to be involved in, such as increased competition enforcement in their own jurisdiction. So, there is also a potential opportunity cost in terms of their own consumers, which also needs to be weighed against the many benefits. Many of these costs are double-edged swords, as they give these advanced NCAs influence within the ICN (see Section 1.3.1).

Note though that there are times when EU/US competition systems do not align.[139] Here there is a risk that competition between them might break out again. The consensus rule was probably a wise addition by the EU/US. This helps in the story that all NCAs choose whether or not to adopt ICN work products (even though we will see that the soft pressure to do so can be immense). It also protects the EU and the USA from ICN rules that they themselves disagree with. In fact, policy conflicts are not normally openly discussed in the ICN. One might have

Network, but similar points apply to the ICN). Similarly, Wälti (n 12) 416; van Waarden and Drahos (n 12) 933.

[137] Raustiala (n 2) 41. In fact, this seems to have been an aim of the ICPAC report suggestion to adopt a network, see the reference in footnote 280. By way of contrast, more classical arrangements, such as treaties and international organizations, are not always optimal for such exchanges. It can be hard and time consuming to agree unanimous, binding rules. This slows things down in fast-moving areas. Negotiations often involve actors with little knowledge of these increasingly complex regulatory areas (such as officials from foreign ministries). Bargains are constructed based around sovereignty, demanding equality, and focusing on the costs and benefits of any change to each state.

[138] For example, the US Federal Trade Commission currently has the equivalent of several permanent employees dealing with ICN-related matters, <www.ftc.gov/policy/international/international-competition> accessed 7 October 2021. When asked, the UK's Competition and Markets Authority said that these costs would be almost impossible to measure, as there as so many people involved in small chunks of ICN work.

[139] Examples of conflicts are evident. For example, think of the disagreements between the USA and the EU (principally Germany) on unilateral effects and digital markets, Oliver Budzinski, 'The Economics of International Competition Policy: New Challenges in the Light of Digitization?' (2020) 26 Ilmenau Economics Discussion Papers 12–13; and the tremendous (unresolved) conflicts in the UCWG on the competition rules' goals, discussed in Section I.3 of this book. See also, Harry First and Spencer Weber Waller, 'Antitrust's Democracy Deficit' [2013] New York University School of Law, Centre for Law, Economics and Organization: Law and Economics Research Paper Series Working Paper No 13–05 41–42.

thought that such a comprehensive grouping of most of the world's NCAs might be an ideal place to have such discussions. Yet, the ICN does not seem to be there to make new policy. Rather, its main role seems to be to impose/encourage others to adopt the existing policies of a small group of established NCAs (particularly the EU and the USA).[140]

New jurisdictions from poorer countries Good competition rules can benefit rich countries, they may be even more important for poorer ones. This is because such countries often have concentrated markets, lack economies of scale and scope, entrenched political links for businesses, etc. However, new jurisdictions have, by definition, new competition rules. Their NCAs often have very limited resources (and powers) with which to take on entrenched interests in their countries. They may also lack well-trained staff in this niche area and have little money for training.[141]

Here we discuss the incentives for less-developed (and less well-resourced) NCAs to participate in the ICN. Many believe that the ICN 'has had an important impact in the development of competition policy in Mexico'.[142] We discuss three key benefits: community support, help building a coherent framework, and support in confrontations with stakeholders back home and raising esteem there. However, the ICN also imposes costs on newer NCAs, including: a lack of rules tailored to their needs, costs of adaptation, and hits to self-esteem. So, the benefits that new jurisdictions seek from their ICN membership are not likely to be the same as those that the EU and USA are pursing. Yet, we have seen that all NCAs must perceive benefits from their ICN membership. Otherwise, they will not expend resources participating.[143]

Less experienced (newer) NCAs are often also keen to participate in transnational networks. Being part of this community can be comforting. It is not easy to introduce a whole new system of regulation into a jurisdiction; especially one that many influential stakeholders resent.

Second, there is assistance in identifying common problems and building and navigating a coherent framework for their nascent competition system. Even better, this comes from esteemed actors in the competition community (actors that often helped their state write its competition rules in the first place). To make things easier (and more efficient), this might all be distilled into best practice

[140] Having said that, this needs to be a dynamic assessment, as the role of the ICN might be changing here. Some important conflicts are being brought within the ICN structure and debated there of late. One example of this is digital issues and competition law, where significant disagreements between NCAs exist. See for example, <www.internationalcompetitionnetwork.org/portfolio/dominance-substantial-market-power-in-digital-markets-survey-report/> accessed 7 October 2021.

[141] Eduardo Pérez Motta, 'The Role of the International Competition Network (ICN) in the Promotion of Competition in Developing Countries: The Case of Mexico' in Lugard (n 7) 217–19.

[142] ibid 219.

[143] For similar examples of asymmetrical contracting in the GATT, see Steinberg (n 125) 348–49. That said, this kind of behaviour by powerful actors may be less important in networks focusing on technical 'best' rules, rather than state bargaining.

guidelines for all to follow.[144] There is also the chance of receiving extra training from 'more advanced' NCAs through the relationships that they build within the ICN. Competition enforcement is a complex area where a lot of the know-how is hidden.[145] So, this support is valuable. As Section 1.3 explains, despite the costs, providing training can benefit advanced NCAs and their stakeholders (and those from the EU and the USA have done a lot). It allows them to focus newer NCAs on 'approved' goals, techniques, and processes. Poorer NCAs appreciate assistance. It develops their staff's techniques (and competence), boosts their self-esteem, and initiates them into the competition epistemic community.

Third, newer NCAs may also be supported in confrontations with stakeholders back home. Facing down local vested interest groups is partly about persuading states of the benefit of a strong competition regime.[146] Such a regime also benefits the EU and the USA if local competition rules are applied in line with their thinking. This is because it should help to open up new markets to entry from EU and US firms. The ICN can support an NCA in many ways which boost the NCA's (and its staff) profile. One example is to hold ICN events in that country.[147] This emphasizes competition's importance and hints to the NCA's government that the international community may take a hostile act against the NCA negatively.

The ICN can also support new jurisdictions in their struggle to get more resources and better powers. Both can help the NCA to be more active in its role (helping the EU/US if the NCA is acting in line with their views on competition). For example, the ICN might write reports arguing that effective enforcement can only be achieved under certain conditions.[148] These might say that NCAs

[144] Svetiev (n 79) 185. Similarly, Slaughter adds, in relation to other regulations, but a similar point is relevant here, that:

> Recommended rules and practices compiled by a global body of securities regulators or environmental officials offer a focal point for convergence. Equally important, they offer a kind of safe harbor for officials the world over looking for guidance and besieged with consultants, who need not only to make a choice but to be able to defend it to their superiors.

Slaughter (n 36) 180.

[145] For example, NCAs might not advertise mistakes that they have made in their notices, but knowing about these mistakes may provide useful learning for other NCAs, helping them to avoid them too.

[146] For example, during the ICN's Annual Conference in 2012, the ICN's (then) Chair, Eduardo Pérez Motta said 'It is time for the ICN to take on a more active role in supporting members, whenever they ask for assistance, in the complicated and politically charged debates they often face at home, for example when advocating improvements to their legislation – or indeed, when resisting regressions to their regimes' <www.internationalcompetitionnetwork.org/wp-content/uploads/2020/01/SpeechChairMottaclosing2012.pdf> accessed 7 October 2021. At this time, Eduardo Pérez Motta was actually asking for ICN support himself as he was 'under fire' from the Mexican government because, in 2011, the NCA that he led imposed a $1 billion fine on Telcel for breaching the competition rules, <www.reuters.com/article/mexico-competition/mexico-agency-mulling-1-bln-slim-fine-gets-new-member-idUSS1E78D2EF20110915> accessed 7 October 2021.

[147] Tavares (n 95) 335. An example was when El Salvador's recently created NCA organized an ICN Cartel workshop in El Salvador. This meant that it could show its government that it has its peers' respect and trust.

[148] The ICN has assisted several NCA members (such as Brazil, India, Jersey, and Peru) when they sought external support for domestic reforms. ICN members want such work to be done more

need: *sufficient funds* to be able to employ well-trained staff and actively enforce the competition rules; *certain powers*, such as an ability to offer leniency sometimes; or it could be an *institutional issue*, like the amount of independence that the competition community considers optimal for an NCA. Of course, such reports, written by NCAs, can only help all of them back in their own jurisdictions, as they generally ask for more money and power.

On the other hand, there are also costs involved for these less developed NCAs, aside from the costs necessary to participate in ICN activities. These come in three major forms: a lack of tailored rules; the costs of adaptation; and hits to self-esteem. The first problem is that the principal origin of the rules that the ICN focuses on and recommends is the competition policy of advanced industrial states (given their predominant influence—see above). The Introduction to this book notes that newer NCAs, especially those in developing countries, may require quite different kinds of competition rules.[149] The size and diversity of the ICN's membership means that one set of recommendations is unlikely to fit all needs. Much ICN activity is likely to entrench the practices of mature regimes, whether or not this was the original intention.[150] The ICN claims to be aware of this. Chapter 4 notes that it is paying more attention to newer regimes' needs, but this is still not a major all-encompassing part of ICN work. This is strange, given the emphasis placed on precisely this issue in the ICN mission statements.[151]

Second, there are costs of adaptation. When deciding whether to implement an ICN work products an NCA will be confronted with several costs and benefits. The NCA might look at the new rule on its merits. Perhaps it generates more consumer surplus, or it does this at a cheaper price of operation than other rules (perhaps it is easier to enforce). It might bring all such rules into line around the world, reducing firms' compliance costs. Such benefits should be balanced against the costs of change.[152] Costs include their firms having to get legal advice (and possibly also

often, ICN Merger Working Group, *ICN Recommended Practices for Merger Notification and Review Procedures: Member Self-Assessment: Report on 2016 Survey Results* (2017) 17–18, <https://www.internationalcompetitionnetwork.org/wp-content/uploads/2019/04/MWG_NPRPssurveyreport2017.pdf> accessed 7 October 2021.

149 Newer regimes might have quite specific substantive and procedural problems (concentrated markets, less experienced staff, difficulty to collate basic data), Michal Gal, *Competition Policy for Small Market Economies* (Harvard UP 2003); Michal S Gal, 'When the Going Gets Tight: Institutional Solutions When Antitrust Enforcement Resources are Scarce' [2009] Antitrust: Antitrust Law & Policy eJournal. See also Svetiev (n 79) 185–89 and the sources cited there.

150 ICN working groups are mainly organized around the competition categories familiar in 'advanced' regimes. The ICN collates information on experiences through questionnaires, NCAs from these richer states are better resourced and so more able to reply (this issue is discussed further in Chapter 4). The ICN does not normally offer divergent choices in its recommended practices, nor does it seek to understand diversity. In fact, ICN benchmarking largely seems to be a tool for entrenchment, Svetiev (n 126) 164–70.

151 See the text around n 103.

152 For insights into costs of change, see ICN Merger Working Group (n 148) 17.

change production and distribution processes).[153] States may also have the economic costs of retraining regulators and constructing new regulatory frameworks. There are also the political costs of getting changes through the legislative system in their own country;[154] there may also be costs of dealing with those that lose out under the changes.[155] As the NCA (especially highly independent ones) is not directly paying the price of many of these costs, it is the state (and firms and consumers), then this might reduce these 'costs' from its perspective. Costs of adaption exist for all NCAs faced with a work product that deviates from its own local practices. That said, they may be relatively low for actors in states whose NCAs' practices have not become too entrenched yet.

A third cost is the potential hit to self-esteem for the new NCA. The more time one spends on attending, the more susceptible one is to influence from competition peers and the less time one has for developing independent policy and doing competition work at home (although ICN membership can assist in getting more competition powers and status at home). While it is theoretically conceivable that they might suggest practices that ICN members unanimously agree to incorporate into ICN recommended practices, the problems and lack of experience of these NCAs limit the chances of this.[156] It seems unlikely, in fact, that advanced NCAs will really treat the NCAs (and their employees) that are learning from them as equals, despite the ICN's promise of equality for all NCAs. Help may breed a kind of dependence, making it harder for disagreements to occur, despite their formal freedom. Having said that, new NCAs do have some, limited power. From the perspective of the EU and the USA, the network's value increases the wider the participation is,[157] as long as these participants adhere to their rules. But there are clearly limits.

In this way, new NCAs form alliances with their more influential peers to 'punch above their weight'. But the nature of this alliance should not be forgotten. Despite the explicit emphasis on equality in the ICN, this is not an alliance of equals. New NCAs know (or they suspect) that valuable offers like these will only come to compliant NCAs (ones that support, and implement, the policy preferences of the

[153] Simmons (n 67) 590.

[154] This means the costs of agreeing to a 'bad bargain' (or not preventing one) might be small and perhaps outweighed by other benefits, such enhanced credibility as being seen to agree with the majority of actors in this area. In any event, we will see examples of competition authorities agreeing to things that do not seem to be in their own self-interest, or that of their consumers or economies.

[155] Drezner (n 66) 845.

[156] Having said that, there are examples of NCAs that have been more active than one might expect. One example is the Pakistani NCA, which seems particularly active for an NCA of its size and wealth. For example, it replied to two out of four ICN questionnaires (2007 and 2009). This is significant because on average, 37 countries replied per questionnaire, out of over 100 members. Why is it doing this? Perhaps, it is seeking recognition from international peers. Or, it may be that it is certain individuals involved that can push this agenda. For example, they had Dr Jo Wilson who is very well respected and so he might have been keen to engage with an international audience. This reinforces the point that one would do well never to forget the individual dimension of the network too.

[157] Hollman and Kovacic (n 26) 58. See also the discussion around n 127.

advanced NCAs). To stand effectively against influential NCAs on a 'good practice' is another matter. You need to be from a reasonably strong and large economy and with strong leadership that is prepared to be isolated. This rarely happens.[158] New NCAs normally have neither the knowledge nor the confidence to take such a stance. They probably also fear that they could not afford the price that such a strategy would involve.

The consensus rule (or requirement) The final thing to assess here is whether the 'consensus rule' for changing the ICN constitution or agreeing the ICN work schedule or new ICN work products is sufficient to protect all NCAs and their states. For important acts, the ICN only works through consensus. So, perhaps there is no need for newer NCAs (and their states) to fear that the ICN could undermine their national interests. Several factors make us question this idea, newer NCAs: lack control over the ICN agenda; lack relevant knowledge; might not be acting in their states' interests (and may not even realize this given the power of the epistemic community); may be overly relaxed in the light of the lack of need for implementation of ICN work products. The combination of these factors may give pause for thought for states considering relying on their NCAs, unchecked. In addition, it is worth noting that 96 per cent of respondents (NCAs and NGAs) in our survey, said that some NCAs are more influential than others in the ICN.[159]

Given their disproportionate control over leadership roles in the organization, Section 1.2.1.2.1 demonstrates that the most technically advanced NCAs have had disproportionate influence to set the ICN agenda, decide which topics should be investigated (and which should be ignored), and to allocate key roles for who should investigate these topics (and setting the 'micro agenda' there too).[160] Then, when the discussions start, they are able to focus attention on the issues and solutions that most benefit them (this might benefit the NCA (or its employees) directly, or indirectly, by helping relevant stakeholders).[161] So, as Chapter 4 explains, the selection and orientation of ICN work products already favours advanced NCAs.

[158] One example of this is when the South African Competition Tribunal went 'against the world' in the UCWG discussions on the goals of the competition rules. Contrary to the mainstream, it said that there are other concerns, such as social integration, that need to be taken into account when enforcing competition law. But the South Africa Competition Tribunal is from a major African economy and, even though it did not have lots of staff, it had a charismatic president (David Lewis) so it felt able (and willing) to go against the mainstream views.

[159] Perhaps it does not matter if some NCAs are more powerful than others. Each state can decide whether to follow an ICN recommended practice, so legitimacy and accountability may be 'preserved'. However, Chapter 2 explains why this bulwark often provides less protection than is attributed to it too.

[160] Scholars stress the importance of these issues in other fora, such as the GATT, Steinberg (n 125) 354–56.

[161] Is there a contradiction between the argument that some powerful states use the ICN to advance their domestic interests and the interests of their 'national champions', and the fact that many NCAs participating in the ICN are insulated from state influence? The answer depends upon the ideology that NCAs employ in the ICN. Where an NCA's ideology is thought to advance its state's domestic interests (including its industrial policy), then its state has less reason to seek presence, or influence, in the ICN (and we will see many good reasons why this might not be in its interests). Here, it is irrelevant whether

Second, while open search for the best ideas sounds meritocratic, ideas can come from anyone; however, it likely favours 'advanced NCAs' and their states. Their large research budgets give them significant advantages in these discussions compared to newer NCAs. Advanced NCAs have had more time to build up experience of a range of problems in different markets to see what works best for them and their stakeholders. This generates opportunities to advance their industrial policy goals through soft extraterritorial advocacy of the rules they favour. In an arena which they dominate, they can dress up their preferences as the best technical solutions. Newer NCAs find these narratives hard to refute. They often do not have the time, competence, or advanced knowledge to question whether the position of the 'advanced NCAs' is right for their own state and will work optimally there.[162] Let us put on one side for the moment the point that these competition systems are not universally accepted in these 'advanced' states. In any event, the solutions that work in their jurisdictions might not be optimal for less developed states (or their NCAs). Different varieties of capitalism, competition goals, histories, and socio-economic frameworks may all impact upon the optimal substantive and procedural competition rules that are wanted/needed.[163]

Third, as Section 1.2.1.2.3 highlighted, the focus on technical issues in the network, rather than on negotiating from a state perspective, may drive a wedge between what NCAs are aiming for and what their states might want. This wedge is likely to be driven further in by the epistemic community (see discussion in Section 1.3.1.2). A particularly powerful effect of policy networks is how they seem to socialize members over time. According to Weber, when actors come together to do technical tasks, a feeling of 'belonging together' can emerge and communal relationships can develop.[164] Identities then can change, through mutual orientation around a common project (due to similar concerns, interests, or aspirations).[165] Network members develop a kind of interdependence. This helps them to fit in but can make it hard to challenge the status quo in any fundamental way.[166]

Some rightly point out that independent regulators (like NCAs) are still subject to national controls. National politicians might appoint senior staff to its NCA, there might also be parliamentary hearings on the NCA's performance, for

the NCA seeks to achieve these state aims, or they are a consequence (by-product) of its own agenda. Richer jurisdictions, like those of the EU and the USA, largely seem to support their NCAs' competition ideology because, from an industrial policy perspective, it is thought to benefit firms from these regions. NCAs do not only consider the effects on themselves. They also consider the effect on their firms. Wilks talks of a surrendering of many areas of government through contracting out or privatization and then subjecting firms to regulation by business-friendly regulatory agencies, Stephen Wilks, *The Political Power of the Business Corporation* (Edward Elgar 2013) 105. The quotations above at n 129 support this point too.

162 This is not to impugn the abilities of the many bright, hard-working, and dedicated staff working in newer NCAs. Their lack of resources (time and equipment) simply handicaps them in this effort.

163 See the discussion around n 149.

164 Max Weber, *Economy and Society* (U of California Press 1978) 41.

165 Thompson (n 1) 30–31; Kohler-Koch (n 6) 140; Djelic and Quack (n 15) 12–13.

166 Schmidt and Radaelli (n 11) 203.

example. This is the case in many NCAs, including those in the USA and the UK, for example. There may also be process requirements on how national guidelines are produced. NCAs may also need to persuade regulatees of the legitimacy of their rules, in order to achieve compliance. Enforcement actions based on such guidelines might also face judicial review.[167] These can be a check (especially as it is hard for the ICN to easily and accurately assess implementation; see Chapters 2 and 4). However, many of the ICN's most influential NCAs have a considerable degree of independence from effective political and judicial control, even in their enforcement decisions. This is especially true for 'best practice' international norms that they 'follow' which have been agreed in fora like the ICN (where regulatees have a major role). This, along with the power of the epistemic community, means that changes in NCAs can be pronounced. Network actors are Janus-faced, having allegiance to their epistemic community (such as the competition community) and also their jurisdictions, for example. These allegiances are often in tension. But the power of networks is so strong that there are many instances of network actors using their specialist knowledge, to marginalize their own national interests (favouring ideas from their epistemic community).[168]

Gaus is right: newer NCAs can formally block the adoption of ICN work products. This tempers the 'advanced NCAs' somewhat, as they cannot be so outrageous in their demands. However, the mere presence of important NCAs from the EU and the USA (in agreement) puts others under great pressure to follow them,[169] bringing many benefits to EU/US stakeholders. In addition, given all the legal transplants and training they provide, it seems quite likely that EU/US views will often be supported by many other ICN members. As Sokol explains:

> When the United States and the EU are behind such norms, there is a powerful snowballing effect; other countries want to join in to be seen as part of the 'club'

[167] Verdier (n 62) 126–29 and 162.

[168] See the text around n 30. There is even some evidence for this in the ICPAC report. When concluding on the 'need' for a new forum it notes that the Asia-Pacific Economic Cooperation (APEC) forum is 'built on this recognition that "peer" pressure is capable of advancing some liberalization and harmonization of practices even without binding legal instruments'. ICPAC envisioned the ICN (as it was to become) as a body where 'nations can usefully explore areas of cooperation in the field of competition policy and facilitate further convergence and harmonization' ICPAC (n 20) 283. Note the reference to 'nations' here, which does not completely chime with the idea of replacing the 'normal' state officials with 'NCA officials' in this policy network.

[169] Best practice 'may carry a cognitive message of convergence' and in environments like the competition one, 'best' might well be defined 'as the oldest rule, the rule on which key jurisdictions have achieved consensus, the rule followed by the majority of jurisdictions, and so on' Svetiev (n 79) 185. This sounds more like entrenching existing habits rather than encouraging learning. Sadly, ICN surveys asking how many NCAs use ICN recommended practices when reviewing their competition systems do not normally identify which NCAs do so: see, for example, ICN Merger Working Group (n 148). Sometimes the EU and USA may change their rules in the light of ICN recommended practices, Carles Esteva Mosso, 'The ICN and Global Competition Convergence: Reflections on Its Origins, Its Achievements and Its Future' in Lugard (n 7) 167; but these instances are few and far between. Probably because ICN rules often follow their existing norms. See also ICPAC (n 20) 22–24. For similar comments in other areas, see Simmons (n 67) 592; Raustiala (n 2) 76.

> because this legitimises their own agency's standing. They also rely on the EU and the United States for technical assistance and capacity building, and US and EU experts will push this agenda. Aid may be contingent upon implementing these norms. There also may be a shaming effect through international institutions.[170]

Furthermore, the more that newer NCAs follow the ICN guidance (and their more established mentors), the more they are seen as a 'success story' and lauded within the ICN. This provides even more reason for advanced NCAs to help them, to offer them this valuable support and protection. There is, of course, also a dark side to this. Newer NCAs often know (or fear) that if they do not follow the relevant norms (or if they try to block norms proposed within the ICN by advanced NCAs), then this help, support, and training may be lost. The result is that they are often persuaded to import the developed NCAs' competition standards. In fact:

> networks do appear to strengthen the power of the already powerful ... the traditionally powerful states play leading roles in networks and it is the weak nations of the world that are adopting many of the regulatory policies of the more powerful. While difficult to evaluate, the resulting convergence process often favors dominant economic actors such as the US.[171]

Obviously, states can intervene if they wish.[172] However, the network actors often tend to work hard to ensure that this does not happen (otherwise they lose power).

The ICN (and the actors there) has constantly emphasized the fact that NCAs (and their states) do not need to implement ICN work products. This is voluntary. As a result, even where NCAs disagreed with a certain ICN work product, they might not have used their veto to block it. Why create that bad feeling and run the risks of less support, when they can just ignore it? However, as we will see in Chapter 2, the ICN has begun to place more emphasis on the need for implementation over the last few years. This may mean that more NCAs use their veto more often in the future. That will not help with the implementation of existing ICN work products. In any event, the factors above also underline how hard such a transition is to make.

In conclusion, while less well-resourced NCAs can certainly benefit from ICN participation, the same can also be said for NCAs from the EU and the USA. The consensus requirement gives a useful air of legitimacy to the ICN project.[173] Despite this, advanced NCAs seem to have been able to more or less control the

[170] Sokol (n 7) 154.
[171] Raustiala (n 2) 24–25.
[172] ibid 24.
[173] Similarly, in relation to the GATT, see Steinberg (n 125) 361.

ICN's outputs. Even better than forcing newer NCAs, they have participated willingly, the mechanisms of this are explored more fully in Section 1.3.

To our knowledge, no NCAs explicitly justify joining the Steering Group or Co-chairing a Working Group to gain power to impact ICN outputs and processes. This is interesting in itself. Managed normative convergence through unifying discourses (legal, market, and depoliticization), has helped to reduce conflicts within the ICN. It may be that this is not a permanent peace. There may come a time when NCAs feel powerful enough vis-à-vis their national administrations such that they no longer need the support of the ICN and other NCAs there (which may be undermining their freedom). Or it may be that national administrations realize that their power is being hollowed out and insist on greater control over their NCAs, pushing back against the ICN and the actions of their NCAs, perhaps to support national regulatory agendas.[174] If redistributional, rather than technical, issues move centre stage, the risk of breakdown is high, especially if the relevant issues have high political salience.[175]

We also need to consider why some NCAs, for example China's NCA, have not joined the ICN.[176] We do not know of any clear reason on this issue from China (or others). It is unclear whether China's NCAs have applied for membership and been rejected (and, if so, on what basis) or whether they have simply not wanted to become members.[177] One possibility is that China wishes to avoid pressure to converge with the EU and the USA (it still has access to the work products via the ICN website). Although China 'has expressed little desire to depart from or challenge the international', competition law norms, its consideration of 'non-competition goals' (such as environmental protection and industrial policy) does present some challenges to the international order.[178] This theory fits with other observations. China does not engage much with the international competition community in other areas either, although it participates in some UNCTAD meetings. While there is some plausibility to this theory, China's lack of engagement may have other

[174] The Netherlands may be an example of this, politicians there have pushed the NCA to consider public policy goals in ways that better fit with national preferences. For a brief discussion of this struggle, see Christopher Townley, 'Co-ordinated Diversity: Revolutionary Suggestions for EU Competition Law (and EU Law Too)' in Piet Eeckhout and Takis Tridimas (eds), *Yearbook of European Law*, vol 33 (OUP 2014) 232–33.

[175] Barbara Gabor, *Regulatory Competition in the Internal Market* (Edward Elgar 2013) 206. Recent action by Austria, France, and Germany has sought to push the European Commission to consider the impact of its enforcement work on national champions, for example. However, a state's ability to interfere in ICN work can be limited. For example, a state (as opposed to its NCA) may not be aware of the current ICN debates and so may not even know they effect matters of importance to it, Christopher Townley, *A Framework for European Competition Law: Co-ordinated Diversity* (Hart 2018) ch 3.

[176] 'The Chinese agencies have not discussed their intentions concerning ICN membership... China's participation in ICN is an important determinant of the organisation's future success' Hollman and Kovacic (n 26) 52. In 2011 Williams opined that it is likely that the Chinese NCAs will become ICN members soon, Mark Williams, 'Enter the Dragon: competition law with Chinese characteristics' in Lugard (n 7) 357.

[177] The fact that such issues are opaque makes it harder to defend the ICN's legitimacy.

[178] Ng (n 10) 13.

causes. These range from structural issues within Chinese competition enforcement,[179] to the possibility that Chinese competition officials may simply not have wanted to more clearly explain their newly blooded competition system (perhaps due to feeling their way at the start and a lack of confidence in explaining a new order, especially one that does not fit the 'normal way of doing' competition policy and enforcement today). Rather than resisting pressure, perhaps China was focusing internally, trying to decide how its competition rules should operate, combined with some 'learning by doing'. If this is the reason, things might be about to change. In 2017 China announced generally (not just for competition law) that it might seek greater engagement internationally, offering an alternative path for developing countries wanting to accelerate their development and maintain their independence. This creates a threat to the EU and the US power over the voice of the international competition community.

One option is for China to join the ICN.[180] If this were to happen, the EU and the USA might lose control of the ICN's agenda to some extent. China's economic power would give it a strong voice. If it decided to be (and were widely accepted as) another pole for competition 'norms' in the ICN this could rapidly undermine the ICN's largely cohesive message (for example on competition goals).[181] Ng suspects that this is unlikely. She thinks that China would find it hard to overcome the dominant voices of the USA and EU (China may also not want to be pushed to match the procedural guaranties offered by even the mildest of the ICN good practice on due process). Another possible route would be for China to seek bilateral or regional arrangements, where it could have more influence.[182] In this way, by acting outside of the ICN, China might start to undermine the ICN (intentionally or not), which would also challenge EU and US power here. This scenario gains traction if NCAs start to feel that the ICN is not working for them (for example

[179] Before 2018, China's competition enforcement system had three NCAs: the National Development and Reform Commission (NDRC), the Ministry of Commerce (MOFCOM), and the State Administration for Industry and Commerce (SAIC). It was generally agreed that it had been hard to coordinate these three NCAs' activities (lack of effective supervision, dispersed functions, and uneven bureaucratic rankings). Although the Anti-monopoly Commission (AMC) in the State Council acted as the supervisory body for these three NCAs, it had not been particularly effective in the past decade. There may have been tensions between the NDRC, MOFCOM, and SAIC about whether or not to join the ICN, especially if they disagreed about what was appropriate, and what they would do there. It may simply have been that, faced with such complex dynamics, doing nothing (not joining) was easier. In 2018 a single NCA replaced them: the State Administration for Market Regulation (SAMR).

[180] There have been some, recent signs, that this may be about to happen. The SAMR released its annual enforcement report in December 2020. There, it said that 'it has been deeply studying on joining the international competition network and the cooperation frameworks of competition enforcement procedures' SAMR, *Annual Report of Anti-Monopoly Law Enforcement in China (2019)* (Law Press China 2020) 5 (in Chinese). An abstract of this report published on SAMR's official website (also in Chinese), makes similar comments in its penultimate paragraph <www.samr.gov.cn/xw/zj/202012/t20201224_324676.html> accessed 7 October 2021.

Our thanks to Chunxu Wu for his helpful insights on the Chinese competition system.

[181] Gerber (n 83) 223.

[182] Ng (n 10) 13–15 (indeed she reports some signs of this, with the BRICS, for example).

developing NCAs may feel ignored or undermined and think that a China-focused body would be more useful).

Another challenge to the ICN might come if many less powerful NCAs, who are already ICN members, organize and assert themselves collectively. The EU and the USA have had to fight various battles on this front already. For example, Brazil (in its capacity as co-Chair of the implementation working group) sought to propose regional ICN groupings, where NCAs might have more in common, culturally and linguistically (as well of in sense of competition problem). The USA seemed to perceive this as a risk to its ICN competition message and resisted the initiative. There is also the core ICN idea of 'informed divergence'. The idea is that NCAs are free to disagree with a certain position, even if many others agree. If either were to become too deeply accepted in too many areas, then they would make it much harder for the EU and USA to push convergence with their rules. So far, the response of the EU and USA suggests that they understand these risks. So far, they have been able to contain them.

There has been some acknowledgement from senior ICN luminaries that power has not been equally shared in the past in the ICN.[183] Some call the first decade a time of EU/US leadership, learning but also persuading others to follow them, noting that many other countries and NCAs had different needs. As we have seen, under Andreas Mundt's leadership, inclusiveness has been a major focus of the ICN's second decade, through more rotation of Working Group Chairs and strengthening the Advocacy Working Group, for example (and more NGA participation). In our opinion, the ICN remains a long way off being a fully inclusive body.[184]

1.2.2 NGAs

Many other actors, potentially affected by the relevant rules, may also be keen to participate in their formation and interpretation. For example, in international financial reporting standards, Perry and Nölke examine the presence (and impact) in the relevant fora of financial institutions (such as large banks) and non-financial firms.[185] Wilks tells us not only to think of economies of scale, but also politics of scale. He adds that many see global governance as a prime (and successful) hunting

[183] See, for example, the speeches by Andreas Mundt (the current ICN Chair and President of the German NCA) and John Fingleton (previously the ICN Chair and now as an NGA), in the introductory session to Day 4 of the ICN 2020 Virtual Conference, 17 Sept 2020, <www.internationalcompetitionnetwork.org/2020vac/> accessed 7 October 2021.

[184] Tembinkosi Bonakele, Commissioner, Competition Commission, South Africa, also highlighted the need for further efforts at inclusiveness in the introductory session to Day 4 of the ICN 2020 Virtual Conference, 17 September 2020, <www.internationalcompetitionnetwork.org/2020vac/> accessed 7 October 2021.

[185] James Perry and Andreas Nölke, 'The Political Economy of International Accounting Standards' (2006) 13 Review of International Political Economy 559.

ground for multinationals. Even though individual multinationals may have little individual influence, together they are a force to be reckoned with.[186]

This section charts NGA involvement in the ICN, breaking this down by the types of actor (businesses, service providers, consumers), their geographic origin and their area of expertise (lawyers, economists, etc). NGAs influence ICN processes and outputs. So, we look at why they say they are involved there, then examine academic theories for their presence and compare the two. NGAs consistently claim to pursue the greater good in the ICN. This is unlikely. External assessment here is hard because there is no clear list of who NGAs are and what they are specifically doing in the ICN. So, we often have to rely on our own knowledge of these processes from participation in ICN meetings. As we will see, NGAs seem to have a lot of influence and so this lack of transparency is, in itself, troubling.

1.2.2.1 Categories of actors

We have seen that non-state actors, such as businesses and law firms, were influential in the ICN's establishment. In fact, it was the International Bar Association (a group of lawyers from around the world) that called the meeting of senior competition officials and practitioners in February 2001 that supported the establishment of the ICN. They have been heavily involved in ICN work since then. We are told that there is not one kind of NGA that:

> is considered a 'gatekeeper', partly to avoid any prioritising between large private sector organisations that operate on a multinational or national basis and also to encourage the objective of the broadest possible participation among NGAs.[187]

That may be true, but major EU and US multinationals, and the lawyers that represent them, seem to have disproportionate voice, in fact. NGAs appear to be principally major multinational firms (and their representatives), such as:[188] Alcan Inc., Barclays Bank, British Telecom, Charles River Associates, Compaq Computer Corporation, General Electric, Goldman Sachs International, Intesa Sanpaolo, Google, Microsoft, NERA, Philips International, Rio Tinto plc, Shell International, Sumitomo Electric Industries, Ltd, the US Chamber of Commerce, Vodafone Group plc, and Walmart. These actors are identifiable because they contributed to ICN discussions as panel speakers. The lack of publicly available attendance

[186] Wilks (n 161) 5 and 43–47.

[187] Goldman and others (n 96) 383–84.

[188] See ICN Merger Review Working Group, *2002–2003 SubGroup Work Plans* (2002) 6–11, previously available at <https://www.internationalcompetitionnetwork.org/uploads/library/doc473.pdf> (broken ICN link, see discussion in Introduction, n 16). NGA Submission, *NGA Report on Implementation of ICN Recommended Practices for Merger Notification Procedures* (2003); ICN (n 56) 27.

sheets for ICN events, as well as a lack of information about precisely who does what in many ICN activities, makes it hard to know which NGAs are active and what they do.

In addition, businesses are nested in a supportive environment of service providers. Being parasitic upon them, these service providers are also dependent upon big firms' continuing success in order to, in their turn, thrive. This could well alter their incentives. The major UK and US law firms, for example, are part of this elite. As Wilks says, rather than reinforcing 'a legal philosophy that controls and limits corporate activity (which German law firms tend to do) they have lubricated corporate strategy and profit seeking'.[189] So, it is no surprise to find the big global law firms, who serve the major EU and US multinationals, present and active in the ICN. It is likely that these law firms tend to protect their clients' interests there (and their own). This may well be at the expense of consumers and the economies of the states involved.

As competition policy and enforcement may have highly redistributive consequences, ICN discussions and outputs are also theoretically of interest to small firms, consumers, employees, and their representatives, such as consumer associations, trade unions (and relevant law firms).[190] Yet, consumer groups (and law firms who represent them)[191] 'are noticeably under-represented'.[192] There are also very few small firms actively involved in ICN work.

When it comes to NGAs' expertise, the main participants are business people from the major multinationals. Perhaps the largest area of expertise is lawyers. Many are employed by these major multinationals directly, or the law firms that multinationals use to defend themselves.

The ICN has said that it is keen to recruit more widely (not just from large firms). It is unclear how many NCAs, especially those from richer states, support this. In their discussions with ICN members, especially those from transition economies, Hollman and Kovacic have heard:

> recurring concerns that ICN must increase participation by non-private sector NGAs (such as academics or officials of consumer groups) to balance the representation of NGAs from companies or law firms.[193]

[189] Wilks (n 161) 82.

[190] See citation at n 13, for example. Particularly as the goal of many competition law regimes is consumer welfare, consumers' voice seems relevant in competition law and policy. 'The ICN works to facilitate improved enforcement and advocacy of competition law, which fosters vibrant competition in open and well-functioning markets and optimizes consumer welfare. This should create conditions that promote lower prices and wider consumer choice' ICN (n 103) 3 and 8.

[191] See the quote at n 197.

[192] Fox (n 9) 125.

[193] Hollman and Kovacic (n 26) 59. Philip Marsden, 'Acta Non Verba: keep "talking shop", don't become another talking shop' in Lugard (n 7) 148, also argues for more diversity among the NGAs.

That said, the results of our survey support the idea of the predominance of law firms (54 per cent), big businesses (14 per cent) and academics (14 per cent) among the most represented NGAs. Consumer organizations and economists are less present (around 6 per cent each). Other groups (international organizations, national courts, members of business confederations, small businesses) make up less than 7 per cent of NGAs.[194] The ICN has challenged economists to get involved.[195] This initiative has not been very successful. There are not many other kinds of service providers (such as: business schools, management consultants and accountants) in attendance either. There is also a lack of political scientists, sociologists, and international relations scholars, who all have something to say about the distributional interests and outcomes of the current rules. Finally, behavioural economists and psychologists would also be interesting additions, as consumers are often not as rational as many competition authorities assume.[196]

Once again, there is no public data that we can find on who has applied to be an NGA, if anyone, from such groups. It is also unclear how extensive any efforts that have been made by the ICN, or its NCAs, to recruit such expertise have been. The ICN certainly seems to perceive a problem with NGAs' current competence distribution. One Working Group has even said:

> It is also important [to] seek input representing a diverse range of viewpoints. Not all lawyers practice at large firms or act for large corporations. Reaching out to practitioners outside of the traditional competition bar is a helpful component of any policy aimed at enhancing consultation and ensuring optimal policy results.[197]

When one looks to see where NGAs are based, many are from Europe and North America. This is not necessarily surprising; it partly reflects the origin of many of the largest firms globally (especially given that Chinese NCAs are not ICN members).[198] We are told that many NGAs are 'from younger jurisdictions such as Armenia, Pakistan, Vietnam and others'.[199] Even if this were true (and ICN opacity

[194] One ICN report says that NGAs are overwhelmingly from the private bar (70 per cent) and academia (15 per cent), as well as business, consumer groups, and international organizations <www.icnblog.org/?p=130> accessed 7 October 2021. A similar picture also emerges from ICN (n 56) 27–29.

[195] Martin Mandorff, 'Engaging Economists in the ICN: Uniting under a Common Language' [2012] Competition Policy International 1–2. This is happening in the UCWG too, Lewis Lagdameo and Heimert (n 98) 295.

[196] For its report, for example, ICPAC solicited input from 'various enforcement officials, business groups, economists, organised labour, lawyers and other interested parties' ICPAC (n 20) Executive Summary 22.

[197] ICN Advocacy Working Group, *Summary of ICN Teleseminar on Building Agency/Bar Relationships* (2009) 3, previously available at <http://internationalcompetitionnetwork.org/uploads/library/doc663.pdf> (broken ICN link, see discussion in Introduction, n 16).

[198] Of the Fortune 500 firms in 2020, for example, about 28 per cent come from the EU and 28 per cent from the USA and Canada. The rest come from China (28 per cent) and Japan (11 per cent) <https://fortune.com/global500/>

[199] Ulf Böge, Closing Speech 4th Annual ICN Conference, 6–8 June 2005, 2.

makes it hard to check), they are unlikely to make up a large percentage of all NGAs present.[200] Furthermore, while presence is important, active influence is more valuable. The ICN itself reports that NGAs from Europe and the Americas were participating in the working groups the most actively.[201]

The ICN also seems to perceive a problem with NGAs' current geographic distribution, saying, 'a gap remains to be bridged in terms of the number of NGAs from Asia, Latin America and Africa'. Nonetheless, according to the ICN, this gap is slowly being filled.[202] Unfortunately, the ICN has not published a database of NGAs.[203] Without giving data to support this (or showing how quickly any transition is taking place), it is hard to comment.

Perhaps this is related to the way in which NGAs are appointed. The ICN states 'NGAs are identified by ICN member agencies, and liaise with and provide input into projects predominantly through these agencies'.[204] An ICN survey from 2010 showed that 74.4 per cent of NGAs got involved in the ICN because their NCA invited them.[205] Hollman and Kovacic note:

> NGAs are [mainly] nominated by their [NCA] ... This gives NCAs the ability to filter out prospective NGAs on various grounds unrelated to their expertise in competition law. For example, we are aware of instances in which it appears that a potential NGA has failed to gain approval from its NCA because the NCA believed the candidate had been insufficiently supportive of the NCA's program.[206]

The kinds of actors involved as NGAs in the ICN, the type of expertise that they bring and their geographic spread are focused around major western multinationals and their lawyers. Admittedly, the ICN often talks about needing a more diverse range of viewpoints and says things are changing, albeit slowly. However, this lack of diversity is relevant, given that ICN claims to legitimacy often rely on assertions of diverse, representative inputs.

[200] Our survey supports the geographical predominance of European (40 per cent) and North-American (25 per cent) NGAs, with Asia (19 per cent), South America (12 per cent), Africa and Oceania (1 per cent) much less represented.

[201] ICN (n 56) 14–15; 20 per cent of the most active NGAs come from North America and 16 per cent from Europe. Only 7 per cent of 'particularly responsive' NGAs, are from Asia and Oceania, and even then, they are mainly from the richer countries there, ibid 26.

[202] ICN SG Working Group (n 13) 6.

[203] Although there is a hint that something of this nature may be published soon <www.internationalcompetitionnetwork.org/working-groups/icn-operations/membership-ngas/> accessed 7 October 2021.

[204] Unilateral Conduct Working Group (n 58) 1. To become an NGA, one can approach one's local NCA, the chair of the Working Group that you want to join, or the ICN Liaison for NGAs. However, if they are approached, the latter two revert to the relevant, local NCA, ICN SG Working Group (n 13) 6.

[205] ICN SG Working Group (n 13) 7.

[206] Hollman and Kovacic (n 26) 76.

1.2.2.2 The reasons these actors (and others) give for their ICN engagement

NGAs are highly integrated into the ICN and its work. Coppola et al provide a helpful explanation of the range of work that NGAs can get involved in (as well as the special, perhaps even unique, nature of their role in the ICN):

> NGAs help identify projects; produce and offer important comments on work product; contribute to the policy dialogue at conferences and workshops; and help disseminate ICN work product and promote its use … In no other government competition fora do non-governmental experts play such an integral role. The network's inclusive approach to membership coupled with the active participation of non-governmental advisors from around the world means that the ICN is truly a reflection of the global antitrust community [although we have just seen that it is actually quite a small part of this].[207]

The ICN believes that NGAs' participation in ICN activity is important,[208] especially in the promotion of recommended practices. Similarly, in their evaluation of their own contributions, lawyers acting as NGAs are extremely positive about their role in the ICN.[209]

So, who are NGAs acting on behalf of in the ICN? Worryingly, the ICN thinks that firms act for the benefit of all 'independence and integrity are key features of the NGA role. NGAs work towards the advancement of the ICN's general interest to the benefit of all stakeholders.'[210] NGAs say similar things:

> The goals of NGAs, and indeed all competition law advisers, are in principle aligned with those of the agencies in that everyone in the competition community wants to promote and encourage competition law and culture. We are all aiming to effect justice by creating and maintaining good systems.[211]

[207] Coppola and others (n 97). See also ICN SG Working Group, *NGA Toolkit* (2020), <https://www.internationalcompetitionnetwork.org/portfolio/icn-nga-toolkit/>, previously available at <http://internationalcompetitionnetwork.org/uploads/library/doc623.pdf> (broken ICN link, see discussion in Introduction, n 16).

[208] Frederic Jenny, 'The International Competition Network and the OECD Competition Committee: differences, similarities and complementarities' in Lugard (n 7) 101. Fostering cooperative links between NCAs/NGAs is a key ICN aim, ICN Cartel Working Group, *2010–2011 Work Plan* (2010) 4.

[209] Speaking for firms, Ronald Stern, 'The Role of the ICN in Fostering Convergence: An NGA's Perspective' in Lugard (n 7) 321–31. Speaking for law firms, Dave Anderson, 'Reflections on the ICN and Its NGAs: Advocacy and Implementation' ibid, 277–85; Goldman and others (n 96) 383.

[210] ICN SG Working Group (n 13) 3. Similarly, ICN SG Working Group (n 207) 5; Advocacy Working Group (n 197) 2.

[211] Anderson (n 209) 279–80.

When asked, NGAs often emphasize networking with enforcers, better understanding them and discussing with them as key benefits of ICN participation.[212]

NCAs often give three reasons for supporting NGAs' presence in the ICN. In their view, NGAs provide: more resources, advice, and increased legitimacy.[213] Looking at these points in turn, NCAs often complain about a lack of resources. So, if NGAs can help to provide ideas, basic research, or secretarial assistance for ICN work products, then this could save NCAs money, while increasing ICN outputs. Second, NCAs are keen to tap into businesses' technical expertise, different perspectives, and information.[214] For example, the ICN notes that competition enforcement generally may impose unnecessary costs (invoking several competition regimes at the same time could potentially multiply this effect).

> Competition enforcement may, at times, impose unnecessary costs and uncertainty on the business community and marketplace. The ICN works to promote sound and principled procedural and substantive standards that minimize such burdens and leave pro-competitive, efficiency enhancing conduct to flourish.[215]

NGAs can be helpful in pointing out where these costs arise and suggesting how they might be reduced (for an actual rule, or a draft ICN recommended practice).[216] This role ties in with ICPAC's original industrial policy aims for the ICN, see book's Introduction. Third, the ICN thinks that more diversity in the types of actors present in the ICN 'enhances the legitimacy and relevance of the ICN, of the work it produces, of the standards it aims to offer'.[217]

1.2.2.3 Academic theories of influence

An advantageous regulatory regime can significantly enhance firms' profitability.[218] Wilks argues that contemporary politics can no longer be understood without an

[212] ICN (n 135) 24. Similarly, Unilateral Conduct Working Group, *2012–2013 Work Plan* (2012) 4, previously available at <https://www.internationalcompetitionnetwork.org/uploads/library/doc843.pdf> (broken ICN link, see discussion in Introduction, n 16).

[213] Bizarrely, the ICN also highlights that NGAs might find it interesting to be in ICN discussions, and they will learn more about competition law and policy, ICN SG Working Group (n 13) 4. Similarly, ICN SG Working Group (n 207) 3.

[214] ibid 2 and similarly, 3, 5, and 8; ICN Steering Group, *Draft Minutes* (2011), 3; ICN (n 135) 24, 33–34; Fingleton (n 101) 10–11. Coen, for example, makes a similar point about the use of firms in the EU, David Coen, 'Business Lobbying in the European Union' in David Coen and Jeremy Richardson (eds), *Lobbying the European Union: Institutions, Actors and Issues* (OUP 2009) 148.

[215] ICN (n 103) 3.

[216] Improving the quality of ICN work products, Tavares (n 95) 345. Similarly, in other areas, Simmons (n 67) 590. This may be particularly true in fast-moving markets (ibid 592).

[217] ICN SG Working Group (n 207) 3.

[218] Private firms might advocate certain types of regulation, or new focus for existing regulation, which might particularly benefit them, see Richard Revesz, 'Federalism and Environmental Law: A Public Choice Analysis' (2001) 115 Harvard Law Review 553. Perhaps their own businesses are better able to operate in this business environment than their competitors, for some reason, for example; or, regulation may raise barriers to entry, better protecting incumbents from new entrants.

account of business influence on regulation.[219] This influence can arise directly, through NGAs' input into the ICN. In addition, the mere presence of NGAs there may distort the incentives of other actors.

The idea that firms might become large enough to influence or even dominate politics has been around for a long time.[220] Zingales highlights three mechanisms which contribute to firms' effectiveness in the political sphere. First, over the last 30 years, the relative size of large (often US) firms has increased. This reduces the number of conflicting interests in each sector. It also makes firms more powerful vis-à-vis consumers. When firms' preferences are heterogeneous, their voice is divided, which reduces their power when arguing for change.[221] Second, the complexity of regulation has increased, making it easier for those with greater knowledge of the industry to tilt rules in their favour (especially in the face of a collective action problem). This is particularly likely to be true in the area of competition and regulation, which are seen as highly complex. Third, politicians on the left get fewer benefits from appearing to be anti-business (by contrast, being 'too friendly' to business is less of a problem).[222]

The more market power firms have the more effective they are likely to be at getting what they want from the political system (and regulators). This should feedback into more market power and an improved ability (and incentive) to protect themselves on the political plane too.

Economists and political scientists have analysed at length the risk that, while independent from politicians, regulators may become 'captured' by those that they are meant to regulate. There is a lot of evidence that firms are highly effective at influencing regulatory processes.[223]

[219] Wilks (n 161) 2.

[220] In 1967, Berle and Means wrote, for example 'The rise of the modern corporation has brought a concentration of economic power which can compete on equal terms with the modern state – economic power versus political power, each strong in its own field. The state seeks in some aspects to regulate the corporation, while the corporation, steadily becoming more powerful, makes every effort to avoid such regulation' Adolf Berle and Gardiner Means, *The Modern Corporation and Private Property* (2nd edn, Harcourt, Brace and World 1967) 313.

[221] There has been a major consolidation of economic (and political) power, leaving relatively few, largely unaccountable, firms: Adil Abdela and Marshall Steinbaum, 'The United States Has a Market Concentration Problem' Brief—Economy & Growth <https://rooseveltinstitute.org/united-states-has-market-concentration-problem/> argue that markets in US industry are increasingly concentrated. Increasing concentration does not necessarily equate with more market power, but there is some evidence that market power has increased too, Bruce Blonigen and Justin Pierce, 'Evidence for the Effects of Mergers on Market Power and Efficiency' [2016] 22750 NBER Working Paper; Simcha Barkai, 'Declining Labor and Capital Shares' [2017] New Working Paper Series No 2 Stigler Center Working Paper. In 2016, Global Justice Now highlighted that of the '100 wealthiest economic entities in the world today, 69 are now corporations and only 31 countries' <www.globaljustice.org.uk/blog/2016/oct/13/standing-90000-people-against-corporate-power> accessed 7 October 2021. This includes firms such as General Electric and Microsoft (both have an active presence in the ICN).

[222] Luigi Zingales, 'Towards a Political Theory of the Firm' (2017) 31 Journal of Economic Perspectives 113 , 124–25. He adds, the interaction of 'concentrated corporate power and politics is a threat to the functioning of the free market economy and to the economic prosperity it can generate, and a threat to democracy as well' ibid 114.

[223] For a review, see E Dal Bó, 'Regulatory Capture: A Review' (2006) 22(2) Oxford Review of Economic Policy 203–25. Respectively, in environmental matters, see eg Peter Cane, 'Standing,

One way that firms seek influence is by openly contesting the creation or application of norms. This is confrontational and involves risks (especially for repeat players in games where they have limited power to compel others). So, especially where power is unevenly distributed (as between large firms and other weaker actors), firms often prefer to operate in the shadows. First, they try to confine 'the scope of decision-making to relatively "safe" issues'.[224] For example, firms might advocate a focus on 'technical' issues in competition law and suggest ignoring public policy. Second, firms seek influence over the media, think tanks, etc to try to foster beneficial beliefs in them (and their audiences), about what is possible/desirable.[225]

In order to assess how easily firms may be able to exercise influence over regulators in a particular field, we need to consider institutional and economic characteristics. As regards institutional characteristics, NCA independence has a role to play. Independence shields them from political protection and makes capture of NCAs particularly valuable.[226] Regulators' prevalent economic and legal ideology is also important. US multinationals have been extremely successful at changing the ideology in the area of competition policy, placing great emphasis on consumer welfare arguments (which is socially acceptable and the long-term version of which benefits big firms) and excluding any perceived 'non-economic' policy concerns (which benefits all firms by ensuring more consistent regulatory outputs). Both these shifts benefit multinational firms at the

Representation, and the Environment' in Ian Loveland (ed), *A Special Relationship? American Influences on Public Law in the UK* (Clarendon Press 1995); Maria Lee and Carolyn Abbot, 'The Usual Suspects? Public Participation Under the Aarhus Convention' (2003) 66 Modern Law Review 80, 105; Thompson (n 1) 153–59.

[224] Peter Bachrach and Morton Baratz, 'Two Faces of Power' (1962) 56 American Political Science Review 947, 948. On the same page they explain that, by 'safe' issues, they mean that power is exercised:

> when A devotes his energies to creating or reinforcing social and political values and institutional practices that limit the scope of the political process to public consideration of only those issues which are comparatively innocuous to A. To the extent that A succeeds in doing this, B is prevented, for all practical purposes, from bringing to the fore any issues that might in their resolution be seriously detrimental to A's set of preferences.

Richard McKelvey, 'Intransitivities in Multidimensional Voting Models and Some Implications for Agenda Control' (1976) 12 Journal of Economic Theory 472 models how agenda control can determine outcomes. Similarly, 'The blocking of efforts to update policies (related to unions, financial regulation, the minimum wage, etc.) have arguably been more important than the passage of new legislation (Hacker and Pierson 2010). Here again, much of the exercise of influence involves "non-decisions".' Paul Pierson, 'Goodbye to Pluralism? Studying Power in Contemporary American Politics' (Presentation at the Wildavsky Forum for Public Policy, Goldman School of Public Policy, April 2015) 25.

[225] Pierson (n 224) 7.

[226] Richard Posner, Lee Epstein and William Landes, 'How Business Fares in the Supreme Court' (2013) 97 Minnesota Law Review 1431; Lee Epstein, William Landes and Richard Posner, *The Behaviour of Federal Judges: A Theoretical and Empirical Study of Rational Choice* (Harvard UP 2013), discussing the relative pro-business orientation of the US Supreme Court's ideology.

Zingales highlights two more institutional characteristics (they are less relevant here): the importance of the media in achieving democratic consensus; and the role of electoral processes in shaping political consensus, Zingales (n 222) 124–26.

expense of smaller firms and others (such as the environment, employment, consumer interests). In terms of the economic characteristics (and given the fact that explicit bribes are often illegal) facilitating firms' ability to influence the political system, Zingales advises investigating firms' ability to: make implicit promises of future career opportunities (for firms that credibly will have economic power in the future);[227] lobby the legislator;[228] (threaten to) challenge unfavourable legislation;[229] lobby the regulator to change its policy or enforcement practices;[230] and hide relevant information.[231] It would also assist firms to align their self-interest with a 'public interest' (such as national security); and to control their image through employment, media links, advertising, research funding, etc.

So, major multinationals may wield influence even when this is not obvious. This raises a challenge for political scientists in general, and studies like this one. If one cannot study what one cannot see, then how can we investigate NGA power? (We have pointed out several times how opaque ICN processes are.) The starting point must be the insight that those with power do not only use it to achieve specific, individual advantages for themselves. They also use it to change the 'rules of the game', to stack the deck in their favour for the future. Stigler says as 'a rule, regulation is acquired by the industry and is designed and operated primarily for its benefit [at the expense of the wider public]'.[232] This:

> suggests the need to recognize that political contestation is *both* a battle to gain control over political authority *and* a struggle to use political authority to institutionalize advantage—that is, to lay the groundwork for future victories. In short, it calls for an appreciation of how political influence is often invested. The exercise of authority is not just an exercise of power; it is potentially a way of generating power.[233]

[227] One example may be Citigroup's work to change a US law which sought to sever ties between commercial and investment banking, Zingales (n 222) 122.

[228] See Pierson (n 224) regarding the healthcare industry; Thomas Philippon, *The Great Reversal: How America Gave up on Free Markets* (Belknap Press 2019), on US competition law.

[229] Zingales (n 222) 124 discusses the US Security and Exchange Commission's decision to drop its rule preventing institutional investors from nominating their own representatives to corporate boards, in the face of litigation from the Business Roundtable.

[230] Thomas Lambert, 'Lobbying on Regulatory Enforcement Actions: Evidence from US Commercial and Savings Banks' (2019) 65 Management Science 2545 calculates that regulators are just under 45 per cent less likely to initiate enforcement actions against lobbying banks.

[231] Firms often have a lot of relevant information about themselves and the market more generally. They may try to withhold adverse information from regulators; lie about it where it undermines what they might want to do; or, manipulate regulatory processes so as to distort both the types of enquiries made of them and the methodologies used to assess them in their own favour. Zingales (n 222) 124, reports that DuPont delayed liability for contaminating the water supply near one of its US factories for over 30 years by hiding information and using trade secret laws.

[232] George Stigler, 'The Theory of Economic Regulation' (1971) 2 Bell Journal of Economics 3, 3.

[233] Pierson (n 224) 11.

This likely reflects a key reason for large multinational firms (and their advisers) actively encouraging the creation of the ICN. It is a forum where they have a special degree of influence, especially compared to fora like the OECD and UNCTAD, for example.

We have discussed firms' potential for influence. It is important, when doing this, to remain aware of the context. This is because the role of firms changes in different economies. Our focus has largely been on theories of Anglo-Saxon-style firms. Yet the role of firms has to be understood in a legal and cultural context. The logic of the firm in Continental Europe and Japan is one where firms operate in partnership with their state. As Wilks explains, in its classic European form:

> neo-corporatism refers to the voluntary sharing of economic governance between businesses, labour and government in the form of negotiated tri-partite agreements over issues such as investment, taxation and wage bargaining.[234]

To make this sustainable, firms need to build some trust and reliability with the government. This translates into a degree of civic responsibility.[235] This is similar to the philosophy underlying coordinated market economies (CMEs). In CMEs, there is more collective discussion between firms; they negotiate collectively with trade unions and other social actors, aiming to safeguard employment, and they participate in funding vocational training so as to maintain a skilled workforce. By way of contrast, in liberal market economies (LMEs), as in the UK and USA, firms focus more on their self-interest and markets are the main way of allocating resources.[236]

These two systems (CMEs and LMEs) are different. The role of firms in them is different too. This is something to take into account when analysing the role of firms within the ICN. One might reasonably ask, where do most firms come from. This should tell us which state's position they might promote. It may also hint at their philosophical orientation; ie are they likely pursuing their own self-interest, or that of other members of their society. Most of the NGAs that are most active in the ICN come, as we have previously seen, from LMEs.

1.2.2.4 Compares reasons given by these actors to the academic theories of influence

We discuss three areas: the redistributive nature of competition policy and enforcement; firms' potential for influence in the ICN; and why some with relevant interests do not join the ICN.

234 Wilks (n 161) 26.

235 ibid 27. Note that this kind of partnership is based on public interest; there may be a 'bad' kind developing based more on private gain, ibid 117.

236 ibid 27.

Firms have a lot to fight for in the competition arena, as these rules are a major threat to some, but can also provide great opportunities. Neo-classical economists emphasize the limits that competition and the 'market for corporation control' impose on firms' power. Competition pushes them to an efficient scale (neither too large, nor too small).[237] Second, inefficient publicly traded firms present an opportunity to corporate raiders to buy them, make them more efficient and then either sell them, or operate them, for a profit.[238] In terms of opportunities, competition law can help to create a level playing field. It can also help open up closed economies to competition, allowing outsiders access to compete (see the ICPAC report).

Competition rules are often drafted widely, leaving a lot of room for interpretation by relevant actors (such as courts and/or NCAs). For example, Article 102 TFEU states:

> Any abuse by one or more undertakings of a dominant position within the internal market or in a substantial part of it shall be prohibited as incompatible with the internal market in so far as it may affect trade between Member States.

Obviously, several key concepts (abuse, undertaking, dominant position, effect on trade between Member States) demand further interpretation. Those interpreting these rules have a lot of power. Firms have two aims when they seek influence. They want to influence NCAs to interpret competition rules in ways which favour them.[239] However, even if firms cannot achieve this, for them 'implementing any of a wide range of stable regulatory regimes is better than the uncertainty of not knowing'.[240] Stability makes firms' investment climate (and consumer preferences) more predictable.

Given this, what sorts of interpretations might firms seek? Firms share some political goals, such as (their) stability and prosperity.[241] In addition to these common values, firms share some generalizable interests, such as flexible labour laws or low business taxes. These interests may conflict with those of other members of society. For example, should competition policy focus on consumer welfare or producer welfare, or even a mixture of these? However, firms' interests can be heterogeneous too.[242] What large firms want can clash with small firms. For example, large firms

[237] Joseph Stiglitz, 'The Economics of Scale' (1958) 1 Journal of Law and Economics 54.

[238] Henry Manne, 'Mergers and the Market for Corporate Control' (1965) 73 Journal of Political Economy 110.

[239] Wilks (n 161) 115. Similarly, see the views of Mr Goldman, a Canadian lawyer, reported in Michal Gal and Simon Evenett, *A Report on the Third Annual Conference of the International Competition Network* (2004) 28, <https://www.alexandria.unisg.ch/22155/> accessed 7 October 2021.

[240] Gary Miller and Andrew Whitford, *Above Politics: Bureaucratic Discretion and Credible Commitment* (CUP 2016) 235.

[241] Wilks (n 161) 41.

[242] For example, in the area of financial reporting, Perry and Nölke argue that in clashes between financial institutions (such as large banks) and non-financial firms and industries, the former are gaining

might emphasize the possibility of economies of scale, and their (potential) importance for price. They might also underline the risks of over-enforcement of competition law and the chilling effect that this could have on innovation, and ultimately consumers. By way of contrast, SMEs (small and medium-sized enterprises) might focus on the benefits of choice and the risk that anti-competitive behaviour, once started, might be impossible to undo.

The redistributive potential of competition policy and enforcement, the fact that most NGAs are major, rich multinationals (or their advisers), and the divergent incentives of these firms from other actors in society is potentially a deadly cocktail.[243]

The ICN does not see this as a risk. In Section 1.2.2.2., we saw the ICN saying that firms act for the benefit of all 'independence and integrity are key features of the NGA role. NGAs work towards the advancement of the ICN's general interest to the benefit of all stakeholders.' NGAs agreed, all are 'aiming to effect justice by creating and maintaining good systems'.

Given NGAs' incentives to influence NCAs, these are extremely troubling statements. The idea that a group of largely major western multinational firms (and their representatives) would act independently, for the benefit of society in general, is, at best, naive.[244] Furthermore, even this independence claim is sometimes watered down. One US NCA (the Federal Trade Commission) explains that this means 'independence from *political* interests'.[245] This is not the same as expecting NGAs to provide value neutral suggestions, or to act in the public interest. This revision is more likely to be accurate (which makes it more troubling).

In Section 1.2.2.3, Zingales advised us, when examining firms' power, to look at both institutional and economic characteristics. We should not just look for open battles where they publicly fight enforcers in individual cases (such as when they appeal competition decisions). We must also be alert to them acting more covertly. Carving out quiet places where they can come into regular and direct contact with NCAs. It seems relevant that a group of NCAs from advanced economies (many without express political authority) came together to make 'best practice' rules at the USA's initiative (after ICPAC argued that this would support US industrial

power. In part, this has happened through (and is reinforced by) changes in the fair value accounting standards that are widely accepted around the world, Perry and Nölke (n 185).

[243] Giuseppe Tesauro, *Opening Speech, ICN First Annual Conference* (2002) 2–3, previously available at <http://www.internationalcompetitionnetwork.org/uploads/library/doc568.pdf> (broken ICN link, see discussion in Introduction, n 16).

[244] Wouter Wils, 'Independence of Competition Authorities: The Example of the EU and Its Member States' (2019) 42 World Competition 149, fn 76.

[245] Russell Damtoft, Bureau of Competition, Lessons Learned in the Delivery of Technical Assistance: The United States Experience, FTC 2. International Competition Network Second Annual Conference, Merida, Mexico, 23 June, 2003.

policy). NCAs did this supported by major, western multinationals (and their advisers). From the start, NGAs were then invited into this policy network (to help design the rules which regulate them).

Major multinationals (and their advisers)[246] have sought to foster helpful beliefs in NCAs about the value of competition (benefits of open markets), what competition rules should be about (efficiencies rather than choice) and who they should benefit (focusing on long-term consumer benefits is often the same as focusing on combined consumer and producer welfare).[247] There is widespread acceptance that the epistemic community (including NCA and NGA employees) has been influential in the competition community for a long time (see Section 1.3.1.2). As one would expect when they sense big benefits, NGAs expend enormous resources in ICN work. In the words of one NGA, they devote lots of time to the ICN because they feel that their 'ideas and views are actively sought and incorporated into work products'.[248] In other words, NGAs think that their lobbying is effective. This is especially problematic, given the unbalanced distribution of NGAs (geographically and by expertise and interests)—see Section 1.2.2.1.

In the NCAs' view, NGAs help by providing resources, advice, and increased legitimacy. Section 1.2.2.3 said that it is unlikely that Anglo-Saxon firms (the ones that predominate in the ICN) are likely to act in line with wider social goals (unless they also benefit them). In terms of the economic characteristics of a firm's ability to get what it wants from the regulatory system, one might highlight their ability to hide relevant information (in their discussions with, one might call it lobbying of, NCAs).[249] NGAs might ignore issues that harm their interests, when suggesting what should be prioritized for ICN action, or try to get favourable perspectives incorporated into draft work products. NGAs also have much to offer NCAs (and their staff), which might help to encourage cooperation (along with states' expectation that their NCA will help their firms). For example, law firms might offer 'likeminded' NCA employees jobs; or send their staff on secondments, as a form of subsidy to compliant NCAs (or as a way of injecting their own views into the NCA)—see Section 1.3.2.3. The ICN offers NGAs the chance to create a partnership where a few firms help NCAs with policymaking and implementation. We have already seen what kind of 'partnership' that is likely to be. As regards greater legitimacy, Chapter 4 explains why 'legitimacy through inclusiveness' is problematic. If all relevant perspectives are neither equally present, nor equally resourced (as happens in the ICN), then policymaking risks becoming distorted in favour of the better resourced, rather than being aligned with the public interest. Whatever that might be.

246 Wilks (n 12) 431.
247 Massimo Motta, *Competition Policy: Theory and Practice* (CUP 2004) 20.
248 Anderson (n 209) 278.
249 Wilks (n 161) 109.

Theoretically, Wils has called it almost inevitable that 'among the different NGAs, those representing (directly or indirectly) the views and interests of big business will end up being most vocal'.[250] In order to study these effects empirically, one needs to examine (over time) the evolution of policy options, examine who favours certain outcomes, what enabled the outcome that won to win (eg context), and the long-term effects of these outcomes on preferences and political resources.[251] A historical perspective is vital here because 'power is something that develops over time and simultaneously becomes less visible as it does so'.[252] This sort of analysis of the ICN is extremely difficult, given the lack of transparency. Having said that, Jenny reports a discussion in the ICN Annual Meeting in 2004. There, some NCAs from developing countries proposed that the ICN start work on recommended practices on abuse of dominance. This idea was flatly rejected. Jenny says:

> Some delegates suspected that the refusal of the ICN to take up the issue of abuse of dominance was due to the reluctance of business-related NGAs who did not want to see competition authorities encouraged to go after large multinational firms using abuse of dominance or monopolisation provisions.[253]

It was another two years before the Steering Group created the UCWG to look at this issue. Even if the NGAs lost the battle in the end, their ability to disrupt ICN work for two years on this point, likely brought considerable extra profits to the multinationals that had been taking illicit advantage of their market power (and their advisers).

These powerful coalitions of multinationals are intervening in the ICN because they care about the outcomes of governance. They want to remake the structures of opportunity (to their own advantage, rather than that of society at large). This is not easy. It requires the capacity:

> to overcome collective action problems, mobilize resources, coordinate actions with others, develop extensive expertise, focus sustained attention, and operate flexibly across the multiple domains of political authority. Moreover, all of this must typically be done over long periods of time, across shifting partisan environments, despite considerable turnover of elected officials, and in the face of dogged resistance from other resourceful actors. These are not capacities we usually associate with voters [or consumers]. They are the comparative strength of organized interests.[254]

[250] Wils (n 244) fn 76.
[251] Pierson (n 224) 15.
[252] ibid 16.
[253] Jenny (n 208) 101.
[254] Pierson (n 224) 13–14.

At the same time, many of these features make it hard to challenge firms that have a longer-term horizon. In order for opposition to be effective, this must be a salient issue for the public (for the media and politicians to invest time in the matter). Relevant knowledge must also be widely dispersed in order to offer skilled 'combat' to counter the arguments of the firms in the relevant industry. Otherwise, firms may well wield disproportionate influence over 'thin' political markets (for example, this is often true of financial reporting and bank governance rules).[255]

Many actors with relevant interests are not present in the ICN (or not as present). There are many potential reasons for this, even if competition policy and enforcement seriously affect them. First, they may not be aware of the ICN as a forum, either what it does, or their potential impact there. Second, they may not be aware of the competition rules, or they may feel alienated by the complex nature/language of these rules and the relatively closed community enforcing them. Third, they may not have the resources to attend the ICN. Fourthly, even if these actors have the resources to attend the ICN, they might feel that these resources could be better spent elsewhere. Perhaps these actors think that the benefits to be derived from ICN participation do not outweigh the costs involved? If so, this could be due to a collective action problem. As producers are normally much more concentrated than consumers, the former face lower organization costs than the latter when promoting their interests. This is because the benefit to each individual producer could potentially be more than for each consumer. Fifth, perhaps these other actors have asked to be involved in the ICN, but the NCA that they approached refused. As we have seen, NCAs are the gatekeepers for NGA participation. In competition policy, independent regulators are often tasked with maintaining profitable firms in managed markets. Wilks says: 'In these fields citizens have become consumers; as voters, like elected politicians, they are self-righteously kept at arm's length.'[256] There is no public data on whether any applicants were refused and, if so, why.

1.3 How actors might exercise influence in a consensus-based organization

Although the ICN operates by consensus,[257] Section 1.2 argued that this does not prevent some having significantly more influence in the ICN. This section shows that powerful NCAs and NGAs use several mechanisms, intentionally or not, to pressure weaker NCAs into accepting ICN processes and outputs, even when they might not be in their best interests. Section 1.3.1 looks at NCAs; then, Section 1.3.2. examines how powerful NGAs use similar mechanisms.

[255] Karthik Ramanna, *Political Standards* (U of Chicago Press 2015).
[256] Wilks (n 161) 255.
[257] ICN (n 103) 2, 6.

1.3.1 NCAs

This section discusses various mechanisms that advanced NCAs can use to get other NCAs to do what they want (and thus capture more benefit for themselves). We examine the following: political and economic power, epistemic community and the technical nature of rules, getting into the debate early, a relative lack of resources, and offers of technical assistance. Whether or not the influence generated through the adoption of these mechanisms is conscious, there are likely effects on those not exercising these techniques or blessed with the advantages of more powerful NCAs. This is often poorer NCAs, from developing countries.

1.3.1.1 Political and economic power

When thinking about power in networks, political scientists often speak of formal power (which might be thought of as power derived from immaterial resources).[258] As we will see in Chapter 3, the view of most NCAs and NGAs is that those in the Steering Group and the Working Group co-Chairs have more influence than NCAs without these formal roles.

It is common to consider structural power of network actors. By this we analyse their role and place in the structure of the network. This often entails looking at the number, quantity, and type of ties an NCA or NGA might have with other network actors.[259] In terms of structural power, the NCAs of the EU (especially DG COMP) and the USA hold particular significance. Not only have they had a disproportionate number of roles (see Section 1.2.1.2, discussing their election to the Steering Group and as Working Group chairs), but they have also likely accumulated more structural power through the cumulative effect of the linkages gained through these multiple, overlapping roles across almost the entire spectrum of ICN activity. Gaus neatly summarizes the overlap of formal and structural power within the ICN like this:

> In terms of structural power at the ICN, which refers to the centrality of members within the network and their linkages with other members, two conclusions emerge based on data that captures the successive chairing of the five ICN thematic working groups and sub-working groups between 2010–2014 ... First, those that have structural power are also those that hold formal roles. This may seem obvious but previous organizational research has shown that there must not always be such a close fit. Quite often and contrary to hierarchies and influential positions established in an organization, it may be others who are central by their

[258] Karin Ingold and Philip Leifeld, 'Structural and Institutional Determinants of Influence Reputation: A Comparison of Collaborative and Adversarial Policy Networks in Decision Making and Implementation' (2016) 26 Journal of Public Administration Research and Theory 1, 2.

[259] Structural power considers the number, quality, and type of ties with other network members that a node (in our case an NCA or NGA) has, ibid 2.

> ability to connect with a large number of people in the organization ... [260] The second conclusion is that even among those where structural power overlaps with formal power, a certain hierarchy in the sense of greater connectivity and influence is visible.[261]

The informal power of other ICN actors has a mediating effect on this formal and structural power. Gaus takes a wide definition of informal power and relates it to three core features: 'At the ICN, informal power is primarily based on the legacy one has in the organization, on connections one brings and on legitimacy one may add to the organization.'[262] He rightly notes that, in terms of legacy, the founding members of the ICN have high status and this adds to the already considerable formal and structural power of (once again) the US NCAs, DG COMP, and a few others. In terms of connections (both within and outside of the ICN), Gaus highlights two sets of actors: the Australian NCA which has been given a 'horizontal role', acting as a mentor and guardian to co-Chairs of the working Groups in defining their annual work programmes; and the NGAs (which we discuss in Section 1.3.2). This horizontal role is powerful as it is the only one that permanently connects an NCA to all Working Group co-Chairs. Gaus claims that the resulting informal power gives this NCA 'far-reaching agenda-setting and control abilities'. The third aspect of informal power that Gaus highlights in the ICN is legitimacy. Gaus reports a striking pattern through his interviews, that smaller NCAs (which he defines as all NCAs other than those that: are in the Steering Group, set up the ICN originally, or are co-Chairs of Working Groups) 'yield increasingly informal power due to their relevance to the stability and legitimacy of the network'.[263] He rightly says that the ICN does not function without 'inclusiveness, cohesion and stability'. This means that the advanced NCAs need the others in order to generate a harmonized competition system. So, he thinks that the smaller NCAs have exceptional power to influence the ICN's stability and legitimacy.[264]

260 Rob Cross and Andrew Parker, *The Hidden Power of Social Networks* (Harvard Business School Press 2004).

261 Gaus (n 108) 15. See also his interesting graphic (ibid 16) and his conclusion (also supported by his interviews) that some:

> Steering Group members hold more central positions than others due to their engagement in a large amount of working groups and the greater amount of connections this allows with smaller but influential ICN member agencies. Most prominent in this regard are the EC [now the EU] and the US Department of Justice, which have not only chaired the most working groups over time but also had the most exposure to agencies outside of the Steering Group that had co-chair roles. Due to this, the EC and US can act much more than other Steering Group members as bridge-builders that allows them to reach other agencies, transmit information faster and in turn have greater influence on key members.

262 ibid 18–20.

263 ibid 18.

264 ibid 20.

We do not deny that some NCAs in the ICN have some power (Gaus highlights how India was able to change the agenda when it joined the ICN and how officials from DG COMP and the US NCAs have never led the ICN because this might undermine the legitimacy of the ICN). However, we think that this kind of power is minimal, often transient, and rarely decisive.[265] Furthermore, informal power structures sometimes, in fact, bolster these formal power structures.[266] It is, of course, true that the ICN would be significantly less able to achieve the advanced NCAs' goals if it had fewer members. As we note below, these advanced NCAs need to consider the effect on other NCAs (and ensure that they generate other benefits as counterweights—see Section 1.3.1.5). But, unless Gaus's 'smaller NCAs' get together as a bloc, united in their determination to exercise power on an ongoing basis, we think that the advanced NCAs will continue being able to exert considerable pressures through their formal and structural roles.[267]

1.3.1.2 Epistemic community and the technical nature of rules

Transnational regulatory networks, like the ICN, create and store relational capital between NCAs. However, Lewis claims that the ICN was never just about institutions. It is about meeting with individuals, building respect, and trust: 'It has become a dense network, not merely of competition agencies, but of deeply committed individuals.'[268] The employees of NCAs and NGAs are part of this community. Their presence in the ICN affects the conversation and brings the concerns and costs of doing business centre stage there.[269] Kennedy agrees, more generally, that we cannot only focus on state actors.[270] We need to look at NCAs, but also competition experts within the NCAs, businesses, etc.

[265] We give several examples throughout the book, but a striking example was the way David Lewis (South Africa) effectively 'stood up against' the epistemic community when it came to the goals of unilateral competition norms. That said, such stories are almost the exceptions that prove the rule.

[266] For example, the ICN Steering Committee designed the 'horizontal role' to reinforce its own power. The aim was to ensure that the Steering Group had more control over the Working Groups (which have always been quite independent in their choice of projects, for example). Through the creation of this role, the Steering Group sought a way to 'control' and 'coordinate' the Working Groups.

[267] Gaus identifies three control mechanisms for exercising power and influence in the ICN 'control is exercised in the short term by managing processes, in the medium term by strategy setting and in the long run by sense-making' Gaus (n 108) 22. We note that this small group of NCAs that we say has the real power and influence within the ICN dominate all three control mechanisms. The only place where Gaus concretely disagrees with this observation is where he argues that 'sense-making' has now been extended to a wider group of NCAs through a new mantra, inclusiveness, ibid 24–25. However, as we point out in Section 1.3.1.4, and Chapter 4, despite speaking about it a lot, especially under Andreas Mundt, we do not think that inclusiveness has had much impact on ICN processes and outputs so far.

[268] David Lewis, 'Some Reflections on the ICN' in Lugard (n 7) 215.

[269] The individuals that work in the NGAs form a managerial elite that works with political elites (and those in the NCAs) in many countries, Wilks (n 161) 33. Those working in the NCAs may also (or instead) pursue their own goals in the ICN, rather than acting solely in their NCA's interests, see discussion around n 295 and Section 1.3.2.3.

[270] David Kennedy, 'Challenging Expert Rule: the Politics of Global Governance' (2005) 27 Sydney Law Review 5, 16–20.

The Introduction to this book showed that there is room for a lot of highly redistributive choices in widely drafted competition rules.[271] Theories narrow the options available to decision makers building upon expert ideas. As van Waarden and Drahos emphasize, ideas are vital in complex areas (like competition) with uncertainty about what is best and how best to achieve it.[272] So, we need to understand experts' impact on NCA decision-making.

This brings us to the topic of what is professional expertise. Experts argue about choices that produce outcomes. To do this they dispute alternate policies and ideas by reference to underlying methods, theories, and politics. Expert knowledge also channels the way we understand problems and the narrow range of potential solutions. There might be a common sense of history (a way of seeing the world and what has caused the problem before them). There might also be a common intellectual history, eg economics as a basis for argument. This can lead to various shared assumptions. 'Expert opinion' (eg that economic analysis in competition rules should not be tainted by public policy concerns)[273] always have a political result, even if those advocating them do not know it (or even aim for it):

> following Gramsci's notion of the organic intellectual (Gramsci, 1971),[274] we view experts as political actors whose preferences set the 'technical' agenda and define the range of possible outcomes in a decision making process. Expert knowledge is itself always political because it is always acquired in a particular social context, and reflects the political–economic structures and social relations which generated and which reproduce that context. Each expert uses his or her own theoretical approach to produce technical solutions, which is why they are seen as

[271] In addition, many NCAs enjoy significant independence from government influence, making them particularly powerful decision makers (subject to appeal).

[272] Ideas are:

> important in complex policies with uncertainty concerning eventual outcomes. Since the effects of competition policy are difficult to measure, ideas matter ... There are various economic schools of thought, with different concepts of competition and different ideas concerning competition policy. In this 'limbo' EU competition policy had the function of 'field experiment' ... It allowed for policy learning concerning the effects of specific competition policies.
>
> van Waarden and Drahos (n 12) 932.

Similarly, William Kovacic, 'The Modern Evolution of US Competition Policy Enforcement Norms' (2003) 71 Antitrust Law Journal 377. By way of example, van Waarden and Drahos add:

> The Dutch and Austrians traditionally believed that strict competition policy would lead to cut-throat competition and decrease competitiveness. For them, EU policy was their first direct contact with a prohibition system, with merger control, and, for Austria, with rules on abusing a dominant position. EU experience taught that a prohibition system does not lead to a breakdown of the economy. This has helped to remove some of the worst fears of its opponents, or to diminish the legitimacy of their arguments.
>
> van Waarden and Drahos (n 12) 932.

[273] Mandorff (n 195) 1.

[274] Antonio Gramsci, Quintin Hoare and Geoffrey Nowell-Smith, *Selections from the Prison Notebooks of Antonio Gramsci* (International Publishers 1971) 3–23.

> experts. As Robert Cox puts it, 'theory is always for someone and for some purpose' (Cox, 1981: 128).[275] In other words, technical solutions are never purely technical; they always have a political purpose even if those propagating the solutions are not fully aware of it.[276]

In terms of identifying the political element in an 'expert opinion', there are three key approaches. First, we could focus on the consequences of expertise, ie who wins or loses as a result; second, we might analyse experts' underlying, shared assumptions, showing how they favour certain groups or ideologies; or, finally, we could ask whether the expert's decision was really compelled, or if she exercised discretion. Most experts flee from this kind of discussion. Transparency would be aided if experts were to admit the gaps and to take responsibility for filling them in the way they do.[277] This first approach for identifying the political (redistributive) element in expert opinion, focuses on the consequences of expertise, ie who wins and who loses when we prioritize one expert view over another. This approach:

> requires an assessment, however crude or incomplete, of consequences—who wins and who loses? Who decides and who submits to the decisions of others? Only by identifying the stakes of expert action can we understand its politics.[278]

The EU and US will focus on the merits of their rules, probably emphasizing liberal, pro-privatization, open markets. Focusing on this type of market-based system has consequences for who wins and who loses. It is not a value neutral position.[279] The EU/US focus on the welfare effects that competition policies have for consumers. For example, they might say that if the NCA in a developing economy were to use competition policy to open up its markets to EU and US firms then this would result in more competition and lower prices (and more choice) for local consumers. However, there are likely to be other winners and losers too, which are not discussed so openly. One set of winners is often EU and US firms themselves. We need go no further than the ICPAC report for an admission of this industrial policy aim:

> U.S. support of new competition policy regimes also creates an opportunity for the United States to share its perspective. This can be important as a means of influencing the legal environment in which U.S. exporters and businesses operate.[280]

275 Robert Cox, 'Social Forces, States and World Orders' (1981) 10 Millennium Journal of International Studies 126.

276 Perry and Nölke (n 185) 578.

277 Kennedy (n 270) 20.

278 ibid 17.

279 There is no consensus that economic efficiency increased in Britain through privatization. There is, however, says Wilks, a consensus that privatization created new interest groups seeking to influence political institutions, Wilks (n 161) 122–28.

280 ICPAC (n 20) Executive Summary 31.

The flip side of this is that probable losers are local firms (and their employees). Some might consider this an acceptable price to pay for the extra consumer surplus (at least in the short term). However, it is one thing to fully debate the consequences of following the EU/US competition paradigm here, including the potential winners and losers, and another thing just to blindly follow what one is told is the technically best policy. The way competition policy is interpreted is highly redistributive. This is usually considered to be a political function. By excluding states from the ICN and encouraging independent NCAs, the EU/US paradigm also seeks to exclude a focus on this redistributive dimension from competition discourse.

The consequences of ideological choices can be hard to establish, concretely. The way things interact are complex and ideologies often favour many groups, or it can be easy to argue that they do, in the abstract. It may be preferable instead to adopt the second approach to highlighting the political element in expert opinion. This is to remind NCAs that technical analysis is not conclusive, and that instead they rely on assumptions that may not always be applicable[281] and are value laden. The focus here is 'the blind spots and biases which skew their choices or place some alternatives altogether out of discussion'.[282]

Let us take two common assumptions of the competition community: protectionism is bad (free trade is good) and consumers are rational. It has been generally assumed that gains from trading with one country accrue to both countries.[283] However, Chang, for example, argues that protectionism can be beneficial to developing countries seeking to shelter their industries, especially if they can quickly become competitive.[284] Competition policy can effectively help to protect infant industries, if required. There may be cheaper ways of protecting these industries than through distortions to competition, but that also depends on the country concerned.

Second, traditional economics makes other simplifying assumptions, for example in relation to consumer preferences, decision-making, and consumer choice. The assumption is that the way information is framed to consumers does not matter and that consumers use all available information when making decisions. Furthermore, it is often assumed that consumers 'engage in fully rational and fully conscious reasoning, weighing up the best course of action. People are skilled at forecasting the future, and over time act in a way that maximizes their lifetime

281 Sol Picciotto, 'Introduction: Reconceptualizing Regulation in the Era of Globalization' (2002) 29(1) Journal of Law and Society, 8–9.

282 Kennedy (n 270) 18.

283 Joseph Stiglitz, 'Participation and Development: Perspectives from the Comprehensive Development Programme' (2002) 6 Review of Development Economics 163.

284 Chang Ha-Joon, 'Kicking Away the Ladder: Infant Industry Promotion in Historical Perspective' (2003) 31(1) Oxford Development Studies 21–32. He also highlights the important role that protectionism, rather than free market, played in the economic growth of today's developed countries. Similarly, <https://sdgpulse.unctad.org/barriers-to-trade/#Ref_Radelet2015>

utility.'[285] However, several interesting studies demonstrate that consumers do not always behave in this way.[286] This is important because it means that competition may not always result in the most efficient firm 'winning', but rather the firm that is better able to manipulate consumer choice. This is now an area which many NCAs are taking seriously in their competition analysis[287] (and in other areas, such as false advertising and wider consumer protection legislation for those NCAs that also work in such areas). Nevertheless, this kind of behavioural economics was ignored for a long time and is still not incorporated by many NCAs.

The third approach for identifying the political element in expert opinion emphasizes discretion in decision-making. A key aspect of experts' claim to power is often that knowledge limits their discretion (ie they cannot respond to conscience, or to political power). In this tradition:

> the key to politics is the experience of responsible discretion. An expert governs when he or she decides—in the sense that they experience a freedom of manoeuvre to go one way or the other—and when their decision has consequences for other people for which they are then responsible.[288]

There are several examples of discretion in the consumer welfare paradigm (indeed selecting this paradigm is itself an example of discretion in many competition regimes, including the EU and the USA). By way of illustration, deciding whether to give more weight to short or long-term consumer welfare, or to balance welfare effects across different relevant markets, and how to trade off choice and price, all demand the exercise of discretion (and are redistributive).[289]

[285] Oxera Consulting Ltd., 'Behavioural Economics, Competition and Remedy Design' (2015) <https://www.oxera.com/wp-content/uploads/2018/07/Behavioural-economics-competition-and-remedy-design-1.pdf-1.pdf> accessed 7 September 2021.

[286] See, for example, Amos Tversky and Daniel Kahneman, 'Judgment under Uncertainty: Heuristics and Biases' (1974) 185 Science; Amos Tversky and Daniel Kahneman, 'The Framing of Decisions and the Psychology of Choice' (1981) 211 Science; Richard Thaler and Cass Sunstein, *Nudge* (Yale UP 2008).

[287] Office of Fair Trading, *What Does Behavioural Economics Mean for Competition Policy?* (2010), OFT 1224, <https://webarchive.nationalarchives.gov.uk/ukgwa/20140402142426/http:/www.oft.gov.uk/shared_oft/economic_research/oft1224.pdf> accessed 7 September 2021. Emanuele Ciriolo, 'Behavioural Economics in the European Commission: Past, Present and Future' (2011) < https://www.oxera.com/wp-content/uploads/2018/03/Behavioural-economics-in-the-EC_1-1.pdf > accessed 7 September 2021; Oxera Consulting Ltd., *Behavioural Economics and Its Impact on Competition Policy* (2013), <https://www.oxera.com/insights/reports/behavioural-economics-and-its-impact-on-competition-policy/> accessed 7 October 2021.

[288] Kennedy (n 270) 23. He continues, 'In this tradition, politicising a decision does not mean translating its terms from an apparently neutral expert vocabulary into a vocabulary of interests and ideologies. It means rendering implausible the expert's presentation of the decision, to himself or herself and to others, as determined rather than "free".'

[289] See discussions in Christopher Townley, 'The Relevant Market: An Acceptable Limit to Competition Analysis?' [2011] 32(10) European Competition Law Review 490; Christopher Townley, 'Remembering Those Not Yet Born: Inter-Generational Impacts in Competition Analysis' [2011] 32(11) European Competition Law Review 580.

So, expert opinion generates redistributive consequences for NCAs. Different expert opinions will have different redistributive consequences and so choosing between them (deciding to prioritize some experts over others) is redistributive too. An exclusive focus on consumer welfare makes the interests of employees and SMEs irrelevant in competition law, for example. Section 1.2.1.1 argued that it benefits economically advanced states to frame competition policy and enforcement as technical disciplines prioritizing economic expertise. Powerful multinationals (and their advisers)[290] also benefit from supporting/influencing such choices.

It is hard for poor NCAs, especially those recently invested with competition powers, to influence arguments about which experts to favour. They often have less legal and economic expertise in the area and find themselves outgunned by technical experts from richer, more established NCAs. In fact, there are some clues that the role envisaged for newer NCAs (at least by the richer ones) is that, rather than seeking influence, they focus on learning.[291]

It is widely accepted that epistemic communities influence what is considered to be relevant expertise in the competition community.[292] An epistemic community is a network of professionals 'with recognised expertise and competence

[290] Much of the theory cautions against trusting in the motivations of such intermediaries, especially private firms (including law firms and economic consultancies). This is because they may exploit/seek to change regulatory systems for their (clients') ends, perhaps modifying compliance in ways that are easy to sell rather than in ways which best achieve regulatory goals, Jeroen van der Hiejden, 'Brighter and Darker Sides of Intermediation: Target-Orientated and Self-Interested Intermediaries in the Regulatory Governance of Buildings' (2017) 670 Annals of the American Academy of Political and Social Science 207; and/or are paid for by the regulatees, as payment offers a temptation to distort one's actions as agents of these regulatees to get future work, Andreas Kruck, 'Asymmetry in Empowering and Disempowering Private Intermediaries: The Case of Credit Rating Agencies' (2017) 670 The Annals of the American Academy of Political and Social Science 133.

One US study, on environmental consultants, argued that two mechanisms may sometimes mean that a more positive picture emerges (it was cautious of assuming such benefits outside of that narrow field). First, environmental consultants 'often strive to operate as trusted facilitators of relationships between regulated businesses [their clients] and regulators'. Second, environmental consultants:

> often embrace the public-spirited values underlying the regulatory programs they implement and view advancing those values as part of their professional role. This *guardian of public values* role was not purely altruistic, and consultants did not pretend otherwise. While they often explained how a personal commitment to environmental protection informs their work, consultants readily acknowledged that they make money from regulation. Nor were consultants as vocal or persistent in their advocacy as environmental advocates from non-profit groups. Nor, finally, are these values universal among environmental consultants.
>
> Dave Owen, 'Private Facilitators of Public Regulation: A Study of the Environmental Consulting Industry' [2019] Regulation & Governance 2, see also 8–11.

[291] 'Certainly the ICN's value to the developing countries cannot solely be judged by their participation in the annual conferences and working groups. They can also benefit from the ICN's guiding principles and recommended practices' Ulf Böge, Speech on the Opening of 4th Annual ICN Conference, 6–8 June 2005, 2.

[292] See Gerber (n 61) 126. We refer to *the* epistemic communities, but there may be several struggling for power, and internally, they are not necessarily uniform, Djelic and Quack (n 15) 25–26.

in a particular domain and an authoritative claim to policy relevant knowledge within that domain or issue-area'.[293] Expert opinion is informed by the epistemic community's own broader world view. It is not objective:

> While epistemic communities provide consensual knowledge, they do not necessarily generate truth. The epistemological impossibility of confirming access to reality means that the group responsible or articulating the dimensions of reality has great social and political influence.[294]

Prioritizing one epistemic community over another produces winners and losers. Once again, this is often done through the intellectual leadership of rich, western academics, competition practitioners and NCAs. Joining the leading epistemic community can benefit individuals[295] and NCAs[296] too. Influence and prestige can be reward in themselves. Influence can also enhance future employment opportunities (for example, the 'revolving doors' in Section 1.3.2.3).

Members of the competition epistemic community are not necessarily motivated by their own self-interest.[297] This community of 'believers' often genuinely thinks that its ideas provide huge benefits to the economy and consumers.[298] Individuals reinforce these beliefs in each other. Years of learning help to deeply embed this perspective.[299] Nevertheless, these political effects often occur even when experts are not motivated by selfish ends.

These choices by the powerful in the ICN matter. The pressure on members to conform with the epistemic community's view can be immense, because the cost of exclusion can be so high.[300] Sections 1.2 and 1.3.1.1 show how powerful actors within them can put weaker actors under pressure to follow their agendas

[293] Haas (n 14).

[294] ibid 23. Similarly, Sol Picciotto, 'Networks in International Economic Integration: Fragmented States and the Dilemmas of Neo-Liberalism' (1996–97) 17 Northwestern Journal of International Law and Business 1014, 1037.

[295] Van Waarden and Drahos (n 12) 929. More widely, see also Imelda Maher, 'Competition Law in the International Domain: Networks as a New Form of Governance' (2002) 29 Journal of Law and Society 1, 117; Palacios Lleras (n 118) 195–96; Haas (n 14) 17.

[296] In fact, NCAs try to bolster their independence (and ultimately their power), through the ICN—see the discussion around n 148 and Chapters 2 and 4. This is not surprising. The ICN explicitly aims to 'facilitate effective international co-operation to the benefit of member agencies' (see n 17).

[297] In fact, if it looks as though they are acting in their own self-interest (rather than their expert knowledge) then experts may lose authority, Mai'a K Davis Cross, 'Rethinking Epistemic Communities Twenty Years Later' (2013) 39 Review of International Studies 137, 142.

[298] Van Waarden and Drahos (n 12) 913–34.

[299] Some, guided by professional norms (from the epistemic community), may prefer to fall on their swords rather than do something outside of the acceptable limits of their community (even if this means they get sanctioned), Mark Pollack, 'Principal–Agent Analysis and International Delegation: Red Herrings, Theoretical Classifications and Empirical Disputes' [2007) Bruges Political Research Papers 7.

[300] Haas (n 14) 20. Specifically in relation to EU competition law, see Van Waarden and Drahos (n 12) 929; Townley (n 175) 154–55.

(perhaps conforming with ICN recommended practices, for example), even if those actors have a power of veto over decision-making. In order to protect their position (and power), epistemic communities often create barriers to entry, which 'help to inure the community to influence from other actors'.[301] For example, those that do not conform might be 'punished' (so they lose help, influence and power);[302] those with different 'world views' might be ridiculed or even find that they cannot enter the community at all. But a really powerful effect is most likely epistemic communities' ability to socialize the opinions of those from poorer NCAs so that they conform to those of their colleagues from richer NCAs. Many believe that this kind of socialization is possible.[303] Where successful this could turn officials from these poorer NCAs (and the NCAs themselves) into EU/US competition cuckoos, embedding these rich world views (and their consequences) into the heart of poorer states.

1.3.1.3 Getting into the debate early

Structural power (economic or political) and an ability to disseminate self-serving ideas may count for little without the ability to influence the debate from an early stage. If true, this explains, in part, why being on the Steering Group is (ever more) important, as well as chairing Working Groups, rather than merely participating in the ICN as most NCAs do.

Lall emphasizes two mechanisms which, taken together, may explain the distributional consequences of regulatory processes for complex, technical matters (such as competition policy and enforcement). These two mechanisms are:

> First, they affect which stakeholders have access to regulatory officials' informal social networks (ISNs)—networks that play a crucial role in determining who claims first-mover position and, thus, sets the agenda . . . Second, they give rise to distinctive increasing returns processes that serve to reinforce and entrench proposals made at an early stage of rulemaking, guaranteeing that first movers exert an enduring influence over the content of international standards.[304]

[301] Maher (n 295) 120–21; Imelda Maher, 'Functional and Normative Delegation to Non-Majoritarian Institutions: The Case of the European Competition Network' (2009) 7 Comparative European Politics 414, 425. Anecdotally, two readers of our first draft chapter on SSRN told us that, although they were senior competition officials, they had never been encouraged to join the ICN. They attributed this to their vocal support of diversity.

[302] Marie-Laure Djelic and Sigrid Quack, 'Overcoming Path Dependency: Path Generation in Open Systems' (2007) 36 Theory and Society 161, 180–81.

[303] For example, Fingleton (n 85) 191.

[304] Ranjit Lall, 'Timing as a Source of Regulatory Influence: A Technical Elite Network Analysis of Global Finance' [2014] Regulation & Governance 125, 126, see also ibid 129; Lall's focus is financial regulation, but competition policy and enforcement are similar in important respects. Lall's argument originally focused on NGAs (see the discussion in Section 1.3.2.2), but it also speaks to issues in our scenario with NCAs. Others agree that sequencing, something employed by the historical institutionalists, is important: Posner (n 64) 648.

The idea here is that regulatory standards are adopted over several phases. They start with agenda setting, then planning, then a discussion paper, consultation, and finally approval.

The technical complexity of the issue affects those who have access to ISNs (which might be linked to the ICN Steering Group, for example) and thus who may get a first-mover advantage. Those involved earlier tend to enjoy more influence than stakeholders arriving later. It is often the richer NCAs and NGAs that have this knowledge, access, and influence. Our focus is NCAs, but similar arguments are relevant for NGAs—see Section 1.3.2.2. Knowledgeable NCAs can see problems in the existing rules and suggest ways of solving them, which reflect their regulatory preferences (or they may ignore gaps where it is not in their interest to point them out). NCAs with 'timely and high-quality information' about the regulatory agenda, may contribute to the setting up of a Working Group or the scoping of a project (or an idea within a project), before others are even aware that the issue is being discussed. This helps them to set or lead the agenda. In addition, because of their specialist knowledge and skills, these NCAs are more likely to be delegated (trusted with) key roles, such as drafting relevant sections of a recommended practice or doing feasibility studies. NCAs from the EU and the USA are likely to propose rules that they both already have, making them more knowledgeable, likely leaders in this area (and better able to win arguments, should any arise). Lall notes, 'regulators often *depend* on the expertise provided by ISN members to develop rules that make operational sense'.[305] Our survey confirms the importance of expertise in granting NCAs influence: 97 per cent consider it 'important' or 'very important'.

So, how does Lall's process work? He thinks there are increasing returns from getting in early. He highlights two processes which tend to reinforce themselves and each other. First, high fixed costs are involved in formulating competition standards, given their technical nature. Developing standards demands extensive 'research, planning, deliberation and drafting'. The sheer size of this task means that many cannot contemplate it; and, once done, the costs of abandoning the proposal is extremely high. The costs of this are even higher where those that led on the drafting of the proposal (the EU or US NCA, for example) originally suggested it. The combination of high sunk costs and pressure from within make discarding proposals at an advanced stage hard. In addition, a second process reinforces entrenchment of proposals. This is because NCAs, not states, are ICN members. If the ICN were intergovernmental:

> rules may be blocked by states during the latter stages of the regulatory process if they are believed to adversely affect some group of domestic constituents.[306]

[305] Lall (n 304) 128.

[306] Indeed, such regimes typically involve a distinct ratification phase in which governments consult with constituents about whether to endorse rules agreed during earlier negotiations.

> Governments are directly accountable for failing to protect domestic stakeholders, creating strong incentives for them to ensure that international rules are acceptable to a broad range of societal interests.[307] Non-state regulatory bodies, on the other hand, have no formal accountability to the citizens of countries under their jurisdiction. Because officials cannot be sanctioned for failing to defend the interests of particular domestic groups, they have little reason to block provisions on public interest grounds during the final stages of the regulatory process. The upshot is that rules proposed at an early point in negotiations—rules in which regulatory experts, subsequently, invest substantial resources—have a high likelihood of eventually being adopted.[308]

Let us ask ourselves how the ICN drafts recommended practices, for example (and who has power). First, the Steering Group decides whether to set up a Working Group in a certain area. It also controls agenda setting, sets the Working Group's boundaries, and reviews the Working Group's work. There are no recorded disagreements on any of these important issues.[309]

Section 1.2 showed that the Steering Group was dominated by those from rich NCAs. This effectively means that potentially important power is concentrated in the hands of well-resourced NCAs. This may not be a coincidence. Note that it was principally well-resourced (advanced) NCAs that established the ICN and decided these constitutional structures.

There certainly is not a lot of publicly available dissatisfaction with the lack of diversity in the Steering Group. In 2011, the ICN produced a vision for its second decade. Members were polled and (according to the ICN people that drafted the report) the feedback indicated:

> relatively little demand for membership of the Steering Group to be broadened. Three members commented that younger agencies and agencies in developing countries should be better represented on the Steering Group, while another (not a Steering Group member) commented that provided the Steering Group's decisions were reflected at working group level and vice versa, the focus on broadening participation in decision-making should centre on the working groups.[310]

Nevertheless, one ICN member did suggest that it was important to rotate more members through the Steering Group. In a nudge to a need for better processes in relation to elections to the Steering Group, two members 'commented that

[307] Robert Putnam, 'Diplomacy and Domestic Politics: The Logic of Two-Level Games' (1988) 42 International Organization 427.

[308] Lall (n 304) 129.

[309] <www.internationalcompetitionnetwork.org/about/steering-group/archive.aspx> accessed 7 October 2021.

[310] ICN (n 135) 19–22.

the elections to the Steering Group should be more clearly advertised and more transparent'.[311]

Once the Steering Group has established a Working Group in an area and that Working Group has suggested a specific topic to investigate (and the Steering Group has agreed), then the Working Group drafts a recommended practice. Pérez Motta says they are drafted:

> by members and NGAs, vetted with the substantive group [by which he appears to mean the Working Group as a whole and then the Steering Group, and then with the ICN membership]. This collaborative and open process, unique in the competition world, provides the Practices with a legitimacy that facilitates their implementation.[312]

This seems to be an open process with lots of opportunities to pull the brake. Having said that, with the benefit of Lall's perspective, one can see that those NCAs and NGAs that are assigned drafting tasks may already have an advantage over others. It is normally advanced NCAs and NGAs doing this. It is also unclear why the work needs to be vetted by the Steering Group. This seems to give further power to the (mainly) advanced NCAs that lead it. Wouldn't a proper discussion in the Annual Conference suffice?[313] However, even here, there are hints that the discussions in the Annual Meeting are not always as full and as open as they might be.[314]

The position in the Working Groups, while less extreme, follows a similar pattern to that in the Steering Group. This is true in terms of the benefits of leadership, as well as the distribution of leadership roles. As noted above, in 2012 the ICN produced a vision for its second decade. Members were polled and several suggested that the ICN should pay more attention to the needs of newer NCAs when it comes to agenda setting in the Working Groups and elsewhere (although others said that this was fine).[315] Formally, any NCA can participate in Working Group activities

311 ibid.

312 Eduardo Pérez Motta, 'A Network of Competition Advocates' (UOKiK's Second International Competition Forum) 2.

313 This is not to say that some preparation is not helpful. Less well-resourced NCAs often do not have the time, expertise, and ultimately the will to do this. However, this is partly the point. Then the large can act, they get in first, and can focus more on what they want. This is not necessarily done in a way so as to exclude, but once these other kinds of actors are not involved (even if they choose this) then their interests tend to be considered less deeply.

314 Note the following quote from one ICN document, for example, when commenting on the ICN Annual Conference 2014, the Steering Group said that there was a good balance of plenary and breakout sessions. There was more room for audience participation in breakout sessions. However, 'room for improvement remained', previously available at <www.internationalcompetitionnetwork.org/uploads/library/doc997.pdf> 1, (broken ICN link, see discussion in Introduction, n 16).

315 'A number of smaller/younger agency members felt they have adequate opportunity to be involved in the ICN and take a leadership role should they choose to do so, one small and new agency noting that "you get out of [ICN] what you put into it. Participation may take some effort, but the rewards are there for those that participate"' ICN (n 135) 19–22.

and products (and Working Group Chairs are encouraged to reflect the ICN diversity in their Working Groups).[316] The criteria for selecting Working Group co-Chairs are basically the same as for the Steering Group mentioned above. Formally then, the path seems reasonably open for more diversity within Working Groups as well as for their leadership.[317] We have seen similar results in who takes these roles. There have also been calls for more diversity in working group discussions/work products; that working groups should encourage free debate on future work and ideas before circulating draft work plans; and that efforts should be made to encourage a broader range of agencies to speak on working group calls.[318]

These comments may indicate ways in which formal equality is being eroded in practice.[319] Since 2014 the Steering Group has asked each Working Group to report to it on the process:

> for creating the work product(s) [which might include recommended practices], including the scope of member and NGA involvement, how the work product fits with the group's long term goals, and any plans to promote the work products.[320]

This may be an indication that the ICN is also worried with this idea. There are, increasingly, limits to the Working Groups autonomy.

> The Horizontal Coordinator reviewed draft versions of the work plans to check for: potential duplication or conflicts between plans; gaps in individual plans; balance of work across the Working Groups; and consistency with the ICN's goals and objectives. Following this review, the Horizontal Coordinator sent comments to each of the respective Working Groups. The Working Groups have since considered those comments and have now submitted final work plans for our approval.[321]

However, what they actually say on these issues is not reported in the Steering Group minutes and it does not entirely deal with the issue of first-mover advantages, the focus being on who is in the discussions, rather than their impact. This

[316] ICN (n 16) 5, (broken ICN link, see discussion in Introduction, n 16).
[317] ibid 6. See also the criteria set out for the Steering Group around n 91.
[318] ICN (n 135) 19–22.
[319] Based on those discussions, the ICN Steering Group members committed to consulting with all of ICN membership—<www.internationalcompetitionnetwork.org/second-decade.aspx> NGA responses were previously available at <www.internationalcompetitionnetwork.org/uploads/2010-2011/responses%20nga%20survey%208.10.pdf> (broken ICN link, see discussion in Introduction, n 16).
[320] Previously available at <www.internationalcompetitionnetwork.org/uploads/library/doc996.pdf> 1, (broken ICN link, see discussion in Introduction, n 16).
[321] ICN Steering Group, *Note from the Chair for the June 13, 2012 Steering Group Meeting* (2012) 1, previously available at <http://internationalcompetitionnetwork.org/uploads/library/doc806.pdf> (broken ICN link, see discussion in Introduction, n 16).

may be a sign of richer states trying to consolidate more power through their dominance over the Steering Group.

1.3.1.4 A relative lack of resources

There is a lot of ICN activity. This has many benefits. However, to actively participate in all activities (answering questionnaires, commenting on draft recommendations, etc) and attend all meetings (including physical attendance at the Annual Meeting) costs a lot. Many poorer NCAs cannot afford this time or money: participation involves substantial opportunity costs.[322] This is even more so for NCAs seeking to constructively engage with the ICN and generate their own views and the evidence.[323] So, poorer NCAs may not be heard. This makes it harder for them to protect their own interests when they clash with those of richer NCAs and NGAs.

The burden becomes even greater when one considers the further cost of being the Chair of a Working Group or even the Steering Group. Fox says that less well-resourced NCAs would find it expensive to be in the Steering Group, or act as a Chair there, or in Working Groups. 'This means that authorities from resource-strained nations have less opportunity to participate in setting the agenda and to write first drafts of recommendations.'[324] Respondents to our survey also identify resources as an important factor in determining an NCA's influence in the ICN: 83.5 per cent of them consider resources as 'important' or 'very important'. We have already seen why these are influential positions; and why an ability to help set agendas and participate in early drafting helps one to better control the outcomes of policy debates.

In addition, if English is not your first language, and you have less technical knowledge, you may also be more silent. This gives more voice to the USA and the EU, the two leading antitrust models in the world whose representatives are normally comfortable speaking, debating and drafting submissions in English.[325] Language then, can be used to exclude. Once again, this is a double-edged sword. If everything is only written in English, then this also reduces the influence of documents, such as the recommended practices. Ideally, if an NCA were looking to exploit its power to the maximum, it would have all discussion and questionnaires and debate in one language, possibly English (reducing the ability of many to intervene). Then, it would push for these recommended practices, etc. to be widely translated. This would allow those working in many NCAs to read and

[322] ICN, 'The Future of the ICN in Its Second Decade, Draft Final Report' (2016) 12. Note that the equivalent discussion in the final version of this report ICN, The Future of the ICN in Its Second Decade, Final Report (2016) 12-14, no longer specifically refers to developing countries here.

[323] This does not only create problems for NCAs from poor countries. Swedish NCA staff have said, for example, that they find 'active participation in all working groups is almost impossible' Sjöblom and Widegren (n 57) 355.

[324] Fox (n 9) 126.

[325] ibid.

understand these documents. In this way, there could be pressure without influence. Unsurprisingly, this is now happening.[326]

There is, of course, a tension here, and a legitimate one. If all of these Working Groups and workshops are needed and doing important work, then one would obviously want to have them. However, once NCAs start being left behind and feel this, then there is a risk that the ICN will not be considered an inclusive forum. If this happens, it may well rapidly lose its status, influence (and thus its meaning). So, there is a delicate balance. The more that richer NCAs can raise this burden, without complaints, the harder it is for poorer NCAs to contribute (and defend their interests). So, the richer NCAs could reserve themselves (yet) more power.

Lewis believes that the weaker, less-resourced NCAs are given a voice. Indeed, he points to active efforts that have been made to help here. In his view, they have been treated as equal members. Those that want to be active are. He still says that there are marginalized NCAs though, normally through a lack of their own resources and information.[327]

The topic has been debated within the ICN itself. For example, it has been suggested that the number of workshops per year should be reduced to allow each NCA to attend as many of them as possible. The point being made that inclusiveness could be undermined if NCAs were forced to miss many of these important events.[328] The Steering Group decided not to formally reduce the number of workshops. Rather, it focuses on preventing conflicts between them, also encouraging Working Groups to try to reduce to less than one workshop per year.[329] Similarly, the Chair of the Steering Group has also said:

> Even member agencies that have a large workforce struggle with keeping up with all work products, especially if they are as resource intensive as Recommended Practices. For the sake of inclusiveness the Working Groups should try to aim to prioritize and limit the overall burden for all members.[330]

One way of helping more NCAs to participate more often, and better, in ICN activities is to reduce the cost of doing this. As a virtual organization, the ICN does a good job of keeping costs down. However, finding ways to avoid the cost

[326] There was an initiative to translate some ICN documents into French and Portuguese (although the working language of the ICN remained English and all documents are originally worked on in English).

[327] Lewis (n 268) 213–14.

[328] Previously available at <www.internationalcompetitionnetwork.org/uploads/library/doc998.pdf> 2, (broken ICN link, see discussion in Introduction, n 16).

[329] Previously available at <www.internationalcompetitionnetwork.org/uploads/library/doc998.pdf> 2, (broken ICN link, see discussion in Introduction, n 16).

[330] Previously available at <www.internationalcompetitionnetwork.org/uploads/library/doc992.pdf> 2–3, (broken ICN link, see discussion in Introduction, n 16).

of international telephone calls and ensuring that the timing of ICN calls (a particular problem for agencies in the eastern part of the world[331]—once again, one suspects the EU/US influence here, given their geography) is not a barrier to participation in ICN activities would help, eg offering toll-free numbers; webinars; posting recordings/minutes of teleseminars/calls on the ICN website.[332]

Calls have been made to address language barriers through: translating ICN work products; having calls/meetings for specific language groups; and/or having some working subgroups for specific language groups.[333] Limited progress has been made in this regard, so far. It must be noted, though, that according to our survey, language is less important than resources in shaping NCAs' influence, as only 46 per cent believe language is an important or very important issue. That said, this is still a high percentage. Perhaps it should have been higher. One wonders whether those without strong English have already been excluded from the debate (and our survey).

If the ICN wants to keep poorer NCAs involved, or preferably even increase their involvement, then it needs to help them to do so.[334] Good examples of this sort of inclusion were twinning of experienced and inexperienced NCAs in the leadership of every working group. Similarly, the USA, Korea, and Japan hosted induction sessions for new NCAs in the ICN explaining what is on offer, helping them to make informed choices about where to devote their energies.[335]

Funding poorer NCAs is another way that their attendance and input at ICN events can be improved. That said, finding an appropriate structure is not easy; 50 per cent of NCAs say that they cannot receive funds from others. First, one must clarify what each NCA considers acceptable.[336] Any funding stream can have negative ramifications if 'abused'. For example, richer NCAs might fund poorer ones; in effect this happens when they offer free technical assistance and training (see Section 1.3.1.5). Those that can may also help with direct money transfers to poorer NCAs and their firms and states (although, when it comes to donating pure money, 80 per cent of NCAs said they could not donate to other NCAs).[337] Another possibility is to get funding from other sources, such as the World Bank, and other institutions (including the ICN itself). Other fora, such as the OECD and UNCTAD, find it easier to generate funds to help pay for travel and other costs.[338] The risk

331 ICN, 'The Future of the ICN in Its Second Decade, Final Report' (2016) 23, <https://www.internationalcompetitionnetwork.org/wp-content/uploads/2018/09/ICN2dDecade2016.pdf> accessed 7 October 2021.

332 ICN (n 135) 19–22.

333 ibid.

334 Lewis (n 268) 207; Tavares (n 95) 346; Operational Framework Working Group, *Report to the Steering Group* (2003) 4, previously available at <http://www.internationalcompetitionnetwork.org/uploads/library/doc457.pdf> (broken ICN link, see discussion in Introduction, n 16).

335 Lewis (n 268) 208.

336 ICN (n 135) 19–22.

337 Operational Framework Working Group (n 334) 7.

338 Hollman and Kovacic (n 26) 71.

here is that funding is often tied to other conditions, such as adopting competition law in a style that ends up favouring richer states, again.[339] Finally, another source of funding might be NGAs. Here, the problems may be even greater: 56 per cent of NCAs have said that they could not get funding from private sources.[340] One can easily see how conflicts of interest might arise. If this sort of funding were to occur, the ICN has said:

> It was also recognized that guidelines would need to be established to identify eligible donors, the type of events that could be sponsored (e.g., should enforcement-related events such as the Merger Workshop on Investigative Techniques be free from sponsorship), and caps on the value of the contribution. There is a potential to receive funds from other interested parties for other, non-conference related purposes. For example, a portion of the cost of setting up the ICN website was defrayed by a contribution from the IBA.[341]

Another idea was to have a small fee for attending the annual conference, as long as this did not put off developing countries.[342] If one is really seeking to help poorer NCAs actively engage with the ICN (without coming under undue influence from others), then it may be sensible to adopt practices that allow similar NCAs from states with similar features to pool resources. It may also help to consider regional arrangements for assistance. Many NCAs are in favour of having regional platforms to address regional interests. This reduces travel time, which is not a major factor in the virtual ICN. However, neighbours often have similar problems, culture, and languages.[343] There is still a risk of undue influence, even here. It is no surprise that the EU and US have not supported such initiatives, which would give them less influence.[344]

1.3.1.5 Offers of technical assistance

Richer NCAs and NGAs can also exercise influence over poorer, inexperienced NCAs through technical assistance. Support of this nature may involve sending employees to the poorer NCA to provide general training to improve their knowledge or systems. It can also mean helping NCAs in their work on specific cases. The US ICPAC Report itself explains why NCAs from the (EU or the) USA might want to use technical assistance to influence poorer NCAs:

[339] Heba Shahein, 'The Development of Competition Law and Policy in Egypt: International and National Factors' London School of Economics, 2009 96.
[340] Operational Framework Working Group (n 334) 7.
[341] ibid 9.
[342] ibid 7.
[343] ICN (n 135) 19–22.
[344] See the discussion following n 182.

> Technical assistance programs may provide the United States with a voice to support the adoption of sound competition principles and promote the rule of law, especially by transition economies. Further, in light of the proliferation of new antitrust authorities, technical assistance can be used to convey practical experience and advice to emerging antitrust regimes, as well as guidance on the formulation of domestic competition policies that make sense in the globalized economy. U.S. support of new competition policy regimes also *creates an opportunity for the United States to share its perspective. This can be important as a means of influencing the legal environment in which U.S. exporters and businesses operate.*[345]

The provision of technical assistance is often expensive. That it appears to be a major act of benevolence only increases its power as a mechanism for influence. Nonetheless, richer NCAs are often eager to offer technical assistance (and they have done a lot of it).[346] In part, because of its power to influence (see the last quote).[347] It is also a good way of increasing ICN participation from younger and smaller NCAs.[348] The ICN increases in value, especially for richer NCAs and NGAs, the more NCAs participate.[349] This is because wider participation effectively widens the scope of the influence of the rich to more jurisdictions around the world.

There are three ways in which the providers of technical assistance programmes can influence. First, they are an additional opportunity to increase pressure from the network and the epistemic community—see Section 1.3.1.2. Second, technical assistance programmes provide a wonderful opportunity to literally 'get inside' the newer NCA, engage with its staff and influence them (including in the ideological underpinnings of the 'best' competition policy and enforcement to apply). The nature of an education program implies that inexperienced actors are receiving the support. This knowledge gap makes it much harder for the newer NCAs' employees to understand (or to even be aware of) the ideological choices that have been made in the advice that they are given, let alone to challenge this advice.[350]

[345] ICPAC (n 20) Executive Summary 31 (emphases added).

[346] Tavares (n 95) 335.

[347] Where networks include training then this may mean that the legal export impacts are longer lasting and greater. There is some debate about the size of this effect, but it seems quite strong, at least in antitrust. Socialization of network members should further enhance this effect (see our discussion of epistemic communities in Section 1.3.1.2).

[348] ICN, The Future of the ICN in Its Second Decade, Final Report (2016) 60.

[349] The link between the interests of the richer NCAs and NGAs should not be lost here. For example, the ICN Training on Demand project was financed by the American Bar Association (and the contact point for this project is the US FTC), <http://www.internationalcompetitionnetwork.org/training/> accessed 7 October 2021.

[350] More generally, Slaughter has said:

> US regulatory agencies offer technical assistance and training to their foreign counterparts to make their own jobs easier, in the sense that strong foreign authorities with compatible securities, environmental, and antitrust regimes will effectively extend the reach of US regulators. It

Finally, providers of technical support can influence newer NCAs (and their employees) through a (often implicit) threat to withdraw such support if newer NCAs become too critical elsewhere. This probably impacts upon the freedom, actual or imagined, of newer NCAs to criticize or disagree (see Section 1.2.1.2.4's discussion of the consensus rule, for example).

All this ICN activity generates an enormous amount of organizational work, both within Working Groups and of the ICN as a whole. It is often the richer NCAs that take on this burden. This exposes the ICN to the risk that the large NCAs may not maintain their level of commitment and support, if they are not getting what they want. As Lewis rightly notes:

> Should one of the US or the EU or Canada significantly downscale its level of commitment, the ICN may well find itself in serious trouble. This is not a comfortable position for an institution that is involved in heavily contested terrain where, on important occasions, national interest rears its head.[351]

This sort of threat probably need not even be vocalized. NCAs from developing states are used to keeping dissent within proper limits (this risk arises in many areas).

1.3.2 NGAs

In his study of the ICN, Gaus acknowledges that NGAs wield influence and power. However, based on the interviews that he conducted, Gaus argues that NCAs significantly curtail this:

> Non-governmental advisors are the second group of actors that yield informal power in the ICN due to their expertise and connections ... Some NGAs are involved long-term in drafting work products, others more ad-hoc on individual issues. This adds resources to the ICN that the national competition agencies may not bring to the table themselves ... Their power is however limited since ICN members do have fine antenneas [*sic*] of detecting undue influence by NGAs as both ICN members and NGAs confirmed.[352]

> also seems clear that if foreign regulators are being trained by US regulators, their practices and procedures are likely to reflect how the United States does things.
>
> Slaughter (n 36) 175; see also Raustiala (n 2) 54–55.

[351] Lewis (n 268) 206. Similarly, Hollman and Kovacic (n 26) 58, state that without the resources of the wealthy NCAs the ICN risks collapse. At the same time, the magnitude of these contributions of the wealthy NCAs (with its implications of control by them) risk making the ICN seem less relevant for other, poorer NCAs. This is a difficult tension. See also Sokol (n 7) 158, 160.

[352] Gaus (n 108) 19.

As we now go on to explain, we think that significantly underrepresents some NGAs' power.

Many of the NGAs' influence mechanisms mirror what we said about rich NCAs. We have already talked about the power of epistemic communities and offering technical assistance in the ICN. Our focus was on NCAs, but similar observations apply to NGAs. Our focus here is on three issues: presence is something; getting in early; and revolving doors.

1.3.2.1 Presence is something

Originally, the power of corporations was held in check by elected governments. Wilks argues that this liberal democratic equilibrium has broken down. If we want to see whether (and how) NGAs (particularly major multinationals) exercise power within the ICN, we have to check their ability 'to participate in political decision-making in respect of public policies', ie assess their impact on regulatory activities that define public priorities and distribute welfare.[353]

> Power over public policy includes direct pressure, indirect influence (agenda setting) and hegemonic power, the ability to secure desired outcomes by creating systems of norms, expectations and meanings.[354]

The ICN relies more heavily on NGAs than other international organizations, such as the OECD, UNCTAD, and the WTO.[355] This 'privatization' of the regulatory space[356] within the ICN gives firms (and their regulatory intermediaries, such as law firms)[357] direct access to competition policy debates and opportunities to exert direct pressure and indirect influence over policymakers and enforcers. Remember

[353] Wilks (n 161) 16–17.

[354] ibid 17.

[355] Hollman and Kovacic (n 26) 76; Wils (n 244) fn 76.

[356] Some argue that using private actors to achieve regulatory goals can be more efficient and innovative, Michael Trebilcock and Edward Iacobucci, 'Privatization and Accountability' (2003) 116 Harvard Law Review 1422. However, others worry that asking private, profit-orientated firms to take over regulatory tasks undermines the public values in regulatory systems, Paul Verkuil, *Outsourcing Sovereignty: Why Privatization of Government Functions Threatens Democracy and What We Can Do about It* (CUP 2007).

[357] Regulatory intermediaries often work between private regulatees and the regulators, examples include auditors, lawyers, and environmental consultants, Kenneth Auld, David Levi-Faur and Duncan Snidal, 'Theorizing Regulatory Intermediaries: The RIT Model' (2017) 670 Annals of the American Academy of Political and Social Science 14. These intermediaries can be useful in terms of transferring information about how markets work from their clients to the regulators, ibid; supplementing regulators' expertise, ibid; and often act as intermediaries between regulators in different systems where they work across multiple jurisdictions or disciplines (Dave Owen, 'Regional Federal Administration' (2016) 63 UCLA Law Review 58). However, much of the theory cautions that these actors, especially private firms, may exploit/seek to change regulatory systems for their ends, perhaps modifying compliance in ways that are easy to sell rather than in ways which best achieve regulatory goals, van der Hiejden (n 290); and/or are paid for by the regulatees, as payment offers a temptation to distort one's actions as agents of these regulatees to get future work, Kruck (n 290). In some narrow areas, this might not be such a problem, Owen (n 290) 2, see also 9–11.

that, given the wide language in many competition rules, the usual distinction between policy and enforcement often collapses.[358]

When it comes to indirect types of influence (such as agenda setting), the ICN has explicitly highlighted NGAs' role in identifying topics for discussion and work. The ICN specifically says that NGAs help to identify topics for discussion and work and may be consulted when Working Groups plan their future work so that they can offer suggestions towards the ICN's substantive agenda.[359] One concrete example that we have already seen, was the way in which NGAs argued against establishing a UCWG in the ICN. This contributed to nearly two years of delay in the creation of this Working Group.[360]

The ICN has also highlighted several other roles which give NGAs the opportunity to exert direct pressure towards their desired outcomes. NGAs contribute to the drafting and reviewing of ICN recommended practices, case-handling manuals, databases, and toolkits. Over 56 per cent of NGAs said they were involved in drafting or reviewing.[361] Section 1.3.2.2 explains why drafting these documents is a significant coup for the major multinationals seeking specific outcomes. NGAs also conduct research and prepare background papers[362] (one can readily see how this might help them to get what they want). Fox gives a concrete example of NGAs (and rich NCAs) applying pressure in relation to the content of rules. At issue was how to assess market power (the discussion took place in the UCWG). The South African NCA wanted to use a market share proxy for market power. It argued that most developing countries do not have the resources for more complex assessments and market share works relatively well as a rule of thumb. However, many major multinationals that were present in that Working Group (as NGAs) and some developed NCAs disagreed. They said that assessing market power is highly complex and market shares mean little in and of themselves. Before any finding of dominance (or equivalent), they said that lots of economic evidence was needed: just focusing on market shares would be over inclusive. Regardless of the merits of this discussion, the method that NGAs favoured would be much more expensive and likely to significantly reduce the amount of such cases that poorer NCAs undertake. Interestingly, the South African NCA bowed to pressure and agreed to the recommended practice. This is strange. If NCAs are so free, why did they not refuse to condone a practice that they disagreed with (unless it was persuaded on the merits, of course)? That said,

358 See discussion around n 239.

359 ICN SG Working Group (n 207) 5. Similarly, ICN SG Working Group (n 103) 4.

360 See the discussion around n 253; David Lewis (Chairman of the South African Competition Tribunal and an active UCWG member): 'At the 5th annual conference held in Cape Town in 2006 it was agreed, *not without some opposition*, to set up a working group on unilateral conduct, or, as it is more commonly referred to, abuse of dominance or monopolisation [our emphasis]' David Lewis, *Enforcing Competition Rules in South Africa: Thieves at the Dinner Table* (Edward Elgar 2013) 241.

361 ICN SG Working group (n 207) 2; and Chapter 3 of this volume.

362 Hollman and Kovacic (n 26) 59.

it won a slight compromise, because market shares were accepted as relevant as part of a bigger picture.[363]

Businesses (NGAs) do not have formal control in the ICN. There are several reasons for this. First, NGAs are not actual ICN members (or members of Working Groups) by right. Nor are they invited to vote on ICN agendas or the adoption of work products in the ICN annual meeting. However, we still believe that NGAs' presence in the ICN makes a major difference. In fact, when asked what they value about their participation in the ICN, NGAs emphasize: networking with NCAs, better understanding NCAs, and discussing with NCAs.[364] Opportunities to influence seem centre stage. So, although major multinationals (many of whom are NGAs) do not have 'legal' power over ICN processes, NGAs' presence gives them power, in fact. We have already seen how they have the ability to exert influence over ICN agendas and outputs.

From a theoretical perspective, structuralism argues that liberal democracy and the market system are structurally biased in favour of firms. According to this theory, the current rules and processes automatically benefit larger firms. This might be because of their economies of scale or due to their better ability to coordinate action to successfully lobby decision makers. In this way of seeing the world, business is privileged, not only because states try to look after them, but also because of the privileged roles they get as participants in policy deliberations.[365]

When we look at what is going on in the ICN, one rapidly gets the feeling that structuralism may be a good way of describing the systemic biases and power imbalances at work. Enhanced contact with decision makers (NCAs) gives NGAs more opportunity to push their aims. It is also another forum for these firms to exercise influence even when they have been unable to get political support for their ideas through the normal, legislative channels. The ability to influence NCAs is particularly important given the wide drafting of many competition rules. This often leaves NCAs with a lot of discretion about how to interpret them.

Lall believes that we must reduce information asymmetries for regulators more generally. There might be a positive obligation to actively engage with all (more) varied, stakeholders. This might mean more consultations with public and private actors from different backgrounds. There might also be a wider distribution of finished work product too. This would help to create 'a more equitable distribution of regulatory capabilities among stakeholders'.[366] His points seem relevant to the

[363] Fox (n 9) 129–30. Lewis Lagdameo and Heimert (n 98) 287, 289. Furthermore, while the recommended practices put forward by the Mergers Working Group contain concrete process-orientated approaches for NCAs to adopt, those from the UCWG propose are more general and analytical approaches. This makes them harder to apply. For NGA recommendations on this issue, see Goldman and others (n 96) 388–89, although they often seem to be referring to academics when it comes to non-partisan points.

[364] ICN (n 135) 24. Similarly, Unilateral Conduct Working Group (n 212) 4.

[365] Wilks (n 161) 28.

[366] Lall (n 304) 19.

ICN, given that NGAs do not represent society's interests as a whole. There is a disproportionate influence of large, rich, western multinationals—see Section 1.2.2.1. These firms are likely (and often legally bound) to represent their own interests above others. NCAs are often quite independent of political power. The lack of general state actors in the ICN, means that there is no viable counterweight to these multinational firms there.

1.3.2.2 Getting into the debate early

Section 1.3.1.3 examined NCAs' ability to influence debates at an early stage in this complex, technical area (competition policy and enforcement). Here, we study the same two mechanisms (access to informal social networks and increasing returns processes) to see if they might also help to explain how NGAs could manipulate the ICN to support their desired distributional consequences (Lall's original study focused on private actors).[367]

The idea here is that regulatory standards are adopted over several phases. They start with agenda setting, then planning, then a discussion paper, consultation, and approval. The technical complexity of competition issues affects those who have access to these important informal social networks (which might be the ICN more generally, or for a special favoured few the ICN Steering Group or Working Group leadership, for example). This might give some NGAs a first-mover advantage. Those involved earlier tend to enjoy more influence.

NGAs are involved in many ICN tasks, including suggesting topics for discussion, drafting, and reviewing recommended practices. Knowledgeable NGAs can see problems in the existing rules and suggest ways of solving them, which reflect their regulatory preferences (or ignore gaps where it is not in their interest to point them out). NGAs with 'timely and high-quality information' about the regulatory agenda, may suggest a new Working Group or the scoping of a project (or an idea within a project), before others are even aware that the issue is being discussed. This helps them to set or lead the agenda. In addition, because of their specialist knowledge and skills, these NGAs are more likely to be delegated (trusted with) key roles, such as drafting relevant sections of a recommended practice or doing feasibility studies. NGAs from the EU and the USA are likely to propose rules that already apply to them (and they are familiar with), making them more knowledgeable, likely leaders in this area (and better able to win arguments, should any arise). One NGA has even suggested that NGAs be given expedited access to potential reforms, so that they can comment early.[368] This desire fits with Lall's theory of the benefits for business of getting in early to the decision-making process. This is reaffirmed by our survey: 77 per cent of our NGA respondents considered being

[367] ibid 6. Remember that his focus was financial regulation, but competition policy and enforcement seem similar in this regard.

[368] Anderson (n 209) 282–83.

involved in drafting at early stages as either 'important' or 'very important'. NGAs only considered 'expertise' to be more influential than early involvement (by 94 per cent of respondents).

Yet, it is not all NGAs that will have such ready (and influential) access. Only a few have close personal relationships with NCA officials, regularly interacting with them. Not many NGAs have sufficient experience of international markets and enough technical knowledge and vision to think of how to improve the rules (and add to NCA knowledge), and so this pool of influential NGAs is limited. Those with influence often work in (or for) large multinationals who have a lot of experience with competition rules from around the world. Some NGAs' expertise can exceed that of NCAs. Lall notes, 'regulators often *depend* on the expertise provided by ISN members to develop rules that make operational sense'.[369] NCAs often ask senior NGAs for input (here is a link between expertise and early involvement, which explains why NGAs consider both so valuable). So, even if consumers and consumer associations became NGAs, they are unlikely to gain much influence if they have limited technical experience.

Lall suggests that the ICN should be wary of delegating crucial regulatory functions to NGAs, to protect the independence of officials. So, NCAs must have resources to attract sufficient expertise from a wide range of disciplines. If delegation cannot be avoided 'regimes should divide functions among several stakeholders to prevent narrow interests from monopolizing regulatory capabilities'.[370] However, in the ICN, they are not currently taking this advice. The current narrow range of interests among the NGAs does not look set to change. Furthermore, existing NGAs are getting more and more influence. For example, the Steering Group said that NGAs' role should further increase, including early access to the agenda:

> A stronger/greater involvement of NGAs in all sessions was supported and may be considered in the early planning stages among the Annual Conference Planning Committee members.[371]

The solution to this issue may also help to solve another problem too. In part, the NCAs are too busy, and this relates to how many Working Groups and other meetings they are going to. If NGAs are given less of a role, this will create more work for the NCAs. As we have seen, this is a problem for many of them. However, if the solution were to create fewer Working Groups and for them to have less activity, we could provide more time for the NCAs to get good solutions.

[369] Lall (n 304) 5. He was speaking here of financial regulation, rather than competition rules.
[370] ibid 19.
[371] Previously available at <www.internationalcompetitionnetwork.org/uploads/library/doc997.pdf> 2, (broken ICN link, see discussion in Introduction, n 16).

At the same time, we would ensure that they maintain quality and control and ensure that access to comment were more equal for the various, representative stakeholders.

1.3.2.3 Revolving doors

In regulation, the expression 'revolving doors' indicates cases in which employees of regulatory agencies work (before or after) in regulated firms. As regulators and regulatees have, in principle, distinct preferences and goals, this may be problematic. Statutes of regulatory agencies usually forbid people who have served there to take jobs in regulated firms for a certain period of time. However, these rules do not usually apply to normal employees. As a matter of fact, employees of NCAs are encouraged to spend time working in firms. Similarly, firms' employees are encouraged to spend time working in NCAs. These policies, which are now common in many NCAs and NGAs, especially in the EU and the USA, consolidate an elite (between NGAs and the NCAs) with collective goals, sharing the fruits of power. Importantly, this further extends rich, western multinationals' influence and power.[372]

There seem to be two processes at work here. First, all good employees working in NCAs know that, when they leave the NCA, there is the potential for employment or consultancy work. Some may be motivated to moderate their behaviour while working in the NCA in order to make these potential, future benefits that they might receive from NGAs (eg law firms, businesses) more likely. This might incentivize them (whether this is intentional or not) to seek out and show deference to NGAs' arguments, in their NCA work. Given their origin, these arguments likely involve (potential) impacts of competition rules on NGAs. They are unlikely to emphasize others' interests unless they coincide with these multinationals' interests too.

The second process arises due to the perceived lack of funds that many NCAs say they face. In order to ameliorate this, and because they see it as good experience for their employees, many major multinational businesses and law firms encourage their employees to go on secondment to NCAs. This is a way of subsidizing NCAs. Obviously, when a firm's employees work inside an NCA on policy or enforcement projects, they are in a prime position to protect and pursue their employers' interests (while conflict rules prevent the most obvious examples of this, more dispersed influence is still there). In addition, spending time in an NCA helps these employees to make connections with NCA employees to facilitate the first process—see above. There is some empirical support for this. Having worked in NCAs is considered 'important' or 'very important' for being an influential NGA by 51 per cent of our survey's respondents.

[372] Wilks (n 161) 78. Similarly, Palacios Lleras (n 118) 195–96.

Lall says that it is important for entities such as the ICN to 'prevent informal social links between officials and regulated interests from becoming too strong'. This demands more distance between NCAs and NGAs. This might mean slowing, or stopping, the revolving door between NCAs and NGAs, or at least ensuring that NCAs recruit more widely. NCAs might also limit the number of secondees, interns, and temporary staff they hire from NGAs.[373] Currently, NCAs seem to have a desire to hire good candidates cheaply, and they can do this, in part, because of the revolving door. If we are to close this, then we might also need more financing from government, in order to make working in an NCA competitive with NGAs.

1.4 Conclusion

The ICN describes its current mission as advocating 'the adoption of superior standards and procedures in competition policy around the world ... [formulating] proposals for procedural and substantive convergence, and ... [seeking] to facilitate effective international cooperation to the benefit of member agencies, consumers and economies worldwide'.[374] Moreover, it claims that this is to be achieved in a forum where 'public and private sectors, and member agencies from developing and developed economies, participate on an equal footing'.[375]

Competition rules are highly redistributive between different stakeholders in society, and different states. 'Superior standards and procedures' are dressed up as value neutral. They are not. For example, if competition rules are used to open up markets in developing countries, who benefits? Western multinationals, local firms, local consumers? Will they all benefit equally, or should the spoils be weighted in favour of one group? Competition rules are generally widely drafted, so, decision makers often have a lot of discretion in how to interpret and apply them.

It matters what ICN work products say. Despite the ICN's formal rule that NCAs (and their states) can choose whether or not to apply them, Chapters 2 and 3 show that they have a lot of influence on the way many NCAs interpret and apply their competition rules. So, it matters a great deal whether some actors in the ICN have more influence than others.

The ICN claims that NCAs participate on an equal footing. Formally, this is true. However, this chapter has argued that NCAs from advanced economies and multinationals have disproportionate influence over agendas and the production of work products in the ICN, in fact.

Network design has a major impact upon how a specific system works. For example, networks with fewer members are often cheaper to participate in (less

[373] Lall (n 304) 19.
[374] ICN (n 17) 3.
[375] Von Finckenstein (n 25) 3–4.

coordination means less cost). However, fewer members may mean fewer new ideas and less ability to persuade others (less benefits). It is likely that their vision for the ICN played a large part in the design that the founding NCAs made to its institutional structure. The aim has always been to encourage wide NCA membership, giving each NCA a veto over many administrative acts in the ICN (such as membership of the Steering Group) and ICN recommended practices. This makes the ICN a great vehicle for persuading others about the benefits of certain rules. The unanimity requirement formally protects all NCAs against practices that they do not agree with. In reality, it principally protects NCAs from advanced economies in this way (there are many ways to pressure poorer NCAs into accepting practices, even when they disagree with them). Framing discussions over the interpretation of competition rules as technical (rather than political), arrived at by a network of 'technical NCA specialists' rather than government officials, is an ingenious way of avoiding focus on the redistributive impact of ICN outputs. Similarly, the decision to allow NGAs into the ICN's heart seems to have been designed to (and, in practice does) help bake the desires of principally rich, western multinationals into this system.

We have argued that the powerful NCAs have many ways to influence (pressure) other ICN members. First, they could use raw political power. The reality is that this is unlikely to be necessary. Formally, in the ICN, all NCAs can raise issues and suggest specific ways of dealing with competition problems. The reality is that poor NCAs tend to be so both in terms of financial resources and in terms of time. So, NCAs from the EU and the USA end up with better opportunities to control the ICN's agenda (through their leadership roles). It also means that poorer NCAs often do not have the time to fully understand and critique the advice that they receive from richer NCAs. For the same reason, they may not be able to properly engage in the ICN. Richer NCAs also work hard to frame competition debates and get into them early, generating more and better opportunities to push discussions to their own advantage, and possibly to the disadvantage of others. Other background factors also facilitate rich NCAs' influence. For example, in their offers of training and assistance, it is easy for emphasis to be placed on rules that help firms from richer NCAs' states. As we have seen, one example might involve using the competition rules to open up markets in developing states to firms from the EU and USA. The (implicit) threat of withdrawing their help may be another route to control.

These factors further reinforce each other. For example, NCAs with limited time and resources, probably become more dependent on training and technical assistance from others. This influence is further enforced through the competition epistemic community. By socializing people into this community, they become part of a club. This makes it increasingly difficult (and costly) to challenge the received wisdom of this club and its members.

As we have seen (and as with NCAs), on issues where influential NGAs speak with a common voice, they are likely to have great weight within the ICN. Their resources and allowing them into the heart of the ICN give NGAs (who are disproportionately multinationals from advanced economies and their lawyers) the opportunity to frame debates (and influence which debates take place).

However, today powerful NGAs (and thus 'their NCAs') disagree on several issues, think of the intersection of digital issues and competition policy, for example. In part this is because many of the 'low-hanging fruit' (such as due process) have already been picked. So, we are left with more obviously distributive topics where influential, rich country NGAs have divergent views. This may mean that NGAs (and even NCAs) start to lose their influence on many newer topics within the ICN over time. Or it might mean that such topics are avoided in the ICN, until there is more consensus. The risk here is that the ICN could start to become irrelevant. We may even be witnessing newer NCAs starting to demand more influence over topic selection.

So, NGAs are seeking common ground again (and more influence). They have consistently said 'that implementation is fundamental to ensuring that the promise of ICN best practices and work products is translated into tangible results'.[376] The next chapter shows that (re)focusing the ICN on the implementation of its existing work products is becoming the new battleground. For similar reasons, this priority fits with the wishes of the richer NCAs.

[376] Anderson (n 209) 277.

2
The ICN's influence in the national systems

2.1 Introduction

The ICN was set up to be a 'project-oriented, consensus-based, informal [virtual] network'.[1] Its 'activities take place on a voluntary basis and rely on a high level of goodwill and cooperation among members'.[2] The ICN has created 'significant momentum' in the international antitrust world.[3] It 'has produced a tremendous body of work including recommended practices, manuals, reports and templates in addition to events like teleseminars, webinars, workshops, and annual conferences'.[4] The ICN work product develops 'sound and principled procedural and substantive benchmarks' that 'can serve as a model for governments and competition agencies looking to develop new laws and policies, and to update current practices'.[5] Its ultimate goal is to promote 'more efficient and effective antitrust enforcement worldwide to the benefit of consumers and business'.[6]

Chapters 1 and 3 show how, despite the ICN's 'consensus rule' for accepting new work products, some NCAs and NGAs have more influence than others when it comes to deciding which areas the ICN will focus on and the content of ICN work products. As a result, ICN work tends to focus on issues of interest to NCAs from advanced industrialized economies (even at the expense of other economies). The same is true for the focus of the resulting work products.

What happens when it comes to the implementation of ICN work products? As discussed in the Introduction of this book, there is a tension at the heart of the ICN. On the one hand, it formulates proposals for procedural and substantive convergence. On the other hand, the ICN is an informal international organization without a rule-making function. Its members are not under the special obligation

[1] ICN, *ICN Operational Framework* (2012) 1(i), previously available at <http://internationalcompetitionnetwork.org/uploads/library/doc784.pdf> (broken ICN link, see discussion in Introduction, n 16).

[2] ibid 1(iii).

[3] Pierre-Hugues Verdier, 'Transnational Regulatory Networks and Their Limits' (2009) 34 Yale Journal of International Law 113, 158.

[4] Kazuyuki Sugimoto, Chairman of the Japan Fair Trade Commission, ICN Work Products Catalogue, September 2020, 2. The ICN Working Product Catalogue (2020), which lists the ICN available material, is 42 pages long.

[5] ICN, *ICN Factsheet and Key Messages* (2009) 5, previously available at <http://internationalcompetitionnetwork.org/uploads/library/doc784.pdf> (broken ICN link, see discussion in Introduction, n 16).

[6] ibid 1.

The Law and Politics of Global Competition. Christopher Townley, Mattia Guidi, and Mariana Tavares, Oxford University Press.
 DOI: 10.1093/oso/9780198859789.003.0003

of a formal international agreement captured by the *pacta sunt servanda* doctrine.[7] Where the ICN reaches consensus on work products, 'it is left to its members to decide whether and how to implement the recommendation'.[8]

Formally then, the ICN cannot force its members to implement its work products. However, the mere fact that the ICN is an informal network and that its working products are not legally binding does not tell us much about its capacity to influence its members to adopt them. The normative difference between a formal, legally binding treaty and a non-binding arrangement is not always that clear.[9] Yet, how is it that an advisory rule of the ICN could have an impact? By definition soft law is voluntary, lacks mutually agreed upon obligations, and does not need to be adopted, transposed, or implemented by national and regional rule-making authorities.[10] Does the ICN (or do others) even try to push ICN members to follow ICN work products? If so, what mechanisms are used to do this? And, are all ICN members influenced in the same way?

In order to answer these questions, it helps to begin by reminding ourselves how changes might be made to competition policy. NCAs can often achieve major substantive and procedural impact just by changing the way in which they implement competition rules. Competition rules tend to be widely drafted, leaving lots of room for different interpretations. Therefore, in principle, NCAs can often follow ICN recommendations even without involving other state actors. However, sometimes, implementing ICN recommendations may require legislative change, for example, where national competition rules explicitly diverge from ICN rules. This is normally not within the gift of NCAs.

Addressing the issue of the impact of soft law, political scientists distinguish between first-order and second-order effects.[11] The analysis of the former focuses on the short-term: coordination and compliance, ie the consequences of soft law that imply the adoption of certain standards, the implementation of recommendations and the compliance with a certain rule.[12] In relation to the ICN, first-order effects include efforts by the ICN itself, ICN members and NGAs to push NCAs (directly or indirectly) to interpret their own competition rules in line with ICN

[7] 'Every treaty in force is binding upon the parties to it and must be performed by them in good faith' (Vienna Convention on the Law of Treaties, art 26).

[8] ICN (n 1) 1(iv).

[9] Binding international treaties have their limits and non-binding arrangements routinely have legal and practical bite, Abraham L Newman and Elliot Posner, *Voluntary Disruptions: International Soft Law, Finance, and Power* (OUP 2018) 16.

[10] ibid 22.

[11] ibid. See also eg Giliberto Capano and others (eds), *Making Policies Work: First- and Second-Order Mechanisms in Policy Design* (Edward Elgar 2019).

[12] Kenneth Abbott and Duncan Snidal, 'Hard and Soft Law in International Governance' (2000) 54 International Organization 421–56; Abraham Newman and David Bach, 'The European Union as Hardening Agent: Soft Law and the Diffusion of Global Financial Regulation' (2014) 21 Journal of European Public Policy 430–52; Paul A David, 'Clio and the Economics of QWERTY' (1985) 75 American Economic Review 332–37.

work products. Where legislative change is needed in order to achieve this in a country, first-order effects would include instances where the ICN helps NCAs to lobby their own states to make such legislative changes.

The analysis of second-order effects, by contrast, takes into consideration a double-dynamic—time and politics—and focuses on the mechanisms which, over time, allow political actors to shift the balance of authority among competing regulatory factions.[13] In relation to ICN work products, this might include their use by litigants in court, or lobbyists in political debates, to move the legitimate parameters of the debate, to define 'best practice', or normal.

This chapter shows how ICN outputs provide a focus for those seeking to influence national competition policies. The ICN uses them to push the implementation of its work products. Others do too. Section 2.2 deals with first-order effects, and Section 2.3 deals with second-order effects. We will see that this principally happens in countries that are not advanced industrialized economies, ie jurisdictions where ICN work products are often not designed to work optimally. Section 2.4 concludes.

2.2 ICN's first-order effects: coordination and cooperation

Research on the first-order effects of soft law focuses on the generation of soft law and compliance with it.[14] Chapter 1 dealt with the generation of ICN soft law and how some ICN members (and NGAs) influence it. Here we focus on how the ICN (and others) seeks to influence ICN members (and their states) in order to secure their compliance with ICN work products.

Soft law provides focal points for political actors with common goals to coordinate their policies. Regulatory coordination has been defined as 'the codified adjustment of national standards in order to recognize or accommodate regulatory frameworks from other countries'.[15] As a result of this process of coordination, transnational cooperation takes place when the policies followed by one nation are regarded by its partners as facilitating the realization of their own objectives, improving their self-perceived welfare.[16] Ultimately, this can result in the convergence of regulatory regimes. Slaughter emphasizes transnational networks' ability

[13] Newman and Posner (n 9) 22.

[14] See, for example, Benjamin William Cashore, Graeme Auld and Deanna Newsom, *Governing Through Markets: Forest Certification and the Emergence of Non-State Authority* (Yale UP 2004); Matthew Potoski and Aseem Prakash, 'Green Clubs and Voluntary Governance: ISO 14001 and Firms' Regulatory Compliance' (2005) 49 American Journal of Political Science.

[15] Daniel W Drezner, *All Politics Is Global: Explaining International Regulatory Regimes* (Princeton UP 2008) 11.

[16] Robert O Keohane, *After Hegemony: Cooperation and Discord in the World Political Economy* (Princeton UP 1984) 51–52.

to foster regulatory coordination and identifies three main mechanisms of influence: convergence/informed divergence, compliance, and cooperation.[17]

Transnational networks influence convergence.[18] They do this by focusing on what they consider to be relevant information and filtering out what they consider to be irrelevant information. Transnational networks give their members the opportunity to exchange information on common problems and actual and potential solutions. As we saw in Chapter 1, the ICN collates information on what its NCA members actually do and what they, its NGAs and others think the best way of conducting competition policy and enforcement might be. We also saw in Chapter 1 how the ICN's most powerful NCAs and NGAs then distil, filter, and disseminate their preferred policies and approaches. In this way, the preferences of the advanced industrialized economies become ICN work products.

Generally, networks disseminate information in a form that enhances its impact. They often present it as 'codes of international best practice', 'model legislation', or a set of 'governing principles' compiled by an elite, global body of regulators working in the public interest. Packaged like this, 'these exhortations become a version of soft law' that offers a focal point for convergence. Best practices and principles are ostensibly an opportunity for everyone to learn. Yet, as we saw in Chapter 1, the ICN (and this is true for many transnational networks) provides a structure for advanced industrialized nations to get their own competition policy and rules adopted as international best practice. As we demonstrate in this chapter, other NCAs and states, particularly from developing countries, are then pushed to align with what has become 'international best practice', ie the existing practices of advanced industrialized states. This benefits the 'rule-makers'. Chapter 1 discussed the important benefits that advanced industrialized nations get from others converging around their competition systems, as well as the benefits that this can generate for their regulators and large multinational firms based in these countries. 'Rule-taking' countries can also benefit. NCAs that are setting up regulatory models from scratch are offered a (supposedly) 'effective and legitimate model' to follow. ICN work products also offer a kind of 'safe harbour' for officials facing complex regulatory choices, who are looking for guidance and who may need to defend their choices to their superiors. States with relatively developed regulatory frameworks of their own, may also prefer to converge around some general model. Even though changing standards can produce costs, a more uniform global set of rules can reduce business costs and increase competition. This is because participants in a regulatory network derive greater benefits from the network if the network expands—(these are called 'network effects'). The more beneficial they become the more actors adopt these standards.

[17] Anne-Marie Slaughter, *A New World Order* (2004) 198.
[18] See discussion in Chapter 1, Section 1.2.

Slaughter stresses that what to do with this information (to converge or not to converge), however, remains the choice of the states. They can acknowledge the standard generated by the transnational network but decide not to adopt it. Within a culture of democratic experimentalism, states ensure efficiency and compliance with international standards by borrowing the then-existing best practices from other states or international actors. When a state decides not to harmonize its rules, this can give raise to 'informed divergence'. This happens 'where a national governmental institution or the government as a whole acknowledges a prevailing standard or trend and deliberately chooses to diverge from it for reasons of national history, culture, or politics'.[19] As we have seen above, the ICN explicitly emphasizes NCAs' (and their states) right to informed divergence from ICN work products.

Without disputing 'informed divergence' as a theoretical possibility, transnational networks can be powerful forces towards convergence. This can be hugely problematic. As Chapter 1 shows, ICN work products are rarely optimally designed for rule-taking states. Furthermore, several mechanisms exist to incentivize rule-taking NCAs to adopt or favour ICN work products even those that are not optimal for their home states and do not conform to policy preferences there.

Transnational networks principally influence through two main mechanisms: self-regulation and improving the capacity of states to comply. Self-regulation occurs because transnational networks help to make reputation matter. They socialize their members, monitor them closely and support them in adhering to 'best practice' norms. In this way, networks build trust, cohesion, and common purpose among their members.[20] At the same time, this monitoring of compliance by members puts those not complying under pressure to justify their divergence or conform. This can be painful, especially for those lacking confidence in the area. A second way for transnational networks to strengthen compliance is to improve the capacity of a government to comply. Often, non-compliance with international rules is not only about the law, it is also about the capacity to comply. Countries often lack sufficient material and human resources to pass, implement, and apply laws effectively.[21] According to Slaughter, networks play an important role here. They can engage in capacity building directly, through training and technical assistance programs, and indirectly, through their provision of information, coordinated policy solutions, and even moral support to their members.[22]

We now analyse these mechanisms in more detail. Section 2.2.1 discusses how the ICN promotes convergence. Section 2.2.2 discusses how the ICN promotes

[19] Slaughter (n 17) 24.

[20] ibid 33. 'Once convinced of a particular path of action or the wisdom of a particular result, the national government officials operating in both horizontal and vertical networks possess hard power to make things happen—as much hard power as they possess within their own domestic political systems' ibid 168–69.

[21] ibid 185.

[22] ibid.

compliance, Section 2.2.3 debates informed divergence and Section 2.2.4 examines whether the ICN influences all its members in the same way.

2.2.1 How does the ICN promote convergence?

Convergence was a key objective when creating the ICN. This goal also sustains the ICN's continuing operations. The ICN summarizes convergence as 'the voluntary adoption of widely-accepted norms of competition policy, substantive standards, procedures and levels of institutional capacity'.[23]

The ICN understands convergence as a three-stage 'process'. In the ICN's own words:

> The first stage is decentralized implementation, as different jurisdictions experiment with diverse processes and substantive standards for solving specific problems. The second stage involves sharing their experiences and building consensus through the identification of best practices and techniques. In the third stage, individual jurisdictions opt in to the consensus norms.[24]

In many ways, the first stage happens anyway, and perhaps this is even the norm without the ICN (although organizations like the OECD and UNCTAD obviously influence 'best practice'). For the ICN, the second stage of the process, experience sharing, is about understanding how NCAs from around the world do things. This allows ICN members 'to identify shared standards and techniques as well as areas of difference'. ICN work products have evolved and diversified over time. Coppola et al. provide the following summary of this evolution:

> The ICN's first wave or '1.0-era' work tended to focus on written work products addressing enforcement fundamentals and the basic underpinnings and benefits of competition law. The ICN's '2.0 era' work incorporates more cross-cutting policy topics that overlap with competition, timely debates, cooperation-oriented tools, and a wider variety of work formats. Both aspects are alive and well today within the ICN, and combine to produce a robust, treasure trove of work for ICN members.[25]

These two stages are discussed in Chapter 1.

[23] ICN, *The ICN's Vision for Its Second Decade* (ICN 2012) 5. <www.internationalcompetitionnetwork.org/wp-content/uploads/2018/07/ICN2dDecade2011.pdf> accessed 7 October 2021.

[24] ibid.

[25] Maria Coppola and others, '(Nearly) A Century with the ICN' (2020) Competition Policy International 4.

Finally, regarding the 'third stage' of convergence, 'opting in to an ICN work product' of some kind, the ICN emphasizes that this is voluntary (although, as we will see 'voluntary' can involve significant arm-twisting). It is 'left to the individual member agencies and, in some cases, national governments to decide whether and how to implement them'.

2.2.2 How does the ICN promote implementation?

For a network that regards the implementation of its work by its members as voluntary, the ICN puts considerable effort into promoting its implementation. Section 2.2.2.1 highlights the ICN's focus on implementation and its internal debate on whether implementation should be a priority, then Section 2.2.2.2 presents some measurement of how much implementation there is of ICN work products. This is based on the two major ICN stock taking exercises to date and also on our own survey, also discussed in Chapter 3. Section 2.2.2.3 explains the techniques the ICN employs to increase the implementation of its work. Finally, Section 2.2.2.4 shows how the ICN is increasing its implementation focus.

2.2.2.1 Taking implementation seriously

In 2002, in the inaugural speech of the ICN, Konrad von Finckenstein, the first chair of the ICN, explained that one of the ICN's hallmarks is:

> the aspirational nature of its work product ... Because the ICN is not a rule-making body, members are under no obligation to ensure their domestic law reflect these practices. It is up to each agency to decide whether, and how, to implement the recommendations.[26]

Yet, behind this rhetoric, the reality is that ICN has been increasingly focusing on the implementation of its work products since its inception.

As von Finckenstein anticipated, 'On a practical level I would expect that as best practice proposals are acted upon by members, a natural peer influence will come to bear on other jurisdictions to do the same.'[27] The following year, in the second ICN annual conference, ICN members agreed on the introduction of an Implementation Session during the ICN's annual conference, 'where the goal is to assess and reflect upon the extent to which ICN members have adopted previously agreed recommendations and principles'.[28] The implementation session

[26] Konrad von Finckenstein, *Introductory Remarks to International Competition Network* (2002) 2, previously available at <http://www.internationalcompetitionnetwork.org/uploads/library/doc566.pdf> (broken ICN link, see discussion in Introduction n 16).

[27] ibid 4, previously available at <http://www.internationalcompetitionnetwork.org/uploads/library/doc566.pdf> (broken ICN link, see discussion in Introduction n 16).

[28] Michal Gal and Simon Evenett, *A Report on the Third Annual Conference of the International Competition Network* (2004) 1.

took place for the first time in the third ICN annual conference and, as per its report, there was a high level of participation. ICN members and NGAs were eager to publicly demonstrate their implementation efforts. For example, it was reported that 'Mr. William Rowley, an NGA from Canada, presented a report of the Merger Streamlining Group that assessed the extent of implementation of the ICN's Recommended Practices on merger review.' Representatives from the European Commission and the Brazilian Secretariat of Economic Law, Ministry of Justice, summarized their experience regarding the implementation of the same ICN Recommended Practices too. A representative from the US FTC, and co-chair of the Working Group (one of the USA's NCAs), also presented a report on the Monitoring and Implementation of the Recommended Practices for Merger Notification.[29]

Another example of the ICN's early efforts to push the implementation of its work products was the creation of a Vice Chair for Advocacy and Implementation, in 2007. This new role involved working with a group of NCAs to launch the Advocacy and Implementation Network and its Support Program (AISUP). This programme encourages NCAs to make better use of ICN work products. It also responds to requests for assistance from NCAs who want to push for legislative change in their national systems. NCAs in many countries benefit from ICN support in lobbying their national legislative bodies in their efforts to bring their national competition systems into line with various ICN work products.[30]

An implementation-focus in not necessarily to be expected in a 'soft law network' such as the ICN,[31] and has been challenged by some of its members. By the time of the 2009 ICN annual meeting, many thought that things needed to change in order for the ICN to remain relevant (and for the powerful actors highlighted in Chapter 1, principally NCAs from advanced industrialized nations and NGAs from these states, to maintain their influence over the agenda). Not everyone agreed, of course. The global financial crisis and the ensuing economic recession undermined political confidence in the ability of competitive markets to deliver positive outcomes. There had been calls on NCAs to take a step back in their enforcement activity and on governments to more actively review competition law.[32] A discussion within the ICN on the role of competition in securing economic growth and the role of the ICN in such a context became inevitable. Clashes between competition law systems and between different approaches to the role of competition were manifest.

[29] ibid 23–24.

[30] ICN, Activity Report on ICN Advocacy and Implementation Network Support Program, previously available at <www.internationalcompetitionnetwork.org/uploads/icn%20vice%20chair%20work%20plans%2020009%202010.pdf> (broken ICN link, see discussion in Introduction, n 16).

[31] See the discussion in Chapter 4, Section 4.3.2.

[32] Philip Lowe, 'Competition Policy and the Global Crises' (2009) 5 Competition Policy International 4; Howard Shelanski, 'Enforcing Competition During an Economic Crisis' (2010) 77 Antitrust Law Journal 229.

The debate on the role of the ICN in such a context turned into a kind of a battle for the soul of the ICN. In January 2009, David Lewis, the charismatic president of the South African Competition Tribunal and then the ICN's vice-chair of Outreach, was appointed as the ICN's interim Chair, until the ICN annual meeting later that year.[33] Lewis took this unique opportunity to, once again, underline what he thought the ICN's role should be. In a controversial opening speech, he said that over the last eight years (since the ICN's creation), it had become clear that its activities and work 'do not necessarily lend themselves to textual consensuses and harmonized implementation'.[34] Lewis went on to ask what role the ICN could play in the context of the severe economic downturn that the world then faced. He said:

> We must ask ourselves whether we are sufficiently flexible to assist our member agencies in responding to radical changes in the social and economic environment in which we work, starkly typified by the global economic crisis. We have to ask ourselves whether the ICN is playing a sufficiently active role on the international stage in informing responses to the crisis.

Lewis did not think that the ICN was playing a sufficiently active or flexible role. He described the work of the ICN as being 'at once, too ambitious and too narrow an approach to deal with the more complex and controversial questions that increasingly characterize ICN work'. It was too ambitious because 'the transmission belt from ICN recommendation to national legislation is bound to be extremely slow and imperfect'. Even recommendations in relatively uncontroversial areas 'have to be tailored to national circumstances and so implementation will always be uneven at best'. It was too narrow because it was constrained by the ICN's 'inflexible founding mantra of "all competition, all of the time"'.

From Lewis's perspective, the answer was clear. On the one hand, the ICN should do more to remain relevant, not just to NCAs, but to a wider group of state actors. He proposed revisiting 'our founding mantra of "all competition, all of the time"'.[35]

[33] David Lewis replaced Sheridan Scott, the Head of the Canadian Competition Bureau and Chair of the ICN from 2007 to 2009, when she left to private practice, <www.engineeringnews.co.za/print-version/tribunals-lewis-appointed-chair-of-global-competition-group-2009-02-05> accessed 7 October 2021; John Fingleton, Closing Speech to International Competition Network (ICN) Conference (2009) 1.

[34] David Lewis, Introductory Address to 2009 ICN Conference (2009) 3.

[35] In Lewis's words:

> Competition law, as a US Supreme Court justice once famously reminded us, is the Magna Carta, the fundamental law, of the market system. As such, it cannot be confined to an island where its relationship with every other branch of economic and social policy—particularly with trade and industrial policy—is studiously ignored. And if anybody seriously believed that this was ever possible, then the financial and economic storm that has battered us all since the latter half of 2007 and the policy responses to these events should have put paid to any such illusions. With industrial policy ascendant and protectionism in the air, can we afford to remain aloof? Must we not rather engage with the concerns of policymakers to ensure that their interventions—many of them necessary—respect and preserve that which is dynamic and creative and democratic in a market system?

ibid 4

This would mean more explicitly confronting the fundamentally political (redistributive) side of competition policy and enforcement.[36] On the other hand, Lewis thought that it made little sense to overly focus upon the implementation of ICN work products. It was unfair to judge the ICN on whether states and other actors followed its lead. Furthermore, it was unlikely that implementation would be high, given the different legal, social, and economic contexts of the ICN's members' states.

Lewis is making two perfectly reasonable descriptive points here (at least in our opinion). Yet, this was a frontal attack on two 'core beliefs' of many influential ICN actors. There was a risk that Lewis's logic could gain momentum, particularly in the specific context of the global economic crisis.[37] This was something that the powerful members of the ICN (like the NCAs from the EU and the USA) could not allow to happen. Confronting the political (redistributive) side of competition policy and enforcement was an attack on their attempts to avoid 'interference' from majoritarian bodies.[38] Admitting to the political side also clashed with core tenants of today's antitrust religion (like maintaining the 'purity' of an exclusive consumer welfare approach). However, perhaps even more importantly, emphasizing the relevance of context and accepting that this could justify a lack of implementation would undermine key objectives of many of those that helped to establish the ICN originally. The idea that there is a 'best way' of doing competition policy and enforcement; and that this 'best way' involves a focus on technical rules. This paradigm gives a core and influential role to NCAs from the EU and the USA and other advanced industrialized countries. It also benefits their large multinationals.[39]

Lewis's proposals could not be allowed to blossom.

The 2009 ICN annual meeting ended on a completely different note. The newly elected chair, John Fingleton, then the CEO of a UK NCA, the Office of Fair Trading, had quite different ideas for the ICN. Fingleton returned to core, traditional ICN themes in his closing speech, the idea of 'opening markets to competition and improving consumer welfare'. This idea was fully aligned with the objectives of the

[36] Section I.3 of the Introduction to this book discusses the redistributive nature of competition policy and enforcement in more detail.

[37] This might happen again under the current leadership. In the ICN's 2020 Annual Conference its current Chair, Andreas Mundt, announced the Third Decade Project. He described this as a full self-evaluation of the ICN, asking whether the ICN was engaging with the right topics or should embrace others, the interface between competition law and data privacy, for example.

[38] Chapter 1, Section 1.2.1 has a more detailed discussion of their attempts to avoid majoritarian scrutiny and how the ICN, as established, was a way for NCAs from the EU, the USA, and others to further achieve this.

[39] Chapter 1, Section 1.2 has a more detailed discussion of this aspect too.

ICN's powerful actors discussed in Chapter 1 and sought to reaffirm their influence and control. Addressing Lewis's concerns regarding the narrow scope of the ICN work product limited by the 'inflexible founding mantra of "all competition all of the time"', Fingleton said:

> if we are to ensure that long term we continue to dismantle trade barriers and protectionism, and ensure that the benefits of international competition flow to final consumers, we must strive for the most effective system of dealing with competition issues that transcended national barriers. This is true whether we look at this through any of the three lenses, economic, democratic and the rule of law.[40]

Under his leadership, said Fingleton, the ICN's focus would remain 'all competition, all the time', Fingleton identified 'continuity' as the first of the four priorities of his tenure as ICN Chair.[41] However, the need for change had become self-evident. Fingleton recognized that:

> a number of complex and controversial questions now characterised the work of the ICN that are different from the concerns that prompted the establishment of the network in 2001. That 'community of interest' that brought us together in 2001 had evolved over time.[42]

In that speech, Fingleton did not focus on the implementation of ICN work products. However, in the following year he urged the ICN to 'think about success in terms of outcomes, rather than in terms of outputs'. He called upon ICN members to 'take stock of what we have done, where we are going, and how we are getting there'.[43] In this spirit he launched the 'ICN Second Decade project'. It was a self-examining exercise aiming at:

> discussing fundamental questions such as: is the ICN addressing the right topics and is it striking the right balance between convergence and divergence? Does the ICN provide value for money; is the input/output ratio correct? Is the current structure of the network fit for purpose? And what do you see as the ICN's 2020 vision?[44]

40 Fingleton (n 33) 3.
41 The other priorities were longer-term vision, governance, and inclusiveness and agency effectiveness.
42 Fingleton (n 33) 2.
43 John Fingleton, 'The International Competition Network: planning for the Second Decade' (9th ICN Annual Conference, 27–29 Apr 2010) 3.
44 ibid 12.

All ICN members were asked to participate and NGAs were also consulted.[45] At that point, it was the most ambitious and comprehensive self-assessment exercise that the ICN has ever performed. Such a core initiative would have not been approved by the Steering Committee without the full support of the powerful members of the ICN. Given his OFT role, this clearly included the UK (as well as the EU, of which the UK was then a member state). In the case of the USA, this support meant the direct involvement of NCA staff. Maria Coppola, Counsel for the International Antitrust at the US Federal Trade Commission, was seconded to the Office of Fair Trading to assist Fingleton in this endeavour.

The results of the ICN Second Decade Project were presented the following year, at the tenth ICN annual conference in a document entitled 'The ICN's Vision for its Second Decade'.[46] The conclusion was that, despite the impressive achievement of the ICN:

> [w]ithout more cooperation and convergence, international competition policy risks failing to address four key sources of consumer harm: i. Private anti-competitive behaviour; ii. Unwarranted public restrictions on competition; iii. Potential chilling effects from differing substantive standards and policies; iv. Unnecessary costs and burdens caused by inconsistent and duplicative procedures.[47]

In 2011, Fingleton announced a new ICN Mission Statement, partly to underline the importance of implementation.[48] This became:

> to advocate the adoption of superior standards and procedures in competition enforcement and policy around the world, formulate proposals for procedural and substantive convergence, and seek to facilitate effective international cooperation to the benefit of member agencies, consumers and economies worldwide.[49]

Fingleton called for three things to achieve this: a relevant portfolio of ICN work, in the interest of all of its members; relevant ICN work products, and 'above all, our work has to translate into real outcomes. This is the core of our vision for the second decade of the ICN.'[50]

Fingleton's focus on emphasizing the importance of the implementation of ICN work products has been embraced by the ICN Chairs that followed in his footsteps.

[45] ICN (n 23) 2.
[46] ibid.
[47] ibid 2.
[48] The ICN's original Operational Framework (2001) only referred to implementation once. It said that where 'the ICN reaches consensus on recommendations arising from a project, it is left to its members to decide whether and how to implement them'.
[49] ICN (n 23) 4.
[50] ibid .

Eduardo Pérez Motta (ICN Chair, 2012–13), in his first speech in this role, 'swore allegiance' to implementation as an ICN priority:

> The ICN's mission statement's first precept is 'to advocate the adoption of superior standards and procedures in competition enforcement and policy around the world'. Taking on a more active role when asked by members for assistance on specific policy initiatives not only supports competition advocacy; it also helps crystallize procedural and substantive convergence on those topics where the ICN has agreed on recommended practices, and thus helps us on our way to achieving our vision for the second decade.[51]

The ICN Chair since 2013, Andreas Mundt, has maintained the network's implementation efforts. His vision statement for the ICN includes implementation as one of three 'key factors' for ICN success, emphasizing that if the ICN wants 'to ensure that the ICN and its work products matter, we need to make our high-quality products available to everyone and continue our efforts to promote their implementation'. Importantly, he has also said that all ICN efforts:

> have of course one key direction: to enhance the implementation of ICN work products. If we want to ensure that the ICN and its work product matter, we need to make out high-quality production available to everyone and continue our efforts to promote their implementation … We should aim to convince stakeholders not only of the benefits of competition but also of the benefits taking inspiration from ICN guidance. All approaches to achieve this are equally important and give the Working Groups and ICN members a variety to choose from.[52]

Today, the focus on the implementation of ICN work products remains of high importance. The ICN's website currently says:

> Promotion, awareness, and encouraging implementation of ICN work product is vital to the network. The first goal mentioned in the ICN's mission statement is an active one: 'to advocate the adoption of superior standards and procedures in competition policy around the world'.[53]

[51] <www.internationalcompetitionnetwork.org/wp-content/uploads/2020/01/SpeechChairMottaclosing2012.pdf> accessed 7 October 2021.

[52] Andreas Mundt, President of the Bundeskartellamt, ICN Chair (2013), <www.internationalcompetitionnetwork.org/wp-content/uploads/2018/07/ICNSGMundtVision.pdf> accessed 7 October 2021.

[53] <www.internationalcompetitionnetwork.org/working-groups/icn-operations/implementation/> accessed 7 October 2021.

2.2.2.2 *Measuring implementation*

The ICN has also made several attempts to gauge how much implementation there is of its work products. The results of the first major stock-taking exercise that took place in 2011, concerning the impact of the ICN (the ICN Second Decade Report), stated that:

> ICN work products have influenced agency practice of many ICN members and have also influenced legal and policy reforms in many ICN member jurisdictions. For example, 39 ICN members have reported using the Anti-Cartel Enforcement Manual to advance their cartel enforcement programmes. Two-thirds of ICN members that made changes to their merger control regimes cited the ICN Recommended Practices for Merger Notification and Review Procedures as having influenced their reforms. More than a dozen agencies have reported using the ICN's Recommended Practices on Dominance/Substantial Market Power Analysis Under Unilateral Conduct Laws in their casework or staff training.[54]

The results of a subsequent exercise, undertaken in 2016, add:

> More than half of the responding agencies use ICN work products (including teleseminars and webseminars) for training purposes. More than half of the respondents also have used ICN guidance documents to develop or revise internal procedures, guidelines and best practices, and are cited in the internal documents of the agencies accordingly. ICN workshops and teleseminars are considered a useful opportunity for the staff to gain additional knowledge on specific topics, discuss real cases and exchange experiences. Attendance at the ICN events has been very useful for the agencies' delegates in building relationships with members of other agencies. Agencies frequently refer to ICN work products when engaging in competition advocacy. Some agencies report that ICN products were an important source of information and inspiration to support, advance, or improve proposals to review or amend national competition laws. In the past this was especially the case for merger control rules (e.g. introduction or amendment of the thresholds), but also cartel investigations (e.g. setting of fines) and leniency programs.[55]

There is some suggestion that implementation of ICN work products has been increasing over time.[56] We are more sceptical about the level of confidence one

[54] ICN, *The Future of the ICN in Its Second Decade—Final Report* (2016) 2. For a further discussion on implementation, see also Chapter 4, <https://www.internationalcompetitionnetwork.org/wp-content/uploads/2018/09/ICN2dDecade2016.pdf> accessed 8 October 2021.

[55] ICN (n 54) 19.

[56] Maria B Coppola and Cynthia Lagdameo, 'Taking Stock and Taking Root: A Closer Look at Implementation of the ICN Recommended Practices for Merger Notification & Review Procedures' in Paul Lugard (ed), *The International Competition Network at Ten: Origins, Accomplishments and Aspirations* (Intersentia 2011) 307–09.

can place in these ICN assessments. Assessing effective implementation is a complex exercise. As discussed in Chapter 4, we have concerns about the accuracy of the ICN's implementation data and the ICN's methodology when it collects it.[57]

In our survey (see Chapter 3), we used several variables to measure implementation that we consider to be a good proxy for 'commitment' in implementing ICN work products. A first variable is the answer to the question 'how often does your competition authority address national legislators to request a change in the legislation following a recommendation from the ICN?' NCAs do not always need to do so. This is because, their national laws may already be aligned with the ICN work or because the NCA itself might be able to follow the ICN recommendation without legislative change. In any case we consider addresses by the NCAs to their legislators as a good proxy of commitment in following ICN work. This does not seem to be a very common practice: 21 per cent answered 'often', 48 per cent reported that they do that 'rarely', and 31 per cent that they never do it. This trend seems to be confirmed by another variable used in our survey to measure NCAs' attitudes towards implementation of ICN recommendations: the answer to the question whether the lack of compliance has a negative impact on the NCA's reputation within the ICN. The expectation is that the higher the importance NCAs attribute to lack of compliance with ICN work products, the more willing they are likely to be to comply with these work products. Only 21 per cent of the respondents think that lack of compliance undermines an NCA's reputation 'a lot'; 32 per cent think it does so 'only slightly' and 47 per cent thinks that not implementing recommended practices has no reputational damage whatsoever.

The ICN seems increasingly keen to measure the implementation of its work products. Perhaps NCAs are increasingly pushing for it to measure its own effectiveness. What seems clear is that measuring the level of implementation of ICN work products is, itself, likely to help to drive implementation of these same work products. This is because it pushes NCAs to confront their level of implementation. The resulting compliance (and non-compliance) will be easily publicly available. This also makes it easier for those keen to push further compliance to monitor what is happening and act upon it.

We saw how the ICN focuses on the implementation of its work since its early stage (Section 2.2.2.1). Also, we presented some results of its efforts and how, through monitoring implementation, it can help to drive compliance (Section 2.2.2.2). In the next sections we show several techniques that the ICN employs for increasing implementation (Section 2.2.2.3) and how its implementation focus has been reinforced (Section 2.2.2.4).

57 See Chapter 4, Section 4.3.2.

2.2.2.3 *Techniques for increasing implementation*

As noted previously, implementation can be done directly by NCAs, when this falls within their discretion (perhaps because it falls within their remit for interpreting national competition rules), or by states (perhaps if implementation requires a change of national laws). As argued by Slaughter:

> [p]art of the genius of government networks is that they marry soft with hard power. The power within the networks themselves—among different regulators or judges, or between a supranational court or parliament and a national court of parliament is soft. Even when, as in a vertical network the supranational entity has formal legal authority over its national counterpart, it has no actual means of enforcing the obligation. Instead it must use everything from expertise to endearments: information, persuasion, socialization ... Once convinced of a particular path of action or the wisdom of a particular result, however, the national government officials operating in both horizontal and vertical networks possess hard power as they possess within their own domestic political systems.[58]

Here we briefly outline some mechanisms that the ICN employs (intentionally or not) which help to drive the implementation of its work products. Then we discuss many of these in more detail through the example of the ICN Recommended Practices on merger notification and review procedures.

In terms of direct NCA activity, the ICN employs several techniques to increase the implementation of its work products, depending upon the changes that are needed. This obviously depends on the existing rules and procedures in each state, as well as its ability to change. Sometimes, changes at the NCA level are enough to implement the ICN work product. Here we highlight five mechanisms: the epistemic community and network effects, monitoring (followed by naming and shaming) and even coercion. The ICN (and its actors) also facilitate implementation with training and capacity building.

An important part of the success of implementation is personal relationships among the individuals that participate in the ICN. This can be seen as a consequence of having people that have the same goals and interests working together and sharing ideas and practices. This is important. It engages actors on a personal level, triggering important social institutions like trust, honour and honesty (as we saw in Chapter 1's discussion of the epistemic community). As Lewis has said:

> I know that when I—and I suspect that this is true of most of us—engage with the US FTC it is not only a 100 years old, all powerful agency of the richest country in the world with whom I engage but it is also Bill or Randy, flesh and blood like the rest of us, just as when I engage with Barbara Lee, it is not a small, island economy

[58] Slaughter (n 17) 168.

> that I see, but rather someone steeped in competition law and policy and whose particular experience can help representatives or even the most sophisticated agencies understand complexities of their world a little better.[59]

So, the implementation (or not) of global 'best practices' that an NCA has not objected to (through the consensus principle), creates a reputational dynamic which pushes actors to implement these 'soft rules'.[60] When choosing whether (or not) to follow the advice of personal contacts, these social institutions are triggered. In dealing on this personal level, NCA employees want to belong to this 'elite club' of experts, they want to fit in. To do so they know that some reasons for disagreement are acceptable and others are not. If they can get their NCA to follow the ICN standard, this will be judged as a success. Something to celebrate with their ICN colleagues. If they can persuade their state to change its rules in line with ICN work products, that too is worthy of trumpeting. On the other hand, if they cannot, or do not, achieve these things, then this may be embarrassing. Excuses are needed.

Some research also highlights the additional role of network effects in bringing about compliance with soft law in transnational networks (here the mechanism can often be similar, but the focus is on the institutional level).[61] These can be extremely powerful too, especially when combined with the pressure of the epistemic community.[62]

However, the ICN does not only rely on the powerful socialization effects of its network to achieve its goals. As we now discuss, the ICN has other ways of pushing NCAs (and their states) to take implementation seriously. To understand the degree of the implementation of their work by its members, the ICN working groups make positive efforts to assess this. We saw an example of this in Section 2.2.2.2. Assessing implementation gives an opportunity to name and shame NCAs that do not comply with ICN work products. Knowing that monitoring will occur, in itself increases the pressure on NCAs to implement ICN work products.[63] Publishing this 'compliance data' also provides a mechanism to try to 'keep NCAs honest', in their reporting of whether or not they are fully complying with ICN work products. This can even be true for data that has been partially aggregated. It also provides a mechanism for

[59] Lewis (n 34) 5.

[60] Daniel E Ho, 'Compliance and International Soft Law: Why Do Countries Implement the Basle Accord?' (2002) 5 Journal of International Economic Law 647–88; Chris Brummer, *Soft Law and the Global Financial System: Rule Making in the 21st Century* (CUP 2011).

[61] Newman and Bach (n 12) 430–52; David (n 12) 332–37.

[62] See also the discussion of these issues and references to relevant literature in Christopher Townley, *A Framework for European Competition Law: Co-ordinated Diversity* (Hart 2018) pt B.

[63] For the relevance of measurement, see, for example, the discussion (in a different context) in Charles Sabel and Jonathan Zeitlin, 'Learning from Difference: The New Architecture of Experimentalist Governance in the EU' in Charles Sabel and Jonathan Zeitlin (eds), *Experimentalist Governance in the European Union: Towards a New Architecture* (OUP 2010). This is not to say that the ICN is a true example of experimentalist governance. For an interesting critique, see Yane Svetiev, *Experimentalist Competition Law and the Regulation of Markets* (Hart 2020) ch 5.

others to highlight any lack of implementation. This is because it allows NGAs to see what NCAs are saying and to 'call them out' if they notice an implementation gap.

Some authors also identify coercion as a mechanism leading to compliance.[64] For example, jurisdictions with large internationalized markets such as the United States and the European Union often use conformity with soft law as a condition of market access. Foreign firms, or their respective governments, then follow soft law or face exclusion from these important markets.[65]

Another way of enhancing the successful implementation of ICN work products is to help to deal with any barriers to this. Examples of such barriers can include both technical knowledge and experience. 'In developed countries, this comes from on-the-job experience and institutional knowledge of the process of trial and error that led to past failures and successes.'[66]

The ICN describes technical assistance as 'the process by which a new competition agency can take advantage of the experience of others as it develops that experience and judgement on its own'.[67] Building domestic governance capacity improves the prospect of (good) compliance.[68] This is important. NCAs from developing economies often:

> face serious constrains when designing and implementing [competition] policy. One of these constraints is related to the fact that, since developing economies have only recently introduced competition legislation and created specialised agencies to enforce it, the available experience and expertise on competition matters is frequently scarce.[69]

To assist with this, the ICN has developed a 'Training on Demand project', financed by the American Bar Association's Section of Antitrust Law.[70] The mission of this project is:

> to create a comprehensive curriculum of training materials to serve as a virtual university on competition law and practice for competition agency officials.

[64] Ethan Kapstein, 'Between Power and Purpose: Central Bankers and the Politics of Regulatory Convergence' (1992) 46 International Organization 265–87.

[65] Tim Büthe and Walter Mattli, *The New Global Rulers: The Privatization of Regulation in the World Economy* (Princeton UP 2011); David Andrew Singer, *Regulating Capital: Setting Standards for the International Financial System* (Cornell UP 2015); Elliot Posner, 'Making Rules for Global Finance: Transatlantic Regulatory Cooperation at the Turn of the Millennium' (2009) 63 International Organization 665–99.

[66] ICN, *Findings Related to Technical Assistance for Newer Competition Authorities* (2007) 1. <www.internationalcompetitionnetwork.org/wp-content/uploads/2018/09/CPI_TechnicalAssistanceFindings.pdf> accessed 7 October 2021.

[67] ibid.

[68] Slaughter (n 17) 185. For further discussion on the impact of capacity building, see Chapter 1, Section 1.3.1.5.

[69] Eduardo Pérez Motta, 'The Role of the International Competition Network (ICN) in the Promotion of Competition in Developing Countries: The Case of Mexico' in Lugard (n 56) 218.

[70] <www.internationalcompetitionnetwork.org/training/> accessed 7 October 2021.

> Training modules, consisting of video lectures and accompanying materials from a diverse group of international academics and practitioners, will provide an on-line interactive educational center for competition authorities from around the world.[71]

As we saw in Chapter 1, Sections 1.2–1.3, many NCAs also send their staff to other NCAs to provide them with training. This has proved to be an invaluable tool (or Trojan horse) for 'educating' staff in developing countries' NCAs about best practice (by which is often meant, the 'techniques that advanced industrialized nations' NCAs would like them to adopt'). Moreover, the ICN organizes a broad range of events, from workshops, teleseminars to annual conferences, giving ICN members the opportunity to share experiences, build trust and develop understanding about the standards and procedures of other members, which at the end might facilitate compliance.[72]

Sometimes, implementation of the ICN work product needs legislative change. This is not normally within the remit of NCAs. However, the ICN counts on its NCA members, and also NGAs, to put pressure on the national legislator both to trigger change and then to guide what that change is (pushing it towards compliance with relevant ICN work products). We outline several examples of this technique, below.

A good example of the use of these different techniques for increasing implementation can be found in relation to the ICN Recommended Practices on merger notification and review procedures. The mission of the ICN Merger Working group is:

> to promote the adoption of best practices in the design and operation of merger review regimes in order to: (i) enhance the effectiveness of merger review mechanisms; (ii) facilitate procedural and substantive convergence; and (iii) reduce the public and private time and cost of multijurisdictional merger reviews.[73]

[71] ibid. Currently, the list of modules includes eight series organized by subject matter, including competition policy fundamentals, horizontal restraints, dominant firm conduct, mergers, competition advocacy, and investigational techniques. Complementing these modules are several 'short form' presentations prepared for the ICN by academics, agency officials, and non-government advisors, which can be found at the end of each series.

[72] The current ICN Chair, Andreas Mundt, has maintained the network's implementation efforts. Importantly, he has said that all ICN efforts: 'On a practical level, implementation may be realised by various means. It can be promoted by presenting work products in teleseminars, using work products or internal training classes, or within the advocacy work of ICN members.' Andreas Mundt, President of the Bundeskartellamt, ICN Chair (2013), <www.internationalcompetitionnetwork.org/wp-content/uploads/2018/07/ICNSGMundtVision.pdf> accessed 7 October 2021.

[73] <www.internationalcompetitionnetwork.org/working-groups/merger/> accessed 7 October 2021.

Multi-jurisdictional merger review has been a priority for the ICN since its creation.[74] It is a good example of an area where there are overlapping interests of both powerful NCAs and NGAs.[75]

The Merger Working Group was one of the first ICN working groups to be created.[76] It was divided into three subgroups: Merger Notification and Procedures, the Analytical Framework of Merger Review, and Investigative Techniques in Merger Review. It has been working on several detailed work products, on merger notification and review since then.[77] Its subgroup on Merger Notification and Procedures included leading merger lawyers from the private sector, who were essential participants and 'became a reliable backbone of the work'.[78] It developed a set of eight Guiding Principles and three initial recommended practices prior to the first ICN annual meeting in September 2002. The Chair of the Merger Notification and Procedures Subgroup, the US FTC, was directly involved in this effort. Many NGAs were also heavily involved, particularly those in the Merger Streamlining Group.[79] This subgroup on Merger Notification and Procedures represents well the network of professionals 'with recognised expertise and competence in a particular domain and an authoritative claim to policy relevant knowledge within that domain or issue-area'[80] that form an epistemic community. They use their strength

[74] Eleanor Fox, 'Linked-In: Antitrust and the Virtues of a Virtual Network' in Lugard (n 56) 159.

[75] In 2011, Fox recalled the 'chaos in merger control' decried by leading members of the bar. 'At the time, approximately sixty-five nations required merger review, and the jurisdictions had different timing, different informational requirements, arbitrary filing deadlines, and often a long-arm reach to mergers with little relationship with the regulating jurisdictions' ibid 161.

[76] The other working group to be created in the early stage of the ICN was the Advocacy Working Group.

[77] The documents produced include: *Guiding Principles* and *Recommended Practices for Merger Notification and Review Procedures* (for example, advising against asserting jurisdiction over a merger unless that merger has an appreciable impact on that jurisdiction); and *Recommended Practices on Merger Analysis* (which, for example, caution on automatically linking market shares and market power). There is also: a *Merger Guidelines Workbook*, with a checklist of topics to be considered in merger guidelines; a *Handbook on Investigative Techniques for Merger Review* (informing NCAs of various tools and techniques and how to use them more effectively and efficiently); a *Merger Remedies Guide* (providing guidance on key principles and tools in merger remedies); and a *Model Confidentiality Waiver for Mergers* (that merging parties and NCAs can use to facilitate waivers of confidentiality protection for information that parties submit in the merger review process). There are also several other guides and reports, including a *Practical Guide* (elaborating on recommended practices and principles of merger review cooperation contained in ICN work products, which is intended to offer: (a) a voluntary and flexible framework for interagency cooperation in merger investigations; (b) practical guidance for agencies seeking to engage in such cooperation; and (c) practical guidance for merging parties and third parties seeking to facilitate cooperation). For more details as well as the documents referred, see n 73.

[78] Fox (n 74) 161.

[79] The Mergers Streamlining Group is a group of international businesses whose membership consists of multinational firms with a common interest in promoting the efficient and effective review of international merger transactions. The current members of the Group include Accenture, BHP Billiton, Bosch, Chevron, Cisco, Danaher, General Electric, Novartis, Oracle, Procter & Gamble, Siemens, and United Technologies. See: <https://assets.publishing.service.gov.uk/government/uploads/system/uploads/attachment_data/file/770678/15._Merger_Streamlining_Group_Redacted.pdf>

[80] Peter Haas, 'Introduction: Epistemic Communities and International Policy Co-ordination' (1992) 46 International Organization 1.

to pressure NCAs and national legislators to conform to the ICN's recommended practices on mergers review.

The Chair of the Merger Notification and Review Procedures subgroup has made direct contact with many NCAs whose states were considering changing their merger rules. The idea was to understand whether these NCAs would welcome ICN support to review the law or to advocate specific (ICN compliant) changes directly to their government. This was the case of Portugal, for example, which, in 2011, was undertaking a review of its competition law, including the merger thresholds. Upon learning of these possible reforms, the Chair of the Merger Notification and Review Procedures Subgroup (Coppola) contacted the Portuguese NCA to offer support in trying to embed the ICN recommended practices in the heart of the Portuguese reform. Similarly, in relation to Brazil, Coppola reports that at the invitation of the Brazilian NCAs:

> ICN representatives supported the merger review provisions in the pending amendments to the Brazilian competition law, first through an in-country visit in 2008, and in 2010 through a formal letter of support.[81]

Many NGAs participating in the Merger Working Group also made direct contact both with NCAs and their national governments in the context of legislative changes to competition law. The Merger Streamlining Group lists extensive contacts with national governments with detailed documents showing how far NGAs are willing to deploy efforts to secure compliance with the ICN Recommended Practices in Merger Reviews.[82] Each contact contains detailed comments benchmarking the

[81] Coppola and others (n 25) 4.

[82] In 2009, for example, there was a letter to the Canadian Competition Bureau regarding the Draft Guidelines on the Revised Merger Review Process. In 2011, there was a letter to the Italian government regarding the Proposed Merger Control Reforms; a letter to the Portuguese government regarding the Stakeholder Consultations on Merger Control Reform Proposals; a letter to the Russian Federal Antimonopoly Service regarding the Third Antimonopoly Package; a letter to the Philippines government concerning the House and Senate Competition Law Reform Proposals; a letter to the Polish Competition Agency regarding Merger Notification Thresholds in Poland; and a letter to the UK government in connection with Stakeholder Consultations on Proposals to Reform the UK Competition Regime. In 2012 there was a letter to the Austrian government regarding Merger Control Reform Proposals; a letter to the Brazilian CADE regarding Stakeholder Consultations on Merger Control Provisions of the New Brazilian Competition Law; and a letter to the Peruvian Congress, INDECOPI regarding Proposed New Competition Law. In 2013 there was a letter to the European Commission regarding Public Consultation on Non-Controlling Minority Shareholdings; a letter to the Australian Competition and Consumer Commission regarding the Draft Merger Review Process Guidelines; a letter to the European Commission regarding the Draft Revision of Simplified Procedure and Merger Implementing Regulation; a letter to the Chilean Government regarding Merger Control Reform Proposals; and a letter to the Taiwan Fair Trade Commission regarding the Proposed Amendments to Taiwan Merger Notification Law. In 2014 there was a letter to the Australian Competition Policy Review Secretariat regarding Competition Policy Review; a letter to the Brazilian CADE regarding the Public Consultation to Amend CADE Resolutions (Nos 2 and 8); a letter to the Cyprus Parliamentary Committee Service, Commission for the Protection of Competition, the Legal Service of the Republic of Cyprus, and Ministry of Energy, Commerce, Industry and Tourism regarding Proposed Amendments to the Control of Concentrations Between Undertakings Law; a letter to the

national initiative against the relevant ICN recommended practice and calling on the national governments to follow it. For example, in the context of the Reform of the UK Competition Regime, the Merger Streamlining Group sent a letter to the UK government in 2011 regarding the Stakeholder Consultations on Proposals to Reform the UK Competition Regime. In this letter the Group criticizes the lack of compliance with the relevant ICN Recommended Practices:

> With respect to the share of supply threshold, the Group believes that thresholds based on shares of supply or market shares introduce unnecessary uncertainty into review processes: such criteria are not objectively quantifiable and may be the subject of dispute between the CMA [a UK NCA] and merging parties. Such a threshold would not be ICN-compliant in a mandatory notification regime (see below) and the Group suggests that it would also be desirable to remove the share of supply jurisdictional threshold if the voluntary regime is continued.
>
> The Group is concerned that the thresholds proposed for a full mandatory notification regime are much too low to be material given the size of the United Kingdom's economy (as required by Recommended Practice I-B), and would require companies to notify transactions that would not have a foreseeable impact on competitive conditions in the UK. Merger notification thresholds in ICN-compliant jurisdictions are often in the range of £35 million and upwards (including in a variety of jurisdictions that have much smaller economies than the UK)…
>
> ICN Recommended Practice I-C provides that determination of a transaction's nexus to the jurisdiction should be based on the activities of at least two parties to the transaction in the local territory and/or based on to the activities of the target business in the local territory. While the proposed £70 million turnover threshold for a hybrid mandatory notification regime meets the requirement (since it is based on the target's turnover in the UK), the Group would encourage the Government to consider adopting a second threshold based on the activities of a second party to the transaction in the UK…

German Bundeskartellamt regarding the Draft Guidance on Domestic Effects in Merger Control; a letter to the Italian Autorità Garante della Concorrenza e del Mercato regarding the Consultation on Prior Notification of Concentrations; and a letter to the European Commission Submission on the White Paper 'Towards More Effective EU Merger Control'. In 2015 there was a letter to the Competition Commission of India regarding the Invitation to Comment on the Proposed Amendments to the Combination Regulations; a letter to Minister of Economic Development and Trade of Ukraine (copied to Chairman of Antimonopoly Committee of Ukraine) regarding Competition Law Reforms; a letter to the Chilean Fiscalia Nacional Economica, Ministerio de Economica, Formento y Torismo, and Camara de Diputados de Chile regarding the Bill amending the Competition Act; a letter to the Israel Antitrust Authority regarding Proposed Amendments to the Restrictive Trade Practices Law, 1988. In 2016 there was a letter to the Indian Ministry of Corporate Affairs regarding the expiration of May 2011 'de minimis' or 'small target' exemption. For the full list, see: <http://mcmillan.ca/files/merger-steamlining-group2016.pdf>. This document was published on the website of McMillan, a Canadian law firm. Since its publication there, the site has changed and we cannot find the document any longer. The old, broken link has been kept in the hope that it may help readers to find the document in a cache.

> Any mandatory filing requirement should be based on a clear standard setting forth the type of transaction that will be considered a 'merger' and, therefore, require a filing. As the Consultation Paper recognizes, the current 'cease to be distinct' standard is too imprecise and should be replaced by a requirement of the acquisition of control of the target or the acquisition of decisive influence over the target. Such an approach would be consistent with ICN Recommended Practice II-A which states that '[n]otification thresholds should be clear and understandable'.
>
> The Group supports the introduction of time limits that conform to ICN Recommended Practices IV-C and IV-D, which state that initial waiting periods in suspensive jurisdictions and initial merger reviews in non-suspensive jurisdictions should expire or be completed within a specified period following notification, and that any extended waiting periods or reviews should expire or be completed within a determinable time frame. However, the first phase time limit recommended by the ICN is 6 weeks and the Group therefore encourages the Government to apply a 30-working day time limit for voluntary as well as mandatory reviews.[83]

Also, in a letter to the Ministry of Corporate Affairs of India, sent in 2016, regarding the expiration of a 'de minimis' or 'small target' exemption, in May 2011, the Merger Streamlining Group commented:

> The cornerstone of the Group's activity has been to work with competition agencies and governments to help implement international best practices in merger control. In particular, the Group focuses on the Recommended Practices for Merger Notification Procedures ('Recommended Practices') of the International Competition Network ('ICN'), of which the Competition Commission of India 'CCI') is an active member and currently a Co-Chair of the Merger Working Group . . .
>
> Consistent with our past submissions, the Group respectfully encourages the CCI to consider the ICN Recommended Practices generally, and the following issues in particular, in any future review of India's merger control laws: (i) the need for greater local nexus requirements in India's merger notification thresholds—(in particular, the avoidance of thresholds based solely on the assets or revenues of the acquiror alone, or the combined activity of the acquiror's 'group' and target entity following the transaction); (ii) the abolition of the current filing deadlines (which are very disruptive to complex global transactions and which are not necessary); and (iii) the unavailability of the 'de minimis' or 'small target' filing exemption for transactions other than asset-only acquisitions.[84]

[83] <https://assets.publishing.service.gov.uk/government/uploads/system/uploads/attachment_data/file/312068/L-O-competition-regime-for-growth.pdf>

[84] <http://mcmillan.ca/Files/188516_MSG%20-%20Submission%20to%20India%20-%20Feb%202016.PDF>. As noted above in n 82, this is a broken link, but has been included in the hope that it helps readers to find a cached version of the document.

Since their adoption, the level of implementation of the ICN Recommended Practices for Merger Notification and Review Procedures has been monitored. The first four recommended practices were approved in 2003 during the second ICN Annual Conference. The following year, two reports on their implementation were presented at the ICN Annual Conference. One was presented by Randy Tritell, Assistant Director for International Antitrust at the US Federal Trade Commission.

> The Recommendations are valuable in so far as they are applied in practice, said Mr. Tritell. The results of the report are quite encouraging, as it seems that most ICN members with merger laws follow most of the Recommended Practices.[85]

The other report on the implementation of the ICN Recommended Practices for Merger Notification and Review Procedures was presented by Mr William Rowley, a lawyer from Canada and an active ICN NGA, representing the Merger Streamlining Group. The Merger Streamlining Group undertook a survey to assess the implementation of these recommended practices. This report was based on responses from a survey of competition agencies and private law firms.

> The recommendations, Mr. Rowley said, have made a remarkably strong start, and it is important that the momentum continue, to influence additional members to change their laws and procedures accordingly. Mr. Rowley stressed the need to promote the work of the ICN to a wider audience, in order to enhance its visibility outside member agencies and advisors.[86]

The ICN Merger Working group undertook a first comprehensive assessment of the ICN work and its implementation between 2010 and 2011.[87] The results were presented during the 10th ICN annual conference.[88] According to the results:

> over the past ten years, more than two-thirds of the ICN's 87 members with merger control have made changes that bring their merger regimes into greater

85 Gal and Evenett (n 28) 24

86 <www.alexandria.unisg.ch/22155/1/seoulicnfinal.pdf> accessed 7 October 2021.

87 Between 2002 and 2006, ICN members adopted 13 Recommended Practices on merger notification and review procedures. The Recommended Practices for Merger Notification and Review Procedures address: (1) nexus between the merger's effects and the reviewing jurisdiction; (2) clear and objective notification thresholds; (3) timing of merger notification; (4) merger review periods; (5) requirements for initial notification; (6) conduct of merger investigations; (7) procedural fairness; (8) transparency; (9) confidentiality; (10) interagency coordination; (11) review of merger control provisions; (12) remedies; and (13) competition agency powers. ICN Merger Working Group: Investigation and Analysis Subgroup, ISCN Merger Guidelines Workbook 2006, <https://www.internationalcompetitionnetwork.org/wp-content/uploads/2018/05/MWG_MergerGuidelinesWorkbook.pdf> accessed 7 October 2021.

88 ICN Merger Working Group, Comprehensive Assessment 2010–2011, <www.internationalcompetitionnetwork.org/wp-content/uploads/2018/05/MWGAssessment2011.pdf> accessed 7 October 2021.

> conformity with the Practices, and more than half of these have indicated that the Recommended Practices played a role in their reforms. In the area of merger thresholds, for example, 39 ICN members are in full conformity with the ICN best practice that prescribes notification only for transactions where at least two parties to the transaction or the target company have material local sales or assets. Eighteen of these 39 jurisdictions conform because of reforms made in the past decade.[89]

The second assessment on the implementation of the ICN Recommended Practices for Merger Notification and Review Procedures revealed the same pattern of high degree of implementation.[90]

The success on the implementation of the ICN Recommended Practices for Merger Notification and Review can also be explained by network effects resulting from their implementation at national level. As Fox argued:

> Nations' implementation of the recommended practices and use of the guiding principles have rationalized the global merger process, reducing costs, eliminating conflicts and facilitating translations.[91]

As discussed in Chapter 4, there are reasons to question the accuracy of this type of monitoring exercise. However, it does allow the identification of those that do not comply and provides opportunities to put pressure on ICN members (and their states) that do not comply.

Of course, formally (legally), compliance cannot be imposed. The ICN lacks this power. However, ICN members may deploy peer pressure or naming and shaming to bring recalcitrant members into line.[92] For example, in 2011, Portugal was in the process of revising its competition act. The new law did not fully respect the notification threshold recommended by the ICN. In a meeting of the OECD Competition Committee, in an ad hoc peer review process, the Portuguese NCA (the AdC) gave reasons for the divergence. It had chosen to diverge based on the findings of a preparatory economic study. This

[89] Maria Coppola, 'ICN Best Practices: Soft Law, Concrete Results' (2011) 1 CPI Antitrust Chronicle 3.

[90] ICN Merger Working Group, *ICN Recommended Practices for Merger Notification and Review Procedures: Member Self-Assessment—Report on 2016 Survey Results* (2017), <https://www.internationalcompetitionnetwork.org/portfolio/guiding-principles-for-merger-notification-review-procedure/> accessed 8 October 2021.

[91] Fox (n 74) 166.

[92] Elliot Posner, 'International Financial Regulatory Co-operation: an experimentalist turn?' in Jonathan Zeitlin (ed), *Extending Experimentalist Governance?* (OUP 2015) 204.

study analysed past mergers that had been contested by the AdC. It showed that the application of an objective notification threshold would not have required the notification of some previous mergers to the AdC. The study argued that such a shift would create an important gap. At the end of the meeting a representative of the US FTC, that chaired the ICN Mergers Notification and Review Procedure Working Group, stated that there was no reason for Portugal not to comply.

Sometimes coercion is also employed. Powerful jurisdictions have been known to use conformity with the ICN recommended practices as a condition to grant access to something another jurisdiction wants. This was the case of the accession of Russia to the OECD.[93] Accession to the OECD entailed 'a thorough 360-degree review of its public policies'.[94] This was done mainly by the different OECD committees, such as the Competition Committee. Though the evaluation was done according to the OECD's own standards, one should not forget that many ICN members represent their states at the OECD Competition Committee. Such is the case of powerful ICN NCAs, such as the US FTC and DoJ. The European Commission also takes part in the work of the OECD, including of its Competition Committee. In 2013, a report on Competition Law and Policy in the Russian Federation was published.[95] It was prepared as part of OECD accession review 'to assist the OECD Competition Committee in assessing the willingness and ability of the Russian Federation to the obligations of membership in the OECD concerning Competition Policy'.[96] This report highlighted 'key challenges facing Russia in its implementation and enforcement of competition policy'.[97] In identifying such challenges, the OECD Report refers to information provided by the ICN on other jurisdictions' thresholds in merger review as a benchmark for Russia's rules.[98] It then formulates several recommendations for 'future action by the Russian Federation', including on merger control procedures. Those recommendations include modifying:

> the merger notification thresholds to conform to the ... international best practices on nexus, to provide that at least two parties to a transaction have sales or assets in the Russian Federation exceeding a certain material threshold with the

[93] In 2007, the OECD Council delivered an invitation to Russia to join the OECD.

[94] <www.oecd.org/about/secretary-general/integration-russia-global-economic-institutions-oecd-accession.htm> accessed 7 October 2021.

[95] OECD, Competition Law and Policy in the Russian Federation, 2013, <www.oecd.org/daf/competition/CompetitionLawandPolicyintheRussianFederation.pdf> accessed 7 October 2021.

[96] ibid 3.

[97] ibid.

[98] ibid 69.

> relevant sales and/or assets of the acquired party limited to the sale and/or assets of the business(es) being acquired.[99]

This recommendation corresponds to the ICN Recommended Practice on Merger Review regarding Nexus to the reviewing jurisdiction.[100] Interestingly, this ICN recommended practice became part of the OECD recommendations that Russia needs to address if it wants to become an OECD member.

Finally, training on merger review and capacity building are also available for those NCAs requiring it. Currently, the ICN's Training on Demand Curriculum includes two models on merger review. One module is on 'Handling Mergers Investigations' and 'addresses competition agency merger investigations, drawing upon concepts from the modules on market definition and market power in the merger context'.[101] The other module is on 'Mergers remedies' and 'explores the principles underlying the need for and identification of remedies appropriate to the anticompetitive concerns in a particular case and addresses more common practical considerations such as timing, elements of the remedy package, challenges in identifying effective buyers, international coordination, and "after the fact" monitoring and compliance'.[102] The Merger Working Group has also organized several workshops for staff on investigative techniques and procedures.[103] For example, during the third ICN Annual Conference, Mr Menzi Simelane, Commissioner, Competition Commission, South Africa, focused on technical assistance. He stressed the critical role that technical assistance has in the creation of an efficient competition regime, and said that technical assistance:

> facilitates an exchange of ideas and tactics to overcome enforcement problems and it enables jurisdictions to have ready access to competition experts and to other competition agencies.[104]

2.2.2.4 *Increasing the implementation focus*

Recent developments show that ICN is taking the drive for the implementation of its work products even more seriously. Here we discuss two examples of the ICN

[99] ibid 9.

[100] According to the ICN Recommended Practice on Merger Review regarding Nexus to reviewing jurisdiction: (i) jurisdiction should be asserted only over transactions that have a material nexus to the reviewing jurisdiction and (ii) determination of a transaction's nexus to the reviewing jurisdiction should be based on activities within that jurisdiction as measured by reference to the activities of at least two parties to the transaction in the local territory and/or by reference to the activities of the acquired business in the jurisdiction, ICN Recommended Practices for Merger Notification and Review Procedures, Part II, A and C. <www.internationalcompetitionnetwork.org/wp-content/uploads/2018/09/MWG_NPRecPractices2018.pdf> accessed 7 October 2021.

[101] <www.internationalcompetitionnetwork.org/training/handling-merger-investigations/> accessed 7 October 2021.

[102] ibid.

[103] For more details as well as the documents referred to, see n 73.

[104] Gal and Evenett (n 28) 23.

reinforcing its monitoring capacity to detect failure to implement ICN work products. First, the ICN has sought to institutionalize the promotion and implementation of its work products. It has done this by creating a specific group, currently named the 'Promotion and Implementation' team (P&I).[105] According to Coppola et al, this was 'the single biggest act of institutionalizing the ICN's commitment to encouraging use and implementation of its work came with the establishment of a group dedicated to implementation'.[106] The P&I team promotes ICN work and the implementation of ICN work products. To achieve its goals, the P&I team coordinates with the Chairs of the ICN's substantive Working Groups to assist NCAs interested in learning more about ICN work products on specific topics. NCA members can also approach the P&I team directly with questions about existing ICN work products and their application. The P&I team also invites NCAs to share stories about how they have used ICN work product 'to help document the ICN's impact and inspire members with implementation ideas from their peers'.[107] Furthermore, the P&I team organizes 'implementation sessions' at the ICN annual conferences to showcase how NCA members make use of ICN work products. The P&I team's work is complemented by the activities of the Vice-Chair Palacios Prieto, Vice-Chair for Young Agencies and Regional Diversity.[108]

Second, the ICN has recently introduced Opt-in Frameworks to its arsenal too. They could provide a major push to the monitoring effort and they have a 'normative bite'. NCAs that opt in to these frameworks are subject to certain obligations, mainly to report how and why they think they are conforming (or not) with the framework. The ICN has promulgated three such frameworks, one on merger enforcement cooperation, one on cartel enforcement cooperation, and one covering procedural fairness principles for NCA procedures. Any NCA can participate in these Opt-in Frameworks, regardless of whether they are ICN members.

The most high-profile and far-reaching of these frameworks is the third one, the 2019 Competition Agency Procedures (CAP) Framework.[109] It includes important

[105] Originally it was Advocacy and Implementation Network. Portugal's AdC, Mexico's COFECE, and the US FTC jointly chair this P&I team.

[106] Coppola and others (n 25).

[107] See n 53.

[108] ibid.

[109] Section 1d of this Framework states that:

> All ICN members and other competition agencies that are willing to adhere to the Principles and to participate in the Cooperation Process and in the Review Process are welcome and encourage to participate and to contribute. Therefore: to participate in the CAP is independent of the ICN membership, and likewise CAP participation does not convey ICN membership. It is the first time an ICN product recognises the separation between framework participation and ICN membership, welcoming 'all' competition agencies whether they are ICN members, or not. This might be an attempt of the ICN to pressure non-members of the ICN, such as the Chinese NCAs to opt in. Remember that Procedural fairness has been identified as a major issue when it comes to antitrust enforcement by Chinese NCAs.

Mary Ma and Daniel Sokol, 'Procedural Fairness in Chinese Antitrust' in Daniel Sokol and Andrew Guzman (eds), *Antitrust Procedural Fairness* (OUP 2019) 71–84

due process commitments regarding, for example: non-discrimination, transparency, timely resolution, confidentiality, conflicts of interest, proper notice, opportunity to defend, access to counsel, and judicial review. O'Brien provides a useful summary on how the CAP Framework works:

> The CAP contains two aspects: 1) an annex of fundamental, consensus principles for sound agency procedures, and 2) implementation tools—a 'cooperation process' and a 'review process'—to help promote use of the principles. While both the substantive and administrative aspects of the CAP (the ICN's third opt-in framework) borrow from previous instruments within the ICN, their combination represents an innovative leap in ICN efforts to promote implementation of its work.[110]

Importantly, for the purposes of our discussion, the CAP Framework has a reinforced monitoring mechanism (which is obviously designed to enhance its implementation):

> any Participant may request that another Participant engage in a dialogue regarding any issue of Competition Law procedure that is material to this Framework. Requests for dialogues are limited to Participants; participation in the Framework does not create rights in third parties to obligate or require a Participant to request a dialogue. A dialogue will only be undertaken for matters that fall within the responsibility of the requested Participant, although Participants may raise broader issues related to Competition Law investigation and enforcement for information purposes.[111]

Interestingly, the CAP Framework started, in 2018, as a unilateral initiative of the US Department of Justice, an NCA (independent from the ICN). This met resistance from other NCAs because:

> many ICN members viewed creating a new forum as confusing or inefficient, as well as unnecessary given the ICN's near-universal membership, established working procedures, and existing work addressing the substantive topics.[112]

[110] Paul O'Brien, 'ICN's Framework for Competition Agency Procedures, Part 1: What Does the CAP Mean for the ICN Today?' (2019) Competition Policy International, < https://www.ftc.gov/system/files/attachments/key-speeches-presentations/obrien_-_icn_column_4-19.pdf> accessed 7 October 2021.

[111] ICN, *Framework for Competition Agency Procedures* (2019) 2, <www.internationalcompetitionnetwork.org/frameworks/competition-agency-procedures/> accessed 7 October 2021.

[112] Coppola and others (n 25).

For example, EU Competition Commissioner Vestager argued that such initiatives should be accomplished through existing multilateral bodies like the ICN.[113] This shows that members do value cooperation within the ICN. It also seems to be an example of the EU using a threat to veto an independent US initiative in the competition domain. The EU did not seem to have a problem, substantively, with the US initiative. The problem seemed to be that it wanted the US to act within existing structures, where the EU has power. An added benefit, from the EU's perspective (and presumably that of the USA's ICN members) was that moving this initiative inside the ICN would help give further impetus to their implementation agenda within the ICN more widely.

2.2.3 Informed divergence

The introduction to this chapter highlighted a tension at the heart of the ICN. On the one hand, it formulates proposals for procedural and substantive convergence. On the other hand, where the ICN reaches consensus on work products, 'it is left to its members to decide whether and how to implement the recommendation'. The ICN explicitly states that it does not seek full harmonization by all ICN members implementing all ICN work products.

Indeed, aiming at full harmonization in a transnational network such as the ICN would be both unrealistic and undesirable as '[v]ariations in the economic traditions, history, legal process (eg civil law versus common law), and political science of individual jurisdictions are enduring sources of differences among competition systems'.[114] Moreover, if one accepts the evolutionary nature of the competition law and policy, individual jurisdictions must be able to test new approaches, introduce new reforms, gain experience and (re)assess results. As Hollman and Kovacic say:

> [t]o insist upon full uniformity across systems, or wait for unanimous approval before any single system undertook an innovation, would rob competition policy of a valuable source of continuing renewal and vitality.[115]

[113] ibid at 13. Coppola et al report that another European Commission official summed up this EU perspective by stating, 'For an agency, I would be probably more willing to join an initiative under the umbrella of the ICN, rather than join now a new self-standing initiative where you don't really know where it will end, what are your obligations, what it will mean in terms of resources and so on.'

[114] Hugh Hollman and William Kovacic, 'The International Competition Network: its past, current and future role' in Lugard (n 56) 278–79.

[115] ibid 278.

According to the ICN:

> where differences are greater due to different domestic economic histories, development and priorities (such as the analysis of unilateral conduct), the ICN facilitates 'informed divergence': identifying the nature and sources of apparent divergence and understanding and respecting any underlying divergent rationale. This greater understanding can offer business and consumers greater clarity and transparency and can lay the groundwork for possible convergence over the longer term.[116]

So, one might think that this tension between convergence and the ability of states not to implement ICN work products, has been resolved through this concept of 'informed divergence'. However, that would be a mistake.

Arguing more generally (and not specifically in relation to competition policy), Slaughter considers 'informed divergence' to be an exercise of 'democratic experimentalism'. States ensure efficiency and compliance with international standards by borrowing the best practices from other states or international actors.[117] When a state, having the choice to harmonize its rules or standards, decides not to do it, it is making 'a statement about the uniqueness of its national tradition or the intensity of its political preference'.[118] Such a choice results in 'informed divergence'. In the context of network governance, informed divergence 'permit[s] any subset of national officials to decide deliberately to affirm their difference'.[119]

Despite their apparent similarity, 'informed divergence' has quite different meanings for the ICN and Slaughter. The ICN says that it 'facilitates' informed divergence.[120] Yet, it is not immediately apparent what 'facilitates' means in this context. It might mean, for example, that the ICN facilitates the exchange of information and knowledge about the reasons behind divergence. In this way, ICN members could decide whether they wish to (continue to) diverge with ICN work products. The ICN certainly facilitates such exchanges (Chapter 4 highlights the value of its efforts here). However, when it comes to, paraphrasing Slaughter, 'states choosing not to harmonise their rules', the ICN does not seem to facilitate this (the idea makes no sense anyway, as divergence is already happening). In fact, the ICN only, temporarily 'tolerates' such divergence.

[116] ICN (n 23) 6.
[117] Slaughter (n 17) 180.
[118] ibid 181.
[119] ibid 182.
[120] For further discussion on informed divergence, see Chapter 4, Section 4.3.2.

The idea of 'informed divergence' was first outlined to the ICN in 2011, during the ICN Second Decade Initiative report. In 2011, Fingleton announced:

> In the next decade, the ICN will continue to seek opportunities for new Recommended Practices. In areas where convergence is not feasible *in the near term*, the ICN will instead seek to foster informed divergence.[121]

This is interesting because, as we saw before, the ICN Second Decade Initiative represented a shift in ICN priorities from work production to the implementation of its work products. At first sight, a focus on implementation and a tolerance for Informed divergence seem to be in contradiction. However, we think they are actually (at least temporarily) compatible and they both reinforce convergence.

According to Fingleton:

> In considering the implications of different substantive standards, it is of course important to recognise that the potential welfare harms will necessarily depend on the conditions in domestic markets.
>
> ... informed divergence is particularly important in the context of moving from a bi-polar to a multi-polar world. In particular, the emergence and development [of] the economies of China, other Asian countries, South America and Africa will see the emergence of new approaches to competition law and policy and will increase the need to consider the economic and other factors giving rise to those approaches.[122]

As already noted, at first sight, informed divergence leaves the door open to diversity in the implementation of ICN work products. As discussed in the Introduction to this book, we believe that diversity in competition law enforcement is a good thing (particularly when it is arrived at conscious of the alternatives). However, it is likely that 'informed divergence', rather than being a mechanism to accept diversity within the ICN, is a powerful and efficient way to control and coerce ICN members that are recalcitrant, pushing them to converge and accept ICN standards. First, informed divergence lowers the costs of reaching a consensus on a proposed ICN standard. Chapter 1 discusses how ICN recommended practices are adopted by consensus. When the consensus rule applies, any NCA can formally block the adoption of the ICN work that it believes does not fit its needs (or that might even clash with its needs). Too much emphasis on implementation of ICN work products may

[121] ICN (n 23) 6 (emphasis added).

[122] John Fingleton, 'Competition Agencies and Global Markets: The Challenges Ahead' in Lugard (n 56) 184 and 200.

undermine agreement in the first place. Yet, an NCA may choose not to oppose the adoption of an ICN work product that it considers to be unsuited for its national context or priorities, if it has (or thinks it has) the possibility to freely diverge. This gives an incentive to NCAs not to oppose the adoption of recommended practices that have the consensual support of other ICN members (even when they disagree with them), especially where the epistemic community is as strong as it is in the ICN.[123]

Second, if an ICN standard exists in a certain area, then NCAs are expected to follow it. NCAs that do not wish to follow the ICN standard, should justify divergence from that standard with reasons.[124] Put another way: members are no longer free to simply decide if they want to converge or not:[125] they must at least provide reasons not to. Furthermore, the reasons that they give in order to justify 'informed divergence' must be considered appropriate by other ICN members. Remember that they are in a close epistemic community here (and being 'judged' by it). As we show below, this does, in fact, seem to be happening. Of course, the sanction where there are no reasons (or the reasons are considered inadequate) is not compulsory convergence. A transnational network is not able to impose that. However, their peers' will evaluate the reasons and critique them. Dragging a 'recalcitrant NCA' into (often unwelcome) arguments. Other NCAs and NGAs may deploy peer pressure or naming and shaming to bring divergent NCAs into line.[126] The ICN does not host peer reviews itself. However, many ICN members meet in different international for a which do host peer reviews, such as the OECD and UNCTAD.[127] Naming and shaming for lack of compliance with the ICN working product can also take place is these other fora, as we will see below for Portugal (and as we have just seen with Russia). Other (often implicit) 'threats' highlighted in Chapter 1 may also be engaged, such as a reduction in the training offered to the recalcitrant NCA, or a lessening of influence in the ICN, for example. Informed divergence has to be earned, it does not come for free.[128]

The following example is a case in point. It concerns a failure to implement the ICN Recommended Practices for Merger Notification and Review Procedures by the Jersey Competition Regulatory Authority (JCRA) and the Israel Competition Authority (IAA), on one hand, and the Portuguese Competition Authority (AdC) on the other. In the ICN report on Competition Law in Small Economies the JCRA

[123] Chapter 1, Section 1.3 discusses the relevant epistemic community in more detail.

[124] Remember that the ICN's definition of 'informed divergence' given above (see text around n 100) refers to the provision of an 'underlying divergent *rationale*' (emphasis added).

[125] Remember the ICN Operational Framework 1(iv), according to which '[w]here the ICN reaches consensus on recommendations arising from a project, it is left to its members to decide whether and how to implement the recommendation'.

[126] Posner (n 92) 204.

[127] The ICN has suggested that its 'Recommended Practices remain a key benchmark in ... the peer reviews conducted within the OECD and the UNCTAD'. ICN Merger Working Group (n 90) 1.

[128] There is certainly room to go further than this with 'enforcement'. The discussion of opt-in frameworks in Section 2.2.2.4 might be a first step in this direction. For further critique of the current ICN position, see Svetiev (n 63) ch 5.

and the IAA report their reasons for diverging from those standards in the following terms:

> Notwithstanding the ICN Recommended Practices for Merger Notification and Review Procedures, some merger control regimes, such as the following competition agencies from Israel, Jersey and Taiwan, continue to employ structural thresholds. Such thresholds are based on market share data or similar (i.e., 'share of supply'). JCRA and IAA, coming from self-proclaimed small 'island' economies, as well, provided reasons for their favoring of such a practice in their respective countries.
>
> Under Jersey antitrust law, the current reportability thresholds are based on each merging party's share of supply or purchase of goods or services supplied to, or purchased from, persons in Jersey. While acknowledging that thresholds may not follow the ICN's Recommended Practice stated above, JCRA explains that such thresholds 'have worked well in Jersey's context, and may be particularly well suited for very small economies. Share of-supply thresholds are more closely related to the central focus of merger control determining whether a proposed acquisition would substantially lessen competition compared to criteria such as the turnover or assets of the merging parties'. Furthermore, based on JCRA's experience, such thresholds '[make] it easier to explain to merging parties, in a jurisdiction where competition law is a new concept, why they must undergo the merger review process'. In addition, JCRA's internal analysis, based on a survey of the past three years, indicates that if the regulatory agency switched to sales turnover thresholds, this would not dramatically reduce the number of merger filings but would materially increase the number of unnecessary filings. IAA voices similar concerns. The Israeli Restrictive Trade Practice Law employs a hybrid test triggering a duty to notify a merger based on either turnover or structural indicia. IAA argues that based on its island economy and inclination towards concentrated market segments, the use of market shares side by side with turnover indicia has proven to be better suited for the protection of competition in small markets, where even a monopoly might be left unchecked if the statutory turnover thresholds were to be the sole criterion. Moreover, empirical studies conducted in Israel demonstrate that its antitrust authority has opposed or conditioned several proposed mergers that were notified solely based on market share threshold that otherwise would have gone forward unchecked. According to IAA, in order to capture such anti-competitive mergers, it would have been forced to adjust its sales turnover thresholds, imposing an unwarranted burden on market participants.[129]

[129] ICN, *Special Project for the 8th Annual Conference—Competition Law in Small Economies* (2009) 36. <https://www.internationalcompetitionnetwork.org/portfolio/guiding-principles-for-merger-notification-review-procedure/> accessed 8 October 2021.

One can see what lengths the JCRA and the IAA have gone to justify their 'informed divergence'. They have done surveys, they have tested the application of the ICN rule in their jurisdiction to see how it would work, and they have underlined the different nature of the competition system where they operate. This divergence was never contested by the ICN.

In the case of Portugal, however, the situation was different. In 2011, Portugal was in the process of revising its competition act. The new law did not fully respect the notification threshold recommended by the ICN. In a meeting of the OECD Competition Committee, in an ad hoc peer review process, the Portuguese NCA (the AdC) gave reasons for the divergence. It had chosen to diverge based on the findings of a preparatory economic study. This study analysed past mergers that had been contested by the AdC. It showed that the application of an objective notification threshold would not have required the notification of some previous mergers to the AdC that it had contested. At the end of the meeting, a representative of the US FTC, that chaired the ICN Mergers Notification and Review Procedure Working Group, in an oral intervention, stated that there was no reason for Portugal not to comply with the ICN standard. Here we can see that compliance is scrutinized and failure to converge is strongly challenged. Portugal had obtained an economic study and gave reasons for its divergence.

There could be several reasons for the ICN not to 'facilitate' informed divergence in the case of Portugal, when it had been prepared to tolerate it by Jersey and Israel. Perhaps it was because Portugal is a member of the European Union and the ICN merger recommended practices aimed, in particular, at achieving more convergence between the US and the EU systems. Having an EU member state diverging from the ICN standard could be perceived as undermining this goal. It may also be because there was an ongoing revision of the law in Portugal there remained the possibility of bringing the law in line with the ICN recommended practice.

Whether divergence is 'informed divergence' (such as the JCRA and the IAA), in which case it would be 'tolerated' by the ICN, or mere 'divergence' (such as that of the AdC), in which case it would not, is a matter of opinion. And the opinion that matters in the ICN is not necessarily that of the NCAs that diverge. In any case, 'informed divergence' is only tolerated on a temporary basis. As seen above, the ICN expects convergence to be possible 'over the longer term'.

2.2.4 Does the ICN influence all members in the same way?

The ICN includes more than 120 NCAs[130] from over 100 jurisdictions around the world. This is a large target for influence. The possibility to influence depends on the

130 ICN, *ICN Statement of Achievements 2001–2013* (2013) 3. <https://www.internationalcompetitionnetwork.org/portfolio/guiding-principles-for-merger-notification-review-procedure/> accessed 8 October 2021.

range of working products available. The variety and breadth of ICN work across the Merger, Cartel, and Unilateral Conduct Working Groups, and a host of operational and institutional matters in the Agency Effectiveness Working Group is impressive. This work is available for free on the internet. In addition, conference hosts and the Steering Group regularly take on special projects to address particular matters of interest, such as competition policy in an economic downturn, competition law and policy in small economies, competition issues involving state-owned enterprises, abuse of superior bargaining position, and disruptive innovation.

However, in the same way that all ICN members (NCAs) and NGAs do not have the same influence in the ICN, the ICN does not have a similar influence on all NCAs (and their states). In terms of influence in the ICN, Chapter 1, distinguishes between 'Advanced NCAs' (specially the NCAs from the EU and the USA) and 'New jurisdictions from poor countries' (although it says there is a spectrum here). Advanced NCAs generally have the capacity to get into the debate early and have the necessary expertise and resources to influence and shape ICN activities and work products.[131] They took several constitutional decisions when establishing the ICN that help to preserve the influence of these 'advanced' NCAs and NGAs from their states. Convergence of the competition rules globally helps EU and US firms to expand into new jurisdictions, as they are familiar with the rules. More uniform rules across different states reduces multinational's costs. Being able to influence the ICN work, these 'rule makers' are unlikely to be (much) constrained by its prescriptions, except when they want to be.[132] In fact, they may use the ICN to push for the adoption of ICN work that reflects a change they advocate at home. However, most ICN work does not require advanced NCAs/their states or NGAs, to act much differently from how they already do. Compliance in this case is best explained by a 'coincidence of interest',[133] rather than by the impact of the ICN work. They use the network to export their own regulatory standards to others—the *rule-takers*.

New jurisdictions from poor countries generally lack knowledge, access, and influence in the ICN. The benefits that they seek from their participation in the ICN membership are related to community support, help building a coherent framework, support in confrontation with stakeholders back home and raising their

[131] Ranjit Lall, 'Timing as a Source of Regulatory Influence: A Technical Elite Network Analysis of Global Finance' (2014) Regulation & Governance 125.

[132] Rule-makers may be interested in changing their own national standards and may use the ICN for that. The success of the implementation of the ICN Recommended Practices on Merger Review provides a good example. As seen above a considerable amount of the ICN members implemented the practices even though many of their own merger laws and practices did not conform to the Recommended Practices. ICN, Merger Working Group, ICN Recommended Practices for Merger Notification and Review Procedures, Member Self-Assessment, Report on 2016 Survey Results, 2017. The Recommended Practices were drafted by the ICN's Merger Notification and Procedures Subgroup. Many of the key players in that group, including Germany, Italy, Korea, and Spain, at that time had laws or procedures that did not reflect the Practices.

[133] Jack Goldsmith and Eric Posner, *The Limits of International Law* (OUP 2006) 12.

own esteem there. Though they can use their veto power to stop the adoption of ICN rules that do not match their existing practice, Chapter 1 emphasized many reasons why rule takers may not do that.[134]

Capacity building can also be done bilaterally, by the offer of technical assistance by an ICN member to another one. As discussed in Chapter 1, technical assistance programs give another opportunity for the ICN to influence. First, assistance programs are an additional opportunity to increase pressure from the network. They also help make available to outside actors the amount of implementation of ICN work products actually taking place. Second, technical assistance programs provide access to the newer NCAs, opportunities to engage with their staff and to influence them. Finally, providers of technical support can influence newer NCAs (and their employees) through an (often implicit) threat to withdraw such support if newer NCAs become too critical elsewhere. This probably impacts upon the freedom, actual or imagined, of newer NCAs to criticize or disagree.

Our survey supports this idea that there are *rule-makers* and *rule-takers* within the ICN. A good proxy to understand the impact of the ICN work in the NCAs is the NCAs' perception of how important the ICN work products are. Younger agencies were more likely to answer 'very important' than older agencies. This is compatible with the fact that younger agencies are less institutionalized and therefore use the ICN work to 'catch up' with the older ones.

The survey also identified other factors which are relevant when it comes to the ICN's influence in its members, such as geographical location and number of staff members. African and Asian NCAs address more often national legislators to support changes in the legislation following a recommended practice of the ICN.

2.3 ICN's second-order effects: empowerment of members and strategic use of ICN work product

Newman and Posner argue that soft law (such as ICN work products):

> is more than simply a coordination mechanism deployed to solve global governance challenges and that its political and distributional consequences extend well beyond the first-order effects discussed in existing accounts.[135]

Even when a transnational network's soft law fails to be adopted in a national context, it often still has the potential to disrupt the balance of political authority between competing regulatory factions.[136] To study this they look at how soft law is

[134] See discussion around n 69.
[135] Newman and Posner (n 9) 30.
[136] ibid 10.

wielded by political actors and regulatory factions and how it changes the legitimacy and power of political bodies over time. They argue that international soft law shapes actors' goals, agendas, strategies, resources, and identities and alters the distribution of political winners and losers. Such consequences are not limited to the weak. Soft law's second-order effects have the potential to recast policy battles inside the most powerful jurisdictions and change the way influential industries engage in global and domestic politics.[137] In sum, international soft law does much more than provide focal points that help political actors with common goals to coordinate and otherwise smooth out the bumps of globalization at single points in time; it disrupts and transforms political landscapes and their participants.[138]

Newman and Posner identify two ways soft law can trigger political change: legitimacy claims and arena expansion. First, soft law provides policy entrepreneurs with new political resources for intervening in, influencing and opening-up domestic fights. In areas where competing regulatory fractions struggle to set the policy agenda, 'skilled political actors take advantage of the various forms of legitimacy associated with the bodies that create it'. This may include piggy-backing on the perceived expertise of a body of 'experts' like the ICN, for example, with its claims to operate the state of the art in a politically neutral and non-partisan manner ('neutral technocratic expertise').[139] Policy actors make claims intended to leverage perceptions of (il)legitimacy as they do political battle. For skilful actors, international soft law can offer a resource that helps to disrupt domestic political contests in their favour.[140]

Second, international soft law is politically disruptive because it involves the expansion of contestation to new arenas. Formal international law is achieved though formal negotiations, often by head of states. Soft law, however, is typically the domain of:

> sub-state officials and private actors including national regulators, international bureaucrats, firms and their associates. The making of soft law thus breaks up the state's monopoly of professional diplomats, allows for transnational alliances of like-minded factions across jurisdictions, and expands policy-making to new arenas.[141]

Like the legitimacy claims mechanism, expanding the arena has temporal effects that bring about political change. Powerful actors like states, regulators from

[137] ibid 4.
[138] ibid 5.
[139] ibid.
[140] ibid 5 and 9.
[141] ibid 5. A great example of this from the ICN is the decision to focus on just competition all of the time, which is not what many states have asked their NCAs to do, see the discussion in Section I.3 of the Introduction to this book and also Chapter 1, Section 1.2.1.3 (discussing the EU, for example).

leading markets, and multinational firms and industry associations not only react to and deploy soft law to achieve political ends. They are also shaped by it. Over time, arena expansion contributes to shifts in policy priorities and to the reorganization of regulatory authorities and interest groups. This can ultimately have wide-ranging repercussions for the rules that govern domestic and global markets.[142]

Eduardo Pérez Motta, as chair of the ICN, articulated well this idea second-order effects of the ICN. In his closing remarks of the INC's Eleventh Annual Conference:

> Competition agencies throughout the world frequently face a very basic collective action problem: our constituencies—in essence, the whole economy—are scattered, while the interest groups resisting competition policy tend to be concentrated and quite powerful politically. This means—as we at the [Mexican competition authority] know from first-hand experience - that allies tend to be scarce and less than fully committed.
>
> One should not underestimate the potential influence of 123 agencies speaking with one voice to support one of their own, on the basis of well-founded and time-tested best practices. It could go a long way towards restoring balance to otherwise lopsided domestic debates.[143]

We illustrate the concept with examples of three different kinds of second-order effects. We start by looking at how NCAs can use ICN work products (and their activities within the ICN) to bolster their status at home. This can be useful as it can help to give them the space and time to adopt reforms that they consider appropriate (as well as protecting their independence, with all the benefits that brings). Second, we have an example of one NCA mobilizing ICN structures to support it in an argument with another NCA about the room for different applications of 'national' competition rules. Third, we provide examples of how ICN work products have been used in courts to justify the taking of a decision in one direction or another, and by NCAs to advance their goals.

Let's start with an example from Mexico, showing how an NCA can use ICN work products (and its activities within the ICN) to bolster its status at home. It has been argued that the ICN, and other international organizations, have helped steer political support for the Mexican NCA (the FCC) in its negotiations with domestic political actors.[144] The recommendations of the ICN were influential in shaping the competition law reforms in Mexico as well as the gradual improvements in the FCC's performance, particularly during the time Pérez Motta was chairman. Pérez

[142] ibid 6.

[143] Eduardo Pérez Motta, 'Closing Remarks for the International Competition Network's Eleventh Annual Conference', 4.

[144] Umut Aydin, 'Competition Law and Policy in Mexico: Successes and Challenges' (2016) 79 Law and Contemporary Problems 18 <https://scholarship.law.duke.edu/cgi/viewcontent.cgi?article=4806&context=lcp>.

Motta knew the power of international organizations and how to use them. He had been ambassador to the WTO. As ICN chair he pledged 'to place a particular emphasis' on improving hands-on assistance to members.[145] He argued that the ICN had a direct impact in empowering the Mexican NCA's push for national reforms of the competition law, including cartels investigation and merger review. He said that 'this impact has resulted in substantial improvements in the effectiveness of its [Mexican] competition policy'.[146]Active participation in the ICN leverages perception of the performance of the NCAs. This is relevant, as it is not only NCAs from developing countries that want to be shielded from state intervention. The Global Competition Review, an internationally recognized competition law and policy journal, considers participation in international fora as a relevant factor to consider when evaluating an NCA's annual performance. For example, in the case of the Portuguese NCA, referring to the rating enforcement of 2009, its engagement in the ICN was considered as a reassuring factor in a transitional period of its leadership.[147] This made it harder for the Portuguese state to intervene in the work of its NCA, when it might otherwise have been tempted to do so.

The ICN has also been used by some powerful NCAs to leverage their positions vis-à-vis other powerful NCAs. In 2006, the European Commission published a discussion paper on the application of a core provision of EU competition law (abuse of a dominant position, now in Article 102 TFEU). The Bundeskartellamt was critical of this initiative. The risk here was that the Commission would use the discussion paper as a basis for a Communication on what it considered to be an abuse of dominance and then seek to influence Member States' interpretation of that provision (including Germany). The Bundeskartellamt considered that, given:

> the different views and approaches on the application of Article 82 EC [now Article 102 TFEU] the possible aim of the Commission to use the discussion paper as basis for guidelines on Article 82 EC seems to be quite ambiguous ... the framework for any kind of guidance is the [European] Court of Justice's interpretation of Article 82 EC.[148]

[145] Pérez Motta (n 143) 3.

[146] Pérez Motta (n 69) 219.

[147] The Global Competition Review specifically mentioned that 'the authority maintains excellent ties with other competition enforcement around the world, sources say, it is active member of the OECD and it hosted an ICN cartel workshop'. Mariana Tavares, 'The ICN: One of the Many International Priorities' in Lugard (n 56) 336.

[148] Written Statement of the German Bundeskartellamt and the German Ministry of Economics and Technology on the DG Competition discussion paper on the application of Article 82 of the Treaty to exclusionary abuses, Bonn, 2006, 2, <www.bundeskartellamt.de/SharedDocs/Publikation/DE/Stellungnahmen/Stellungnahme%20-%20On%20the%20Application%20of%20Article%2082%20of%20the%20Treaty%20to%20exclusionary%20abuses.pdf?__blob=publicationFile&v=3> accessed 7 October 2021.

That same year, a new ICN working group on Unilateral Conduct was proposed. After lobbying, the Bundeskartellamt was made a co-chair, together with the US FTC. As discussed in Chapter 1, acting as a chair gives an NCA a lot of opportunity to influence the agenda and direction of a working group.[149] This role served the purposes of the Bundeskartellamt. It was a platform which it could use to show the European Commission (and others) that there are many possible approaches for dealing with the unilateral conduct of dominant firms. While we do not argue that this was the only factor which discouraged the European Commission from a discussion of the substantive rules on Article 102 TFEU, this was part of the Bundeskartellamt's strategy to oppose the European Commission initiative and we think it was important. The European Commission ended up adopting a Communication on Guidance on its *enforcement priorities* in applying Article 82 EC Treaty (ie where it would target its limited resources), rather than substantive guidance on the interpretation of that provision.[150]

Our third example of second-order effects of the ICN, is how ICN work products have been used in courts to justify the taking of a decision in one direction or another. For example, to support his argument for the importance of proof of the possibility of recoupment in predatory pricing cases, AG Mazák referred to, among other things, similar views from the OECD and an ICN survey.[151] Also, in Chile, the Competition Tribunal revealed that when discussing and drafting a decision, the Tribunal says its members study ICN guidelines, along with other relevant legal and economic literature.[152]

ICN documents have also been used in efforts to define what is normal or appropriate in many other situations. For example, in private submissions to state consultations on the possible changes to the national competition rules,[153]

149 'In Phase I, the group would examine the objectives of competition law pertaining to unilateral conduct of dominant firms and the definition and assessment of dominance. In Phase II, the group would examine dominant firm conduct.' ICN, Unilateral Conduct Working Group, Discussion Paper on Initial Work Product and Organization, May 2006.

150 Communication from the Commission, Guidance on the Commission's enforcement priorities in applying Article 82 of the EC Treaty to abusive exclusionary conduct by dominant undertakings (2009/C 45/02).

151 Opinion of AG Mazák in Case C-202/07 P *France Télécom SA v Commission*, EU:C:2008:520, para 75, particularly fn 55 where he says 'For a recent general overview of 35 jurisdictions, see International Competition Network, Report on Predatory Pricing, prepared by Unilateral Conduct Working Group, Presented at the 7th Annual Conference of the ICN, Kyoto, Apr 2008, <https://www.internationalcompetitionnetwork.org/wp-content/uploads/2018/07/UCWG_SR_PredPricing.pdf> accessed 7 October 2021. That said, this is the only reference to ICN work that we can find in EU court judgments and opinions.

152 Francisco Agüero and Santiago Montt, 'Chile—The Competition Law System and the Country's Norms' in Eleanor Fox and Michael Trebilcock (eds), *The Design of Competition Law Institutions: Global Norms, Local Choices* (OUP 2012) 174.

153 Law firms and others often refer to ICN surveys and other work products as a means of pointing to what is 'normal' in other jurisdictions or 'objectively' best practice. This was the case in two responses to a UK government enquiry into reform of its competition system, see for example: <https://assets.publishing.service.gov.uk/government/uploads/system/uploads/attachment_data/file/312063/D-F-competition-regime-for-growth.pdf>; <www.lawscot.org.uk/media/10534/comp-lss-response-to-hol-im-sub-com-brexit-competition-inquiry_sep-17-2.pdf>.

and justifications for considering certain elements in legislative proposals.[154] Concerning the ICN Recommended Practices on Merger Review specifically, the ICN reports that:

> ICN members have also used the Recommended Practices as a stamp of legitimacy for changes the agency wanted to make. Agencies have used the Recommended Practices to convince the legislative body of the soundness of proposed reforms, because they conform to international standards. For example, in Germany, the Practices are cited in official documents for the legislature as a rationale for change. In Ireland, the Competition Authority cited the ICN Recommended Practices in a consultation document on proposed reforms, saying the reforms would make the Irish regime consistent with international standards. Many other agencies, such as those in Belgium, Brazil, Finland, Mexico and Portugal have used the Recommended Practices to promote their reforms with the legislature: for instance, in May 2012, Brazil has introduced a drastic overhaul to its merger regime which now envisages, in line with the ICN practices, a pre-merger notification regime, with a fast track system for non-problematic mergers and new notification thresholds. These and other agencies (e.g., Zambian Competition Commission) have used the Recommended Practices to build support with the private sector as well, by showing how proposed changes would measure up to best practice.[155]

2.4 Conclusion

This chapter has reinforced our argument that the ICN matters, and that what it does has an impact.

We have seen that the ICN's impact on NCAs and their jurisdiction can take the form of both first- and second-order effects. The former refers to attempts by actors within the ICN to incentivize implementation through several tools: promoting measurement of implementation that allows for benchmarking and 'naming and shaming'; setting-up monitoring mechanisms; reinforcing institutions in charge of pushing for implementation. The latter occurs when domestic actors (most notably

[154] For example, justification for the consideration of certain elements in market power assessments in digital markets Commission Staff Working Document Impact Assessment Report Accompanying the document Proposal for a Regulation of the European Parliament and of the Council on contestable and fair markets in the digital sector (Digital Markets Act), SWD(2020) 363, para 73; or the need for confidentiality provisions in cooperation agreements between NCAs, Proposal for a Council Decision on the conclusion of an Agreement between the European Union and the Swiss Confederation concerning cooperation on the application of their competition laws, COM(2012) 245, para 2, similarly, Commission staff working paper accompanying the Communication from the Commission to the European Parliament and Council—Report on the functioning of Regulation 1/2003 {COM(2009)206 final}, SEC(2009) 574, para 307.

[155] ICN (n 130) 18.

NCAs, but also private actors) use ICN membership or work products to advance their goals. Second-order effects prove that even international fora like the ICN, which lack substantive authority and rely on voluntary cooperation, can alter the 'balance of power' domestically.

The ICN's impact helps to preserve the influence of richer NCAs and NGAs—the *rule-makers*, that use the network to export their own regulatory standards to others—the *rule-takers*, or to advocate for domestic changes they support. As the ICN is not neutral in terms of the content of its recommendations, neither it is in the advantages or disadvantages it produces. Chapters 1 and 2 have shown how ICN actors have several instruments in their toolkit for driving a wedge between the interests of NCAs and the interests of their states. As a consequence, it cannot be assumed that an NCA is necessarily acting in what its own state would perceive as the national interest when it agrees to ICN work products (Chapter 1) or when it agrees to implement them at home (Chapter 2).

This is particularly relevant, as this chapter showed that the ICN has shifted its main focus from the production of recommended practices and other work products (which still takes place) towards pushing the implementation of its work products. Implementation has become part of the DNA of the ICN. ICN cooperation is disarmingly aimed at proposing 'superior' standards and procedures in competition policy (by consensus); proposing substantive and procedural convergence (informed diversity); and aiding international cooperation. Depending upon the choices made, welfare is pushed between different groups. This chapter has also shown that, although the ICN explicitly emphasizes NCAs' (and their states') right to informed divergence from ICN work products, it is likely that rather than being a mechanism to accept diversity within the ICN, 'informed divergence' is a powerful and efficient way of controlling and coercing ICN members to converge around ICN standards.

Feedback from the ICN members supports this shift towards an 'implementation focus'. They say that the ICN should '[c]ontinue to aim for convergence'. More convergence is also supported by the NGAs. Many would like the ICN 'to reach greater convergence of national competition laws, practices and procedural rules, as well as more inter-agency cooperation in the future'.[156] NGAs would also like more uniform implementation of the ICN Recommended Practices and other guidance. Yet, there is reason to question how appropriate such choices are. The Introduction to this book highlighted the redistributive nature of competition policy and enforcement. Furthermore, diversity in competition law enforcement has many benefits (not just costs). It is not obvious that the ICN is the right forum for making such choices. Nor is it obvious that the mechanisms of influence highlighted in Chapters 1 and 2 are appropriate for these highly political judgements

[156] ICN (n 54) 39.

(especially, although this depends on the values in the state concerned, where there is a lack of oversight by majoritarian institutions).

The ICN has now entered into its third decade. Its Chair, Mundt, has announced the ICN Third Decade Project, a fundamental review of the ICN's activities. The stakes are high in the battle for the ICN's soul. Chapter 4 investigates the legitimacy, effectiveness, and efficiency of the ICN. Before that, Chapter 3 offers a quantitative analysis of various ICN actors' opinions of how the system works.

3
Measuring interests and influence in the ICN (and of the ICN)
A quantitative analysis

3.1 Introduction

As we have seen in the previous chapters, the ICN is an organization characterized by voluntary membership (national competition authorities participate because they wish to do so, not because they have to), consensus-based decision-making (decisions are made when there is a sufficiently large agreement, so that no member formally opposes the adoption of an ICN work product, such as a recommended practice), and voluntary implementation (NCAs that approve a work product from the ICN are not bound to follow it in their day-to-day activity). Put it in this way, one could even argue that there is little interest in studying such an organization. After all, the ICN does not force its members to do anything. One could even argue that ICN members do what they would do anyway, even if the ICN did not exist.

This relates more broadly to the emergence and increasing diffusion of transnational networks. Why are non-binding prescriptions preferred to binding ones? What are the effects (at national and transnational level) of international soft law? Why do countries comply or fail to comply with these prescriptions? How does international soft law change the behaviour of relevant decision-making actors in the long run? Assuming that the NCAs that promoted the creation of the ICN and the ones that joined the organization afterwards behave somewhat rationally, we must recognize that they did so because they have some goal(s)—something that they thought they would not achieve without the ICN (or not as easily or cheaply). This does not imply that all ICN members have joined the organization for the same reasons and with the same objective, of course. Depending on their power, resources, preferences, different NCAs might expect to obtain different benefits from their membership. In the same fashion, the participation (and influence) in ICN decision-making activities will vary across members, and so will their willingness or ability to implement what is decided.

In the previous chapters, we have analysed the main charactertistics of the ICN's membership and decision-making processes, as well as the impact of its decisions when it comes to implementation. We also looked at the ICN's capacity to influence domestic and cross-border debates on the market rules. In Chapter 1, we have

The Law and Politics of Global Competition. Christopher Townley, Mattia Guidi, and Mariana Tavares, Oxford University Press.
 DOI: 10.1093/oso/9780198859789.003.0004

shown that, despite a formally egalitarian setup, in which all NCAs have the same powers, and consensus-based decision-making, doubts exist regarding the actual power that some members of the ICN can exert over others. Similarly, we have argued that the role of NGAs demands scrutiny, as they are probably more influential than superficial evidence would suggest. In Chapter 2, we have seen that a framework based on voluntary cooperation does not prevent the ICN from actively promoting regulatory convergence among its members. There is evidence that ICN's guidelines are increasingly cited by its members as a source when explaining changes that NCAs have made in their rules of procedure. An aspect to investigate here, which relates directly to the issue of agency autonomy, is to what extent NCAs are free to implement ICN guidelines without passing through democratic checks (national government or parliament).

Thus, on the one hand we have raised questions pertaining to *power* and *influence* within the ICN. These questions imply asking whether some NCAs actually have more power than others, how this power is perceived, how it is exerted, what it is based on, and where it is seen. On the other hand, we have questions pertaining to *implementation* of ICN work products. In this respect, we want to know how much of what the ICN recommends is actually implemented, whether there are differences between different NCAs that explain why some implement more than others (geography? resources?), and ultimately what drives the decision to implement (or to not implement).

The previous two chapters have explored these issues using documentary sources. In this chapter, we seek to complement the evidence illustrated before with quantitative analyses of data coming from an anonymous survey that we administered to members of NCAs and NGAs participating in the ICN in 2018. In this survey, we asked respondents a series of questions related to influence and power on the one hand, and implementation on the other. It is worth stressing that, for all the questions asked in our survey, we assume the respondents' answers were overall correct[1]—ie we did not check the factual accuracy of all responses. In some cases, it would have been possible but impractical (for instance, checking how many staff members in a NCA regularly deal with the ICN, or whether each NCA implemented, or did not implement, a given recommended practice, as declared in the survey); in other cases, it would have just been impossible, as many questions refer to *perceptions* of influence, or of what matters, according to the respondents, in making some agencies more powerful than others.

In this chapter, we will try to identify the perceived benefits ICN participants obtain from membership, what they find more useful and whether and how their influence varies (despite the consensus requirement, noted above). We do not expect all ICN members to have the same influence, and we want to investigate who

[1] Statistically speaking, we assume that the error (the difference between what we measure and reality) is randomly distributed, and does not affect our estimation.

is more influential, and why. On the other hand, we want to assess the impact of ICN decision-making: what is demanded of members? Who implements more and why?

Our results show that several factors (such as geographical location, staff size, institutionalization and length of ICN membership) explain to a large extent the variation of both different NCAs' level of influence within the ICN and their implementation of ICN work products. For example, some NCAs report being more actively involved in determining the content of ICN recommended practices, while others participate mainly for networking and to acquire expertise. Our main conclusion, which we document in detail in the following sections, is that ICN members can be divided in two groups: *rule-makers* and *rule-takers*. The former are the most experienced and staffed NCAs, which can greatly shape the content of the ICN recommended practices. These agencies *upload* their rules and practices at the ICN level and, in doing so, they *export* these rules and practices to other jurisdictions. The latter, the *rule-takers*, are agencies that lack the resources, the connections, and the expertise to effectively shape the ICN's outcomes. Therefore, the main benefit of membership for them is acquiring expertise and socializing with more prestigious NCAs. In the remainder of this chapter, we first explain how we measure influence and implementation. Then, we describe how we collected the data. Subsequently, we show the main results of the data analysis, focusing on some factors (geographical location, number of staff members, number of staff members dealing with the ICN, seniority in the ICN) that help us highlight differences between NCAs.

3.2 Influence within the ICN and implementation of ICN work products: definitions and measurement

In this section, we detail how we define and measure the main concepts whose interaction we want to test with our survey. We start by listing the factors that may explain why influence and implementation vary among members (Section 3.2.1) and then we illustrate the variables measuring the phenomena that we want to explain (Section 3.2.2).

3.2.1 What explains influence in the ICN and the likelihood of a state implementing ICN work products?

Before we started collecting and analysing data, we asked ourselves which of the theoretical puzzles we identified in the previous section could have been addressed with survey data. We can start by noting that, for obvious reasons, none of the hypotheses that relate to the long-term effects of the establishment and institutionalization of the ICN can be analysed with a survey like ours. The data that we collected is a snapshot, that is, it gives us information about facts, practices and perceptions relating to the specific time (the summer of 2018) in which it was gathered. Some questions, as we will see in the remainder of this chapter, reveal information that refers to events that happened before the data collection, but, in any case, the survey is not a tool primarily designed to assess whether some things have changed or evolved through time.

That said, the survey contains a lot of useful information. It lets us appreciate differences in the way NCAs and NGAs participate in the ICN. As regards NCAs, we can analyse the impact of several background factors[2] on a series of variables that, from different angles, aim to measure influence within the ICN. Let us see these factors.

One important aspect we look at is the *geographic location* of NCAs. Of course, we cannot posit that differences are due to a country's position *per se*, but rather to being embedded in an area that is characterized by certain political, legal and economic institutions. The importance of market and competition, the evolution and enforcement of economic rights like private property, the level of economic development, the presence of supranational institutions (like the European Union) that foster some principles—all of these variables can play a role.

Another factor that we analyse is the *number of staff members* of NCAs. This is a rather accurate proxy for the size of the authority. A big authority is often more important, more powerful, more institutionalized than a small one. This applies to the domestic environment, but also to the international one. Bigger authorities are more likely to have more staff that can prepare documents, proposals, and lobby for them in an international arena like the ICN. Also, they may have more capacity to carry out research and training on their staff, with obvious spillover effects.

Together with size, we can also assess the impact of the degree of institutionalization. As a proxy for institutionalisation we use the *number of years since the NCA was established* (ie the life of the NCA). There are numerous contributions from various disciplines that show how bureaucratic institutions tend to grow and stabilize over time,[3] and on how political institutions are 'sticky' and benefit from

[2] These factors, in the language of social sciences, are what can be called 'independent variables'. With this term, social scientists mean that such variables cannot be affected by others on which they may have an impact. For instance, we can hypothesize that geographic location has an impact on perceived influence within the ICN, meaning that NCAs from some areas of the world perceive themselves as more influential. If we find that NCAs from a certain area perceive themselves as less influential than NCAs from another area, we can be confident that the difference is due to the factor we are exploring (geographic location), and that the direction of causality is the one hypothesized. Indeed, while it is possible that geographic location either affects perceived influence or it does not, it is certainly not possible that perceived influence affects geographic location.

[3] WA Niskanen, *Bureaucracy and Representative Government* (Aldine, Atherton 1971); WA Niskanen, *Bureaucracy: Servant or Master?: Lessons from America* (Institute of Economic Affairs 1973).

increasing returns.[4] For the purpose of this analysis, suffice it to say that authorities that were established earlier in time have higher chances of having developed the political and diplomatic skills that allow them to better promote their interests, especially in environments like the ICN, in which informal power is key.

Finally, we cannot avoid considering the *length of ICN membership*, measured as the time passed since a certain NCA joined the ICN. There is no need to repeat what has been said above regarding the effect of time and institutionalization. Let us just add that in a relatively 'young' organization like the ICN this impact could be particularly significant. On top of that, there is no doubt that a decisive role has been played by the NCAs that have actively participated in shaping the organization from the very beginning. And among the oldest members, the agencies that created the structure and the 'constitution' of the ICN are probably the most influential, even today. In general, older members of the ICN have a much higher chance of being rule-makers rather than rule-takers, compared to NCAs that have joined more recently.[5]

As regards NGAs, our survey is less systematic in investigating their influence in the ICN. On the one hand, because we have less precise information about who they are; on the other, because their participation and role is, if possible, even more informal than that of NCAs. NGAs are not members of the ICN; they do not participate in decisions; they do not hold chairs. However, we are interested in knowing more about why they participate. What is valid for NCAs (if there were no advantage in participating, they would not participate) is true for NGAs too. Evidently, NGAs get something out of their participation, be it information, networking capacity, or ability to influence the outcome of ICN work products. Our survey aims to elucidate these aspects too.

3.2.2 How can we measure influence within the ICN and implementation of its work products?

In Section 3.4, we will seek to test the impact of the factors illustrated above (geographic location, number of staff members, institutionalization, length of ICN membership) on a series of variables that may signal how authorities perceive influence, participation and compliance in the ICN. These factors, derived from questions asked in our survey, can be divided in two groups, which are meant to answer the two broad questions recalled at the beginning of this chapter: first, what generates influence in the ICN, and second, what influences more or less

[4] BD Jones, T Sulkin and HA Larsen, 'Policy Punctuations in American Political Institutions' (2003) 97 American Political Science Review 151; P Pierson, 'Increasing Returns, Path Dependence, and the Study of Politics' (2000) 94 American Political Science Review 251.

[5] Section 3.4.1 presents an overview of these factors.

implementation in the ICN. A full list of all questions asked in the survey is available in the Appendix.

To measure influence, we mainly rely on the following questions.[6] First, we look at the number of people that an NCA normally allocates for dealing with the ICN and its related activities. Our expectation is that NCAs having more people dealing with the ICN will have more influence on the selection (and content) of ICN activities and work products (such as recommended practices).[7] A third variable measuring influence is what we could define as the degree of engagement with the ICN, measured with the question 'How often is your competition authority in touch (at a distance or at conferences) with other ICN participants for ICN-related issues?' Here again, the expectation is that, all else equal, being in touch more often leads to more influence.[8] We also have a series of questions that measure how useful each NCA perceives certain ICN activities or work products to be. Although we cannot link these variables directly to influence, we can infer that NCAs that find certain ICN activities and work products particularly useful are likely to be rule-takers rather than rule-makers. Finally, we have a series of questions that more explicitly asked about perceptions of influence exerted in the ICN: we asked whether respondents perceive that some NCAs are more influential than others and what this influence is due to in their view.

To measure implementation, we use several variables too.[9] The first one is the answer to the question 'How often does your competition authority address national legislators to support changes in the legislation following a recommendation from the ICN?'. There are a few reasons why an NCA might not address its national legislators in these circumstances: the ICN norm might already be part of its rules (rule-makers often seek to push their own rules to save costs, see above); it might be able to follow the ICN norm without legislative change (competition rules are often widely drafted, leaving lots of discretion to NCAs); or the NCA might not be in favour of following the ICN norm (either in itself or because it has other priorities). Nonetheless, while accounting for these other possibilities, we consider addresses by NCAs to their national legislators to be a good proxy of commitment in following ICN work products. A second variable, which measures the importance attached to implementing ICN recommended practices, is the answer to the question whether lack of compliance undermines an NCA's reputation within the

6 For an overview of the responses to these questions, see Section 3.4.2.

7 We must acknowledge that our question referred generically to 'people'. For example, we did not ask respondents to quantify the full-time equivalent units employed in the NCA in general or dealing with the ICN on a regular basis. Such calculations would have been difficult to make for many respondents, and we were concerned that they would affect the response rate. We preferred to have more responses with an approximate measure than fewer more precise ones (knowing that the accuracy of the FTE calculations could have been questioned too).

8 Not all contacts with other ICN members are equal, of course, and it might be that some NCAs are often in touch with a 'proactive' attitude while others that are often in touch with ICN members take a more 'passive' stance.

9 For an overview of the responses to these questions, see Section 3.4.3.

ICN. Our expectation is that those authorities that see lack of compliance as problematic are those that are more willing to comply with ICN work products. Finally, we included four questions in our survey that asked NCAs about their implementation of specific recommended practices regarding procedural, substantive and institutional aspects in core areas of competition policy and enforcement: cartels, unilateral conduct and mergers. The recommendations on which we asked about NCAs' compliance were:

- the use of 'markers' in leniency applications—a procedural tool conceived to facilitate both national and cross-border cartel investigtions;[10]
- the presence in the NCA of staff dedicated to digital evidence gathering—an institutional aspects regarding cutting-edge evidence gathering technics employed to uncover and investigate competition law infringement;[11]
- the criteria used to assess a dominant position in a market—a substantive aspect of unilateral conduct laws;[12]
- the criteria on which mandatory notification thresholds are based—a procedural aspect with substantive implications regarding mergers control.[13]

For each of these ICN recommended practices, we gave respondents the reference to the specific manual or recommended practices and we asked whether the NCA had implemented it or not. On top of that, we asked to those which had

[10] The introductory text of the survey (see Appendix of this book) read as follows: 'The ICN Anti Cartel Enforcement Manual (at p. 12) states that "It is good practice to use markers in the leniency application process". A marker system:

> under a leniency policy is a means for leniency applicants to reserve their place in the queue for a defined period of time whilst they conduct further internal investigations and attempt to perfect their application for leniency prior to the competition agency determining the first eligible leniency applicant. Markers are often sought and granted with initially incomplete information or evidence provided by the leniency applicant'.

[11] The introductory text read as follows: 'The ICN Anti Cartel Enforcement Manual (at p. 33) establishes that '[i]t is good practice: to have a dedicated internal organisation or staff capacity to undertake digital evidence gathering'.'

[12] The introductory text read as follows: 'The ICN recommended practices on "Dominance/Substantial market power analysis pursuant to unilateral conduct laws" (at p. 2) state that "[a]gencies should use a sound analytical framework firmly grounded in economic principles in determining whether dominance/substantial market power exists. [...] Properly assessing whether a firm possesses dominance/substantial market power, is a complex and multi-faceted analysis".'

[13] The introductory text read as follows: 'The "ICN Recommended Practices for Merger Notification and Review Procedures" (at p. 6) state that: "[m]andatory notification thresholds should be based on objectively quantifiable criteria. [...] Examples of objectively quantifiable criteria are assets and sales (or turnover). Examples of criteria that are not objectively quantifiable are market share and potential transaction-related effects. Market share-based tests and other criteria that are inherently subjective and fact-intensive may be appropriate for later stages of the merger control process (e.g., determining the scope of information requests or the ultimate legality of the transaction), but such tests are not appropriate for use in making the initial determination as to whether a transaction requires notification".'

implemented *how* they had done so, and to those which had not implemented *why* they had not.

3.3 Data and descriptive statistics

In this section, we illustrate the dataset that we employ for our empirical analysis, and we also present some descriptive statistics drawn from our data, which were collected with a survey conducted between May and September 2018 among ICN participants, both members of NCAs and NGAs. The survey was sent out to 1,480 email addresses, in three waves (May, July, and August). In total, 145 responses were collected, of which 74 are from NCAs, 68 are current NGAs, and three were NGAs in the past.

The survey was divided into several sections. Some sections contained questions that were only posed to NCAs, others contained questions that were only posed to NGAs; some sections were submitted to both NCAs and NGAs. At the beginning of the survey, we collected general information about the respondents. For NCAs, this included questions about the year the NCA was established, the territory in which it operates, the year in which the authority joined the ICN, and the number of staff members that the authority employs for competition enforcement.[14] For NGAs, general information sought included whether the respondent was an NGA in the past or whether it is currently an NGA, the type of NGA (to be selected from a list including law firm, academia, consumer organization, big or small business, etc), the country in which the NGA is based and the number of years the NGA has participated in the ICN.

One important statistical issue with every survey concerns the extent to which the sample is representative of the population. In our case, we have indeed two samples (NCAs and NGAs) taken from two distinct populations (all the members of the ICN, and all the NGAs participating in ICN activities, respectively). If the general characteristics of the sample differ too much from those of the population, the survey cannot provide useful information about the population—which is what we ultimately want. Since some types of respondents are more likely to answer questionnaires than others (for example, one might think that well-staffed NCAs are more likely to have the time to answer surveys), this is a fairly common problem. The way in which researchers conducting surveys usually deal with this issue is by building *weights* for the observations in the dataset.

[14] We asked this question instead of a generic one about the number of personnel because several NCAs in our sample also have other (non-competition) functions, like regulation of specific sectors (energy, telecommunications, etc). In cases like these, the total number of staff members would have given a biased figure of what we are interested in.

Each respondent is assigned a weight that is lower than one if that type of respondent is *over-represented* in the survey, and greater than one if that type of respondent is *under-represented*.[15]

To build our weights for NCAs, we used two variables: geographical area (the continent in which the authority is located) and the level of economic development of the country in which the authority is based (measured through GDP per capita). Since we know how these variables are distributed in the population, we can compare the survey's distribution to the population's distribution and build weights accordingly.[16] Unfortunately, we cannot do the same with NGAs, because we do not have a list of all NGAs (the ICN does not publish this information which, in itself, raises concerns); in other words, we do not know the population of NGAs. For this reason, observations referring to NGAs are not weighted (ie their weight is equal to 1). To the best of our knowledge, however, the geographic distribution of NGAs in our sample matches the actual distribution quite closely.

3.3.1 Background factors

As concerns the number of staff members that NCAs employ for competition enforcement, we observe a considerable variation. While one authority from North America reports more than 1,100 staff members dealing with competition enforcement, some small NCAs report only three staff members for the same task (admittedly to regulate a smaller economy). If we exclude NCAs from North America and Oceania, for which the number of respondents does not provide a representative sample, we can calculate the mean number of staff members for each continent. In this respect, we have fairly similar numbers in Europe (102 staff members reported on average), Asia (101), and Central and South America (99). African NCAs appear to have the least staff (most of them are probably understaffed, according to our data), with an average number of staff members of 53.

The geographic distribution of respondents, grouped by continents,[17] is shown in Figure 3.1. We can notice some differences between NCAs and NGAs. In particular, for several continents, there is an evident disproportion between the number of NGAs and the number of NCAs. Take North America for example, which, in terms of number of respondents, has 4 per cent in NCAs and 25 per cent

[15] For instance, in our survey NCAs from Asia are significantly under-represented, and so are (although to a lesser extent) NCAs from North America and Oceania. Similarly, NCAs from countries with a low GDP per capita are slightly under-represented in our sample.

[16] We calculated weights and then 'capped' them to range between 0.3 and 3.

[17] We have intentionally split respondents from America into Northern American and Central and Southern Americans.

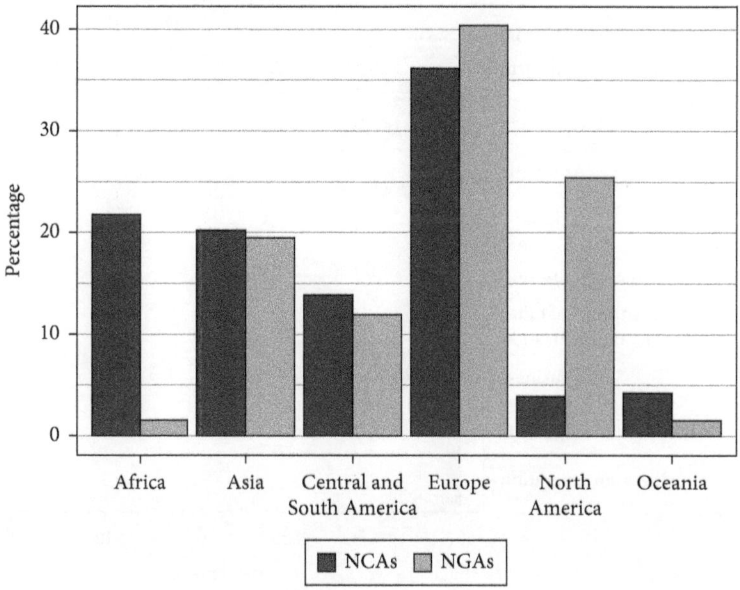

Figure 3.1 Geographic distribution of NCAs and NGAs

in NGAs. Africa shows instead a reversed proportion—22 per cent of NCAs and only 1.5 per cent of NGAs. Other continents have instead a roughly similar proportion in both groups. Europe is the continent that is most represented in our sample, having almost 40 per cent of the total number of respondents. In terms of possible influence on the debates and discussions taking place within the ICN, these distributions suggest that some continents are over-represented when it comes to NGAs' participation (notably North America), while others like Africa are under-represented.

We also collated information about the background of NGAs. This is quite varied. As we can see in Figure 3.2, law firms are the largest 'providers' of NGAs in the ICN, followed by big business employees and academics. Other categories are less represented.

Another interesting descriptive statistic that we can analyse is the average value of NGAs' answers to the question 'For how many years have you been an NGA?'. Excluding continents from which we have only one NGA responding (Africa and Oceania) there do not seem to be substantial differences among Asia (7.38), Central and South America (8.14), Europe (7.07) and North America (6.41). Similarly, we can look at the average length of ICN membership for NCAs. Here substantial differences emerge. The continent with the highest average length of membership is, as was easy to expect, North America (17 years), followed by Europe (13.4 years), Central and South America (11.5 years), Asia (10.6 years), and Africa (7.7 years).

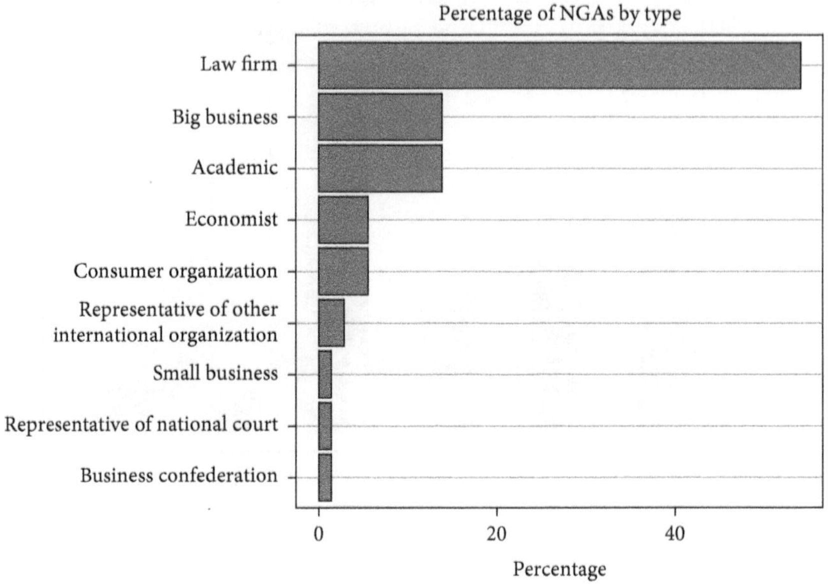

Figure 3.2 Percentage of NGAs by type

For the purpose of identifying which geographical areas are more or less influential on the ICN activities, we propose a summary index of 'continental relevance' derived from these statistics. The index is a combination of:

- mean length of ICN membership for NCAs from a certain continent (the higher the length of ICN membership, the higher the relevance);
- mean number of years NGAs from a certain continent have participated in the ICN (the higher the number of years, the higher the relevance);
- percentage of NCAs participating in the ICN from a certain continent (the higher the number, the higher the relevance);
- percentage of NGAs participating in the ICN from a certain continent (the higher the number, the higher the relevance).[18]

The results of this exercise are shown in Table 3.1, which ranks the continents from the most to the least influential based on the indicators proposed above.[19] As we can see, Europe appears to be the continent with the highest presence, followed

[18] These percentages are calculated as the ratio between the number of NGAs from a certain continent, based on our dataset, and the total number of NGAs present in our dataset.

[19] The index has been calculated as follows. The four variables have been normalized to have mean equal to 0 and standard deviation equal to 1. Then, the mean of these variables has been calculated. The resulting index has been rescaled to range between 0 and 1.

by North America. Asia and Central and South America are in the middle of this ranking. Oceania and Africa appear to be last continents on this scale.

Table 3.1 Relevance of geographic areas within the ICN

Continent	Mean length of ICN membership (NCAs)	Mean number of years of participation (NGAs)	Percentage of NGAs participating	Percentage of NCAs participating	Summary index
Europe	13.5	7.07	40.3	36.24	1
North America	17	6.41	25.4	3.86	0.52
Asia	11.4	7.38	19.4	20.18	0.48
Central and South America	10.8	8.14	11.9	13.85	0.36
Oceania	1	15	1.49	4.19	0.08
Africa	8.27	2	1.49	21.67	0

Note: Continents are ranked from the most to the least influential, according to the index.

3.3.2 Variables measuring influence in the ICN

We now turn to some descriptive statistics regarding the variables that we employ to measure influence within the ICN. In Figure 3.3 we show the distribution of responses for the number of staff members and also the number of staff members dealing with the ICN reported by each authority. As we can see, in terms of total number of staff members there are two big 'outliers' with much more personnel than all the others. In terms of staff members dealing regularly with the ICN, the differences are less striking, but still notable. The majority of NCAs reported a number between one and six, but some respondents report higher numbers. From this figure we deduce that only a few people in most authorities regularly interact with the ICN. Not many NCAs can afford to have a lot of employees dedicated to this task. It is very likely that NCAs with a lot of staff dedicated to the ICN are more influential than average on ICN activities.

Similarly, we see in Figure 3.4 that most authorities get in touch with the ICN a few times a year, while much fewer do so on a monthly or even a weekly basis. This suggests a 'divide' between a small group of very active members and a majority of less engaged ones.

One survey question asked how important NCAs find ICN work products. We then had more specific questions concerning working groups and ICN products and practices. From the responses to the general question, which asked to assign importance on a scale going from 1 ('Not important at all') to 5 ('Very important'), we can conclude that most authorities find ICN work products very important: 89 per cent responded 4 or 5, while only 11 per cent responded 2 or 3 (none responded 1). This does not explain *why* an NCA finds ICN work products important, of course. An NCA that uses the ICN to export its own norms and another NCA that needs help importing others' norms, might both have answered 'very important' to this question. We unpack these issues in more detail below.

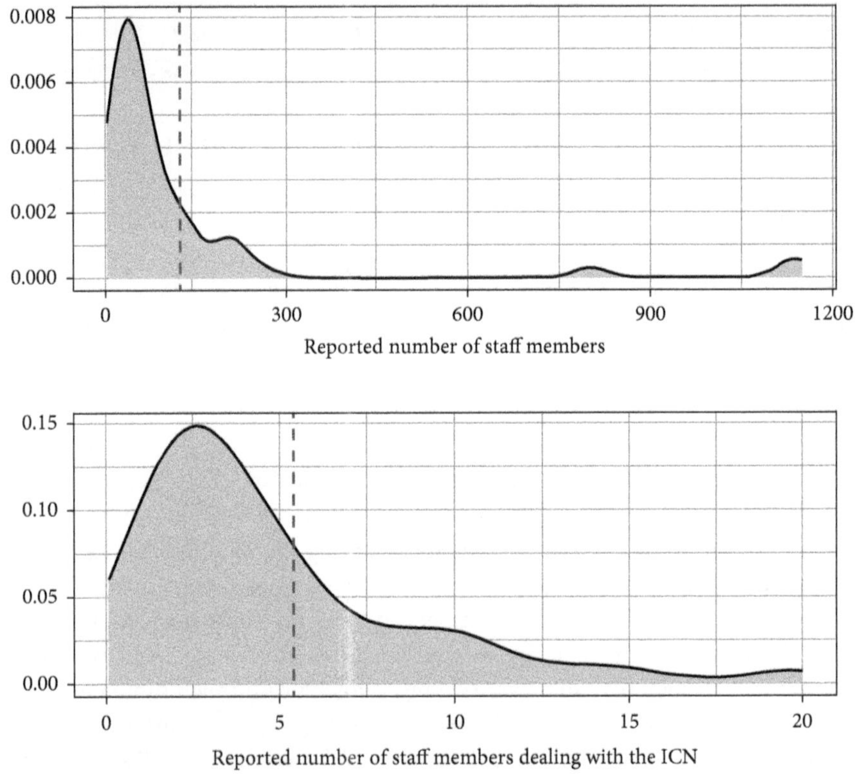

Figure 3.3 Distribution of the responses for the number of staff members and the number of staff members dealing with the ICN
Note: Dashed vertical lines represent the average values

For the more specific questions on ICN working groups (see Figure 3.5), we see that these are generally regarded as important by NCAs. Two working groups that 'stand out' with higher 'percieved importance', namely the Cartel and the Merger Working Groups; although we do not observe particular differences among the other working groups in terms of perceived importance. The working group with the lowest perceived importance is the Agency Effectiveness Working Group.

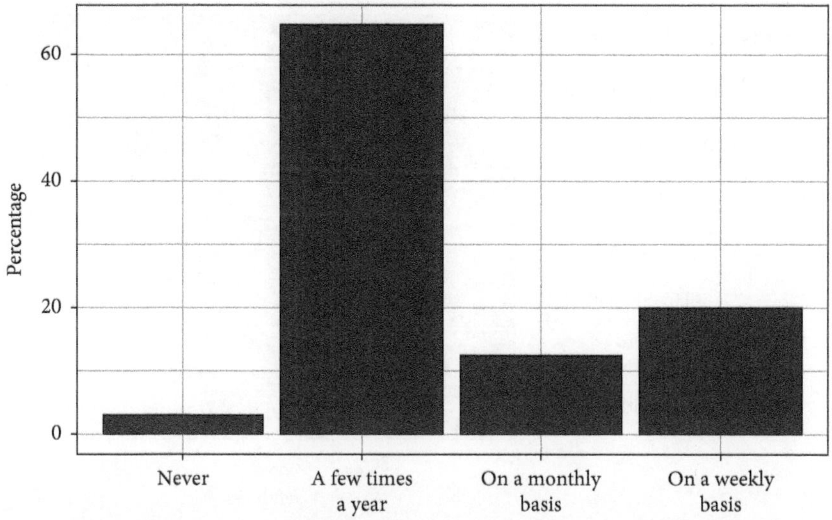

Figure 3.4 Distribution of the responses for the question 'How often is your competition authority in touch (at a distance or at conferences) with other ICN participants for ICN-related issues?'

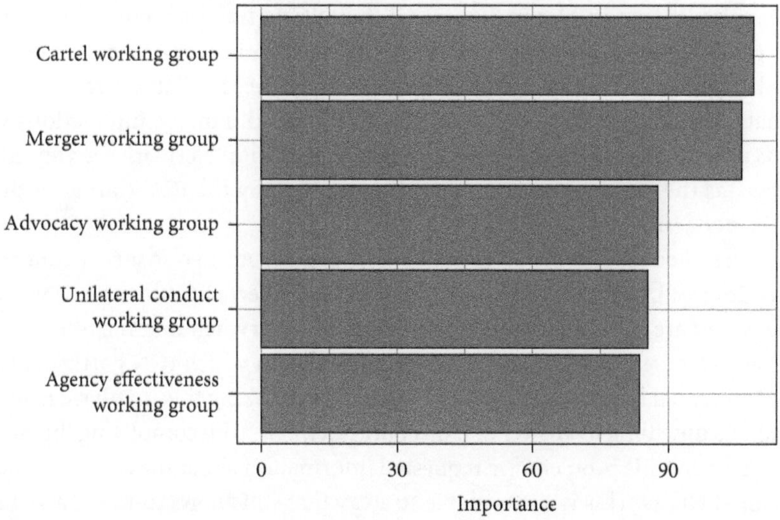

Figure 3.5 Distribution of the responses for the variables 'For your authority, how important are the following ICN working groups?'

Looking again more in detail, an interesting battery of questions in our survey regarded the degree to which NCAs found certain publications or exchanges useful for their activities. We provided a list of activities and asked respondents to give each of them a score going from 1 ('Not useful') to 5 ('Very useful').

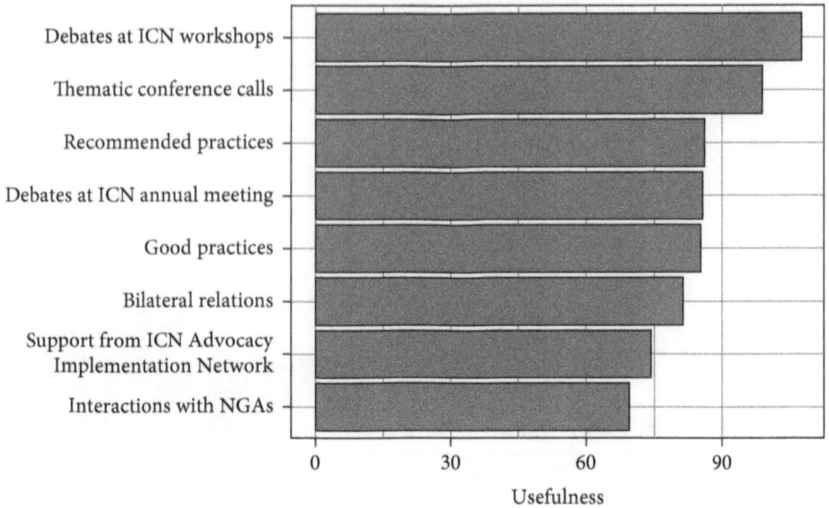

Figure 3.6 Distribution of the responses for the variables 'To what extent does your competition authority find the following publications or exchanges useful for its activities?'

The results, shown in Figure 3.6, reveal that NCAs find particularly useful, on average, debates held at the ICN annual meeting and workshops, closely followed by good practices and recommended practices. Bilateral relations and thematic conference calls are found to be less useful. Finally, interactions with NGAs and support from the Advocacy Implementation Network are viewed, on average, as the least useful opportunities provided by the ICN (but even this is over 70 per cent).

A series of questions, posed to both NCAs and NGAs, in our survey concerned perceptions of influence within the ICN and what affects it. When asked whether some NCAs are more influential than others, an overwhelming majority (96 per cent) answers 'yes'.[20] While we were also interested in which ICN participants are more influential than others, we feared that directly asking this may have made respondents unwilling to answer and discouraged them from completing the survey. To circumvent this problem, we requested information about the *characteristics* of influential NCAs. This is a reasonable strategy that still allows us to identify a sort of 'profile' of influential NCAs. The responses to these questions are illustrated in Figure 3.7. Expertise is deemed to be more important than anything else (more important than resources, notably) when it comes to making an NCA influential. Resources are the second most important factor. The two other factors, according

[20] Notably, all of the NGAs responded 'yes'.

to our respondents, are less relevant: duration of ICN membership and the ability to address colleagues in their own language. Most respondents only see them as moderately important in determining influence.

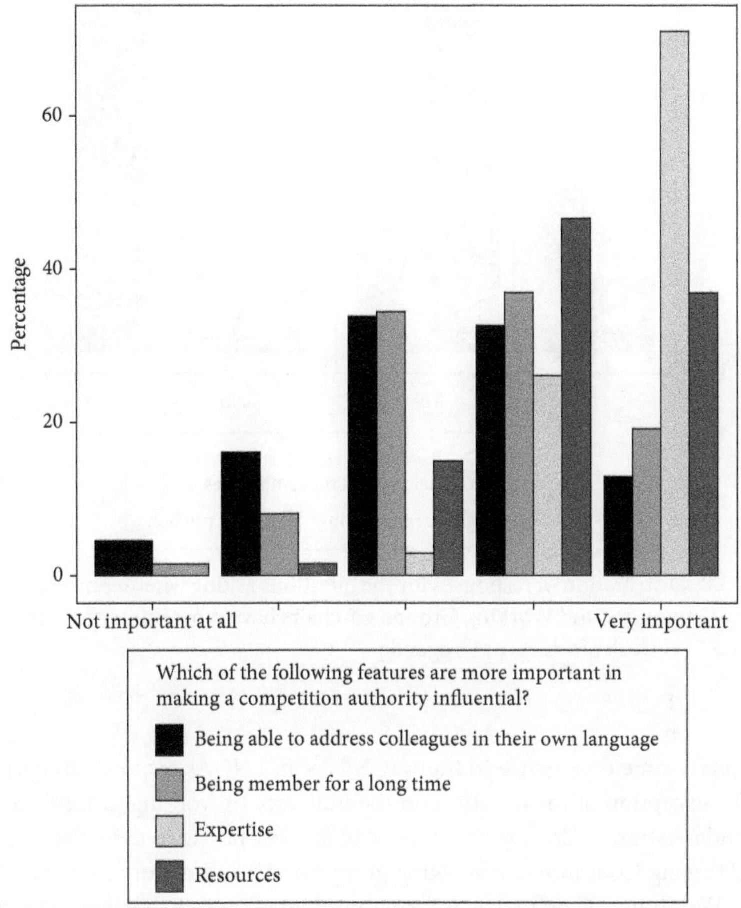

Figure 3.7 Distribution of the responses for the variables 'Which of the following features are more important in making a competition authority influential?'

Another group of questions asked more specifically about the influence exerted by authorities sitting in the Steering Committee or acting as co-chairs in working groups on ICN work products and more generally on the ICN's agenda. The results presented in Figure 3.8 show that, overall, authorities holding these roles are perceived by a large majority as more influential than ordinary members. This influence is perceived as higher in agenda-setting than in the drafting of ICN work products, and there do not seem to be notable differences between the percieved influence of the members of the two groups. It is worth noting that in these questions

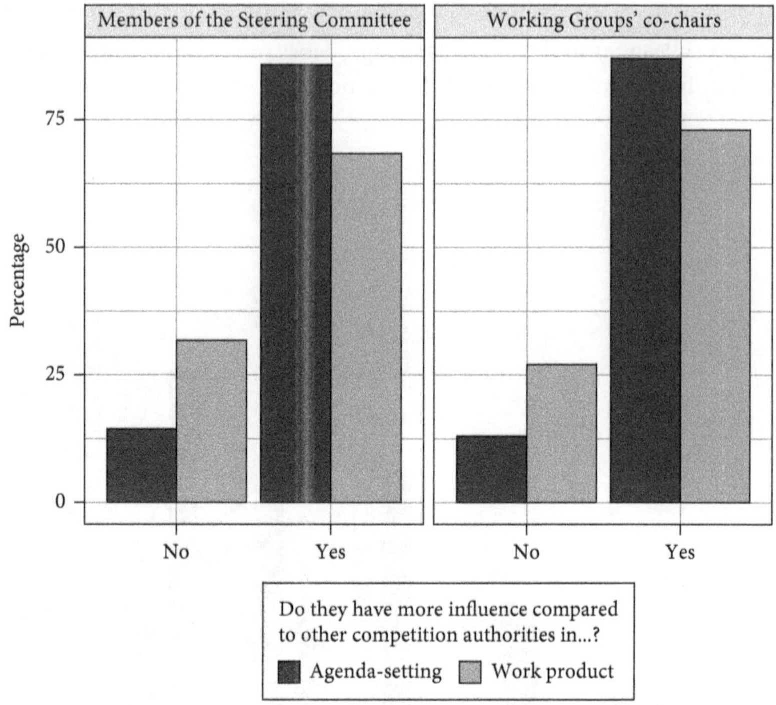

Figure 3.8 Distribution of responses for the questions asking whether members of the Steering Committee and Working Groups' co-chairs have more influence than other NCAs on ICN work products or its agenda

we observe some divergence in the way NCAs and NGAs respond. In particular, with the exception of the question on the influence of working groups' co-chairs on agenda-setting, NCAs are more likely to answer 'no' (ie to deny that members of the Steering Committee or working group co-chairs are more influential) than NGAs. We do not have further information that allows us to speculate more on this finding, but it might be that NGAs (which are external observers) are more 'outspoken' than NCAs (which might show some self-restraint when judging the influence of their colleagues).

Finally, we investigated the extent to which authorities push for the adoption of common standards. According to 78 per cent of the respondents, some NCAs do so (22 per cent disagreed). We went further by asking whether some authorities ever pushed for the adoption of *their own* standards. To this question, 50 per cent responded 'yes' and 50 per cent responded 'no'. So, it seems that the adoption of common standards is something for which NCAs exert pressure in the ICN, but there is no clear perception that this takes place in favour of one authority's own regulatory practices. Besides, even in the cases in which this occurs, most respondents perceive that NCAs do so because it is in the general interest (70 per cent) and not because there was a preference of domestic actors in this direction (30 per cent). These responses give the general impression of an organization in which decision-making is rather consensual. Perhaps respondents' perceptions (such as that NCAs push their own rules when this is in the general interest) are correct. However, it may also be an example of how powerful (and successful) the discourse of the powerful NCAs (the rule-makers) in the ICN is. Have they persuaded others that they are purely motivated by expertise, rather than the 'politics' of favouring firms and other stakeholders from their own jurisdiction (as discussed in Chapter 1)? If so, this has likely been a remarkably successful strategy. As we shall see below, these perceptions are strongly affected by the NCA's characteristics.

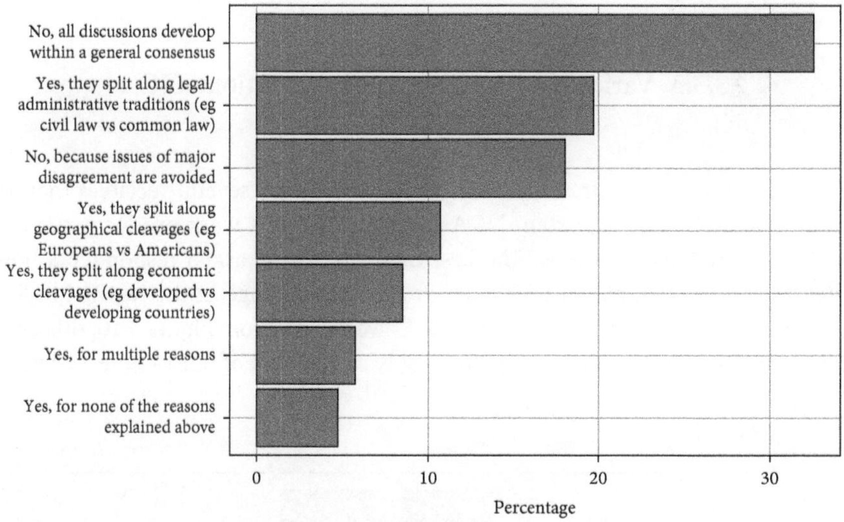

Figure 3.9 Distribution of responses for the question 'Do competition authorities openly disagree among themselves within the ICN?'

Having said that, responses to the question about whether NCAs openly disagree among themselves within the ICN confirm a mixed picture, as can be observed in Figure 3.9. Overall, 49 per cent of respondents stated that they do not perceive open disagreement in discussions and debates in the ICN, while the remaining 51 per cent answered that they observed such disagreement. Unpacking the answers, we can see that, among those reporting that NCAs openly disagree among themselves, the most frequent cleavage seems to be the legal tradition, followed by geographical and economic cleavages.

In sum, NCAs engage in ICN decision-making with different endowments, especially in terms of dedicated personnel. Also, there are notable differences between authorities that are more and less active: most of them interact with ICN activities only sporadically. Most work products and activities are considered useful, but some are not—interaction with NGAs in particular. In this respect, it would be interesting to investigate whether such interaction could be improved. When it comes to perceived influence, there is a clear indication that some authorities have a greater impact on ICN activities than most of the other members, and the perception is that this is due mainly to expertise and resources. Being members of the Steering Committee and co-chairing Working Groups' also seems important (as Chapter 1 explained, appointments to these positions also purportedly takes account of an NCA's expertese and resources). Those positions allow a high degree of influence on ICN products and agenda-setting. Decision-making is mainly consensual but only to a certain extent: there are authorities that push for their own standards at the expense of others', and there are splits across several types of cleavages.

3.3.3 Variables measuring implementation of ICN work products

As we have already illustrated in Section 3.2.2, there are several variables that we used to measure to what extent NCAs implement ICN's work products, such as ICN recommended practices. The first that we analyse asked respondents how often they address national legislators to request a change in the legislation following a recommendation from the ICN. As we can see from Figure 3.10, this does not seem to be a very common practice: only 21 per cent of our sample answered

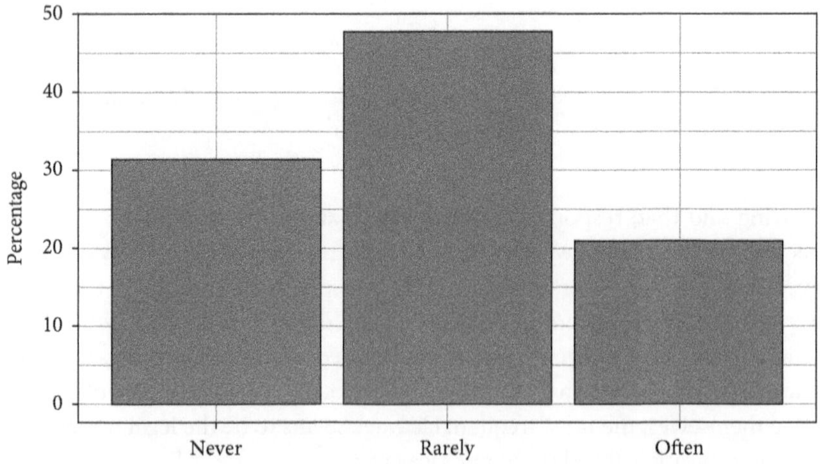

Figure 3.10 Distribution of responses for the question 'How often does your competition authority address national legislators to support changes in the legislation following a recommendation from the ICN?'

'often'; 48 per cent reported that they do so rarely, and 31 per cent that they never do so. From such data, one could conclude that what gets recommended in the ICN almost never reaches national policymaking. Yet, we cannot infer too much from this information. As a matter of fact, a relevant part of the implementation (as we shall see below) does not require changes in legislation. Also, some authorities might address legislators rarely because they have succesfully transformed their domestic standards into ICN recommended practices: therefore, they do not need to change their legislation because their legislation already incorporates what is recommended.

The importance NCAs attribute to lack of compliance with ICN's recommended practices seems to corroborate the impression derived from the previous variable. Looking at Figure 3.11, we can observe that only 21 per cent of the respondents think that lack of compliance undermines an NCAs' reputation 'a lot'; 32 per cent think it does so 'only slightly'; 47 per cent think that not implementing recommended practices yields no reputational damage whatsoever. Again, this picture casts some doubts on how faithfully and effectively NCAs implement ICN's recommended practices and, above all, on how seriously they take them. Although this variable does not tell us exactly how much is implemented, it is unlikely that NCAs answering 'no' to this question have implementation of ICN's recommended practices as their priority. The next variables, which provide information on concrete recommendations to be implemented, help to clarify these issues.

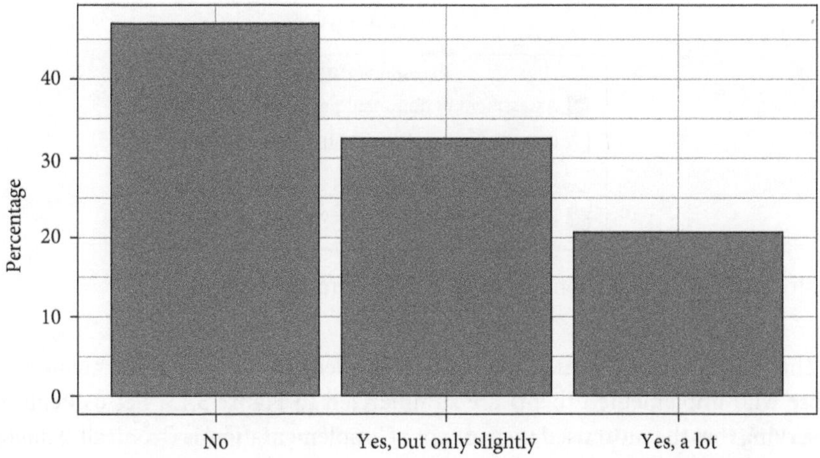

Figure 3.11 Distribution of responses for the question 'Does a lack of compliance with ICN's recommendations undermine a competition authority's reputation?'

As was explained in Section 3.2.2, we asked NCAs if they had implemented four specific ICN recommended practices. Figure 3.12 shows that the degree to which these recommended practices were implemented varies considerably. Two of them (the recommended practice on the use of 'markers' in leniency applications and the one on the objective criteria for mandatory merger notification thresholds) have been implemented by a majority of NCAs (72 per cent and 67 per cent respectively), and two recommended practices (the one on digital evidence gathering and the one on the assessment of dominant positions in the market) were implemented by 38 per cent and 24 per cent of our sample.

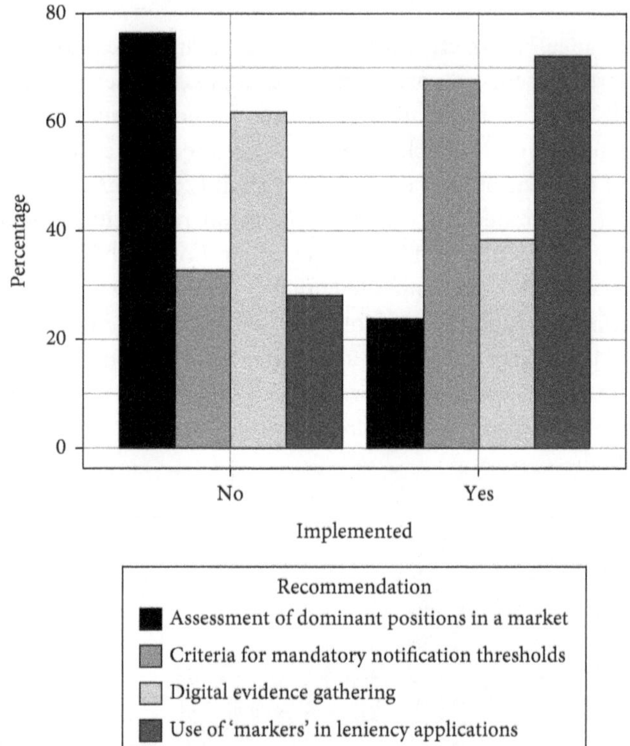

Figure 3.12 Implementation of specific ICN's recommendations

The means through which the four recommendations were implemented (by those who implemented them) are summarized in Figure 3.13. Let us begin by observing that the most used instrument of 'implementation' is (ironically) having adopted a certain measure before it was recommended. If we exclude these cases (which cannot be properly defined as implementation), it is clear that domestic changes triggered by ICN's recommended practices are rather rare. An exception is the recommended practice on the use of markers in leniency applications, which is the most implemented of the four measures that we selected (see Figure 3.12). It was introduced by a majority of countries after it was recommended. We can also observe that the most common means of adoption is autonomous implementation by the competition authority: implementation seems more likely when NCAs can introduce changes on their own.

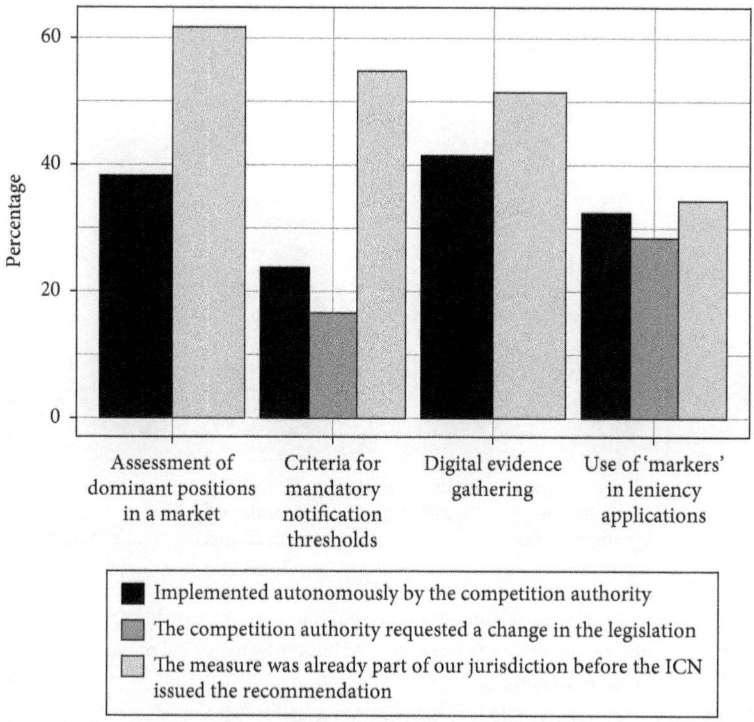

Figure 3.13 How ICN's recommendations were implemented

If we move to analysing NCAs' responses for the cases in which ICN recommended practices were not implemented, the picture is more mixed and more dependent on the specific recommendations. In fact, in these questions, besides offering a number of answers to be selected, we allowed respondents to specify their own answer if none of the ones presented applied to their case. The results are shown in Figure 3.14. Most of the authorities that did not implement the recommended practice on the assessment of dominant positions in the market did so because they 'autonomously decided not to implement'—this means they could have implemented it, but preferred not to do so because they were probably not convinced about the substance of the recommendation (which is interesting, given that they chose not to object to it in the ICN annual meeting).[21]

[21] Some NCAs might have accepted not having influence in deciding the content of recommended practices, understanding that they did not have to implement everything after all. It remains to be seen if this equilibrium will hold now that the ICN seems to push more strongly for implementation.

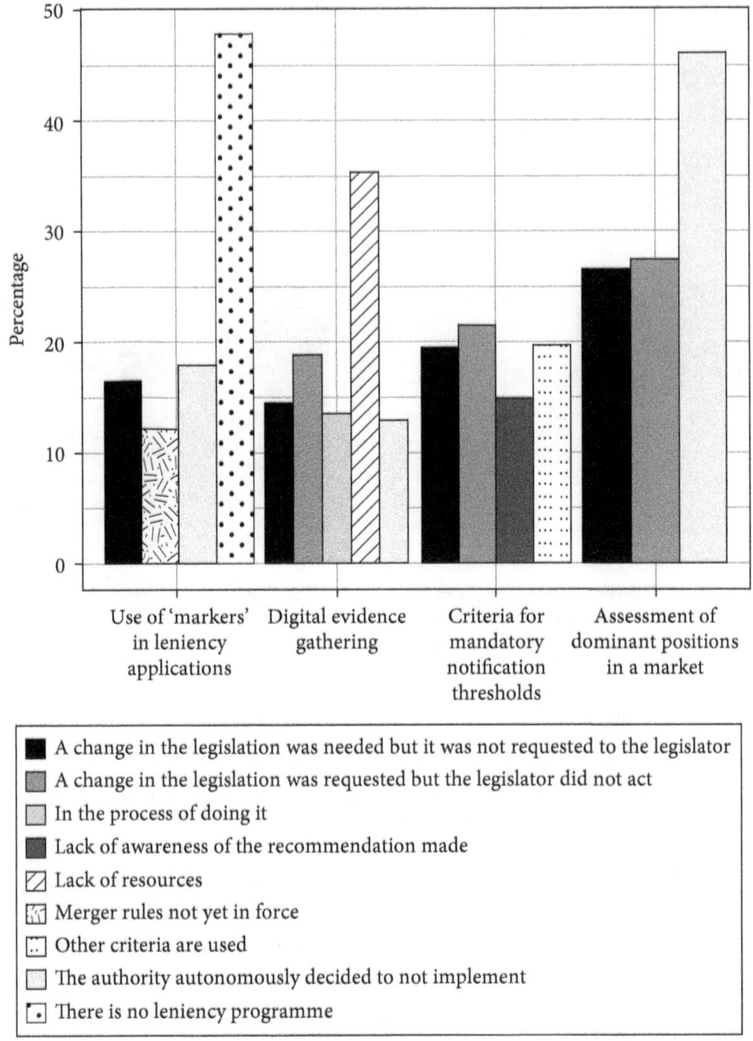

Figure 3.14 Why ICN's recommendations were not implemented

Similarly, 19 per cent of the 'non-implementers' reported that a change in the legislation was needed but was not requested, which reveals a very similar pattern of behaviour: given that governments do not follow closely what happens in the ICN, and that participation in the network is 'outsourced' entirely to NCAs, if they do not ask for a change in the legislation, it seems unlikely that the government will pass measures to implement some ICN recommendation. This is a helpful reminder that, in organizations producing international soft law like the

ICN, the fact that some decisions are taken with general consensus does not necessarily mean that everybody agrees and will implement them. If there are disagreements, one can avoid vetoing a recommended practice (and the potential confrontations that this might generate) and simply not implement. Apparently, this option was widely used in this case.

In the second case, that of criteria for mandatory merger notification thresholds, the answer given by most NCAs is that 'other criteria are used' or that a change was not requested to the legislator, which is very similar to saying that the authority decided autonomously not to implement. As concerns the recommended practice of having a unit in charge of digital evidence gathering, the most common reason for not implementing is lack of resources. This is something that can probably be implemented in most cases autonomously, but if the NCA does not have space in its budget, it may be unable to create such a unit. Finally, with regard to the advice of using markers in leniency applications, lack of implementation is mainly due to the fact that there is no leniency programme—that is, since the authority has not even implemented the recommended practice of having a leniency programme (which is a precondition), it certainly cannot implement the one specifying a particular procedure for leniency applications.

3.3.4 Variables measuring the reasons behind NGAs' participation in the ICN

Before analysing in detail what affects NCAs' influence within the ICN and their capacity to implement ICN work products, we can illustrate some further descriptive statistics that we collected about NGAs participating in the ICN (in addition to the ones already illustrated in Section 3.3.1). A section of the questionnaire was specifically devoted to investigating the NGAs' incentives in participating in the ICN, the frequency of their interactions, their perceptions of reciprocal influence and the reasons for it.

We addressed the issue of the incentives for participating in the ICN in the question 'What is the incentive in participating to the ICN for NGAs?'. Three options were proposed: 'Checking the ICN decision-making process', 'Having a chance to influence policies they have to comply with', and 'Networking'. It is important to specify that respondents could select from just one to all of these options. For each option, we calculated how many selected it (vis-à-vis those who did not select it). Figure 3.15 shows how responses were distributed. 37 per cent of NGAs responded that they participate because they expect to influence the decisions that the ICN will make; 31 per cent responded that they are interested in networking opportunities, be they with other NGAs or with NCAs; only 18 per cent are concerned with checking how the ICN decides. These data give us a picture of NGAs that do not wish to be involved just as 'spectators', but rather want to influence the outcome of ICN's work.

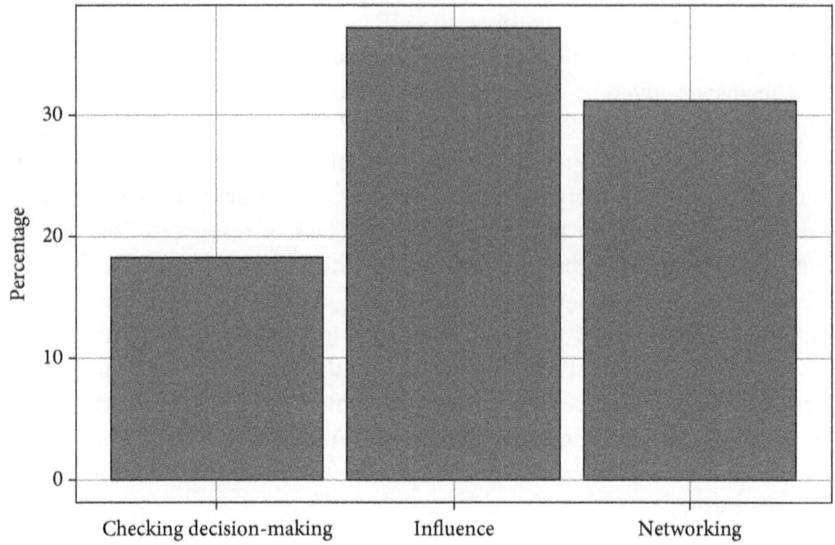

Figure 3.15 NGAs' incentives for participating in the ICN

That said, NGA's participation is somewhat less frequent than that of NCAs. If the percentage of NCAs that reported to be in touch with other ICN participants a few times a year was around 45 per cent (see Figure 13.4), for NGAs it is 75 per cent—and only 22 per cent report to be in touch on a monthly basis.

Another interesting aspect to analyse is whether the influence that NGAs exert in the ICN decision making process (which, as we have seen, is their primary reason for being involved) varies among participants. When asked whether some NGAs are more influential than others, 93 per cent of NGAs thought that some NGAs are more influential than others. By way of comparison, 95 per cent of NCAs thought that some NCAs are more influential than others.

In a subsequent question, we asked which factors are more important in making an NGA influential. The responses to this question are illustrated in Figure 3.16. The factor that most respondents indicate as important or very important is personal expertise, followed by early participation in drafting. The two are closely connected: a precondition for being involved at earlier stages of selecting projects and drafting outputs is having something to offer in terms of suggesting what could be the consequences of a certain decision (in terms that is relevant to those organising the ICN, ie the Steering Committee and Working Group co-Chairs). Revolving doors are seen as less important and nationality is, according to the respondents, the least important factor.

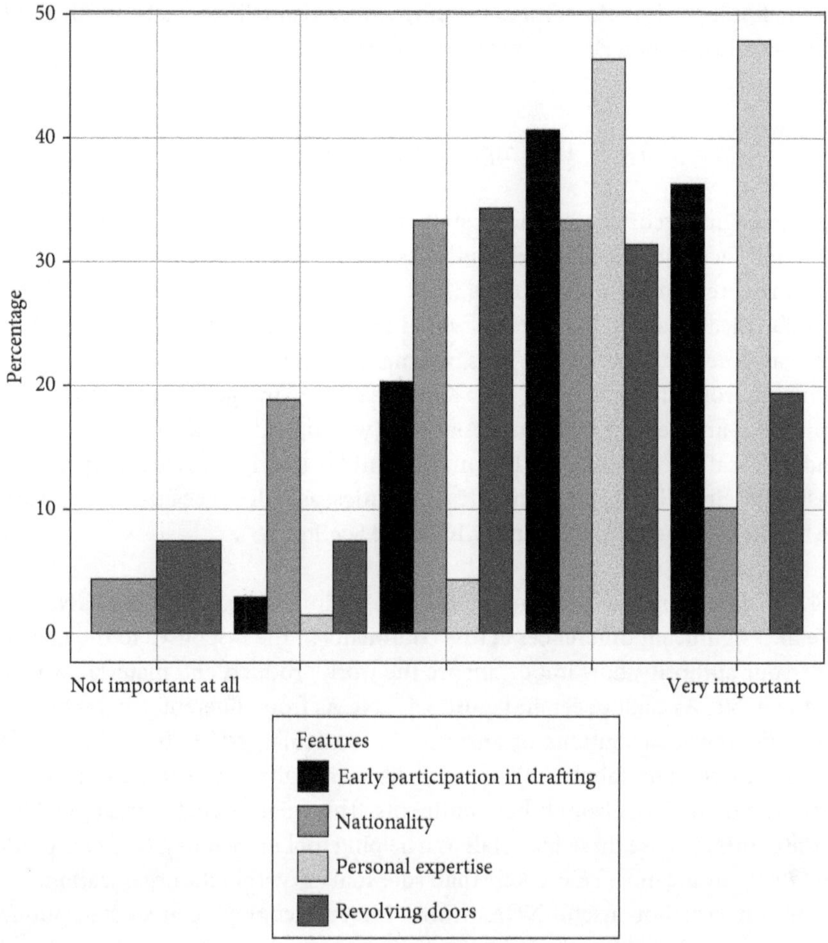

Figure 3.16 Distribution of responses to the question 'Which of the following features are more important in making an NGA influential?'

3.4 Empirical analysis

We now analyse the impact of the factors illustrated in Sections 3.2.1 (geographic location, number of staff members, number of staff members dealing with the ICN, and length of ICN membership) on the variables measuring perceived influence and implementation (presented in Sections 3.2.2 and 3.3.3). Our empirical strategy consists in proceeding, for each of the four main factors, to a statistical testing of its impact on influence (within the ICN) and implementation of ICN work products, looking at all the variables that we have identified. As we analyse many combinations of variables, we do not have enough space to fully report all the findings. Therefore, for some of them we report the results in full and for others we just summarize what we have found.

3.4.1 The impact of geographic location

To test the impact of geographic location, we divide NCAs into four groups: Africa; Asia and Oceania; Central and South America; and Europe and North America. The main reason for doing this is that, with a rather limited number of cases, the statistical analyses that we run would not be accurate if too few observations were assigned to each group. Thus, we merge some continents to achieve a certain numerosity in each group. Asia and Oceania are merged for geographic proximity,[22] as are Central and South America (which, by the way, also have cultural and political similarities); North America and Europe, instead, are merged on the basis of their political and economic similarities, as well as because they appear to be the most influential NCAs in the ICN (see Section 3.3).

3.4.1.1 The impact of geographic location on influence within the ICN

We find significant differences across continents in the responses to the question 'For your authority, how important are the work products and material provided by the ICN?'. As can be seen in Figure 3.17, NCAs from different geographic areas have different distributions of answers. In particular, NCAs from Central and South America and (above all) Africa attribute a higher importance to ICN work products than NCAs from other continents. This might signal that authorities in these continents use these materials as a helping tool in their day-to-day activities, and that they are more rule-takers than rule-makers within the organization.

As concerns how useful NCAs from different geographic areas find publications or activities within the ICN, we also have some interesting findings. Despite some variation across items, we have a consistent pattern in all responses: two areas (Africa and Central and South America) find ICN publications or activities significantly more useful than others, and one (Asia and Oceania) find them less useful. To get a sense of this pattern, we summed up all the responses for all publication and activities, and then divided the respondents into three groups, based on whether they reported overall a low, medium or high level of 'usefulness' for the products and activities proposed. The results of this summary are shown in Figure 3.18. It is rather striking that not a single NCA from Asia or Oceania positions itself in the 'high usefulness' group.

Responses are also distributed unevenly across geographic areas for the questions dealing with the influence of members of the Steering Committee and

[22] Let us note that we have only one response from Oceania.

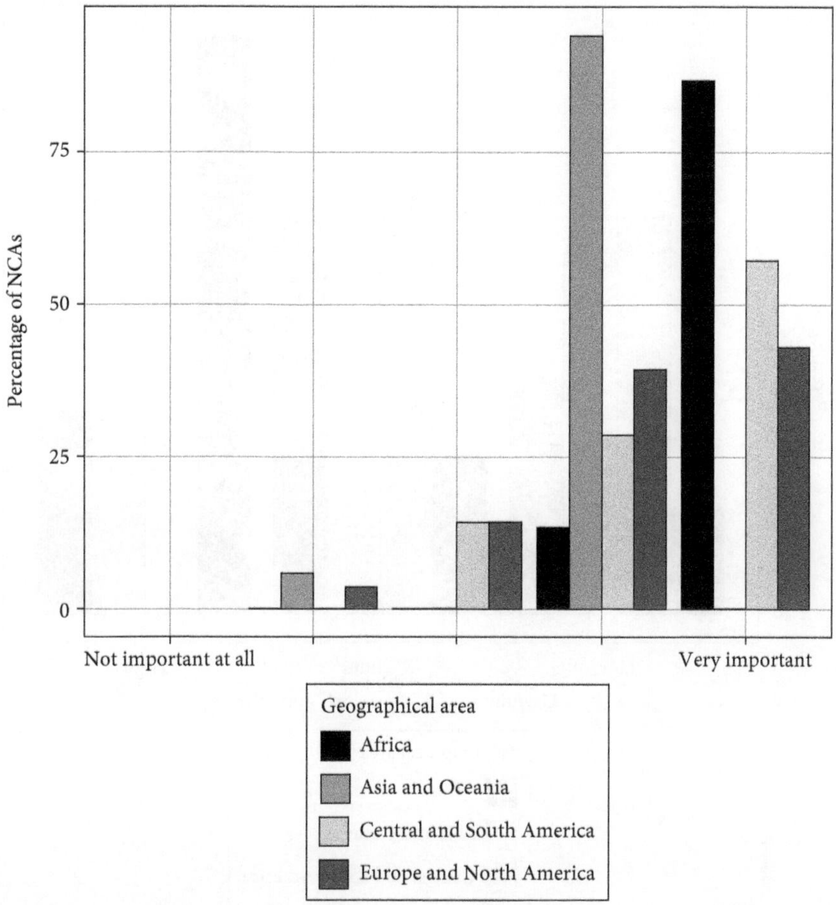

Figure 3.17 Importance of ICN work products by geographic areas (percentages are calculated among the total number of responses from each area)

Working Groups' co-chairs. For both groups, we asked whether they had more influence than other members on ICN work products and agenda-setting (see Figure 3.8). If we disaggregate the results by geographical area, African authorities split almost evenly among those who say that these members are more influential (49 per cent) and those who say they are not (51 per cent), in all other areas there is a strong majority (between 74 per cent and 87 per cent) saying that these members are more influential.

Finally, there is an interesting result (see Figure 3.19) regarding the question on whether NCAs openly disagree among themselves: a majority of NCAs from Europe and America answer positively to this question, while authorities from Africa, Asia and Oceania tend to say that there is *not* open disagreement. If all NCAs interpret the question in a similar way, we must deduce that not all

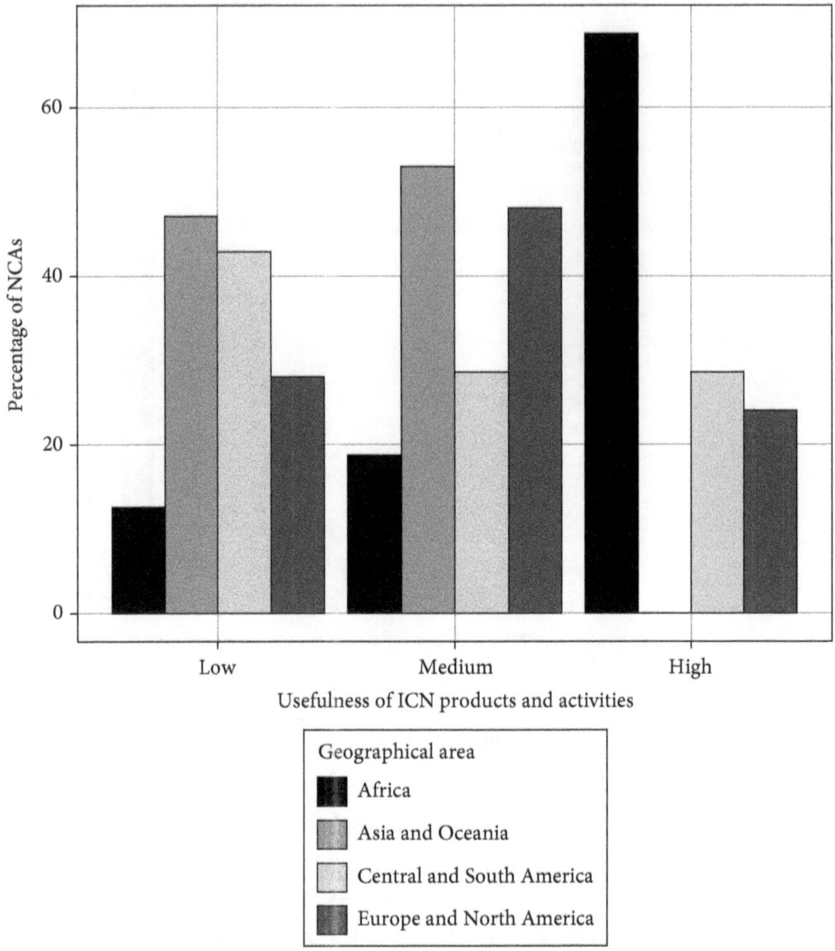

Figure 3.18 Utility of ICN's products and activities by geographic areas (percentages are calculated among the total number of responses from each area)

authorities witness disagreement to the same extent. Do the discussions that matter, those in which contrasting views come to surface, take place only among some authorities, and not all of them? If so, perhaps this might also explain the different perceptions noted above. Perhaps African and Asian NCAs, for example, are excluded from such discussions and so miss the power of the core NCAs and the disagreements between them. Or, it might be that disagreements are present, but not within the ICN. Given the ICN's consensus requirement, it may not be seen as the right body to deal with highly contentious matters, as Chapter 1 argued. Contentious matters (or those that are percieved to be so) might be filtered out by the Working Group Co-Chairs, before they propose projects to the Steering Committee (or by the SC when deciding what projects to accept and focus on in the coming years). It may be that arguments take place within those groups, but not more widely in the ICN? This might explain the different answers between those within those groups (SC and WG co-Chairs) and those outside them.[23]

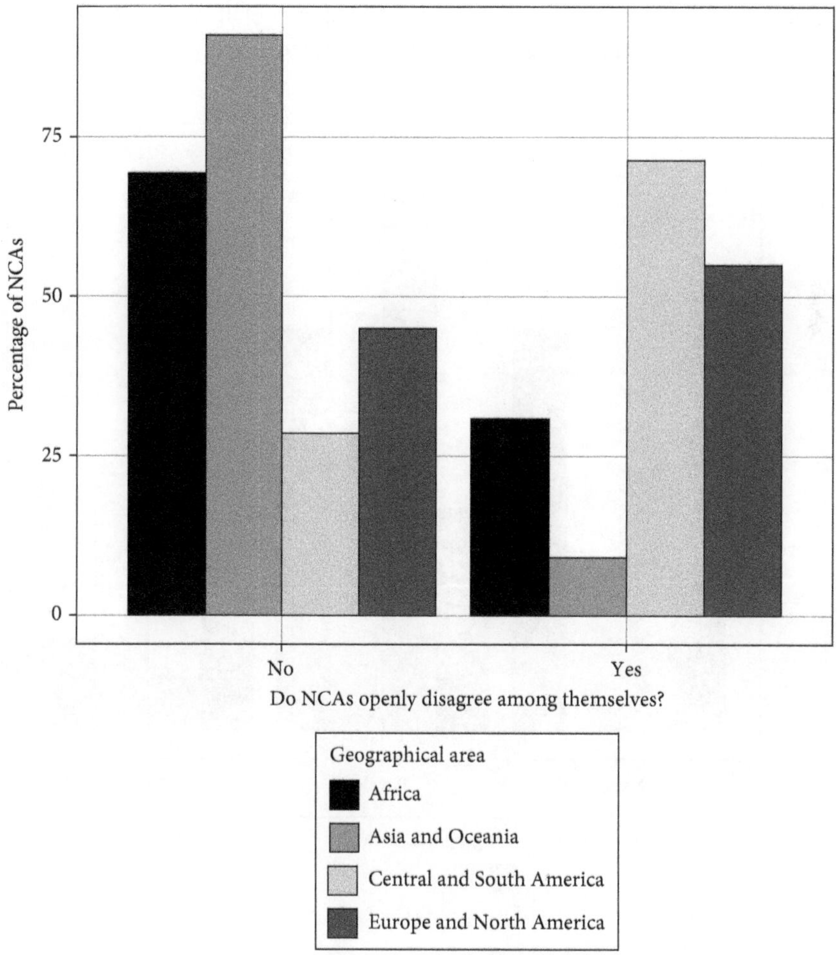

Figure 3.19 Distribution of responses, by geographical area, for the question 'Do competition authorities openly disagree among themselves within the ICN?' (percentages are calculated among the total number of responses from each area)?

[23] We cannot rule out that cultural reasons play a role too, in the sense that it is probably easier for European and North Americans to openly recognize that there are disagreements.

3.4.1.2 The impact of geographic location on implementation of ICN's recommended practices

We now analyse how geographic areas may affect the extent to which NCAs implement ICN recommended practices, and how they do so. Looking at Figure 3.20, we can see that authorities from all areas, except Africa, say that they rarely address national legislators where new laws are needed in their jurisdiction for it to align with ICN recommended practices (44 per cent of African NCAs rarely or never address national legislators, whereas for other areas this percentage

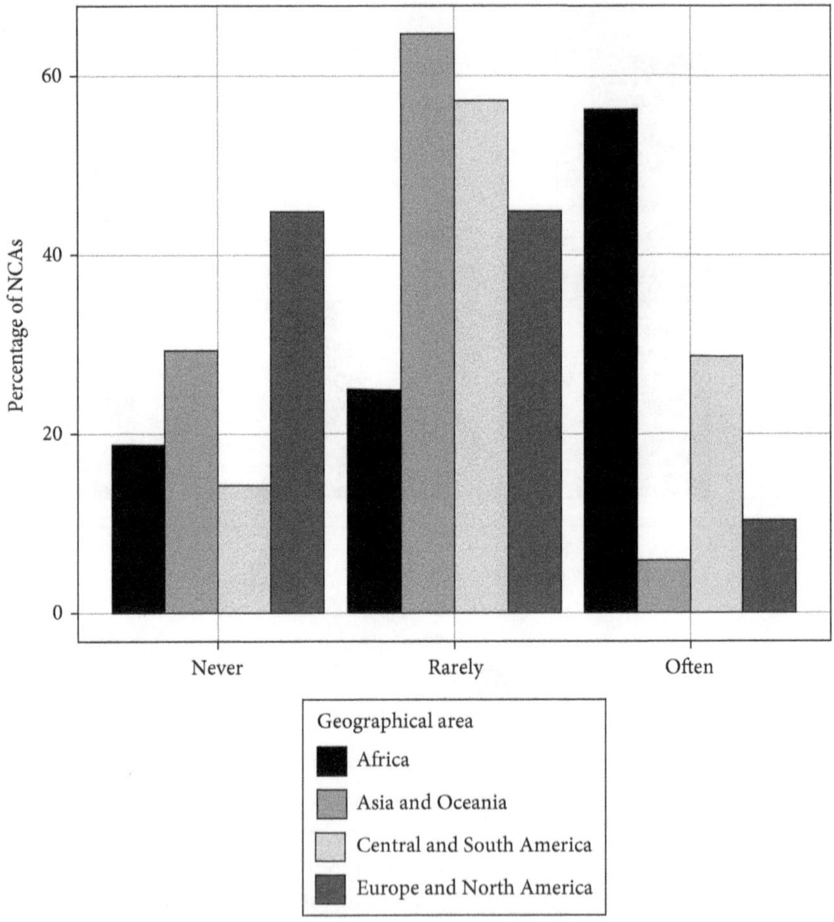

Figure 3.20 Distribution of responses to the question 'How often does your competition authority address national legislators to support changes in the legislation following a recommendation from the ICN?' by geographic area (percentages are calculated among the total number of responses from each area)

ranges between 71 per cent and 92 per cent). However, the interpretation for this finding could also be that national competition laws of African countries are more distant from what is recommended (or some measures might be missing altogether), and therefore that they need to request more substantial changes. This might mean that they need legislative changes more often than NCAs from other areas and it might also mean that change is more costly for firms or other stakeholders in their systems. Another possible interpretation is that African competition laws are less flexible and so it requires legislative changes more often.

Turning to the questions which asked about the implementation of specific recommended practices, the one about the use of markers in leniency applications (Figure 3.21) reveals that, although the level of implementation is approximately the same in all areas, not all NCAs had to do the same effort. In particular, authorities from Europe and North America with this recommendation basically 'exported' a feature that most of them already had. Most likely the recommendation originated from this group of countries. Other areas have instead very similar patterns of responses in this question: they either implemented autonomously or asked to change the relevant legislation.

Concerning the second recommended practice (that of having a unit for digital evidence gathering), we have on average lower levels of implementation, as already seen in Section 3.3.3. However, in America and Europe almost half of the authorities have implemented it, while in Asia, Oceania and Africa fewer NCAs (23 per cent and 33 per cent respectively) have implemented this recommended practice. Moreover, when it comes to how the measure was enforced by those who implemented it, most NCAs from Europe and North America report that the measure was already part of the domestic jurisdiction before the recommended practice was issued. In this case as well, such pattern suggests that the recommendation originated from this area.

Also, the levels of implementation of the third recommended practice reported in our survey show a clear 'implementation divide' between Europe and America on the one hand and Asia and (above all) Africa on the other (see Figure 3.22). Regarding the fourth recommended practice, about using objective criteria for mandatory merger notifications, the geographic area that is characterized by lower implementation (37 per cent) is Asia and Oceania, with other areas reporting implementation with higher percentages (between 57 per cent and 81 per cent).

What emerges from the analysis of the impact of geographic areas on implementation, overall, is that NCAs from Europe and America are more likely to already have in their jurisdiction those measures that are recommended by the ICN. There is a high chance that this happens because NCAs (and probably NGAs

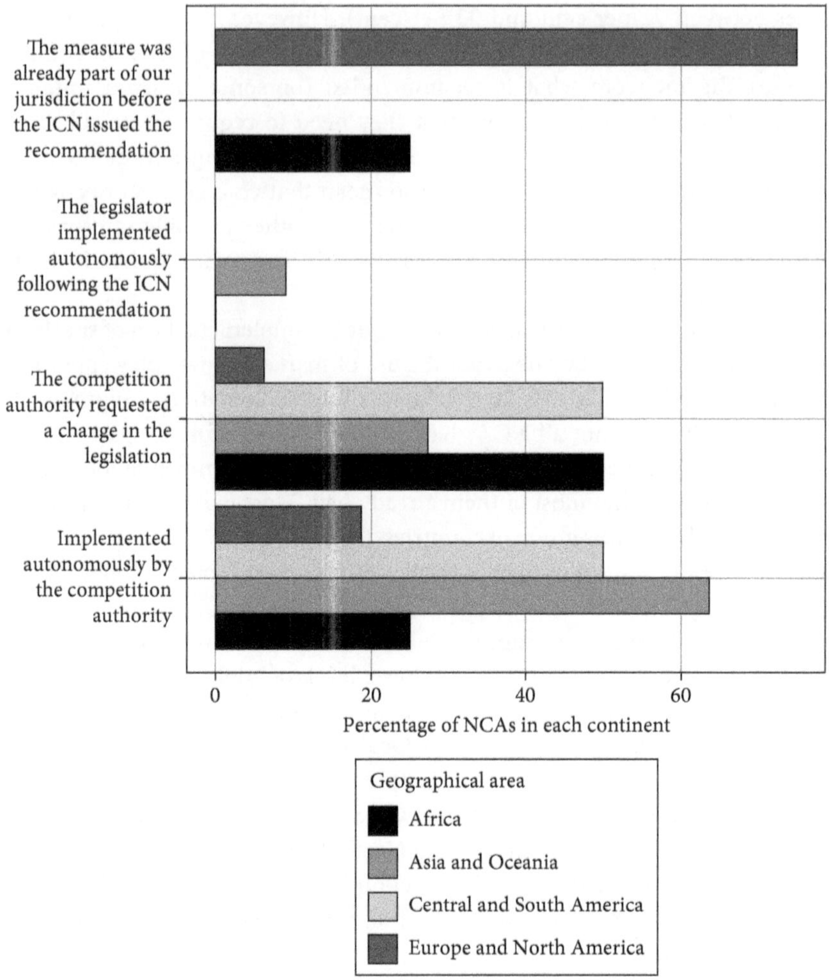

Figure 3.21 How was the recommendation on the use of markers in leniency applications implemented (percentages are calculated among the total number of responses from each area)?

too) from those areas pushed for the inclusion of their own rules in ICN work products in the first place (as a kind of industrial policy designed to harmonise the competition order worldwide around their own norms). Even when this does not happen, European and American authorities are those with the highest levels of implementation, which suggests that they are overall better equipped (in terms of personnel, know-how, links with policymakers) for enforcing ICN recommended practices.

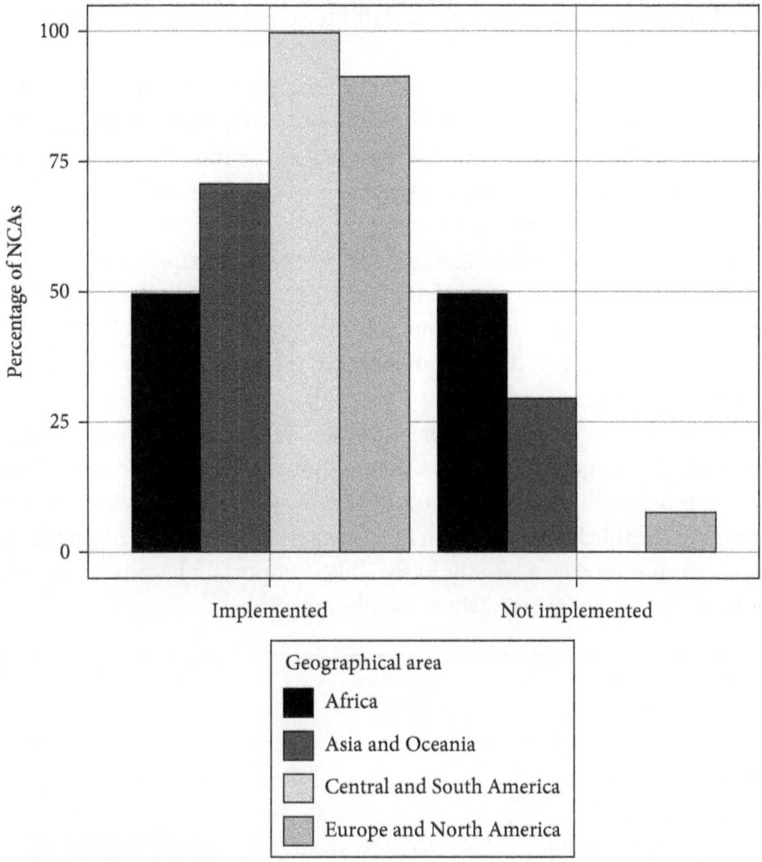

Figure 3.22 Implementation of recommendation on assessment of dominant positions in a market (percentages are calculated among the total number of responses from each area)

3.4.2 The impact of the number of staff members

In this section, we analyse whether, and to what extent, the number of staff members of an NCA affects its influence within the ICN and its implementation of ICN work products. As anticipated in Section 3.3.1, we expect bigger authorities to have better means to influence ICN activities and work products. If bigger NCAs have more influence in the ICN, they are also more likely to be the ones whose practices end up being recommended (Chapter 1 explained why this benefits NCAs and their stakeholders). At the same time, the number of employees may also positively affect their capacity to implement recommended practices when needed (or lobby for legislative change).

3.4.2.1 The impact of the number of staff members on influence within the ICN

There is a significant correlation between the number of staff members of an NCA and the number of employers that, in the same authority, deal with the ICN. This relationship is summarized in Figure 3.23: the bigger the size of an NCA's personnel, the higher the number of people assigned to work with the ICN. To perform the following analyses, we divided the sample into three groups of equal size ordered on the basis of the number of staff members. In the first group (low number of staff members) we have the NCAs with fewer than 32 members; in the second (middle number of staff members) we have NCAs with a staff comprised between 32 and 100 members; in the third (high number of staff members) we have the authorities with more than 100 employees.

One of our findings is that bigger NCAs are 'in touch' more often with other ICN participants. Figure 3.24 shows that, although most authorities report that they are in touch with colleagues of the ICN only a few times a year, bigger NCAs (and those in the third group in particular) have a higher share of respondents that are on a monthly, or even a weekly, basis. This is important because, as we explain below, larger NCAs are more likely to be rule-makers.

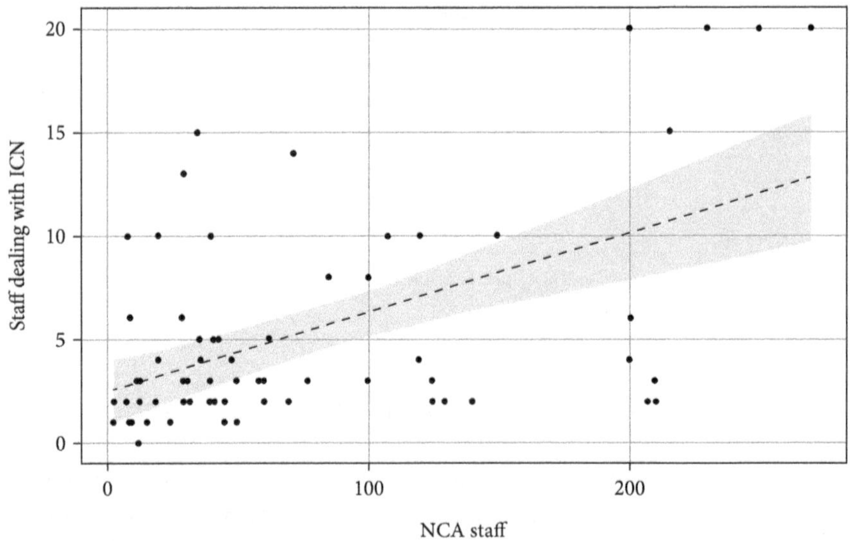

Figure 3.23 Relationship between NCA staff and number of staff members that regularly deal with the ICN

While we have no statistical evidence that size affects the importance NCAs attach to ICN work products or working groups, we have some interesting findings as regards two activities (bilateral relations with other ICN members and interaction with NGAs). Bigger NCAs consider these two activities the most useful.

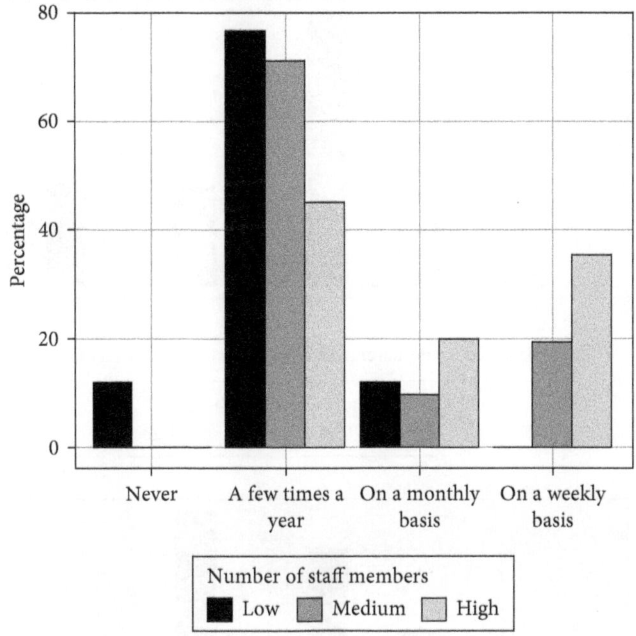

Figure 3.24 Distribution of responses, by group, for the question 'How often is your competition authority in touch (at a distance or at conferences) with other ICN participants for ICN-related issues?' (percentages are calculated among the total number of responses from each group)

These two activities are not among the most useful overall (see Figure 3.6). These are probably the kind of practices that authorities can take more advantage of only if they have enough resources to invest. Figure 3.25 illustrates how big authorities (those with more than 100 staff members) are the majority among those who find useful or very useful these activities. Developing bilateral relations and interacting with NGAs are not of utmost importance; they are something more compared to participation in meetings, conference calls, working groups—which we could consider as more 'basic' activities. They are something that can be achieved only informally when attending the annual meeting or certain workshops. Yet, for the NCAs that can afford to develop these relations, there is certainly some utility that others are excluded from. Bilateral relations could be a good way of influencing other NCAs. Similarly, if an NCA uses the ICN for industrial policy, it might want to hear from relevant firms. Small NCAs might need less this type of interactions or see it as technical and less relevant. Chapter 1 argues that this is precisely what one would predict, in terms of the influence of bigger, more advanced NCAs.

When we ask which features are more important in making an authority influential within the ICN, we observe further differences between smaller and larger

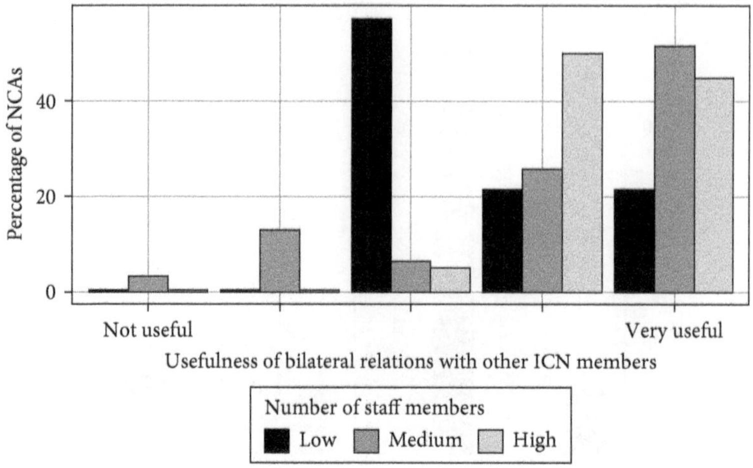

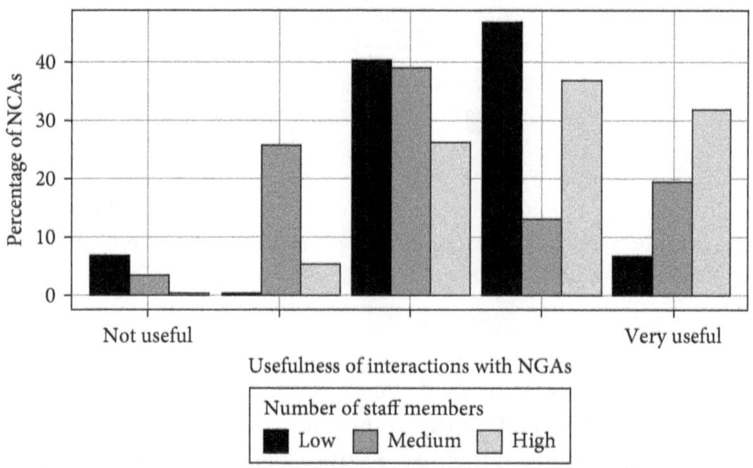

Figure 3.25 Distribution of responses, by group, for the question 'To what extent does your competition authority find the following publications or exchanges useful for its activities?' (percentages are calculated among the total number of responses from each group)

authorities in two answers in particular. Figure 3.26 shows how responses are distributed for the answers regarding resources and length of ICN membership. In both cases we can observe that smaller authorities tend to attribute a higher importance than bigger ones to these two factors. Regarding resources, one might be tempted to say that better resourced NCAs (staff is certainly a valuable resource) tend to downplay the importance of resources, while less resourceful authorities do the opposite. Looking at the length of ICN membership, the pattern is less clear, but it is nevertheless curious that larger authorities (which, by the way, tend to be the ones that joined the ICN earlier) do not consider very important this asset of theirs. This is despite the fact that, as pointed out in Chapter 1, Section 1.2.1.2.1, resources and length of ICN membership are both relevant in the selection of candidates for the ICN's two most influential sets of posts (the Steering Group and Chairs of Working Groups).

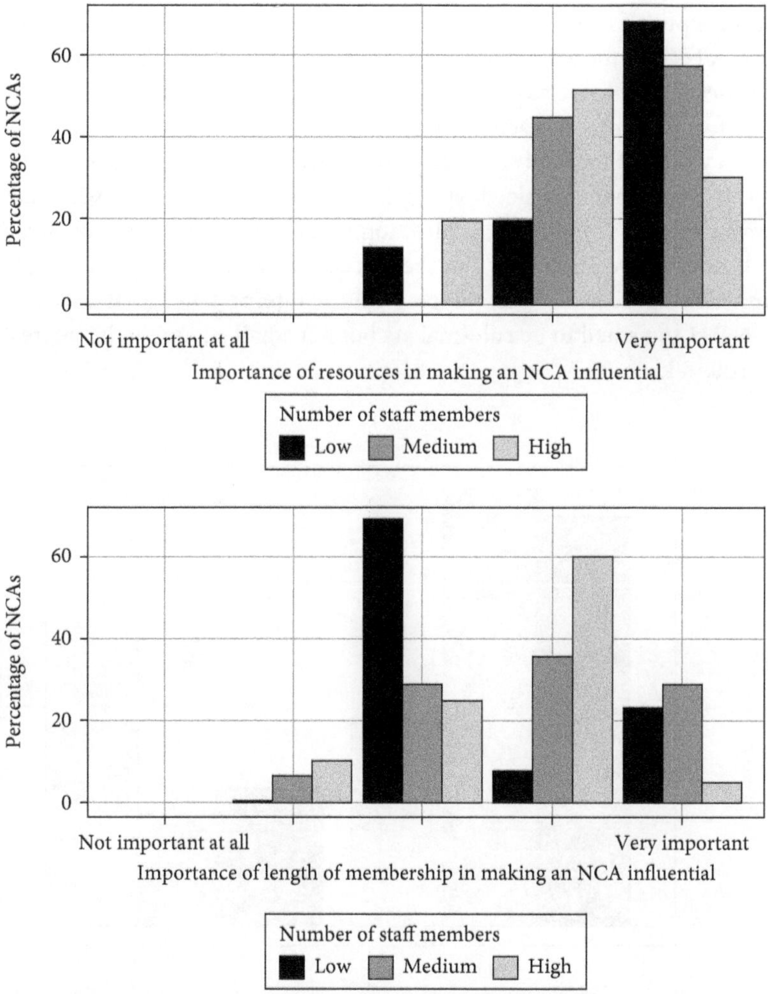

Figure 3.26 Distribution of responses, by group, for the question 'Which of the following features are more important in making a competition authority influential?' (percentages are calculated among the total number of responses from each group)

Even more interesting findings come from the analysis of the questions concerning authorities pushing for the adoption of their own standards. Figure 3.27 shows a strong divide between small and medium NCAs on the one hand, and big ones on the other. While among the former a majority answered that NCAs pushing for their own standards never happened, most big authorities stated the contrary. This result is not straightforward to interpret. It could be that bigger authorities are the ones that have disagreements most often over standards, and therefore that they perceive this situation as more common than others do. At the same time, bigger authorities are also the least likely to report that, when some authorities push for their own standards, they do so because there is preference of national economic actors for this (see Figure 3.28). It looks like medium-sized authorities are the most 'suspicious' regarding the reason why some standards are pushed for: does this happen because they report what actually goes on or because they are not listened to? This picture seems to suggest that one of the two groups (big and medium-sized NCAs) is not reporting accurately what happens. However, with this type of data collection we have no means to know where the truth lies. What we observe is that there is certainly a tension between these two groups. This figure is also compatible with the interpretation that sees medium-sized NCAs too small to be rule-makers but not small enough to be interested in being rule-takers.

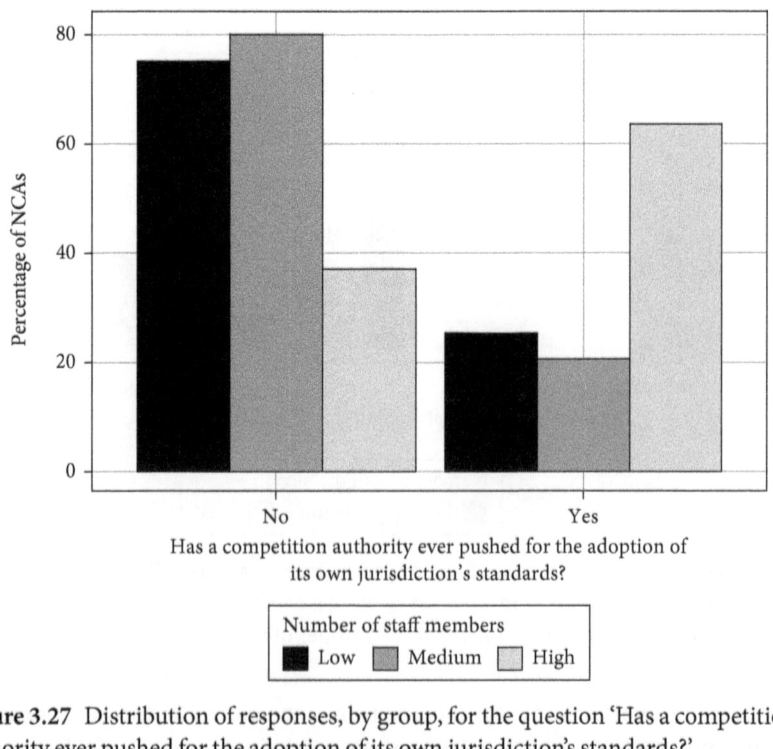

Figure 3.27 Distribution of responses, by group, for the question 'Has a competition authority ever pushed for the adoption of its own jurisdiction's standards?' (percentages are calculated among the total number of responses from each group)

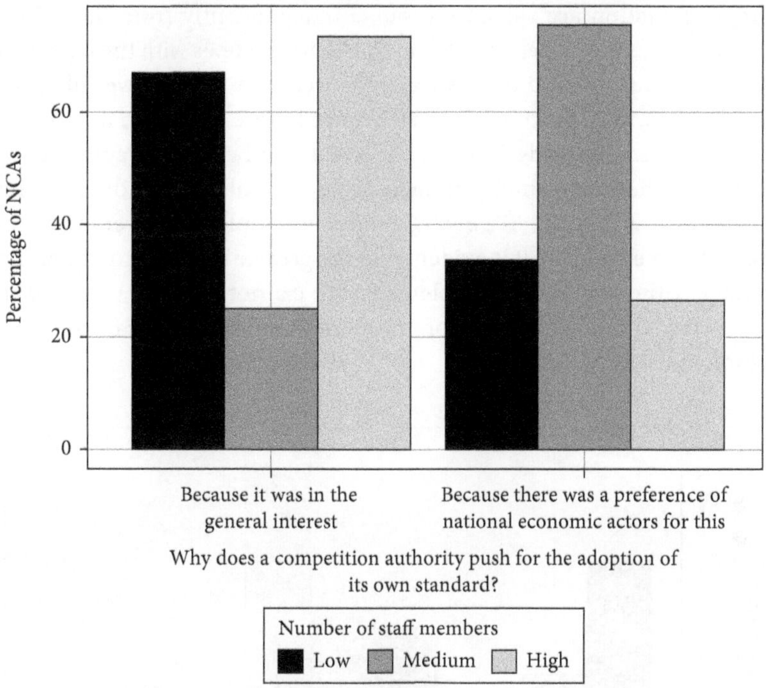

Figure 3.28 Distribution of responses, by group, for the question asking why an NCA pushes for the adoption of its own standards (percentages are calculated among the total number of responses from each group)

3.4.2.2 The impact of the number of staff members on implementation of ICN's recommended practices

When considering all the variables that are related to implementation of ICN recommended practices, we do not find a particularly strong association with the number of staff members, with a few exceptions. The first regards the variable indicating how often NCAs are in touch with national legislators for demanding changes in response to ICN recommended practices. As we can see in Figure 3.29, small NCAs are the ones that address national legislators less often, followed by medium-sized NCAs and big ones. Thus, it seems that size has an impact on the tendency to address policymakers. Whether this is due to more resources for doing so, or to a higher standing (and therefore higher chances of success) is something that we cannot ascertain at this stage. Probably both factors play a role. The next question that we analyse seems to lend credence to the second hypothesis.

If we look at Figure 3.30, we can observe that big authorities distinguish themselves from the other two groups when perceptions of reputation are concerned: most of them, contrarily to smaller NCAs, finds that failure to implement results in reputational losses. If we assume that all instances of non-implementation are valued the same, independently from the NCA, this could be explained considering that big NCAs are the ones with the highest reputation, internationally and domestically (as well as a more powerful epistemic community); so, they perceive they have more to lose if they do not implement what the ICN recommends. However, it could also be that big authorities have more eyes on them: if a small authority from a small country does not implement, few peers will notice; if a big NCA does not implement, everybody knows. Whatever the mechanism, it is evident that the greater is the size of the authority, the greater is the incentive to implement. We cannot rule out that, with these responses, big NCAs signal their commitment to strengthen the focus on implementation in the ICN.

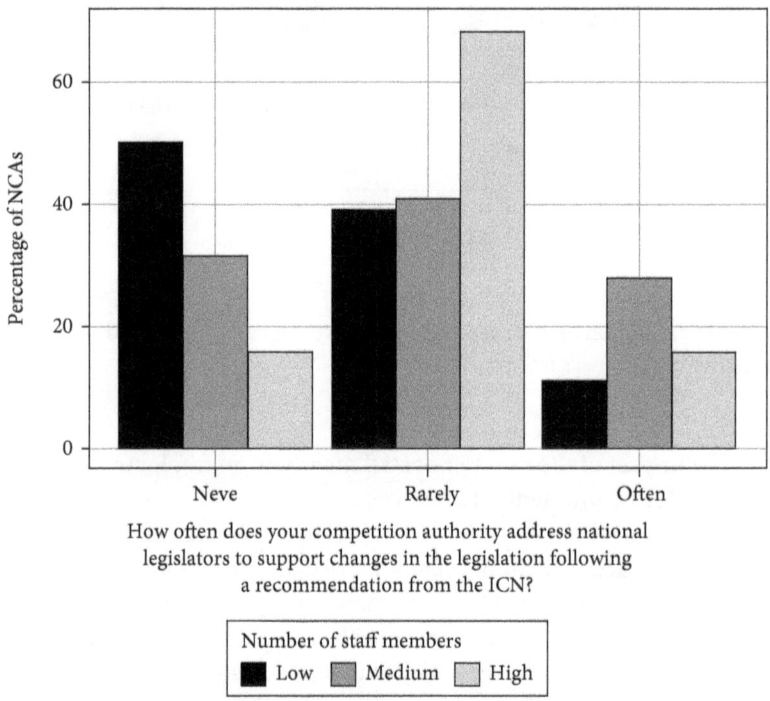

Figure 3.29 Distribution of responses, by group, for the question 'How often does your competition authority address national legislators to support changes in the legislation following a recommendation from the ICN?' (percentages are calculated among the total number of responses from each group)

If we analyse the levels of implementation for specific recommended practices, this intuition appears to be reinforced. Figure 3.31 shows that both for the use of markers in leniency applications and for the setting up of a unit for digital evidence gathering, there is a linear relationship between size and tendency to

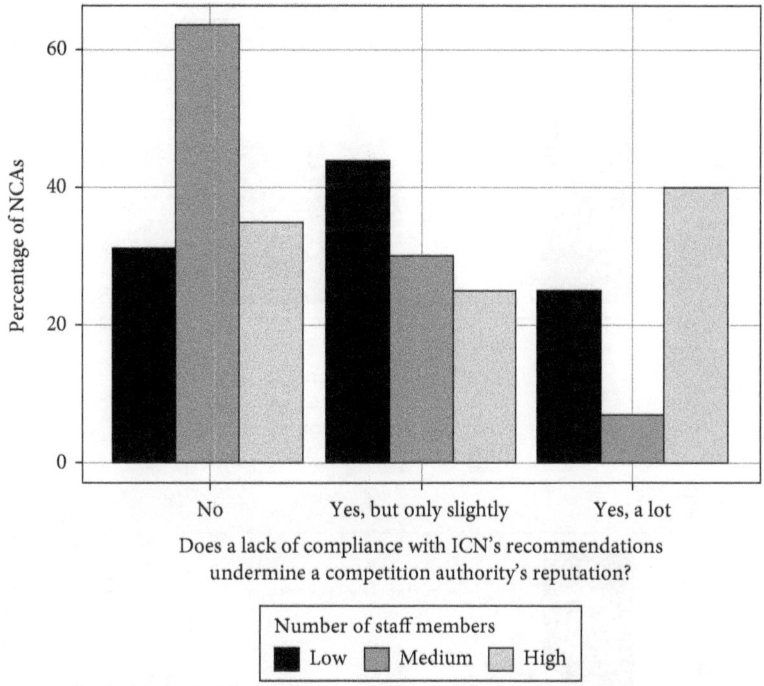

Figure 3.30 Distribution of responses, by group, for the question 'Does a lack of compliance with ICN's recommendations undermine a competition authority's reputation?' (percentages are calculated among the total number of responses from each group)

implement.[24] It is therefore confirmed that bigger authorities tend to implement more. In this case, bigger NCAs' higher implementation rates did not arise because they already had certain measures in their jurisdictions before the recommended practice was issued. Thus, we must conclude that greater implementation is due to their higher ability to do so.

3.4.3 The impact of institutionalization

The third variable that we employ to explain what determines influence within the ICN and implementation of recommended practices is institutionalization, which we measure as the 'age' of the NCA. The hypothesis is that an NCA that has been

[24] For the two other policies, we did not find significant differences across NCAs of different size.

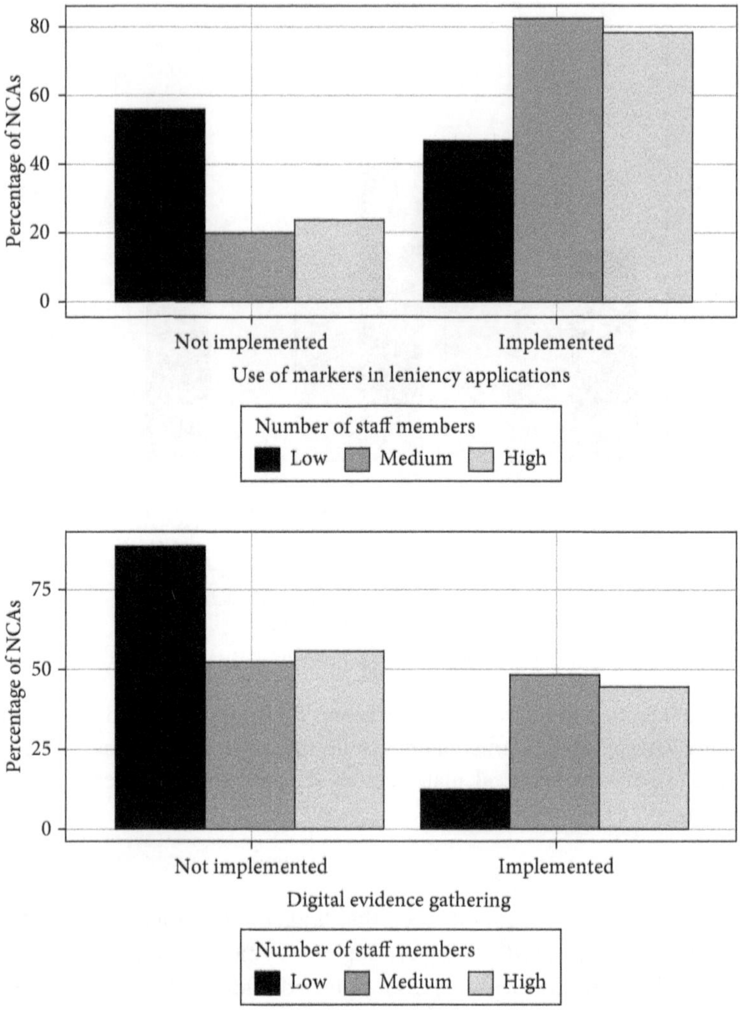

Figure 3.31 Implementation of the recommendation about granting markers in leniency applications and of the one on digital evidence gathering (percentages are calculated among the total number of responses from each group)

operating for more years has more expertise, a better reputation (both domestically and internationally), as well as better links with national policymakers and other national authorities.

To perform our analyses, we ordered the NCAs in our sample on the basis of their age, and we created three groups of equal size: a first group, with authorities that have existed for fewer than 14 years; a second group, including NCAs with age comprised between 14 and 25 years; a third group, with authorities more than 26 years old.

3.4.3.1 The impact of institutionalization on influence within the ICN

The first finding that we present regards the authorities' perception of how important ICN work products are. As explained before, this is a good proxy for how much NCAs are 'dependent' on the work of the ICN—to what extent they are rule-takers rather than rule-makers. Figure 3.32 shows that, although NCAs find ICN work products overall important or very important, younger authorities are more likely to answer 'very important' than older authorities. This is compatible with our hypothesis, in that younger authorities are less institutionalized and therefore use the ICN to 'catch up' with the older ones. It also supports Chapter 1's hypothesis that some of the more established NCAs use the ICN to export their own competition rules to other countries.

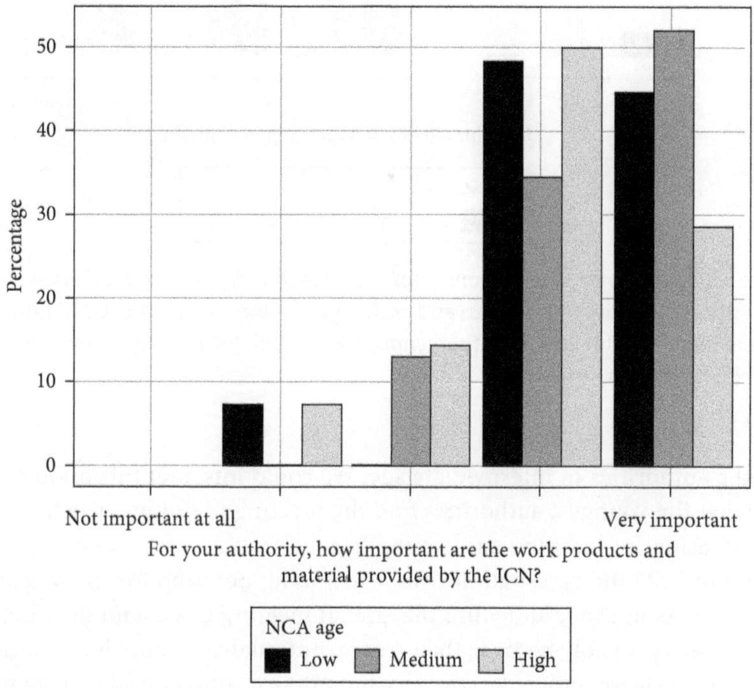

Figure 3.32 Distribution of responses for the question 'For your authority, how important are the work products and material provided by the ICN?' (percentages are calculated among the total number of responses from each group)

A further confirmation comes from the result illustrated in Figure 3.33, which shows that less institutionalized authorities see the ICN annual meeting as more useful than other authorities. The logic guiding this response is probably similar to the one above. One interesting finding that can be appreciated from this graph is that, after the youngest NCAs, the oldest find the annual meeting more useful

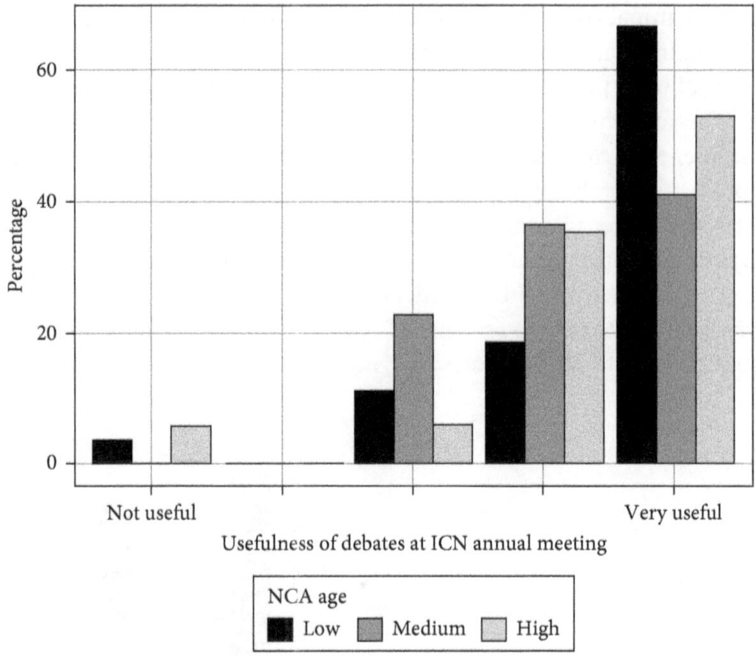

Figure 3.33 Distribution of responses for the question 'To what extent does your competition authority find debates and exchange of views during the ICN Annual Meeting useful for its activities?' (percentages are calculated among the total number of responses from each group)

than the authorities of intermediate age. We could interpret this finding in the sense that the youngest authorities find the meeting useful because for them it is an occasion for learning and getting in touch with more established NCAs, while (most of) the oldest authorities use it as an occasion for influencing the debate. NCAs in the middle find the annual meeting less useful than both the other groups probably because they are institutionalized enough to not need it as a chance to learn and make contacts, but not institutionalized enough to lead the debate.

The youngest authorities also seem to be the ones that have more difficulties in being part of the debate. This is reflected in the responses illustrated in Figure 3.34, according to which the youngest NCAs find being able to address colleagues in their own language overall more important for being influential. This could be explained with the fact both that authorities in this group are less able to take part in discussions due to language barriers and that it takes them an extra effort (which involves being fluent in English) to be involved.

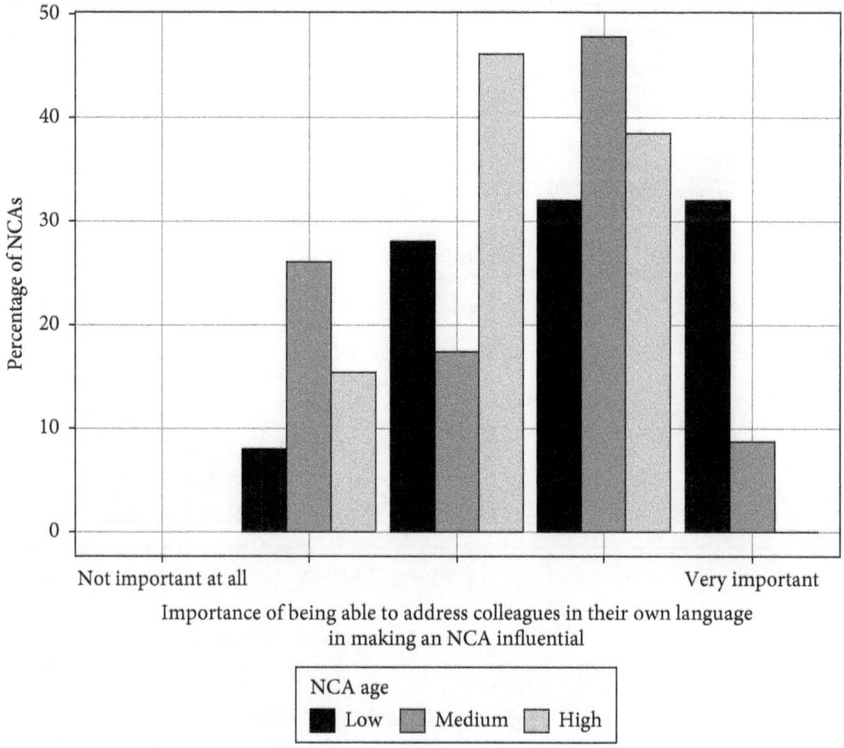

Figure 3.34 Distribution of responses for the question 'How important is being able to address colleagues in their own language in making a competition authority influential?' (percentages are calculated among the total number of responses from each group)

3.4.3.2 The impact of institutionalization on implementation of ICN's recommended practices

For what concerns implementation, we find that the perception of loss of reputation due to a lack of compliance is higher among older authorities than among younger ones (see Figure 3.35): this pattern is similar to the one we found for the number of staff members. In this case as well, we see a correlation between how serious NCAs think it is to not implement, and how much they implement: the more they implement, the more they perceive lack of compliance as damaging their reputation, and vice versa.

More specifically, we observe that older authorities have a better record, especially regarding the two recommendations that showed a different implementation pattern in Section 3.3.3 as well. The two recommendations are the one on granting markers in leniency applications and the one on digital evidence gathering; the first

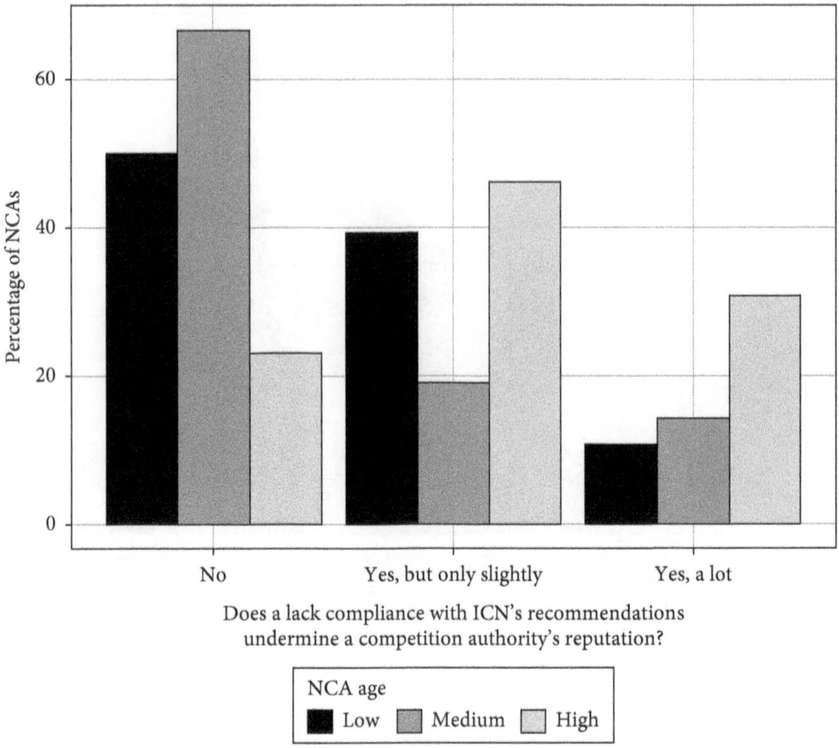

Figure 3.35 Distribution of responses, by group, for the question 'Does a lack of compliance with ICN's recommendations undermine a competition authority's reputation?' (percentages are calculated among the total number of responses from each group)

is a recommendation that most NCAs (71 per cent of them) implement, while the second could be classified as a 'harder' one, since it is implemented by only around 38 per cent of the authorities.

As we can see in Figure 3.36, as the authority's age grows, the chances that an NCA has implemented both recommended practices increase. As we do not find differences between groups regarding the way in which the two recommendations were implemented, we conclude that, in this case, this has not to do with having those measures already in their legislation: apparently, more institutionalized authorities were better able to implement these ICN recommended practices.

3.4.4 The impact of the length of ICN membership

NCAs can be in the ICN for various reasons: to improve their ties with other authorities, to extend their influence by pushing for the adoption of their own

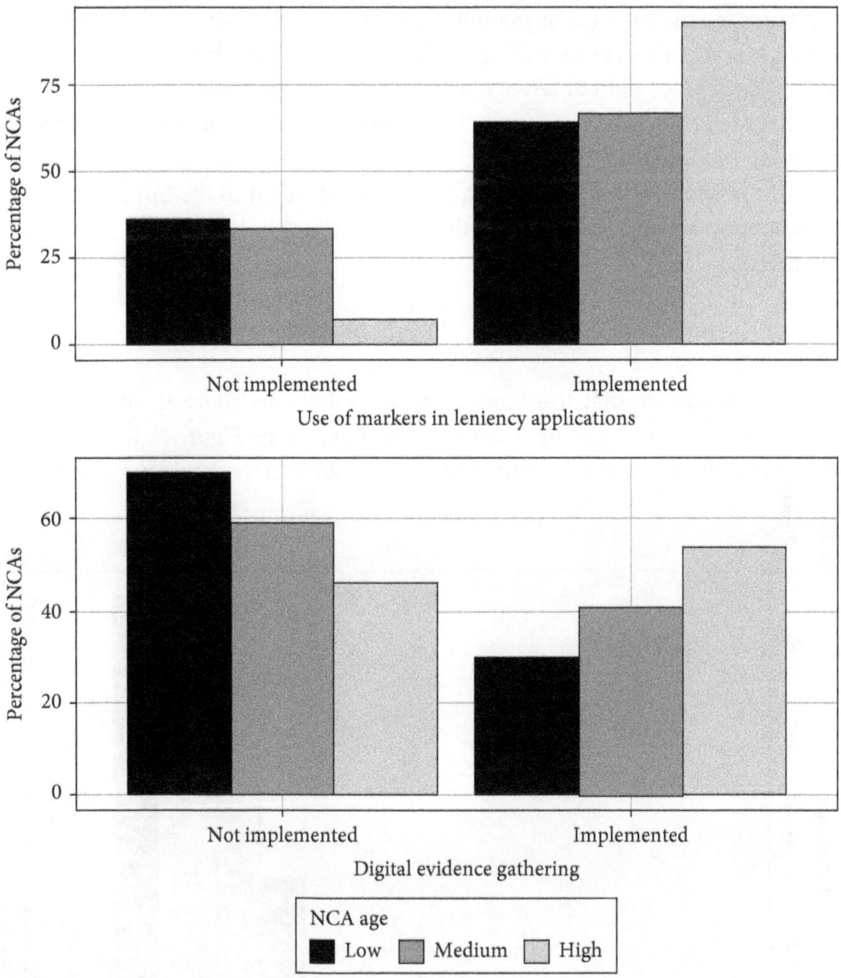

Figure 3.36 Implementation of the recommendation about granting markers in leniency applications and of the one on digital evidence gathering (percentages are calculated among the total number of responses from each group)

standards, to learn from more experienced agencies. In this section, we analyse to what extent having joined the ICN earlier or later makes a difference. Our expectation is that authorities that were in the ICN since the beginning are the ones that are more active as rule-makers, while most recent members have less experience (and less 'authority') to carry out that function, and they participate in the ICN mainly to 'catch up' with the other NCAs. It is worth mentioning that there is a relevant correlation (r = 0.51) between NCA age and length of ICN membership, which means that the oldest members are on average also the most institutionalized authorities.

We ordered the NCAs in our sample on the basis of their length of ICN membership and created three groups of equal size: a first group with authorities that have been in the ICN for eight or fewer years, a second group of authorities whose membership lasted from nine to 16 years, and a third group of authorities that have been members for more than 16 years.

In this section, we will not have a subsection devoted to the impact on implementation, as we did not find any discernible effect of length of ICN membership there.

3.4.4.1 The impact of the length of ICN membership on influence within the ICN

Our expectation (ie that the most recent members are more likely to be rule-takers) seems to be confirmed by what we observe in Figure 3.37. NCAs that have joined the ICN later attribute more importance to work products than other

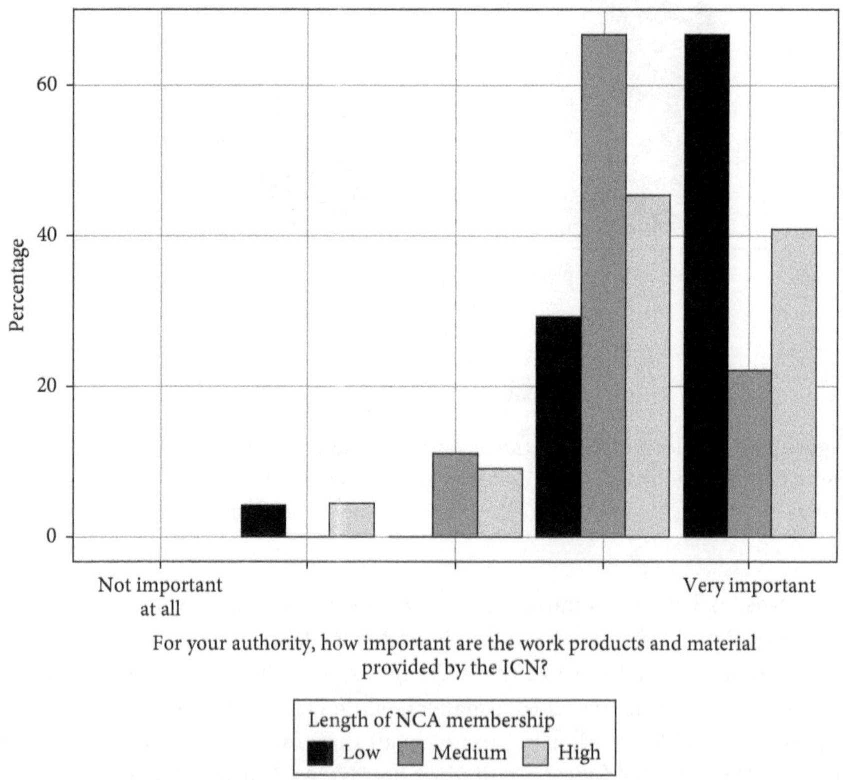

Figure 3.37 Distribution of responses, by group, for the question 'For your authority, how important are the work products and material provided by the ICN?' (percentages are calculated among the total number of responses from each group)

authorities. It is rather curious that the second group assigning the highest importance to ICN work products are the 'founders' of the ICN. Probably they do so because they feel themselves more involved in the process, while NCAs with intermediate length of ICN membership lack both the benefit of learning and that of being involved in decision-making—in other words, they are neither rule-makers nor rule-takers.

That authorities with a longer membership are more involved in the ICN's informal decision-making process is confirmed by the amount of time NCAs report dedicating to the ICN during the year. As shown in Figure 3.38, almost 80 per cent of the members that have joined more recently report an involvement of a few times a year; in this group, very few report to be involved on a monthly or on a weekly basis. As Chapter 1 argued, this makes it less likely that newer NCAs will be active participants in the Steering Committee or as Working

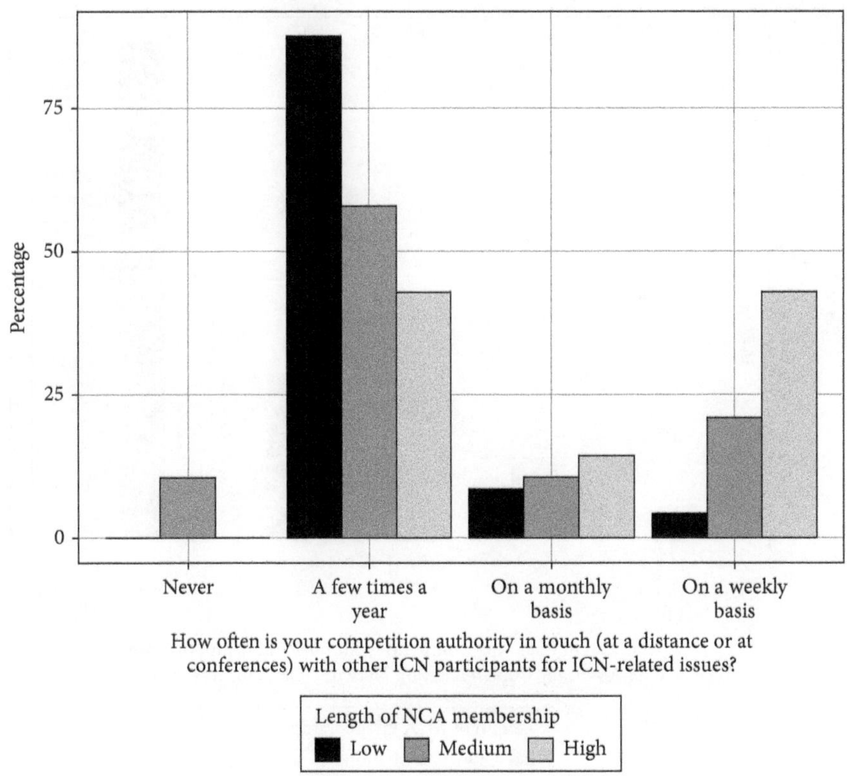

Figure 3.38 Distribution of responses for the question 'How often is your competition authority in touch (at a distance or at conferences) with other ICN participants for ICN-related issues?' (percentages are calculated among the total number of responses from each group)

Group Chairs. The implication is that, once again, newer NCAs are rule-takers not rule-makers. NCAs in the intermediate group dedicate more time to ICN-related activities, although many of them participate rarely. Among the oldest members we observe the highest share of authorities reporting a weekly involvement. Figure 3.38 also shows that regular participation in ICN-related activities is not something that *all* the older members do: there are roughly the same number of NCAs that report an involvement on a weekly basis and a few times a year. The authorities that really shape ICN decision-making are a subset of the oldest members.

Another indication of the fact that the most recent ICN members use the organization mainly to take advantage of the guidance provided by work products, or by other members informally, can be found in Figures 3.39 and 3.40. Figure 3.39 shows that there is positive correlation between the length of ICN membership

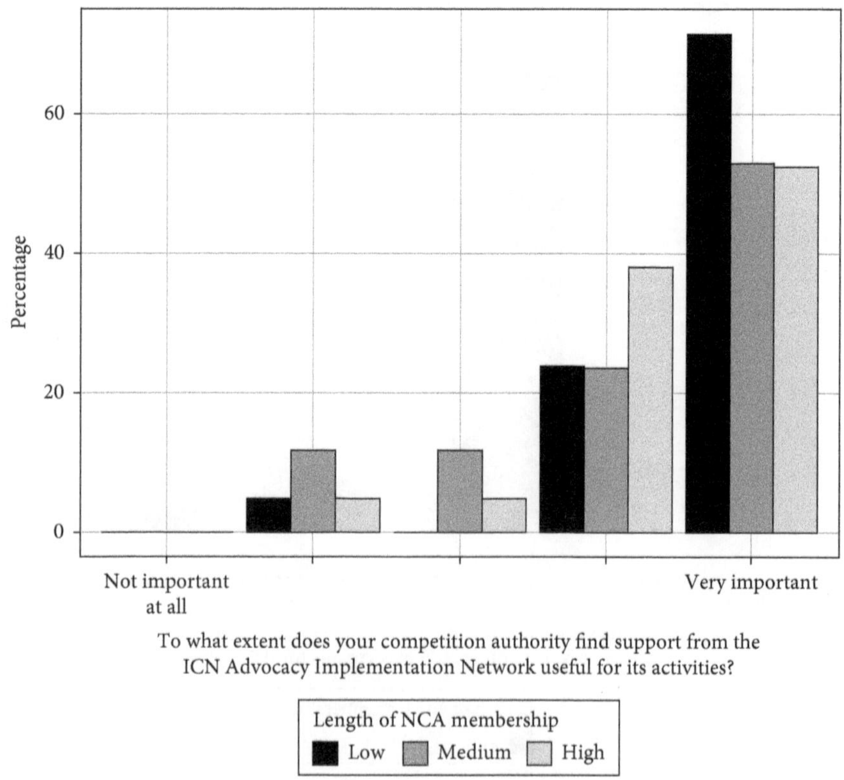

Figure 3.39 Distribution of responses for the question 'To what extent does your competition authority find support from the ICN Advocacy Implementation Network useful for its activities?' (percentages are calculated among the total number of responses from each group)

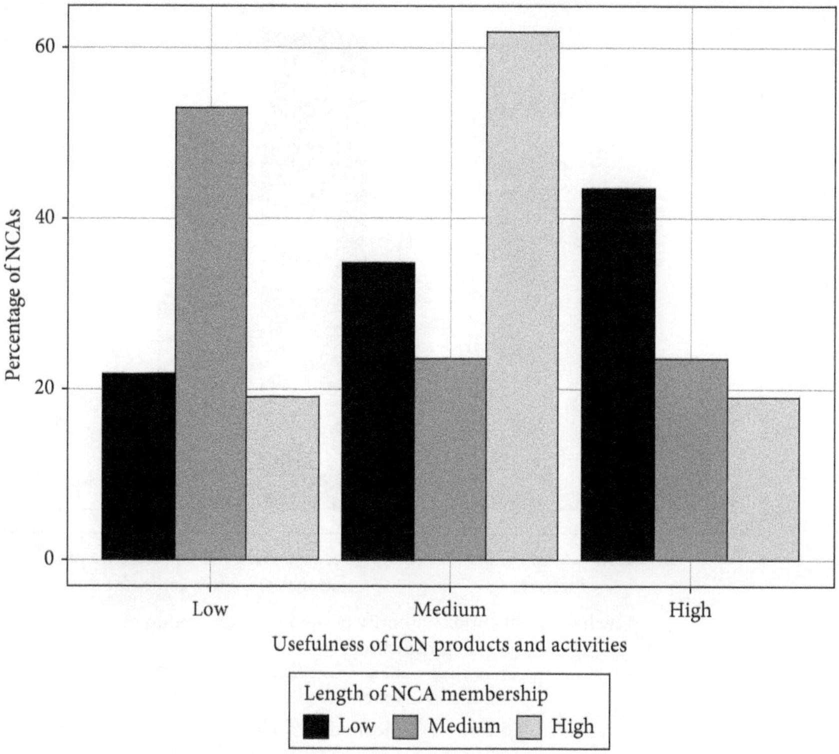

Figure 3.40 Distribution of responses for the utility of ICN publications or exchanges (percentages are calculated among the total number of responses from each group)

and the degree to which respondents find the ICN Advocacy Implementation Network useful. This network was designed exactly to assist the younger members in catching up with the implementation of ICN recommended practices, so it does not come as a surprise that the target group find it particularly useful. Figure 3.40, on the other hand, illustrates a divide between recent members and all the others in how much they find ICN publications or exchanges useful.

This does not necessarily mean that the oldest members' influence in ICN decision-making is viewed as neutral of solely concerned with the general interest. When asked whether the fact that some authorities (oldest members most likely) push for the adoption of their own standards because it was in the general interest or because there was a preference of national economic actors for this, NCAs split quite clearly between short-membership authorities on the one hand and intermediate- and long-membership ones on the other. As Figure 3.41 illustrates, those who are more excluded from the decision-making process perceive the influence of private actors to be much higher than the rest of the authorities.

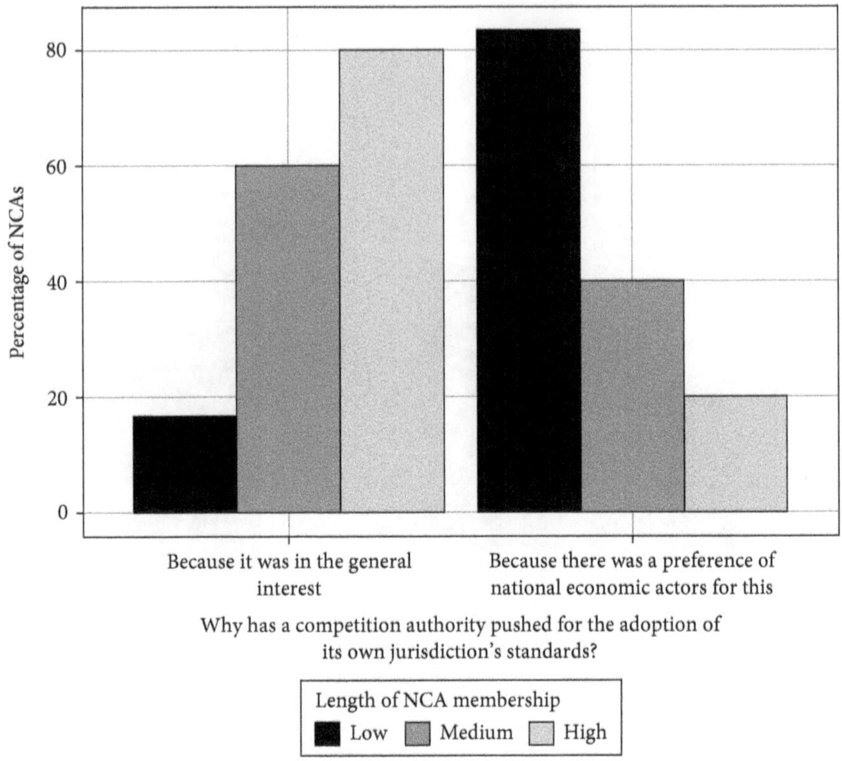

Figure 3.41 Distribution of responses, by group, for the question asking why an NCA pushes for the adoption of its own standards (percentages are calculated among the total number of responses from each group)

3.5 Discussion of results and conclusions

Table 3.2 offers a summary of the findings with respect to the two main dependent variables (influence and implementation) and the four independent variables (geographic location, number of staff members, institutionalization and length of ICN membership) around which we have organized the empirical analysis.

As concerns geography, we have found that NCAs from Africa and Asia tend to distinguish themselves from the rest in terms of influence within the ICN. NCAs from these continents are usually less experienced, they find ICN work products (and recommended practices in particular) more useful than the other authorities. At the same time, we find that European and American authorities tend to perceive more the existence of open disagreement among ICN members, while African and Asian authorities do this to a lesser extent: this suggests a different degree of involvement of NCAs from different groups in actually participating in (and influencing) the selection and production of ICN work products and actvities. As regards

Table 3.2 Summary of the results of the empirical analysis

Factor	Influence	Implementation
Geographic location	• African and Asian NCAs find ICN work products more important than NCAs from elsewhere • African NCAs find ICN products and activities more useful than NCAs from elsewhere • European and American authorities state that NCAs openly disagree among themselves more than is reported by Asian and African NCAs	• African NCAs address more often national legislators to support changes in the legislation following a recommendation from the ICN • European and North American NCAs have a better implementation record because they often have measures already in their legislation before they were recommended
Number of staff members	NCAs with more staff members: • have more members dealing with the ICN • are more often in touch with other ICN members during the year • find the bilateral relations with other ICN members and interaction with NGAs more useful • perceive that other authorities push for the adoption of their own standards NCAs with a medium number of staff members perceive that authorities push for the adoption of their own standards because this benefits their national economic actors NCAs with fewer staff members perceive that: • resources and being an ICN member for a longer time are more important for being influential	NCAs with more staff members: • address national legislators more often to support changes in the legislation following a recommendation from the ICN • perceive that lack of compliance with ICN recommendations harms an NCA's reputation Authorities with medium and high number of staff members have a higher chance of having implemented the recommendations on the use of markers in leniency applications and on digital evidence gathering
Institutionalization (age)	Compared to other NCAs, younger NCAs: • find ICN work products more important • find the ICN annual meeting more useful • perceive that being able to address colleagues in their own language is more important for being influential	• Older NCAs perceive that lack of compliance with ICN recommendations harms an NCA's reputation • The older the NCA, the higher the chances that recommendations on leniency applications and digital evidence gathering are implemented

(continued)

Table 3.2 *Continued*

Factor	Influence	Implementation
Length of ICN membership	Compared to other NCAs, younger NCAs: • find ICN work products more important • find support from the Advocacy Implementation Network more useful • find ICN publications and exchanges more useful • perceive that authorities push for the adoption of their own standards because this benefits their national economic actors Older ICN members are more often in touch with other ICN members during the year	No discernable effect from the survey

implementation, European and North American NCAs do better, but mainly because they already have in their legislation the measures that are recommended by the ICN (in other words the ICN is a mechanism for pushing harmonisation around their own standards). Among the other NCAs, only African authorities address national legislators to support changes in the legislation more often.

The number of staff members has also proved to be an important factor. Authorities with more members can better follow (and actively participate in) ICN activities and benefit more from their membership, as they have more dedicated staff that can interact more often with other colleagues within the ICN. Authorities with fewer members report that resources (ie what they miss) are crucial in making an NCA influential, and that standards that are pushed for by the ICN are demanded by national economic actors of more involved NCAs. More staffed authorities confirm that NCAs pushing for the adoption of their own standards is a real phenomenon. Implementation is also affected by staff size. Better staffed authorities perceive that lack of compliance with the ICN recommended practices harms an authority's reputation, and they tend to address legislators to demand changes in the legislation more often. We also find that recommended practices on leniency applications and digital evidence gathering have a higher chance to be implemented if the NCA has more staff members.

Institutionalization (that is, an NCA's age) correlates with whether an NCA is likely to be a rule-maker or a rule-taker. Younger authorities find ICN work products more important, which is unsurprising given that they are those to whom these products are principally addressed. They also find the ICN annual meeting more useful than other NCAs. As regards factors determining influence, younger authorities report that resources (something that they often lack) are important. For example, newer NCAs report that being able to address colleagues in their own language is very important for influence. We also find that older NCAs have a higher perception that lack of compliance with ICN recommended practice harms an authority's reputation; understandably, these authorities also have a better implementation record, particularly as regards recommendations on leniency applications and digital evidence gathering. Also, given that they are often rule-makers, seeking to export their own rules to others, it is unsurprising that many emphasise the importance of implementation.

Finally, the last factor that we considered (length of ICN membership) seems to affect influence within the ICN similarly to the other variables. Among the authorities that find ICN work products more important we find the ones that have joined the organization more recently. They find the Advocacy Implementation Network particularly useful. Older members of the ICN, not surprisingly, are more often in touch with colleagues, as they are with all evidence the ones that influence ICN activity and outputs the most. In line with what we have found for previous factors, younger ICN members also share the perception that the ICN's recommended practices are influenced by economic interests residing in other members' countries.

In sum, our survey seems to support the hypothesis that the most influential NCAs are those from Europe and North America. These NCAs tend to have more staff, have been established earlier and they often joined the ICN earlier (or even helped to establish the ICN). Geography, staff size and institutionalization also affect implementation. The big picture shows a small number of influential NCAs (which we have called 'rule-makers') that, because of their size and expertise, manage to shape to a great extent the outcome of ICN's work products and recommended practices. What ends up being recommended is often already part of their legislation. This means that the more 'passive' members (which we have called 'rule-takers') are not only largely excluded from the decision-making, but have also a harder time catching up with implementation.

It is also worth mentioning that between the two groups there seems to be a sort of 'gray area' of NCAs that are neither rule-makers nor feel the need to be rule-takers. These NCAs are the ones investing the least time in participating in the ICN, and they are probably more interested in venues where they can either be more influential (like regional networks) or acquire more prestige (like the OECD).

Overall, our findings do not necessarily reveal that some 'conspiracy' is going on. It is common that the NCAs from countries that have had competition regimes established for a longer time, and that have more resources, take the lead in an organization like the ICN. It is also common that NCAs from other countries do not primarily take part in the ICN as rule-makers, but rather to build relationships, get support, and be exposed to inside knowledge that they would otherwise lack, and that they can also use to enhance their status in their home country (they can, after all, find the ICN work products online even as non-members). However, it is interesting that (and this calls for further investigation) most 'rule-takers' perceive that ICN recommended practices (and potentially other ICN work products) are not solely guided by a genuine interest in sharing best practices, but also influenced by the interest of private economic actors in the rule-makers' jurisdictions (ie the perception is that, for these larger NCAs, the ICN is partly about industrial policy rather than 'objective' expertise exercised in the interest of the world). The instrument that we employed for collecting this information, an anonymous survey, prevents us from finding out whether this is true or not, but the simple fact that such perception exists should invite scholars to pay closer attention to how decisions are made within the ICN (which is what Chapter 1 sought to do) and how ICN work products are implemented (see Chapter 2).

Competition policy is not a field in which international standards have to be set from scratch. National traditions and approaches exist, and they predate the process of internationalization that has led to the establishment of the ICN. So, using the language of game theory, the type of interaction that we observe can hardly be considered a 'coordination game'. In this context, some countries have an incentive to use the ICN as an instrument to 'export' their regulatory model to other countries. As Chapter 1 pointed out, this, among other things, benefits their firms operating in foreign jurisdictions. Therefore, it is not surprising that NCAs that are in a position to be rule-makers maximize the benefit of their ICN membership by influencing the content of recommended practices (and other ICN work products). Chapter 1 also explained that NCAs that are not in a position to be rule-makers, and play the rule-taker role, still have an incentive to be part of this system as long as it allows them to acquire expertise, status and de facto independence at home. Nonetheless, this might not be in the best interest of their states (or their states' citizens), as Chapters 1 and 4 explain.

In this respect, rule-makers are mainly interested in the practical content of recommendations, and their implementation among all members, while rule-takers, who are unable to reap the benefits of direct influence, are more interested in increasing their reputation and acquiring instruments for increasing their influence at home.

4
Legitimacy, effectiveness, and efficiency of the ICN

4.1 Introduction

Previous chapters analysed how the ICN has been established, which goals it is supposed to pursue, how it decides and what are the consequences (in terms of implementation) of its outputs. This chapter uses the information of the previous chapters (as well as additional sources and empirical evidence) to assess how the ICN performs in terms of legitimacy, effectiveness, and efficiency.

We start by recognizing that, following the democratic principle, power must always be exerted in the interest of the people. This often means control by political (majoritarian) bodies. Nevertheless, it does not exclude making recourse to bodies that enjoy some degree of independence from politics, if this is necessary to improve outputs in some fields (for example, many scholars and practitioners say this for competition enforcement). However, in such areas, because regulatory independence entails some loss of control of the voters on the course of action of public bodies, the performance of 'independent' agencies should be precisely defined and constantly scrutinized by majoritarian actors. This is even more important where, as in the case of the ICN, independent bodies (national competition authorities (NCAs)) design and establish a supranational network and then associate within it, and states are not allowed to participate.

There are trade-offs between some goals that international fora like the ICN aspire to achieve and democratic principles. To recall Rodrik's trilemma, it is impossible to maximize at the same time democracy, national determination, and economic globalization.[1] We can maximize combinations of two of the three goals, but not all three of them together. We believe that this trilemma applies to the ICN too. It aims to create a level playing field of competition worldwide, promoting the diffusion of uniform competition rules in different jurisdictions (ie it strongly favours economic globalization), but it gives little weight to national peculiarities, and so far it does not allow for democratic control either.

This matters. Competition policy is not value neutral; it has strong redistributive implications.

[1] Dani Rodrik, *The Globalisation Paradox: Democracy and the Future of the World Economy* (Norton 2011) xviii.

The Law and Politics of Global Competition. Christopher Townley, Mattia Guidi, and Mariana Tavares, Oxford University Press.
 DOI: 10.1093/oso/9780198859789.003.0005

The ICN might counter that it can ignore the trilemma. Even if it focuses on economic globalization, other bodies can consider democracy and national determination. This is because NCA members set ICN rules by consensus. These NCAs are, one assumes, acting in the interest of their own states when they operate within the ICN. Furthermore, these NCAs (and their states) can then decide whether or not to implement ICN work products at home (taking the trilemma into account at that stage).

Yet, Chapter 1 showed that a small group of NCAs and NGAs, mainly from advanced industrial states, has a strong influence over the ICN agenda and work products. ICN 'best practice' is often tailored for these advanced economies and might be less useful in developing countries. It also showed how the ICN's 'consensus rule' offers little protection for such states. This is because several features of the ICN drive a wedge between the interests of newer NCAs and their states (such that these states can no longer assume that NCAs necessarily act in the interest of their states). Chapter 2 also underlined how NCAs can implement many ICN work products themselves. Even when wider state actors (such as legislators) need to be involved, Chapter 2 highlights the considerable pressure that the ICN, its NCAs and NGAs put on them to adopt ICN 'best practice'. All of this might matter less if the ICN had been established by majoritarian actors. However, as we have seen, it was set up by a small group of NCAs (supported and encouraged by several multinationals). They also chose its rules and continue to dominate the ICN.[2] So, an assessment of the legitimacy, effectiveness, and efficiency of the ICN (and states' use of its work products) is particularly necessary.

Among the questions that this chapter attempts to answer, the most important are: did the procedures used by NCAs to join the ICN take democratic bodies' input into account? Do national democratic bodies (and parliaments in particular) scrutinize what their NCAs do within the ICN? Does the ICN assess what it does in terms of effectiveness and efficiency?

Currently, the majoritarian actors with the greatest legitimacy claims are national, rather than global. That the ICN increases interdependence without involving national majoritarian actors, without being open to all those affected by its work, and without incorporating properly the input from all its members is, we argue, undesirable. To put it another way, globalization demands politics that are less domestic, while there is the risk that greater 'emphasis on deep economic integration' reduces 'the room for national differences in social and economic arrangements', and 'the space for democratic decision making at the national level'.[3]

[2] The lack of transparent ICN processes, highlighted in the Introduction to this book, exacerbates these problems.

[3] Rodrik (n 1) 205; see also 189–90 and 200. Joining treaties is a sovereign national act. There need not be a conflict between international commitments and national democracy (international commitments can even enhance national democracy through wider influence, ensuring minority representation or other factors). It is just that international commitments do not necessarily enhance national democracy either.

Nevertheless, as the Introduction to this book noted, rather than focusing on what we think is the most appropriate balance of legitimacy, effectiveness, and efficiency, we adopt some middle-level theorizing here. One's view of legitimacy (and its appropriate relationship with effectiveness and efficiency) links to one's model of democracy. There are different models. As a result, there are different ways of legitimizing these processes, some of which overlap. We believe that each state should assess the ICN and its outputs (as well as how they should be used in that state). This assessment should be shaped by that state's understanding of democracy. Many states (and thus assessments) are potentially relevant. They may also change over time. So, we consider it more useful to provide states (and others) with a toolbox which they can use to make their own assessments.

This chapter proceeds as follows. Section 4.2 presents the theoretical framework guiding our analysis. Section 4.3 then asks how the ICN performs in relation to legitimacy, effectiveness, and efficiency. In particular, asking whether a select sample of NCAs complied with their national rules when setting up and participating in the ICN. Then, it assesses how ICN outputs perform on these measures when it comes to implementing them (or not) in the states. Finally, Section 4.4 outlines our conclusions.

4.2 Theoretical framework

In this section, we lay out the theoretical framework that we adopt in the empirical analysis of this chapter. Since our main goal is to understand if the ICN guarantees minimum standards of legitimacy, we begin by tracing in the literature the criteria that international bodies should adhere to in order to be considered as legitimate, and we discuss to what extent they can be applied to the ICN. These criteria will allow us to give an overall assessment in the conclusions. We then develop the lower-level framework that we employ for our detailed analysis of the ICN. To do this, we identify two potential 'paths' to legitimacy: one that ensures legitimacy by linking the powers and actions of a body to a democratic mandate that this body must have received (input legitimacy), and one that sees legitimacy as a function of a body's *performance* (output legitimacy). This distinction will allow us to evaluate how the ICN tries to build its legitimacy, and if it succeeds in doing that.

4.2.1 Criteria for assessing transnational networks, like the ICN

The concepts of legitimacy, effectiveness, and efficiency have been defined in various ways, depending on the purpose and the perspective of the scholars using them (for a detailed discussion of the three terms see Section 4 of the Introduction). In their broader sense, these concepts are employed to assess how political institutions work. Indeed, the first question to ask is why we should be interested in this exercise in the first place. To answer this question, we must first understand what institutions *do*.

As has been summarized by Moe, institutions do not only 'help mitigate collective-action problems, particularly the commitment and enforcement problems',[4] but they are also 'weapons of coercion and redistribution'. Institutions are '[. . .] the structural means by which political winners pursue their own interests, often at the great expense of political losers'.[5] In other words, institutions are not necessarily efficiency-enhancing; institutions are also a means to exert power (also see the discussion in the Introduction to this book, Section I.2, reaching a similar conclusion through empirical insights).

Moe's insights apply to political institutions that can impose behaviours and sanctions on their members and others (such as the European Commission and the US Federal Trade Commission (FTC) in some areas of competition enforcement). Does it also apply to institutions that, at first sight, miss this feature, like the ICN? We believe it does, because, as we have shown in the previous chapters, *informal* powers are often as important as *formal* ones. And there is no doubt that the relationships between ICN actors (both in terms of the content of ICN work products and their later use), entails the presence of power.

Given the power of some actors over others, many states may want to check whether this power is used in a way that they consider appropriate. As we will see in the remainder of this section, scholars have attempted to set a series of principles, or criteria, that international organizations or similar bodies should aspire to fulfil. We do not see this as a checklist, but rather as a series of guidelines that can help us assess the ICN with respect to legitimacy, effectiveness, and efficiency. As noted above, every state should make its own assessment of the benefits and costs of participation in the ICN.

A first check that should always be performed on international organizations (including transnational networks) is whether their existence is preferable to a status quo in which countries produce their own policies autonomously. This is not a trivial point. We all know that democratic checks are difficult to exercise at the international level. Delegating formal or informal powers to organizations 'above' the state can take decisions away from the control of the voters (see below). And, given the enormous growth of international organizations in the twentieth and twenty-first centuries (see Section I.2 of the Introduction), it is legitimate to ask

[4] The *commitment problem* refers to a state's (or a groups of states') inability to make reciprocal promises, while the *enforcement problem* arises when promises are not kept because there is not an authority than can sanction actors that do not enforce what they have pledged to do. In both cases, international organizations can be useful in overcoming these problems, as they make interactions regular (thus making non-enforcement more costly in terms of reputation) and have bodies that can monitor and (sometimes even directly) sanction member states.

[5] TM Moe, 'Political Institutions: The Neglected Side of the Story' (1990) 6 Journal of Law, Economics, & Organization 213.

whether they always respond to a logic of enhancing cooperation, coordination, and ultimately efficiency of interstate interaction (or whether 'inappropriate influence' dominates).

The ICN underlines its own importance by highlighting how competition rules in multiple jurisdictions can impact upon the same arrangement. This raises costs for firms (and their customers) and sometimes even generates conflicting regulatory requirements for them. The ICN claims that:

> With an increasing number of investigations that involve cross-border effects and concurrent reviews by multiple agencies, competition agencies need to collaborate with each other to reduce the risk of: (i) sub-optimal enforcement, and (ii) inconsistent outcomes. The ICN helps to facilitate cooperation and convergence, where appropriate.[6]

Yet, Dani Rodrik recalls that, although '[v]irtually any domestic policy has some implications on the other side of the border',[7] homogenizing national rules comes with the cost of compressing national diversities—considering that the nation state is still the organization where the highest democratic influence is possible. In other words, homogenizing rules at the supranational level has both benefits and costs.

Traditionally, international organizations have been seen as a response to the provision of *global public goods* or to mitigate the risk of *beggar-thy-neighbour policies*. Global public goods are policies that, by definition, will not be provided adequately in the absence of state coordination. The logic is similar to what happens domestically. Domestic public goods are policies like national defence, or environmental policies, which economic theory defines as *non-rivalrous* and *non-excludable*. Non-rivalrous means that the supply of the good is not influenced by the number of people who enjoy it: for instance, if an environmental policy improves the quality of air and water in a country, it does so regardless of the number of citizens that live in the country. Non-excludable means that it is impossible to exclude some people from enjoying some good. If we think about national defence, an army will protect all citizens in a country, regardless of whether some of them want it or not. Because of these characteristics, it is unlikely that these goods will be provided in sufficient amounts if citizens have to do that individually. The cost for a single contributor would be very high, and the benefit would be spread on the whole population anyway. Something similar happens at the international level. Goods like carbon control policies for climate change are already difficult to provide in the presence of coordination, but they would be impossible to provide

[6] ICN, *ICN Factsheet and Key Messages* (2009) 1, previously available at <http://www.internationalcompetitionnetwork.org/uploads/library/doc608.pdf> (broken ICN link, see discussion in Introduction, n 16).

[7] Dani Rodrik, 'Putting Global Governance in Its Place' [2019] NBER Working Paper 26213 2.

without it. Imagine if every country should reduce its emissions autonomously: it would know that it would bear the entire cost of the reduction, but the benefits would be enjoyed by other states too, even states that do nothing in this respect. This is why international coordination is the most efficient way of providing global public goods. 'Beggar-thy-neighbour' policies are also an inconvenience of international politics that cooperation aims to contain or avoid. These are policies that produce a gain for the home country at the expense of others. An example are tax havens, small countries that prosper by depriving many other countries of their tax base and leading to an undesirable equilibrium internationally. In these cases, as well, international cooperation can achieve a better *global* equilibrium.

However, Rodrik notes that 'many policies have become "internationalized" through happenstance or the operation of political lobbies [. . .] rather than on account of principled distinctions'.[8] For example, we have regimes with very little institutionalization in policies where they would be most useful (reducing greenhouse gas emissions) and we have very institutionalized regimes in policies like trade. International trade policy or global financial regulation are not global public goods: they provide, first and foremost, *domestic* benefits.

Applying this logic, it is questionable whether competition policy demands global regulatory convergence. The main incentive for a domestic competition regime is balancing the economic interests of incumbents, newcomers, consumers *at home*. Of course, like all domestic policies, this has international spill-overs, and these spill-overs are higher the bigger the country is. Chapter 1 discusses why large multinationals often prefer a more uniform competition rules globally. We saw the influence of many of these firms in the establishment of the ICN. This chimes with Rodrik's reference to 'political lobbies rather than principled distinctions'.

In cases like this, even if influence abroad does not necessarily require a global regime (because they are not a response to the provision of global public goods or mitigating the risk of beggar-thy-neighbour policies), an international network could help all its members to better appraise their interdependence. Yet, even here, there are many reasons why individual states might want to diverge from 'global' best practice. According to Rodrik, '[f]irst, there may indeed be market failures or distortions at home that justify the use of such policies, as second-best remedies even if not first-best ones'. A horizontal agreement among some firms in a market might protect employment or safeguard national production in strategic sectors. 'It is not obvious', Rodrik continues:

> that trade negotiators or international bureaucrats are better placed than domestic legislatures and policy makers to make the right call in complex cases. Second, there may be overwhelming non-economic considerations—social,

[8] ibid 3.

> environmental, health, national security or moral—that trump economic costs and benefits. Once again, the relevant trade-offs are better evaluated at the national level, within pre-existing democratic decision-making bodies, than via delegation to international agencies.[9]

The author also notes that countries should be able to 'make their own mistakes', and that:

> there is no presumption that global governance institutions are more immune to capture by special interests than domestic policymaking. Indeed, large corporations, international banks, and big pharma have exercised disproportionate influence on global economic governance. It would be naïve to presume that they have prioritized the public interest over their particular interest in shaping global agreements in line with their needs.[10]

Part of the tension between global governance and national democracy derives from the fact that the national community constitutes (in most cases) a *demos*—a core political unit (the EU may be an exception here). The demos constitutes a group of people who, through historical, cultural, or other bonds tend to be more willing to share resources, and in which some are prepared to lose in favour of others (the case of redistribution). Of course, the procedures for 'agreeing' redistribution within the demos can only take place in accordance with the agreed principles for that demos. For example, such decisions are often made by decision makers who are democratically elected in accordance with agreed national processes. Legitimacy is more difficult on the international plane, given the lack of demos at that level and the absence of mechanisms for legitimately 'agreeing' redistributions. Usually international cooperation is justified on the ground that it generates Pareto improvements (ie no one loses). If everybody gains (or no

[9] ibid 19. A similar argument is made by Morgan and Yeung:

> Even where it is possible to identify broader community consensus in support of the collective goals lying at the heart of a voluntary regime, this does not prevent the emergence of competing priorities to collective well-being. Yet the possibility of such conflict demands the making of political trade-offs which the limited expert community cannot claim to make on behalf of the broader global community affected by the relevant activity. Moreover, the legitimacy of expert-based consensus is called further into question in circumstances where the community of experts establishing consensual standards does not rest on any strong formalised institutional foundation with associated mechanisms for ensuring transparency and accountability. In other words, even in circumstances where the law's facilitative capacities are enrolled to provide binding force to the consensual basis of supranational regulatory structures, underlying political tensions may remain unresolved, so that the social and political cohesion that the law's expressive force may contribute to national regulation is not reflected in the role which it plays within the supranational context.
>
> Morgan Bronwen and Karen Yeung, *An Introduction to Law and Regulation* (CUP 2007) 318.

[10] Rodrik (n 7) 20.

one loses), if international cooperation is a positive-sum game, then the lack of democratic legitimacy is at least partially compensated (see Section 4.3). But if international decisions create winners and losers, if they (albeit implicitly) redistribute, then we cannot avoid asking on behalf of which demos are those decisions taken and what made the mechanism by which this distribution was agreed legitimate. As we will see, it is possible to generate more legitimacy at the supranational level. For example, this might happen if a group of states (each acting under a democratic mandate) agree to establish a body to act on the international plane. Legitimacy could be further enhanced where each redistributive decision of this supranational body were unanimously supported by the nationally legitimate officials.

In any case, even if states decided that an international regime were needed (along with more uniform implementation of it), this would not automatically mean that the ICN structure is the most preferable. For example, it might be better to have one with more democratic oversight, such as the OECD and UNCTAD. On top of that, it should be justified why another regime (the ICN) is needed when we have these two already. As Chapter 1 pointed out, this has never been properly done for the ICN.

Against this background, it is useful to recall some criteria that have been put forward by scholars for checking on the legitimacy of international institutions where they are considered desirable. Buchanan and Keohane list three of them: minimal moral acceptability, comparative benefit, and institutional integrity.[11] The first refers to 'not committing serious injustices'; the authors refer here mainly to actions against human rights. Over the last 20 years or so, the increase in challenges to NCA action which undermines the human rights of firms has been a booming area. The second states that, to be legitimate, international institutions must 'provide benefits that cannot otherwise be obtained' (this is similar to Rodrik's claim that no international institution might be preferable in some cases). The third requires that the formal procedures put in place by member states are followed.

Pauwelyn, Wessel, and Wouters,[12] referring to *informal* international law-making (the case of the ICN), stress the importance of two additional criteria. The first is some involvement of legislatures, which 'ought to be informed and be given

[11] A Buchanan and RO Keohane, 'The Legitimacy of Global Governance Institutions' (2006) 20 Ethics & International Affairs 419.

[12] J Pauwelyn, RA Wessel and J Wouters, 'When Structures Become Shackles: Stagnation and Dynamics in International Lawmaking' (2014) 25 European Journal of International Law 733. On the following page authors add '[f]ormal international law is stagnating in terms both of quantity *and* quality' and 'increasingly superseded by "informal international lawmaking"'. In their view, this does not imply that coordination in the form of soft-law should be exempted from legitimacy checks. On the contrary, it must 'be kept accountable, through tailor-made accountability mechanisms, especially towards stakeholders not involved in the network but affected by it'.

a minimum of oversight (albeit indirectly through administrative agencies) in respect of all international cooperation that affects public policymaking and individual freedom'.[13] The second criterion is *transparency*. In their words:

> To the extent that lawmaking powers are delegated to administrative agencies, transparency, reason-giving, and notice and comment procedures should apply to both the domestic and international activities and norm-making of these agencies, whether norms are binding under international law or not.[14]

In democracies, transparency is of utmost importance. Citizens need proper information on why and how certain measures were adopted. For this reason, it has been highlighted that even non-majoritarian bodies can increase their legitimacy by increasing the *transparency* of the decision-making.[15] Practices of transparency can include 'commitments to the publication of annual reports and complaints procedures, the creation of websites with information on the task, structure, products, and performance of organizations, and periodic evaluations by an external committee of professional peers'.[16]

What characterizes these practices is their voluntariness. For this reason, in deciding whether to adopt them or not, organizations compare costs and benefits. Among the costs, we can mention the time and personnel necessary to collect, organize and disseminate information, and also the risk that openness could result in negative press and damage the organization's reputation.[17] Among the benefits, the most important is that of meeting the expectations of legislators, who are responsible for the organizations' funding and independence: by acting in accordance with what legislators desire, organizations secure their funding and their status, which could otherwise be in danger.[18] Obviously, these voluntary practices cannot substitute 'traditional' accountability and monitoring by democratically elected

[13] ibid 747. See also A Flückiger, 'Keeping Domestic Soft Law Accountable: Towards a Gradual Formalization' in Joost Pauwelyn, Ramses Wessel and Jan Wouters (eds), *Informal International Lawmaking* (OUP 2012) 409 ('the validity of restrictions [imposed through informal or soft law] to these fundamental rights [of individuals] must be judged based on the same criteria as those applied to legal [hard law] restrictions, which means that they are subject to the requirements of legal basis, public interest and proportionality').

[14] Pauwelyn and others (n 13) 751–52.

[15] D Curtin and AJ Meijer, 'Does Transparency Strengthen Legitimacy?' (2006) 11 Information Polity 109.

[16] C Koop, 'Theorizing and Explaining Voluntary Accountability' (2014) 92 Public Administration 565. Scholars like Koop refer to these practices as 'voluntary accountability', distinguishing it from 'mandatory accountability'. For clarity's sake, we prefer to talk of accountability only when the agency's response is demanded by the political principal (so it is mandatory), and consider all voluntary acts that provide more information, explanation, or disclosure as transparency. Obviously, transparency is not relevant for independent agencies only, but for governments as well; see J Fairbanks, KD Plowman and BL Rawlins, 'Transparency in Government Communication' (2007) 7 Journal of Public Affairs 23.

[17] Koop (n 16) 566.

[18] ibid.

bodies—exactly because organizations could still be unwilling to reveal information that they fear could be used against them.

Transparency is supposed to enhance legitimacy by making citizens, and the relevant epistemic communities in particular, more aware of the decisions adopted by independent agencies and the reasons for them. Since no body in a democracy enjoys *full* independence, the assumption is that the initial act of delegation can always be modified if the political principal thinks that the agency has not made good use of its independence. Such decisions, however, can be taken only if citizens, experts, political parties have full information about the agency's conduct.[19]

The requirement of transparency does not only concern the participation of public actors (like government officials or state agencies), but also the involvement of private actors. Chapter 1 showed that the ICN invites non-governmental advisers (NGAs) to its meetings, and that some NGAs were influential in the establishment of the ICN as well. NGAs do not formally participate in decision-making (they do not vote), but given that there are no formal voting procedures and everything is agreed by consensus, participating in the discussion is certainly relevant. Scholars that have addressed this issue warn against the risk of considering the participation of experts and private actors as 'neutral'. Freeman argues that 'many private actors participate in governance in ways that are rarely recognised by the public, acknowledged by politicians or carefully analysed by legal scholars'.[20] Chapters 1–3 also confirm this in relation to the ICN.

Like bureaucrats serving in independent agencies (see also Section 4.3.1.1.1), private actors are not elected. However, while bureaucrats are expected to serve the public interest, private actors are not, and they remain 'relatively insulated from legislative, executive and judicial oversight'.[21] The involvement of private actors in regulation and democratic decision-making in general relies on a pluralistic perspective, according to which all actors in a society must be able to articulate their interests in the political system, leaving to democratic institutions the decision on how to 'balance' all interests.[22] But this perspective must consider that not all actors are endowed with the same resources and capabilities to access decision makers.

[19] This does not mean that more transparency is always desirable. As Weiler argues, '[t]ransparency and access to documents are often invoked as a possible remedy [. . .]. But if you do not know what is going on, which documents will you ask to see?' Joseph Weiler, 'To Be a European Citizen: Eros and Civilisation' (1997) 4 Journal of European Public Policy 495, 512.

[20] Jody Freeman, 'The Real Democracy Problem in Administrative Law' in David Dyzenhaus (ed), *Recrafting the Rule of Law* (Hart 1999) 331.

[21] Freeman (n 20) 335.

[22] An argument in favour of the participation of firms in decision-making is put forward by Zingales, who argues that this helps to counter the power of states that are too strong (Luigi Zingales, 'Towards a Political Theory of the Firm' (2017) 31 Journal of Economic Perspectives 113, 125). However, if business power is too strong, businesses might become able to shape legal protections in their own interests, rather than those of society at large.

Notably, firms tend to be in a strong position: they have resources, they provide jobs, they are fewer compared to workers (so better able to coordinate among themselves). This makes it possible for some of them to have preferential access to policymakers.[23] Our survey has shown (see Chapter 3, Section 3.3.1) that most NGAs participating in the ICN are either representatives of big business or lawyers from law firms (who most likely assist big business in competition matters). So there is probably a bias in the access that different private actors have to the ICN.

As private actors participate in decision-making first and foremost to advance and defend their interests, we should pay close attention to the information they provide (and most importantly the information that they *do not* provide). According to Freeman, the fact that:

> a public entity […] retains ultimate authority over a decision-making process does not make per se that process acceptable or legitimate. When an agency adopts without deliberation a private standard setting organisation's safety standards, for example, we might rightly doubt that the mere fact of agency incorporation ensures the legitimacy of the standards. Formal legal procedures and agency oversight may provide the appearance of adequate accountability, but informal mechanisms and private parties play an important and undervalued role legitimising public–private arrangements.[24]

This does not mean that private actors should be cut out from public processes, of course, but there must be transparency about who participates, what information she or he brings, and how this information is used by decision makers.

To sum up, based on the literature review illustrated above, we can list the following criteria for checking the legitimacy of a transnational network like the ICN:

1. minimum moral acceptability (not committing serious injustices, principally human rights abuses);
2. comparative benefit—the Rodrik criterion (the transnational network must provide some benefit that would not be provided, or would be more costly if the network did not exist);
3. institutional integrity (the network must adhere to its own rules of procedures);
4. involvement of legislatures (the activity of the network should be controlled by national legislatures);

[23] Stephen Wilks, *The Political Power of the Business Corporation* (Edward Elgar 2013) 24–26. On the influence firms can have on regulators, see also Johanna Stark, *Law for Sale: A Philosophical Critique of Regulatory Competition* (OUP 2019) 103.
[24] Bronwen and Yeung (n 10) 287.

5. transparency regarding:
   a. decisions (the network should publish information about how decisions have been made, and about which principles were followed in decision-making);
   b. the involvement of private actors (the network should publicize information about private actors who participate in decision-making, and what is their role and input).

While we will structure our detailed assessment of the ICN's legitimacy, effectiveness, and efficiency according to the distinction illustrated in the following section (and the definitions set out in the Introduction to this book, Section I.4), we will get back to these criteria in the Conclusion, highlighting whether and how these criteria are fulfilled by the ICN. As noted at the beginning of this section, we find it useful to 'unpack' the different ways in which organizations can achieve legitimacy, which are often conflated at the expense of conceptual clarity. By distinguishing between input (democratic) legitimacy and output legitimacy, we can more clearly assess the ICN. Moreover, most debates on the ICN focus on the concept of efficiency and effectiveness, and it is useful to refer to these discussions explicitly. Our insight is that those who assess efficiency and effectiveness imply that both can increase a body or organization's legitimacy. In Section 4.2.2, we clarify the link between these three concepts. In a nutshell, we argue that there is, to some extent, a trade-off between democratic legitimacy and output-based legitimacy (ie legitimacy based on supposed efficiency or effectiveness). The lack of the former can be compensated by increasing the latter, and vice versa. This argument has been proposed for justifying the establishment of independent regulatory agencies, for instance. At the same time, no body in a democracy can be legitimized by effectiveness and efficiency considerations only. By analysing them separately, scholars and policymakers (and, in the ICN's case, individual states) can assess if the 'balance' they reach is satisfactory.

4.2.2 Democratic (input-based) and output-based legitimacy

In this section, we discuss the distinction between a view of legitimacy based on an organization's link with the 'will of the people' (democratic legitimacy) and a view of legitimacy, used frequently in the context of non-majoritarian institutions, as justified by a superior policy outcome that an organization may grant (often described in terms of effectiveness and efficiency).

A core principle of democracy is that political institutions are legitimate because they respond to the 'will of the people'. In this respect, democracies can be understood as 'chains of delegation': voters elect representatives (members of parliaments and, in some systems, heads of states), representatives elect or appoint prime ministers and governments, governments appoint bureaucrats, and so forth.[25] Delegation implies *accountability*, which has been defined by Bovens as 'a relationship between an actor and a forum, in which the actor has an obligation to explain and to justify his or her conduct, the forum can pose questions and pass judgement, and the actor may face consequences'.[26] Using the example above, bureaucrats are accountable to ministers in governments, governments are accountable to representatives in parliaments, representatives are accountable to voters. Accountability means that, when a body delegates power to another body, it will set up a series of procedures that enable it to control how the agent operates (for example through reports, or obliging the agent to legally justify its conduct), to request information, to possibly intervene or sanction the behaviour of the agent if the 'delegation contract' has been breached, and so on.

In the end, power comes from the people, although it requires delegation to be exercised effectively—millions of voters would find it impossible to adopt decisions themselves. This last point is crucial. There is an inherent tension between delegation and accountability. Delegation is necessary for reasons of *efficiency* of decision-making: since it would be too cumbersome to reach an agreement among millions of decision makers, societies rely on representation. A few hundreds of decision makers can take decisions more efficiently, and more effectively. However, the power they exercise does not *belong* to them. They exercise power on behalf of those who elected them. In the language of principal–agent theory, they are the agents, voters are the principals.[27]

Everyone understands that this representation is overly simplistic. The fact that accountable actors will 'face consequences' for not complying with the will of the forum to whom they are accountable is seldom observed in politics, especially when it comes to the most important 'link' in the chain of delegation, that between representatives and voters. Sanction is possible through elections—if voters are not satisfied with their representatives, they can elect others—but elections take place at regular intervals (and involve myriad issues). Unsatisfied voters cannot just change their representatives when they want. The reason why this happens is again related to the complexity and expense of holding elections in societies with millions of voters.

However, there is more than that in the justification of the use of power, and this concerns regulation in particular. Taking inspiration from economic studies on the independence of central banks,[28] a number of political scientists (and

[25] T Bergman, WC Müller and K Strøm, 'Introduction: Parliamentary Democracy and the Chain of Delegation' (2000) 37 European Journal of Political Research 255; K Strøm, 'Delegation and Accountability in Parliamentary Democracies' (2000) 37 European Journal of Political Research 261.

[26] M Bovens, 'Analysing and Assessing Accountability: A Conceptual Framework' (2007) 13 European Law Journal 450.

[27] Y Karagiannis and M Guidi, 'Principal–Agent Models and EU Policy-Making' in Nikolaos Zahariadis and Laurie Buonanno (eds), *The Routledge Handbook of European Public Policy* (Routledge 2017), 13.

[28] See FE Kydland and EC Prescott, 'Rules Rather than Discretion: The Inconsistency of Optimal Plans' (1977) 85 Journal of Political Economy 473; RJ Barro and DB Gordon, 'Rules, Discretion and

Giandomenico Majone in particular) have argued that democratic accountability is not always desirable in regulation.[29] According to this view, there are cases in which democratically accountable politicians may adopt decisions that are not in the interest of the people, but only of their re-election. In the field of monetary policy, (hyper)inflation has usually been interpreted as the result of politicians' incentive to 'pump' money into the economy; this has the effect of sustaining state expenditure in the short term, but it damages the government's credibility in the long term, leading to expectations of high inflation for the future. In the field of competition policy, this dilemma could be framed as a politician's incentive to protect a few uncompetitive 'national champions'. This might protect national jobs in the short term, but it might also damage consumers and potential competitors, and thus discouraging investment in the longer term.

One solution to these drawbacks of democratic accountability has been identified in insulating some policymaking from the democratic 'chain of delegation', ie making decision makers *independent* from governments and parliaments. The expansion of regulatory policymaking carried out by independent agencies, which has accelerated between 1990 and the early 2000s,[30] is a consequence of this paradigm shift that has characterized all advanced democracies. Independent agencies have been established in policy fields as diverse as competition, financial markets regulation, telecommunications, environmental protection, food safety, and so forth.

This novel justification for the establishment of political institutions introduces a new type of legitimacy, not linked to the 'will of the people', but to *performance*. Performance is the reason why some bodies are insulated from democratic control (independence is needed because otherwise elected policymakers would interfere in suboptimal ways). In this respect, scholars have talked of 'output legitimacy'[31]

Reputation in a Model of Monetary Policy' (1983) 12 Journal of Monetary Economics 101; K Rogoff, 'The Optimal Degree of Commitment to an Intermediate Monetary Target' (1985) 100 Quarterly Journal of Economics 1169.

[29] G Majone, 'Temporal Consistency and Policy Credibility: Why Democracies Need Non-Majoritarian Institutions' (1996) RSCAS 1996/57 EUI Working Papers; G Majone, 'From the Positive to the Regulatory State: Causes and Consequences of Changes in the Mode of Governance' (1997) 17 Journal of Public Policy 139; G Majone, 'Two Logics of Delegation: Agency and Fiduciary Relations in EU Governance' (2001) 2 European Union Politics 103; G Majone, 'Nonmajoritarian Institutions and the Limits of Democratic Governance: A Political Transaction–Cost Approach' (2001) 157 Journal of Institutional and Theoretical Economics 57. See also M Guidi, 'Delegation and Varieties of Capitalism: Explaining the Independence of National Competition Agencies in the European Union' (2014) 12 Comparative European Politics 343; M Guidi, 'The Impact of Independence on Regulatory Outcomes: The Case of EU Competition Policy' (2015) 53 JCMS: Journal of Common Market Studies 1195; M Guidi, *Competition Policy Enforcement in EU Member States: What Is Independence For?* (Palgrave Macmillan 2016).

[30] See J Jordana, D Levi-Faur and X Fernández i Marín, 'The Global Diffusion of Regulatory Agencies Channels of Transfer and Stages of Diffusion' (2011) 44 Comparative Political Studies 1343.

[31] Output legitimacy is opposed to input legitimacy, that is legitimacy based on the process of appointment and delegation of the decision makers. See F Scharpf, *Governing in Europe: Effective and Democratic?* (OUP 1999); JHH Weiler, 'In the Face of Crisis: Input Legitimacy, Output Legitimacy and the Political Messianism of European Integration' (2012) 34 Journal of European Integration 825.

to emphasize that, in the absence of democratic accountability, these regimes, bodies or institutions derive their legitimacy from their capability to deliver. This, however, immediately raises three further questions: first, do these independent bodies deliver or not? Second, who sets the parameters of what a satisfactory 'delivery' is? Third, even if they deliver, is this enough to make them legitimate or is some form of democratic control also important, regardless of the effectiveness and efficiency gain? If democratic control is important, how much is sufficient and what type of control should this be? Evidence of a relationship between independence and performance of regulatory agencies is very limited.[32] In the field of competition policy as well, studies have pointed to mixed evidence.[33] This suggests that the promise of 'performance through independence' might not have been kept.

Of course, there are many ways of measuring performance. In the definition of what is performance, two important concepts are those of *effectiveness* and *efficiency* (see Section I.4 of the Introduction). When we ask ourselves whether a body or organization is effective, we ask ourselves: does this organization do what it is meant to do? Does it achieve its goals? Are its actions consistent with its mandate? Differently, when we ask ourselves whether a body or organization is efficient, we ask ourselves: does this organization achieve its goals making a good use of its resources? Do the benefits it brings about outweigh its costs? These questions suggest that independent actors need to be controlled to make sure that their independence is ultimately justified.

According to Majone, independence is justified and desirable when policy-making has to pursue *efficiency* rather than *redistribution*. The rationale behind this distinction is that redistributive policies are zero-sum games (someone gains, someone loses), and therefore only representatives with a popular mandate can make those choices. Vice versa, policies aiming at efficiency are positive-sum games (everybody gains). In these policies there would be no space for partisan consideration, but only the need to choose the most efficient equilibrium—which, Majone argues, can be done by independent experts. While Majone's distinction is theoretically appealing, it is very hard to distinguish between redistributive and efficiency policies in practice. As a matter of fact, redistributive policies (eg

[32] See eg D Sutherland and others, 'Public Policies and Investment in Network Infrastructure' (2011) 2011 OECD Journal: Economic Studies 1; AR Vining, C Laurin and D Weimer, 'The Longer-Run Performance Effects of Agencification: Theory and Evidence from Québec Agencies' (2015) 35 Journal of Public Policy 193. More evidence of the link between independence and performance has been found in the field of monetary policy, see eg V Grilli, D Masciandaro and G Tabellini, 'Political and Monetary Institutions and Public Financial Policies in the Industrial Countries' (1991) 6 Economic Policy 341; A Cukierman, SB Webb and B Neyapti, 'Measuring the Independence of Central Banks and Its Effect on Policy Outcomes' (1992) 6 World Bank Economic Review 353; A Alesina and LH Summers, 'Central Bank Independence and Macroeconomic Performance: Some Comparative Evidence' (1993) 25 Journal of Money, Credit and Banking 151.

[33] See Guidi (n 29) 138ff for an overview. In its comparative analysis of the impact of independence on competition enforcement, Guidi finds no significant relationship between independence and performance. See Guidi (n 29) 1195.

shifting the tax burden from poorer to richer citizens) can enhance the efficiency of the economic system, and regulatory policies that seem aimed at pursuing efficiency (like breaking or not breaking a monopoly) have huge redistributive implications for the actors involved. Moreover, multiple equilibria potentially exist not only for redistributive, but also for regulatory policies. The regulator's discretion in favouring certain equilibria at the expense of others can be, in practice, huge, and questionable. Advocates of regulatory independence often assume that the regulator is given a clearly specified goal (that is set by democratic bodies) and then it just has to choose the best instruments to achieve it. This representation is overly simplistic, and practically never met.[34] We therefore believe that a clear-cut distinction cannot easily be drawn, and that the legitimacy of independent decision makers must rely on more solid criteria, like the ones we have illustrated in the previous section.

4.3 Legitimacy, effectiveness, and efficiency and the ICN

In Section 4.2.1, we argued that international networks like the ICN should fulfil certain criteria to be considered legitimate. For this reason, the creation, development, and activity of the ICN, while not self-evidently problematic, should be carefully scrutinized. The fact that many of its members are agencies that already enjoy some degree of independence from politics in their own countries; the limited parliamentary scrutiny that the ICN receives (and received when the ICN was established); the opacity of its decision-making process; the involvement of private actors—all these aspects call for further inquiry.

How, then, should an assessment of the ICN be carried out? Since the ICN does not have the power to impose decisions on its members, we cannot discuss its legitimacy as we would discuss the legitimacy of a body with policymaking powers in a nation state. However, we can assess its status and actions from several viewpoints, which pertain both to the 'input side' of legitimacy and to the 'output side'. We can also examine the legitimacy of the ICN system as a whole (including the ICN, but also the NCAs and other actors which participate in it and their states).

As regards input legitimacy, it is important, first of all, to assess the origins of the ICN's *mandate*. When we analyse public bodies in nation states, we can trace how they position themselves in the chain of delegation: who created them? With which purpose? Ultimately, even if a body is not democratically accountable (meaning

[34] Consider the quintessential independent bodies, central banks. They were the first to be studied by scholars who noted that they had a clearly defined goal (controlling inflation) and they just had to choose the policy tools to obtain it. This could have been true in periods of sustained economic growth like the 1980s and 1990s. But when economic crises have emerged (the post-2008 crisis, and the COVID-19 crisis as well), and inflation has ceased to be a problem, central banks have not only changed tools: they have redefined their goals, mostly autonomously.

that its members cannot be sanctioned, removed, or replaced if they do not act in the interests of their principals), we still know why it is so. When an independent agency, for instance, is created by law, there has been an act of a legislative body which recognized the necessity to establish the agency, and which also concluded that it is in the interest of the country to give independence to that body. We can certainly discuss whether this decision is right or wrong, but it is clear when such decision was taken, by whom, and on which grounds.

In the case of the ICN, who are the actors who established it? Formally, the creators of the ICN were (some) competition authorities. Did they act on behalf of the legislators that established them? Or was their decision autonomous? Did they follow any explicit national rules for the establishment of such bodies? As NCAs are given a certain degree of independence, we can expect that they do not need to consult parliaments and governments for every decision they take (where there are not explicit rules). Yet, this creates a potential problem when independence is not used to carry out the functions *for which independence was initially conceded*, but to adopt new, different, not initially foreseen decisions. In the political science literature, such phenomena are defined as 'unintended consequences of delegation'.[35] This concept is employed to explain why and how bodies that are created with a certain purpose, and that have been given autonomy and discretion to pursue such purpose, use at a later stage their autonomy to pursue different goals, or simply to expand their powers.[36] In sum, when assessing some NCAs' decision to establish the ICN, others' decision to join it once it was created, and each member's decision to continue participating (instead of abandoning it, for instance) we must ask the following questions: what level of democratic control over the ICN was established? What goals were set for the ICN (this is necessary to assess whether the ICN is effective and efficient)? Were these decisions taken in consultation with democratic bodies or were they autonomous? Were they decisions aimed at better implementing NCAs' mandates (in which case one could argue that it was coherent with the initial act of delegation) or not?

Another aspect related to input legitimacy concerns the *nature* of the ICN. While for NCAs we know for sure that they are *public* bodies, which perform their functions on behalf of all citizens, when it comes to organizations like the ICN this identification is much more blurred. The ICN sometimes calls itself an

[35] J Tallberg, 'Delegation to Supranational Institutions: Why, How, and with What Consequences?' (2002) 25 West European Politics 23.

[36] This approach is rather popular among scholars who study European integration. The way the Commission, with the help of the European Court of Justice, managed to overcome member states' resistance to deepen integration in certain policies, or to create European competences that were not specified in the Rome Treaty (think of the power to authorize mergers, conferred on the Commission with Regulation 4064/89). For an application of this approach, see MA Pollack, *The Engines of European Integration: Delegation, Agency, and Agenda Setting in the EU* (OUP 2003) 281–99; SK Schmidt, 'Commission Activism: Subsuming Telecommunications and Electricity under European Competition Law' (1998) 5 Journal of European Public Policy 169.

'international organization', placing itself in a similar category to the OECD and UNCTAD.[37] Yet, while it has been established by public bodies, the ICN is not a 'standard' public international organization. This is because, unlike the OECD and UNCTAD, the ICN was not created by states themselves. It was designed and created by organizations (NCAs) within those states—organizations that are often highly insulated from political influence. As we will see, at least some of these NCAs acted without a direct (or even indirect) mandate to create and then participate in an international organization like the ICN. Those founding the ICN also chose to mainstream the input and influence of NGAs into its activities (although they are not full ICN members). Although the ICN cannot impose behaviours on its members (in this respect it is like the OECD and UNCTAD), as Chapters 1–3 demonstrate, it certainly has some power and influence: it makes recommendations, and it investigates compliance with these recommendations, for example. What is the ground for these actions? Where do these powers come from? Are they legitimately controlled?

Turning to output legitimacy, the main aspects to analyse regard, as we have illustrated above, the *effectiveness* and the *efficiency* of the ICN. One might find that the ICN's input legitimacy is weak, and yet conclude that what it does is beneficial to all its members—in this case, its output could justify its existence ('could', because consequentialist arguments are not always sufficient in all states).

As we argued above, effectiveness concerns being able to deliver. But to deliver what? Who sets the goals of the ICN? Are these goals clearly specified so that it is possible to compare expectations and reality? Assuming that this is the case, we should assess: (a) whether the ICN has allowed and enabled its members to achieve the objectives they set when they created it; (b) whether new goals were progressively added; (c) if these goals were coherent with the initial mandate (or generated following the correct 'constitutional' method for changes).

Regarding efficiency, it is useful to analyse the relationship between costs and benefits of membership. While participation in the ICN can entail direct costs, such as the money used to participate in ICN meetings, or to hire people that must deal with ICN's activities, most costs and benefits that must be assessed are indirect—more specifically, political, social, and economic. An NCA could benefit from participating in the ICN because this allows it to improve its competition enforcement and therefore to attract investments that benefit the whole country. This is probably the main benefit that most NCAs expect from ICN membership. Could there be also political benefits? NCAs participating in the ICN could introduce in their country best practices that could be adopted by other bodies. In

[37] See, for example, ICN Vice-Chair for Young Agencies and Regional Diversity, Lessons to Be Learnt from the Experience of Young Competition Agencies: An Update to the 2006 Report (2019) 3, <https://www.internationalcompetitionnetwork.org/wp-content/uploads/2019/06/SGVC_YoungerAgenciesReport2019.pdf> accessed 8 October 2021.

theory, this is possible. What about costs instead? Could ICN membership imply an economic cost for a country? Again, in theory it is possible that the implementation of ICN recommended practices makes it possible for some multinationals to take decisions that damage a country's economy (for instance, a merger that raises costs for consumers, or a takeover that leads to a relocation of workforce to another country). However, as the (expected) benefits are probably mainly economic, the likely costs are probably mainly political. In democratic terms, anything that reduces the voters' control on policymaking can be seen as a cost, a loss. These costs can be worthwhile. To recall the example made above, voters lose power by delegating decision-making to a parliament, but the gain in efficiency and effectiveness can outweigh this cost. Similarly, if delegating a power to an independent bureaucrat allows democratically elected politicians to better pursue their goals, independence (a loss of control in its strict sense) can be worthwhile.[38] However, if NCAs, which were given independence for achieving certain goals, use the ICN to gain even more autonomy, and to be less accountable than they already were, one might doubt that such loss of control is reasonable (especially when they use their powers to favour policies which are counter to the long-term preferences in their states). In sum, the key exercise in assessing effectiveness and efficiency is comparing costs and benefits, and seeing which prevail. This 'calculation', of course, might be different from country to country. Some countries might find it beneficial to participate in the ICN, some might not. This is one reason why the ICN should make value judgements it makes explicit. It is also why we think that states (not just NCAs) should examine the costs and benefits within their own legal order of ICN participation, as well as their use of each ICN work product.

In the remainder of this section, we will analyse to what extent the ICN conforms with principles of democratic (input) legitimacy as well as with criteria relating to effectiveness and efficiency—which (as we have shown) can provide an output-based legitimacy for an organization. When analysing democratic legitimacy, we will focus both on the decision to join the ICN and to that of continuing to participate; moreover, we will check the ICN's democratic legitimacy both in the *creation* of rules (or, better said, recommended practices) and in their *implementation*.

4.3.1 Input legitimacy and the ICN

Discussions about democratic accountability often focus on two kinds of democracy: liberal and deliberative. Liberal theories consider active citizen engagement in each issue unnecessary. Citizens elect politicians to engage for them (unelected people should not do this, as they are not accountable). Different liberal democracy

[38] See for instance J van 't Klooster, 'The Ethics of Delegating Monetary Policy' (2020) 82 Journal of Politics 587.

models demand that politicians be: directly involved in competition policy and enforcement (given the highly redistributive nature of enforcement),[39] indirectly involved by pushing their NCA to act in specific ways, or to appoint those in charge of NCAs, so that citizens can punish these officials at the ballot box if they act contrary to citizens' wishes. Disputes about the 'best' model arise even in established democracies. In part, this is because, as we discussed above, many scholars have argued that we should insulate regulatory agencies (and their outputs) from democratic oversight to some degree. From the citizens' perspective, political accountability should improve the quality of regulatory agencies' policy outputs.[40] Deliberative theories focus on citizens' liberty to participate in politics. Those affected by an issue should have equal participation rights, so that relevant issues (for them) will be debated, and debates are accessible to them, with their resources being considered when assessing this.[41]

Section 4.3.1.1 starts by examining the input legitimacy at the creation of the ICN itself. Then, it discusses states' ability to control ICN-related inputs. Our analysis focuses on deliberative theories of democracy and then liberal theories. Section 4.3.1.2 discusses the input legitimacy of states' use of ICN outputs. States might use ICN outputs in NCA competition decisions or as part of a national legislative process. Even if input legitimacy is missing in the other two levels, it might be recovered here.

4.3.1.1 Input legitimacy (when joining the ICN and ongoing participation)

We do not know what was specifically agreed between the first NCAs when they created the ICN. However, we can access the ICN website as it was on 14 January 2002 (shortly after the ICN was set up). It told NCAs seeking ICN membership to send a letter saying that they had read the *Memorandum on the Establishment and Operation of the International Competition Network* and noting that their membership would be governed by its terms.[42] Given the timing, it seems likely that the original NCAs were also bound by the same, or similar, rules. This *Memorandum* sets out the ICN's mission and aims. Certain things seem binding. For example, as we have already seen, it will be:

> a project-orientated, consensus-based, informal network of antitrust agencies from developed and developing countries that will address antitrust

[39] See Christopher Townley, *A Framework for European Competition Law: Co-ordinated Diversity* (Hart 2018) 97ff.

[40] Anne-Marie Slaughter and David Zaring, 'Networking Goes International: An Update' (2006) 2 Annual Review of Law and Social Science 211, 220.

[41] Tanja Börzel and Diana Panke, 'Network Governance: Effective and Legitimate?' in Eva Sørensen and Jacob Torfing (eds), *Theories of Democratic Network Governance* (Palgrave MacMillan 2008) 164–65, and the references cited there; Eva Sørensen and Jacob Torfing, 'Theoretical Approaches to Democratic Network Governance' ibid 2 34–35, and the references cited there.

[42] ICN, Become a Member (n.d.), <http://web.archive.org/web/20020114184234/http://www.internationalcompetitionnetwork.org/mem4.html> accessed 8 October 2021.

> enforcement and policy issues of common interest and formulate proposals for procedural and substantive convergence through a results-orientated agenda and structure.[43]

In its letter, the prospective NCA member also signs up to a binding set of *procedural* rules. These contain obligations like what types of actors can be ICN members (as well as their voting rights and contributions) or who else can participate in the ICN as non-members (how they are appointed and their rights). It also outlines issues like: how topics are selected for study by the ICN, who selects these topics (along with rules for the election to ICN leadership roles, the length of the leaders' mandate, etc), and how ICN work products will be agreed. It seems reasonable to call these 'binding procedural rules'. This framework was updated in 2012. However, the changes in the 2012 version of the framework make no difference to our analysis, except insofar as this is explicitly noted below.

On the other hand, there are also hints that ICN membership is not necessarily envisaged as generating binding, ongoing *substantive* commitments. ICN activities are voluntary. Furthermore, the ICN 'is not intended to replace or coordinate the work of other organizations, nor will it exercise any rule-making function'. And, when the ICN reaches agreement on work products, individual states must decide whether and how to implement them.[44] Chapters 2 and 3 showed that NCAs can sometimes unilaterally follow ICN work products. At other times, changes require input from other actors too, for example where new legislation is needed. Having said that, as Chapter 2 also noted, there is increasing emphasis on checking the implementation of the ICN work products (which seems designed to 'encourage' states to implement too).

Different states have different ways of injecting sufficient democratic legitimacy into competition policy and enforcement (and what is 'sufficient' depends on each state's system). For illustrative purposes, Section 4.3.1.1.2 examines a spectrum of approaches to input legitimacy in the ICN, through a liberal democracy lens. Before that, Section 4.3.1.1.1 adopts a deliberative democracy perspective.

4.3.1.1.1 Deliberative democracy

There is little discussion about the 'input' legitimacy of the ICN and its outputs. However, for those that reflect upon this issue, Fox provides a helpful expression of

[43] Applications must also be approved by the ICN Steering Group, ICN, *ICN Operational Framework* (2012) s 2, previously available at <http://internationalcompetitionnetwork.org/uploads/library/doc784.pdf> (broken ICN link, see discussion in Introduction, n 16).

[44] ICN, Memorandum on the Establishment and Operation of the International Competition Network (n.d.), <http://web.archive.org/web/20030420143508/http://www.internationalcompetitionnetwork.org/mou.pdf> accessed 8 October 2021.

the logic. According to Fox, the ICN's legitimacy 'is built around notions of participation and transparency'. She explains it like this:

> All antitrust jurisdictions of the world are invited to belong to the ICN. Representatives of all authorities are invited to attend the annual meetings and workshops and to take part in all working groups. A substantial number of non-governmental advisors (predominantly from the defense bar and business but also some academics and others) actively participate ... The ICN prides itself on its open, inviting, inclusive, and transparent process.[45]

The ICN has gone to some lengths to increase the number, geographic origin, and range of expertise of its participants. However, Chapter 1 showed that ICN members are NCAs (that are often largely independent of political influence), rather than states. NGAs are not ICN members but can also participate in ICN activities when invited. Many actors can be NGAs, such as private practitioners, consumer groups, academics, and companies. That said, most stakeholders are not represented in the ICN. Immediately after the previous quote, Fox herself highlights many weaknesses with her 'inclusiveness' characterization. For example, she notes that consumer groups and representatives of the plaintiffs' bar are noticeably under-represented.[46] She adds, other than the core 'mature' NCAs, participation is 'predictably limited' by a lack of funds, time, expertise, and language (all these limitations have been confirmed by the analysis we carried out in Chapter 3). This, Fox explains, 'may produce' greater voice for NCAs from the USA and the EU. In other words, there are not necessarily a diverse range of actors involved and, even to the extent that there are, there are large disparities in their 'voice'. In fact, Chapters 1 and 3 highlighted that the NCAs and NGAs with most influence tend to be from rich, 'Western' states.

[45] Eleanor Fox, 'Linked-In: Antitrust and the Virtues of a Virtual Network' in Paul Lugard (ed), *The International Competition Network at Ten: Origins, Accomplishments and Aspirations* (Intersentia 2011) 125–26. See also Daniel Sokol, 'The ICN in the Context of International Antitrust Institutions' ibid 159; John Fingleton, 'Competition Agencies and Global Markets: The Challenges Ahead' ibid 195 and 199; ICN Merger Working Group, *ICN Recommended Practices for Merger Notification and Review Procedures: Member Self-Assessment—Report on 2016 Survey Results* (2017) 1, <https://www.internationalcompetitionnetwork.org/wp-content/uploads/2019/04/MWG_NPRPssurveyreport2017.pdf accessed 8 October. Others have even narrower conceptions of this type of legitimacy, such as increased legitimacy through participation of NCAs from mature and newer competition systems, Merit Janow and James Rill, 'The Origins of the ICN' in Paul Lugard (ed), *The International Competition Network at Ten: origins, accomplishments and aspirations* (Intersentia 2011) 37); David Lewis, 'Some Reflections on the ICN' ibid 213. Still others imply that adding political input increases legitimacy but do not think this adds much, Philip Marsden, 'Acta non verba: Keep "Talking Shop", Don't Become Another Talking Shop' ibid 144.

[46] By way of contrast, others believe that 'the ICN has proved unique in its capacity to engage all relevant actors on all issues of competition law and policy' Maria Coppola and others, '(Nearly) A Century with the ICN' [2020] Competition Policy International, <https://www.competitionpolicyinternational.com/nearly-a-century-with-the-icn/#_ednref6> accessed 8 October 2021.

It is possible that when Fox highlights the lack of wider consultation by the ICN, she is hoping that, if wider consultation could be achieved, it would increase legitimacy through some deliberative democracy model (although this is unclear). This is a powerful idea in regulatory theory. Under such a rubric, the solution to the ICN's partial membership and unequal power relationships is to widen the range of actors (firms, NGOs, citizens, etc) involved there and to support the less influential to develop their ideas and to make them known. If this is her hope, then there is a deeper problem. This is because increasing *democratic* legitimacy through deliberative democracy does not just demand a wider range of voices. It demands a wide range of relevant voices (ie those *citizens* that will be affected by the relevant measure). Chapter 1 showed the ICN effectively ignoring citizens. As Wilks cogently argues, under such a model, there now seems to be government by the people and corporations. Government by regulation is a very different proposition to government by hierarchy. It replaces command and control with negotiation and persuasion.[47] Firms can exercise political influence in a body where political control is less. This seems almost certainly true for the ICN, given the role and prominence firms have there (see the discussion in Chapter 1).[48] It is curious that we give firms this access and influence in policymaking when they are not individuals with moral values.[49] This is especially true for firms in the Anglo-Saxon mould, who are only focused on their own interests (this is essentially all that UK company law allows normal firms such as these to consider); unless one thinks that this selfish action will benefit society in general (which might undermine the need for the ICN at all). If we give firms power, should we also ask that they exercise some political responsibility?[50] If so, it might also be worth checking that this actually happens, given how unlikely it seems (see Chapter 1).

States, and others, looking to increase the ICN's democratic legitimacy through a deliberative democracy model would need to engage with a wide range of affected citizens through the ICN. Furthermore, due to likely problems of resourcing, language, gaps in understanding, and other problems, those citizens that got involved would likely need significant support. The level of engagement required under such a model would radically alter the nature and cost of the ICN. Changes of this magnitude, if they are even possible, seem unlikely to happen any time soon.

Even if more 'inclusion' does not necessarily increase legitimacy, it may (by taking account of a wider range of ideas) facilitate a higher quality of policy output, increasing effectiveness (although fully engaging with a wider range of stakeholders could undermine the efficiency of the system).

47 Wilks (n 23) 145.

48 The risk of regulatory capture is already great. See discussion and references in Wouter Wils, 'Independence of Competition Authorities: The Example of the EU and Its Member States' (2019) 42 World Competition 149, s VI.

49 Wilks (n 23) 11.

50 ibid 17.

4.3.1.1.2 Liberal democracy

Input legitimacy might matter less if the ICN had no power. Yet, as we have seen in the previous chapters of this book, the ICN actually wields considerable 'soft' power. So, if we cannot justify the ICN framework through deliberative democracy mechanisms, what is left for input legitimacy?

There is a widespread view that NCAs' competition enforcement should be largely independent of politicians (albeit still accountable).[51] Even if a state thought that such independence were necessary for NCAs (and we have questioned this),[52] it might still consider it problematic (democratically) that its NCA unilaterally joins an international forum like the ICN and then helps to produce influential (albeit non-binding) work products. Especially if the NCA then applies these work products itself; or, encourages others in the state to do so. Of interest here, more specifically, are questions such as, did the NCA act in consultation with democratic bodies in its home state or not? Insofar as an NCA acted autonomously, was it acting within the limits of its existing powers? Was creating the ICN a decision aimed at better implementing each NCA's mandate (if so, one could argue that it was coherent with the initial act of delegation) or not? Policymaking by technocrats may be more legitimate in this highly redistributive area if it had been explicitly (or even implicitly) endorsed by majoritarian actors from the relevant states in the ICN's 'constitutional moment' (alongside other elements of the ICN's 'constitution', such as ignoring public policy concerns and 'non-discrimination').[53]

In fact, even today there are some hints that many states do not automatically accept ICN recommended practices and other work products (even when they have been endorsed by their NCAs).[54] This is, potentially, an important

[51] See, for example, William Kovacic and Marc Winerman, 'The Federal Trade Commission as an Independent Agency: Autonomy, Legitimacy, and Effectiveness' (2015) 100 Iowa Law Review 2085.

[52] See the discussion in the Introduction to this book, Section I.2.

[53] As we saw in Chapter 1, who is present in a network (and who is not) matters. It can change the nature of the debate, who actors think they represent and affect who controls the debate. Sometimes majoritarian state actors set up networks (for example, the WTO). Sometimes regulatory officials set up networks themselves (think of the Basel Committee and the ICN). 'The image of national regulators coming together of their own volition and regularising their interactions either as a network or a networked organisation raises the spectre of agencies on the loose, unrestrained by democratic accountability' Anne-Marie Slaughter, *A New World Order* (Princeton University Press 2004) 48. There are also implications for network legitimacy, where a group of non-state actors seem to have been influential (often large US and EU multinational firms, with the ICN) and this is not effectively balanced, at a very minimum, by other relevant voices and interests in the relevant domain.

[54] In one ICN survey, for example, NCAs were asked about the main barriers to their state's implementation of ICN recommended practices. Sixteen said the cost/difficulty of legislative change; 15 said it was hard to build external consensus on specific areas for reform; 10 mentioned the difficulty of building external consensus on need for reform; 91 per cent of respondents said ICN should be more active in promoting its recommended practices, eg 46 respondents said help with seeking external support for domestic reforms; 42 respondents also wanted the working group to provide in-depth technical assistance to NCAs on how to identify reforms and overcome barriers to implementation. ICN, *The Future of the ICN in Its Second Decade—Final Report* (2016) 15–17, <https://www.internationalcompetitionnetwork.org/wp-content/uploads/2018/09/ICN2dDecade2016.pdf> accessed 8 October 2021.

area of discord between states and their NCAs. It also implies that many ICN outputs are not considered acceptable by states for some reason (although one cannot be certain as states might not even implement practices that they agree with if their legislative calendar is already too busy, for example). Of course, NCAs may be able to implement many ICN work products themselves without legislative help. Some states might consider that this makes a legitimate political check of all ICN work important before any actors from that jurisdiction implement it.

In this section we turn to liberal democracy to see whether some form of control of competition policy by politicians might help generate input legitimacy here. The choices that a state makes about how much leeway to give its NCA over competition policy are likely driven by some combination of: its understanding of the role of its NCA, the reasons for delegating responsibility to the NCA, the political salience of competition issues in that state, and how important active political intervention is perceived to be there. Different states will have different views on democratic legitimacy here (and what is 'appropriate' depends on each state's system and context).

For illustrative purposes, we examine a spectrum of three different approaches to input legitimacy, for the kinds of ICN engagement at issue: the constitutional inability for the NCA to unilaterally join and participate in the ICN without consultation and approval of political actors (the EU); general, explicit political empowering of the NCA to act unilaterally on the international stage, within certain limits (Portugal); and more indirect control of the NCA's decision-making regarding the ICN (the USA, UK, and South Africa).

Constitutional inability for the NCA to unilaterally join and participate in the ICN without consultation and approval of political actors (the EU) In some jurisdictions, only by following explicit constitutional norms in collaboration with actors with wider democratic (input) legitimacy, can an NCA join and participate in arrangements like the ICN. Although there is some debate on the subject, this seems to be the position for the EU (and DG COMP).

The legal framework for EU external action is complex.[55] Complexity is driven by, on the one hand, Member States seeking to preserve their control over EU external action, and, on the other hand, their desire to 'enhance the EU's external effectiveness and consistency'.[56] To achieve this, the Member States limited the EU's power to act in the international arena and formalized procedures to follow when action is authorized. These procedures pursue effectiveness and efficiency

[55] Annex 4.1 (see end of this chapter) provides examples as well as further details on the arguments and reasoning here. Note that the EU definitions are not based on the Vienna Convention or other international rules.

[56] Geert de Baere, 'EU External Action' in Catherine Barnard and Steve Peers (eds), *European Union Law* (2nd edn, OUP 2017) 711.

by allowing the EU to negotiate as one in some areas (normally through the Commission), but they preserve the Member States' control over policy by giving the Council (made up of the Member States) the ultimate sign off on EU external action (legitimacy).

The EC Treaty, and others, governed the European Community (the Community) when the ICN was formed, in 2001. The Lisbon Treaty was signed by the Member States of the European Union (EU) on 13 December 2007. This replaced the EC Treaty, and others, with two new treaties, the Treaty on European Union (TEU) and the Treaty on the Functioning of the EU (TFEU). We apply Community law to the decision to join the ICN (although we explain any EU law differences where relevant) and EU law to later 'agreements' by DG COMP to ICN work products.

To establish which procedure to use, one has to follow the legal basis for each policy area, as some areas have different procedures. Getting this choice wrong could invalidate the act concluding the international agreement, vitiating the EU consent to be bound by the agreement it had signed.[57] The EU is empowered to conclude international agreements in the competition area.[58] The relevant legal bases (cited in the preceding note) determine the appropriate procedure for doing this. In 2001, this was art 228 EC (now TFEU, art 218),[59] which set out the following procedure:

> Where this Treaty provides for the conclusion of agreements between the Community and one or more States or an international organization, such agreements shall be negotiated by the Commission. Subject to the powers vested in the

[57] Opinion 2/00, EU:C:2001:664, para 5.

[58] When assessing the correct legal basis, one can start by checking whether the EU has an internal power to act in the relevant ways. If it does, then this internal power can often be 'mirrored' into an external power to agree such measures with other jurisdictions. When producing internal substantive and procedural competition rules the EU has often relied on EC, art 83 (now TFEU, art 103 plus TFEU, art 3(1)(b)). For extra issues related to international agreements covering mergers, see Annex 4.1, n 285. By way of contrast, when recently agreeing internal rules for the effective enforcement of the EU competition rules (including matters relating to the European Competition Network (ECN)), the EU relied on a combination of TFEU, arts 103 and 114 (EC, old arts 83 and 94). In terms of the powers, the ECN is a rough equivalent of the ICN, although it also deals with enforcement), see, for example, European Parliament and Council, Directive 2019/1/EU to empower the competition authorities of the Member States to be more effective enforcers and to ensure the proper functioning of the internal market (2019). Article 33(2) of that directive says, for example, that 'The European Competition Network shall be able to develop and, where appropriate, publish best practices and recommendations on matters such as independence, resources, powers, fines and mutual assistance.' Relying on these internal powers and their use in adopting provisions laying down common rules, the EU can likely conclude international agreements in the same areas, Case C-22/70 *Commission v Council ('ERTA')*, EU:C:1971:32, paras 13–14. See also Joined Cases C-3/76, etc *Cornelis Kramer and Others*, EU:C:1976:114, paras 17–18. Specifically, in the area of competition, see Case C-327/91 *France v Commission (EC/USA competition agreement)*, EU:C:1994:305 (by implication).

[59] The procedure set out in art 218(2)–(8) TFEU largely follows that in art 228 EC. However, there are some important differences. For example, art 218(2) says the Council authorizes the opening of negotiations (as well as their conclusion).

Commission in this field, such agreements shall be concluded by the Council, after consulting the European Parliament where required by this Treaty.[60]

The EU has made many international agreements using this procedure in the competition area.[61] However, in many areas (not just competition), EU directorates-general (DGs) have ignored EC art 228, directly making 'non-binding' international arrangements themselves, often with no input from other EU institutions or the Member States. Some speculate that the aim of these agreements was to increase effectiveness and efficiency.[62] DG COMP (the Directorate General of the EU Commission which deals with competition) has also concluded many 'non-binding' competition arrangements without following EC, art 228.[63] It did this when joining the ICN, for example. It continues to ignore art 228 EC and similar provisions when 'agreeing' to ICN recommended practices at the ICN annual meeting.

When asked to rule on the legality of such arrangements, the ECJ[64] is effectively determining whether possible increases in effectiveness and efficiency justify reductions in 'input' legitimacy. The answer is unlikely to be 'yes', in the EU legal order. DG COMP's 'agreement' to join the ICN is probably an international agreement.[65] It does not seem to matter that ICN outputs do not bind ICN members. The implication from the ECJ's case law is that it is sufficient that that the ICN's procedures and institutional rules are intended[66] to bind DG COMP (and

[60] If the ICN arrangements are held to fall within the EU's Common Commercial Policy (CCP), then this art 228 EC (not art 218 TFEU) procedure should be further modified. Annex, especially in n 290, explains why this is possible and what the procedural modifications are. We ignore the 'enhanced' CCP procedures here because they do not change our underlying point which is that DG COMP has strayed from the right procedures (if the CCP is relevant, then DG COMP has strayed even further from the right procedures).

[61] For example, Decision 95/145/EC of the Council and the Commission, *Concerning the conclusion of the Agreement between the European Communities and the Government of the United States of America regarding the application of their competition laws*, OJ 1995 L95/45.

[62] See the discussion in Ramses Wessel, 'Normative Transformations in EU External Relations: The Phenomenon of "Soft" International Agreements' (2020) 43 West European Politics 4.

[63] Valerie Demedts, *The Future of International Competition Law Enforcement: An Assessment of the EU's Cooperation Efforts* (Brill Nijhoff 2018) s 4.1.3(A), lists several examples of these, such as with Brazil, Chile, Russia, and China. Available here <https://ec.europa.eu/competition/international/bilateral/index.html>

[64] The ECJ stands for the Court of Justice, the most senior of the two Courts of Justice of the EU, art 19 TEU. The Courts of Justice of the EU ensure the interpretation and application of the EU treaties. To be clear, when the ECJ comments on the 'legality of such arrangements' it does not directly analyse the legality of international arrangements themselves (it cannot as these are not EU acts). Instead, it analyses the legality of the act whereby the EU actor decided to enter into this arrangement (or was authorized to do so), *France v Commission* (n 58) paras 13–17.

[65] ibid para 27, where the ECJ held 'As the Court explained in Opinion 1/75 of 11 November 1975 ([1975] ECR 1355), Article 228 uses the expression "agreement" in a general sense to indicate any undertaking entered into by entities subject to international law which has binding force, whatever its formal designation'. A similar position persists under art 218 TFEU, Joined Cases C-103/12 and C-165/12 *Parliament and Commission v Council (Venezuelan Fishing Rights)*, EU:C:2014:2400, para 83.

[66] The ECJ held that the 'intention of the parties' is the decisive feature in assessing whether an arrangement is binding, Case C-233/02 *France v Commission (Transatlantic Economic Partnership)*, EU:C:2004:173, paras 40–46.

other ICN members) when participating in ICN activities.[67] So, when concluding these kinds of international agreements in the competition area, the Commission (and DG COMP) should have followed the EC, art 228 (now TFEU, art 218) procedure.

It is possible that the ECJ will not classify DG COMP's agreement to join the ICN as a binding international agreement. However, competence allocation is still likely to be relevant. The ECJ seems to demand that actors basically follow the formal procedure for adopting binding international agreements seen above, even for non-binding international arrangements. Some deviation from the relevant formal procedure seems possible, although how much is not entirely clear. The implication is that the EU institution in charge of policy in the relevant area must still set this for non-binding arrangements (this would be the Council for our purposes). Furthermore, where the procedures for creating binding international agreements demand that the Council should be involved, it must at least be kept informed and given ample time for comment (and perhaps also the chance to stop the conclusion of the non-binding arrangement).[68,69]

The ECJ demands input legitimacy for binding international agreements and non-binding international arrangements. Whichever joining the ICN is considered to be, DG COMP was probably not competent in EU law to conclude it. At a minimum, ICN membership should have been negotiated by the Commission (not just DG COMP) and then concluded by the Council, after consulting the European Parliament. DG COMP did none of this. As far as we can tell, it acted alone. Failure to follow the correct procedure means that the act where DG COMP decided to join the ICN (or was authorized to do this) is likely void.

Let us now turn our minds to ICN recommended practices, from an EU perspective. This time our focus is the legal position of the EU 'agreement' today

[67] By way of example, in one competition case, the Commission argued that it did not have to follow the art 228 EC procedure even for binding international agreements. The agreement there was between the EU Commission and both the Antitrust Division of the United States Department of Justice and the US FTC. The aim was to promote cooperation and coordination between the Commission and the US NCAs and lessen the possibility or impact of differences between them (art I). Article IX of the agreement explicitly provided that 'nothing in this Agreement shall be interpreted in a manner inconsistent with the existing laws, or as requiring any change in the laws, of the United States of America or the European Communities or of their respective States or Member States'. Nevertheless, the ECJ disagreed with the Commission and found that there was a binding international agreement, given the procedural arrangements, *France v Commission* (n 58) paras 32–43.

[68] As the Annex demonstrates, see n 307, some argue that the European Parliament only has a role in binding international agreements (not these non-binding international arrangements).

[69] In one case the Commission 'agreed' a (non-binding) arrangement with the USA. When assessing the legality of the procedure, the ECJ took into account 'the division of powers and the institutional balance' that the Treaty established in the relevant substantive area (there the CCP). The ECJ endorsed the Commission process, noting that the Council had approved both the wider strategic partnership and action plan that the Commission was working under, and the Commission had kept the relevant Council committee (art 133 Committee) regularly informed of its progress in the negotiation. These procedures were in line with those for concluding a binding international agreement except that there the Council authorized signing of the arrangement and concludes it, art 133 EC, *France v Commission* (n 66) para 41.

(rather than in 2001). If the correct procedures are followed, agreeing ICN work products is possible from an EU law perspective (as long as they do not conflict with the EU treaties or EU court judgments). The relevant competences and legal bases are the same as set out above, so our focus here is on the relevant procedures today.[70]

In terms of the relevant procedure, debate remains. Agreeing work products within the ICN (such as recommended practices) may be seen as agreements between the EU and third countries (TFEU, art 218(1)). In which case, the procedure to follow is explicitly laid down (see TFEU, arts 218(2)–(6)). In broad terms the Commission submits recommendations to the Council, which shall adopt a decision authorizing the opening of negotiations (it may also address directives to the negotiator and designate a special committee in consultation with which the negotiations must be conducted). It is often the Commission that actually negotiates. The Council, on a proposal by the negotiator, adopts a decision concluding the agreement (after consulting the European Parliament).

It seems unlikely that ICN work products are international agreements, given the extensive statements that the parties to them do not intend them to be binding (although this is increasingly questionable, given the rising focus on implementation—see Chapter 2). Nevertheless, even for non-binding international arrangements, we have seen that the EU institutions normally have to follow a similar procedure to this formal one. In either case (whether ICN work products are held to be international agreements or non-binding international arrangements), DG COMP probably did not follow the right procedure. Failure to do this means that the act where DG COMP decided to act in this way (or where it was authorized to) is likely void. At best, this will be a major political embarrassment for the EU.

However, the Lisbon Treaty introduced a new procedure that seems designed to be used when bodies set up by an agreement (like the ICN) are called upon to adopt acts having legal effects (which might include the production of ICN recommended practices). The relevant parts of TFEU, art 218(9) read:

> The Council, on a proposal from the Commission ... shall adopt a decision ... establishing the positions to be adopted on the Union's behalf in a body set up by an agreement, when that body is called upon to adopt acts having legal effects. [art 218(10) adds 'The European Parliament shall be immediately and fully informed at all stages of the procedure']

[70] Once again, this chapter's Annex provides examples and further details on the arguments and reasoning. Furthermore, as noted in n 60, the procedures discussed below may (once again) need to be further modified by those from the EU's CCP. The Annex, especially in n 290, explains why this is possible and what the procedural modifications are. We ignore the 'enhanced' CCP procedures here for the same reason set out in n 60 (it simply makes our underlying argument stronger).

Article 218(9) TFEU demands a shift in focus from the binding nature of an arrangement (the position that we saw under EC, art 228), to its legal effects in the EU legal order.

One might question how mere (non-binding) recommended practices of an international body could have 'legal effects' in the EU order. Nevertheless, this is possible. In one case, for example, the ECJ held that non-binding recommendations from the International Organisation of Vine and Wine (OIV) were 'capable of decisively influencing the content of' EU rules (and so they 'have legal effects').[71]

The limits of 'legal effects' remain unclear at this early stage of interpreting TFEU, art 218(9).[72] However, 'soft law' such as ICN recommended practices, can have considerable legal effects, by inducing actors to modify behaviours.[73] By way of comparison, according to the Commission, a non-binding OECD recommendation is capable of having legal effects.[74]

Several potential causal mechanisms have been suggested (some are more controversial than others). For example, international soft law (like ICN recommended practices) often has legal effects in the international order 'on the basis of the principle of good faith, and it will generate, at the least, expectations between the parties with regard to the compliance with those political agreements'.[75] The EU is bound by the international consequences of the conclusion of even non-binding agreements.[76] Alternatively, legal effects may be found, given the interpretative role that (even non-binding) ICN recommended practices likely have.[77] By agreeing to ICN recommended practices, DG COMP (and national NCAs) may be taken as showing how they think the EU competition rules should be interpreted there

[71] Case C-399/12 *Germany v Council*, EU:C:2014:2258, paras 59–64.

[72] Does it apply, for example, to cases:

> where the EU tends to adapt its legislation in a given policy field on the basis of developments internationally spearheaded by legally non-binding instruments of an international organization, but does not do so expressly. Thus, it will come as no surprise if the Court is confronted with other cases with similar facts in the near future and is asked once again to interpret Article 218(9) TFEU.

Thomas Ramopoulos and Jan Wouters, 'The Institutional Structure' in Takis Tridimas and Robert Schütze (eds), *Oxford Principles of European Union Law*, vol I (OUP 2018) 1083

[73] Wessel (n 62) 6.

[74] European Commission, *Proposal for a Council Decision on the position to be taken on behalf of the European Union in the OECD Public Governance Committee and the OECD Council on the draft Recommendation on Countering Illicit Trade: Enhancing Transparency in Free Trade Zones* (2019) s 4.

[75] Paula García Andrade, 'The Distribution of Powers between EU Institutions for Conducting External Affairs through Non-Binding Instruments' (2016) 1 European Papers 115, 119 (her comments specifically related to Case C-660/13 *Council v Commission (Swiss MoU)*, EU:C:2016:616, but they seem generally applicable).

[76] Opinion of AG Sharpston, Case C-660/13 *Council v Commission (Swiss MoU)*, EU:C:2015:787, para 69.

[77] More details of the following mechanisms, in relation to EU recommendations/guidelines, can be found in the Opinion of AG Bobek, in Case C-16/16 P *Belgium v Commission*, EU:C:2017:959, paras 89–95.

('regulation by information'). By following such statements, firms and national courts may hope to minimize their legal risks (even non-binding guidelines can be guides).[78] Soft law may generate parallel sets of rules which pre-empt the legislative process and thus impact the institutional balance. ICN recommendations, in fact, influence Commission action.[79]

ICN recommended practices are definitely *capable* of having legal effects. This is increasingly likely as the ICN augments its monitoring of the implementation of its recommended practices and raises the pressure on its members to converge. So, the EU courts may insist on input legitimacy for ICN recommended practices (as the DG COMP 'agrees' to them). As a consequence, TFEU's art 218(9) procedure would have to be followed when negotiating and agreeing them. Even if ICN recommended practices are incapable of having 'legal effects' to this standard, the ECJ may hold that competence allocation is still relevant (given the potential effects noted above). Recent treaty changes bolster the emphasis on input legitimacy vis-à-vis effectiveness and efficiency.[80] If the ECJ emphasizes input legitimacy, it could stipulate a procedure for international agreements without legal effects which is similar to that in TFEU, art 218(9).

The procedures that DG COMP has followed in 'agreeing' the ICN recommended practices so far fall far short of either of these TFEU, art 218 standards (not even involving the Commission, let alone the Council and the European Parliament). So, DG COMP may be acting outside of its powers.[81] If the right procedures are followed, the legitimate actors may retroactively mend this legal error. This has been done in previous cases.

The second approach that we examine on this spectrum is that of general, explicit political empowering of the NCA to act unilaterally on the international stage, within certain limits (the case of Portugal).

[78] Case C-226/11 *Expedia Inc. v Autorité de la concurrence and Others*, EU:C:2012:795, para 32.

[79] For example, Proposal for a Council Regulation on the control of concentrations between undertakings /* COM/2002/0711 final—CNS 2002/0296, para 63; Commission Staff Working Paper accompanying the Communication from the Commission to the European Parliament and Council, Report on the functioning of Regulation 1/2003 (COM(2009)206 final), paras 169–79; Explanatory Memorandum for the *Proposal for a Council Decision on the conclusion of an Agreement between the European Union and the Swiss Confederation concerning cooperation on the application of their competition laws* (COM(2012) 245) point 2.

[80] Case C-660/13 *Council v Commission (Swiss MoU)*, EU:C:2016:616 (Grand Chamber) paras 31–43.

[81] Some argue that a third kind of arrangement is possible (ie there are not just binding international agreements and non-binding international arrangements), Eva Valle Lagares, 'International Agreements Regarding Co-operation in the Field of Competition: The New Strategy of the European Commission' (2010) 1 Journal of European Competition Law and Practice 155, 155; Valerie Demedts, 'International Competition Law Enforcement: Different Means, One Goal?' (2012) 8 Competition Law Review 223, 243. They call these administrative arrangements. We do not discuss administrative arrangements. First, because the ECJ has shown little appetite for using this classification so far (see *France v Commission* (n 58)); and, second, because we do not see agreeing ICN recommended practices (and joining the ICN itself) as operational matters for the Commission (see TFEU, art 335). For more detail see the discussion in Annex 4.1 around footnote 329.

General political empowering of the NCA to act on the international stage (Portugal) In Portugal, the NCA's by-law entitles it to represent the Portuguese state internationally.[82]

Since its creation in 2003, the Portuguese Competition Authority received a legal mandate to (a) establish cooperation relations at the EU level and internationally in matters of competition policy[83] and (b) secure technical representation of the Portuguese state in the EU and internationally.[84] The reform of its by-law in 2014 left these competences unchanged.[85]

These provisions give the Portuguese NCA a general, explicit legal mandate to join and participate in international bodies without any need for further, specific authorization either from the national Parliament or the national government. The NCA relies on this power to legitimize its activities in the ECN, the OECD, and UNCTAD. In addition, this power covers the Portuguese NCA's participation in the ICN as well as in other international networks, such as for example the Lusophone

[82] From an EU law perspective, one needs to consider whether the Member States can act on the international stage in this area. If the EU has an exclusive right to act on the international stage (we have seen that the EU can act there, but not discussed the exclusivity of this) then Member States cannot 'make unilateral proposals, even for non-binding acts' Peter Jan Kuijper and others, *The Law of EU External Relations: Cases, Materials and Commentary on the EU as an International Legal Actor* (OUP 2015) 726. This might include agreeing ICN recommended practices. See, for example, Case C-45/07 *Commission v Greece*, EU:C:2009:81, paras 20–23.

In 2001, competition was an area of shared legislative and executive competence. Some claim that, under the current version of the EU treaties, competition is now an area of exclusive EU legislative competence. See, for example, Giorgio Monti, 'Legislative and Executive Competences in Competition Law' in Loïc Azoulai (ed), *The Question of Competence in the European Union* (OUP 2014) 106–07 , and the references given there; Robert Schütze, 'From Rome to Lisbon: "Executive Federalism" in the (New) European Union' (2010) 47 Common Market Law Review 1385; Lucia Serena Rossi, 'Does the Lisbon Treaty Provide a Clearer Separation of Competences between EU and Member States?' in Andrea Biondi, Piet Eeckhout and Stefanie Ripley (eds), *EU Law After Lisbon* (OUP 2012) 99. If this is correct, then Member States can only act when authorized to do so by the EU, art 2(1) TFEU. For example, where 'agreements are entirely dedicated to competition law, [as ...] competition law is an exclusive competence of the Commission' the Member States should not be involved, Demedts (n 81) 241.

We do not discuss this issue in-depth here (because it is not likely to be of major interest to many of our intended readers). However, briefly put, we think that Member States also have the right to participate in the ICN. This is because, while art 3(1)(b) TFEU says that the EU has exclusive competence in 'the establishing of the competition rules necessary for the functioning of the internal market' this still leaves plenty of scope for legislative and executive competence by the Member States in relation to competition, see, for example, Townley (n 39) ch 10; Mariana Tavares, 'A Constitutional Analysis of Multi-jurisdictional Conflicts in the EU Legal Order Confirms that Diversity Is Possible in EU Competition Law' King's College London 2018. Some of these areas seem to be areas of exclusive competence for the Member States. The existence of arrangements that cover exclusive competences of both the EU and the Member States means that all should sign. 'EU law requires the conclusion of a mixed agreement only in the event that that agreement includes a part which falls under the competence of the European Union and a part which falls under the exclusive competence of the Member States, without any of those parts being ancillary to the other', the Opinion of AG Szpunar in Case C-600/14 *Germany v Council (OTIF)*, EU:C:2017:296, para 85 (the ECJ did not discuss this).

[83] Article 6(1)(d) Portuguese Competition by-law approved by the Decree-law 10/2003, of 18 January 2003, Diário da República 15/2003, Série I-Am 2003–01–18, no longer in force.

[84] ibid art 6 (1)(h).

[85] See arts 5(i) and 6 Portuguese Competition by-law approved by Decree-law 125/2014, of 18 August 2014, Diário da República 157/2014, Série I-A, 2014–08–14.

Competition Network.[86] In this context, the Portuguese Competition Authority is also competent to establish its priorities regarding EU and international cooperation.[87] For example, with the aim to promote the discussion and implementation of international best practices in competition policy, the Portuguese Competition Authority has established among its priorities for 2018 its participation in the EU Merger Control Working Group and in two ICN working groups: Advocacy Working Group and Promotion and Implementation Group.[88]

The Portuguese NCA's annual budget proposal (that has to be approved by the Ministry of the Economy) includes an estimate of how much the NCA's international representation activities will cost during the relevant period. The Annual Report and Accounts for each financial year reports on the expenditure in relation to the EU and international cooperation and technical representation of the Portuguese state. This annual report is presented and discussed before the national Parliament.

An intermediate position—indirect control over NCA treaty-making (USA, UK, and South Africa) The third and final approach that we examine on this spectrum is a more ambiguous, indirect control of the NCA's decision-making regarding the ICN.[89] Some states do not seem to have directly considered whether (and how) their NCAs should be able to act within global networks. Depending upon how one interprets their existing rules, this may or may not be possible. By way of example, we briefly examine the powers of NCAs from the US, the UK, and South Africa (all founding ICN members).

Both the US FTC and the US Department of Justice (DoJ) claim inherent authority to cooperate with NCAs from other jurisdictions, bilaterally and in networks like the ICN. This would legitimize, from a political perspective, their ICN engagement. The political nature of senior appointments in both NCAs and the ICN-related statements that they have made further support this. It is instead questionable whether the UK's Office of Fair Trading (OFT) had the power to help establish this network then, at least in relation to merger policy. This is problematic from a UK perspective. In the beginning, the ICN almost exclusively focused on mergers. From April 2014, the OFT was superseded. Relevant powers and duties were transferred to the Competition and Markets Authority (the CMA), which is an independent non-Ministerial government department. While there is still room for doubt, the UK's principal NCA now seems to have the power to legitimately

[86] The Lusophone Competition Network was created in 2004 with the Rio Declaration, and its members are the entities responsible for competition matters in the Portuguese-speaking countries: Angola, Brazil, Cape Verde, Guiné Bissau, Mozambique, Portugal, São Tomé e Príncipe e East Timor.

[87] See the Portuguese Competition Authority's plans of annual priorities for 2013–2021, <www.concorrencia.pt/vPT/A_AdC/Instrumentos_de_gestao/Prioridades/Paginas/Prioridades.aspx>

[88] See the Portuguese Competition Authority Priorities Plan for 2018, <www.concorrencia.pt/vPT/A_AdC/Instrumentos_de_gestao/Prioridades/Paginas/Prioridades.aspx>

[89] Our thanks to Liat Davis for her research assistance on the law and actions in South Africa.

debate competition policy within the ICN. Whether it has the power to agree recommended practices and other ICN work products remains more questionable. From the perspective of the South African NCAs, joining the ICN is seen as equivalent to joining a conference and did not need parliamentary approval.

Taking the position in the USA first, remember that the FTC and DoJ were both founding members of the ICN. In addition, as we discussed in the Introduction to this book, the influential International Competition Policy Advisory Committee (ICPAC) Report which ultimately led to the establishment of the ICN, was originally set up by the US Attorney General in 1997. Both the FTC and the DoJ claim to have an inherent mandate to conduct both bilateral and multilateral competition cooperation.

> 'The Agencies' [the FTC and the DoJ] authority to cooperate with foreign authorities is inherent in their ability to act in furtherance of their mandates. The Department and FTC, therefore, each has the discretion to cooperate, including when it furthers its enforcement interests. Cooperation can be facilitated by bilateral and multilateral arrangements.[90,91]

If correct, their mandates (set by actors with explicit political authority (and thus legitimacy) in the US system) could justify their lead role in establishing the ICN and their participation in it since 2001 (including agreeing recommended practices and other work products).

[90] For example, the United States or the Agencies have bilateral cooperation agreements with 11 jurisdictions or competition agencies: Germany (1976); Australia (1982); the European Union (1991); Canada (1995); Brazil, Israel, and Japan (1999); Mexico (2000); Chile (2011); Colombia (2014); Peru (2016). The Agencies also have entered into memoranda of understanding with the Russian Federal Antimonopoly Service (2009), the three Chinese antimonopoly enforcement agencies (2011), the Indian competition authorities (2012), and the Korea Fair Trade Commission (2015). These arrangements are available at <www.justice.gov/atr/antitrust-cooperation-agreements> and < https://www.ftc.gov/policy/international/international-cooperation-agreements > both accessed 8 October 2021. Multilateral arrangements include the Recommendation of the OECD Council Concerning Co-Operation on Competition Investigations and Proceedings, and the ICN Framework for Merger Cooperation. Organisation for Economic Co-operation & Development, Recommendation of the OECD Council Concerning Co-Operation on Competition Investigations and Proceedings (2014), <www.oecd.org/competition/international-coop-competition-2014-recommendation.htm> accessed 8 October 2021; International Competition Network, Framework for Merger Cooperation (2012), previously available at <www.internationalcompetitionnetwork.org/uploads/ library/doc803.pdf> (broken ICN link, see discussion in Introduction, n 16).

[91] US Department of Justice and Federal Trade Commission, *Antitrust Guidelines for International Enforcement and Co-operation* (2017) s 5.1.3. When the FTC and DOJ enter into binding agreements on behalf of the US government, they must first be authorized by the State Department under the terms of the Case-Zablocki Act of 1972 (even if they are not binding international treaties in public international law). The texts of international agreements other than treaties must then be transmitted to Congress and printed in the United States Treaties and Other International Acts series (also available at <https://www.state.gov/tias/> accessed 8 October 2021); Robert Dalton, 'National Treaty Law and Practice: United States' in Duncan Hollis, Merritt Blakeslee and Benjamin Ederington (eds), *National Treaty Law and Practice* (Brill 2005) 767ff. This was not done for the ICN, which may be because the US NCAs (and Secretary of State) did not consider it to be binding.

Further legitimacy for the US NCAs' involvement in the ICN project comes from the support garnered for the network by senior political appointees. In 2001, the incoming President George W Bush was impliedly supportive given the candidates he appointed there—the US president appoints the Assistant Attorney General in charge of the DoJ's antitrust division as well as the five FTC commissioners (subject to confirmation by the US Senate). In June 2001, the US Senate confirmed Bush's appointment of Charles James as the DoJ's Assistant Attorney General for Antitrust. Soon afterwards, James affirmed his support for the global initiative.[92] Similarly, Timothy J Muris, Bush's appointment as the new head of the FTC, made the ICN one of his top priorities. James and Muris both endorsed the ICN concept in summer 2001.[93] Both the FTC and the DoJ were founding members of the ICN. From the point of view of democratic legitimacy, the newly appointed officials (and the NCAs they led) seemed to have at least an implicit mandate to continue with the ICN's establishment and work. This is not surprising given the US hopes for the network after the ICPAC Report discussed in the Introduction to this book.

By way of contrast, the legitimacy of the UK's NCA in this area is slightly less certain (we know of no internal or external NCA studies on these issues, which is itself surprising).[94] The UK follows the definition of a binding international agreement in the Vienna Convention on the Law of Treaties 1969, although it includes agreements concluded between agencies (such as between its NCA and other foreign NCAs). Where an agreement falls within this definition, the legal advisers of the Foreign and Commonwealth Office (FCO) must be given the opportunity to comment on the form and substance of any drafts. Whether an agency-to-agency agreement is considered binding depends upon its content:

> that is to say, whether or not the agreement creates rights and obligations taking effect under international law. More often than not, these agreements concern minor and technical matters and do not create such rights and obligations.[95]

It seems unlikely that joining the ICN would, from a UK perspective, demand FCO involvement.[96]

[92] Janow and Rill (n 45) 31–32.

[93] US FTC, 'U.S. and Foreign Antitrust Officials Launch International Competition Network' (2001) <www.ftc.gov/news-events/press-releases/2001/10/us-and-foreign-antitrust-officials-launch-international> accessed 8 October 2021.

[94] Thanks to Alex Schofield (CMA) and Tony Penny (CMA) for their assistance here. Their observations are gratefully acknowledged as their own in this instance, as opposed to those of the CMA. Thanks too to James Grant and David Elliott. Any errors here are, of course, those of the authors of this book.

[95] Ian Sinclair, Susan Dickson and Graham MacIver, 'National Treaty Law and Practice: United Kingdom' in Hollis and others (n 91) 729–30.

[96] The focus seems to be on substantive commitments, rather than procedural ones, by way of comparison, see the discussion of this issue relating to the EU, around n 66.

In addition, in English law, public actors must not act outside of their powers.[97] Their powers can be derived from specific regulatory instruments (such as statutes). These powers also 'extend to a range of ancillary and incidental administrative powers not expressly spelt out in' these acts.[98]

In 2001, the OFT was led by the Director General of Fair Trading (DGFT).[99] Several statutes empowered the DGFT (rather than the OFT itself) in his conduct of competition enforcement work (such as merger enforcement). While we can find no explicit legal mandate for it, the OFT also engaged in policy work itself (and on behalf of the UK through international organizations like the OECD and UNCTAD), including in the merger area.[100] As far as we can see, the DGFT had no explicit power to collaborate or research internationally on merger policy. In 2001, such activities (including joining and participating in the ICN) were likely outside of his (and thus the OFT's) express or incidental powers.[101] The position may have been different for competition provisions on anti-competitive arrangements and abuse of dominance (which were also applied by the DGFT through the OFT in 2001). While the relevant statutes gave the DGFT no explicit power to collaborate or research internationally, he had an explicit duty to publish 'general advice

[97] *Boddington v British Transport Police* [1999] 2 AC 143, 171 (Lord Steyn).

[98] *R (on the application of New London College Limited) (Appellant) v Secretary of State for the Home Department (Respondent)* [2013] UKSC 51, para 28 (Lord Sumption, with whom Lord Hope, Lord Clarke, and Lord Reed agreed). As noted by Lord Sumption, in addition to this, there is some recognition 'that the Crown possesses some general administrative powers to carry on the ordinary business of government which are not exercises of the royal prerogative and do not require statutory authority, see BV Harris, 'The "Third Source" of Authority for Government Action Revisited' (2007) 123 Law Quarterly Review 225. The extent of these powers and their exact juridical basis are controversial'. See, for example, Lord Carnwath in the same case, para 34. One issue is how incidental such actions can be. As an authority like an NCA becomes more independent of political influence, its actions might need greater explicit justification. Especially when they incur significant extra costs.

[99] Fair Trading Act 1973, s 1. The DGFT was appointed by the Secretary of State for Trade and Industry.

[100] In 2001, the Department for Trade and Industry's (DTI) Competition and Markets Group (with its Competition Policy directorate) also had a policy focus, including on merger policy. By accessing the archive of the DTI's website at that time one can see examples of the merger policy issues being dealt with by that directorate then, matters such as reform of the UK and EC merger regime and responses to consultations on UK merger fees, <http://web.archive.org/web/20010618033955/http://www.dti.gov.uk/CACP/cp/default.htm> accessed 8 October 2021. Having spoken to officials present at the time, the demarcation between what the OFT and the DTI did in terms of policy work does not seem to have been clearly delineated in a way that bears much legal scrutiny.

[101] That said, it is conceivable that a wide interpretation of the DGFT's powers allowed him to report on the creation of the ICN and include details of ICN recommended practices in his annual review. In relation to mergers, the DGFT had many functions, including keeping under review commercial activities within the UK from a merger perspective. He also had to produce an annual report. Section 125(1) of the Fair Trading Act 1973 directs the DGFT to produce an annual report including (s 125(2)): 'a general survey of developments, during the year to which it relates, in respect of matters falling within the scope of the Director's duties under any enactment (including any enactment contained in this Act, other than this section)'. The Secretary of State would then lay this report before Parliament (s 125(3)). As the focus of the DGFT's merger work (and by implication that of the OFT) principally related to reviewing 'commercial activities within the UK' from a competition perspective, his annual report most likely should have been on surveying what is happening, rather than designing or debating competition policy and making these things happen himself.

and information' on the application and enforcement of the UK provisions on anti-competitive arrangements and abuse of dominance (including how he expected them to operate).[102] In so doing, the DGFT could consult those he considered appropriate. This likely allowed him to consult others, even in bodies like the ICN, on the best way to apply and enforce these UK competition provisions (but not mergers). Whether such provisions (or their implied extensions) empowered him to help to establish the ICN is questionable (especially as the OFT was already in the OECD and UNCTAD where it could consult others if needed). That said, this is arguable.

Some aspects of the OFT's (and now the CMA's) participation in the ICN has been on a much more secure footing, from a legitimacy perspective, since 2002. This is because of much more explicit support for it to research and fund better competition policy (including in mergers). ICN participation is not explicitly endorsed even here but there is lots of support for the CMA to be able to debate competition policy with other NCAs and NGAs in all areas of its work.[103] There is also reason to believe that the ICN can help NCAs from developing countries, both within the ICN and externally.[104] What is less clear is whether the CMA can agree ICN recommended practices or other ICN work products;[105] however, even this may be considered to be 'ancillary and incidental' to the CMA's explicit powers.[106]

In 2000 and 2001 the DGFT was extremely transparent about his vision for helping to establish the ICN (or a body of this nature).[107] The CMA often

[102] Competition Act 1998, s 52.

[103] It is now explicitly instructed to obtain, compile, and keep under review 'information about matters relating to the carrying out of its functions'. One aspect of this has been to ensure that it has enough information to take informed decisions and to carry out its functions effectively. To do this it may 'carry out, commission or support (financially or otherwise) research'. The NCA also has to provide information on matters relating to its functions to the public and Ministers (including proposals, information, or advice as to any aspect of the law), Enterprise Act 2002, ss 5–7.

[104] The CMA's mission is 'to promote competition, both within and outside the United Kingdom, for the benefit of consumers' Enterprise and Regulatory Reform Act 2013, s 25. As the public and consumers are not defined it seems possible, given the precise phrasing of the relevant clauses, that this relates to competition policy and consumers worldwide, rather than just in the UK.

[105] Enterprise and Regulatory Reform Act 2013, sch 4, para 20, says 'The CMA may do anything that is calculated to facilitate, or is conducive or incidental to, the performance of its functions'.

[106] This is especially insofar as ICN work products are not coercive and do not affect the legal rights of others. That said, it is problematic if they are out of line with other CMA duties (and may be problematic if they are out of line with existing CMA guidance), *R (on the application of New London College Limited) (Appellant) v Secretary of State for the Home Department (Respondent)* [2013] UKSC 51, para 29 (Lord Sumption, with whom Lord Hope, Lord Clarke and Lord Reed agreed).

[107] In the OFT Annual Report 2000 11 the DGFT reported on various issues, including 'moves towards a global competition forum'. In wider international initiatives, it briefly refers to work in the WTO, UNCTAD, and the OECD (ibid 88). In its Annual Report 2001 the ICN is mentioned directly. In his Foreword to this report the DGFT said:

> We play a full part in international initiatives, working with a number of other national authorities and international bodies active in competition and consumer protection issues, and we have cooperated on action on cross-border cases wherever possible. For example, we have been involved in discussions with the European Commission on the modernisation of EC competition law and the reform of EC consumer law. And we play a leading role ... in OECD

talks explicitly about its ICN work.[108] Nevertheless, we can find no explicit UK Parliamentary or ministerial support for the DGFT/OFT's decision to help to establish the ICN (although there is some support for its continuing engagement there).[109] This provides some political cover. CMA accountability is also increased through scrutiny from many bodies (such as the National Audit Office and Parliament).[110] Still, such support and accountability cannot, on their own, legitimize actions beyond the CMA's powers. The reports that we have seen provide little comfort that those reviewing the CMA have a detailed understanding of what goes on in the ICN.

In 2001 the South African Competition Tribunal and the Competition Commission took a joint decision to join the ICN. They seem to have considered

> work, and in the new International Competition Network. As markets become more global, so must our perspectives and working practices.

for archived versions of the OFT's Annual Reports (2000–2012/13), see <https://webarchive.nationalarchives.gov.uk/20140402160246/http://www.oft.gov.uk/OFTwork/publications/publication-categories/corporate/annual-report/> accessed 8 October 2021.

[108] CMA, *Annual Report and Accounts 2017/18* (2018) 65–66, <https://www.gov.uk/government/publications/cma-annual-report-and-accounts-2017-to-2018> accessed 8 October 2021.

[109] Searches in Hansard on 26 April 2020 for HC419 (OFT Annual Report 2000) and HC773 (OFT Annual Report 2001), 'ICN' and 'International Competition Network' revealed no relevant discussions in 2000 and 2001. Having said that, the OFT's Annual Report 2001 highlights the OFT's Service Delivery Agreement with the Treasury. There it committed to achieving 13 objectives in 2001/02. It says that each objective is underpinned by performance targets. One such target seems to have been to 'work effectively with international partners to ensure effective competition enforcement'. In terms of this it highlights some relevant things such as participation in EC Advisory Committee meetings for cases and assisting DG COMP with dawn raids. However, it adds participation 'in UK examination of OECD Regulatory Reform Project . . . [and] in the development and operation of the International Competition Network'. These are not directly relevant to *enforcement* (although one could argue that policy development is indirectly relevant to this). Also, no further information given here. Another target was to 'Communicate clearly in order to: show how competitive markets that work well are important for consumers, fair dealing businesses and economic performance; explain our decisions transparently; promote compliance by explaining to business what the law is and how the OFT will apply it; promote consumer awareness and confidence; and coordinate effectively with enforcement partners locally, nationally and internationally' although the ICN is not mentioned there.

That said, there is some later support for its role within such networks more generally (and presumably, by implication the ICN). See, for example, 'In terms of the CMA's international influence, BEIS [the UK Department for Business, Energy and Industrial Strategy] said that the CMA had "a strong track record of effective engagement" in the development of global competition policy through international networks, which the Government would expect the CMA to maintain after Brexit' House of Lords European Union Committee, *Brexit: Competition and State Aid, Chapter 7: Determining the UK's Future Institutional Framework* (2018) para 248, <https://publications.parliament.uk/pa/ld201719/ldselect/ldeucom/67/67.pdf> accessed 8 October 2021.

[110] Relevant reports can be found at <www.nao.org.uk/report/the-uk-competition-regime/> accessed 8 October 2021. In terms of transparency and its activities, including with the ICN, the CMA now has to produce an Annual Plan, after a public consultation, setting out its objectives and priorities for the year. This must be laid before Parliament: Enterprise and Regulatory Reform Act 2013, sch 4, paras 12–13. There is also an agreement between the CMA and the UK government on a performance management framework, which provides some external accountability that the CMA is providing value for money to taxpayers (including reporting on its collaboration with partner agencies at home and abroad) <www.gov.uk/government/publications/competition-and-markets-authority-performance-management-framework> accessed 8 October 2021.

that this decision falls within the function of the Commission and did not need parliamentary approval. This joint decision was communicated to the then line department, the Department of Trade and Industry, who supported the decision.[111]

One of the purposes of the South African Competition Act 1998 (No 89), s 2(d), is 'to expand opportunities for South African participation in world markets and recognize the role of foreign competition in the Republic'. In its annual reports, the Competition Commission sets out what it has done to achieve the six objectives set out in s 2 of the Act. With regard to s 2(d), the Competition Commission lists all the conferences it attended or organized as well as any other international initiatives it has been involved in. One such initiative is the ICN.[112] Moreover, in its annual reports the Competition Commission sets out the international expenditure that it has incurred in order to attend competition conferences, such as ICN or OECD conferences.[113]

As regards the nature of ICN outputs in South Africa, they are not binding on the Commission or the Tribunal but rather provide persuasive authority. In accordance with s 1(3) of the Act, appropriate foreign and international law may be considered when the Act is being interpreted. The Commission may prepare guidelines that indicates its policy approach to a matter within its jurisdiction, but such a guideline is not binding on the Commission, Tribunal or Competition Appeal Court in the exercise of their respective discretion, or their interpretation of the Act (Competition Act 1998, s 79). Should an ICN proposal conflict with the Competition Act or require the Act to be amended to take into account such a proposal, the Commission would need to report this to the Minister who would then need to table it in the National Assembly (Competition Act 1998, s 21). To date, no changes to legislation have been made based on ICN work products.

If joining the ICN (or later actions within it) were considered to be a formal international agreement, the department in charge of South African NCAs would be required to table this before Parliament and it would need to be approved by a resolution in both houses of Parliament as per the South African Constitution, s 231. Chapter 5 of the 'Constitutional Handbook for Members of the Executive'

[111] This was set out by the then Minister of Economic Development on 5 March 2013, <https://pmg.org.za/question_reply/431/> accessed 8 October 2021.

[112] See for example the Commissions annual reports for 2002/03; 2005/06; 2006/07.

[113] Competition Act 1998, s 40 deals with financing. Under s 40(3), the Commissioner of the Competition Commission submits to the Minister of Trade and Industry a statement of the Commission's 'estimated income and expenditure, and requested appropriation from Parliament, in respect of the next ensuing financial year'. The Commissioner and the Head of the Tribunal present their respective annual reports and annual performance plans to the Portfolio Committee on Trade and Industry who can ask questions about it. Few published meeting reports mention the ICN, see for example, the meeting of 8 November 2006 (at: <https://pmg.org.za/committee-meeting/7591/>); 6 October 2009 (at: <https://pmg.org.za/committee-meeting/10849/>); 13 October 2010 (at: <https://pmg.org.za/committee-meeting/12122/>); 3 May 2017 (at: <https://pmg.org.za/committee-meeting/24259/>). The DTI then includes this information in its departmental budget which will eventually be submitted to the National Treasury and be included within the national annual budget which is then introduced to the National Assembly.

provides guidelines on how section 231 will be implemented. It says that 'technical, administrative and executive agreements' require 'the department responsible for processing the agreement to determine, (in conjunction with the Law Advisors of Justice and Foreign Affairs)' whether such agreement falls within the category of international agreements as set out in s 231(3) of the Constitution. We have found no record of any consultation on this matter. The South Africa NCAs seem to have concluded that ICN membership is like joining a conference or a workshop.

In conclusion, when it comes to input legitimacy (when joining the ICN and their ongoing participation), it is unlikely that deliberative democracy will provide much support. When it comes to liberal democracy arguments, we have seen that some jurisdictions have taken decisions on the amount of direct political oversight needed for the NCA when it does things like joining or participating in the ICN. Some, such as Portugal, have explicitly empowered its NCA to represent the state; others, such as arguably the EU, have explicitly decided that the Commission (not just DG COMP) can act, but only if appropriately supported by EU institutions with greater political legitimacy, such as the (European Parliament and the Council). Other states, such as the US, the UK, and South Africa seem to fall somewhere in between. Other states might reflect upon where they stand on this spectrum and review their NCA's participation in the ICN in the light of this assessment.

4.3.1.2 Input legitimacy of 'states' use of ICN outputs

In the *ICN Factsheet and Key Messages* document (2009), the ICN claims to be 'a unique source of international best practice and benchmarks for governments looking to introduce reforms and/ or strengthen their competition regime'.[114] States use ICN work products a lot, adds the ICN:

> According to a recent outreach survey,[115] 96% of competition agencies surveyed make use of ICN work products and materials, and 94% distribute them inside the agency. 77% use ICN materials for reference purposes, 46% for staff training and 40% for outreach. 69% of all agencies say they are pro-actively working towards applying ICN Recommended Practices (71% of newer and 65% of established agencies).[116]

This section discusses the input legitimacy of ICN outputs by 'states'. This is important. Even if input legitimacy is missing in the other two levels, it might be recovered here. As Chapter 2 highlights, 'states' might use ICN outputs in many ways,

[114] ICN (n 6) 7, see also 4 for the following quote.

[115] Previously available at <http://www.internationalcompetitionnetwork.org/media/library/mergers/Vice_Chair_1.pdf?bcsi_scan_A2018E0826 464712=0&bcsi_scan_filename=Vice_Chair_1.pdf> (broken ICN link, see discussion in Introduction, n 16).

[116] Section 4.3.2.2 discusses how much implementation there is of ICN work products in more detail.

for example, in their NCA's competition decisions or as part of a national legislative process of reform by a majoritarian institution.

When a state is considering changing its competition regime, one question that may arise is whether its new rules can (or should) simply follow relevant ICN recommended practices. The ICN's position on this is confused. On the one hand, it points out that ICN recommended practices are not binding. It is up to states to decide whether or not they want to implement them. In the past, the ICN has also highlighted that there is a place for 'informed divergence'. On the other hand, the ICN is ever more actively seeking to encourage the implementation of its ICN outputs, whether this is through legislative change in states, or through its NCA members implementing these changes themselves in their own policy statements and enforcement decisions (see discussion in Chapter 2, Section 2.2).

Of course, every state must conduct its own assessment of whether following ICN work products is appropriate. Our own view is that when a state (including an NCA) considers making changes to its competition regime, it is worth considering ideas from ICN work products (as well as from the OECD, UNCTAD, and others). However, these work products should be fundamentally reassessed every time, and not just blindly followed. This reassessment of whether the ICN work products have the same aims as required in the national order, undermine important values that are respected there or fit appropriately into the national regulatory framework are all important in themselves. In addition, they may help to restore some level of national input legitimacy, which many legal orders consider valuable. In part, this is because there is room for reasonable disagreement about the optimal competition rules in a specific time and context and whether it is appropriate to crystalize around one set of highly uniform norms. It is also important for states to remember that the ICN is a powerful force in realigning the interests of its ICN members (NCAs) towards a core set of values. As a result, NCAs do not necessarily act in their own state's best interests within the ICN. The same applies when NCAs return to their national sphere and decide whether to follow ICN work products in their own outputs; or advocate following ICN work products in debates about national legislative change.

Let's discuss these two points in turn. There are seven core reasons why it is not always appropriate for a state to crystalize around one set of highly uniform norms. As highlighted in this book's Introduction, there is space for reasonable disagreements about the best goals for competition policy, the best way of achieving these goals (even where we agree on the goals), and procedural issues relating to competition policy and enforcement. These disagreements are driven by many things, such as different views about the role of firms (which may be related to the variety of capitalism in a certain state and, thus, the kind of competition rules needed to 'steer' this); adherence to different economic schools of thought; as well as a rigorous evaluation of what works (or not) in different state contexts. There is some convergence around a narrow set of ideas in the 'competition community', although there is certainly not just one perspective, even there.[117] The amount of convergence rapidly diminishes outside of this small clique. So, what might seem like optimal solutions to competition lawyers and economists (when discussing in their silos), the rest of society might consider suboptimal. Choosing to emphasize some issues over others (such as short-term consumer welfare over long-term consumer welfare, or price over choice), demands choices which are often highly redistributive. Even if not following ICN recommended practices generates efficiency losses (which is by no means always certain), then this is a legitimate, *political* choice that each state is (and should be) free to make.

Second, one must not forget that ICN outputs are partial, even on their own terms. From the start, the ICN took the decision to focus exclusively on 'competition all of the time'. But states need to do more than this. They must consider how they want their competition rules to interact with other policies.[118] Different views on this issue may legitimately drive different views of how useful some ICN work products are and whether there are benefits from implementing them.

The third reason why a state (including an NCA) might question whether it should follow an ICN work product, is because the ICN is changing as a body (remember that ICN work products are adopted by consensus). In its early years, nearly all of the emphasis in the ICN was on producing work products. There was little focus on implementation (in fact, it was made clear that this was not necessary, see Chapter 2, Section 2.2). So, even if an NCA did not agree with (or understand) an ICN work product put before them for 'approval' in the Annual Meeting, it may have been happy not to object to it. Silence would allow it to save face and avoid awkward discussions and disagreement. And agreement did not mean a cost. Even if the ICN work product was against its own interests (or those of its state), allowing it to become official ICN policy not really matter as the ICN work product did not have to be implemented. Why stop others from agreeing something in the ICN if they valued it? However, Chapter 2, Section 2.2 also shows that, implementation is considered increasingly important by the ICN leadership today. So, now there is growing emphasis on pushing states (including their NCAs) to implement

[117] There are many examples of difference even within the competition clique. Compare, for example, the EU's predominantly administrative system of competition enforcement to the US system, which emphasizes a court-based model. There are many substantive differences too. One example is the different national attempts to deal with price parity clauses by online travel agents. See the discussion in Townley (n 39), 8–9. Chapter 1, Section 1.2, emphasized that ICN activity often focuses on areas where leading ICN lights (such as the NCAs from the EU and USA) are in agreement. As also pointed out there, the fact these advanced industrialized nations agree on a competition rule does not mean that it is in the interests of all states.

[118] For example, should competition policy ignore trade policy and environmental policy, or should those issues be weighed (where relevant) within competition policy. In the former route conflicts between different policy areas are dealt with by delimiting the reach of each policy area. In the latter approach, conflicts are brought inside each policy area and considered in enforcement decisions. For more details of this distinction (and an example of how it is resolved in EU law), see Christopher Townley, *Article 81 EC and Public Policy* (Hart 2009) ch 2 and pt B.

ICN work products. This includes ICN work products that NCAs may have agreed to, even though they did not consider them to be in their own interests (or perhaps the NCA was not even an ICN member when the item was discussed). The ICN does revisit its outputs to update them, but one can see how the climate is different today and the consensus model is not protecting some.

Fourth, there is a rich comparative law scholarship which highlights how rules can operate in different ways when transplanted into different cultural, historical, and social contexts.[119] What is 'optimal', theoretically (or in some economies), does not always operate in the way intended in another place and time. So, in order for a competition rule to be 'optimal' in a specific context, in fact, it might need to be different from the ICN's theoretically optimal paradigm (even without disagreements on goals, methods, or procedural and institutional structures).

In addition, there may also be costs for the 'competition system' as a whole if the competition rules and related procedures are interpreted uniformly (ie if all states follow them, even if they think that they are the best rules). Diversity has several benefits (for example, think of Hayek's knowledge problem and the coordination of competition law experiments) which may be lost if all states follow the ICN recommended practices (and we get one uniform way of dealing with issues). This might be a cost worth considering for every state when deciding whether to follow the ICN.[120]

Sixth, as noted in Chapter 1, Section 1.1.2, changing the competition rules in a state in itself creates some costs. It is worth assessing whether the benefits of the change itself outweigh these costs. Such assessments can be difficult, but they can make it more difficult to argue for change, especially because the costs of change often seem clear, immediate and to fall on local actors, whereas the benefits are often more obscure, predicted in the medium term and often falling to external actors. Remember that many ICN work products normally simply reflect what those leading the ICN are already doing (NCAs from the EU and the USA, for example). So those states do not face these costs.

As a result of the above, states may find fundamental reassessment of ICN work products along with appraisal of the likely impacts in that state important (before they are adopted at home). This is even more so when that state has not controlled (or has been unable to control) its NCA's inputs into ICN work. However, state reassessment could even be important where the state has had complete control over its NCA's actions in the ICN and been able to stop it accepting ICN recommended practices where they undermine perceived state interests. This is because the 'politics' of competition law policy and enforcement changes over time—the

[119] See, for example, Thomas Cheng, 'How Culture May Change Assumptions in Antitrust Policy' in Ioannis Lianos and Daniel Sokol (eds), *The Global Limits of Competition Law* (Stanford Law Books 2012).

[120] Townley (n 39) 10, 272–74.

same is true of knowledge (law and economics). So, when the state comes to consider or implement a certain change (even one recommended by the ICN) then it might find it more legitimate to assess again, in that context and moment, whether it is desirable,[121] rather than blindly following (and being pushed to follow) the ICN model.

The second main point that we wanted to make here was that states can find the assessment of such things particularly difficult. This is because, states would often turn to the experts in their NCAs for advice in such moments. However, as Chapters 1 and 2 explain, states should be cautious about doing this. In part this is because many NCAs work hard to disguise the value judgements involved in competition policy and enforcement work (as a way of justifying their continuing independence). This makes it hard (and unattractive) for them to clearly point out all of the value choices being made. Highlighting these value judgments is a core part of helping majoritarian bodies to make informed choices here. It is questionable whether non-majoritarian bodies are appropriate vehicles for dealing legitimately with the highly redistributive questions demanded in enforcement, but also policy work.

Furthermore, as we now outline, a state cannot be sure that its own NCA is acting in that state's best interests (at least as perceived by the state). Once again, we should emphasize (as we did in the Introduction to this book), that this is not all necessarily some nefarious plan. Many of these results simply arise because of the structure of the ICN, the independence of many NCAs, etc.

Given the power of the network and the epistemic community at work within the ICN (in combination with knowledge gaps that inevitably arise between the NCA and its state), it may be worth checking that the NCA really did act in line with perceived state interests within the ICN (and also later). Chapter 1 argued that while all NCAs may be formally equal, it is likely that organizing the ICN as a group of experts where technical, rather than political, issues are discussed enhances the power of a small group of technically advanced NCAs (principally many of the ICN's founding members) and NGAs. This may have allowed these same powerful actors to co-opt the ICN's agenda and work products for their own ends. These may overlap with the interests of developing countries and others. That said, sometimes they do and sometimes they do not. The problem is exacerbated because NCAs from outside of this powerful group, often have incentives to align with the powerful group, around a core set of values. These are often the values espoused by those NCAs and NGAs 'controlling the network'. In the ICN we have argued that this tends to be NCAs and NGAs from advanced industrialized economies, such as the EU and the USA. NCAs from outside this powerful group may have the incentive to align with the powerful NCAs and NGAs. So, NCAs from developing

[121] The ECJ makes a similar point about political oversight of the Commission in external relations here Case C-660/13 *Council v Commission (Swiss MoU)*, EU:C:2016:616, paras 31–43.

countries, for example, may not protest ICN work products (and even apply them) against their own state interests.

As noted in Chapter 1, states do not meet in the ICN (only their NCAs). State interests can diverge from those of their NCAs. This is all the more likely as the independence of each NCA from political influence increases. This is, after all, a key *aim* of independence, from an NCA perspective,[122] and, we have argued that reducing state influence is likely a key reason why NCAs sought to establish their own competition network outside of the OECD and UNCTAD (see Chapter 1, Section 1.2.1).

The reason that the values of all NCAs may be realigned (even when this is not in the interests of their states) is because of the other incentives that 'good' ICN participation can bring to NCAs, separate from their state (help with training, for example, see Chapter 1, Sections 1.2 and 1.3). So, we suggest that all states thoroughly check that ICN recommended practices are in their own interests before adopting them. This even includes advanced industrialized states with powerful NCAs. Their NCAs likely established their own network (the ICN) so that they could work outside the OECD and UNCTAD structures and escape their own state influence to some degree. One wonders why.

So, NCAs are not necessarily acting in their own state's best interests within the ICN. The same can be true when these NCAs return to their national sphere and contemplate following ICN work products in their own outputs; or advocating following them in debates about national legislative change. This means that, many states cannot trust that their own NCA is acting in what that state perceives to be its own best interests in relation to ICN matters. As a consequence, we strongly recommend getting external advice. This might be from another ministry, or academics outside of that community. State (rather than just NCA) involvement in competition policy is relatively uncontroversial.

Some may question whether states should intervene in competition enforcement (that probably depends upon whether enforcement is seen as the granting of political licences, or the checking of legal rights and obligations). Even if states do not want to intervene in enforcement we suggest that they make more active efforts to understand what their NCAs are doing in enforcement and to see whether this is what states desire. If it is not, then legislative or policy change may be needed. State involvement of this sort may go a long way to improving the legitimacy of competition systems.

4.3.1.3 Input legitimacy: conclusions

It seems important that each state assess whether the goals, procedures, and institutional structures that the ICN injects into its work products are appropriate for

[122] As we have seen, there is a feedback loop here, the ICN itself has a keen interest in promoting the independence of NCAs, see the discussion in Chapter 1, around n 148.

that state (do they match its competition law's requirements). This applies both at a formal level (ICN 'constitutional principles' such as non-discrimination and no public policy in competition law must be followed) as well as seeing what happens in practice. Chapter 1 showed how there is much to fight over in this highly redistributive area and that advanced NCAs are likely to be able to ensure that joint rules favour them.[123]

The outcome of these enquiries should help each state to decide whether its NCA should be an ICN member, whether it agrees to certain work products, and whether or not (and how) these work products should be implemented in that state (either by its NCA or through other means).

When it comes to input legitimacy, we have observed that deliberative democracy arguments are unlikely to help. Adopting a liberal democracy perspective, we have seen that some jurisdictions have taken explicit decisions on the amount of political oversight needed for the NCA when joining or participating in the ICN. Some, such as Portugal, have explicitly empowered its NCA to represent the state for such matters; others, such as the EU, seem to have explicitly decided that the Commission (not just DG COMP) can act, but only if supported by EU institutions with wider political legitimacy, such as the (European Parliament and the Council). Others, such as the USA and the UK, seem to have adopted intermediate positions.

States might reflect upon where they stand on this spectrum and review their NCA's joining of the ICN and its participation in the ICN in the light of this assessment. What is particularly concerning though, with the ICN, is the lack of a general 'political moment', even at its inception, where wider state interests elected this course (unlike the OECD, for example). Even those that favour these sort of transnational networks, normally see such a 'constitutional moment' as crucial for legitimacy.[124]

It may be possible to recover legitimacy later, through oversight of NCAs' actions within the ICN (although this is not easy, especially for those NCAs with a great deal of independence) or through greater scrutiny of the adoption (or not) of ICN work products in states later on. Legitimacy concerns are likely to be particularly acute for states that automatically adopt ICN work products without wider scrutiny (often the case for their NCAs); and even more so for poor countries with weakly developed institutions of domestic accountability, and dependent upon assistance from ICN actors.[125]

It is important to stress that states always retain the power to 'fight back', demanding access to the ICN, more transparency, conducting informed political

[123] Similarly, Pierre-Hugues Verdier, 'Transnational Regulatory Networks and Their Limits' (2009) 34 Yale Journal of International Law, 162.

[124] See, for example, Robert Keohane, Stephen Macedo and Andrew Moravcsik, 'Democracy-Enhancing Multilateralism' (2009) 63 International Organization 1, 1–2.

[125] See, for example, ibid 22 and 27.

scrutiny of ICN work products before they are used in the state concerned and even introducing politics into the ICN (by insisting on a reformulation of its membership from NCAs to states). States might (also) achieve this through more general political scrutiny of their NCAs, perhaps through reducing their independence. Whether states will do this depends, on the one hand, on each jurisdiction's view of the importance of input legitimacy in this area. On the other, this is also likely to be affected by the effectiveness and efficiency of the ICN, to which we now turn.

4.3.2 Output legitimacy: effectiveness and the ICN

Section 4.3.1 highlighted several potential (even, major) gaps in input legitimacy, which might cause concern in some jurisdictions. So, we move on to discuss two important types of 'output legitimacy', effectiveness (here, Section 4.3.2) and efficiency (in Section 4.3.3). We explain that a lack of clarity over how ICN goals should be balanced effectively makes it impossible to conduct either an effectiveness or an efficiency assessment. As we further explain below, the position is exacerbated by problems with the way in which the ICN collates its 'data'. Transparency is an important ingredient in our assessment here. Section 4.3.2.1 highlights that a lack of transparency can make assessments difficult (we give several examples below). So, the best that we can do in the rest of Section 4.3 is to raise issues for states to consider when they conduct their legitimacy, effectiveness, and efficiency assessments (if they choose to do them).

Following Héritier and Lehmkuhl, in the Introduction to this book, we defined 'policy effectiveness' as the extent to which a policy achieves the goals defined for it.[126] We propose adapting this for the ICN to look at the extent to which that organization's policies achieve its goals.[127] Slaughter reports that networks can improve the effectiveness of the solutions to specific problems. In part this is through encouraging the sharing of information, dialogue (even positive conflict), and collective learning. As the actors involved are actually key to the implementation process (either directly or through persuading national rule makers to change their rules), involving them in formulating solutions can help to ensure their support. Networks can help make regulation matter by socializing network members into a common way of seeing the world and through use of reputation to encourage implementation. Having said that, for Slaughter, this all seems to be premised on the

[126] Adrienne Héritier and Dirk Lehmkuhl, 'Governing in the Shadow of Hierarchy: New Modes of Governance in Regulation' in Adrienne Héritier and Martin Rhodes (eds), *New Modes of Governance in Europe: Governing in the Shadow of Hierarchy* (Palgrave Macmillan 2011) 66.

[127] We do not discuss the appropriateness of the ICN's goals here. That was relevant in the legitimacy discussion and for states considering whether to use ICN work products (if states want different goals, ICN work might not help them). So, states may want to assess whether the ICN ship is sailing in the right direction (for them)—see discussion in Section 4.4.

idea that (to some extent) informed divergence is possible, and it must be guided by legitimate norms.[128] So, this effectiveness assessment is normally in addition to some measure of legitimacy—see Section 4.3.1.

This book's Introduction also referred to many possible aspects of an 'effectiveness assessment'. First, should the focus be on the ICN's effectiveness as a discussion forum, learning about insights that others have had, comparing methods and systems, debating what is best? Or, should the focus be on whether the ICN produces policies and generates changes that solve the problems that it was designed to address? This is a process versus outputs discussion, although they are likely to interrelate to some degree. To answer the 'outputs' question, we would also need to know what the ICN's goals are, whether they are clearly specified and how they are supposed to interrelate when they conflict. A second aspect of an 'outputs' assessment relates to the extent and nature of ICN outputs. On the one hand, there is an issue of speed and quantity. Has the ICN effectively produced sufficient policy output in a timely manner? On the other hand, the value of the ICN outputs is also relevant. For example, the ICN might be effective at generating consensus in a few 'easy' areas. Is it also able to achieve meaningful consensus where disagreements run deeper? A third set of issues arises when measuring 'output' effectiveness. Is mere production of ICN recommended practices and other work products sufficient? Or, is implementation of these ICN outputs needed too (implementation might become more important as it becomes a more central ICN preoccupation)?[129] At a further level of abstraction, is the issue of evidence. Can we simply assume that states actually achieve their goals with ICN work products if they use them? In other words, are we content to assume ICN benefits once its outputs are used or do we want evidence that ICN outputs actually improve NCA effectiveness? If we demand evidence, empirical or even anecdotal, how accurately should (or can) this be assessed?

We start by discussing how effective the ICN is at achieving its declared goals. The ICN is preoccupied with effectiveness, making significant (increasing) efforts to assess this on some dimensions. As far as we know (and, as explained below), the ICN has never clearly articulated how it trades its goals off against each other. This essentially makes it impossible to assess the ICN's effectiveness using the benchmark that we have set (does it achieve its goals). So, as a second-best assessment, we ask how effective the ICN is at achieving some of its different aims. The ICN's overall message is that it is an effective organization that largely achieves its goals.

[128] Slaughter (n 53) 169–70, 197–8, and 209–14.

[129] Lugard talks of a 'natural tendency' to judge the ICN's effectiveness by reference to implementation of its work products. On the other hand, 'on a strict interpretation of its purposes, ICN activities are not meant to extend to implementation [for example, the Memorandum on the Establishment and Operation of the ICN]. The ICN does however assist in the implementation of best practices.' Lugard (n 45) 12–13.

In some areas, such as the production (and, to a lesser extent, the implementation) of its work products, the ICN does seem to be fairly effective, although it does not achieve *all* of its goals equally (and it is difficult to be certain given the apparent flaws in the methodologies of assessment used). Furthermore, as previous chapters have argued, different actors have different aims for the ICN (not all of which align with the explicit ICN goals). Despite the 'consensus requirement', many agree that ICN structures and practices favour a narrow set of rich, often 'western' states. Finally, it should be pointed out that, for an organization that claims to be 'results-based', the ICN spends remarkably little time and effort assessing the results of its actions (eg when its work is implemented by NCAs/states, do superior outcomes occur there and at what cost?).

When analysing effectiveness, commentators often highlight that the ICN provides a 'place' for competition officials and NGAs to meet and discuss competition concerns.[130] The aim is to facilitate consensus on substance and procedure,[131] and ultimately bring enforcement practices into greater alignment.[132] Real strength comes from the ICN's 'wide membership, wide geographic, diverse coverage and plurality of views'.[133] The ICN also facilitates the mentoring of newer NCAs by more experienced authorities.[134] Judged by its own aspirations, many think that the ICN 'had been an enormous success'.[135] The literature gives a real sense of 'ICN effectiveness'.

We are more sceptical. A good starting point is to ask how the ICN assesses its own effectiveness. In many statements the focus is placed upon the many different types of ICN work products that have been produced and the wide range of different topics that they cover. In 2009, for example, the ICN wrote:

> The ICN has produced a series of practical recommendations and other tools on best practices, investigative techniques and analytical frameworks, which have significantly contributed to cooperation efforts among competition agencies. Notable achievements have been made in the areas of mergers, cartels, unilateral conduct, advocacy, and competition policy implementation, through a variety of practical products and outputs. These include recommended practices, case-handling and enforcement manuals, reports, templates on legislation and rules in different jurisdictions, databases and toolkits, and workshops.[136]

[130] Fox (n 45) 123–24; William Rowley and Omar Wakil, 'The ICN Five Years On' [2007] Global Competition Review 29, 29; Coppola and others (n 46); Fingleton (n 45) 196.

[131] Fox (n 45) 123–24; Coppola and others (n 46); Fingleton (n 45) 196.

[132] Fox (n 45) 123–24; Rowley and Wakil (n 130) 29; Coppola and others (n 46).

[133] Carles Esteva Mosso, 'The ICN and Global Competition Convergence: Reflections on Its Origins, Its Achievements and Its Future' in Lugard (n 45) 169. Similarly, Fingleton (n 45) 196.

[134] Fox (n 45) 123–24.

[135] ibid 123. Similarly, Rowley and Wakil (n 130) 29.

[136] ICN (n 6) 3–4, see also 8–15.

Some go further in linking effectiveness to real world implementation. For example, a 2005 ICN statement comments on the work products and adds:

> But these work products are not achievements in themselves, but only intermediate steps towards achieving the goal of improved enforcement and advocacy. In order to become achievements, the work products must influence changes for the better in the real world.[137]

So, our effectiveness assessment starts by discussing the production and the implementation of ICN work, which is what the ICN principally focuses on itself (but we will look more widely than this as well). We will see an ICN that makes a lot of effort to assess its effectiveness under both dimensions. It is certainly possible to conclude (as the ICN does) that it is highly effective at both (and it is still trying to improve on both measures). However, we point out several weaknesses in the ICN's efforts to define and measure its own effectiveness which undermine these self-assessments.

4.3.2.1 Effectiveness within the ICN

If one focuses on the number (and different types) of ICN work products that have been produced, one can easily conclude that the ICN has been extremely effective. For example, in relation to mergers (the ICN's busiest area), the Merger Working Group has produced (and updated) many documents, as well as running several workshops and other events.[138]

[137] A Statement of Missions and Achievements up until May 2005, 3. We could not find this document, but we have used a citation from Ronald Stern, 'The Role of the ICN in Fostering Convergence: An NGA's Perspective' in Lugard (n 45) 325.

[138] The documents produced include: *Guiding Principles* and *Recommended Practices for merger notification and review procedures* (for example, advising against asserting jurisdiction over a merger unless that merger has an appreciable impact on that jurisdiction); and *Recommended Practices on merger analysis* (which, for example, caution on automatically linking market shares and market power). There is also: a *Merger Guidelines Workbook*, with a checklist of topics to be considered in merger guidelines; a *Handbook on Investigative Techniques for Merger Review* (informing NCAs of various tools and techniques and how to use them more effectively and efficiently); a *Merger Remedies Guide* (providing guidance on key principles and tools in merger remedies); and a *Model Confidentiality Waiver for Mergers* (that merging parties and NCAs can use to facilitate waivers of confidentiality protection for information that parties submit in the merger review process). There are also several other guides and reports, including a *Practical Guide* (elaborating on recommended practices and principles of merger review cooperation contained in ICN work products, which is intended to offer: (i) a voluntary and flexible framework for interagency cooperation in merger investigations; (ii) practical guidance for agencies seeking to engage in such cooperation; and (iii) practical guidance for merging parties and third parties seeking to facilitate cooperation). As noted above, the Merger Working Group has also organized several workshops for staff on investigative techniques and procedures; and 60 NCAs have completed *Merger Notification and Procedures Templates* providing background on their merger laws, rules, and procedures. See for more details as well as the documents referred to, <www.internationalcompetitionnetwork.org/working-groups/merger/> accessed 8 October 2021; Coppola and others (n 46) discuss how ICN work products have changed over time, noting a shift from focusing on enforcement fundamentals to a wider range of topics, a loose hierarchy of work products and an expansion of the type of work products used.

Yet, a thorough effectiveness assessment may also consider the 'quality' of ICN work products. We highlight two dimensions of quality, neither of which is considered in the ICN's own analysis. First, myriad tensions within and between the ICN's goals make it unclear precisely what the ICN is ultimately aiming to achieve. This makes it impossible to assess whether individual work products actually hit their target. Second, when looking at outputs, have ICN working groups focused on the 'easy topics' where agreement has been relatively forthcoming (if so, the future looks less rosy)?

Taking these two quality dimensions in turn, our starting point is that measuring the effectiveness of ICN work products is currently impossible. There are myriad tensions within[139] and between[140] the ICN's goals. A meta goal is necessary in order to rationally balance conflicting goals.[141] The ICN has not specified one. Furthermore, to establish how effective the ICN is at achieving its goals, we also need a meta goal

[139] Tensions arise within individual goals because they are insufficiently specified. For example, the ICN has said that it works to optimize consumer welfare. The ICN 'works to facilitate improved enforcement and advocacy of competition law, which fosters vibrant competition in open and well-functioning markets and optimizes consumer welfare. This should create conditions that promote lower prices and wider consumer choice' ICN (n 6) 3. Yet, the consumer welfare goal demands trade-offs between different groups (perhaps vulnerable consumers versus others, today's consumers over those of tomorrow, or consumers in one's own jurisdiction over others abroad). See, for example, Christopher Townley, 'Remembering Those Not Yet Born: Inter-generational Impacts in Competition Analysis' [2011] European Competition Law Review; Christopher Townley, 'The Relevant Market: An Acceptable Limit to Competition Analysis?' [2011] European Competition Law Review; Okeoghene Odudu, 'The Distributional Consequences of Antitrust' in Philip Marsden (ed), *Handbook of Research in Trans-Atlantic Antitrust* (Edward Elgar 2007). The ICN does not explain how it has chosen between these different groups in its work products.

[140] Tensions also arise between ICN goals. For example, the ICN says it works for the benefit of NCAs and consumers. Conflicts between consumer and NCA goals are clearly possible, possibly affecting access to justice and other issues (think of the amount of work that an NCA is prepared to do to 'understand' a consumer complaint; or how ready NCAs are to tell complainants to take private actions rather than helping them). Of course, this is also linked to NCA resources, something not entirely within the control of most NCAs, but it is also linked to deeper issues such as the NCA's priorities and how it sees itself and the role that it performs in society.

Chapter 1 showed some ICN statements implying that the ICN works for other beneficiaries too. For example, the ICN also works to facilitate: 'the task of firms and their representatives in working with several competition agencies simultaneously, especially with regard to merger notifications. Antitrust enforcement at times may impose unnecessary costs and uncertainty on the business community and marketplace. The ICN works to promote sound and principled procedural and substantive standards that help minimize such burdens and leave pro-competitive, efficiency enhancing conduct free to flourish', ICN, *A Statement of Mission and Achievements up Until May 2006* (2006) 1, previously available at <http://www.internationalcompetitionnetwork.org/library.aspx?page=37> (broken ICN link, see discussion in Introduction, n 16). Sometimes these do not clash. 'Unnecessary costs and [business] uncertainty' might undermine the interests of consumers, leading to higher prices (although it seems unlikely that the costs of these 'one off events' would have pronounced effects on prices). Yet, the above quote's focus is not on consumer benefits, but rather on saving firms' money. This can mean conflicts. Reducing business costs can mean less comprehensive application of the competition rules, possibly reducing consumer welfare. ICN work makes such choices, without explicitly explaining the existence of these trade-offs or how they are assessed. An example of this arose in the discussions on the proper nexus between the reviewing jurisdiction and the parties in mergers, see ICN Merger Working Group, *ICN Recommended Practices for Merger Notification and Review Procedures* (2002 (amended 2017)). Drafting the nexus requirement too widely means extra costs for firms (and NCAs). Drafting it too narrowly may result in consumer harm, with problematic mergers missed. These problems can be reduced in certain ways (as those drafting these recommended practices sought to do), but the tension likely remains to some extent, see Fox (n 45) 128–29.

[141] On the need for a meta goal for rational balancing, see Townley (n 118) ch 8.

against which its outputs can be measured. Perhaps even more problematically, the ICN normally does not even note that these conflicts exist or explain how its work products resolve relevant tensions. In part, this feeds into a wider NCA narrative of how they like to steer clear of 'political issues'. This is, as the Introduction to this book and Chapter 1 point out, impossible. Competition policy and enforcement are highly redistributive. It is also ironic, given that the ICN has entered some highly political areas, where this fits with richer NCA and NGAs' wider industrial policy aims.[142]

This lack of openness also impacts upon the legitimacy of the ICN project. Not all NCAs participate equally in the production of ICN work products (indeed some NCAs were not even members when certain ICN work products were produced). These NCAs may not even be aware of the existence of conflicts in ICN work products, or how they have been resolved and at what cost (states, as opposed to their NCAs, have even less insight). This does not seem legitimate if NCAs are then encouraged to lobby for the introduction of ICN outputs at home (or the ICN does that). As a minimum, the ICN should select a meta goal; and, in each work product, highlight any conflicts and explain how they have been dealt with there.[143] This would alert potential users to the political dimensions of ICN work and allow them to adopt different policy formulations where appropriate in their jurisdictions.

The second dimension, when looking at the 'quality' of ICN outputs, is whether the ICN (and its working groups) principally focus on the 'easy topics' where agreement is relatively forthcoming. There is a tension between outputs' quantity and the quality. Gerber says:

> The ICN has been highly influential as a forum for the exchange of ideas and experience and for the development of an international competition law

[142]

> As the organization matured and its membership rapidly grew to encompass almost every competition agency in the world, it began to consider whether, in addition to working on internal agency policies and practices, it could assert a common voice more widely to advocate procompetitive policies. Although there was some concern about venturing into a realm that could be more political and could intersect with other Ministries in members' governments, ICN leadership understood that the collective breadth and expertise of the ICN membership could be an important voice for consumers. The value of moving the ICN in this direction was heightened by the realization that there was no comparable international body that could speak with the authority of the ICN as a voice for competition. Moreover, it became clear that the proposition that competition policy should be a key organizing principle for national economies in many cases needed buttressing and in some cases was under serious challenge.
>
> Coppola and others (n 46)

> The ICN thus began to spread its wings in several directions. There were occasions when members' legislatures were considering reforms that involved issues on which the ICN had adopted recommended practices, particularly regarding merger review procedures. When the ICN determined that its intervention would likely be welcome and effective, it submitted letters on behalf of its Steering Group urging that the legislative body enact rules that were consistent with international standards as reflected in the ICN's recommended practices.
>
> ibid

[143] We also suggested this in Chapter 1, Section 1.3.1.2.

'community'. Its most direct influences on competition law development have probably related to procedures for enforcement against international cartels and to merger law enforcement ... These efforts to enhance convergence have been of much value in moving toward a more effective normative framework for global competition ... Nevertheless, their success and potential should not be overdrawn. In many major substantive areas such as dominant firm conduct and vertical restrictions, there is little evidence that they have made great strides towards convergence or that they have overcome significant differences among competition law systems.[144]

The ICN does not include this 'quality' dimension in its effectiveness assessments either. There is certainly some evidence that the ICN seeks to avoid controversy. The Merger Working Group's early work, for example, on merger notification and review procedures was intentionally picked for its 'non-controversial and practical nature'.[145] Potential projects have to fight for limited resources (the time of working group members). It should be said that, even where ICN work products have been relatively easy to agree, they may still be extremely valuable. Furthermore, focusing on the 'easy wins' seems like a sensible strategy for a new network, as it helps it to build cohesion and momentum. The critique might be stronger if a tendency to avoid controversial topics persists some twenty years later.

Some argue that this is now changing and that the ICN focuses on more complex issues today.[146] For some time there has been a wider debate about whether the ICN *should* actively seek to engage with more controversial issues, at least in part.[147] By way of example, Fox argues that the ICN should take on more controversial topics (such as nationalistic aspects of financial rescues, jurisdictional clashes, etc). On the other hand, while he accepts that these are all important issues, Marsden warns against such siren calls, at least in some areas. For example, he advises against the ICN moving into linkage areas, such as a focus on economic development (fundamental to developing countries) or nationalization. Marsden fears that discussions on these matters will degenerate into talking shops with less useful work product and duplicate existing good work done by others, respectively for these topics, UNCTAD and OECD. In addition, Marsden argues that there are 'many unfinished enforcement-related matters closer to home that the ICN should focus on and which are better suited to its

[144] David Gerber, *Global Competition: Law, Markets and Globalisation* (OUP 2010) 116. Similarly, Sokol (n 45) 159; Fox (n 45) 133.

[145] Fox (n 45) 120.

[146] Coppola and others (n 46).

[147] 'Part of effective enforcement is addressing challenges presented by new issues, markets, and theories. Member agencies have brought these challenges to a shared dialogue within the ICN', ibid. Similarly, see the sources in n 148.

skills, and its demand for results'.[148] We see the problems raised by Marsden, and share some of his concerns. The Introduction to this book noted that the ICN's Unilateral Conduct Working Group has struggled in relation to topics such as the goals of unilateral conduct rules, excessive pricing, and discriminatory pricing, for example. Nevertheless, there is some evidence that the ICN is more open to entering controversial areas (as noted above), although it seems to be doing this timidly.

One place to look for evidence here is in the Merger Working Group's work plan for 2020–21.[149] Several potentially controversial topics are opened here (such as joint ventures). These areas have not been selected for recommended practices at this stage, but the focus is rather on a stock-taking exercise. Furthermore, in '2015–2016 the ICN Chair initiated a "Town Hall" discussion series for all members and NGAs on topics at the intersection of competition and other policies'.[150] Starting with a stock-taking exercise before entering controversial areas seems like a sensible preliminary step, before recommending practices. However, even if other policy goals are discussed, if the ICN only discusses 'competition all of the time' and is effective at pushing the implementation of its work products, then this will likely favour competition over other goals that states might also want to promote. This is one reason why we suggest that all states conduct a deep assessment of all ICN work products before deciding whether to implement them (this also applies to implementation by the NCA). As the ICN moves into more complex spheres, it is also imperative that it explains how it balances competition with other 'non-competition' policy goals within its meta framework, as we argued above.

[148] Marsden makes both comments in Marsden (n 145) 137. Fox's points are in Fox (n 45) 133.

[149] This lists five projects: Joint Ventures (aiming to produce a comparative and informational survey and report on joint ventures); Regional webinar series on merger control in times of crisis (on how NCAs have responded and adapted their merger review processes in reaction to the COVID-19 pandemic and aiming to produce a report on this); Global webinar series on merger remedies (focusing on how NCAs approach merger remedies, such as divestiture and behavioural remedies and aiming to produce a report on this); Update of the merger notification and procedures template (reviewing the template and updating it as to reflect recent developments in merger assessment); and Working Group dialogue, implementation, and outreach (including a workshop in 2021 and continuing to promote the implementation of its recommended practices, such as through designing more model templates). Previously available at <www.internationalcompetitionnetwork.org/wp-content/uploads/2020/09/Workplan2020–23MWG.pdf> (broken ICN link, see discussion in Introduction, n 16).

[150] ICN (n 54) 7. The so-called ICN 2.0 initiative has been explained in this way:

> The discussion of hot topics is a purposeful decision by the ICN to facilitate experience sharing and take part in shaping global competition law dialogue. Examples of this 'ICN 2.0' line of topics have included disruptive innovation, competition advocacy in an economic downturn, online vertical restraints, public interest standards and industrial policy, and implications of the digital economy. These types of topics often are recognized as not ripe for consensus recommendations, but the ICN has valued member discussion and exchange on new developments.
>
> Coppola and others (n 46)

4.3.2.2 Effectiveness in the implementation of ICN work products

As we have noted above, one needs to understand the hierarchy of ICN goals in order to judge how effective it is. One issue here is the relative importance that the ICN assigns to the implementation of its outputs (particularly recommended practices) versus seeing the ICN as a forum whose focus is discussing, interacting, and better understanding each other's approaches and perspectives.[151] Many feel that implementation is crucial to the ICN's success. Hollman and Kovacic, for example, say that routine monitoring of implementation 'is important to determine whether the network is fulfilling the objective that most strongly inspired its formation'. They add that this will also enhance convergence (and assessing what is working and what is not). This is helpful for organizing experimentation.[152] Measuring implementation (as they suggest, and we support) is not the same as making implementation a key parameter for judging the ICN. Hollman and Kovacic do not advocate this, but the ICN's emphasis on implementation as an additional effectiveness measure is increasing over time, alongside efforts to persuade states to implement its work products (see Chapter 2). In 2011, the ICN even changed its mission statement to raise implementation's profile.[153]

An implementation-focus is not necessarily to be expected in a 'soft law network'. In such networks, by definition, members give no commitment (and have no

[151] Although the ICN does not necessarily accept such a distinction. For example, 'The ICN provides a forum for competition agencies to work together, exchange experiences, and develop a deeper understanding of each other's policies, procedures, and analytical approaches [eg all WG have workshops and teleseminars with experience sharing]. This experience-sharing is a step on the path to convergence' ICN (n 54) 4–5. This also seems to be the implication from the merging of categories on page 42 of the same report.

[152] Hugh Hollman and William Kovacic, 'The International Competition Network: Its Past, Current and Future Role' in Lugard (n 45) 78. See also, Coppola and others (n 46).

[153] The ICN's original *Operational Framework* (2001) only referred to implementation once. It said that where 'the ICN reaches consensus on recommendations arising from a project, it is left to its members to decide whether and how to implement' them. In 2011, Fingleton announced a new ICN *Mission Statement*, partly to underline implementation. This was 'to advocate the adoption of superior standards and procedures in competition enforcement and policy around the world, formulate proposals for procedural and substantive convergence, and seek to facilitate effective international cooperation to the benefit of member agencies, consumers and economies worldwide' John Fingleton, 'The ICN's Vision for Its Second Decade' (ICN Annual Conference 2011) 4. Fingleton called for three things to achieve this: a relevant portfolio of ICN work, in the interest of all of its members; relevant ICN work products, and 'above all, our work has to translate into real outcomes. This is the core of our vision for the second decade of the ICN' ibid 5. The ICN website currently says 'Promotion, awareness, and encouraging implementation of ICN work product is vital to the network. The first goal mentioned in the ICN's mission statement is an active one: "to advocate the adoption of superior standards and procedures in competition policy around the world"'. In his vision statement for the ICN's second decade, Andreas Mundt (ICN Chair) proposed three goals: focus, inclusiveness, and implementation. On the latter point he said 'All the efforts mentioned above have of course one key direction: to enhance the implementation of ICN work products' <www.internationalcompetitionnetwork.org/wp-content/uploads/2018/07/ICNSGMundtVision.pdf> 4, accessed 8 October 2021. Summarizing after one survey in 2015 the ICN said 'More effort should be done to ensure **implementation** of ICN work products'. ICN (n 54) 25, see also 5, 42 ('There is a broad consensus that the ICN should focus on implementation' 48–51). See also www.internationalcompetitionnetwork.org/working-groups/icn-operations/implementation/ accessed 8 October 2021.

obligation) to follow recommendations. Many agree that measuring implementation is important, while arguing that a key parameter of ICN effectiveness should not be the implementation of its work products by others. Lewis, for example, says that ICN effectiveness assessments should not revolve around implementation. It is likely to be slow and imperfect, so the ICN would be constantly falling short (especially in more contentious areas). He adds that an implementation focus would also be too narrow because an organization that does not focus on producing binding rules should not be judged by those standards. The development of soft law 'is rooted in consensus, rather than majority; in persuasion through shared experience, rather than coercion; in understanding and celebrating differences, rather than suppressing them'.[154]

There is a risk that too much of an implementation focus undermines the importance of the ICN as a forum for simply exchanging ideas, discussing and better understanding others.[155] This would be unfortunate as it is potentially valuable work. NCAs highlight the importance of the 'softer' kinds of engagement that the ICN facilitates,[156] as does the ICN.[157] Merely focusing on the production and implementation of ICN work products likely underestimates the ICN's effectiveness on this less concrete, but potentially really important, dimension. Ironically, this is an area in which the ICN may really claim to make a major contribution by regularly bringing so many NCAs together (although, scholars have questioned the efficacy and accountability of this unstructured learning in the ICN).[158]

[154] David Lewis, Introductory Address to 2009 ICN Conference (2009), <www.internationalcompetitionnetwork.org/wp-content/uploads/2020/01/SpeechChairIntroLewis2009.pdf> accessed 8 October 2021. See also Lewis (n 45) 209. Implementation is not the 'only or the best' way to judge ICN success. Relationships between members are also important. That said 'Most observers and participants nonetheless agree that implementation of the Recommended Practices is one important indicator of the Network's success', Maria Coppola and Cynthia Lagdameo, 'Taking Stock and Taking Root: a closer look at implementation of the ICN Recommended Practices for Merger Notification & Review Procedures' in Lugard (n 45) 299. Fox (n 45) 125 says that ICN effectiveness assessments should not revolve around implementation (although she does not explain why).

[155] For example, one ICN report says 'This experience-sharing is a step on the path to convergence' ICN (n 54) 4.

[156] 'According to the member interviews that the Steering Group carried out, opportunities for networking and experience sharing are the biggest benefits arising from ICN membership' Fingleton (n 153) 3. See also Esteva Mosso (n 133) 169; Lewis (n 45) 214–15; Dan Sjöblom and Monica Widegren, 'ICN Membership: Opportunities and Challenges for a Competition Authority' ibid 352 and 354; Mariana Tavares, 'The ICN: One of the Many International Priorities' ibid 335.

[157] ICN, *ICN Report on OECD/ICN Questionnaire on International Enforcement Co-operation* (2013) 8–11, <https://www.internationalcompetitionnetwork.org/wp-content/uploads/2018/09/ICNOECDCooperationReport2013.pdf> accessed 8 October 2021.

[158] This is because 'the often unstated beliefs, assumptions or approaches that emerge in the context of closed epistemic communities are treated as tacit knowledge, which is not made explicit and so cannot be scrutinised by outside actors.[fn For some evidence on the limitations of purely informal in the ICN, see Yane Svetiev, 'The Limits of Informal International Law: enforcement, norm generation, and learning in the ICN' in Pauwelyn and others (n 13) In such informal exchanges, officials from established regimes typically adopt the role of teachers, with new adopter officials doing the learning, even where their enforcement contexts and problems greatly differ.[fn ibid 286–87]', Yane Svetiev, *Experimentalist Competition Law and the Regulation of Markets* (Hart 2020) 162–63.

An increased implementation-focus could have other unintended consequences. There is likely to be an interrelationship between NCAs' ability (and willingness) to agree to ICN work products and how demanding the ICN (and the wider ICN membership) is about the implementation of these work products by NCAs (and their states).[159] Rather than getting fixated on narrow metrics one needs to assess effectiveness in the round.

In any event, as we have seen, the ICN has made implementation a key parameter of effectiveness. Many ICN working groups go to great lengths to 'nurture, promote and advocate' the implementation of their outputs.[160] So does the ICN as a whole.[161] Hollman and Kovacic say that compliance with 'recommended procedural practices should be amenable to effective measurement'.[162] The ICN often tries to measure this and is often extremely positive in its self-assessments. There are certainly signs that ICN work products have influenced several NCAs and their states. For example, the ICN's 2010–11 Second Decade review included interviews with most ICN members and reported that:

> ICN work products have influenced agency practice of many ICN members, and have also influenced legal and policy reforms in many ICN member jurisdictions. For example, 39 ICN members have reported using the Anti-Cartel Enforcement Manual to advance their cartel enforcement programmes. Two-thirds of ICN members that made changes to their merger control regimes cited the ICN Recommended Practices for Merger Notification and Review Procedures as having influenced their reforms. More than a dozen agencies have reported using the ICN's Recommended Practices on Dominance/Substantial Market Power Analysis Under Unilateral Conduct Laws in their casework or staff training.[163]

[159] Lugard (n 45) 16. Similarly, Fox (n 45) 133 talks about how it limits the discussion of more complex, controversial issues. This might explain Chapter 3's finding that, compared NCAs with over 100 personnel, a higher percentage of smaller NCAs (that responded to our survey) agree that a lack of compliance with ICN recommended practices does not undermine an NCA's reputation (these are recommended practices that they have 'agreed' to but tend not to have participated in drafting). Perhaps this is what is being referred to when saying 'despite, or maybe thanks, to this non-binding nature, this common approach has become in many areas of competition policy the worldwide accepted standard' Esteva Mosso (n 133) 165.

[160] See Coppola and others (n 46); Hollman and Kovacic (n 152) 79, for example.

[161] 'The single biggest act of institutionalizing the ICN's commitment to encouraging use and implementation of its work came with the establishment of a group dedicated to implementation. The ICN established an 'Advocacy and Implementation Network' later renamed the Promotion and Implementation ('P&I') team. The P&I team is made up of Working Group chairs and other interested members. It coordinates network-wide implementation initiatives, being the first stop for questions from members about existing ICN work and its application. P&I encourages ICN member implementation stories to help inspire members with ideas from their peers about how to use ICN work. It also coordinates ICN advice to members that are contemplating changes to laws, rules, or practices that may be informed by ICN recommendations or other work' Coppola and others (n 46). There are also regular efforts made to survey ICN actors to understand barriers to implementation and deal with them, ICN (n 54) 17.

[162] Hollman and Kovacic (n 152) 78.

[163] ICN, 'The ICN's Vision for Its Second Decade' (2012) 1–2.

While there is some suggestion that implementation of ICN work products is increasing over time,[164] many point out that there is still a lot of work to do. In 2005, two private practitioners, Rowley and Wakil, welcomed the increasing efforts of the Merger Working Group and others to push implementation but said that more efforts were needed. They reported insufficient traction of implementation, especially in regimes where it is most needed. Both point to many regimes introducing new laws and ignoring ICN recommended practices, even basic ones like jurisdictional nexus. It is unclear why, but they postulated that it was due to a lack of awareness and failing to see compliance as a priority.[165] Similarly, when commenting on a 2011 analysis of the implementation of four ICN recommended practices in the merger field, FTC officials noted that only 25 per cent of NCAs with merger control complied with all four of them. In this same study the authors conclude by noting that 'the current landscape suggests that there is considerable divergence with the ICN's best practices and the majority of ICN members'.[166] While it is hard to discern, given the changes in the questions asked and the methodology adopted, a similar position seems to emerge in ICN surveys today.[167]

Furthermore, ICN assessments of its own effectiveness are questionable because the methodology that they adopt is insufficiently specified. We also question how robust it is. Assessing effective implementation well is hard, complex work. Many methodological questions need to be considered prior to the analysis. For example, what is the appropriate area of ICN work where implementation is required? Second, what is the best way to collect data on effective implementation? Assessment, in public policy studies, is taken very seriously, and it normally includes *ex ante* assessment (why some measure is needed), *interim* assessment (how implementation is progressing once the law (or, in this case, the recommendation) has been adopted) and *ex post* assessment (have the goals specified ex ante been achieved?).[168] The ICN, apparently, does not do this systematically. This could be due to lack of interest in carrying out proper assessment (because, after all, ICN work products are not binding) or to a lack of resources needed to collect and analyse the data needed for such effort. Also, we cannot discard the hypothesis that proper assessment is not carried out because it is a double-edge sword: if assessment proves that ICN work products are not implemented or, when implemented, do not work as expected, some members could question the usefulness of the ICN.[169]

164 Coppola and Lagdameo (n 154) 307–09.
165 Rowley and Wakil (n 130).
166 Coppola and Lagdameo (n 154) 303 and 315.
167 See, for example, ICN (n 54) 18–21.
168 See E Bozzini and J Hunt, 'Bringing Evaluation into the Policy Cycle' (2015) 6 European Journal of Risk Regulation 57.
169 A similar point is made about the EU by Majone. See G Majone, *Dilemmas of European Integration: The Ambiguities and Pitfalls of Integration by Stealth* (OUP 2005).

Taking these points in turn, there is a tension between demanding implementation and accepting that, at times, 'informed divergence' is acceptable (as the ICN does). Presumably, where 'informed divergence' is appropriate, then implementation is unnecessary, and may even be undesirable. In a 2016 ICN discussion, participants recognized that 'total uniformity is not the goal but that the ICN can continue to help bridge gaps in particular areas. In areas where principles and practice differ among jurisdictions, informed divergence may also be helpful and constructive.'[170] This is helpful, but the borders of appropriate 'informed divergence' need to be mapped, because they mark the appropriate limits of the implementation push.[171] Even when 'informed divergence' is explicitly accepted, this is often undermined by a push to implement anyway.[172] We need to know when (and how much) 'informed divergence' is appropriate (and how to demonstrate this) before we can know how much implementation there 'should be'. This tension is at the very heart of ICN work. Until this is openly discussed and the limits mapped, it is impossible to rationally assess the appropriate limits of implementation (and thus to measure the effectiveness of this aspect of the ICN project). There is a lot at stake. Pushing too hard for implementation may generate unwanted outcomes.[173]

Second, we have concerns about the ICN's methodology when it collects implementation data. By way of example, consider three issues: who provides the data,

[170] ICN (n 54) 51. In this same report, while emphasizing that there is a 'broad consensus that the ICN should focus on implementation' and placing some emphasis on convergence, the ICN adds that if implementation is not likely then it welcomes ways in which informed divergence can be used to minimize problems:

> continue developing Recommended Practices and periodically update them; help younger agencies to implement international best practices; focus on relevant topics and practical materials that can facilitate soft convergence; develop comparative work to identify differences among jurisdictions and evaluate how to bridge the gaps they create; develop case studies showing the efficiencies and benefits resulting from adopting Recommended Practices; circulate ICN new products and updates directly within the relevant divisions of the agencies; cooperate more closely with international organizations (UNCTAD, OECD, ICC, BIAC) to increase awareness and promote implementation of ICN work products; encourage interaction between agencies and NGAs to discuss the use and/or implementation of the ICN work products; collect and share successful implementation stories; perform self-assessment exercises.
>
> ibid 42–43

In an earlier study, Lugard supported the Unilateral Conduct Working Group's emphasis on informed divergence where consensus was not attainable, saying that it is still useful to see what others think and to test and analyse their views. He did see a risk that, once the areas of difference have been identified less than optimal efforts may be 'applied to eventually eliminate the existing divergences. This would be regrettable' Lugard (n 45) 16.

[171] An example of different NCAs' positions on informed divergence was previously available at <www.internationalcompetitionnetwork.org/uploads/library/doc990.pdf> 2, (broken ICN link, see discussion in Introduction, n 16).

[172] For example, ICN Merger Working Group, *Guiding Principles For Merger Notification and Review* (2002) <https://www.internationalcompetitionnetwork.org/portfolio/guiding-principles-for-merger-notification-review-procedure/> accessed 8 October 2021. Principle 1 says 'Jurisdictions are sovereign with respect to the application of their own laws to mergers', yet, Principle 7 says 'Jurisdictions should seek convergence of merger review processes toward agreed best practices'.

[173] See discussion around n 159.

what sort of implementation is relevant, and the implementation of what. The answers to these questions affect the quality of the data and the assessment of how much implementation has taken place. They also relate to the 'kind of ICN' that we want. Let us start with who provides the data. The data going into the 'statistical sausage machine' may not be wholly accurate. For example, the Merger Working Group has been particularly active when it comes to checking on the implementation of its outputs. It provides a good illustration of the difficulties. The Merger Working Group predominantly relies on self-reporting by NCAs in its assessments.[174] While understandable, the ICN has no permanent secretariat, and self-reporting may distort the data. NCAs have an incentive to exaggerate their compliance when reporting back to a network where the epistemic community is as strong as it is in the ICN (especially as ICN surveys are not anonymized). NCAs that have not implemented may also be less likely to reply to surveys (and, in fact, many do not).[175] This 'sample bias' reduces the field of experiences and context that those relying on the survey will consider; it also limits the learning potential of the survey exercise.[176] Such biases could further distort the sample, undermining our confidence in any conclusions we draw from such work.[177] NCAs that feel under pressure to 'demonstrate implementation' may even mislead in their self-reporting. A further issue is that these 'reporting issues', may not arise in a uniform cross-section of ICN members. Poorer, newer NCAs are more likely to feel under more pressure to comply with ICN edicts, see Chapter 1 (although smaller NCAs, which are often poorer, when answering our *anonymous* survey in Chapter 3, tended to say that they did not to consider a lack of implementation damages an NCA's reputation). There is also a problem of causality. Even if states change their rules in ways

[174] After completing its *Recommended Practices for Merger Notification and Review Procedures*, the Merger Working Group looked at NCAs' implementation of them. It produced a report which identified some implementation problems NCAs had had and how they had overcome these, ICN Report on Implementation of the Recommended Practices for Merger Notification and Review Procedures (2005) available at <www.internationalcompetitionnetwork.org/portfolio/implementation-of-the-merger-notification-and-review-procedures-rps> accessed 8 October 2021. A 2010 assessment of the use of Merger Working Group work reported that 'over 90% of responding agencies indicated that they used MWG work product—dozens reported the use of MWG RPs contributing to change in their merger regimes' ICN Statement of Achievements (2001–13) 14–15. The Merger Working Group also introduced self-assessment tools which NCAs can use to benchmark their own practice against ICN recommended practices, ICN Merger Notification and Procedures Self-Assessment Tool (2011) and ICN Merger Analysis Self-Assessment Tool (2019).

[175] Svetiev reports that in most cases about 30–40 NCAs respond to surveys, Svetiev (158) 165.

[176] ibid 165–66.

[177] A standard assumption in empirical work is that those that do not answer are randomly distributed. If this is not true then it affects the conclusions one can draw from the data (which may be the case with these ICN surveys for the reasons noted). For example, in 2016, the Merger Working Group looked at the implementation of the ICN's Recommended Practices for Merger Notification and Review Procedures again. All ICN members with merger control regimes were asked to identify whether and how their merger systems conform. 80 of the 100 jurisdictions surveyed responded (by the time the analysis was done). This lack of response could radically affect the analysis. For example, 52 of the 80 NCA respondents claimed to use recommended practices to review their own merger regimes (65 per cent). This figure could fall to almost 50 per cent if all those that did not respond did not use recommended practices for this purpose, ICN Merger Working Group (n 45) 16.

that better conform with ICN work products (or NCAs do this in their administrative practices), this is not necessarily as a result of the ICN. For example, the EU often applies significant pressure (on non-Member States) to adopt competition rules and then to apply them in defined ways, as do peer reviews by the OECD and UNCTAD. The effects here are further complicated because ICN work sometimes influences these actors (although, at other times, the causality runs the other way).[178]

To reduce this problem, one paper (by a current and previous co-Chair of the Merger Working Group, writing in a personal capacity) augmented the 2011 survey that they conducted with personal research of the various regimes (except for two regimes, Fiji and the Kyrgyz Republic where information was 'unavailable'). This was likely arduous and time-consuming; but we hope that others follow this example. But even this approach does not eliminate problems. Given their lack of access to data (and their inability to see inside many NCAs) the authors of the 2011 survey limited the recommended practices that they studied, focusing on only four (out of thirteen). This was because these four lent themselves 'to a mostly objective evaluation of whether or not agencies confirm to them'.[179]

The second issue raised above is what sort of data is relevant. The ICN produces a lot of 'concrete' work products. Some NCAs might be able to implement some of these themselves through changes in their administrative practice. Sometimes though, some states require legislative changes.[180] Legislative changes can be easier to 'see' than changes in administrative practice (often hidden from view), although it can be harder to convince 'external actors' (ie those not in the ICN) to follow ICN work products.[181] That said, the law on the books is not always the same as

[178] Coppola and Lagdameo (n 154) 307. Noting the influence of ICN work on UNCTAD and OECD work products and practices, see, for example, ICN Merger Working Group (n 45) 1.

[179] Coppola and Lagdameo (n 154) 300–01 (the four 'objectively verifiable' recommended practices were the nexus between merger effects and reviewing jurisdiction, objective criteria for notification thresholds, timing of notification, and merger review periods). By contrast, the 2016 study examined all recommended practices, ICN Merger Working Group (n 45).

[180] The ICN has, for example, advised officials in India's new competition regime (they did the same for China, even though it is not an ICN member). The American Bar Association Antitrust and International Law Sections and the International Bar Association have also given advice to China and India based in the ICN recommendations. India explicitly linked revisions to its draft merger rules to the ICN recommendations.

[181] Chapter 3 showed, for example, that the most common 'mode' of implementation of ICN work products was autonomous implementation by the NCA. NCAs often asked for legislative changes to align them with ICN work products (although in the areas we examined not as often as autonomously implementing ICN work products themselves). Presumably reluctance was also driven by a belief that the legislator would not act. Even when there was a request by the NCA to implement an ICN work product, in the areas we examined, the legislator often did not act (ranging from 5 per cent to 30 per cent of the time).

Similarly, back in 2011, Ron Stern (who used to be the General Counsel for General Electric) said that many of the changes that have been made as a result of the recommended practices are things that the NCAs could do themselves, rather than legislative changes. Some legislative changes have been made in line with the recommended practices. However, 'implementation has proven to be slower, more difficult, and uneven where statutory provisions are required' Stern (n 137) 329–30.

what actually happens on the ground.[182] Once again, this raises methodological data collection issues.

Linked to this too is the wider kinds of implementation that risk being overlooked if we focus exclusively on implementing concrete work products (and are hard to record and verify). ICN work is likely to affect NCAs in myriad, often small ways. Perhaps an ICN training video, or a discussion in a workshop affected the way an NCA's staff choose which cases to focus on and why. Perhaps reviewing the ICN good practice manual changed the way in which evidence was gathered or a specific national provision was interpreted, in practice, by an official. ICN reviews of the 'effectiveness' of its work products likely struggle to capture such effects, which may even be subconscious. There have been efforts by the ICN to measure this more diffuse kind of implementation, which we welcome. For example, in 2009 the ICN noted:

> According to a recent outreach survey,[183] 96% of competition agencies surveyed make use of ICN work products and materials, and 94% distribute them inside the agency. 77% use ICN materials for reference purposes, 46% for staff training and 40% for outreach. 69% of all agencies say they are pro-actively working towards applying ICN Recommended Practices (71% of newer and 65% of established agencies).[184]

But while the ICN encourages NCAs to share information about how they use ICN work product and materials, this is information is often hard to collect, making the ICN's full impact hard to measure (possibly leading to under-reporting of this kind of influence).[185]

The final point that we want to discuss in relation to effectiveness is whether the ICN is more effective at achieving the interests of rich, 'western' NCAs, than newer, poorer NCAs. Their interests sometimes overlap, but they often have different priorities. There is a real risk that richer NCAs will be favoured, given the ICN's origin, and the mechanisms of influence highlighted in Chapter 1 and confirmed by Chapter 3's survey. The ICN's 'consensus requirement' is unlikely to counteract this.

Some are confident that the ICN effectively works for newer jurisdictions too. Fox reports that 'the leaders of the ICN have shown consistent resolve to include,

[182] One might question how 'fair' it is to judge the ICN on a lack of implementation through legislative reform because it cannot control states' legislative agendas—see above. However, as the ICN 'markets' itself, in part, on the implementation of its work products, then it needs to be able to persuade other stakeholders of the value of these work products. In fact, the ICN has made several organizational changes in order to help it to persuade 'external stakeholders' (such as states) about the value of ICN work. So, with this in mind we use its perspective.

[183] Previously available at <http://www.internationalcompetitionnetwork.org/media/library/mergers/Vice_Chair_1.pdf>bcsi_scan_A2018E0826 464712=0&bcsi_scan_filename=Vice_Chair_1.pdf> (broken ICN link, see discussion in Introduction, n 16).

[184] ICN (n 6) 3–4, see also 8–15.

[185] See Coppola and others (n 46), for example.

involve, and respond to all voices'.[186] Coppola et al list many initiatives, that the ICN has undertaken, aimed at being more inclusive. One dimension of this work was encouraging more engagement from newer NCAs. They claim that the ICN's efforts 'intensify the presence and degree of participation of young agencies in the activities of the ICN, including the governance structures, the working groups, and the various conferences and workshops.[187]'[188] The same authors make similar claims about inclusiveness in project selection.[189] Lewis has also said that, where newer NCAs have been able to seize the initiative (and had the confidence to demand this), their efforts have been tolerated, even welcomed.[190]

[186] Fox (n 45) 130.

[187] New and young agencies have regularly hosted ICN events, such as working group workshops and the ICN's annual conference, bringing an important voice to the organization and content of such events. For example, agencies in Morocco, Botswana, Ukraine, El Salvador, India, Poland, Mauritius, Colombia, Czechia, Panama, Singapore, and Turkey have all hosted ICN events.

[188] Coppola and others (n 46).

[189]

> Still other parameters, such as project selection, reflect ICN's commitment to inclusiveness. Every working group, and every ICN project, is open to the participation and input of all members. The network's earliest projects addressed advocacy and capacity building, selected intentionally for their widespread relevance and responsiveness to the needs of younger agencies. The ICN regularly has used its resources to examine and address the needs of new and younger agencies. For example, in 2006, it produced a report that identifies the type of challenges young agencies experience and the measures these agencies have applied to address the challenges.
>
> [ICN Report, Lessons to be Learnt from the Experiences of Younger Competition Agencies (2006), <www.internationalcompetitionnetwork.org/portfolio/lessons-learned-from-the-experience-of-young-competition-agencies/> accessed 8 October 2021.]
>
> In 2019, the ICN revisited the topic, with an update to the 2006 report. [ICN Report, Lessons to be Learnt from the Experiences of Younger Competition Agencies, An Update to the 2006 Report (2019), <www.internationalcompetitionnetwork.org/wp-content/uploads/2019/06/SGVC_YoungerAgenciesReport2019.pdf> accessed 8 October 2021.] The ICN's Training on Demand online compilation of training videos also includes a module on competition policy in developing countries. [ICN Training on Demand, Developing Countries and Competition, available at <www.internationalcompetitionnetwork.org/training/developing-countries-and-competition/> (accessed 8 October 20210)] and one offering advice for new and young competition agencies [CN Training on Demand, Advice for New and Young Competition Agencies, <www.internationalcompetitionnetwork.org/training/advice-for-new-and-young-competition-agencies/> (accessed 8 October 2021)] in addition to many on the fundamentals of enforcement.
>
> The ICN has continued its commitment to diversity by addressing a wide portfolio of work: investigative fundamentals and more sophisticated enforcement subjects across the Merger, Cartel, and Unilateral Conduct Working Groups, and a host of operational and institutional matters in the Agency Effectiveness Working Group. In addition, conference hosts and the Steering Group regularly take on special projects to address particular interests such as competition policy in an economic downturn, competition law and policy in small economies, competition issues involving state-owned enterprises, abuse of superior bargaining position, and disruptive innovation.
>
> Through these concerted efforts that touch on every aspect of the network, today the ICN has mainstreamed the participation of its younger agencies—a reflection of the additional experience gained by the agencies once considered 'younger', but equally proof of ICN's integration of members large and small, old and young. The network's approach to membership, participation, leadership roles, work product, and communication has created a fully inclusive body. Coppola and others (n 46).

[190]

> From the first days of the ICN a number of young agencies from the developing world and the emerging market economies [in the same article he later calls this 'a clutch' of their

But there are reasons to be cautious about such positive stories. In 2011, Hollman and Kovacic noted that topics of particular importance to newer NCAs may be ignored unless richer NCAs are also interested.[191] In the ICN's 2016 survey report, newer NCAs were still requesting 'more products and trainings targeted at young agencies and/or new staff'.[192] Many commentators note the importance of listening to smaller (including richer) NCAs and giving them more influence.[193] The ICN has been saying the same itself, for many years (and still is today).[194] Furthermore, while making the points, noted in the previous paragraph, Fox and Lewis both caveated them. Fox said that, unsurprisingly the 'voices of the major players in the developed world are likely to be more influential than the voices of developing and small economies'. Lewis too added that there are marginalized NCAs, normally through a lack of their own resources and information.[195]

To be fair to the ICN (and its leadership), on many occasions it has sought to understand why newer NCAs are often less active in the ICN.[196] Furthermore, in our experience, silence from newer, less experienced (and confident) NCAs is often the norm, even in smaller networks such as the ECN. In terms of barriers to participation for NCAs, surveys find:

> NCAs] demanded a very active role in its work. They have chaired working groups, they have submitted papers to and participated in debates in working groups, they have hosted conferences and workshops and they have hosted and participated in the network's successful teleseminars.
>
> Lewis (n 45) 213–14

Similarly, by implication, Lewis (n 154) 2.

[191] Hollman and Kovacic (n 152) 60.

[192] ICN (n 54) 18. See also, in the same report, the ICN reporting on its 2015 survey about desired goals in five years' time for the ICN, said:

> Many agencies also feel that the ICN should encourage more active participation of younger agencies in the ICN in order to widen the perspectives informing ICN work and broaden its reach. The ICN should ensure that younger agencies have the opportunity to effectively contribute to the work products, participate in the teleseminars, but also, if possible, take leadership roles within working groups and project teams. More engagement from younger agencies can help ensure that the ICN addresses the needs of all its members, solicit open and candid discussion at seminars and promote convergence. Given that the ICN work is consensus-based, contributions by a larger number of diversified members will only continue to strengthen the network.
>
> ibid 22

[193] Tavares (157) 346; Sjöblom and Widegren (n 156) 355.

[194] <www.internationalcompetitionnetwork.org/wp-content/uploads/2018/07/ICNSGMundtVision.pdf> 3, accessed 8 October 2021. By implication, for example, one ICN Report (2016) said ICN 'should promote more active participation: agencies and NGAs agree that smaller and younger agencies should participate more effectively in the activities of the ICN' ICN (n 54) 42.

[195] Respectively, Fox (n 45) 130; Lewis (n 45) 213. Similarly, by implication, Lewis (n 154) 2, <www.internationalcompetitionnetwork.org/wp-content/uploads/2020/01/SpeechChairIntroLewis2009.pdf> accessed 8 October 2021.

[196] In 2016 the ICN conducted a major survey, for example, which among other things asked about this, ICN (n 54) 22. Coppola and others (n 46) report several other efforts to canvass ICN members and NGAs.

> The lack of sufficient resources that members are able to devote to the ICN and the demands of other (unidentified) priorities were the top identified barriers to participation in the ICN. Approximately one-fifth of respondents also indicated that time-zones make it difficult to take part in calls and seminars. [Other NCAs] ... specified that lack of resources in terms of money, staff and time is a barrier to participation, but also the difficulty of engaging case handlers in the ICN activities and of finding expert speakers for the teleseminars.[197]

The ICN has also sought ways of remedying the situation to some extent. Fingleton said that the best way to ensure that the ICN's work meets NCAs' needs 'is to have the broadest possible participation in our agenda-setting.'[198] In 2011, when he was ICN Chair, the ICN sought to open up new leadership roles in order to widen NCA engagement, increasing the number of such roles, requiring working group leaders to rotate and widening the criteria for selecting new Working Group co-Chairs to 'explicitly include considerations around the geographic and economic diversity of ICN members.'[199] The ICN emphasizes that NCAs can participate in all projects and working groups. The introduction of 'Town Hall' sessions and features like the ICN blog, open to all NCAs and NGAs, also sought to encourage a wider and more inclusive feeling in participants. There have been some successes, as a result. However, leadership roles have often gone to small, rich NCAs (such as Finland), rather than those from developing countries (South Africa and India being obvious exceptions).[200]

It should also be pointed out that many of the reasons why NCAs say that they cannot actively participate either are not the direct fault of the ICN or are due to the ICN's 'success' as a body. The active input of ICN members means that working groups hold many events each year. So, smaller NCAs (even those that are relatively well financed, like the Swedish NCA) can struggle to participate in all ICN events, let alone actively participate (without even considering the further strain from OECD/UNCTAD, etc meetings). Some NCAs have suggested reducing such activities, so that smaller NCAs can participate (and input into) a higher percentage of ICN work product. The ICN leadership is reluctant to accede to this. It prefers to focus on better timetabling, to limit clashes between events in different working groups and to better coordinate with OECD and UNCTAD events.[201] This reduces, but does not remove, the problem—which undermines the ICN's claim to truly speak for all NCAs.[202]

197 ICN (n 54) 14.
198 Fingleton (n 153) 5.
199 ibid 6.
200 ICN (n 54) 7.
201 Previously available at <www.internationalcompetitionnetwork.org/uploads/library/doc998.pdf> 2, (broken ICN link, see discussion in Introduction, n 16).
202 This is a further illustration raised by the lack of transparency in the ICN. Because the ICN reports tend not to link specific ideas with specific actors, it is not easy to see whose opinions are being routinely ignored. It is fairly easy to ignore voices if the ICN wants to. For example, after one survey the ICN says

Nevertheless, several criticisms can be levelled at the ICN and its approach here. First, while the ICN makes some effort to help newer NCAs to take an active role in selecting new areas for ICN focus and to input into the creation of these work products, they have been largely ineffectual. The number of newer NCAs with staff in key roles has increased, but not significantly. Newer NCAs' input into ICN work products is still marginal. And, many ICN work products still hold little interest to newer NCAs. We believe that significantly more (and better) effort could be made in this direction.

Unfortunately, the ICN seems to see its main role, with respect to newer NCAs, as being to educate them and to help them to implement ICN work products (rather than supporting them to take an active role in their own development).[203] The

> The suggestions on specific topics that the ICN should address are very diverse. A full list of all topics that were mentioned by the responding agencies can be found in Annex 2. The top mentioned topic was the interaction of competition and intellectual property rights [supported by six NCAs]. Among the topics that were mentioned by more than one agency are: vertical restraints, non-hard core horizontal agreements and joint ventures, two-sided and multi-sided markets, remedies in mergers, agreements and abuse of dominance cases, enhanced cooperation techniques in anti-cartel enforcement, ex-post assessment of the effectiveness of advocacy efforts, and how to deal with digital evidence. Several agencies suggested more guidance and practical tools for international cooperation and coordination, in merger and cartel investigations. Some agencies would like more guidance on how to deal with sector regulators and, more specifically, with bodies that have concurrent jurisdiction over competition matters.
>
> ICN (n 54) 18

With such a range it is easy for the Steering Group to choose the ones it prefers and ignore those it does not like. Chapter 1 pointed out that the Steering Group is still dominated by richer, 'western' NCAs.

[203] The ICN is quick to note that it is of value to both established and newer NCAs. It describes the ICN as: 'a forum for newer agencies to draw on the experiences and support of more established agencies, for example as they seek to advocate a competition culture in their jurisdiction, where there may face vested local interest groups' ICN (n 6) 7. Similarly, ICN work products 'promote the adoption of the ICN's preferred norms and approaches, but also help to support the ICN's less experienced agencies to mature quickly and leapfrog over the failures of others' Coppola and others (n 46).

In its 2016 report, the ICN lists the following things it has introduced since 2011 in terms of helping newer NCAs. Nearly all of them are implementation-focused:

> The ICN implemented a working group leadership 'rotation' plan that includes clear criteria for more involvement by a broader range of members. A number of members such as Finland, India, Norway, and South Africa have become first-time WG co-chairs since 2011; the ICN established a welcome track for new members; Working Groups, such as the MWG, have a work stream dedicated to 'outreach' to new members as part of their annual planning; the Vice Chair for Implementation started an initiative to collect successful implementation stories from across the network to inspire others to consider implementation and to demonstrate the real impact of ICN's work; and more ICN content has been translated into other languages such as Spanish and French.
>
> ICN (n 54) 7

Similarly, in the Washington and Singapore discussions about how to respond after the ICN's 2016 survey report participants made several suggestions of what to do here, most seem aimed at helping newer NCAs learn from existing NCAs and materials (although the last bullet point on page 53 says 'devote greater attention to issues which are relevant for younger agencies (benefits of competition, privatisation, bid-rigging) and/or to broader policy questions'. However, the topics selected for priority include none of particular interest to newer jurisdictions, although are going into more controversial areas, like the interface between competition and public interest considerations and vertical restraints, ibid 52–53 and 56.

ICN goes to great lengths to assist with implementation in many, imaginative ways. For example, in order to deal with the difficulty of its growing membership, a Vice Chair for outreach was created in 2007. Specific structures were also set up to support engagement through the Promotion and Implementation team. They aim to raise awareness of ICN work product and promote its implementation, engaging NCAs, working groups, and NGAs. It is important to help newer NCAs become more effective enforcers.[204] Education and implementation assistance sometimes help here. However, we are sceptical about whether the focus on helping newer NCAs to implement ICN work products that they have often not input into (and may well disregard their specific needs) is quite as selfless as the powerful actors in the ICN suggest.[205] Similar enforcement practices benefit large multinationals operating in the states of these newer NCAs (see Chapter 1, Section 1.2.1.1.3). Before the impact on newer NCAs (and their states) is conclusively declared, it might be better to thoroughly assess the outcomes of the use of ICN work products.[206] Yet, despite claiming to be 'a results-based, project-orientated organisation'.[207] The ICN makes very little effort to actually check the empirical results of its activities. Until newer NCAs are inputting into the ICN agenda and ICN work products on

[204] For example, Pérez Motta notes that competition enforcement is particularly important in developing countries because they often have more concentrated markets, there may also be institutional endowment issues, with powerful business groups able to protect their interests, etc they often have less experience and expertise in their NCAs (but also judiciary, law firms, etc) as well as limited resources. He then discusses how the ICN has helped Mexico, saying it has clearly had an important impact on the development of competition policy there and 'this impact has resulted in substantial improvements in the effectiveness of its [Mexican] competition policy' Eduardo Pérez Motta, 'The Role of the International Competition Network (ICN) in the Promotion of Competition in Developing Countries: the case of Mexico' in Lugard (n 45) 219, see also 217–18. He gives examples in cartels, mergers, and advocacy, including using ICN work products to push for legislative changes in Mexico. Similarly, Sokol says that ICN outputs 'have helped to increase the capacity of younger agencies to effectively address international cartels and to improve their domestic cartel capacity' Sokol (n 45) 158.

[205] While they clearly emphasize the importance of being more inclusive (more on this below), this quote from Coppola et al encapsulates the idea that, even if they have not contributed to it, there is still value in newer NCAs implementing ICN work:

> The ICN's work product is strengthened by the diversity of views that underlie its creation. Broad-based project participation ensures that the work reflects sound approaches applicable across various legal traditions and experience levels. This further reinforces the relevance of ICN work product, promoting support by newer and more mature agencies as well as NGA community, and thus ready advocates for the adoption and implementation of such work product. [fn Agencies and individuals unable to participate in the ICN's day-to-day work still benefit from ICN work product, which is available free-of-charge, on the ICN's website, and the network, including discussion of work product and issues with experts from around the world either remotely or via participation in the ICN's annual conference.]
>
> Coppola and others (n 46)

[206] The Introduction and Chapter 1 note that the different contexts, experience of competition, knowledge, understanding of capitalism, etc might also affect the kind of competition that works best (and can be most readily accepted) in a jurisdiction. Pushing states to implement ICN work products may not give adequate regard to this (especially where, as noted above, newer jurisdictions are often less influential in the content of these work products). By way of example, Svetiev refers to the experiences of South Africa and China, Svetiev (n 158) 167–68.

[207] ICN (n 6) 1.

something like an equal footing, it may be appropriate for the ICN to limit its efforts to encourage the implementation of ICN work products in the jurisdictions of newer NCAs.[208]

In conclusion, networks (and the epistemic communities participating in them) can be effective sites for sharing information, devising norms and persuading (or even pressurizing) others to follow them. The ICN appears to have been highly effective as a discussion forum. It has also helped to create an epistemic community of competition enforcers that has largely accepted a narrow set of issues, which is often out of step with wider public opinion in many of the states in which these actors operate. This achievement is often overlooked by the ICN itself. Its main focus when assessing its own effectiveness is to examine the number of ICN outputs created and whether they have been widely implemented.

We welcome the ICN's efforts to assess its effectiveness. However, for the reasons set out above, we do not think that they are likely to be accurate. Indeed, it will be hard to rationally make such assessments at all until some of the deeper tensions at the heart of the ICN are resolved. In order to measure effectiveness rationally, the ICN needs to define a meta goal, properly explain when conflicts arise in its work and how it deals with them. We caution against placing too much emphasis on implementation of ICN work products, as it might undermine 'agreement' in the first place (undermining ICN effectiveness elsewhere). We also question whether an implementation focus makes sense, given the ICN's lack of control over outside actors. If the ICN is to persist with this focus, we think that NCAs need to spend more time reflecting upon (and openly discussing) the appropriate limits of 'informed divergence' to better map the appropriate limits of implementation. As regards the ICN's methodology, we are worried that placing too much reliance on self-reporting through surveys that are not anonymized is likely to lead to inaccuracies and distortions in the data set, a particular risk where some members feel under pressure to conform. It is worth adding that surveys might not be the best way to measure implementation. Even if they are perfectly anonymized, they might suffer from the so-called 'social desirability bias'[209]—a bias that leads respondents to answer in ways that are 'socially desirable' (in the case of the ICN, social desirability consists in being a 'good implementer' of its recommendations). This bias holds regardless of anonymity, and might lead, in our case, to overestimate the degree of implementation.

But above all, we think that there is a fundamental gap in the assessments that the ICN undertakes. The ICN architecture does not really seek to understand why

[208] This suggestion is against the tide. 'There is a broad consensus that the ICN should focus on implementation: Working groups should verify the effectiveness, usefulness and influence of their work, but also better promote existing work and planned events' ICN (n 54) 42.

[209] See eg P Grimm, 'Social Desirability Bias' *Wiley International Encyclopedia of Marketing* (Wiley 2010).

states diverge from ICN work products. Are they intentionally (or unintentionally) ignoring them? Don't these work products 'fit' in that jurisdiction? Nor, for example, does it check whether, when states bring their rules into line with ICN work products (or NCAs adapt their administrative practices to align), they end up with superior outcomes from their standards and procedures? If this is true at all, is it true for all states, only advanced industrial states, or also those with newer NCAs? We do not know because the ICN rarely checks or invites its members to do so (the Opt-in Frameworks that we described in Chapter 2, Section 2.2.2.4 are an exception to this). As Svetiev points out:

> In the absence of a systemic focus on reporting and reviewing implementation efforts ... ICN deliberations may neither distinguish between these reasons for divergence, nor use such divergent approaches in a recursive process of revising recommended practices.[210]

This absence is particularly remarkable because these sorts of checks are widely supported. Checking is particularly important, given the impact of different contexts on the way norms operate in fact.[211]

A deeper discussion is also needed in the ICN about its apparent bias in effectiveness when it comes to achieving the interests of rich, 'western' NCAs and NGAs (over poorer, newer NCAs). The ICN itself acknowledges this risk and has made efforts to understand and address it. Many agree that ICN conferences have become increasingly diverse over time, with more frank exchanges of views from a broader range of agencies.[212] However, the ICN's efforts still seem insufficient. Until this issue is dealt with, it seems hard for the ICN to claim that it works for all its members equally. It is also questionable whether the ICN should be pushing the implementation of its work products so hard before the issue of bias is dealt with. This might give pause for thought to states (and their NCAs) who unquestioningly

[210] Svetiev (n 158) 168.

[211] Assessing the actual effectiveness of competition interventions is important, UNCTAD, *Criteria for Evaluating the Effectiveness of Competition Authorities* (2007) <https://unctad.org/system/files/official-document/c2clpd59_en.pdf> accessed 8 October 2021; OECD, *Reference Guide on ex-post Evaluation of Competition Agencies' Enforcement Decisions* (2016) <https://www.oecd.org/daf/competition/Ref-guide-expost-evaluation-2016web.pdf> accessed 8 October 2021. Here our focus is on assessing the actual effectiveness of policy intervention, rather than evaluator assumptions for accountability purposes, see OECD, *Guide for Helping Competition Authorities Assess the Expected Impact of Their Activities* (2014) <https://www.oecd.org/competition/guide-impact-assessment-competition-activities.htm> (accessed 8 October 2021) and references made there. These studies provide many examples of NCAs actively trying to measure the effectiveness of their various activities (and of other state actors trying to measure the effectiveness of their NCAs too). These assessments need to be made in the states implementing ICN work products (and those that do not) to assess the effects of specific practices 'on the ground'. This is because work products can have different effects in different contexts, so practices that work well in one jurisdiction might not work at all in another. UNCTAD makes this point for developing countries at paras 85–88 of the previous paper, for example.

[212] ICN (n 163) 19–22.

adopt ICN work. The lack of proper transparency also needs to be dealt with before a proper stock-taking can begin.

The idea is that taking on wider viewpoints would benefit those NCAs and other actors that so far have felt somehow marginalized within the ICN[213] (that they have felt marginalized makes sense given the industrial policy aims of the NCAs that set up the ICN). Being more inclusive could further strengthen the ICN too. It might make ICN work products relevant for an even wider audience;[214] and further engaging a wider group of NCAs might also help persuade them to value ICN work products more.[215] Widening true participation might also help to see off a risk to the future of the ICN itself. As Lewis rightly notes, many organizations have found their authority weakened as they seemed to just be about EU and US power (such as the WTO, G7, IMF, World Bank). 'The ICN must treat this responsibility with the seriousness and the courage that it demands.'[216] More deference to the interests of a wider group of NCAs is likely particularly important if the ICN does have power.[217]

4.3.3 Output legitimacy: efficiency and the ICN

Here we discuss the second key type of 'output legitimacy', efficiency. As with effectiveness, one needs to consider two levels: the efficiency of the ICN itself, and how efficient 'states'' use of ICN work products is. For the reasons highlighted in the effectiveness discussion (such as the lack of a clear meta goal for the ICN and a lack of internal transparency), it is impossible to make a full efficiency assessment of the ICN. So, we have decided to highlight several issues that states might want to consider when assessing the ICN themselves. We also suggest some ways to improve efficiency.

The Introduction to this book highlighted many 'efficiency' issues. Efficiency has several dimensions; so, optimally efficient structures are unlikely to be unique, but a result of trade-offs.[218] By way of illustrative example, here we discuss four issues from an efficiency perspective. They are: the efficiency of the ICN as a body for sharing information; possible overlaps between the ICN, the OECD, and

[213] More engagement from younger agencies can help ensure that the ICN addresses the needs of all its members, solicits open and candid discussion at seminars, and promotes convergence. Given that the ICN work is consensus-based, contributions by a larger number of diversified members will only continue to strengthen the network' ICN (n 54) 22.

[214] See ICN (n 163) 24.

[215] Although newer NCAs do not normally block the adoption of ICN work products they often ignore them in their own work and they often fail to lobby their states to make relevant legislative changes (Chapter 3).

[216] Lewis (n 45) 214.

[217] Fox (n 45) 128 and 131–32.

[218] Liesbet Hooghe and Gary Marks, 'Does Efficiency Shape the Territorial Structure of Government?' (2009) 12 Annual Review of Political Science 225, pp 226–27.

UNCTAD; who should be setting competition policy; and implementing ICN work products. As we point out below, all of these efficiency discussions also have trade-offs with effectiveness and legitimacy. This is crucial to assess what is the 'best' organizational structure and actor to be making (even soft) policy in this area highly complex and political. Different states are likely to come to different assessments about what is most appropriate for them. This assessment will likely impact upon their willingness to use ICN work products in their jurisdiction without a prior check.

4.3.3.1 Efficiency within the ICN

We start by thinking about the efficiency of the ICN as a body for sharing information. Our effectiveness discussion highlighted the potential importance of this role (although we noted that the ICN does not emphasize it). We also noted how effective the ICN is at facilitating information sharing, and how it is less effective at integrating insights into recursive improvements.[219] As noted above, different states are likely to have different views on how much this all matters.

The benefits of information networks are hard to assess. They facilitate the transfer of information between network members. Information networks have network effects, which can increase efficiencies in relation to information dissemination.[220] Many believe that more information is automatically better, but too much information can also create problems. NCAs (and businesses) can easily be overwhelmed by the sea of data out there, not all of which is relevant or accurate. Moreover, giving meaning to data is hard and can be controversial. So, knowing the origin of information can be important when assessing its quality and relevance.[221] This can be particularly valuable in competition policy and enforcement, where a lot of relevant information is not public (such as ideas that NCAs considered but did not use because they did not work).

Networks in general, and the ICN in particular, are highly efficient conduits for information sharing. They provide regular, repeated, and structured opportunities (both online and in person) for relevant actors to share information about how (and why) they do (or do not do) things. These exchanges are open to most NCAs around the world, as well as many other relevant actors in the competition community. What is more, by narrowing the kinds of actors present in the network (away from wider state actors, for example) the ICN helps to facilitate conversations, by ensuring that all those present share a narrow 'economic perspective' (language).

[219] See the discussion around n 176.

[220] Slaughter (n 53) 176–77; Kal Raustiala, 'The Architecture of International Co-operation: Transgovernmental Networks and the Future of International Law' (2002) 43 Virginia Journal of International Law 1.

[221] Keohane and Nye call this 'the paradox of plenty. A plenitude of information leads to a poverty of attention' Robert Keohane and Joseph Nye, 'Power and Interdependence in the Information Age' (1998) 77 Foreign Affairs 81, 89.

The ICN supports these exchanges through its annual (in person) meeting as well as many different online/telephone discussions in the various working groups about a whole range of specific issues. In addition, these meetings provide regular prompted opportunities for actors to discuss their own specific competition issues. They also facilitate personal relationships between actors which can lead to information sharing (either general policy work or in specific enforcement contexts) outside of ICN meetings. It should be noted that for those not speaking this language, and/or those interested in the wider impact of competition policy, the ICN is not an efficient body as it largely bypasses them.

The costs of the ICN do not fall equally on rich and poor. Many of the costs of setting up and supporting the ICN itself have been borne by the richer NCAs.[222] That said, the ICN is a relatively efficient body, it does not have a permanent secretariat and most of its meetings are conducted online (although the annual meeting of all NCAs is done in person). Second, there are the costs of participating in ICN activities, such as the Steering Group, or on the various Working Groups. This can involve a lot of resources even for 'rich' NCAs. For example, the US FTC currently has the equivalent of several permanent employees dealing with ICN-related matters.[223] Once again, we have seen that richer NCAs tend to be the ones taking up these Steering Group roles and leading Working Groups. This demands more resources, but it leads to more influence, as Chapter 1 explained (which, in turn, raises effectiveness and legitimacy issues). Efficiency questions also arise where newer NCAs participate in a forum whose focus, most know-how and work products focus around the needs and practices of advanced NCAs. These might be useless for, impossible to implement by, or even harmful to newer NCAs, especially those from developing countries with very different contexts.

Tavares adds that there are lots of international competition fora (ICN, OECD, and UNCTAD, for example) and it costs NCAs a lot in order to achieve effective international representation,[224] even for those not on the ICN Steering Group or leading a Working Group. This results in a complex trade-off for NCAs' time that so far has not been particularly clearly articulated by NCAs, at least in public. It is another illustration of why each state may want to consider the costs and benefits of the ICN to it (and may evaluate them differently).

This brings us to our second illustrative example in relation to efficiency, possible overlaps between the ICN, OECD, and UNCTAD. Once again, the efficiency issues also interact with effectiveness and legitimacy assessments in complex ways. Some

[222] Many smaller NCAs, such as the Swedish NCA, note this with gratitude, Sjöblom and Widegren (n 156).

[223] <www.ftc.gov/policy/international/international-competition> accessed 8 October 2021. These sorts of costs are hard to establish from the outside. By way of contrast, and admittedly writing over ten years ago, Lewis has said 'To the best of my knowledge, there is not a single person—even in the best resourced agencies with large international departments—who is engaged in a full time capacity on ICN work' Lewis (n 45) 205.

[224] Tavares (157) 335–36 and 342.

believe that there are overlaps between the ICN, the OECD, and UNCTAD.[225] The ICN certainly seems to foresee a risk of overlaps;[226] and we agree with this (although it is contested by some).[227] This generates efficiency issues, often with only marginal gains in effectiveness. There are also legitimacy losses (given that the ICN's input legitimacy is less than the OECD and UNCTAD). These effects in individual cases are compounded due to the lack of a clearly articulated strategy for precisely when the ICN can be most efficiently and effectively deployed. If the ICN comes to the same conclusions as the OECD or UNCTAD, one wonders whether this is efficient and effective.[228] If it comes to different conclusions, one wonders whether this work is legitimate.[229] The only way out seems to be if the ICN starts something additional, new, and fundamentally valuable for the states (and not just the NCAs) involved. In which case, it is important to demonstrate that this work could not be more efficiently, effectively, and legitimately performed by the OECD or UNCTAD.

One example is 'impact assessment' (providing 'input to policymakers by evaluating the competition impact of a given policy measure and making recommendations to help mitigate negative effects').[230] The OECD has done a lot of work here, its *Competition Assessment Toolkit* runs to three volumes: principles of competition assessment (including the benefits of competition); technical guidance on key issues to consider; and specific step-by-step issues.[231] The OECD and

[225] For example, Hollman and Kovacic (n 152) 60 and 62–63.

[226] See, for example, ICN Agency Effectiveness Working Group, *Report on Agency Effectiveness through Organisational Design* (2019) 7–8 <https://www.internationalcompetitionnetwork.org/wp-content/uploads/2019/05/AEWG-Organisational-design-2019-report.pdf> accessed 8 October 2021; the ICN said 'In drafting the recommended practices, the Advocacy Working Group replied [presumably this should have been relied] on the OECD's extensive work on competition assessment, including the OECD Competition Assessment Toolkit' <www.internationalcompetitionnetwork.org/working-groups/advocacy/comp-assessment/> accessed 8 October 2021.

[227] Fox, for example, writes that, while many thought that overlaps would occur, this has not materialized:

> The ICN is doing work that neither the OECD, nor the UNCTAD, nor the WTO could do or could do as well, given the nature, the constituency, and the orientation of each of these bodies. The ICN's unique networking approach, which harnesses immense energy of private stakeholders, is a distinguishing feature. Also, there is a complementarity among the organisations. The ICN's active and dynamic work has acted as a competitive spur to enliven the competition policy work of the OECD.
>
> Fox (n 45) 125

[228] See the discussion around n 201, for example.

[229] As noted above, see the discussion in section 4.3.1.1.2., the ICN has a narrow focus which has not been legitimated through the political fora of many states (although this works in the interests of some states, see Chapter 1). So, one questions whether ICN work products are focused on the right aims. This is compounded by the narrow subset of stakeholders (and their interests) that typically influence ICN work (here we mean NCAs, but also the kinds of NGAs active there)—see Chapters 1 and 3.

[230] ICN Advocacy Working Group, *ICN Advocacy Handbook: Approaches to Identify Policies for Competition Assessment* (2019) 1 <https://www.internationalcompetitionnetwork.org/wp-content/uploads/2020/08/AWG-Handbook-Approaches-to-Identify-Policies-for-Competition-Assessment.pdf> accessed 8 October 2021.

[231] The OECD toolkit was first introduced in 2007, the last substantial revision was in 2019, <www.oecd.org/competition/assessment-toolkit.htm> accessed 8 October 2021. The OECD's work aims at

UNCTAD have also conducted many country studies on this (the latter particularly focuses on developing countries).[232] Despite this, the ICN has introduced three 'impact assessment' work products. These largely overlap with the OECD toolkit, but are less structured, generally less comprehensive and, one imagines, less useful. The ICN's *Recommended Practices on Competition Assessment*,[233] has 13 recommended practices. Some are uncontroversial.[234] Others are potentially extremely controversial.[235] Many issues overlap with the OECD's toolkit, which deals with them in a more nuanced way. The ICN's *Framework of Competition Assessment Regimes*[236] provides an overview of different competition assessment regimes and processes. It has six tables which compare competition assessments in different regimes and NCAs' remit to undertake impact assessment work. It also provides one-page summaries of competition assessment regimes in 25 jurisdictions. Once again, one wonders why. The tables cover similar ground (and examples) to that set out in the OECD's toolkit.[237] The ICN case studies overlap to some extent with more comprehensive and insightful OECD and UNCTAD case studies (without cross-referencing, which could have been useful).[238] Over half of the third ICN document simply summarizes and reproduces bits of the OECD toolkit. It then suggests 'innovative approaches to ex officio identification of candidates for competition assessment' for NCAs (rather than states).[239] Other than screening (the OECD's focus), it suggests six approaches, such as public hearings and better media engagement.

The ICN explicitly acknowledges[240] that it has not added much to the OECD's outputs, suggesting a possible efficiency loss. Sometimes the ICN has minor useful

helping 'governments to eliminate barriers to competition by providing a method for identifying unnecessary restraints on market activities and developing alternative, less restrictive measures that still achieve government policy objectives'.

232 Available at <https://unctad.org/topic/competition-and-consumer-protection/voluntary-peer-review-of-competition-law-and-policy> and <www.oecd.org/competition/assessment-toolkit.htm>, both accessed 8 October 2021.

233 ICN Advocacy Working Group, *Recommended Practices on Competition Assessment* (2014) a mere 11 pages, <https://www.internationalcompetitionnetwork.org/portfolio/recommended-practices-on-competition-assessment/> accessed 8 October 2021.

234 For example, recommended practice I says that the competition assessment 'should include the identification of a proposed or existing policy that may unduly restrict competition and an evaluation of its likely impact on competition' and the need for transparent processes.

235 For example, recommended practices II and VI suggest NCAs 'lobby for' more competition, yet there is no discussion about how independence of an NCA might impact on what appropriate limits might be relevant in this advocacy function.

236 ICN Advocacy Working Group, *Framework of Competition Assessment Regimes* (2015).

237 See link to the OECD Toolkit in n 231, particularly the Principles volume, chapter 3.

238 Unlike the OECD, for example, <www.oecd.org/daf/competition/reducingregulatoryrestrictionsoncompetition/competitionassessmentdocumentsandlinks.htm> accessed 8 October 2021.

239 ICN Advocacy Working Group (n 230) a mere 14 pages long. The ICN also organized events on this and related topics, such as a December 2018 AWG (Advocacy Working Group) teleseminar. Impact assessment was also one of the issues explored at the AWG Workshop in Kiev and the topic of one of the break-outs at the 2019 ICN Annual Conference.

240 See the ICN statement in n 226.

additions, such as the *Framework of Competition Assessment Regimes*' six tables' more comprehensive list of relevant jurisdictions (aiding contacts between NCAs). Even here, one wonders whether such work could have been more efficiently and effectively included in the OECD discussions and report.[241] It seems likely that the OECD's state focus makes it the more legitimate and effective venue for discussing things like impact assessments, which may involve NCAs, but also implicate many other state actors. Even if it is useful to 'translate' the OECD's work into practice and discuss it in NCAs, it is hard to see why the OECD's Competition Forum could not have been a more efficient and effective place for this. The ICN's work also completely ignores UNCTAD's extensive work on competition assessments. It is surprising that the ICN should ignore this expertise in helping developing countries, since the ICN claims to want to help developing countries too. In addition to the efficiency and effectiveness concerns, ICN work raises significant legitimacy issues which may concern states, as we have already seen in this chapter. ICN outputs in this area clearly illustrate this point (as well as the ICN's failure to highlight such issues). For example, there are major legitimacy implications when (often independent) NCAs unilaterally deciding to adopt a competition advocacy role in their interactions with others (which the ICN *Recommended Practices* advocate).

Unfortunately, it seems unlikely that the ICN, OECD, and UNCTAD by themselves will resolve these turf battles. For some this might be an existential fight. We might not even want this kind of 'market sharing'. Nevertheless, poor NCAs find these costs hard to bare, such that they may not be able to effectively participate in all three organizations. Many states might consider it worth reflecting upon the overlaps between these 'institutions' in terms of their legitimacy, effectiveness, and efficiency.

On top of this, participation in the ICN generates substantial opportunity costs. Reasonably senior, knowledgeable staff often generate the highest respect in the ICN, yet these are precisely the sorts of people that would often produce the biggest impact doing case work back home. The size and importance of these costs likely varies for different jurisdictions, depending on things like the number of (full time equivalent) staff involved in ICN work and the amount of traveling involved, and so forth. These opportunity costs also need to be weighed against the many benefits. Many of these costs (such as leadership roles) are what gives the EU and US influence within the ICN (and they open new opportunities for training for poorer NCAs), see below. Nevertheless, large costs can be incurred. One would expect clearly articulated assessments by an NCA about how much participating in the ICN would cost, compared to the benefits that it expects, that it could not otherwise achieve (remember that ICN work products are public). Furthermore, given that the OECD and UNCTAD already dealt with competition policy at the time of

[241] It is noteworthy that Hilary Jennings, an independent competition consultant, is thanked for her contribution to the drafting of the ICN *Framework*. Hilary used to work for the OECD.

the ICN's creation, one would expect clearly articulated explanations about why they are insufficient (and how the ICN will fill these gaps) as well as why merely reforming these institutions to achieve these goals would not work. We are not aware of any such estimates.

Some, belated efforts are being made to reduce the inefficiencies here. For example, the ICN created the role of Horizontal Coordinator to help enhance coordination across the ICN's working groups (for example in relation to the scheduling of calls). Similarly, some efforts are made to schedule ICN meetings (in both time and place) alongside OECD and UNCTAD meetings. Although more could be done, the ICN now has a direct liaison with the OECD to consider cooperation opportunities. For example, in 2012 the ICN and OECD did a joint enforcement cooperation survey.[242] The ICN also works with other international organizations, such as the World Bank and the African Competition Forum.[243]

As we saw in the effectiveness discussion, question marks arise when it comes to what should be done with information shared through the ICN. There is a tension between seeing the ICN as a vessel for informed divergence and as a more active conduit for aligning competition systems around the world. Different network structures may be needed in order to efficiently and effectively achieve these two aims. So, choices are needed. As we saw in our effectiveness discussion, a key problem is the lack of definition of a meta goal for the ICN, as well as a lack of explanation about how different goals should be traded off against each other. If we do not know precisely what the ICN is trying to achieve (informed divergence or harmonization), we cannot assess how efficiently it is achieving that end.

The first point to make here is that, if ICN work products are going to be used to push convergence, then it becomes even more important to participants to effectively push their understanding of the 'best' practice (Chapter 1 highlighted many efficiency benefits for states in keeping their existing rules in place, all other things being equal). Effective participation of this kind is even more costly than mere participation.[244] For NCAs that are unable to persuade others to follow their lead, these costs might be largely considered wasted (given that the ICN recommended practices are public documents and can be downloaded for free, even by non-participants). In the last ten years, the ICN has been trying harder to facilitate

[242]

> The ICN will also seek to coordinate better with other international networks concerned with competition policy. These various networks often address similar or complementary issues (albeit with different areas of focus) and have many common participants. By exploiting these complementarities, avoiding unnecessary duplication of work, and cross-promoting one another's work products, we can help our members to make the best use of the resources they contribute to the ICN.
>
> ICN (n 163) 11–13

[243] ICN (n 54) 8 and 21.

[244] Tavares (157) 335–36 and 342.

the efforts of those that want to be more actively involved. It does this by providing clearer information to NCAs and NGAs on how to get involved in the ICN, including criteria for becoming a Steering Group member or Working Group co-chair and introducing processes to rotate those positions. We saw that this has not made much concrete difference yet (in terms of who is getting senior roles). Ten years ago, the ICN also promised to improve transparency, by publishing Steering Group agendas, minutes, and notes from the Chair.[245] Few have been published on the ICN's website yet and, where they are, they are often opaque, offering few helpful insights. In the light of such problems, it seems unlikely that NCAs' efforts for better representation are efficient.

Second, efficiency trade-offs arise when considering who should be setting competition policy. It may be more efficient for competition experts to outline 'best practice' competition policy and enforcement techniques. Relying on policies produced by these experts may also lead to better competition decisions, and thus fewer appeals and disputes (and thus more efficient competition enforcement).[246] If one were to rely solely on 'competition experts' to devise competition policy, this might include all those working in the NCAs (and those working in the ICN's NGAs). Such a focus could be much more efficient than devising competition policy in parliaments, for example. This is because those in the competition community often have similar backgrounds and beliefs, making it easier for them to agree what the best norms are. In this vein, it may be even more efficient to restrict input to an even smaller, more homogeneous, group of experts, rather than involving the wider ICN community. A smaller more homogeneous group with significant technical expertise, such as the NCAs and NGAs from the EU and North America, may proceed even more efficiently.

At first sight, relying on a smaller, more homogeneous group, of experts does not seem possible in an organization like the ICN, where decisions are taken by consensus of all NCAs. However, the reality is somewhat different. There is a widespread perception within the ICN (both of those in NCAs and NGAs) that a narrow group (largely from rich, western) NCAs and multinationals do in fact wield more influence than most ICN members. This view is reflected in Chapter 3's survey. Relying on law, political science, and international relations theory, Chapter 1 explains how various factors, such as the homogenizing influence of the competition epistemic community and the inequality in knowledge and resources between NCAs, make it possible for this narrow group of richer NCAs to strongly 'encourage' other NCAs to support their initiatives even when they disagree. In part this might be because there is also a powerful perception that technical expertise

[245] ICN (n 153) 11–13.

[246] Although, Townley (n 39) chs 6 and 7, notes that networks of experts can be less tolerant of change and difference. This, in itself, can undermine the efficiency and effectiveness of the systems that they control (depending upon the instructions they have been given). Fundamental legitimacy concerns can also arise with technocracy (see discussion earlier in this chapter).

and resources are the most important determinants for making an NCA influential in the ICN (see Chapter 3).

On the other hand, if actors that have not been consulted are less likely to accept ICN recommended practices, any increased disputes may, in the long term, reduce systemic efficiency. This could apply to NCAs that felt ignored (especially if a smaller group of NCAs were thought to hold more influence and they did not listen to others). Similarly, even if all NCAs could be carried along on the promise of the best technical norms imaginable, this might not be sufficient for states. This is because states might not feel that all the goals that they consider important are reflected in ICN recommended practices. In such circumstances, states might not be willing to legislate to copy such norms, where this is required. They might even be prepared to intervene against their own NCAs if they are not acting sufficiently in line with state preferences where these differ from ICN ideals. In this way one can see how efficiency and effectiveness need to be properly aligned at some point. As discussed above, one can see, relatively easily, how these tensions also raise effectiveness and legitimacy issues too.

4.3.3.2 Efficiency in the implementation of ICN work products

This brings us to the role of the ICN in relation to the implementation of ICN work products. The ICN makes extraordinary efforts to disseminate its views on myriad competition issues in order to achieve convergence (to ICN members but also to those outside of the ICN, such as China, for example). If richer NCAs are using the ICN to push their policies more widely, then the ICN's ability to effectively push implementation may justify its costs to them. In response to members' feedback, the ICN has reworked its website, to make ICN work products more visible. Working Groups are making more efforts to push their own recommended practices in their meetings as well. NCAs are also encouraged to refer to ICN work products in their communications and work back home. Efforts such as these are relatively cheap (efficient) ways of raising the profile of ICN work products.

According to Slaughter, harmonization networks help to improve order in the world (through encouraging convergence).[247] They aid actors in their efforts to standardize their rules in areas where they think that this advances their common interests. Slaughter adds that:

> Recommended rules and practices compiled by a global body of securities regulators or environmental officials offer a focal point for convergence. Equally important, they offer a kind of safe harbor for officials the world over looking for guidance and besieged with consultants, who need not only to make a choice but to be able to defend it to their superiors.[248]

[247] Slaughter (n 53) 167–68.
[248] ibid 180.

Chapters 1 and 3 showed how this is also the perception of ICN actors and this seems to have, in fact, occurred within the ICN. This is despite the consensus requirement (and the ICN's efforts at better communication, see above). Competition rules have, to some extent, converged around ICN rules. This can reduce costs for firms operating in markets where competition rules become aligned, which increases the efficiency of trade.[249] It might also make the fight to implement such rules at home more effective and efficient. Agreed international rules of this kind can give weaker NCAs an international standard. This can then help weak states to build capacity and can lead to deeper cooperation that would not otherwise be possible.

Networks can be powerful tools for a small group of well-resourced actors to influence the agenda and outputs. As Raustiala points out, strong states use networks to export their rules to weak states.[250] As we saw in Chapters 1 and 2, stronger NCAs and NGAs have been extremely successful at co-opting the ICN to export what are predominantly their own rules to others, with 'expertise' acting as the clothing through which the 'political' wolf enters the policy framework of poorer NCAs and their states. By rephrasing the choices faced as technical (rather than political), those with enhanced influence over such technical interpretations have a relatively efficient tool for encouraging wider adoption of their preferred rules. 'Agreed international best practice' provides cover for these richer NCAs to efficiently and effectively expand their field of influence, spreading rules that favour them and their own firms abroad.[251]

When the proponents of ICN work products are regularly a small group of fairly homogeneous, rich, 'western' NCAs, one might wonder about how fair this is. There has been some acknowledgement that wider active participation in the ICN is desirable. In 2016 the ICN, reporting on its survey about desired goals in five years' time for the ICN said:

> ICN members list several concrete ideas on how to facilitate participation in the ICN. As financial constraints are the main barrier to participation, members

[249] That said, it may be hard to ensure identical interpretations of the rules, especially if enforcers seek to avoid the central policy. Furthermore, as competition law is normally applied in the legal and economic context then the size of economies of scale and reduced transaction costs should not be exaggerated. One will need to assess all relevant markets, which may make a big difference, especially where geographic markets are small.

[250] Raustiala (n 220).

[251] Also relevant here is the efficiency of the ICN's decision-making rules when it comes to the adoption of ICN work products. One might question whether 'consensus decision-making' is the most efficient kind of rule-making that it could have used. In principle, this demands that all NCAs must be convinced before the ICN adopts a recommended practice. In practice things do not work like this. First, the ICN does not demand that all accept such practices, just that no NCA objects to them. Second, many NCAs accept recommended practices that diverge from their own national rules. Third, when it comes to spreading norms worldwide, it may be more efficient to rephrase things as technical expertise, rather than to use political pressure. As Chapter 1 explains, this turns NCAs into Trojan horses in their own jurisdictions. Having said that, as we discuss in the effectiveness section, there is likely a link between how willing NCAs are to accept rules that they do not entirely agree with and the pressure the ICN applies to implement its recommended practices.

> suggest a number of ways to reduce costs. One suggestion is consideration of geography and timing when deciding the venues for the workshops, taking into account the diversity of members' location, as well as a better distribution of workshops throughout the year. Other suggestions are to limit the number of workshops per year, for example by holding workshops on a biannual basis; organising 'shared workshops' (i.e. combining two topics); concentrating several events in one location; and organising joint events with the OECD, other international organizations, or members such as the European Commission. Another suggestion would be to organise teleseminars and meetings in all regions for members to have the opportunity to connect with or attend nearby events. Another way to reduce the burden for agencies in terms of time and staff could be an increased involvement of NGAs in the drafting and commenting of work products. A couple of agencies point out that financial constraints are a problem not only for jurisdictions that are currently eligible for funding, but also for other agencies with limited budgets.[252]

As noted previously, the ICN response to these suggestions has not achieved much, in terms of widening the active participation in the ICN. From the perspective of the powerful NCAs, this seems to make sense.

Increasingly, this is followed up by harder pushes to implement ICN work products too. One particularly effective and efficient way that information networks push convergence is through technical assistance and training. There is still a high demand from newer NCAs for this kind of training today. The ICN has created many structures to efficiently and effectively encourage technical assistance and training, particularly in accordance with ICN work products. This includes twinning new NCAs with more experienced ones, setting up the 'ICN university', with lectures on various kinds of competition rules and their interpretation. The ICN also encourages its Working Groups to offer workshops to discuss implementation of ICN work products.

The relationship between information networks and implementation is complex, though. Better information may encourage convergence, but better information might also provide reasons to continue to diverge.[253] However, the efforts that the ICN makes to push implementation seem to have efficiently and effectively pushed the equilibrium towards convergence rather than informed divergence. Although senior ICN figures have often said that informed divergence can be acceptable, there are relatively few institutional efforts to promote this view, or to publish this agenda. For example, one approach with the ICN recommended practices would have been to use a format where policy choices were highlighted

[252] ICN (n 54) 22.
[253] Slaughter (n 53) 171–83.

and examples given of regimes going in different directions.[254] Instead, most ICN work products just refer to one 'best' answer, rather than signalling reasonable options.[255] This makes the ICN's efficiency as a forum for circulating 'valid' alternative options and ideas questionable.

As the focus turns to the state level, of interest to us is whether the benefits of ICN membership outweighs the costs. This is particularly relevant as non-members can freeride on ICN recommended practices. Even if the socializing benefits and (potential) to influence ICN work products occurs, are these efficiently serving the interest of the citizens of the NCA's country, or just the interests of the NCA itself (Chapter 1 hinted that it could well be the latter)? This is likely to be an important assessment for each state to make when examining its NCA's ICN-related costs. It is also tied in with a state's assessment of the value of ICN work products in that state. If, for example, ICN work products do not pursue the same goals as are desirable in that state, or they are not framed within the realm of what is technically or empirically possible in that state (especially if its NCAs on certain points have not been engaged with), then it will be harder to justify the costs of ICN membership.

Chapter 1 noted that there are also costs involved for less developed NCAs, aside from the costs necessary to participate in ICN conferences and meetings. These come in two major forms: the costs of adaptation and possible damage to their self-esteem, if they feel patronized or feel that they need to ingratiate themselves to get assistance (see Section 4.3.2 above). When deciding whether to implement an ICN recommended practice an NCA will be confronted with several costs and benefits. The NCA might look at the new rule on its merits. Perhaps it generates more consumer surplus, or it does this at a cheaper price of operation than other rules (perhaps it is easier to enforce). It might bring all such rules into line around the world, reducing firms' compliance costs. Such benefits should be balanced against the costs of change.[256] Costs include firms in their jurisdictions having to get legal advice (and possibly also change production and distribution

[254] This is the technique adopted in UNCTAD, *Model Law on Competition—Draft Commentaries to Possible Elements for Articles of a Model Law or Laws* (2020), for example. Available at <https://unctad.org/system/files/official-document/tdrbpconf5d7.en.pdf> accessed 8 October 2021.

[255] Rare exceptions to this general rule include: on substance—ICN Merger Working Group, *Project on Merger Guidelines* (2004) previously available at http://www.internationalcompetitionnetwork.org/uploads/library/doc488.pdf (broken ICN link, see discussion in Introduction, n 16), on some techniques, for example (at 13), for supply-side substitution and market definition; ICN—Unilateral Conduct Working Group, *Report on the Objectives of Unilateral Conduct Laws, Assessment of Dominance/ Substantial Market Power, and State-Crated Monopolies* (2007) (where there was a major argument) <https://www.internationalcompetitionnetwork.org/wp-content/uploads/2018/07/UCWG_SR_Objectives.pdf> accessed 8 October 2021; on investigatory techniques and procedural issues—ICN Merger Working Group, *ICN Investigative Techniques Handbook for Merger Review* (2005) ch 1, <https://www.internationalcompetitionnetwork.org/wp-content/uploads/2018/05/MWG_HBInvestigativeTechniques.pdf> accessed 8 October 2021.

[256] For insights into costs of change, see ICN Merger Working Group (n 45) 17.

processes).[257] States may also have the economic costs of retraining regulators and constructing new regulatory frameworks. There are also the political costs of getting changes through the legislative system in their own country.[258] Finally, there may also be costs of dealing with those that lose out under the changes.[259] As the NCA (especially highly independent ones) is not directly paying the price of many of these costs, it is the state (and firms and consumers), then this might reduce these 'costs' from its perspective. Costs of adaption exist for all NCAs faced with a recommended practice that deviates from its own local practices. That said, they may be relatively low for new NCAs, as their practices might not be so entrenched yet.

4.4 Conclusions

In this chapter, we have illustrated which standards of legitimacy, effectiveness, and efficiency we should expect from an international forum like the ICN, and we have assessed what the ICN has done in this respect and what is still lacking. In this section, we present some conclusive remarks, going back to the five criteria that we have identified in Section 4.2.1.

As regards the *comparative benefit* criterion, which states that an international organization is legitimate if it improves the status quo, our discussion has cast doubts on the actual benefits of the ICN. We have shown that there are considerable overlaps with organizations like the OECD and the UNCTAD. Chapter 1, Section 1.2.1.1 argued that the few points raised to justify establishing the ICN in 2001, despite the existence of these other bodies, are largely unconvincing. This is, of course, from the perspective of states (and their citizens); we saw benefits for NCAs, NGAs, and their employees, especially those influential leaders of the organization. Otherwise, it is often unclear what the added value of the ICN is. The ICN itself does not appear to be particularly interested in making this argument. This is understandable from the point of view of the organization: if its members believe that it would be difficult to justify the ICN, based on the comparative benefit criterion, they will likely avoid this point altogether. Furthermore, since NCAs are not obliged to participate, some may regard it as self-evident that, if

[257] Beth Simmons, 'The International Politics of Harmonization: The Case of Capital Market Regulation' (2001) 55(3) International Organization 589, 590. NCAs do not only consider the effects on themselves. They also consider the effect on their firms. Wilks talks of a surrendering of many areas of government through contracting out or privatization and then subjecting firms to regulation by business-friendly regulatory agencies, Wilks (n 23) 105.

[258] This means the costs of agreeing to a 'bad bargain' (or not preventing one) might be small and perhaps outweighed by other benefits, such enhanced credibility as being seen to agree with the majority of actors in this area. In any event, we will see examples of competition authorities agreeing to things that do not seem to be in their own self-interest, or that of their consumers or economies.

[259] Daniel Drezner, 'Globalisation, Harmonisation, and Competition: The Different Pathways to Policy Convergence' (2005) 12 Journal of European Public Policy 841, 845.

they participate, it is because they see something valuable in what the ICN does. Even NCAs that might participate just because they find that it is important to be there—for reasons of reputation, status, networking—ultimately perceive that they gain something from participation. There seems to be enough evidence to claim that NCAs, which created the ICN, mostly benefited from it (or think that they do). It is less obvious if the citizens those NCAs act on behalf of also benefit from the ICN. The evidence that the ICN has improved the life of ordinary citizens within ICN members' jurisdictions is hard to collect. Nevertheless, it is for them that the *comparative benefit* principle should be primarily assessed. If the ICN turned out to be a project that only enhances the power and the reputation of NCAs (even of all of them) and NGAs, it could hardly be seen as legitimate.

The second criterion, that of *institutional integrity*, is not adhered to by the ICN satisfactorily. Given how informal its organization and procedures are, it is difficult to make sure that all voices are heard when it comes to making decisions. We cannot but restate what we have said above (and in Chapters 1 and 3) about the disproportionate influence that some NCAs and NGAs have over the ICN work product. It is well documented that informality in decision-making advantages the most powerful actors.[260] In this respect, there is a lot to gain from making ICN procedures more standardized and transparent. Even if the introduction of a proper voting system were not accepted, the network could at least work on providing more information about the issues that are debated and the disagreements that arise among participants (as well as making it clearer which individuals and organizations have input into each ICN initiative, what they have input and when)—we know from Chapter 3 that disagreements occur regularly. More clarity would be welcome also as regards the request to implement work products (about what is asked, how implementation is assessed, and what is done in case of non-compliance). Chapter 2 shows that this is often confusing.

The (lack of) *involvement of legislatures* within the ICN is also an issue that weakens the legitimacy of the ICN, as we have documented in Section 4.3.1. It is not clear if NCAs participating in the ICN have received a clear mandate to do so from their legislatures. In many cases, this has not happened. In some cases, we can deduce that some political input has been provided informally (eg for the USA); in other cases (eg Portugal), the authority has been granted in its statute a general power to participate in international cooperation fora, including the ICN. Other NCAs, such as the EU's DG COMP, seem to have breached their basic 'national' constitutional principles when joining and engaging with the ICN. In many other instances, it is hard to trace any political input. This seems to fundamentally undermine the legitimacy of the involvement of many NCAs. What is more, even where there has been an *initial* political input, there is very little political follow-up.

[260] See eg J Tallberg, 'Bargaining Power in the European Council' (2008) 46 JCMS: Journal of Common Market Studies 685.

Parliaments see what NCAs do in the ICN as something *technical*, and they do not debate it. This could be due to a lack of interest (the legislature thinks it is irrelevant and therefore it does not spend time scrutinizing it), but our own opinion is that autonomous implementation (by NCAs) of ICN recommended practices is not politically irrelevant or neutral. Even where legislative change is needed and forthcoming in a state, we often see limited scrutiny of ICN proposals. Chapter 1 argued that NCAs have an interest in marking some issues as technical, as this helps to depoliticize them. This can help the NCA to avoid political interference. However, such 'value neutral' claims should never be taken at face value. Obviously, any legislature is free to decide whether it wants to scrutinize its NCA more closely or not. Given our analysis, we suggest that this might often be worthwhile. Furthermore, as will have been apparent in Chapter 2, there is often a lack of involvement of legislatures when deciding to implement ICN work products in national jurisdictions. The lack of scrutiny at this level further undermines the legitimacy of the use of ICN work products in national policy or enforcement decisions. We highlighted another criterion in Section 4.2, that of *minimum moral acceptability* (not committing serious injustices). This principally relates to ensuring that the order does not commit human rights abuses. As such assessments are often national, this also emphasizes the importance of involving legislatures to check the content of ICN work products is compatible with their assessment of this criterion.

Finally, there is the *transparency* criterion, which regards both how decisions are made and who participates (especially with regard to private actors). As can be seen from Section 4.3, it is always difficult to trace back the timing and the rationale of ICN decisions. There may certainly be a reason why a certain issue is dealt with before another, or why something ends up being recommended instead of alternative options. But the current set up of the ICN does not allow external observers to collect this information, simply because this information is not made available. We understand that this way of proceeding can allow frank exchanges of views without fear of publicity, but it can also allow subtle mechanisms of influence to take place. In several instances, we were left speculating about the real reasons behind certain choices. This way of proceeding and communicating hides all disagreements and all issues relating to *divergence* between NCAs, giving an overall impression of consensus and unanimity. This is particularly worrying given the widespread lack of legitimate political influence. Reaching (and communicating) unanimity is certainly a respectable strategy, but it might weaken the ICN's ability to 'mature'. The involvement of NGAs also needs to be considered more carefully. Private actors and stakeholders can bring different views to the table, and this is something to encourage. But this must come with transparency about who participates. Only transparency can allow external observers to assess how *diverse* and *representative* are the views that participants listen to. Our analysis in Chapter 3 has indicated that NGAs come disproportionally from North America and Europe, and equally disproportionally from law firms. This information should definitely be made public. Also, we would welcome increased transparency in documenting the NGAs' contribution to the ICN. Chapter 1 argued that the reasons that NGAs give for their ICN participation (help the common good) are unlikely to predominate over more self-serving motivations. Increased transparency would also allow observers to see which motivations, in fact, dominate.

Despite the critiques that we have illustrated, it would be unfair not to acknowledge the potential merits of the ICN. The logic guiding its creation was that economic globalization is likely to produce many more competition investigations involving more than one jurisdiction. In this scenario, NCAs need to be able to cooperate with each other to reduce suboptimal enforcement where an NCA only sees part of the puzzle and inconsistent outcomes. The ICN was meant to facilitate cooperation and convergence where appropriate. This can potentially bring benefits for NCAs, governments, businesses, and consumers.[261]

Networks like the ICN, because of their flexibility, are a good way of linking state bodies in ways that supplement the normal national democratic institutions.[262] They might give states the power to influence (even if they cannot control) what happens beyond their boundaries, which could also give their actions more efficiency and effectiveness (for example, through agreements to take into account externalities and economies of scale, as well as other issues such as coordinating experiments).

We can also say that the ICN can be good for NCAs as it encourages dissemination of experience and best practices,[263] and it can also be good for governments, as it may facilitate the building of markets that benefit businesses and consumers. ICN products also help governments implementing new laws (or changing them) as they provide examples of pro-competitive rules.[264]

We have also seen that an argument that is often used to mitigate concerns about the lack of democratic accountability and transparency of bodies like the ICN is that it does not have binding powers. As Fox puts it, '[t]he ICN was designed *not* to be antitrust governance'.[265] National governments and parliaments are free to do whatever they want. If an NCA, implementing some ICN recommendation, adopted acts that the parliament deems to be against the public interest, nothing prevents it from amending national legislation to avoid it. It must also be mentioned that the consensus rule (nothing is agreed unless everyone agrees) mitigates concern about the dominance of some actors (public or private) in the decision-making process.

One question to ask is whether the ICN aims at promoting innovation, pushing its member to come up with the best competition rules, or whether it merely tries

[261] ICN (n 6) 2.
[262] eg Rhodes (n 13) 9.
[263] ICN (n 6) 3, see also 7.
[264] ibid 3, see also 7–8.
[265] Fox (n 45) 123.

to spread one set of rules to achieve overall consistency. These two distinct goals refer to two types of learning identified in the literature: *exploitation* (refining and extending existing paradigms) and *exploration* (experimenting with new alternatives).[266] Both are vital in the long-term, and they are often traded off against each other. Different network structures incentivize different types of learning: closed, dense networks facilitate exploitation, less densely connected networks facilitate exploration.

Among these two ideal types, the ICN is certainly closer to the first. It is a network that meets regularly and often, quite homogeneous and protected from outside influences, and whose members share similar views of the world and of what they are trying to achieve. The ICN's constitutional DNA is based on bringing many competition experts together to generate improvements in policy. This, however, comes at a cost. Where complex solutions are necessary, networks like the ICN may fail to achieve learning in the long term, as they often quickly coalesce around one solution.[267] The risk is that closed networks become cliques, stifling change, and difference in the end. Such networks can start off efficient and effective, but this is unlikely to last once the initial set of information transfers happens. Furthermore, this strategy of promoting convergence may not help where constantly evolving firms respond differently in different states; nor where different states have different preferences for their competition rules. The multiple economic crises that have occurred in the last 12 years can only increase the (actual and pursued) divergence among states.

[266] In his seminal paper on the topic, March defines them as follows: 'The essence of exploitation is the refinement and extension of existing competencies, technologies, and paradigms. Its returns are positive, proximate and predictable. The essence of exploration is experimentation with new alternatives. Its returns are uncertain, distant and often negative' James March, 'Exploration and Exploitation in Organizational Learning' (1991) 2 Organization Science 71, 71, 85 and also 73. See also, in relation to competition networks, Townley (n 39) ch 7.

[267] Some define convergence in the ICN as something more nebulous 'the broad acceptance of standards concerning the substantive doctrine and analytical methods of competition law, the procedures for applying substantive commands, and methods for administering a competition agency' Hollman and Kovacic (n 152) 54. In part, this is because they see 'harmonization' as unattainable (given the different histories, economic conditions, and legal processes) and undesirable (given its impact on evolutionary experimentation) (ibid 54–55). In an interesting study, Lazer and Friedman model different network structures to examine the trade-off between exploitation and exploration. They found that highly interconnected networks led to rapid convergence on the best existing solution, but quickly drove out diversity, performing poorly at exploration. On the other hand, where nodes (for us this is NCAs) were connected less densely, this seemed to slow down their ability to exploit the learning of others in the short term, but it meant that they typically found better solutions in the end through exploration. It seemed to be more important how the nodes were organized in these experiments rather than how many nodes were working on a problem at any one time (ie how many NCAs there are). Furthermore, asking nodes to consult each other less frequently increased the amount of 'exploration' that they did (although this comes at the expense of the amount exploitation that they do) and thus raised their long-term results at the expense of their short-term results (this process was also aided by allowing more mistakes, encouraging diversity etc). Caveman networks, which group small clusters of NCAs into totally connected networks and then linked these mini-networks together through weak, irregular links, achieved more exploration in the end, but there is also quite a lot of exploitation.

In this respect, until the ICN has a clear focus, it will struggle to be clear about the kind of learning that should predominate. However, its current structure favours exploitation at the expense of exploration. This may be understandable given the quick benefits that exploitation can produce, but it is not a good long-term strategy (neither for NCAs nor for the ICN as a whole). Changes to network structure, actors' orientations, the autonomy of actors and network dynamics may all be needed to get a better balance. Also of fundamental importance, as Sections 4.3.2 and 4.3.3. of this chapter also highlight, is that until the ICN clearly articulates how its competing goals interact, then properly assessing its effectiveness and efficiency will not be possible.

Our analysis has highlighted that there is a question mark about whether the ICN is optimally designed, in terms of efficiency and effectiveness. Even if a focus on exploitation was deemed important in 2001, it may be that today increasing the amount of exploration is more valuable. This might produce a better balance of efficiency and effectiveness in the longer term, which could encourage NCAs to accept structural change.[268] This argument may also go in the direction of allowing regional 'ICN networks' to develop, as many NCAs have suggested.[269]

That being said, one must acknowledge that NCAs seem to appreciate the ICN, as its survival and growth of membership prove. This means that it serves some purposes that NCAs consider important. Damro, in this respect, argues that the choice of joining the ICN can be explained as a case of venue-shopping—NCAs choose it because they do not have to share their inputs with governments.[270] One might say that this characteristic (together with its international coverage, including both developed and developing countries) is what allows the ICN to remain popular among NCAs. This also means that the input legitimacy of the ICN is low, not only in the decision-making, but also in the implementation stage. In particular, the more an NCA is independent, the higher its autonomy in both stages will be.

At the same time, networks of independent technocrats may generate legitimacy problems because they make power away from elected officials and into the hands of enterprising bureaucrats, without the approval of their elected superiors. This may generate suboptimal outcomes if technocrats lose sight of potential trade-offs with other areas. This phenomenon is not restricted to competition

[268] David Lazer and Allan Friedman, 'The Network Structure of Exploration and Exploitation' (2007) 52 Administrative Science Quarterly 667. This study is applied to the European Competition Network in Townley (n 39) ch 7.

[269] See the discussion in Chapter 1, around n 182.

[270] Chad Damro, 'The New Trade Politics and EU Competition Policy: Shopping for Convergence and Co-operation' (2006) 13 Journal of European Public Policy 867. According to Damro, NCAs' choices are likely affected by five features: the international coverage of the body concerned, how binding its outputs are, the primary target of its activity (just developed countries, or developing ones too), fora where competition is the only consideration; and the role of the NCA within that body (is it constrained by other 'state' actors).

policy, obviously. It is a trend that we observe in many areas, including health and safety, networks of central bank governors, and economic regulation more generally.[271]

Networks give states the chance to exert their influence beyond their borders in potentially fruitful ways. But this has at least three downsides. First, members may seek to transfer costs to those outside of the network (eg environmental problems or issues of workers' rights might be left outside). Second, networks often exclude potentially relevant members, either in fact or in practice (for example, states, environmentalists—including environmental economists, and psychologists all have relevant things to input, see Chapter 1). Third, networks are often guided by informal structures. They are flexible, but they also lack accountability mechanisms. These problems may become even more pressing as network goals often arise over time.[272]

Morgan and Yeung observe that, '[w]ithout denying [that] the effectiveness in achieving regulatory goals is an important component of [...] legitimation, it is widely accepted that it is not the only dimension of legitimation'.[273] The authors also note that in a network like the ICN 'there are no clear existing structures such as courts, legislative committees, national auditors, ombudsmen, and so on, to which recourse can be made to render them accountable; they have no clear jurisdictional boundaries; and there is no easily identifiable set of potential democratic participants in their processes'.[274] Such bodies are also criticized on the grounds that 'they develop outside national constitutional settlements or at the transnational level outside the treaty system, they escape accountability through the mechanisms of consent of either domestic or international law. Moreover, they are criticized as non-transparent; as lacking, or only having very attenuated, consultation processes; as undemocratic; and as failing to have adequate, or any, systems of redress: those affected by their decisions are excluded from the decision-making process and have no way of calling them to account politically or legally'.[275] These problems are less acute for transgovernmental networks, such as the OECD or UNCTAD (networks in which governments are represented), because, since they 'are made from national officials, they are more closely linked to states and thus, in theory, bound by the same accountability mechanisms that control national governments. By giving states a way to solve transnational problems

[271] See, for example, Alisdair Roberts, *The Logic of Discipline* (OUP 2010), discussing central banks, fiscal rules, tax collectors, autonomous main ports, network regulators and long-term infrastructure contracts, for example; Christoph Ossege, *European Regulatory Agencies in EU Decision-Making* (Palgrave Macmillan 2016), discussing food safety, medicines, and chemical experts.

[272] Townley (n 39) 234–35.

[273] Bronwen and Yeung (n 10) 237.

[274] ibid 138.

[275] Julia Black, 'Constructing and Contesting Legitimacy and Accountability in Polycentric Regulatory Regimes' (2008) 2 Regulation & Governance 137, 141.

directly, governmental networks elide a potential legitimacy problem that bedevils many other areas of global governance.'[276]

Solutions to these legitimacy problems can come from mechanisms of accountability. In this sense, accountability must not be understood just as 'the duty to give account for one's actions to some other persons or body'.[277] Scott speaks of 'extended accountability' to both public and private actors on both a vertical (markets, grievance mechanisms or user consultations) and a horizontal plane (auditors, third party accreditation of standards or supervision by public interest groups), given the increasingly decentred nature of regulation. He also suggests that regulators should be accountable to one another, to minimize the risk of capture of a particular regulator.

When it comes to implementation, Morgan and Yeung warn against the risk that networks like the ICN might pressure countries to adhere to their guidelines without considering the bigger picture. Even if a recommendation has been agreed within a restricted group of (like-minded) technocrats, the actors that are subject to implementation might have reservations, and might not have a channel to voice their discontent.[278] In other words, unelected technocrats run the risk of ignoring citizens' social, economic, and political concerns. If this happens, then a supranational network might undermine national democratic legitimacy and thus citizens' national preferences.

One of the key reasons, originally raised by the USA, for starting an international competition network, was to achieve industrial policy aims. Through the various mechanisms that we have highlighted, we believe that the rich NCAs have the means and the motive to pursue their own aims. This may coincide with the needs and wishes of less well-resourced states. Equally, it might not. We have tried to show how it will be hard for less well-resourced states to fight back. They lack the control over the ICN agenda, and the ability to control Working Groups, where most policy is debated and recommended practices are generated. Moreover, they do not have the technical expertise, time, and resources to actively engage in the myriad debates taking place throughout the ICN. This means they may lack the ability to adequately protect their own interests, in the face of the policy goals of the richer countries.

We have seen that competition law is not merely a value-neutral, technical set of rules. For all their technical complexity, competition rules have major policy and redistributive impacts. And given that it is the NCAs, rather than their states, that are represented in the ICN, there is an additional problem. When it comes to dealing with the political consequences of the best practices that they generate,

[276] Anne-Marie Slaughter and Thomas Hale, 'Transgovernmental Networks and Multi-Level Governance' in Henrik Enderlein, Sonja Wälti and Michael Zürn (eds), *Handbook on Multi-Level Governance* (Edward Elgar 2010) 364; Fingleton (n 45) 192–93.

[277] Colin Scott, 'Accountability in the Regulatory State' (2000) 27 Journal of Law and Society 38, 38.

[278] Bronwen and Yeung (n 10).

the level of independence of some NCAs may insulate them from a wider group of stakeholders in their own states. Where the views of those working in the NCAs, which are increasingly socialized around the views of those in the richer NCAs (and NGAs) who monopolize the policy debates, diverge from the prevalent views in their own states, they still have a lot of freedom to act, since most of them are quite independent from their governments. The fact that competition laws are often drafted in very general terms facilitates this ability.

What can we conclude, then, about the ICN? From a legitimacy perspective, technocratic networks can be even more problematic when (as with the ICN) states were not involved in their creation. Remedies are possible, for example in the form of more transparency and participation, or by using legislative networks as a more effective counter-weight to regulatory networks and to oversee them.[279] We can say that the ICN lays on 'shaky ground' in terms of its *raison d'être* and legitimacy. It partially compensates for this by not imposing anything on its members, both in terms of decision-making within the ICN (formally based on consensus) and of implementation (NCAs/states implement if they want/can). However, if participation in the ICN (including in terms of its comparative advantage vis-à-vis other fora, like the OECD and UNCTAD) is not openly debated in countries and decision-making is de facto in the hands of the most powerful NCAs, we have a problem if firms or other actors start to use ICN decisions in national courts. As we saw in Chapter 2, of late the ICN has been working harder to push the implementation of its key work products and pressuring NCAs and states into compliance. Either implementation remains strictly voluntary and there is no pressure on countries to uniformity (but then what would the ICN be there for?), or states might find it preferable to introduce some checks—if not of democratic accountability, at least of transparency and voluntary accountability. In our view, it is also highly desirable for states to thoroughly review the value positions adopted by ICN work products before adopting them (or before allowing their NCAs to adopt them either).

We now make some suggestions on these issues in the concluding chapter.

[279] Slaughter and Hale (n 276) 364–65.

Annex 4.1

The constitutional inability for DG COMP (the EU's 'NCA') to unilaterally join and participate in the ICN

The legal framework for EU external action is highly complex.[280] Complexity is driven by, on the one hand, Member States seeking to preserve their control over EU external action; but, on the other hand, wanting to 'enhance the EU's external effectiveness and consistency'.[281] To achieve their aims, the Member States limited the EU's power to act in the international arena (a legal basis must authorize action in an area) and formalized procedures to follow when action is authorized. In outline, these procedures ensure effectiveness and efficiency by allowing the EU to negotiate as one in some areas (normally through the Commission), but they preserve the Member States' control over policy by giving the Council (made up of the Member States) the ultimate sign off on EU external action.[282]

To establish which procedure to use, one has to know the right legal basis for each area (some areas have different procedures).[283] Getting this choice wrong could invalidate the act concluding the international agreement, vitiating the EU consent to be bound by the agreement it had signed.[284]

When assessing the correct legal basis, one can start by checking whether the EU has an internal power to act in the relevant ways. If it does, then this internal power can often be 'mirrored' into an external power to agree such measures with other jurisdictions. When producing internal substantive and procedural competition rules the EU has often relied on EC, art 83 (now TFEU, art 103 plus TFEU, art 3(1)(b)), also combined with EC, art 308 (now TFEU, art 352) for mergers.[285] By way of contrast, when recently agreeing internal rules for the effective enforcement

[280] Consolidated versions of these treaties are available at <https://eur-lex.europa.eu/collection/eu-law/treaties/treaties-force.html> accessed 8 October 2021. Annex 4.1 provides further legal support for our claims, around n 56, that the incorrect procedures were followed (from an EU perspective) when DG COMP joined, and now continues to participate in, the ICN.

[281] De Baere (n 56) 711.

[282] The Lisbon Treaty was signed by the Member States of what became the European Union (EU) on 13 December 2007. The EC Treaty (and others) which applied back in 2001 to the European Community (Community) were replaced with two new treaties, the Treaty on European Union (TEU) and the Treaty on the Functioning of the EU (TFEU). We apply Community law to the decision to join the ICN (although we explain any EU law differences where relevant) and EU law to later 'agreements' by DG COMP to ICN recommended practices.

[283] Alexander Türk, *Judicial Review in EU Law* (Edward Elgar 2010) 106–67 and references there.

[284] Opinion 2/00, EU:C:2001:664, para 5.

[285] As a legal basis for the creation of legal rules, to the extent that this was possible, given EC, arts 81 and 82 (now TFEU, arts 101 and 102), art 83 EC (now TFEU, art 103) was sufficient unless mergers were also included, in which case EC art 308 (now TFEU, art 352) was also needed, see, for example, Council Regulation (EC) No 139/2004, On the control of concentrations between undertakings, OJ 2004 L24/1.

of the EU competition rules (including matters relating to the ECN), the EU relied on a combination of TFEU, arts 103 and 114 (EC, old arts 83 and 94).[286] Relying on these internal powers and their use in adopting provisions laying down common rules, the EU can likely conclude international agreements in the same areas.[287]

As noted above, once we know that the EU is competent to make external arrangements of this kind, then we have to determine the appropriate procedure for doing this. In 2001, EC, art 228 (now TFEU, art 218)[288] set out the following procedure:

> Where this Treaty provides for the conclusion of agreements between the Community and one or more States or an international organization, such agreements shall be negotiated by the Commission. Subject to the powers vested in the Commission in this field, such agreements shall be concluded by the Council, after consulting the European Parliament where required by this Treaty.

The EU has made many international agreements using this procedure in the competition area.[289] In fact, the EU often uses a procedure with even more political oversight for its international work. One example, is when it prepares its (non-binding) submissions to the OECD's Competition Committee.[290]

[286] In terms of the powers of the EU's competition network (this ECN is a rough equivalent of the ICN, although it also deals with enforcement), the legal bases are EC, art 83 (now TFEU, art 103) and EC, art 94 (now TFEU, art 114); see, for example, Parliament and Council, Directive 2019/1/EU to empower the competition authorities of the Member States to be more effective enforcers and to ensure the proper functioning of the internal market. Article 33(2) of that directive says, for example, that: 'The European Competition Network shall be able to develop and, where appropriate, publish best practices and recommendations on matters such as independence, resources, powers, fines and mutual assistance.'

[287] *Commission v Council ('ERTA')* (n 58) paras 13–14; *Cornelis Kramer and Others* (n 58) paras 17–18. Specifically, in the area of competition, see *France v Commission* (n 58) (by implication).

[288] The procedure set out in TFEU, art 218(2)–(8) largely follows that in EC, art 228. However, there are some important differences. For example, article 218(2) says the Council authorizes the opening of negotiations (as well as their conclusion).

[289] See, for example, Decision 95/145/EC (n 61); Decision 1999/445/EC of the Council and Commission, *Concerning the conclusion of the Agreement between the European Communities and the Government of Canada regarding the application of their competition laws*, OJ 1999 L175/49; Council Decision 2003/520/EC, *Concluding the Agreement between the European Community and the Government of Japan concerning cooperation on anti-competitive activities*, OJ 2003 L183/11; Council Decision 2009/586/EC, *Relating to the conclusion of the Agreement between the European Community and the Government of the Republic of Korea concerning cooperation on anti-competitive activities*, OJ 2009 L202/35.

[290] This is because, in some areas, rather than relying on an assessment of an internal power and then 'mirroring' this into an external one, the EU has explicitly been empowered to make international agreements. One such area is the CCP, see EC, art 133 (now TFEU, art 207). The CCP includes tariff and trade agreements, as well as other related matters, such as the commercial aspects of intellectual property and competition arrangements. In order to be classified as a CCP arrangement, a measure must unequivocally form part of the liberalization of trade between the EU and other jurisdictions (rather than the harmonization of the laws of the EU Member States or to trade between them—as the internal market has another legal basis and set of procedures). See, for example, Opinion 2/15, ECLI:EU:C:2017:376, paras 131–38 and 257–79.

Whether or not this is the case obviously depends on the specific arrangements in question. There is room for debate about whether or not these arrangements to establish the ICN (and then the ongoing

Having said that, in many areas (not just competition), EU DGs have been testing the boundaries of the possible in EU law (the European Commission has 33 DGs). It is increasingly common for DGs to seek to bypass the formal treaty procedures,[291] directly making 'non-binding' international arrangements themselves, often with no input from other institutions (sometimes the Commission as a whole does not even input). They do not often explain why they are doing this, but some speculate that it is to increase the effectiveness and efficiency of international arrangements.[292]

DG COMP (the Directorate General of the Commission which deals with competition) is no different. While we noted that many international competition agreements had followed the art 228 EC procedure (and EU competition submissions to the OECD even follow the 'enhanced' CCP procedure), DG COMP has also concluded many 'non-binding' arrangements in this area without following EC, art 228.[293] It also did this when joining the ICN. It continues to do this when 'agreeing' to ICN recommended practices at the ICN annual meeting.

participation there) fall within the CCP. We do not take a view on this here (although we note that this the basis upon which the EU prepares its submissions to the OECD's Competition Committee, for example, Damro (n 270) 876—see also, the consistency requirement, in TEU, art 21(3)).

If ICN arrangements fall within the CCP, then EC, art 228 (now TFEU, art 218) procedure set out above must be modified in line with EC, art 133(3) (now TFEU, art 207(3)):

> The Commission shall make recommendations to the Council, which shall authorise it to open the necessary negotiations. The Council and the Commission shall be responsible for ensuring that the agreements negotiated are compatible with internal Union policies and rules. The Commission shall conduct these negotiations in consultation with a special committee appointed by the Council to assist the Commission in this task and within the framework of such directives as the Council may issue to it. The Commission shall report regularly to the special committee and to the European Parliament on the progress of negotiations.

For further discussion, see Panos Koutrakos, 'The Decision-Making Process' in Tridimas and Schütze (n 72) 1161–63. We ignore the 'enhanced' CCP procedures in the rest of this chapter because, even if they are relevant, further discussion is not necessary for our underlying points that: the EU legal order has explicitly laid down the appropriate procedures to follow; and DG COMP has strayed even further from the right procedures.

[291] García Andrade (n 75) 115. Kuijper and others (n 82) 95, agree but say that there are some (minor) hints today that this is becoming a little less common.

[292] This:

> may respond to different reasons, such as the need to increase the efficiency of external action, to allow greater smoothness in negotiation and conclusion of the instrument, or to enhance the margin of discretion of the signatories in the fulfilment of commitments. In addition, non-binding agreements may be more suitable to the political sensitivity of the subject of the agreement or to its changing nature. In the case of the EU, it could further be argued that the signing of political instruments may forestall the complications inherent to the conclusion of mixed agreements.
>
> García Andrade (n 75) 116

See also discussion in Wessel (n 62) 4.

[293] Demedts (n 63) s 4.1.3(A), lists several examples of these, such as with Brazil, Chile, Russia, and China—see:<https://ec.europa.eu/competition/international/bilateral/index.html>

Many arrangements describe themselves as 'non-binding'. Nevertheless, Wessels observes that one might question the legal effect of such arrangements in the EU legal order. He continues:

> To what extent does a transformation from 'hard' agreements to 'soft' arrangements matter in that respect? And, to what extent does the Union have a choice to either opt for a formal international agreement or to choose an informal arrangement (thereby perhaps bypassing certain procedural rules and guarantees on for instance transparency and democracy)?[294]

The risk is that 'choosing informality' might undermine the legitimacy of the arrangement and may breach EC law. When asked to rule on the legality of such arrangements,[295] the ECJ[296] is effectively determining whether possible increases in effectiveness and efficiency justify reductions in 'input' legitimacy.

It is in this context that we first analyse the legality of DG COMP's joining of the ICN and then its 'agreement to' ICN recommended practices. DG COMP's agreement to join the ICN would likely count as an international agreement,[297] given the intention[298] that the ICN's procedures and institutional rules[299] would bind DG COMP (and other ICN members) when participating in ICN activities.[300]

In the area of competition, the Commission has argued that it did not have to follow the art 228 EC procedure even for binding international agreements. It said

[294] Wessel (n 62) 4.

[295] To be clear, when the ECJ comments on the 'legality of such arrangements' it does not directly analyse the legality of international arrangements themselves (it cannot as these are not EU acts). Instead, it analyses the legality of the act whereby the EU actor decided to enter into this arrangement (or was authorized to do so), *France v Commission* (n 58) paras 13–17.

[296] The ECJ stands for the Court of Justice, the most senior of the two Courts of Justice of the EU, TEU, art 19. The Courts of Justice of the EU ensure the interpretation and application of the EU treaties.

[297] *France v Commission* (n 58) para 27, where the ECJ held 'As the Court explained in Opinion 1/75 of 11 November 1975 ([1975] ECR 1355), Article 228 uses the expression "agreement" in a general sense to indicate any undertaking entered into by entities subject to international law which has binding force, whatever its formal designation'. A similar position persists under TFEU, art 218, *Parliament and Commission v Council (Venezuelan Fishing Rights)* (n 65) para 83.

[298] The ECJ has held that the 'intention of the parties' is the decisive feature in assessing whether an arrangement is binding, *France v Commission* (n 66) paras 40–46. Many now think that this is the rule: see, for example, Council of the European Union (legal service), *Procedure to be followed for the conclusion by the EU of Memoranda of Understanding, Joint Statements and other texts containing policy commitments, with third countries and international organisations* (2013) fn 2.

[299] 'So far as concerns the nature of the obligations set out in the Agreement [the Community/ US cooperation agreement for competition rules], it is sufficient to reiterate that they are, as stated earlier, instrumental and procedural obligations, that is to say obligations binding on the parties and therefore on the Community, and which undoubtedly make up an international agreement', Opinion of AG Tesauro in *France v Commission (EC/USA competition agreement)* (n 58) para 20 (although the issue was not explicitly discussed by the ECJ, it, too, held that this was an international agreement, which provides implicit support). AG Tesauro's Opinion was cited favourably by AG Alber on this point in his Opinion in *France v Commission* (n 66) para 56 (although, he opined that the arrangement there should *not* be treated as an agreement because of its lack of binding nature, paras 57 and 58 (the ECJ agreed)).

[300] NCA members of the ICN agree to be bound by these rules, see the text around n 43 and Chapter 1.

that the EC Treaty conferred on it special internal powers in this area which (by implication) empowered it to conclude international agreements. According to the Commission, the reference in EC, art 228 to 'Subject to the powers vested in the Commission' meant that, in areas such as these (which it thought should be interpreted widely), other procedures could be used (in competition the Commission claimed it could act unilaterally). The Commission added that it had concluded international agreements in the past.[301]

The ECJ disagreed with the Commission's argument.[302] In addition, the ECJ held that this art 228 EC exception ('Subject to the powers vested in the Commission') 'derogates from the rule empowering the Council to conclude international agreements'. The implication being that, as an exception, it should be interpreted narrowly (a classic rule of treaty interpretation in the Community which still persists today). Furthermore, even if such a practice had been allowed in the past, the ECJ held that 'a mere practice cannot override the provisions of the Treaty'. The ECJ did not accept the Commission's specific competition argument either. It held that:

> Even though the Commission has the power, internally, to take individual decisions applying the rules of competition, a field covered by the Agreement, that internal power is not such as to alter the allocation of powers between the Community institutions with regard to the conclusion of international agreements, which is determined by Article 228 of the Treaty.[303]

The ECJ underlines the importance of input legitimacy for external relations in the competition area. The Commission (not just DG COMP) had the power, internally, to take individual decisions applying the competition rules. However, that did not alter the allocation of powers between the Community institutions when concluding *international* agreements. Article 228 EC (possibly modified if this is held to fall within the CCP)[304] determines that power allocation through a specific procedure.

Assuming that joining the ICN is an international agreement, DG COMP was not competent in EU law to conclude it. Under EC, art 228 membership should have been negotiated by the Commission (not just DG COMP) and then concluded by the Council, after consulting the European Parliament. DG COMP did

[301] *France v Commission* (n 58), paras 21–22. We noted that it has made international agreements without following EC, art 228 (see the text around n 293).

[302] *France v Commission* (n 58) paras 32–43 (in part this was because of its interpretation of other language versions of the treaty).

[303] In his Opinion in this case AG Tesauro agreed, adding that the Commission's interpretation undermines EC, art 228. More specifically, in the competition area, AG Tesauro noted that the Commission did not have the power to make law, just to apply EC, arts 85–86; see EC, art 89 (now, respectively, TFEU, arts 101, 102, 105). Only the Council (EC, art 87) has legislative power. AG Tesauro adds more detail, paras 35–42.

[304] See the discussion in n 290.

none of this. As far as we can tell, it acted alone. Failure to follow the correct procedure means that the act where DG COMP decided to join the ICN (or was authorized to do this) is likely void. In any event, as we now argue, even if joining the ICN counts as an 'informal arrangement', the method followed by DG COMP is likely to have breached Community law in any event.

Informal arrangements, are less strictly regulated. There is a risk that using them circumvents certain EU actors' rights.[305] However, even if joining the ICN were not held to be a binding international agreement, then the 'decision' to allow it is likely still void, once again for failing to follow the correct procedure. The ECJ accepts the possibility of non-binding arrangements on the international plane.[306] However, competence allocation is still relevant. It still seems necessary to basically follow the formal procedure for adopting binding international agreements in the relevant area. Some deviation from the relevant formal procedure seems possible, although how much is not entirely clear.[307] The implication is that the EU institution in charge of policy in the relevant area must still set this for non-binding arrangements (this would be the Council for the purposes of such arrangements). Furthermore, where the procedures for creating binding international agreements demand that the Council should be involved, it must at least be kept informed, given ample time for comment (and perhaps also the chance to stop the conclusion of the non-binding arrangement).[308] So far, the ECJ maintains the importance of

[305] See the discussion around n 294; Wessel (n 62) 5.

[306] *France v Commission* (n 66) para 41.

[307] Similarly, García Andrade (n 75) 117 and 120–21. *France v Commission* (n 66) para 41. While many agree that the Commission and the Council's roles remain largely the same, the same may not also be true for the European Parliament:

> Thus the role of each of the two institutions, the Council and the Commission, is broadly comparable in the negotiation and conclusion of agreements that contain a political commitment and are not purely administrative, irrespective of their binding or non-binding nature. However, it seems that this is not the case with the European Parliament, which only has a role in binding agreements.
>
> Ramopoulos and Wouters (n 72) 1085

[308] In one case the Commission 'agreed' a (non-binding) arrangement with the USA. When assessing the legality of the procedure that the Commission had used, the ECJ took into account 'the division of powers and the institutional balance' that the Treaty establishes in the relevant substantive area (there the CCP). The ECJ endorsed the Commission process, noting that the Council had approved both the wider strategic partnership and action plan that the Commission was working under, and the Commission had kept the relevant Council committee (art 133 Committee) regularly informed of its progress in the negotiation. These procedures were in line with those for concluding a binding international agreement except that there the Council authorized signing of the arrangement and concludes it, EC, art 133, *France v Commission* (n 66) para 41. Larik and Wessel say that the ECJ 'confirmed that the prerogatives of the Council had been duly respected by the Commission through approval of the overall Action Plan with the USA (another soft law instrument), and by regularly informing the working party responsible for Common Commercial Policy', Joris Larik and Ramses Wessel, 'Instruments of EU External Action' in Ramses Wessel and Joris Larik (eds), *EU External Relations Law: text, cases and materials* (2nd edn, Hart 2020) 105. Chamon and Demedts make a similar point, adding that 'the Commission had respected the principle of sincere cooperation by keeping the Article 133 EC (now Article 207 TFEU) committee informed', Merijn Chamon and Valerie Demedts, 'Constitutional Limits to the EU Agencies' External Relations' [2017] TARN Working Papers (online), 7.

input legitimacy even for non-binding international competition arrangements. If joining the ICN is considered a non-binding international arrangement then the ECJ is likely to want to ensure that the art 228 EC procedure was largely followed. As we have seen, DG COMP fell well short of this standard, not getting approval from the Council or the Commission.

Let's now turn our minds to the status of ICN recommended practices, from an EU perspective. Here, our focus is the legal position today (rather than in 2001). If the correct procedures are followed, agreeing ICN work products is possible from an EU law perspective (as long as they do not conflict with the EU treaties or EU court judgments). As before, the relevant legal bases are TFEU, arts (1)(b) and 103 (possibly also TFEU, art 114 depending on the measure, and TFEU, art 352 if the merger rules are relevant).[309] Once again, it should be possible to 'mirror' this internal competence in the external sphere.[310] As before, this may even be explicit if these arrangements fall under the EU's Common Commercial Policy ((CCP) TFEU, art 207).

In terms of the relevant procedure, debate remains. Agreeing work products within the ICN (such as recommended practices) may be seen as agreements between the EU and third countries (TFEU, art 218(1)). In which case, procedure to follow is explicitly laid down (see TFEU, arts 218(2)–(6)). In broad terms the Commission submits recommendations to the Council, which shall adopt a decision authorizing the opening of negotiations (it may also address directives to the negotiator and designate a special committee in consultation with which the negotiations must be conducted). It is often the Commission that actually negotiates. The Council, on a proposal by the negotiator, adopts a decision concluding the agreement (after consulting the European Parliament).[311]

It seems unlikely that ICN work products are international agreements, given the extensive statements that the parties to them do not intend them to be binding. Nevertheless, even for non-binding international arrangements, we saw that EU

[309] Some argument that other policies must be integrated into EU external action as a result of TFEU, art 205 (and where relevant TFEU, art 207) and TEU, arts 3 and 21. Krajewski writes, for example, that as pursuing the goals mentioned in TEU, art 21 (such as environmental protection, sustainable economic development and the social and economic development of developing countries) is a binding obligation the Council and Commission need to explain and justify a particular external policy measure 'with reference to the objectives and goals mentioned in TEU, art 21. This could be supported by the requirement of environmental, social and development impact assessments of all trade agreements and unilateral measures', Markus Krajewski, 'The Reform of the Common Commercial Policy' in Andrea Biondi, Piet Eeckhout and Stefanie Ripley (eds), *EU Law After Lisbon* (OUP 2012) 297. Krajewski's focus is the CCP, but, if the point is relevant there then Article 205 TFEU seems to extend the argument to all external action considered here. This has not been happening when the EU (DG COMP) works in the ICN, given the unitary focus on competition, ignoring other goals, see the Introduction to this book and Chapter 1.

[310] See the sources in footnote 287 and TFEU, art 216.

[311] If the agreement falls within the CCP, this procedure is further modified see footnote 290 and TFEU, art 207(3). We do not explore this issue in detail as, in either case, DG COMP did not follow the correct procedure.

institutions normally have to follow a similar procedure to these formal ones. In either case (whether ICN work products are held to be international agreements or non-binding international arrangements), DG COMP probably did not follow the right procedure. Failure to do this means that the act where DG COMP decided to act in this way (or where it was authorized to) is likely void. At best, this will be a major political embarrassment for the EU.

However, the Lisbon Treaty introduced a new procedure that seems designed to be used when bodies set up by an agreement (like the ICN) are called upon to adopt acts having legal effects (which might include the production of ICN recommended practices). The relevant parts of TFEU, art 218(9) read:

> The Council, on a proposal from the Commission … shall adopt a decision… establishing the positions to be adopted on the Union's behalf in a body set up by an agreement, when that body is called upon to adopt acts having legal effects. [art 218(10) adds 'The European Parliament shall be immediately and fully informed at all stages of the procedure]

This demands a major shift in focus from the binding nature of an arrangement (the position that we saw under EC, art 228), to its legal effects in the EU legal order (under this TFEU, art 218(9)).

One might question how mere (non-binding) recommended practices of an international body could have 'legal effects' in the EU order. Nevertheless, this is possible. In one case, for example, the ECJ held that non-binding recommendations from the OIV were 'capable of decisively influencing the content of' EU rules (and so they 'have legal effects').[312]

The limits of 'legal effects' remain unclear at this early stage of interpreting TFEU, art 218(9).[313] However, 'soft law' such as ICN recommended practices, for example, can have considerable legal effects, by inducing actors to modify behaviours.[314]

[312] *Germany v Council* (n 71) paras 59–64. These provisions must also be must reasoned and indicate the substantive legal basis on which they are founded, Case C-370/07 *Commission v Council (CITES)*, EU:C:2009:590, paras 37–62.

[313] Does it apply, for example, to cases:

> where the EU tends to adapt its legislation in a given policy field on the basis of developments internationally spearheaded by legally non-binding instruments of an international organization, but does not do so expressly. Thus, it will come as no surprise if the Court is confronted with other cases with similar facts in the near future and is asked once again to interpret Article 218(9) TFEU.
>
> Ramopoulos and Wouters (n 72) 1083

[314]

> Despite their presumed 'non-legal' nature, such international soft legal agreements thus cannot be ignored in the EU legal order. They may form the interpretative context for legal agreements and may even commit the Union through the development of customary law or as unilateral declarations. While they are usually described as 'political commitments' rather than legal commitments, this may be confusing… soft and hard law instruments can be both politically and legally important.
>
> Wessel (n 62) 6

By way of comparison, according to the Commission, a non-binding OECD recommendation is capable of having legal effects.[315]

There are at least five potential mechanisms for ICN work products to produce legal effects (some are more controversial than others). First, international soft law (like ICN recommended practices) often has legal effects in the international order 'on the basis of the principle of good faith, and it will generate, at the least, expectations between the parties with regard to the compliance with those political agreements'.[316] The EU is bound by the international consequences of the conclusion of even non-binding agreements.[317] Second, EU legislation may incorporate ICN recommended practices or instruct the Commission/ Member States to 'base' their competition decisions on (among other things) them.[318] Third,[319] the Commission may be held to have limited its discretion in the way it would apply the EU competition rules in line with ICN recommended practices that it 'agrees', as is the case with its own guidelines[320] (and other

[315] European Commission (n 74) s 4.

Using this analysis would help to bring the procedure for ICN recommended practices in line with that of the adoption of (even non-binding) competition recommendations in UNCTAD and the OECD. Damro says if DG COMP decided to pursue an EU initiative in UNCTAD 'it would invite political intervention because of its need to obtain approval from the Council of Ministers via the Article 133 Committee [now an Article 207 TFEU Committee]'. The same is true for the OECD. Before making submissions there, he adds 'the Commission must obtain approval of the Council of Ministers via clearance from the Article 133 Committee. [fn Interview with a Commission official, Brussels, 11 April 2005.]', Damro (n 270) 875 and 876.

[316] García Andrade (n 75) 119 (her comments specifically related to Case C-660/13 *Council v Commission (Swiss MoU)*, EU:C:2016:616, but they seem generally applicable). The ECJ has held that 'the primacy of international agreements concluded by the Community over provisions of secondary Community legislation means that such provisions must, so far as is possible, be interpreted in a manner that is consistent with those agreements'. Case C-61/94 *Commission v Germany*, EU:C:1996:313, para 52. By analogy, might this also mean that, where the Commission has 'agreed' ICN recommended practices, it should follow them in its decisions (even amending its own guidelines in their light), as long as they are not contrary to the EU courts' interpretation of the EU treaties?

[317] Opinion of AG Sharpston, Case C-660/13 *Council v Commission (Swiss MoU)*, EU:C:2015:787, para 69.

[318] In one case, the ECJ held in one case that non-binding recommendations from the OIV were 'capable of decisively influencing the content of' EU legislation (and so they 'have legal effects', TFEU, art 218(9)). This was because some EU legislation incorporated OIV recommendations (eg Reg No 1234/2007, article 120g); or, instructed the Commission to 'base itself' on the OIV's recommendations (among other things) when authorizing certain practices (eg Council Reg (EC) No 1234/2007, art 120f). In that case, it was unclear whether EU provisions of this kind are necessary. The ECJ also highlighted that OIV recommendations sought to aid international harmonization and that the OIV monitored the implementation of its recommendations in liaison with its members (as for ICN recommended practices), *Germany v Council* (n 71) paras 59–64.

[319] More details of the following three mechanisms, in relation to EU recommendations/ guidelines, can be found in the Opinion of AG Bobek, in *Belgium v Commission* (n 77) paras 89–95.

[320] The Commission has a wide discretion in the application of the competition rules. It uses substantive and procedural guidelines to explain how it will exercise this discretion more transparently and predictably (within the limits of the EU treaties and secondary EU law). Guidelines are not statements of law. They cannot bind the EU courts (although they may form a useful point of reference), nor other EU institutions, Case C-310/99 *Italy v Commission*, EU:C:2002:143, para 52. However, their legal effect is so strong that the Commission may not depart from them in subsequent decisions, without reasons (which must be compatible with the EU principles of equal treatment, protection of legitimate expectations and legal certainty), Joined Cases C-189/02 P, etc *Dansk Rørindustri A/S and others*

statements).[321] Fourth, the interpretative role that (even non-binding) ICN recommended practices likely have. By agreeing to ICN recommended practices, DG COMP (and national NCAs) may be taken as showing how they think the EU competition rules should be interpreted there ('regulation by information'). By following such statements, other actors (such as firms and national courts) hope to minimize their legal risks (even non-binding guidelines can be guides)[322] ICN recommended practices may even be 'better than' Commission guidelines at modifying behaviour within the EU. This is because the Member States' NCAs have also 'agreed' them (Commission guidelines just come from the Commission). Fifth, soft law may generate parallel sets of rules which pre-empt the legislative process and thus impact the institutional balance.[323] ICN recommendations, in fact, influence Commission action.[324]

ICN recommended practices definitely seem *capable* of having legal effects in all five of these ways (although one could also say, if they are genuinely not meant to have any binding effects, they may not).[325] This becomes even more likely as the ICN increases its monitoring of the implementation of its recommended practices and raises the pressure on its members to converge. This might push the EU

v Commission, EU:C:2005:408, paras 209 and 211. Legitimate expectations, legal certainty, and equal treatment principles transform them into enforceable legal provisions, Herwig Hofmann, 'Negotiated and Non-negotiated Administrative Rule-Making: The Example of EC Competition Policy' (2006) 43 Common Market Law Review 153, 163.

321 The EU courts cast their nets quite widely here. As well as applying this principle to Commission guidelines, they have held the Commission to its statements in both its (annual) Report on Competition Policy (Case T-190/00 *Regione Siciliana v Commission*, EU:T:2003:316, para 100 and in the *Bulletin of the European Communities* (Case C-457/00 *Belgium v Commission*, EU:C:2003:387, paras 6–10, 79, and 97). If the ECJ were going to include ICN recommended practices in this list it would help to have some kind of 'rule of recognition' to know what kinds of Commission (and DG COMP?) statements were included. The ECJ appears to recognize this as a problem more generally, Case C-325/91 *France v Commission*, EU:C:1993:245, para 26.

322 Case C-226/11 *Expedia Inc v Autorité de la concurrence and Others*, EU:C:2012:795, para 32.

323 The ECJ has noted that guidelines are often adopted when institutions 'do not have the power under the Treaty to adopt binding measures or when they consider that it is not appropriate to adopt more mandatory rules' Case C-322/88 *Grimaldi v Fonds des maladies professionnelles*, EU:C:1989:646, para 13. Furthermore, in *Belgium v Commission* (n 77) paras 89–95, AG Bobek noted that EU recommendations may also impact on the institutional balance within the EU by providing routes for circumventing the normal legislative process; and by reducing the range of options around which actors will coalesce if a legislative process is later organized. In legal theory many call this the 'hardening of soft law'.

324 For example, Proposal for a Council Regulation on the control of concentrations between undertakings (COM/2002/0711 final—CNS 2002/0296) para 63; Commission Staff Working Paper accompanying the Communication from the Commission to the European Parliament and Council, Report on the functioning of Regulation 1/2003 (COM(2009)206 final) paras 169–79; Explanatory Memorandum for the *Proposal for a Council Decision on the conclusion of an Agreement between the European Union and the Swiss Confederation concerning cooperation on the application of their competition laws* (COM(2012) 245) point 2.

325 To put it another way, if DG COMP does not intend to follow ICN 'best' practices, why spend so many resources developing them? Chapter 1 argued that a core focus may be industrial policy. But, even then, ignoring the ICN recommended practices likely undermines this strategy too as other NCAs will notice.

Courts to insist on more input legitimacy, especially for international instruments that the EU signs up to such as the ICN recommended practices. If it did, then the procedure in TFEU, art 218(9) (potentially modified by any CCP procedures from TFEU, art 207) should be followed when negotiating and agreeing ICN recommended practices.

However, even if ICN recommended practices are incapable of having 'legal effects' to this standard, we hope that the ECJ will hold that competence allocation is still relevant (given the five potential effects just discussed). If anything, recent treaty changes bolster the emphasis on input legitimacy vis-à-vis effectiveness and efficiency, also demanding a Council mandate before the Commission starts negotiating. Further effort has been made to define Council and Commission roles in this process (TEU, arts 16–17), emphasizing that the Council is in charge of policy in areas such as competition.[326] If the ECJ emphasizes input legitimacy as we advocate, it could stipulate a procedure for international agreements without legal effects which is similar to TFEU, art 218(9) for concluding international agreements with legal effects (perhaps modified by TFEU, art 207, the CCP). This might engage important continuing rights for the European Parliament in the process too.[327]

The procedures that DG COMP has followed in 'agreeing' the ICN recommended practices so far, fall far short of the art 218(9) TFEU standard (not even involving the Commission, let alone the Council and the European Parliament). It is likely acting outside of its powers. If the right procedures are followed it may be possible to retroactively mend this legal error. This has been done for previous errors of this kind. That said, if TFEU, art 218(9) is deemed to be the appropriate process here, this implies that more emphasis should be placed on the input legitimacy in setting up the ICN itself.[328]

It should be pointed out that some argue that a third kind of arrangement is possible.[329] They call these administrative arrangements. They get some support for this idea from TFEU, art 335, which says that the EU 'shall be represented by each of the [EU] institutions, by virtue of their administrative autonomy, in matters relating to their respective operation'. Could ICN recommended practices be administrative arrangements? We do not discuss this, as agreeing ICN recommended practices (and joining the ICN itself) is not an operational matter for the

[326] Case C-660/13 *Council v Commission (Swiss MoU)*, EU:C:2016:616 (Grand Chamber) paras 31–43.

[327] On this point, see the discussion in Wessel (n 62) 12–15, although see the contrasting comment in n 307.

[328] Remember that the art 218(9) TFEU procedure is only appropriate to the production of work products in 'a body set up by an agreement'. The art 218(9) TFEU procedure established a simplified procedure to be used to decide on the position to be adopted by the EU in such bodies (unless they are 'decisions supplementing or amending the institutional framework of the agreement'). This seems to create a kind of hierarchy.

[329] Valle Lagares (n 81) 155; Demedts (n 81) 243.

Commission. The Council Legal Service (rightly, in our view) distinguishes between arrangements 'for practical cooperation ... with a third country or organisation' and arrangements which contain 'policy statements'.[330] An agreement to cooperate with another (non-EU) NCA in relation to enforcement actions might fall within TFEU, art 335. However, 'operational matters' do not seem to include cooperation on substantive and procedural policy matters, especially when these are not within the remit of DG COMP (and are not normally within the remit of the Commission).[331] This is what happens in the ICN. It would be open to the ECJ to add such a category of arrangement. Some authors think it should.[332] We do not favour such a strategy given the input legitimacy issues.[333] The ECJ has shown little appetite for this so far.[334]

The legal position for agreeing arrangements, like those within the ICN, are unclear. There are strong arguments that even non-binding arrangements should closely follow the procedures for binding ones, in order not to undermine the EU's institutional balance. It would also enhance the consistency of internal and external EU actions, although it would undermine flexibility to some degree.[335] While it is not certain, there is reason to believe that the EU Courts are pushing for similar procedures here. If this is the case, DG COMP's joining and participating in the ICN falls well short of these standards.

330 Council of the European Union (n 298) paras 4–6.
331 Townley (n 39) 252–53.
332 Demedts (n 63) 137–38.
333 Similarly, Opinion of AG Tesauro in *France v Commission* (n 58) para 22; Opinion of AG Alber in *France v Commission* (n 66) paras 64–65.
334 *France v Commission* (n 58).
335 On this point, see the discussion in Wessel (n 62) 12–15.

Conclusion

The conclusion to this book starts with a brief summary of the main lines of argument discussed in the previous chapters. Then, it offers some points of reflection for potentially improving the legitimacy, effectiveness, and efficiency of the ICN.

C.1 Summary of the book

Businesses and their value chains increasingly affect many countries. So do anti-competitive arrangements that they adopt. There is a bewildering array of substantive and procedural competition rules for businesses to follow. This has costs, in terms of a loss of efficiency, for companies operating across different countries. It can also have benefits from a democratic and public interest perspective, as each jurisdiction can (try to) protect the values that it holds dear.

Some jurisdictions have sought wider influence for their own competition systems. Sometimes this has been through the extra territorial application of their competition rules, developing joint substantive and/or procedural competition rules or working procedures, and (largely unsuccessfully) attempting to develop multilateral competition rules. Many international organizations have also entered the competition arena—such as the Organisation for Economic Co-operation and Development (OECD) and the United Nations Conference on Trade and Development (UNCTAD).

Many in the competition community thought that things could be better, and that a new approach was needed. The result was the International Competition Network (ICN), launched in 2001. This transnational network includes most NCAs from around the world (such as influential NCAs from the US and the EU and recently established NCAs from developing countries with little experience of competition policy). The ICN focuses exclusively on competition law and policy, both substance and procedure. Non-governmental actors (NGAs), such as major corporations, the law firms that support them, and academics, also contribute to ICN discussions. International organizations, such as the World Bank, UNCTAD, and the OECD are often involved too. However, only NCAs can be ICN members.

The ICN is a forum where competition experts discuss ways to improve competition policy. The ICN also produces many work products, including an array of surveys, guides, model forms, principles, and recommended practices. ICN work products and proposals for new work streams are adopted by consensus of all ICN

The Law and Politics of Global Competition. Christopher Townley, Mattia Guidi, and Mariana Tavares, Oxford University Press.
 DOI: 10.1093/oso/9780198859789.003.0006

members. States then decide whether to implement ICN outputs in their own jurisdiction. This makes the ICN appear like an innocuous organization, driven by some kind of neutral best practice principles, operating in everyone's favour. The same might be said of ICN work products (otherwise why would all NCA members have agreed to them?). In any event, states can refuse to implement ICN best practices where they perceive that they do not favour them for some reason.

This book has had four core tasks. First, given the lack of transparency of the ICN and how it really works, a key aim has been to more clearly chart what happens there. Despite the formal consensus requirement, Chapter 1 argues that some NCAs (and even some NGAs) have considerably more influence, over the ICN agenda, which work products are produced and their content, than others (Section 1.2). Influential actors tend to be from advanced industrialized nations, such as the EU and the USA. Sometimes their interests (and those of their states) diverge quite radically from those of other NCAs (and their states). Yet, these influential actors often use their influence to favour their own interests, and often ignore others' interests, especially when they conflict with the interests of the advanced industrialized nations. Chapter 1 also explains (Section 1.3) how these actors exert such influence given the ICN's consensus requirement. An important part of this has been to (intentionally or not) drive a wedge between the interest of some NCAs and the interests of their states. The theoretical findings in Chapter 1 are supported by a survey that we conducted on NCAs and NGAs (see Chapter 3). In fact, similar results are found for trans-national networks in other areas too.

We also saw the argument that the implementation of ICN work products is voluntary for states. However, Chapter 2 argues that, in fact, many states, and their NCAs, face considerable (and increasing) pressure to implement ICN work products, particularly the recommended practices. The fact that many competition provisions are widely drafted provides NCAs with a lot of discretion. So, NCAs are often able to implement ICN work products without consulting their own states and without checking whether these ICN work products are in the national interest, as understood by wider state actors (Section 2.2). This becomes important where a wedge has been driven between the interests of some NCAs and the interests of their states (see above). NCAs, and many NGAs, also put wider state actors under immense pressure to adopt legislation implementing ICN work products, where 'necessary'. Furthermore, if one considers political dynamics and the impact of institutions in time, the ICN and its outputs provide policy entrepreneurs with new resources for influencing domestic political struggles (Section 2.3). Once again, the theoretical findings in Chapter 2 are supported by the survey that we conducted on NCAs and NGAs (see Chapter 3).

Taken together, Chapters 1–3 demonstrate a powerful mechanism for transmitting influence. In our view, and acting in their own self-interest, some (often rich, economically advanced) states use the ICN to push specific competition rules (and their interpretations of them) onto some (often weaker) states. We show that this has happened even when the recipient states resist this (and even when it is not necessarily in their best interests). In the ICN, there is a group of NCAs that are almost exclusively 'rule-takers', while a group of powerful NCAs (mostly from Europe and North America and supported by some NGAs) are the main 'rule-makers'.

While improvements could be made to this system, many believe that the ICN and its work products significantly increase the efficiency and effectiveness of the competition system worldwide. The second core task of this book, specifically Chapter 4, was to critically examine such claims. This is important work. Not only is the ICN widely lauded by the competition community, but it is often cited as a model that other regulatory areas should follow.

The ICN is preoccupied with efficiency and effectiveness, making significant (and increasing) efforts to assess them. As far as we know, the ICN has never clearly articulated how it trades off its many conflicting goals against each other (such as tensions between effectiveness and efficiency). This makes it impossible to assess whether the ICN efficiently and effectively achieves its goals. So, as a second-best assessment, we ask how efficiently and effectively the ICN achieves some of its different aims. In some areas, such as the production (and, to a lesser extent, the implementation) of its work products, it can be argued that the ICN is both effective and efficient, although it does not achieve all of its goals equally (and it is difficult to be certain as the ICN's methodologies of assessment could be flawed). Furthermore, for an organization that claims to be 'results-based', the ICN spends remarkably little time and effort assessing the results of its actions (eg when its work is implemented by NCAs/states, do superior outcomes occur there and at what cost?). In addition, different actors have different aims for the ICN (not all of which align with explicit ICN goals). As noted above, despite the 'consensus requirement', the ICN's main focus is on a narrow set of issues, principally in favour of advanced industrial economies. The specific kinds of effectiveness and efficiency of interest to these kinds of economies seems to be most often pursued in ICN work.[1]

However, participation in the ICN is voluntary. ICN work products are adopted by consensus and need not be actually implemented. So, one might ask whether there is a need to look any more widely (than efficiency and effectiveness) for justifications for bodies like the ICN. We believe that this is important. As noted above, some NCAs have great influence over the focus and content of ICN work products and they push many others to follow them. This matters because, given their different cultures, socio-economic backdrops, and legal and institutional endowments, ICN work products principally designed by experts

[1] To repeat, this is not to say that all individuals participating in the ICN (or even all those from economically advanced states) consciously work to some nefarious agenda. Many, believe that they are doing good (and this may often be true). That is partly the point. Once the 'right institutions' are in place, then individual agendas matter less, because discordant voices are less influential (by design).

from advanced industrial economies (which largely reflect the categories and approaches there), are unlikely to be optimal for other (particularly developing) countries too.

In line with this belief, the third core task of this book has been to argue for a change in the way we think about competition rules. Legal and economic insights have been extremely valuable and will continue to be so. However, many in the competition community have lost sight of the redistributive impact of these rules (the Introduction, Section I.3, sought to set the record straight in this regard). One size fits all solutions are unlikely to be optimal. When reminded of this, we are often told that redistributive impacts generated by the application of the competition rules is an issue for other areas of law to deal with. This may be an appropriate response in some legal orders. However, we believe that the competition community needs to move away from the idea that there is a one-size-fits-all system of competition. Many good competition systems are possible (many bad ones are too). When considering whether to use ICN work products, 'states' ought to work out what impact they are likely to have in their own legal orders and to reflect upon whether that is desirable in the context of their own systems, norms, culture, and traditions. Competition rules need to be re-politicized, as they are not just technical rules. So, we need more political scientists too. Democratic processes should be followed, winners and losers considered (not ignored). Diversity needs to be actively explained, acknowledged, and (more often) accepted. States should also take responsibility for this political dimension; rather than leaving major policy choices to 'independent' NCAs. If states did this, then we suspect that they would choose to amend (or even ignore) many more ICN outputs.

As a consequence, the fourth core task of this book has been to argue that efficiency and effectiveness are not enough. Using insights from law and political science (and from Chapter 3's survey) Chapter 4 also assessed the system's legitimacy (and trade-offs between legitimacy, effectiveness, and efficiency). In part, this demands that we check whether NCAs are acting within their powers in their ICN work. Different NCAs have been given different powers. For many states, the legitimacy requirements related to their NCA's actions when establishing the ICN and acting within it are unclear. This raises troubling questions. Even more seriously, some actors, such as the EU's DG COMP, seem to have breached their 'national' constitutional arrangements when acting within the ICN. There is also the issue of the legitimacy of the processes for deciding whether to implement redistributive ICN work products in the national legal orders. Should NCAs be allowed to do this, should wider state actors be actively involved in such decisions, and when is one method better than the other?

Legitimacy has been largely ignored in discussions about the ICN. States are likely to assess the need for 'political input' in competition policy in different ways.

So, rather than declaring the ICN legitimate (or not) we have highlighted several potential legitimacy issues that we hope some states will find useful when making their own assessments of the ICN (which is something that we encourage).

Legitimacy issues are likely to be particularly acute the more states' economies differ from those of the key ICN influencers. This is even more problematic for those that automatically adopt ICN work products without wider scrutiny (perhaps through their NCAs); and even more so for countries dependent upon assistance from ICN actors (especially those with weak institutions of domestic accountability). As Chapter 4 explains, the ICN's design means that states may not be able to trust their NCAs to act in (or ICN work products to be in) their national interest. This all raises highly troubling questions of accountability for the ICN in particular, and more generally for trans-national networks and those that they influence.

The ICN is now entering its third decade. In the ICN's 2020 Annual Conference its current Chair, Andreas Mundt, announced the Third Decade Project. He called this a 'top-to-bottom review of the ICN's working methods and substantive coverage with recommendations for the future of the network'.[2] He encouraged all members, NGAs and others to contribute to this project. We think it is a great idea. It is hoped that this book provides a useful, critical perspective of the ICN that will help NCAs, NGAs, states, and others as they input into what could prove to be a fundamental review.

C.2 Suggested points of reflection for potentially improving the legitimacy, effectiveness, and efficiency of the ICN

Our analysis thus brings us to the issues that we suggest the ICN, NCAs and states (those whose NCAs already participate in the ICN and those whose NCAs are considering joining) should discuss, both collectively and individually. Given the current rethinking of its role by the ICN itself, it is a good time for such a review. It should not be forgotten in this process, that reform efforts are also likely to be met by strong opposition by those with most to lose.[3] Remember, this is a battle for the ICN's soul.

Given the tensions between democracy, national determination, and economic globalization, we believe that the first issue to discuss is whether the ICN is necessary at all. Then, those that consider that it is, might reflect upon how to make it more legitimate, effective, and efficient. This is a relevant exercise even

[2] <www.internationalcompetitionnetwork.org/2020vac/> accessed 8 October 2021.

[3] Ranjit Lall, 'Timing as a Source of Regulatory Influence: A Technical Elite Network Analysis of Global Finance' (2014) Regulation & Governance 125.

for those that perceive no problems in the current set-up (things can always improve).

While conducting such an exercise, each actor is advised to establish the best balance between legitimacy, effectiveness, and efficiency for it; and then to decide how much it is willing to compromise here to achieve wider agreement with others. This is likely to be hard. It may also be controversial. But this just shows the importance of the debate. Further issues arise regarding transparency.

In addition, when proposing change, one needs to think dynamically. What will the effect of any proposed change be on the ICN (and its participants)? Might change mean the end of the ICN, if so, is this better than it continuing in its current form?

Here are our points—we hope that they prove helpful.

C.2.1 Establishing or keeping the ICN

1. Does competition policy need global regulatory convergence? Is the ICN necessary at all, given that it is not really a response to global public goods or major beggar-thy-neighbour policies? (Chapter 4, Section 4.2.1.)
2. Given the redistributive issues at stake, is ICN membership optimal? In this regard:
   a. Should states be allowed to be ICN members, rather than just their NCAs?[4] (Chapter 1, Section 1.2.1.) Or, is it better to preserve NCAs' autonomy and keep the focus on narrow technical issues? Is this possible? Even if states do not become members, should they insist on a greater level of overview of their NCAs' actions within the ICN? (Chapter 1, Section 1.2.1.) How would this overview be attained?[5]
   b. If NCAs are to participate in the ICN, should they be there as national experts or as technical experts? (Chapter 1, Section 1.2.1.) Who should their primary allegiance be towards?
3. Regarding the coexistence of the ICN with other networks:
   a. If we want international regulatory convergence, is the existence of the ICN preferable to producing competition policy nationally, or through

[4] Indeed, some states have even sought to join the ICN in other guises. For example, the Brazilian Ministry of Development, Industry and Trade has actually been accepted as an NGA in the ICN and makes representations in this capacity there, ICN, *The Future of the ICN in Its Second Decade—Final Report* (2016) Annex 3 <https://www.internationalcompetitionnetwork.org/wp-content/uploads/2018/09/ICN2dDecade2016.pdf> accessed 8 October 2021.

[5] This might mean states exercising more direct control over their NCAs, either by reducing their discretion, or by monitoring the use of NCA discretion more closely. Slaughter has suggested, for example, that a parallel, global network of governments or legislatures might be a good way of monitoring and counterbalancing the ICN and the actors there: Anne-Marie Slaughter, *A New World Order* (Princeton University Press 2004) ch 3 and 237–39.

other organizations like the OECD and UNCTAD, where national political actors are more involved? (Chapter 4, Sections 4.2.1 and 4.4.)
   b. Would a parallel, network of NCAs from developing countries (or some other formulation) allow them to group together their research and knowledge as a better means of monitoring, holding to account and counterbalancing the work of the more powerful actors (NCAs and NGAs) in the ICN?
   c. Is there space for enabling ICN regional networks to develop? If so, what would be their role vis-à-vis other actors in this space? (Chapter 4, Section 4.1.)
4. Concerning the informal nature of the ICN, are the reasons that drove NCAs to create an informal organization still valid today? Is it appropriate to formalize the ICN in a constitutional moment with input from majoritarian actors from its various members' states? (Chapter 1, Section 1.2.1.)
5. If changes to the informal nature of the ICN are introduced (including any of the changes below), what impact would that have on the ICN? For example, would it be disbanded, or would many NCAs leave (or individuals stop participating), such that it would become unviable, or even much less worthwhile? (Chapter 1, Section 1.2.1.2; Chapter 4, Section 4.3.2.)
6. Are the trade-offs between legitimacy, effectiveness, and efficiency in the ICN now (or in any changed state) acceptable in all countries' legal orders? (Chapter 4, Section 4.2.1.)

C.2.2 Legitimacy

1. If a deliberative democracy model is relevant in a country's legal order:
   a. Are all relevant stakeholders adequately represented, in fact, in the ICN? (Chapter 4, Section 4.3.1.1.) Are more efforts needed to increase the diversity of the NGAs, geographical origin and expertise within the ICN? (Chapter 1, Section 1.2.2.)
   b. Are all relevant stakeholders adequately represented, in fact, in the resulting national discussions? (Chapter 4, Section 4.3.1.1.)
2. If a deliberative democracy model is not followed in a country's legal order, does ICN work map on to its liberal democracy model? In other words, is the country's national legislature informed and given an appropriate level of oversight commensurate with that required in its legal order (even if this is through the NCA) in respect of ICN cooperation and implementation? (Chapter 4, Section 4.2.1.) Or, is there another model that a country uses and has this been adequately followed both within the ICN and in the resulting discussions? (Chapter 4, Section 4.3.1.1.)

3. Have ICN goals have been sufficiently delineated and have the tensions between various goals and interests been adequately explained? This applies at an ICN 'constitutional level', with its 'non-discrimination' and 'competition only' principles. It also applies when producing individual ICN work products. How do these goals map on to the goals set for a country's NCA and national competition policy? (Chapter 4, Sections 4.3.1 and 4.3.2.1.)
4. Are countries aware of the impacts on relevant values of discussions within the ICN (and the work products that might result from them)? Are they aware of the various choices that could be taken in ICN discussions and when drafting ICN work products? (Chapter 4, Section 4.2.1.)
5. Are countries able to diverge from ICN work products, both in principle, and in practice? (Chapter 4, Sections 4.2.1 and 4.3.1.2.) If not, or if this is difficult, what is constraining countries and (how) can they remedy this?
6. Does the ICN support informed divergence adequately? (Chapter 2, Section 2.2.3.)
7. In terms of the ICN work products that influence states' actions (as well as training and technical assistance that NCAs may be provided with by other ICN members):
   a. Does it impact upon other values and interests in a national system (including human rights)? Is it preferable for national competition rules to pursue an exclusive competition goal? (Chapter 4, Section 4.2.1.)
   b. Even if countries consider an exclusive competition goal preferable, is the competition goal pursued in the ICN work product the specific competition goal that states favour in their system, such as consumer welfare, for example? (Chapter 4, Section 4.2.1.)
   c. In case countries decide to implement some ICN recommendation, has there been an appropriate public discussion in that state? (Chapter 4, Section 4.2.1.) and have the implications of using an ICN work product been fully debated before it has been adopted?[6] (Chapter 4, Section 4.1.)
   d. Do states understand what influence NCAs and NGAs have had over the relevant ICN work product and the impact of this influence? (Chapter 4, Section 4.2.1.)
   e. Have national governments, parliaments or courts been pressured by ICN members, or others, to follow an ICN work product? Has this been done in cooperation with the NCA? (Chapter 1, Section 1.2.2.3.)

[6] Critique needs to be part of a wider build-up of civil society. This means supporting competition curricula in local universities, for example, Christopher Townley, Heba Shahein and Richard Whish, 'Teaching and Researching Competition Law and Economics in New Competition Jurisdictions' in Richard Whish and Christopher Townley (eds), *New Competition Jurisdictions: Shaping Policies and Building Institutions* (Edward Elgar 2012), 291. It may also involve things like engagement with law firms in the local law societies, consumer organizations, trade associations, environmental groups.

8. In terms of relationships between NCAs and the ICN:
   a. Do NCAs follow all relevant national procedures when establishing, joining, and operating within the ICN? Do they act within the limits of their powers there? (Chapter 4, Section 4.2.1.)
   b. Is it clear to NCA officials who they are acting for within the ICN (for example, do they represent the national or the international community and whose benefits are they working for)? How can they be pushed to focus on the appropriate benefits? (Chapter 1, Section 1.2.1.2.)
   c. Do any revolving doors between those within NCAs and state organizations in other countries, or private firms (or the potential for them), need to be reviewed where they could be having an adverse influence on the incentives of those working in NCAs? (Chapter 1, Section 1.3.2.)
9. In terms of NGAs' participation in the ICN (Chapter 1, Section 1.2.2):
   a. Should the ICN formalize the criteria for being an NGA, rather than leaving this up to local NCAs (given the risk of undue influence)?
   b. Should NCAs be the gatekeepers for allowing NGAs in their jurisdiction to participate in the ICN (as well as encouraging potential NGAs in their jurisdiction to participate), or should this power be devolved to some other actor, and if so, who?
   c. Should a list of all NGAs in the ICN be provided and a list of all the work they do (and have done) there?
   d. Should the body that appointed the NGA to this role explain publicly why and how they were chosen (and should this appointment process be formalized)?
   e. Should NGAs draft ICN work products?
   f. Should NGAs finance ICN's initiatives, such as, for example, training?
   g. Should the NGA be obliged to disclose what its influence has been? For example, is it appropriate to insist that all NGA submissions clearly refer to the name of the entity doing this work, so that inputs are transparent? More efforts could also be made to track changes in draft ICN work products to better see how NGAs influence them and to publicize this. In fact, a more transparent effort to track unseen influence may be helpful at all levels of the ICN.
   h. Are there other ways in which NGAs influence NCAs within the ICN (or elsewhere)? Do these need to be controlled? (Chapter 1, Section 1.3.)
10. In terms of increasing the influence of developing countries (and others with reduced influence) within the ICN, one needs to start by fully understanding the barriers to fuller engagement by NCAs from developing countries (or some other group). As experts in understanding these themes,

people at UNCTAD may be useful partners here.[7] Once this understanding has been developed, then it is worth considering whether it would increase legitimacy to do the following:

a. Encourage more research and participation by NCAs from developing countries within the ICN. This is in meetings, but also responding to ICN surveys,[8] taking more senior posts within the ICN hierarchy, allowing them to get into debates early (Chapter 1, Sections 1.2.1.2 and 1.3.1). In addition, are mechanisms needed to more actively facilitate full participation by these actors? The aim here is to ensure that their ideas and issues are more fully considered (Chapter 1, Section 1.2.1.2).
b. Create an advisory council of NCAs from developing countries.[9] They could better review together (perhaps proposed ICN agendas, draft ICN work products, etc), generating economies of scale and gaining greater confidence to challenge those that already have influence within the ICN. Alternatively, a group of independent experts could be tasked with assessing the impact of specific policies on developing countries.
c. Explicitly demand that the needs and interests of small jurisdictions and newer NCAs be integrated into all ICN work products (and that this be demonstrated).
d. Make the use of languages other than English more widespread in the ICN and its work products.
e. Encourage and support (financially and otherwise) more twining between NCAs from similar jurisdictions.

11. Would the introduction of a secret system for NCAs voting on whether to accept proposed ICN work products make the ICN more legitimate? (Chapter 4, Section 4.4.)
12. Should there be a maximum time duration for the mandate of the ICN Chair?
13. Given the highly redistributive nature of competition policy and enforcement, and what we know is happening in the ICN (and in terms of implementation), is the trade-off achieved between delegation and accountability for NCAs appropriate in all countries' legal orders? (Chapter 4, Section 4.2.2.)
14. Finally, it is important that potential conflicts between legitimacy, efficiency and effectiveness are properly assessed in a country's legal order. Is this done? If it is not done, why is it so?

[7] Absent such a deep engagement there is a real risk of making matters even worse. For example, in 2016 the ICN, reporting on its survey about desired goals in five years' time for the ICN reports one suggestion (without saying who made it) 'Another way to reduce the burden for agencies in terms of time and staff could be an increased involvement of NGAs in the drafting and commenting of work products' ICN (n 4) 22. Chapter 1 explains why this might make matters worse.

[8] Newer NCAs tend to respond less to ICN surveys (being less well resourced, they often do not have the time). For example, see the related responses (ibid Annexes 1 and 3).

[9] ICN, *The ICN's Vision for Its Second Decade* (2012) 19–22.

C.2.3 Effectiveness

1. How should ICN effectiveness be measured (the extent to which the ICN achieves its goals)? Should one focus on quantitative or qualitative indicators? (Chapter 4, Section 4.3.2.1.) How can these different methodologies be combined effectively? (Chapter 4, Section 4.3.2.1.)
   a. Should one focus on both administrative and legislative outputs, or even just greater consensus on issues within the relevant communities? (Chapter 4, Section 4.3.2.2.)
   b. What would be the impact of focusing on one at the expense of others? For example, would more focus on implementation undermine ICN members' willingness to agree ICN work products? (Chapter 4, Section 4.3.2.2.)
   c. When NCAs offer free or cheap technical assistance and training to other NCAs, is this being used as a Trojan horse to push uniformity through 'blind' adherence to inappropriate ICN work products?
   b. Is the ICN (and its work products) more effective at achieving the interests of advanced industrialized nations (and their NCAs) than of poorer nations and their NCAs? Are the impacts on consumers and other relevant actors in these states assessed? What efforts are being made to ensure that all can contribute more equally and are these sufficient? (Chapter 4, Sections 4.3.2.2 and 4.4.) Could this be improved?
   c. If states diverge from ICN work products, is this problematic? (Chapter 4, Section 4.3.2.2.) If so, why? If it is not problematic, is this always true, or only sometimes (if so when). Also, is this clear to all relevant actors?
   d. Is it more effective to establish regional hubs for providing training and assistance to NCAs from developing countries, especially in places where the language, culture and the competition problems faced are similar?[10] 'Western experts' might just export their own jurisdiction's competition system without sufficient understanding of how it will transplant in these very different systems, for example.
   e. Have regular and recent effectiveness assessments of ICN related actions been made and are they considered to be of an acceptable quality? Is an

[10] In 2016 the ICN, reporting on its survey about desired goals in five years' time for the ICN, noted that one suggestion was 'to organise teleseminars and meetings in all regions for members to have the opportunity to connect with or attend nearby events' ICN (n 7) 22. There is some suggestion that some ICN members maybe even be rethinking their reluctance to allow regional groupings. Summarizing after one 2015 survey, the same ICN report says:

> As mentioned above, the ICN's comparative advantage is its broad reach to agencies around the world and all perspectives in the competition community. ICN's accessibility to all can be strengthened through more interaction at regional level, for example by cooperating with other international or regional organisations, by organising teleseminars focussing on regional issues or by facilitating cooperation on regional basis, i.e. by giving opportunities for

appropriate and robust methodology used? How effective is the ICN and its outputs on this basis (eg when its work is implemented by NCAs/states, do superior outcomes occur there and at what cost?), both absolutely and when compared to other actors? (Chapter 4, Section 4.3.3.1.) Finally, it is important that potential conflicts between legitimacy, efficiency and effectiveness are properly assessed in a country's legal order. Is this done? If it is not done, why is it so?

C.2.4 Efficiency

1. Efficiency can be assessed on many dimensions and trade-offs are likely between these dimensions. For example, one might assess how efficient each of the following are (and whether cost savings could be made in each area):
   a. Is the ICN considered to be an efficient body for sharing information? This could be a factor of the number of members (more members increases efficiencies of scale but may mean more conflicts), how judgmental it is seen to be (which might discourage honest and open dialogue), how closely tied members' interests are perceived to be (are there big divergences and how much does diversity matter), how clear the (trusted) provenance of certain information is (is information circulated by the ICN trusted or is it just adding extra noise?), etc (Chapter 4, Section 4.3.3.1).
   b. Are there efficiency benefits in terms of keeping ICN work separate from the OECD, UNCTAD and others, or is there largely inefficient duplication? (Chapter 4, Section 4.3.3.1.) Can this be improved? For example, if all these bodies continue to exist, should they focus on different types of issues?
   c. Is it worthwhile to participate in the ICN, or could the money saved be more appropriately used for other things, such as more competition enforcement? (Chapter 4, Section 4.3.3.1.) This is particularly relevant given that ICN outputs are available to all, even non-members.
   d. Have NCAs or states that will potentially follow ICN work products considered the costs to them and their firms and consumers (and other

networking and discussions at ICN events. Interaction with regional networks and at regional level may have advantages: it can broaden the reach and awareness of ICN work and promote convergence; can encourage members from the same region, as well as members from different regions, to share common experiences with ICN work and discuss challenges; it can decrease or spread out costs of participation; and it can inform or inspire the discussion of ICN work and topics in regional initiatives.

ICN (n 7) 24–25.

There is some theoretical support that work products should be easier to agree in smaller more homogeneous groups, Kal Raustiala, 'The Architecture of International Co-operation: Transgovernmental Networks and the Future of International Law' (2002) 43 Virginia Journal of International Law 85.

relevant stakeholders) of adaptation to new rules as well as the potential hit that 'rule-taking' NCAs might take to their self-esteem? (Chapter 4, Section 4.3.3.2.)

2. Is the ICN (and its work products) more efficient at achieving the interests of advanced industrialized nations (and their NCAs) than of poorer nations and their NCAs? If so, what efforts are being made to ensure that all can contribute more equally and are these sufficient? (Chapter 2, Section 2.2.4; Chapter 4, Section 4.3.3.2.)
3. Have regular and recent efficiency assessments of ICN related actions been made and are they of an acceptable quality? Is an appropriate and robust methodology used here? How efficient is the ICN and its outputs on this basis (eg when its work is implemented by NCAs/states, do superior outcomes occur there and at what cost?), both absolutely and when compared to other actors? (Chapter 4, Section 4.3.3.1.) Finally, it is important that potential conflicts between legitimacy, efficiency and effectiveness are properly assessed in a country's legal order. Is this done? If it is not done, why is it so?

C.2.5 Transparency

1. Are states fully informed of the processes and specific discussions within the ICN which might be relevant for them, including what issues were debated there, what disagreements occurred—and between whom and why? The influence of specific NCAs and NGAs within the ICN on matters of interest to you, what they have input into and when? (Chapter 4, Sections 4.2.1 and 4.4.)
2. Insofar as states delegate extensive enforcement powers (including discretion in the application of the competition rules) to an NCA, are there appropriate transparency, reason-giving, notice, and comment procedures, and are they being followed? (Chapter 4, Section 4.2.1.) NCAs might not be acting in their state's best interests? (Chapter 4, Section 4.3.1.2.)
3. Have regular and recent transparency assessments of ICN related actions been made and are they acceptable in your legal order?

As can be seen above, there are many potential issues. There are lots of points to discuss. The recent launch of the ICN's Third Decade project is a great opportunity to have a joint, deep, and far-reaching reflection about these issues.

Differences will emerge. While offering minor tweaks, some will likely tell us that there are no realistic alternatives to the current structures. It is worth reflecting upon this (as well as thinking about who makes these claims and what they have to fear from change). This is not just an issue for competition policy and enforcement. Wider questions of the role of trans-national networks of this kind, whose interests those working in national regulators should be pursuing, and the way that transnational networks interact with majoritarian state actors now exist across many regulatory fields.

Things do not need to be like this.

Even if the ICN were considered necessary, states can demand access to it and more transparency for the work done there, who exercises influence, and how. This could allow states to conduct more informed political scrutiny of ICN work products before deciding whether to use them in the state concerned. They might even introduce more political oversight into the ICN (by insisting on a reformulation of its membership from NCAs to states). States might (also) achieve this through more political scrutiny of their NCAs (both their work within the ICN and also 'back home'), perhaps through reducing their independence. How states actually respond will depend, in part, on each jurisdiction's view of legitimacy's importance (and how they define legitimacy). They may also need to consider how such demands may affect the viability of the ICN as well as, ultimately, its effectiveness and efficiency.

There is a lot to think about and, in our view, many improvements can be made. Given the recent launch of the ICN's Third Decade project, we hope that these suggestions provide helpful input for the ICN process (as well as national reviews).

Appendix

Survey on participation in the International Competition Network

1. Do you work at a competition authority or are you a non-governmental advisor?
   I work at a competition authority *(Skip to question 5)*
   I am currently a non-governmental advisor *(Skip to question 2)*
   I have been a non-governmental advisor in the past but I no longer am *(Skip to question 2)*

General information about NGAs

2. What type of NGA are you?
   Law firm
   Academic
   Consumer organization
   Representative of national court
   Big business
   Small business
   Representative of other international organization
   Other: ______________________________

3. From which country?
   ____

4. For how many years have you been an NGA?
   ______________________________ *(Skip to question 48)*

General information about NCAs

5. When was your competition authority established?
   ____

6. In which country is your competition authority based?
   ____

7. When did your competition authority join the ICN?
   ____

8. How many staff members (approximately) does your authority employ for competition policy and enforcement?

____

Relationship between NCA and the ICN

9. How many staff members of your competition authority regularly deal with ICN?

____

10. For your authority, how important are the work products and material provided by the ICN?

Not important at all 1 2 3 4 5 Very important

For your authority, how important are the following ICN working groups?

11. Advocacy Working Group

Not important at all 1 2 3 4 5 Very important

12. Agency Effectiveness Working Group

Not important at all 1 2 3 4 5 Very important

13. Cartel Working Group

Not important at all 1 2 3 4 5 Very important

14. Merger Working Group

Not important at all 1 2 3 4 5 Very important

15. Unilateral Conduct Working Group

Not important at all 1 2 3 4 5 Very important

16. How often is your competition authority in touch (at a distance or at conferences) with other ICN participants for ICN-related issues?
A few times a year
On a monthly basis
On a weekly basis
Other: ______________________________

17. How often does your competition authority address national legislators to support changes in the legislation following a recommendation from the ICN?
Never
Rarely
Often

To what extent does your competition authority find the following publications or exchanges useful for its activities?

18. Recommended practices

Not useful	1	2	3	4	5	Very useful

19. Good Practices and other Practical Tools

Not useful	1	2	3	4	5	Very useful

20. Debates and exchange of views during the ICN Annual Meeting

Not useful	1	2	3	4	5	Very useful

21. Debates and exchange of views during ICN workshops

Not useful	1	2	3	4	5	Very useful

22. Thematic conference calls organized during the year by ICN Working Groups

Not useful	1	2	3	4	5	Very useful

23. Support from the ICN Advocacy Implementation Network

Not useful	1	2	3	4	5	Very useful

24. Development of bilateral relations with other ICN members

Not useful	1	2	3	4	5	Very useful

25. Interaction with NGAs

Not useful	1	2	3	4	5	Very useful

26. Does a lack of compliance with ICN's recommendations undermine a competition authority's reputation?
    Yes, a lot
    Yes, but only slightly
    No

For your authority, alongside the ICN's work products, how important is the material provided by other organizations and networks?

27. United Nations Conference on Trade and Development (UNCTAD)

    Not important at all 1 2 3 4 5 Very important

28. Organisation for Economic Co-operation and Development (OECD)

    Not important at all 1 2 3 4 5 Very important

29. Your regional network (e.g. ECN, Latin American and Caribbean Competition Forum, ASEAN, Southern African Development Community, Common Market for Eastern and Southern Africa, etc.)

    Not important at all 1 2 3 4 5 Very important

30. Why does your competition authority refer to the work products of other organizations and networks?
    Linguistic reasons
    Local forums are more influential
    Local problems are more relevant
    Other: ______________________________

Implementation of specific ICN recommendations
In the following sections, we will ask whether four specific ICN recommendations have been implemented in your jurisdiction, and how.

Use of "markers" in leniency applications
The ICN Anti Cartel Enforcement Manual (at p. 12) states that "It is good practice to use markers in the leniency application process". A marker system "under a leniency policy is a means for leniency applicants to reserve their place in the queue for a defined period of time whilst they conduct further internal investigations and attempt to perfect their application for leniency prior to the competition agency determining the first eligible leniency applicant. Markers are often sought and granted with initially incomplete information or evidence provided by the leniency applicant" (p. 11).

31. Can a marker be granted to a leniency applicant under your competition authority's leniency programme?
    Yes *(Skip to question 32)*
    No *(Skip to question 35)*

Implementation of recommendation on the use of "markers" in leniency applications

32. How was the ICN's recommendation on the use of "markers" in leniency applications implemented in your jurisdiction?
    Implemented autonomously by the competition authority
    The competition authority requested a change in the legislation
    The measure was already part of our jurisdiction before the ICN issued the recommendation
    The legislator implemented autonomously following the ICN recommendation
    Other: ______________________________

(Skip to question 36)

Implementation of recommendation on digital evidence gathering

33. How was the ICN's recommendation on digital evidence gathering implemented in your jurisdiction?
    Implemented autonomously by the competition authority
    The competition authority requested a change in the legislation
    The measure was already part of our jurisdiction before the ICN issued the recommendation
    The legislator implemented autonomously following the ICN recommendation
    Other: ______________________________

(Skip to question 37)

Lack of implementation of recommendation on digital evidence gathering

34. Why was the ICN's recommendation on digital evidence gathering not implemented in your jurisdiction?
    A change in the legislation was requested but the legislator did not act
    A change in the legislation was needed but it was not requested to the legislator
    The authority autonomously decided to not implement
    Other: ______________________________

(Skip to question 37)

Lack of implementation of recommendation on the use of "markers" in leniency applications

35. Why was the ICN's recommendation on the use of "markers" in leniency applications not implemented in your jurisdiction?
    A change in the legislation was requested but the legislator did not act
    A change in the legislation was needed but it was not requested to the legislator
    The authority autonomously decided to not implement
    Other: ______________________________

(Skip to question 36)

Digital evidence gathering

The ICN Anti Cartel Enforcement Manual (at p. 33) establishes that "[i]t is good practice: to have a dedicated internal organisation or staff capacity to undertake digital evidence gathering".

36. Does your competition authority have a dedicated team to undertake digital evidence gathering?
    Yes *(Skip to question 33)*
    No *(Skip to question 34)*

Assessment of dominant positions in a market

The ICN recommended practices on "Dominance/Substantial market power analysis pursuant to unilateral conduct laws" (at p. 2) state that "[a]gencies should use a sound analytical framework firmly grounded in economic principles in determining whether dominance/substantial market power exists. [...] Properly assessing whether a firm possesses dominance/substantial market power, is a complex and multi-faceted analysis"

37. Are market shares a stand-alone criterion to assess dominance under your competition law?
    Yes *(Skip to question 39)*
    No *(Skip to question 38)*

Implementation of recommendation on the assessment of dominant positions in a market

38. How was the ICN's recommendation on the assessment of dominant positions in a market implemented in your jurisdiction?
    Implemented autonomously by the competition authority
    The competition authority requested a change in the legislation
    The measure was already part of our jurisdiction before the ICN issued the recommendation
    The legislator implemented autonomously following the ICN recommendation
    Other: ______________________

(Skip to question 40)

Lack of implementation of recommendation on the assessment of dominant positions in a market

39. Why was the ICN's recommendation on the assessment of dominant positions in a market not implemented in your jurisdiction?
    A change in the legislation was requested but the legislator did not act
    A change in the legislation was needed but it was not requested to the legislator
    The authority autonomously decided to not implement
    Other: ______________________

(Skip to question 40)

Criteria for mandatory notification thresholds

The "ICN Recommended Practices for Merger Notification and Review Procedures" (at p. 6) state that "[m]andatory notification thresholds should be based on objectively quantifiable criteria. [...] Examples of objectively quantifiable criteria are assets and sales (or turnover). Examples of criteria that are not objectively quantifiable are market share and potential transaction-related effects. Market share-based tests and other criteria that are inherently subjective and fact-intensive may be appropriate for later stages of the merger control process (e.g., determining the scope of information requests or the ultimate legality of the transaction), but such tests are not appropriate for use in making the initial determination as to whether a transaction requires notification".

40. Does your competition authority only use objective quantifiable criteria (such as assets, sales or turnover, and not market share) for mandatory notification thresholds?
    Yes *(Skip to question 41)*
    No *(Skip to question 43)*

Implementation of recommendation on criteria for mandatory notification thresholds

41. Which criteria does your competition authority use? You can select more than one option
    Assets
    Sales
    Turnover
    Other: ________________________________

42. How was the ICN's recommendation on the assessment of dominant positions in a market implemented in your jurisdiction?
    Implemented autonomously by the competition authority
    The competition authority requested a change in the legislation
    The measure was already part of our jurisdiction before the ICN issued the recommendation
    The legislator implemented autonomously following the ICN recommendation
    Other: ________________________________

(Skip to question 44)

Lack of implementation of recommendation on criteria for mandatory notification thresholds

43. Why was the ICN's recommendation recommendation on criteria for mandatory notification thresholds not implemented in your jurisdiction?
    A change in the legislation was requested but the legislator did not act
    A change in the legislation was needed but it was not requested to the legislator
    The authority autonomously decided to not implement
    Other: ________________________________

(Skip to question 44)

Questions about Non-Governmental Advisors (NGAs)

44. How does your competition authority choose potential NGAs?
    Potential NGAs ask the authority to be invited
    We select autonomously NGAs
    Both
    Other: ______________________________

45. Your competition authority selects NGAs because...
    They provide expertise your authority does not possess
    They can contribute to discussions with different perspectives and points of view
    Other: ______________________________

46. Has your competition authority ever refused an application from a potential NGA?
    No
    Yes, because it did not have the necessary expertise
    Yes, because there were already too many accredited NGAs sponsored by us and we could not sponsor more
    Other: ______________________________

47. What type of NGAs has your competition authority sponsored? You can select more than one option
    Law firms
    Academics
    Consumer organizations
    Representatives of national courts
    Big businesses
    Small businesses
    Representatives of other international organizations
    Other: ______________________________

(Skip to question 56)

Questions for Non-Governmental Advisors (NGAs)

48. What is the incentive in participating to the ICN for NGAs? You can select more than one option
    Having a chance to influence policies they have to comply with
    Networking
    Checking the ICN decision-making process
    Other: ______________________________

49. How often are you as an NGA in touch (at a distance or at conferences) with other ICN participants for ICN-related issues?
    A few times a year
    On a monthly basis
    On a weekly basis
    Other: ______________________________

50. Do NGAs in the ICN openly disagree among themselves?
Yes, they split depending on their backgrounds (e.g. firms vs. consumers)
Yes, they split along economic cleavages (e.g. developed vs. developing countries)
Yes, they split along geographical cleavages (e.g. Europeans vs. Americans)
No
Other: ___________________________

51. Are some NGAs more influential than others?
Yes
No

Which of the following features are more important in making an NGA influential?

52. Early participation in drafting of ICN work products

Not important at all 1 2 3 4 5 Very important

53. Having been members of authorities (revolving doors)

Not important at all 1 2 3 4 5 Very important

54. Personal expertise

Not important at all 1 2 3 4 5 Very important

55. Nationality (being from an influential country)

Not important at all 1 2 3 4 5 Very important

Influence within the ICN

56. Are some competition authorities more influential than others in the ICN?
Yes
No

Which of the following features are more important in making a competition authority influential?

57. More resources

Not important at all 1 2 3 4 5 Very important

58. More expertise

Not important at all	1	2	3	4	5	Very important

59. Being a member for a longer time

Not important at all	1	2	3	4	5	Very important

60. Being able to address colleagues in their own language

Not important at all	1	2	3	4	5	Very important

61. Do members of the steering committee have more influence in ICN agenda-setting compared to other competition authorities?
Yes
No

62. Do members of the steering committee have more influence over the ICN work product compared to other competition authorities?
Yes
No

63. Do working groups' co-chairs have more influence in ICN agenda-setting compared to other competition authorities?
Yes
No

64. Do working groups' co-chairs have more influence over the ICN work product of that working group compared to other competition authorities?
Yes
No

65. Do some competition authorities try to push for the adoption of common standards?
Yes
No

66. Has a competition authority ever pushed for the adoption of its own jurisdiction's standards?
Yes
No

67. If yes, why has it done that?
Because it was in the general interest
Because there was a preference of national economic actors for this

68. Has a competition authority ever pushed for the adoption of standards that would require a change of its own?
    Yes
    No

69. If yes, why has it done that?
    Because it was in the general interest worldwide
    Because it was in the national interest

70. Do competition authorities openly disagree among themselves within the ICN?
    Yes, they split along legal/administrative traditions (e.g. civil law vs. common law)
    Yes, they split along geographical cleavages (e.g. Europeans vs. Americans)
    Yes, they split along economic cleavages (e.g. developed vs. developing countries)
    No, all discussions develop within a general consensus
    No, because issues of major disagreement are avoided
    Other: ______________________________

Index

References to notes are indicated after the page number by an n followed by the note number.
Tables and figures are indicated by *t* and *f* following the page number.